The Monsters of Babylon

Gregory Delaney

The Monsters of Babylon

How the Jews Betrayed Mankind

VOLUME ONE

Gregory Delaney

SSPress

— 2024 —

SSPress, LLC

Special Services Press, LLC, is a non-profit educational publisher.

Library of Congress Cataloging-in-Publication Data

Delaney, Gregory
The Monsters of Babylon: How the Jews Betrayed Mankind (volume one)
Reprint of original 2014 edition

p. cm.
Includes bibliographical references

ISBN 978-1963-1430-41
(pbk.: alk. paper)

1.   Jews, history of

2.   Anti-Semitism, history of

Printing number: 9 8 7 6 5 4 3 2 1

Printed in the United States of America on acid-free paper.

"We Jews have spoiled the blood of all the races of Europe. Taken as a whole, everything is Jewified. Our ideas animate everything. Our spirit reigns over the world. We are the Lords."
– Dr. Kurt Munzer, *The Way to Zion*

"If Satan himself, with all of his super-human genius and diabolical ingenuity at his command, had tried to create a permanent disintegration and force for the destruction of the nations, he could have done no better than to invent the Jews."
– Willis Carto

"Jewry once again reveals itself as the incarnation of evil, as the plastic demon of decay, and the bearer of an international culture-destroying chaos."
– Joseph Goebbels

"Planetary master criminals of the most modern modernity."
– Martin Heidegger

Acknowledgment

The editors would like to acknowledge Ryan Cavallius for his extensive assistance in text preparation. His work is most appreciated.

CONTENTS

VOLUME ONE

VOLUME TWO

INTRODUCTION

Much can be learned about any people, if you know who their heroes are. It is their heroes to whom the people look for inspiration and as examples to teach their children. The heroes of a people typify all of the qualities to which the people, themselves, aspire.

So, one may ask, who are the heroes of the Jews? Murderers, thieves, swindlers, rapists, child molesters, assassins, spies, hypocrites, liars, deceivers, betrayers, criminals, perverts, and sociopaths of the worst sort – these are the heroes of the Jews. You can read all about it in their main book of instruction known as the *Hebrew Bible* or the *Old Testament*.

Most certainly, the *Hebrew Bible* is a book of instruction. Every rabbi and Christian preacher will tell you that. But the rabbi is a liar and the Christian is usually his dupe. While they both tell you that the *Old Testament* is a book of instruction, the Christian claims that it is a foundational teaching of Jesus and the rabbi tells you that it is the very word of God given to his Holy Chosen Ones. But the Christian preacher is a deceived fool and the rabbi is a deceiving liar. Both are wrong, as you will learn in the following pages.

The *Hebrew Bible* is a book of instruction for a nation of criminals. Through its pages, one can learn the tricks and swindles for subverting other people; the blessings that the demon god of the Jews gives to them when they murder and destroy; and the hypocritical methods for hiding their mayhem and larceny behind a veil of self-righteousness, deceit, and pseudo-religiosity. The *Hebrew Bible* teaches the Jews how to destroy and subvert other people and to consume the wealth and steal the land of their murdered victims. Yet, for all of this, the Jews could easily be the world's biggest clowns, if they didn't take themselves so seriously in their criminality.

Presiding over the fate of the superstitious Hebrews whom they had deceived, the ridiculous old rabbis and Jewish priests performed their deceptive street theater to impress the Canaanite yokels. For example, if Hymie Swartz, the goat rustler, ate a bite of goat meat and washed it down with a cup of milk, those ancient frauds would perform a chorus line of rabbinical charades. The rabbis, sitting in judgement of poor old Hymie, would simultaneously jump to their feet, scream at the top of their lungs, rip their own clothes into ribbons, while in unison loudly beseeching the heavens to have mercy and not open the earth beneath their feet to swallow the whole city or to send down lightning bolts to blast them all into tiny little pieces. For eating a bite of goat meat and a cup of milk, the rabbis, wide-eyed with feigned terror, trembling and shaking in unison – like a chorus line of stinking, bearded, old show girls – those hairy-faced fraudsters would then point their accusing fingers at the terrified Hymie Swartz, sentence him to be flogged, or stoned to death, or strangled or molten lead poured down his throat so as to "banish such sins from Israel." With such terrorism did the rabbis control the Hebrews.

But with such horrible punch lines to all the practical jokes played upon Hymie Swartz and the millions of other Hebrews who have been deceived by the rabbis, it is impossible for the Jews to be the world's biggest clowns. So, instead of being the world's biggest clowns, the Jews have chosen instead to be the world's biggest liars, something that they take very seriously. For financing their lies, the Sumerian Swindle has provided them with limitless wealth – truly limitless wealth. And limitless wealth buys limitless power.

But of what benefit is it to Mankind when limitless wealth and limitless power are in the hands of the world's biggest liars, thieves, murderers, and betrayers? No good has ever come from such a congruence. No good has ever come from the Jews.

As you saw in Volume One (*The Sumerian Swindle*), it is not a magic wand that creates money out of nothing; it is an arithmetical trick that steals wealth from its unwary victims and loots it from its unwilling opponents. The Sumerian Swindle creates wealth for the subterranean banking elite who practice it and it creates poverty and servitude for the rest of the world. Therefore, those who practice it are very cautious that their criminality is not discovered; and that the mechanism of the Sumerian Swindle remains concealed; and that no one ever learns the basic philosophy of the bankers and financiers which is: "Many must suffer and die so that a few may live in luxury."

Volume One explained the history and the application of the Sumerian Swindle. The present volume, *The Monsters of Babylon*, describes who those criminals are and how they have used a veneer of religion to hide their depredations upon Mankind and to protect themselves from discovery and from justice. The Sumerian Swindle is the basis for the moneylenders' thievery but, over the centuries, the bankers have developed many other ways to steal your wealth, to enslave you to unending toil, to betray and destroy your country and to suck your very life force into their vaults. That most of those monsters are Jews, is more than just a coincidence. That those liars, deceivers, hypocrites, and murderers, those very children of the devil, use religion to hide behind – religion, the most revered and holy of Man's pursuits being used to conceal the vilest of creatures! – that, is the only real joke of the Jews. But only the Jews are laughing while the entire world and all of its people cry out in pain as many suffer and die so that a few Jews may live in luxury.

For the Jews, this is as it should be: all of Humanity suffering while the Jews laugh and dance and sing. After all, that's what their "holy scriptures" claim that their demon god wants for them – pitilessly devouring other people and other people's goods and then singing and dancing on their graves. You can read about it yourself in the *Hebrew Bible*.

*****

This is a difficult book to read because it covers such a long time span and is so varied in subject matter. But it includes everything you need to know about How the Jews Betrayed Mankind between the years 1200 BC and 1000 AD. So, if one chapter does not interest you, skip to the next chapter. The chapters are written both for the interested reader as well as for the specialist researcher. Warning is given in some chapters so that the interested reader may skip over them, to return later and become a specialist researcher.

CHAPTER 1
BIG MONEY SPAWNS THE CHOSEN ONES

Everything about Judaism is a lie. Yes, there is a god, but God did not do any of the things that the Jews claim that He did in the Hebrew Bible. Ask yourself: Who tells lies about God other than devils? The founders of Judaism were not even Hebrews!

They were Babylonians. Terah and his son, Abraham, and his grandson Isaac and great-grandson Jacob, incestuously married their Babylonian relatives in order to keep their wealth within the family. They were the four generations of Babylonians who founded "Judaism." Although they were Semites, the founders of Judaism were not Hebrews, they were schemers! Babylonian schemers.

"How can we be anything other than the Chosen Ones of God?" Terah must have asked himself during his ruminations concerning his tribe in 1200 BC. They were at the top of the social ladder, they owned slaves, estates, farms, mines, ships, villages, huge sections of entire cities. They ate the choicest foods and luxuriated in the most expensive brothels and spas. Even the kings came to them for loans. As long as no one knew that they had acquired their wealth through fraud and theft and murder, then who could *not* accept them as the best of people, the very apple of God's eye? Subterfuge, deceit, hypocrisy and lies kept the moneylenders wealthy and powerful. But something was amiss. The larcenous system of the Sumerian Swindle was breaking down and needed some additional bolstering up to keep Terah and his family of thieves well supplied with gold. The great contending empires of Egypt, Assyria and Babylonia could at any time seize Terah's treasures and lands.

All the ancient Near East – from Phoenicia and Greece to Babylonia and India – functioned with the commercial transfer of silver and gold as a form of money to make trade and manufacturing flourish. The moneylenders had silver and gold in plenty, thanks to the secret mechanics of the Sumerian Swindle where compound interest allowed every moneylender the real potential to own the entire world with nothing more than an initial offering of a tiny loan. But like all problems of owning wealth, how to keep what they had swindled, was the rub. Taxes by the kings, plunder of invading armies, theft by burglars and relatives, losses from donations to temples, and confiscation by outraged victims of their Crimes Against Humanity, all led to losses of their bullion and set-backs in their schemes. And what was worse, the kings had understood what a threat that the private accumulation of silver was to the state and had restricted such hoards only to the palace and the temples.

Yes, Terah and his gang of bankers, loan sharks, merchants, and enforcement goons – no different than any of the other merchant-moneylender families – in the rest of the known world – had been able to impoverish both kings and the common folk. But to keep what they had stolen and to perpetuate themselves as the special and most blessed of people, these bankers needed a subterfuge, a lie, a very clever lie that would deceive both kings and common folk. After all, a larcenous business such as moneylending and banking cannot be protected with truth because truth would destroy it. Neither bankers nor other criminals can thrive if they tell the truth about their crimes.

Only with lies and deceit can criminal ventures be perpetuated. What Terah needed to protect his wealth and that of his family was the power of delusion over the minds of Men. Delusion is most easily engendered through the dark power of lies and deceit.

As patriarch of the moneylender guilds of Ur and Harran, how could Terah solve the serious problems that he perceived arising during his days around the thirteenth century BC? He needed not just one lie but many lies to safeguard both his wealth and the success of his extended tribe of loan-sharks, slaver drivers and import-export swindlers. If kings and commoners knew the truth about banking and moneylending, they would rise up and hang Terah and his entire family.

So, truth would not save his treasures or his tribe. But behind a veil of lies, great wealth and great evil can be hidden. So, Terah invented the Biggest Lie Ever Told and, over three thousand years later, we modern people are still suffering from that ancient curse of the Monsters of Babylon.

Modern archaeology proves that the Biggest Lie Ever Told is without doubt the Hebrew Bible, known to us as the Old Testament. It spawned and it is followed in second place by the Quran of the Muslims. Proving that the Jews are The World's Biggest Liars, is easy. Proving the Muslims to be liars, is even easier. Modern archaeology proves that the Jews are liars and frauds.

In his very excellent collection of ancient translations, James Pritchard states:

> The ancient Near East, until about a century ago, had as its chief witness the text of the Hebrew Bible.
>
> Relatively insignificant was the evidence recovered from sources outside the Bible; that which had been found had not been sufficiently understood to serve as a reliable historical source. Through explorations and excavations carried on within the last century in Egypt, Mesopotamia, Asia Minor, and Syria, a wealth of new information has become available.
>
> This new light from extra-biblical texts has served not only to enlarge immeasurably the horizon for a knowledge of the ancient Near East, but it has also sharpened considerably the understanding of the content of the Bible itself.

And so, for 2,500 years, the People of the West as well as the Near East have had to accept mainly the word of the Jews for our historical perspective of those ancient times and places. And it has only been in the last 150 years, that the ancient mounds of buried cities have been excavated and the cuneiform tablets, the papyrus scrolls and the ancient leather books have been deciphered. Those ancient archives reveal that the word of the Jews, is the word of Liars. Yes, God has done wonderful things, but God never did any of the things that the Jews claim that He did. And who tells lies about God other than devils?

Thanks to archaeology, the people of the 21ˢᵗ Century AD have available to us the facts about the Jews that our forefathers did not have. We are now able to better judge the Jews with historical documents that the Jews did not counterfeit, themselves. Indeed, as the ancient rabbis burned the books of the peoples that their subtle deceit had conquered, as the ancient Jewish priests smashed the clay tablets of the historical archives and ground them into dust, as the old Pharisees burned the papyrus manuscripts and torched the libraries of the peoples around them, they rested in confidence that no one would ever venture to dig up the mounds of the ancient cities or to excavate the burned and demolished libraries of their hated and slandered enemies – thus, leaving only the word of the Jews to tell their tall tales about how wonderful they all are.

The ancient cities of the near East were built of mud bricks. When the walls became eroded from time and weather or smashed from siege and warfare, the citizens simply leveled the buildings, saved the wooden roof beams and built another city of mud brick on top of the old. In this way, many layers of many cities were built up into dirt mounds upon which a new city of mud brick stood. (See Figure 1) The libraries, streets, treasures, and storehouses of many previous cities spanning hundreds and thousands of years were buried, layer upon layer, beneath the city, awaiting only someone to dig down into the rubble to discover the history of the people who had lived there.

Figure 1: City Mounds

In the Old Testament, the Jews brag about committing genocide upon hundreds of towns and villages, burning, looting, raping, and destroying the temples and sacred writings of the people whom they had exterminated.

> You must destroy completely all the places where the nations
> you dispossess have served their gods, on high mountains, on
> hills, under any spreading tree; you must tear down their altars,
> smash their pillars, cut down their sacred poles, set fire to the
> carved images of their gods and wipe out their name from that
> place. (Deuteronomy 12:3)

With the scriptures and teachings of all opposing religious and historical views destroyed, those supreme betrayers and liars stepped forth and presented to the world the writings that they had plagiarized and forged, claiming them to be the very word of their mighty Yahweh-god, a god of lies and destruction. Confident that they would never be found out, convinced that no one would ever dig into the hundreds of feet of rubble of the smashed cities to find proof against their lies, the Jews have promoted themselves right up into modern times as icons of morality and virtue. But both science and religion prove the Jews to be frauds.

How could the ancient Jewish rabbis look into the future and see that a people would exist who would, indeed, dig up those ancient ruins in search for something besides gold and silver. Modern archeologists would excavate the ancient cities in search of knowledge written in the dust, a knowledge that the foul rabbis had thought that they had destroyed and buried.

It is only because of the discoveries of modern archaeology, that the stories the Jews tell about God are proven to be lies. *Not a single tale in the Old Testament is anything more than a lie*, a fiction posing as history, a plagiarized document stolen from other peoples or an out-and-out forgery. Yes, God has done in the past and He is doing in the very present far more wonderful things than what the lying Jews claim. God is great.

No doubt about that. *But as great as God is, He didn't do any of the things that the lying Jews claim that He did.* The Jews are liars, deceivers, hypocrites, and murderers, just as Jesus said that they are. This present volume that you are reading of How the Jews Betrayed Mankind, proves this. Think about this: Devils tell lies about God. Herein, you will discover how and why this fraud known as Judaism was developed by the ancient moneylenders of Assyria and Babylonia into the parasitic plague of murderous, blood-sucking leeches that it is today.

As I showed in my book *The Sumerian Swindle*, the Babylonian carnival barkers and loan-sharks long ago discovered that if only one of them told a lie, few people would be deceived. But if all them told the same lies, then, through force of numbers, their lies became better able to overcome the doubts of those who looked distrustfully into their soulless eyes and sly grins. This was and still is the Jewish method even into modern times, all the Jews braying through their gruntles that they are God's Chosen People and offering up as "proof," hoary old scriptures that they have counterfeited themselves. Even against the foreground of their own criminality, this background lie has been perpetuated for so many centuries that even the Christians have been deceived by it, simply because the Jewish Lies "have always been here."

Therefore, as you read the following pages, I must give you one warning, Dear Reader, if you are a Christian. Do not be too hasty to throw this book aside if it irritates your Old Testament prejudices. The greatness of Christ and of Christianity is certainly upheld in this book. But pagan knowledge is also recommended herein since there is much to be learned from the knowledge of those ancient people who have been maligned by ignorant Christians, perfidious Jews and lying Muslims alike. The teachings that I express herein have never before graced the pages of any other history book ever written. As I demolish both Judaism and Islam, all that you will find remaining is an even greater understanding of Christianity as well as an appreciation for what the pagans knew. Many of the things that Jesus taught were previously well known by those who came thousands of years before him.

As the archaeologists excavated such ancient cities as Eridu of Sumeria (see Figure 2), the proofs that the Jews are liars have slowly come to light. Adam and Eve, the Garden of Eden, Noah and the Flood, the Creation Myths, were all plagiarized from the Sumerians and Babylonians. Archaeologists have unburied the original cuneiform texts to prove this. The wisdom that the lying rabbis claim as their own, was plagiarized and stolen from the Egyptians and Babylonians. We have excavated the original clay tablets and papyrus to prove this. Baby Moses in a reed basket, set adrift on the Nile, to be raised to adulthood by Pharaoh's wife, was an Akkadian story of Sargon the Great and substituted with a Hebrew name and storyline. We have unburied the ancient libraries of cuneiform tablets to prove this. The Jews pilfered the cuneiform libraries of Babylonia and the papyrus libraries of Egypt for those tales and claimed them as their own. Archaeological discoveries, translations of the original cuneiform texts and linguistic studies, prove this. Such tales about Moses performing magic tricks for Pharaoh and parting the Red Sea, all are tales that were known in Egypt a thousand years before Moses was alleged to have lived.

Figure 2: Eridu

According to the proofs of archaeology, Moses, the wanderings of the patri-archs, Exodus from Egypt, wandering in Sinai for forty years, conquest of Ca-naan, the empire of David and Solomon, the Lost Ten tribes, and the rise and fall Israel and Judah were all inventions, fictions. There were no patriarchs, no Exodus, no conquest of Canaan, no prosperous united monarchy under David and Solomon. So what can be said about the so-called "History of Israel and the Jews" as found in the Five Books of Moses and in Joshua, Judges and Samuel? Since these books are fictions, what then is there about Judaism that is true? And what can be said about the Jews today who persist in telling such lies? When every story upon which a religion is based is nothing but lies, then how true can such a religion be? Judaism cannot be true and neither can Islam. But Jesus demonstrated the truth about God, so the Jewish liars killed him and the Muslim liars are betraying him to this very day.

What can be said about an entire people who have been telling monstrous lies for the past three thousand years? What can be said about the entire Jewish People, who claim to be the greatest and most blessed of Mankind but who persist in using this illusory scam of well-advertised and much-touted "great virtue" as a means of concealing all manner of larcenies, thefts, murders, sex slavery, subversions, and genocides against other peoples? What can be said about the Jews that has not already been said by their victims? As you read these pages, I am sure that you will have your own things to say about the hypocritical monsters known as Jews.

With the Sumerian Swindle and compound interest as their primary mon-ey-making engine, the *tamkarum* [merchant-moneylenders] of Babylonia and Assyria gained enormous wealth through usury, fraud, swindles, grand lar-ceny, monopolization of resources, cartel control of businesses, price fixing, war profiteering, murder, slavery, prostitution, gambling, and alcohol. All in a day's work for the moneylenders of the ancient Near East! The moneylender families of ancient times had stolen the wealth and debauched the people in every city and village across all the ancient Near East. The merchant-moneylenders of the ancient Near East were nothing but criminals and perverts, very wealthy criminals and perverts. Limitless wealth bought them limitless power, just as it does for the moneylenders and swindling bankers of modern times.

However, the wealth of the merchant- moneylenders did not make them in any way a generous or a good people. Rather, their wealth from the Sumerian Swindle and business monopolies only allowed them to increase their despotism over every society among whom they lived. As wealthy loan sharks and criminals, they wallowed in their homosexual perversions and the degradation of their female slaves. Their wealth gave them the power to bribe high officials and corrupt both kings and priests. Through the arithmetical sleight-of-hand of the Sumerian Swindle and the juggling of account books – that to this very day are the basic techniques of modern business and finance – those ancient fiends amassed such huge piles of gold and silver that they were at a quandary of how to keep it both safe from confiscation by the kings and out of view from the poverty-stricken victims of their crimes.

Basically, anyone who lends money at interest gets back more than he lends. This is obvious. What is not at first obvious about moneylending, is that by getting back more than they lend at compound interest and then lending it out again, ad infinitum, eventually what they get back is ownership of the entire world and everybody on it. All for the offer of a paltry loan, no matter how small! This is a basic fact of banking and usury that is kept secret from the People even today.

However, swindling the entire world away from and enslaving the People living on it only works under two conditions (1) that the People do not know that they are being swindled and thus give away their wealth to the moneylenders out of a misunderstood, personal honesty and (2) the rich can only keep their wealth by taking it away from and then hiding it from the poor. Making money is only half of the method; keeping what you make is the other half. And to keep it, the gold and silver must be hidden, concealed, and transmuted into other kinds of wealth. Thus, the rich must be both clever and stealthy so that the poor do not take back what was stolen.

Terah, the Patriarch of the Babylonian moneylender guilds with main offices in the cities of Ur and Harran, founded a dynasty of moneylenders originally based in those two Babylonian cities. Terah conceived of a method for both swindling the world's wealth and then keeping what he and his relatives had stolen. But for that, he needed a powerful god to frighten both victims and thieves away from his treasure house. And he needed a base of operations immune from the confiscation of kings.

Both Ur and Harran boasted large temples dedicated to Sin, the Moon God, the god of the moneylenders, the god of darkness and secrecy, the god upon whose moon cycles were based the Babylonian calendar in which interest payments and mortgages were calculated. And since those two cities were the terminus of both the main international sea lane shipping (Ur) and the international overland trade routes of Mesopotamia and beyond (Harran), then those two cities were the logical choice for controlling the entire wealth of the ancient world. And yet, financial control alone was never enough for a banker because with money comes power. Those who have one, always desire the other.

Terah moved his main offices to Harran to take advantage of its tax-free status and its exemption of the citizens from military duty. And then he sent away Abram, his youngest son, to Canaan. Abram's wealth was hidden not just as silver among his goats but as the goats, themselves. In those days, a rich shepherd was one who had a lot of goats for sale or trade.

Among the poor Canaanites, silver and gold often was not as useful in trade as goats or sheep that could be eaten or the wool of sheep that could be spun and woven. To guard his son, Abram, and to secure the land around the proposed fortress city of Urusalem, Terah sent his armed guards and henchmen, the tribe of Binu-Yamina (Benjamin) to trade with the locals, buy property or to murder and steal what they could not buy and during the trade and bartering sessions, to collect the genealogies of the Hebrew tribes. Terah's scheme was to dispossess the Hebrews and Canaanites and to place his own family as the Patriarchs of all Hebrew tribes. It was a simply fraud of writing his own name into the records and so setting the entire future religion of Judaism firmly upon a criminal foundation of counterfeited and forged documents. A clever underpinning for the Biggest Lie Ever Told!

CHAPTER 2
BABYLONIA, CRADLE OF JUDAISM

The center of the merchant-moneylender power was not in Judah where there was nothing but scrub bushes and goats but in Babylonia and Assyria where the money was. Those areas of irrigated lands supported large populations as gifts of the Tigris and Euphrates rivers. And they were at the crossroads of international trade between India, Persia, Egypt, North Africa, Anatolia, and Europe with connections to Arabia, the Spice Islands and the Far East including, at a later time, China.

For nearly the entire civilized time period of the Sumerian, Babylonian and Assyrian Empires, the highlands of Palestine were mere country bumpkin remote goat farms. The crocodile still inhabited the Jordan River. The lion, tiger, bear, antelope, wild ox (*Bos primigenius*), the Mesopotamian fallow deer (*Dama mesopotamica*), the ostrich, crocodile, and hippopotamus, all gradually became extinct in Palestine from extensive hunting.

The Mediterranean Climatic Zone of Palestine is a narrow belt of land, no more than a couple of hundred miles wide. It is characterized by a short and wet winter, with an annual total of between 400 - 1200 mm (15.5 - 47.25 in.) of rainfall, and a long, dry summer. It originally supported a vegetation of evergreen woodlands and high scrub vegetation which has now largely been destroyed by processes of land clearance and warfare. Deforestation and the removal of vegetation has resulted in many eroded landscapes.

In certain regions, the regeneration of tree growth and vegetation has been inhibited by the widespread browsing and grazing activities of sheep and goats.

Once the grasses, bushes and trees were cut back, burned, and dug out, then the rains washed away the humus and topsoil, leaving Palestine what it is today, an arid and desert-like moon scape inhabited by Jewish and Muslim assholes.

Babylonia and Assyria were also arid regions but irrigation canals from the Euphrates and Tigris Rivers gave an abundance of grain and vegetables to support large populations. Grain was the major exportable trade item from this bread basket of the Near East.

But it was a trade good that was controlled by those who controlled the international markets and trade routes. Buying cheap grain in Mesopotamia – cheap grain raised by impoverished farmers and slaves – and shipping it to Persia or Arabia or to the Black Sea regions, allowed not only huge profits in grain but huge profits in metals. Grain, its price suppressed by the merchant-moneylenders of Mesopotamia through slave labor, cheap immigrant labor and tenant farming, could be traded for valuable copper in the grain-hungry lands of those merchant-moneylenders who controlled the copper monopolies in distant countries. Thus, a double profit could be made by buying expensive copper with cheap grain, essentially getting the copper for next to nothing.

Hungry men digging copper out of unyielding rock, look upon an abundance of grain kindlier than they do upon the inedible metal in their hands. International corporations and cartels kept the People impoverished at both ends of the trade routes, while the middlemen thrived. Many must suffer and die so that a few elite may live in luxury.

Always, the merchant-moneylenders made use of the Twenty-One Secret Frauds of the Sumerian Swindle. Secret Fraud #8 "Large crime families are more successful than lone criminals or gangs; international crime families are the most successful of all." Dealing in international trade requires many helpers. Who is more reliable than one's own family members working both ends of the trade routes? Secret Fraud #11 "Dispossessing the People brings wealth to the dispossessor, yielding the greatest profit for the bankers when the people are impoverished." Keeping wages low both for the farmer and the miner through subversion of labor by slavery, requires large networks of conspiring family members and cartel allies setting the labor rates and bribing the kings. But the technique only works when immigration of foreigners or slaves can be used to displace native labor so as to force the freemen into working like slaves. Secret Fraud #18 "When the source of goods is distant from the customers, profits are increased both by import and export." Controlling both ends of a trade route also means controlling the transportation between markets. So, the early Mesopotamian merchant-moneylenders were a well-organized gang who were related by marriage alliances and who operated ships, caravan pack animals and barges.

When we speak of the Ages of Man from the Stone Age, we speak of the Copper Age, the Bronze Age and the Iron Age for the simple reason that these basic metals made huge changes in society. The usual history books speak as if these metals benefited everybody, which they did. But they never speak about who benefited the most.

As you learned in Volume One (*The Sumerian Swindle*), the importation of copper into Mesopotamia was a monopoly of the big moneylenders and business moguls. It was a closed shop; no outsiders were allowed to deal on the wholesale level without being either related by marriage or to a partner via gifts and bribes. Either way, business could only be conducted by permission of the guild patriarchs and under license of the kings. Only the big money *awilum* [the Haves] could afford the expenses; and could negotiate the various territories of kings and tribal bandits; and could hire the ships to transport such a profitable and a heavy merchandise as copper and bulky grain. And since they also managed the loan rates and the secret frauds of the Sumerian Swindle, they could ensure that the copper mines were well supplied with slaves to be worked to death from not paying their debts to the moneylenders – cheap labor digging cheap copper to be sold for a premium price in Mesopotamia for cheap grain raised by starving farmers who were in debt to those same devils. When societies were ruled by the very rich and labored by the very poor, only the very rich prospered.

But copper, itself, had no value unless it could be sold and shipped to where it was manufactured into weapons, tools, and utensils of various sorts. Thus, the big import-export merchants and their relatives and partners within Mesopotamia, controlled the prices and availability of copper from the earliest times. With this control, they also managed a large percentage of and the outright monopolies over the manufacturing of copper into saleable goods such as pots and kettles, tools, and mace heads. This monopoly became even more ruthlessly administered after it was discovered how much more useful copper was when alloyed with tin and thus made into bronze.

Even without owning the copper mines, themselves, the Assyrian and Babylonian merchant- moneylenders could control the prices of copper simply by controlling the foreign merchants and the transportation of the raw copper. They leased or owned their own ships. They could hire large caravans of donkeys, servants, and armed guards. Copper ingots were shipped both overland from the Iranian plateau and from the Zagros mountains or by ships on the Persian Gulf from Magan (Oman), Dilmun (Bahrain), and Melukhkha (the Indus Valley) as well as from Crete. This was too perilous and expensive for the small-time operator. These international, import-export merchant-moneylenders were at the top of Mesopotamian commercial society. Everybody worked for them either directly or indirectly since they controlled the goods and prices for those goods upon which all society depended – metal and grain. In the Bronze Age, the same people who had controlled the copper supplies automatically controlled the even more important and valuable bronze. And they were not about to let anyone interfere with either their profits or their power. Certainly, the kings administered society in both peace and war – just as today – but it was the ones who controlled the gold and silver and the essential trade goods such as copper and bronze who controlled the kings – just as today.

Thus, the same families of merchant-moneylenders who controlled the basic supply of the metals for the Copper Age before 3000 BC, were directly in control of the entire Bronze Age in the ancient Near East beginning after 3000 BC. Up until the advent of the Iron Age around 1000 BC, these same super-wealthy families controlled the metals that created the Bronze Age. However, the copper from the Sinai Peninsula was controlled by Egypt, making that country an even greater target for subversion by the Hyksos and moneylenders of Babylonia than the lure of its gold alone would warrant, great though that hoard of gold was. Those particular Mesopotamian merchant-moneylenders became wealthy and powerful through the application of Secret Fraud #18 "When the source of goods is distant from the customers, profits are increased both by import and export" and Secret Fraud #21 "Control the choke points and master the body; strangle the choke points and kill the body." They controlled the sources and distribution of copper from all the mining regions as well as the grain supplies.

In economic terms, this was equivalent to the modern-day merchant-moneylenders who control the distribution of oil and gas and grain in the West. Today, these *awilum* [the Haves] wear pin-striped suits and drive Ferraris rather than wearing goat-hair garments and driving two oxen from a wagon. But their control of society was the same. The ratio of their wealth is comparable. And their ruthless greed is identical.

This was the beginning of the Bronze Age (~3000-1000 BC), a whole new era among Mankind where the strength and durability of bronze increased Man's power through better tools and more efficient weapons. It was a new age for Mankind and a new profit opportunity for the same Treasonous Class who controlled the bronze supplies because they controlled the copper supplies. Mankind took a step forward but the same parasites were sucking the blood from his veins.

In the Bronze Age, the metalworker was a specialist whose products transformed society by their effect on agriculture, warfare, and transportation. Anatolia had the richest copper ore deposits in the whole Near East. Though naturally occurring metallic copper was already known as early as the Neolithic period, the actual smelting technology was developed during the fourth millennium BC. Native copper could be found in numerous deposits in a belt of mineralization extending across southeastern Anatolia into northern Iraq. In the early third millennium BC the Sumerians suddenly switched to the Persian Gulf trade for copper since their extensive river and canal system made it easier to transport such a heavy item from overseas.

Considerable amounts of copper were involved in this trade. A single cuneiform text from Ur, dated to the reign of Rim-Sin of Larsa (1822-1763 BC), recorded the receipt of copper in Dilmun (Bahrain) which weighed, according to the standard of Ur, 18,333 kilograms. One-third of this copper was earmarked for delivery to Ea-nasir of Ur, a merchant who had close connections with the Dilmun and Magan (Oman) copper trade. Only the *awilum* [the Haves] could deal with such large quantities.

Bronze was an elitist metal not only because of the great distances that it traveled through monopolistic trade channels controlled by a very few capitalists, but because it required a certain technical ability to create molds and to pour the molten metal into those molds. When Bronze tools or weapons broke, they could not be repaired. So, the broken pieces could only be sold as scrap, transported to manufacturing sites where it was melted down and again poured into molds. Bronze was an international product controlled by a few industrial monopolists.

But with the discovery of iron, the Iron Age began.

Iron was found everywhere and once its methods of smelting and forging were disseminated, iron became the common man's metal, superior in strength and cutting power, lighter and easier to work than bronze and holding a sharper cutting edge. When iron implements broke, they could be welded back together and forged over bellows-charged charcoal fires and beat into shape with hammer and anvil, turning them into steel.

With the Iron Age, the elitist control of the Mesopotamian trade networks weakened. Iron plows opened up vast expanses of the European rocky soils and Russian heavy soils to farming. This increased food supplies and resulted in increased populations. Increased populations meant that the moneylenders could work the Sumerian Swindle upon many more people and thus increase their profits through mercantile pursuits including usury, slavery, and warfare. But as the ages passed, the ones who controlled the copper, tin, gold, silver, iron, and bronze, remained the same families of schemers. Through multiple wives, incest and adoption, the same Semitic families perpetuated themselves and maintained their control of these lucrative monopolies and cartels in league with other merchant-moneylender families centered in other cities and other countries. Even across international borders, it was their business interests that bound them together and these were often sealed with marriage contracts. The wealth, the properties, the ships, the mines, the manufacturing facilities, the moneylending activities, the slave markets, the brothels, the taverns, etc., were all operated by family members or trusted cartel- or guild-member allies of the family.

All businesses were kept in the family and not allowed to dissipate through deaths and bequeaths because they used the Semitic moneylender's ploy of incestuously marrying their near relatives. So, when one marriage partner died, the other did not take the family fortune back to their parent family because husband and wife came from the same, extended family of incestuous Semites, marrying their sisters and nieces so that they could keep all their gold.

With such methods as polygamy, incestuous marriages and adoption, these families persisted through the ages while promoting only the most ruthless and sly sons to be heads of their extended gangs of business moguls.

Later examples of those crime families are such banking firms as the House of Egibi in Babylon and the Ea-iluta-bani family of Borsippa during the Neo-Babylonian and Persian periods. They operated throughout Babylonia and even into Iran. Besides operating the Sumerian Swindle for their own profit, they acted as real estate managers by renting fields for absentee landlords, rich landlords who had already swindled the farmers and needed someone else to collect the rents so that they could avoid the very real possibility of being murdered by their impoverished victims. Landlords whose business investments were so extensive that family members alone were not enough to manage the estates, hired out the management to a banking firm when necessary.

For the dispossessed and under-employed people of the ancient Near East who had suffered from two thousand years of the Sumerian Swindle engineered by the ruthless and insatiable greed of the merchant- moneylenders, wages were kept low and rents were kept high. For those who had no mud-brick house of their own; the least they could expect to pay in rent was half a silver shekel per year, but the average price was a whole shekel (8 grams of silver). On taking possession they paid a deposit which sometimes amounted to one-third of the whole sum, the remainder being due at the end of the year. The leases lasted, as a rule, merely a twelve-month, though sometimes they were extended for terms of greater length, such as two, three, or even eight years. During this Old Babylonian Period (2000 - 1750 BC), the average wages paid for hired labor was 10 shekels per year for a twelve-to-fourteen-hour day. But actual wages gradually were reduced to two liters of bread and two liters of beer per day, barely enough to share with a wife. The very rich knew how to starve the very poor into submission.

The archives of the House of Murashu of Nippur have also been found. They were in the banking business in the last half of the fifth century BC.

Working in league with the kings, they rented royal lands to tenant farmers and acted as agents in converting agricultural profits into metal. The Egibi and the Murashu families dominated the entire region. Although most of the archives found so far, were from the beginning of the Persian period (the latter part of the sixth century BC), these archives were often a continuation of those begun under the Neo-Babylonian kings. Remember, it was traditional from the days of Sumeria that archives and records were ceremonially destroyed and stomped into dust when they had been fulfilled. That the extant archives are continuations from an earlier era only means that the same system was perpetuated from the Sumerian times of 3000 BC. These private archives showed a large sector of the population was involved in financial and commercial operations. Like the bankers and financiers of today, they did no actual work but merely manipulated money and people for their own profit.

Once coinage was invented which increased the speed and convenience of commerce, private banking flourished on a scale previously unknown in Babylonia, and from the late 6th century onwards the dynastic banking houses of the Egibi family in Babylon and the Murashu in Nippur, made colossal fortunes by lending money at exorbitant rates of interest.

In regions to the west, the Babylonian practice of charging interest on certain types of loan was regarded as ungentlemanly. That is, it was "ungentlemanly" for *awilum* [the Haves] to charge each other interest but it was business-as-usual to charge interest to everyone else. Thus, this letter from Ugarit (on the Syrian coast): "Give the 140 shekels which are still outstanding from your own money but do not charge interest between us – we are both gentlemen!" The *awilum* [the Haves] made a profit from everyone, but among themselves, they loaned each other silver and gold interest-free.

Just as today, the moneylenders had seized control of society and maintained that control through their extended family connections. But whether Assyrian, Babylonia, Phoenician, Arabian, Yemenite or Hebrew, they were all working the same Sumerian Swindles and monopoly import-export. They all belonged to the trade guilds that specialized in these occupations because no one in Mesopotamia could do business without the help and the permission of the monopolist clans who had been there for millennia.

They all knew one another either personally or through correspondence. In the first place, all business in Mesopotamia was based on import-export since there was nothing other than water, dirt, sunshine, and agriculture possible in those dusty plains lacking natural resources. Anything other than that had to be imported. Import-export was only possible on a large scale.

Travel in summer was usually undertaken at night.

For security purposes to avoid bandits, merchants usually formed joint caravans. In mountains and deserts, guides and armed escorts were hired. The track taken by a road depended on the locations of water, food supplies, mountain passes, river fords, and ferries. The rise of a new political center deflected some roads at the height of their power.

All these conditions and events were discussed and the information shared and made available at the guild halls of the merchant associations, just as they are today. Having the latest geographical, political, and commercial information often meant the difference between good profits and total disaster. But all these merchant associations were in competition with one another. The individuals from these divergent associations were divided in their religious loyalties among the many and various gods and temples of their cities. Thus, the secrets of one guild would be shared with the brothers of another guild who followed a different god. There were many business guilds. Every city had at least one for the moneylenders in addition to those representing the various other occupations of merchants and craftsmen. Doing business without being a member of a guild was impossible, the guild patriarchs and their strong-arm henchmen guaranteed that and the laws of the kings enforced such uniformity. Strong arm enforcement of trade sources, trade channels and both the wholesale and retail trade, was the venue of each guild since there were no laws to protect people from violent tactics. The merchant- moneylenders could afford body guards and small gangs of enforcers.

Business was standardized across the entire ancient Near East. All values were based on shekels of silver.

So, whether businessmen came from Babylonia, Elam, Iran, Phoenicia, or Assyria, they all practiced the same business methods handed down from the earliest times from Sumeria. This included careful control of labor and the hours worked versus the stingy handful of grain paid to a worker for a twelve-hour day.

The merchant-moneylenders kept careful count of the time that their laborers worked. The foreman and his scribe were always early to record the arrival and departure time of the workers. An Ur III archive from around 3000 BC from the temple at Ur, showed that a number of different crafts were responsible to a single administrative officer. Labor was recruited and supervised. For example, texts recorded the amounts produced by potters, listing the exact time needed to make each type of pot. This was also true for other crafts, such as the textile industry, in which types and grades of cloth were precisely listed and recorded together with the work days required. Materials were regularly recycled in palaces and temples. The temple supplied raw materials which were kept in a special storehouse for manufacture. Finished goods were distributed to their destinations. Furnaces were designated specifically for the recycling of metal into assayed ingots which would be redistributed as needed; both archaeological and textual sources have confirmed this process. And all it was supported by accurate book keeping by professional scribes.

The Ur craft archive listed raw materials and finished goods, both balanced by records of labor. Some daily accounts showed that the same craftsmen came to work regularly, though occasionally they were recorded as "sick" or just absent. The rations issued to state employees in the Ur III period consisted mostly of grain, wool or cloth, and oil, but other commodities were sometimes included. The texts clearly differentiated between workers according to age and sex. The level of remuneration was correlated with the kinds of service performed, so that foremen of labor teams, or workers on better quality cloth, received more pay. Long-term workers, whether freemen or slaves, received rations on a monthly basis. The wool ration issued to temple employees of the third millennium BC implied that these workers were expected to spin and weave their own garments. For example, 600 tons of wool were turned over to a factory at Lagash, where over 6,000 workers toiled, the majority being women and children. After the Ur III period, there was less evidence for large-scale centrally controlled production. This is because the numerous private and family businesses began to control all trade through their guilds. As in modern times, the merchant-moneylenders had bribed the officials into allowing them to buy up public work places from the temple factories and to "privatize" industry. No longer were the people working for God, doing the common labor to benefit them all, but they were working for the *tamkarum* [merchant- moneylenders] doing the common labor to benefit the merchants and moneylenders. It was a very sophisticated system of factories, crafts, farms, and transportation monopolies, all operated by related families and interlocking trade guilds. The modern world has basically the same ancient system, only more complicated, and operated by much sneakier and more ruthless merchant-moneylenders.

Mesopotamian trade was run by family firms. The head of the family lived in a large city such as Ashur, and a junior member of the family would be the resident agent in the guild at an outlying trade center such as Kanesh. The family capitalized these ventures, but sometimes partnerships were formed to raise the necessary capital. The merchant colonies were self-governing, but under the aegis of local princes to whom they paid taxes. The guilds had their own legal status separate from the rest of society. Besides merchants involved in large-scale trade, there were plenty of retail merchants and jobbers who operated as small-scale peddlers. Like in modern times, trade was organized like a tree where the source of wholesale goods distributed to smaller and smaller sub-contractors all the way out to the door-to-door salesman riding his donkey into the distant villages.

After 1850 BC the caravan traffic between Assyria and its trade colonies in eastern Asia Minor, centered at Kanesh, was documented by thousands of records and letters from the houses of the merchant colony at Kanesh. These records described the resolution of disputes between Kanesh merchants and their counterparts at the home base at Ashur, the formation of partnerships to provide capital, the adjustment of business debts between both parties, family business such as inheritance arrangements, requests for assistance in private or business matters, and reports of taking interest and compound interest.

Tablets also documented events from their journeys and distribution of goods within Anatolia. So, you see, there was no difference between them and the intelligence level of modern businessmen. The levels of business sophistication were comparable.

The Assyrians lived outside the walled city of Kanesh in their own quarter, called the *karum*, a word from Babylonia originally meaning "quay" or "wharf," where canal traffic was unloaded and business transacted. But whether in Assyria or Babylonia, a *karum* referred to the association of merchants with its own legal status, a kind of trade board, and was applied by the Assyrians there in the heart of Anatolia even though there were no navigable rivers or harbors.

The traders were royal envoys as well, bringing valuable gifts from one ruler to the next. Treaties guaranteed their safety. Luxury items were important for maintaining the prestige and position of the royal palaces and temples. Because of the expense and risk involved in obtaining these rare materials, their acquisition remained almost exclusively the business of kings and queens, powerful governors, and wealthy temple estates, all whom depended upon the merchants for supply; the same merchants whose guilds and international trade channels extended far beyond the view of kings; the same merchants who could supply rare imported luxuries not only at a high price, but also as a way of soliciting kingly favors.

All these merchants practiced Secret Fraud #18 of Sumerian Swindle: "When the source of goods is distant from the customers, profits are increased both by import and export." So, a rare and beautiful oyster pearl that had cost no more than a basket of barley and a couple of metal fishhooks to the merchant stationed at the trade center on Dilmun (Bahrain), might carry a price in silver that only a prince or a king in distant Anatolia or Assyria could afford.

Small, easily concealed, items with a high mark-up value were especially esteemed by the merchants. Not only could they be smuggled past the tax collector and the thieves, but they produced enormous profits in a tiny cargo space. Certainly, all imported goods have a huge mark-up from their original source. But this same pearl could be used to bribe a prince or a king into declaring or, even better, into passing a law giving the merchant and his family of thieves exclusive rights to some commercial scam or some other advantage that no one else had. Thus, incredible commercial and monetary advantages could be had by bribing officials.

And though the prince or other official believed that he had accepted a rare and expensive pearl in exchange for betraying his people to the merchant-moneylenders, in fact, he had betrayed his people and allowed these Monsters to swindle his entire nation for a total cost to them of a basket of grain and a couple of fishhooks. Secret Fraud #18 has many uses.

Bribery was a way of life throughout the entire history of the ancient Near East even into modern times. There was no sense of moral obligation of leaders protecting their people. The appointment of officials was a system of patronage and nepotism. A provincial governor considered his province to be his personal property, from which he tried to obtain as much profit as possible. The concept of "integrity of office" did not exist; bribes or gifts were routinely given to influence a decision. Public office was a potential source of personal wealth, and provincial governorships were the most lucrative offices. It was not that the ancient societies were corrupt, but rather, that they had been corrupted. After many millennia of the rich getting richer by stealing from the poor, the old temple-based teachings of the priests and monks had been set aside by those who controlled the wealth. By controlling the wealth, even the vilest and most evil could pay the price of whoever would do their bidding.

The beer halls and taverns had long been under the control of the merchant-moneylenders. In these places, profits were not only made in excess but the laborers could be anaesthetized from their hard life of poverty with cheap beer and prostitutes – cheap beer and prostitutes, all a spin-off of the Sumerian Swindle. Clay bas-relief plaques excavated from these taverns depict women leaning against a mud-brick tower, perhaps the town walls, where prostitutes usually lived and worked – women desperate to sell their bodies for the price of beer and bread. In some tavern scenes, one or more persons are shown drinking from vases or cups. The taverns, run by the women known as *sabitum* [alewife-moneylenders] were houses of pleasure where men drank, listened to music, and had intercourse with prostitutes. The walls of the tap room were decorated with clay plaques of naked women performing erotic acts. Ishtar, the goddess of love, was the patron of taverns. And, not coincidentally, she was one of the gods of the moneylenders. The consort of the Hebrew-Canaanite god, Yahweh, was Ishtar (a.k.a., Asherah or Astarte).

Thus, it is very clear that the people who operated the Sumerian Swindle throughout Mesopotamia, the people who controlled the silver and gold, the copper and bronze, the grain supplies, the control of labor, the manufacturing, the wholesale and retailing of both finished goods and raw materials, the import-export of all trade goods, the creation and sale of slaves and promotion of slavery, the taverns, brothels, brewing and wine production, the weaving and garment industry, the importation of luxury items and the bribery of officials, were all the same clans and families of conspirators. They were known, in general, as the *tamkarum* [merchant-moneylenders]. They belonged to the highest social class known as the *awilum* [the Haves]. And they considered themselves to be "gentlemen," those who did no work but bought and sold and invested and hired others to do the work for them. They were very ruthless in extracting profits from the *muskenum* [the Have-Nots] and would enslave entire families who fell under their debt. But among their own social class of "gentlemen," they gave each other loans without interest. By the time Terah, the Babylonian, had envisioned his own special swindle, these *awilum* [Haves] were an entire class of people who had been betraying and robbing everybody around them for over two thousand years because "that is how it had always been."

The actual records of their activities, written on the enduring rock-hard clay tablets, were excavated by the archaeologists. They show the innumerable promissory notes, the receipted accounts, the contracts of sale and purchase – those cunningly drawn up deeds which have been deciphered by the hundreds – reveal to us a people greedy of gain, exacting, litigious, and almost exclusively absorbed by material concerns. These were the kinds of people whom Terah, the patriarch of the moneylender guilds of Ur and Harran represented. These were people who wrote extremely binding contracts for their victims and their business partners. They knew how to write an air-tight deed or a business contract so that there would be no doubt as to who was required to do what, and who would benefit and who would pay, all with the appropriate times and amounts stipulated and carefully recorded.

They called themselves "gentlemen," the *awilum* [the Haves]. They were never in debt even to one another because they only charged the enslaving interest of the Sumerian Swindle to the *muskenum* [the Have-Nots], those working and suffering people for whom they had only contempt. The *muskenum* lower classes truly had nothing that they could call their own. They labored on the farms that the "gentlemen" had stolen. They bought their beer in the taverns that the "gentlemen" owned and screwed the whores who were the slave property of the "gentlemen." The wages that the "gentlemen" paid them was only grain to live on and it was never enough to feed their wives and children because the "gentlemen" brought in immigrant aliens and slaves to compete with and dispossess the resident farmers. And when a farmer went broke from the high interest rates, the "gentlemen" sold the farm to foreigners who pushed aside the local people with the help of the king's soldiers. Then, these "gentlemen" put their slaves to work for no pay other than a piece of bread. What else could the free working man do except work for the same wages as a slave or hire himself out to the king as a soldier, a soldier who would be ordered to dispossess his own people if so ordered by a king who had been corrupted and bribed by the "gentlemen"?

What little that the "Have-Nots" made with their labor, they had to give to the "gentlemen" to whom they owned interest. And this debt could never be repaid under the Sumerian Swindle of compound interest because the workers never made enough to pay it off. And the skyrocketing interest soon made it impossible to ever pay it off. So, they were trapped by an eternal debt and by an unending labor owed to those high and mighty "gentlemen" who would steal their wives and children and clap them into slave collars instead of accepting their paltry bowls of grain as their only ability to pay.

Those "gentlemen" had such disdain for the laboring and indebted muskenum classes who would fall at their feet, bowing and pleading for mercy, that the word muskenum [the Have-Nots] did not fully express their contempt. No, that name would not do at all. A new name was coined from their Aramaic language and used privately among themselves. It was standardized in the Hebrew language to fully define those people who were beneath the contempt of the moneylenders. And it is a word that is used to this very day. These "gentlemen" – behind the backs of their victims or laughing up their sleeves as they spoke – began to define their victims and to speak about them in private among themselves as the goyim, a word that means "lowly insects" or "stupid cattle."

And so, by the time that Terah had conceived his clever hoax, the ancient Sumerian class of citizens known as the tamkarum [merchant-moneylenders], belonging to the upper class of kings, priests, and administrators, who were all together known as the awilum [the Haves], no longer looked upon the muskenum [the Have-Nots] as fellow humans who owed them money. They no longer looked upon them as fellow humans whom they had purposely reduced to starvation, prostitution, drunkenness, poverty, and slavery. To refer to someone as a muskenum [Have- Not] no longer contained the contempt, derision, distain, hatred, and malice that these upper classes of moneylenders and merchants – these "gentlemen" – had for the ragged, dirty, malnourished, poverty- stricken slum-dwellers who had been the victims of the moneylenders' very profitable Sumerian Swindle and who had arrived at their wretched condition because of these very same parasitic "gentlemen".

To keep the goyim (lowly insects, stupid cattle) forever in his debt and to put himself and his tribe of moneylenders and con artists at the top of the social and commercial heap, Terah and his scribes devised the Biggest Lie Ever Told. It was a binding, one-way contract based upon two thousand years of merchant-moneylender cunning. But it was more than a legal contract because it also used the Aramaic and Semitic sorcery known as abracadabra, which means "I create as I speak," that is, whatever lie was told came into creation because the speaker created it in his imagination and uttered it through his mouth. In this case, what was written as the "word of God" became the word of God simply because no one could say otherwise. With abracadabra, the priests of Terah's Temple could declare any law and that law became binding because it was declared to be a "law of God." Laws give power to the lawgivers; so write your own laws and gain all the power. And when – Abracadabra! the laws are declared to be the "laws of God" then Abracadabra! – those who write the laws have the power of God.

What happens when greedy, vicious, deceitful, malicious, murderers, rapists and pedophiles speak forth with an abracadabra that says, "This is the word of God"? Then, their evils become concealed behind the alleged "words of God." They are protected by an illusion.

Terah, the Babylonian Patriarch of the moneylender guilds of Ur and Harran, devised the Greatest Lie Ever Told. His family of swindling moneylenders and thieves, polished and perfected that Great Lie over the next three thousand years until it became the Judaism that we know today. Written into the Contract of this genealogical swindle is Terah's name at the very root of the tribal tree, the name of the founder of Judaism – a monster of Babylon.

To establish a home base for his new swindle, a place where all his stolen treasures could be stored and protected from fellow thieves and kings, Terah sent his youngest son, Abraham, to Canaan in order to swindle the property of the Canaanites. And why Canaan? Because located in that inconsequential territory was a rocky promontory surrounded by ravines where a bank could be built inside of a stone temple, surrounded by stone walls, protected by cruel, cunning, perverted creatures with hearts of stone. And to frighten away all who would even so much as look at his piles of gold, Terah conjured up with abracadabra, a monster of a god who would bring havoc and death to the world through the connivance of his little devils wearing beanies and sidelocks while pretending to be holy.

CHAPTER 3

THE CORRUPTING IMPACT OF JUDAISM
ON TRUE RELIGION

It is easy for modern people to look down upon the ancient people as being unsophisticated and primitive. But, as demonstrated in Volume One, there is no difference between them and us. Our entire civilization is built upon what the ancient people invented and we still use many of their inventions today, five thousand years later, without change from their original function. The wheel, mathematics, iron, brass, weaving, metal casting, brickmaking, plowing, and the list goes on for a long length – including the ancient Sumerian Swindle of both simple and compound interest on a loan, used today by the bankers to enslave the world and to bring us endless impoverishment and warfare. So, we must not assume that the ancient days are gone, because we are still the same people, using the same kinds of inventions that were conceived by Mankind at the end of the recent Ice Age.

However, it would be well to more thoroughly understand the kinds of people who developed that false religion and betrayal of Mankind known to us as Judaism, because the Jews are the same devils today that they always were, only worse! Understanding *who they were* and *why* they did what they did will allow us to accurately analyze the strategies of their demented descendants in the light of present times. Just because the ancient citizens of Sumeria, Babylonia and Assyria lived in cities built of mud bricks does not mean that they were primitive people. Even today, mud bricks are really the best building materials for certain arid climates, having served as the basis of advanced civilizations for over five thousand years. Mud bricks are still used today in modern buildings around the world.

Of course, they did not have paper in those early days, but relied upon damp clay tablets to write their letters and documents with incised cuneiform script. Once dried or baked, those clay tablets made more durable archives for documents than even modern inventions in the computer age have been able to equal. Translations of their letters give us great insight into those ancient people in ways that our modern archaeologists seem to have overlooked. The archaeologists have done Mankind a great service in the work that they do, so it is no demerit if they themselves do not understand some of the artifacts that they have excavated from the ancient cities.

The following translation of a clay tablet inscribed a thousand years before Christ tells of the unassailable position of the moneylenders in Mesopotamian society. As is usual for the times, it was written by one scribe to be read aloud by the receiving scribe. So it begins with the standard form of "Tell so-and-so this."

"Tell Ahu-kinum that Awil-Amurrim sends the following message: Immediately after you left for the trip, Imgur-Sin arrived here and claimed: 'He owes me one-third of a mina of silver.' He took your wife and your daughter as pledges. Come back before your wife and your daughter die from the work of constantly grinding barley while in detention. Please, get your wife and your daughter out of this."

The moneylenders had a legal right to enslave even the wives and children of those to whom they had lent silver. Notice that *only the word* of the moneylender was necessary to seize those women. But, by Mesopotamian law, his word had to backed up with a clay tablet documenting the terms of the loan. So, Imgur-Sin was within his rights by the ancient laws traditional within all of Mesopotamia; laws that gave the merchant-moneylenders power over everyone else. Imgur-Sin's name shows that *Sin*, the Moon God, was his god, the god of the moneylenders.

And from the moneylenders most people had to borrow at one time or another. The merchant-moneylenders kept prices high and wages low – just as the merchants and bankers do today – not because they were qualified or entitled to do so, but because with their clever and deceitful engineering of the law and of commerce, they were able to swindle entire ancient societies.

However lucrative a man's occupation might be, in the artificially created poverty of Mesopotamia, both tradespeople and workers were obliged to run into debt to supplement their means. When they had once fallen into the hands of the moneylender, the exorbitant interest which they had to pay kept them a long time in his power. If there was nothing to meet it when the bill fell due, it had to be renewed under still more disastrous conditions, because the pledge given was usually the homestead, or the slave who assisted in the trade, or the garden which supplied food for the family. The debtor was reduced to the extreme of misery if he could not satisfy his creditors. This swindle of simple and compound interest was not, moreover, confined to the towns; it raged with equal violence in the country, and the farmers also became its victims. Just as it is today.

The following cuneiform letter shows how silver was transferred. Is this any different than in modern times?

"Tell Lustammar-Zababa that Belanum Hammurapi sends the following message: 'As to Sin-anaDammar-lisu, the son of Maninum, whom the enemy has taken prisoner: deposit ten shekels of silver in the temple of *Sin* for the merchant dealing with his case, and thus get him released.'"

The ancient temples where everyone worshiped their gods were also the banks of ancient times. The only difference between the two is that the modern banks of today want to be the temples where everyone worships the banker. Notice also that in matters of prisoner ransom it was not the warring government who ransomed its people from the enemy, it was a private affair between the relatives of the prisoner with a merchant-moneylender acting as the middle man. War has always been a particularly profitable investment for the merchants and moneylenders, from the most ancient times until today. Notice that the temple of *Sin*, the god of the moneylenders, was where the silver was deposited and where the transfer of the funds was obtained by the merchant in the case. How could a mere merchant handle a case of prisoner transfer and ransom unless he had connections within the camps of both warring parties? The merchant was obviously a middleman, but whom did he work for?

The following letter was written on a clay tablet excavated from the Assyrian merchant colony in Anatolia (~1300 BC).

> "A message from Silla-Labbum and Elani: 'Tell Puzur-Assur, Amua, and Assur-samsi: Thirty years ago you left the city of Assur. You have never made a deposit since, and we have not recovered one shekel of silver from you, but we have never made you feel bad about this. Our tablets have been going to you with caravan after caravan, but no report from you has ever come here. We have addressed claims to your father. But we have not been claiming one shekel of your private silver. Please, do come back right away; should you be too busy with your business, deposit the silver for us. Remember, we have never made you feel bad about this matter but we are now forced to appear, in your eyes, acting as gentlemen should not. Please, do come back right away or deposit the silver for us. If not, we will send you a notice from the local ruler and the police, and thus put you to shame in the assembly of the merchants. You will also cease to be one of us."

This letter indicates that by 1300 BC, among the merchant-moneylender guilds of Mesopotamia, there was a system of interest-free loans based solely upon the trust among the guild members. A loan made thirty years previously would appear to be lost. And yet, these merchant-moneylenders still had hope that by appealing to the three brothers' sense of honor as *gentlemen* (that is, as *akum*, the leisure class in Mesopotamian society), the loan would be repaid. This letter differentiates between the business silver and the private silver of these merchants, carefully keeping the two separate. And most importantly, it indicates that silver could be deposited in the temple treasury of one city and transferred to the temple treasury of another city. Thus, at a very early time, all of the attributes of a modern bank had already been invented and housed within the temple of a god.

These various methods of business, finance and banking had been developed in Sumeria beginning around 3500 BC. What was missing was the criminal genius necessary to turn such an ancient system of banking into the fine-tuned system of larceny that it is today. Such a criminal genius was Terah, the father of Abraham and patriarch of the moneylender guilds of Ur and Harran.

Almost every major religion has been established by a single individual. Zoroastrianism, Odinism, Hinduism, Buddhism, Christianity, Taoism, Islam and many others can be traced back to a single individual as their founder or primary theoretician. So, it should not come as a surprise that Judaism can be traced back to Terah and his Babylonian family of merchant-moneylenders.

From Ur in Babylonia and Harran in Assyria, Terah and his gang of moneylenders, merchants, strong-arm enforcers, smugglers and slave drivers were in a position to control the entire economy of the ancient Near East, buying, selling, loaning and enslaving both kings and common people. But, certain problems stood in the way of actually achieving this.

Terah had identified Fifteen Secret Problems of the Moneylenders that had prevented his guild of thieving loan sharks from completely owning the ancient world. Those recurring problems had become crystal clear during the Hyksos invasion of Egypt and during the subsequent expulsion of that bandit army.

The Fifteen Secret Problems of the Babylonian Moneylenders were as follows:

Problem #1: Wealth attracts robbers, so how can it be hidden?

Problem #2: The gods do not protect *tamkarum* (merchant-moneylender) wealth.

Problem #3: When the strongest city is not strong enough, where can one go for safety?

Problem #4: Wealth escapes into the gods' temples.

Problem #5: Guild members follow different gods.

Problem #6: Close relatives are lured away by the gods.

Problem #7: What keeps people loyal?

Problem #8: Genealogies link tribes, but without a root.

Problem #9: The kings gain wealth by taxing both rich and poor.

Problem #10: Kings are targets, so it is better to hold the target in your hands than to be a king.

Problem #11: We *tamkarum* (merchant-moneylenders) promote warfare and thereby profit enormously. But while inveigling others to do the fighting, how can we avoid military service without invoking the wrath of our victims?

Problem #12: Armies are expensive, so how can they be induced to fight for free?

Problem #13: When conquering a country, how can it be secured? (Assyrian deportation? Genocide? Slavery?)

Problem #14: Moneylenders are despised. Yet, how can we have honor and prestige?

Problem #15: The Sumerian Swindle is both a secret and a
      mystical gift of the *tamkarum* gods. How can it be protected
      forever as a possession of the *tamkarum* families alone?

The solutions to these problems were both ingenious and simple for the
greedy, vicious and ruthless father of Abraham.

Solution for Problem #1: Wealth attracts robbers, so how can it be hidden?

In the ancient world, there were only two safe places to hide gold and silver
from thieves – either buried in the ground or deposited in the temple treasuries.
Anyone could bury their hoard in the ground. But such a location had the disadvantages of being discovered by thieves and of being inconvenient to the
miser. In order for gold and silver to grow in amount, they needed to be fluid
and easily added to or subtracted from. Any dirt or dust clinging to them would
instantly alert potential thieves as to their possible hiding place. Also, if the
gold or silver were too thoroughly concealed, it could not be accessed for
business use without taking time-wasting precautions. In the event of the death
of its owner, the hoard would be lost to his progeny. So, temple treasuries were
the most convenient and the safest place from thieves. The treasure could be
deposited and withdrawn as necessary. It could be bequeathed to his heirs. And
it was protected by the king and his army, by the temple guards, by the priests,
and by the mighty god of the temple, all four of whom must be as violent and
bloodthirsty as possible.

"How much treasure is there and where is it hidden?" These have always
been the two most important questions to which thieves and burglars want the
answer. Is there enough there to make the effort and danger of getting it
worthwhile? Congruently, these have also been the favorite questions of the
kings' tax collectors. "How much is there and where is it hidden?" Both
thieves and kings have always been the banker's greatest fear, second only to the
fear that the People will rise up and hang the moneylenders for their swindles.

Certainly, the People realized that the bankers and moneylenders betrayed and defrauded them. But as you saw in Volume I, *The Sumerian Swindle*, the moneylenders neutralized this danger with restrictive laws enforced by
the kings' soldiers that made stealing from or murdering a moneylender into a
high crime – appealing though it was. However, no laws of the king or even
platoons of armed guards could entirely protect a banker from thieves. Therefore, armed might is less important to a banker than sly sneakiness and deception. Shrewdness for a banker is more profitable than wisdom. *Concealing the
treasure is more important than guarding it.*

Even in modern times, the armed guards, bulletproof delivery trucks and
vaults with foot-thick walls of solid steel protected by every electronic, acous-
tic and laser technology, are still no guarantee that thieves cannot steal the
banker's treasure. No matter how sophisticated, no technological protection

has ever proven to be superior to the determined penetration of relentless thieves and burglars who know how much and where a treasure is located.

But, if thieves can't find the treasure chest, they can't steal the treasure. True this is in modern times, but how much truer was this in ancient times when the moneylender's walls were not made of steel, but packed mud, and the bullion and gemstones were not hidden in bulletproof delivery vans, but in leather packs and clay jars tied to the backs of donkeys and camels? Even if his hoard was protected by no more than a rock rolled over a hole in the ground which any child could unbury, as long as no one knew where the hoard was located, not even an army of thieves could steal it. And so, for the bankers and moneylenders, armed might has always been second to skill in secrecy, concealment, lies, deception and stealth. Bankers have always been lying deceivers.

Although tax collectors may know where the treasure is hidden, if they do not know how much is there, then they can't tax it. So, the tax man backed by the might of the king's army had both a counting house where some of his wealth was made available for accounting and a secret lair where the unknown and untaxed wealth accumulated from his secret business ventures. Bankers have always been swindlers, smugglers and thieves. This is true of modern bankers and this was true of the ancient bankers and this was especially true for the most wicked moneylender and sly deceiver of them all – Terah of Ur and his son, Abraham, who developed a system of finance that hid not only the gold and silver, but concealed the entire bank as well.

Solution for Problem #2: The gods do not protect *tamkarum* (merchant-moneylender) wealth.

No matter which gods the moneylenders and merchants of Babylonia and Assyria prayed to, and no matter how many sacrifices and gifts to the temples they made, eventually the bullion that was on deposit in the temples was stolen. The mighty kings would sometimes dare to insult the gods by confiscating the temple treasuries, or the soldiers of an invading army would loot the cities and temples. Thus, it was obvious to Terah and his family of con artists that the gods of Mesopotamia were not partial to the moneylenders, because their fortunes were just as apt to be stolen as anyone else's who entrusted it on deposit with the gods at the temples.

So, Terah realized that if the gods of Mesopotamia were not partial to the merchant-moneylenders, then perhaps the merchant-moneylenders were worshiping the wrong gods. To the thinking of an ancient man, it was obvious that *some* god *somewhere* loved the moneylenders because *how else could they be so blessed* with the fantastic profits from the compound interest of the Sumerian Swindle, and in such abundance, and with so little effort? In addition, this unknown god *blessed the moneylenders with wealth wherever they went.* All of the moneylenders from India to the Pillars of Hercules, were making fantastic fortunes. So, this god had to be a very powerful god, since he also had power to bless the merchant-moneylenders throughout the known world.

Therefore, Terah and his merchant-moneylender family must find the god of the moneylenders and worship that god alone, while abandoning those gods of Mesopotamia who did not protect them or their treasure. But where could that god be found? Since their profits from moneylending could be made everywhere, then obviously the god who was blessing the moneylenders was also everywhere. Thus, no matter where they built a temple, their god would bless them there. The most secure place for their gold would therefore be the holiest place in the holiest land for the god of the moneylenders.

Solution for Problem #3: When the strongest city is not strong enough, where can one go for safety?

The cities of Babylonia and Akkad had all been overrun and looted many times during the two thousand years of their existence. Their walls and buildings and temples were constructed of mud bricks. Though such materials were solid, they were not durable enough to withstand a determined army, armed only with crowbars, picks and shovels. Even the biggest mud brick cities in Mesopotamia were not strong enough to protect the treasures of the moneylenders. A stronger location was required, a location where stone and solid rock could be used as building material. The armies in those days could break through the mud brick walls of any city in Mesopotamia, but none of them at that time had the technology to break through solid rock. Thus, Terah concluded that a city made of stone would have to be founded somewhere to protect his growing treasures, a city of stone built in a defensible location.

Solution for Problem #4: Wealth escapes into the gods' temples.

This was a continuing problem for Terah and his fellow Patriarchs of the moneylender guilds in Ur and Harran. Both family wealth and company wealth would be donated to the temples by religious family members who sought the good graces of the gods. Gold and silver that could have been used to generate more gold and silver by lending it at interest was simply given away to the gods. Terah realized that if he could establish his own temple, dedicated to the god of the moneylenders and safely located somewhere inside a rock fortress, all of that donated treasure would become his. It would not be siphoned off by religious family members into the temples of unsympathetic gods, because it would be donated to his own temple and to his own god and controlled by his own family-owned organization.

Besides having a secure place for his personal treasure, Terah wanted a temple where the people could make donations of their silver and their gold to *his* god, deposited into *his* treasury. All of this free bullion could also be loaned out at interest! With his own temple and his own god, Terah could protect his wealth as well as gain the wealth that would otherwise be donated to other temples.

Solution for Problem #5: Guild members follow different gods.

When the moneylender guild members follow different gods, they dilute the corporate power of the guild. Different gods have different festivals, which interrupts the coordination of business and siphons off funds to a variety of temples. Common to every religion in the ancient Near East, no work was done and no business was transacted during religious festivities. So, when the various members of his guild were off at different times, celebrating festivities to different gods, business came to a standstill. Having many guild members absent and away at different times celebrating a variety of festivals was very inefficient for making profits.

Also, the worship of a variety of gods did not allow either his family or his business the harmony necessary for ultimate secrecy. Moneylenders are privy to secrets of kings and high officials as well as to the affairs of ordinary borrowers and clients. Petty jealousies and arguments between guild members over religious doctrine could easily lead to the revealing of secrets as a way of harming an opponent. Therefore, for the sake of business secrets and internal harmony, Terah determined that the members of his moneylender guild should all worship the same god.

But, the god of his own guild both in Ur and in Harran was *Sin*, the Moon God, who had proven to be a god who didn't especially care about the wealth of the moneylenders. The temples of *Sin* had been raided by kings and looted by armies many times. Terah had lost confidence in the safety of the temples of *Sin*. And the temples of *Sin* were open to anyone who wanted to worship *Sin*, whether they were merchant-moneylenders or not. Terah wanted to find a god who could be monopolized, who was partial to the merchant-moneylenders alone and who protected his own guild members and no one else. A god who protected just one people would have in return those one people protecting the dwelling place of that god as well as the treasury of that god. Terah's god would be an inherited god so that children of the guild members would have no choice but to serve the same god as did their fathers. This could only be accomplished through a careful regard for genealogical descent and written laws within a special, members-only Contract.

Solution for Problem #6: Close relatives are lured away by the gods.

This is similar to Problem #5, but more personal. In this case, family members must be induced to follow the same god as the other guild members. Thus, both family and members of the merchant-moneylender guild would all be members of the same religious community of merchants and moneylenders, with no one allowed any other choice under penalty of death. Secrecy, business dealings, political machinations, clever strategies and cons, and all of the other methods for making a profit and bribing kings – these methods could not be allowed to leak out. Close relatives who wanted to worship other gods and to carry away with them and to inform outsiders of guild secrets, could not be allowed. To disallow trusted family members from joining monastic retreats, early marriage between families was encouraged. There would be only one god for all of them to follow, with one set of rules to be followed, which would be to the benefit and perpetuation of the merchant-moneylender guild, its treasures and its secret methods of operation. With execution as the alternative, no one would be allowed to worship other gods than theirs or potentially to inform other guilds of the secrets of the merchant-moneylenders.

Solution for Problem #7: What keeps people loyal?

Terah knew that loyalty could be bought. As a rich moneylender and businessman, he had plenty of employees and friends who were loyal to him as long as they got some sort of benefit or profit. A regular allotment of grain kept his field-workers loyal. A percentage of the profits kept his partners loyal. Regular gifts to the temples kept the priests loyal. Paying his taxes and giving rare, imported gifts kept the king friendly and loyal. So, a certain kind of loyalty can be bought.

But there is another kind of loyalty that comes from inner conviction. Loyalty to one's city when threatened with war brings farmers and merchants alike to the city walls in defense. No pay is involved, since mutual benefit or mutual destruction is the invigorating stimulus. Loyalty to one's god is an even higher kind of loyalty, because there is no earthly reward involved, no wealth, no cities to defend, nothing but an unattainable god to please.

Terah realized that he could solve Problems #5, #6 and #7 and keep his guild members loyal by using two interlocking methods, both of equal importance. First, each guild member would profit from their individual initiative in their own private business enterprises. And second, the greatest profits could be achieved as members of a single, internationally-connected, intelligence-gathering organization, designed for business spying and product acquisition, and all of it coordinated by the priests of the one temple. The priests' job would be to tie it all together through their self-interest in a percentage of all profits. Membership in such an exclusive, centralized organization would be very profitable, so outside clan members would *want* to join.

Whether religious or secular, every organization requires operating capital. To receive the benefits of his new temple-guild, members would be required to donate a percentage of their profits into the temple treasury. In exchange for business intelligence, free loans, the protection of deposits by the temple's god, deferment from military service and the various other benefits of membership, a ten percent tax or tithe was reasonable, since the benefits of membership were so great. By donating into a central temple treasury, no trail of the funds would be obvious to the outside observer nor would anyone other than the chief priests ever know how much was in the Temple treasury. Such funds could be disbursed by the priests to any members of the Temple guild who could be of profit in some way to the whole membership or who was in need of assistance due to business or political disasters. Dues-paying members were thus enrolled in a banking and insurance system not available to outsiders. Even the poorest members among them could provide service to the whole membership merely by concealing the scam behind their own bodies and behind their own numbers, by being the eyes and ears of the temple wherever they went, by feeding the priests and filling the coffers with donations. The more loyal members that could be enrolled, the better.

All of the temples in the ancient Near East were established primarily to worship the gods. Banking was only a sideline. But, Terah's temple would primarily be a bank hidden within a temple, so worship of the god would be the sideline. Only members could obtain interest-free business loans or receive aid directly from the Temple. Outsiders were forbidden access to the treasury as well as to any assistance that they could not pay for. Such loans to members would be required to be repaid, of course, but repaid with zero interest. The profits to the Temple from business loans would come in the form of a ten percent tithe on all profits. So, the Temple could lend money to its members without interest and still profit from what the borrowers did with the silver.

Thus, the principal of the interest-free loan was repaid plus ten percent of all business profits generated from that loan, and over the lifetime of the borrower, this could be very profitable, indeed! Under such a system, members of Terah's temple became wealthy by obtaining interest-free loans from the temple and then loaning that money out at compound interest to nonmembers who prayed to other gods. Even the poorest among them could become rich with the Sumerian Swindle and would have a huge financial advantage over all people in every country where they were allowed to live. It takes money to make money. So, even a poor Jew could become wealthy by borrowing the interest-free money from the Temple corporation and either investing it in some profitable trade or loaning it out at interest to the *goyim* (lowly insects, stupid cattle).

Because not everyone is interested in or has the slyness for business, there are always artisans, agricultural workers and laborers who often need life-sustaining aid. These are very important for filling in the ranks of worshipers, because their donations of food add to the wealth of the temple and the feeding of the priests. Well-fed priests are less likely to pilfer from the treasury. And masses of these lower echelon members provide protection with their living bodies between enemies of the Temple and the banker-priests who operate the it.

To identify all members of this private temple-bank and to prove that they were of the same guild, worshiping the same god, a "membership card" was needed. A membership document could be lost, stolen or forged, but a mark on the body would be permanent. With a special mark, these particular Semites, living in lands already overpopulated with Semites, could recognize one another anywhere in the world. But, being tattooed or branded like a slave would not do, since both can be counterfeited.

Therefore, to solve this problem while continuing the perverted lifestyle of the Babylonian moneylenders and merchants, Terah decreed that they would continue to use the perversion that they had acquired when they had been looting Egypt. All male members of the new Temple would have to be circumcised. The men would also wear a distinctive hair style of sidelocks so that they could recognize one another in the street. With circumcision, they could all be recognized as fellow members and could never defect from their membership since they would be marked for life. Their circumcised penises proved their membership to the holy temple and to its god. Even a modern Jew proves how "holy" he is by showing you the holiest part of a Jew. "Oy Gevalt! Did you ever see anything so holy?"

Solution for Problem #8: Genealogies link tribes but without a root.

Because Terah was a Semite, he thought in terms of family relationships and tribal genealogies. All of the gods of Mesopotamia were genealogically related to one another, one big family of gods ruling all of Mesopotamia, each from their individual city temples. The Sumerian gods' names had been translated into the Babylonian and Assyrian languages, but they were all the identical family line of related gods.

To tie together his new religion of moneylenders with their families, tribes and clans, Terah did not want to be genealogically associated with any of the Mesopotamian gods or partial to any king who prayed to those gods. Whether from a king or a commoner, the moneylenders had learned how difficult it was to collect loans from those who prayed to the same god as they. Debtors pleaded mercy, since they and the lender were both members of the same temple, in the hands of the same god. Priests pleaded mercy and forgiveness of the debts of their temple members, because as priests it was their duty to apply whatever holy influence and social leverage that they could for the mutual benefit of everyone. But, Terah could make higher profits when there was no mercy for the debtor and no forgiveness of debts. For a moneylender who practices every evil, forgiveness of debts is the only sin.

To have power over the kings and the people and the very gods of these kings, Terah devised a method whereby the genealogy of his own family was traced back to the very first man and woman created by God – Adam and Eve. In this way, by not having any genealogical link to either their gods or to their tribes, he could achieve the greatest power over all of them. No one could claim an older pedigree than Terah and his family of swindlers if their genealogy stretched back to the original creation of the world and to a god who was not a part of the Mesopotamian pantheon. With such a god of the moneylenders, they would be free of any and all obligation to the gods or to the temples or to the kings or to the people of the entire world. Whatever morality their god decreed would be the morality of the moneylenders. Thus, he could use the Sumerian Swindle to enslave the world to his temple and to his tribe without any concerns about the morality of anyone other than themselves. Under Terah's system, only the members of his temple would be free of debt, while the entire world would be enslaved to the moneylenders of the Temple forever. And he could write their doom into a Contract.

Terah rewrote the tribal genealogical relationships that already linked so many Semitic tribes. He intended for all members of his guild to be beholden to himself and his family of thieves. With Terah and his family at the root of the genealogical tree, he could tie any number of tribes to him in fealty. This would require forgery and deceit, but after all, Terah was a Babylonian banker. Who is better than a banker at forgery and deceit?

Solution for Problem #9: The kings gain wealth by taxing both rich and poor.

The kings only have one higher than themselves, that is, the high priest of the temple serving the temple's god. So, to avoid taxation, Terah proposed that his own temple would have a family member as the high priest, delegating authority to whatever king. Let a king do the fighting while the priest does the praying and gathering in of donations, sacrifices and taxes, all the while guarding the Temple Treasury where the bullion of the bankers, moneylenders and merchants was on deposit.

With such vast wealth gathered in as ten percent of all business activities, in addition to the free-will religious donations to the temple, taxes on such a great fortune by the kings would have to be avoided as much as possible. Taxes are usually a percentage of accounted wealth. To avoid taxes, Terah would avoid accounting of his total wealth. If the kings didn't know how much wealth was on deposit, they couldn't tax it. Hiding it from kings was only a part of what the priests would do.

To avoid paying taxes to the king was only one problem, but to make sure that the common members paid their taxes to the Temple and did not hide it from the priests, was many problems. So, a system of snoops, spies and busybodies would have to be incorporated into the priesthood whose sole job and whose only income was to be derived by enforcing the laws and tithes of the Temple and its Treasury. Terah's family had made huge fortunes as tax farmers. Why not incorporate such a system into the workings of the temple? The Temple would hide its deposits from the kings, but the people could not be allowed to hide their wealth from the Temple. The Temple must be too holy to allow access to lay kings. And its priests must be so holy and terrifyingly powerful that none of the people would dare to oppose their tax levies. Indeed, they could not do so even if they tried, as long as temple snoops and spies were living among them disguised as priests.

Solution for Problem #10: Kings are targets, so it is better to hold the target in your hands than to be a king.

Obviously, with a high priest as the king's advisor, one can control a kingdom without actually being a king. And if an assassin wants to eliminate the leader of a country, it will be the king rather than those who control the king who will be killed. In any such event, the same high priest and the same advisors can step forward to "loyally" serve and guide the new king. In the ancient world, the high priest was more powerful than the king. So, Terah cleverly chose to build his own Temple rather than build his own kingdom. Temples can be built with free labor using only promises of a god's reward, while kingdoms can only be built by paying the workmen and soldiers in hard silver.

Solution for Problem #11: We *tamkarum* (merchant-moneylenders) promote warfare and thereby profit enormously. But, while inveigling others to do the fighting, how can we avoid military service without invoking the wrath of our victims?

While living in Harran, Terah saw the supreme advantage of having a god-ordained deferment from soldiering and military duty. While the battles raged and tens of thousands of soldiers, farmers, merchants, laborers, craftsmen and people of all occupations and social status, were all killed or maimed in the other cities, he and his family of moneylenders and his fellow citizens of Harran lived safely. The citizens of Harran had been granted freedom from military duty, an arrangement that had been ordained by a god long ago and agreed to both by the kings and by tradition.

Terah and his fellow moneylenders promoted warfare, because it was so profitable if you were on the winning side. The loot always brought in more than war costs. Loans to the kings were repaid, plus interest with the seized booty. Even the booty that was seized by the soldiers eventually became the property of the merchant-moneylenders through their system of taverns, brothels, gambling, booze, pawn shops, slavery, control of the grain market, mercantile sales of various goods and, of course, loans. And if you were on the losing side and could stay out of harm's way and keep your treasure safely hidden, war was still profitable by lending shekels of silver to the desperate survivors on the losing side. Staying alive was the most important tactic during a war, so getting a military deferment was a prime advantage of Terah and his guild of con artists and loan sharks living safely in Harran and Ur.

Because they knew the relative strengths of all kingdoms through their extensive economic spy networks, the big merchants and moneylenders usually knew in advance which side to support in a war and where to move their bullion to safety. But, regardless of the safety of their treasures, only Harran had complete military deferment. How could this advantage be extended to all of his guild members no matter where in the world that they lived? It seemed like an impossible question to answer, since Mesopotamians believed that every god resided in its own city. Yet the solution to this problem for obtaining exemption from military service was simple.

All armies and their soldiers must be ready to fight 24/7, at all times, on all days. The most dangerous element in any army was cowardice and insubordination of the soldiers. Soldiers who refused to fight invited others to also take the path of insubordination and cowardice. This was fatal for morale.

Such soldiers had to be weeded out before battle or executed during battle. Weeding out the cowards and traitors before battle was the most efficient and safest way. However, a soldier who refused orders *because his god command-ed him to refuse orders*, was a pious person who could not be blamed. Only his god could be blamed. And who could punish a god?

To ensure that the members of Terah's guild could avoid military service, he decided that while an entire army had to be ready to fight every day of the week, Terah and his guild of moneylenders would all be officially insubordi-nate malingerers for just one day per week. By building into his religion one day per week where all of the guild members, wherever they lived, all refused to do any work of any kind, he guaranteed that they would all get military de-ferments. Every army is weak and vulnerable when one day per week its sol-diers lay down their arms and refuse to fight, especially when, predictably, it is on the same day per week. Such soldiers could be the death of any army.

Terah devised the Sabbath observance so that all of his guild members could take a rest from their occupations and could have the same god-decreed military deferment as the people of Harran enjoyed. When the kings or gener-als demanded proof that such-and-such a soldier was not fit for military duty because he belonged to this special religious cult, they could merely salute that king or general with their circumcised penises. That's all the proof that they needed.

To further induce the kings and generals to acquiesce to this subterfuge, the rabbis could offer them substantial bribes. The bribe made the kings and generals enthusiastic supporters of the demands of this religion's mighty god. By bribing the kings, the outraged citizens who protested special military de-ferments for the moneylender guild could be suppressed and silenced by the king's own soldiers.

It was the perfect scam utilized from Secret Fraud #17 of Sumerian Swindle: "Kings are required to legitimatize a swindle but once the fraud is legalized, those very kings must be sacrificed." With the moneylender guild immune to serving in the army, they could support whatever army best served their profits even while betraying the very king who granted them military exemptions – all based on a "commandment from God" to sit on their asses for one day per week and refuse to do any work or any soldiering.

Solution for Problem #12: Armies are expensive, so how can they be in-duced to fight for free?

Terah knew that loot and land was the main goal of Mesopotamian wars. *Just as in modern times, the moneylenders were the main cause of those wars.* As the moneylenders worked the Sumerian Swindle and defrauded entire king-doms of their wealth, this gave the kings the necessary inducement to steal the wealth of other kingdoms through warfare. In those days, "paying the national debt" had the same causes and solutions as are offered today – borrow from the moneylenders and when you can't pay the interest of the Sumerian Swindle, steal the extra money from somebody else through high taxes. When the people can no longer pay the taxes, then lead them off to war to steal the loot from some other people. That is how kings did it then because that was "how it had always been" and that is how the modern world of presidents and dictators do it today – all because of the ancient Sumerian Swindle and the demons who control the scam.

But Terah, the merchant-moneylender, wanted an army that he didn't have to pay. To inveigle even simple farmers or shepherds to go to war, all that was required was a promise. A promise, really, is only empty words. Yet, a promise carried a great reward if the agreed upon action was accomplished. Unlike a paid army, with just the mere *promise* of reward nothing needs to be paid out. The reward is given after the promise is made, but *only if* the task is accomplished. And all of this at no cost to the one making the promise. Thus, promises are cheap and work is accomplished without paying out silver for the labor. Yes, it's true. Armies can be induced to fight for free, *simply by promising a great reward*, such as booty.

But, if the reward is not material, such as land or silver, but is merely *the promise of a god's benevolence*, then nothing at all need be paid to the people who fight for the sake of the god whose commands are voiced by the priests of the Temple. The promises of a mighty god could induce fools into outrageous acts – and all at no cost to the one who makes the promise. (Mohammad would later make use of this very technique.) Armies are expensive, but those who fight out of religious conviction will fight for free. Thus, Terah wanted to protect his treasure and attack his opponents with fighters who didn't ask him for pay. They would fight and die, but their only reward would be the empty promise of an invisible god.

Solution for Problem #13: When conquering a country, how can it be secured? (Assyrian deportation? Genocide? Slavery?)

As demonstrated in *The Sumerian Swindle*, the Hyksos had conquered Egypt by promising the Hebrew shepherds of Canaan plenty of loot. Other than for a few loaves of bread, the shepherds essentially had fought for free. Since they already had plenty of land in Babylonia, the moneylender guilds had not been interested in securing the land of Egypt as their own. They wanted to steal the wealth of Egypt and take it back to Babylon. So, they did not take enough precautions against a resurgent Egypt and were thus expelled.

Terah wanted his guild not only to conquer their own lands, but to secure them as their own for all time. He had already seen the shifting boundaries of the Mesopotamian kingdoms. And he had read in the cuneiform archives of the obliteration of kingdoms that were built only upon the strength of kings. He had already decided on the location of his new temple treasury at Urusalem. But what to do with the Canaanites who were already living on the land? They could not be deported, because he had nowhere to move them. They could not be enslaved, because Babylonia already had more than enough slaves. To Te-

rah, the Babylonian banker who counted sacks of grain and cages of slaves on
the same accounting tablet, the solution was genocide. They would all have to
be murdered.

The main danger to this was that all Semites were ingrained with the lust
for revenge as a part of their culture. But, by blaming a god for the slaughter of
entire tribes and cities, the inevitable Semitic revenge could be blunted. Terah's god could order their extinction and thus leave the killers innocent of the
crime. With a god commanding their acts of genocide, they could be much
more than merely innocent of murder, they could be entirely pious and holy by
committing genocide "in the name of the Lord." And that "Lord" would be
whatever god Terah could find who loved the moneylenders best.

Solution for Problem #14: Moneylenders are despised. Yet, how can we have honor and prestige?

Prestige was always a desire of the *tamkarum* (merchant-moneylenders) from
the earliest days of carrying trade goods on donkey-back to distant villages.
Kings who coveted their spices and pearls and wines gave them prestige and
honor. This was a type of prestige not built upon their personal merit – which
among merchant-moneylenders is nonexistent – but rather upon what they
owned and what the kings wanted. Among the common people, the merchants
were hated for their high prices when they sold and for their low prices when
they bought, taking advantage of the buyers' greed and the sellers' need. As
moneylenders, they were hated by everybody. The moneylenders could never be
loved by those whom they had debauched, betrayed, enslaved and swindled.

To protect their very lives, moneylenders needed a king's special and
strict laws to keep themselves safe from assaults and murder at the hands of
their impoverished victims. How could the moneylenders avoid such hatred
and be respected and honored, while still exacting a profit from their victims? No
matter what they did, it was impossible for the moneylenders to ever be loved or
to ever be respected. It was impossible to turn hatred for them into love.

The only solution for this problem was to turn hatred into pity. And from
pity, some measure of empathy and, perhaps, kindness could be elicited. If the
moneylenders themselves could be *perceived* by their victims as fellow victims
who were at the mercy of a powerful and wrathful god, then *the real victims* of
their Crimes Against Humanity could perhaps look upon them as fellow suf-
ferers. If the moneylenders could be *perceived* as the victims of a powerful and
wrathful god, then that perception would hide their own wicked deeds behind
the commands of a mighty and wrathful god. They could be innocent of all
crimes by putting the blame on the god.

Therefore, Terah's religion would have to have restrictive laws and god-
ordained rituals that permanently tied its members to a strict and vengeful god
who ordered them to be thieving and murdering fiends against their will. They,
the world's most diabolical slave drivers, could be *perceived* as slaves to a
wrathful god who gave them no choice, because *they* did not choose to wor-

ship him, *the god chose them*. They were the Chosen Ones of the god. They had no choice in the matter other than to suffer the wrath of the god if they didn't obey his orders.

Terah's religious hoax was an incredibly ingenious scam and con job. Cringing in fear at the altar of a terrifying god could bring them pity, even if the cringing was only a theatrical show. But, who would know the difference if the actors were convincing and if they all wailed and whimpered as if their very lives and the success of their fraud depended upon such a show? Who would know that it was nothing but sly street theater, if their victims would see the worried looks on their hypocritical faces, or be convinced by the loud sighs and moans as they schlepped their way morbidly through life? In this way, pity for them could be changed into sympathy and from sympathy to kindness. And through eliciting kindness from the kindhearted and gullible *goyim* (lowly insects, stupid cattle), the *goyim* might accept from the moneylenders just one more enslaving loan or buy just one more overpriced import or pawn yet another treasure to them for a pittance.

It was certainly better to be pitied than to be hated, because if they were pitied, they could get away with their frauds, thefts and betrayals. Pity evokes tender and sometimes slightly contemptuous sorrow or empathy for people who are in pain, misery or distress. Pity produces a human feeling of protection or a paternal feeling and desire to help them. Thus, whining could have its benefits, if the whining had a goal, if the whining had a purpose, if the whining could give them even greater profits. And who is more pitiful than a whining Jew? And who else "deserves" more sympathy and kindness and special favor? How can it be called a character flaw or a sign of weakness if those who use this sly technique can take the property of and bask in the sympathy and blessings of their victims? Whining was never better used as a weapon than when it was used by the sly merchant-moneylenders of Terah's trade guild.

Solution for Problem #15: The Sumerian Swindle is both a secret and a mystical gift of the *tamkarum* gods. How can it be protected forever as a possession of the *tamkarum* families alone?

To keep the Sumerian Swindle of lending at both simple and compound interest as the private moneymaking engine of the moneylender families alone, lies and deceit would have to hide the truth about the criminality of the swindle. All-out subversion and war would have to be waged against anyone or against any kingdom that wanted an honest money system. Therefore, all of the activities of the new religion of the moneylenders and its Temple would have to be couched strictly in a system that was open only to its own members and closed to all outsiders. It would have to pretend the highest morality so as to deceive outsiders as to its purpose. It would practice the impoverishment and destruction of all of Mankind for the profit of the Temple members alone, because this is what the Sumerian Swindle inevitably leads to. And best of all, all of their thieving could be blamed on God!

To those who practice it, the Sumerian Swindle guarantees ownership of the entire world. How else could Terah's moneylender guild own the entire world unless *everyone else* gave up their wealth and became Terah's vassals and slaves? A dishonest and criminal scam like the Sumerian Swindle could never be protected with *truth*, because when the People know the truth about how they are being cheated, they won't borrow from the moneylenders for any amount of interest, no matter how small. And worse, they will demand a re-fund of all swindled properties and hang the moneylenders in the bargain.

No, truth could not protect Terah's wealth or his new Temple-based, criminal enterprise. The Sumerian Swindle and the priests of the secret bank inside the Temple, could only be protected with lies. And who else were better liars than the Patriarch of the merchant-moneylender guild and his family as they established Abraham's First National Bank and Pawn Shop in the fortress city of Jerusalem? Terah, the patriarch of the merchant-moneylender guild of Ur and Harran, solved the Fifteen Secret Problems of the Babylonian Money-lenders and devised the Greatest Lie Ever Told. And only his family of swin-dlers and con artists would profit thereby.

Although Terah had devised a solution to all of these problems while living in the Sumerian city of Ur, the problems were so big that he needed a lot of help. Big business requires a big workforce. The most reliable workforce is one made up of close relatives. So, to seal his bargain with the Patriarch of Harran's moneylender guild, Terah adopted that man's son whom he named Haran after the boy's native city. He left his adopted son, Haran, along with his oldest son, Nahor, to manage the guild offices in Ur. Then, with his youngest son, Abram, he moved his main offices to Harran to take advantage of its reli-giously decreed tax-free status and its freedom from military service for its residents.

Before leaving Ur, however, Terah sent his hired servants, the tribe of Binu-Yamina (Benjamin) to Canaan to begin trade relationships with the Hyk-sos (Hebrew) tribes who were in possession of the loot that they had stolen from Egypt. This looted gold and silver Terah wanted to gather into his own treasury. Since the Hyksos were both shepherds and thieves, they weren't in-clined to borrow money from him, but they were greatly in need of the trade goods that his teams of peddlers could supply, such as copper cooking pots and bronze weapons. These Binu-Yamina (Benjamin) mercenaries and hirelings had the additional task of occupying the territory around the fortress city of Urusalem (Jerusalem). Although Jerusalem had no agricultural lands worth having, and although it was not situated on any major trade routes, because of its geographical location on a steep ridge surrounded by waterless ravines, its stone walls were easily defensible against even the most powerful military technology of the times.

The land for his prospective temple could not be the gift of any king, since gifts of kings could also be taken back by kings. Nor could it be con-quered from any of the existing empires of Assyria, Egypt, Babylonia or Hatti-land, because anything once captured could be recaptured by kings in return.

Only if the land was claimed to be the gift of an angry and an all-powerful god, and this god proclaimed "his" land to be a "holy land," would even the kings fear to take it away.

The moneylender families of Babylonia had already experienced two thousand years of shifting national boundaries between the empires of Mesopotamia. In trying to anticipate where their loot would be safest, all of them had already moved it from one temple treasury to another countless times and from one empire to another. Therefore, the captured land for Terah's proposed Temple had to be away from the great empires and inhabited by people who could be bought out, swindled, murdered and otherwise dispossessed with relatively few soldiers.

Jerusalem was close enough to the trade routes to make the transfer of bullion easy enough. It did not need to be at the center of busy trade, it only needed to be remote and safe enough for the deposit and concealment of bullion. Jerusalem was a location that only the moneylenders coveted. It was an out-of-the-way country town whose main attraction was that it was the perfect place to establish a secure bank hidden inside of a temple and protected by the god of the moneylenders, a mighty and terrifying god who was jealous of his territory and of his Temple.

Gold and silver bullion is heavy. It is best hoarded in a permanent location from where it doesn't have to be moved. Unlike any other trade goods, gold and silver did not have to change hands directly for business to take place. By this time of 1300 BC, letters of credit and receipts of deposit could be used between merchants based upon actual deposits within a temple treasury. A clay tablet or papyrus letter stating that such-and-such a merchant authorized the payment to the bearer of so many shekels of silver from his account, was as good as the silver on deposit. The bearer of the letter could withdraw the silver from the temple or sell or trade the letter at a discount to some other merchant who would in turn sell or trade it, until finally some merchant, as the bearer of the letter, withdrew the silver from the original account. Thus, the letters of credit became a form of money among the wealthier merchants. They were lighter to carry than gold and less likely to be stolen by illiterate robbers who couldn't read what value they could transfer.

As long as the gold and silver remained safe in the Treasury, the merchants could do business with contracts and bills that were promises to pay at future dates based on actual deposits. No gold or silver needed to be exchanged and the actual bullion on deposit could be later withdrawn upon presentation of the forgery-proof clay tablet receipt or with the cylinder-sealed letter of credit. Thus, many, if not most, of the mechanisms of modern banking were in place by 1500 BC, well before Terah conceived his schemes.

In other religions, the god resided in the local temple and the temple's income depended on the local people. In Terah's new religion, there was to be only one temple to which all donations were sent no matter where in the world its members lived. Thus, there was a greatly larger net of wealth available to be loaned to its members. Terah's businesses were international, extending beyond the borders of any kingdom. So, his new temple would also be international, accepting donations from beyond the borders of any kingdom, and gathering in the tithes on all profits as well as gathering in commercial and military intelligence.

Even if disasters struck the Temple and the city of Jerusalem, unlike similar disasters being visited upon the temples of other gods of other peoples, the Temple at Jerusalem had a constant and secret funding from the merchant-moneylenders who were circumcised members living in far off countries. Disaster brought ruin to temples that were supported only by the local populations which they served. But, like a poison mushroom with its system of vast underground mycelium roots supporting the aboveground fungus cap, Judaism survived until the present day, not because of the power of its god or the piety of its congregations, but because of the financing of its worldwide net of moneylenders and the deceits of its criminal priests and gangster rabbis. As empires rose and fell, the merchants and moneylenders wearing beanies and sidelocks, always had the financial support drawn from a concealed international network of loan sharks to recover from financial setbacks. Even when disaster struck the people around them, the Jews could still do business, financing both sides in wars to both buy the booty of the victors cheaply and fleece the precious treasures of the starving survivors – all the while avoiding combat in the very wars that they had fomented themselves.

Judaism is an ingenious swindle. With both the Biggest Lie Ever Told to deceive the people of the world and the biggest supply of gold with which to leverage power over the kings, the Jews were always able to take advantage of the people among whom they were allowed to live. It was very profitable to be a Jew and to enjoy all of the benefits that such a secret, members-only, financial, criminal organization offered. It was very profitable to be a Jew as long as one didn't object to being a lying, deceiving, thieving, murdering Betrayer of Mankind. And with such huge profits as their reward, what Jew could object to such minor details as that? No Jew ever did. The few Jews who had some misgivings throughout their entire history or who objected to bringing suffering and death to the non-Jews were murdered by their fellow Jews. Such murders of Jews were blamed on those horrible anti-Semitic *goyim*, those non-Jews who hated the Jews, not because the Jews are evil monsters, but because the Jews are the Holy Chosen Ones of God. And the *goyim* are just jealous of Jewish holiness, so they deserve to be blamed!

CHAPTER 4
SECRET POWERS OF THE ANCIENT PEOPLE

Note: This chapter contains a lot of technical data about the powers of ancient pagan people, especially in ancient Europe. It is
meant to give background information about the kinds of spiritual
and religious knowledge that Jewish lies have destroyed. Skip this
chapter if it is not to your liking and move on to the next; then
come back later to find the secret knowledge of Mankind.

To better put their betrayals of Mankind into perspective and before further
studying the Monsters of Babylon, you should first know some of the incredible secret powers and mystical knowledge that have remained hidden from
both modern Man and from modern science. Archaeologists admit that they do
not understand many of the ancient artifacts that they have unearthed. Ordinary, mundane artifacts that they dig up – such as spoons and dishes and hair
combs – are easy to understand. But those mysteries that science cannot fathom – such as auras and swastikas and sun wheels and Celtic spirals – are from
the religious and spiritual knowledge of ancient Man, a knowledge that can be
experienced rather than merely "thought about." So, of course, scientists are
stumped. They do not understand religion in even their own modern lives. Therefore, scientists are disqualified from understanding the ancient mysteries of antiquity, many of which are presented in this book for the first time in 2500 years.

We will have to rely upon the archaeological record because the various
discoveries of the ancient peoples were never written into books or explained
in an organized religious teaching. This record is found in petroglyphs, picto-
graphs, sculptures, paintings, drawings, and bas-reliefs which anyone can see
for himself. The archaeological record is, however, not continuous across any
single culture. So, I am going to combine the various archaeological discoveries of the ancient people into a single montage spanning all cultures and all
times while being as concise as possible. Hopefully, you will not be confused
by this approach. I will try to link everything logically even though I will have
to jump around between cultures and distant time frames. You will find that
this will lead us to an understanding of the differences between true religion
and the false religions promoted by the lying Jews, the deceiving Muslims, and
the atheistic scientists.

Modern scientists are blinded and deafened to the mysteries of the Universe because they put a telescope over one eye, a microscope over the other
eye, put ear buds in their ears to better hear the static, fill their noses with after
shaves and vapor rubs, turn the air conditioner on to low cold or high heat, fill
their stomachs with instant noodles, hamburgers, and fries, and consider them-

selves superior to the ancient peoples. Our modern inventions steal our common sense while dulling our innate human awareness.

The ancient peoples did not rely upon the scientific instruments that blind so many of us modern people. Instead, they used the most powerful of all instruments the human mind. The human mind is what has given us our modern inventions, our scientific and our technological achievements. But modern scientists cannot see the mystery just beyond the tip of their noses because they are looking outward at the distant stars and not looking inward at the marvels of their own inner being. In an infinite universe, infinity is also found within us. We don't have to look infinitely far to find it.

Long before there were any lying Jews, thieving bankers or swindling financiers, there were holy people who found joy in the good things of life. A natural abundance of fresh air, clean water, good food, loving spouses, giggling children, all provided everything that anyone could desire, except for one thing – knowledge of God. Unlike modern people who have their minds filled with Jewish debauchery spewing out of their television sets and radios or headlined as filth across Jewish newspapers and magazines, the ancient peoples had the tranquility of clean air, starry nights, bright water and unpolluted earth. Unencumbered with vast hordes of furniture, binding clothes, and flashing lights, those people sat quietly around the family fire or stood stoically beneath the moon, breathing freely and thinking deeply. Within the quiet of one's own Mind, the Infinite can be perceived. It is simultaneously the Great Beyond and the Great Within and is not separate from us.

Mankind became established on this beautiful planet without any kind of synthetic devices or inventions of any sort. Even when we walked around completely naked, the Earth provided our food and our shelter quite simply without agriculture and without even the invention of simple tools. Even before we discovered the uses of fire and stone tools, we were in harmony with Nature. Our bare feet carried us wherever we wanted to go; and we were perfectly suited to live anywhere on this planet.

Earth is a planet of heaving oceans, aurora lights, flashing lightning, grumbling earthquakes, spinning stars, blinding sunlight, and cleansing rains. It is a fantastic and living planet that evolved all creatures upon it with an orchestral arrangement of cosmic energies and terrestrial powers. Mankind is one of those powers. Men and Women can plug into and use those cosmic and planetary energies for personal power with no instruments other than our own minds and inner sensitivities.

Ancient Man could harness the powers around him without using any physical devices of any kind because the human mind is more powerful than any computer; and the human awareness of the natural universe is more sensitive than any device. Scientists with their instruments may dispute this, but their instruments are not alive. Their instruments only pick up one frequency and are not attuned to the multi-channel combination of holographic frequencies as is the human Mind. The lost mystic skills of the ancient peoples can be achieved by modern man. Scientific instruments are useless for such a quest.

As an introduction to my methodology, here is an easy-to-understand example from ancient times. I use this example to show you how to see what the ancient people were telling us. Have a look at this sculpted bas-relief for a moment. This is the 25,000-year-old "Venus from Laussel". (see Figure 3) Can you understand what these ancient Europeans of 25,000 BC are telling you? Look at it for a while with your eyes and listen to it with your Mind. Can you understand the message?

Figure 3: Venus of Laussel

This limestone bas-relief tells us much about the mysteries of Life. The woman has no face because the ancient people did not recognize individuals but only fellow tribe members, fellow humans. Thus, she represents all women. She is very fat and healthy for producing and nurturing healthy children. Her fatness tells us that she has attained at least the first seven of the Eight Necessities of Life. The woman is holding aloft a morphological puzzle, an actual example of rubber-sheet geometry. It is the hollow horn of a European bison.

Such a shape is geometrically very mysterious and mind-boggling because this same shape simultaneously forms both a hollow, round, interior hole containing empty space as well as an exterior, jutting point. It is simultaneously both female and male, yin and yang, hollow like a vagina and erect like a penis, all contained within the same shape.

A European Bison horn is naturally smooth but this one is incised with thirteen notches. These notches correspond with the thirteen moons or the number of menstrual cycles in one year. This indicates the awareness of the prehistoric cave people of the relationship of a woman's periods to the cycles of the moon, a mystery of female reproductive abilities congruent with the celestial moon cycles. While she is holding this union of two sexual symbols in one hand, her other hand rests over her womb to indicate the connection to or the result of the union of this mystery.

"Look!" she says, "This hollow horn combines two amazing wonders to create a third miracle. The union of the horn (penis) and the hollow (vagina) creates the miracle of conception in my womb! The mystery of birth! I, a woman, can do this." And thus, we know that she has attained all eight of the Eight Necessities of Life – mystical knowledge of the universal power of Creation.

This is a simple message from prehistoric times, passed along through the media of a limestone sculpture, telling of the amazing potential of a woman to conceive. We do not have to know how to read and write to understand the message. But we must know how to understand what the ancient peoples were telling us through their graphic arts because that is how they communicated. That is how they recorded their observations of Reality. And that is how you will learn the hidden secrets described in this book.

Here is another example of my methodology in showing you what the ancient people knew about the secrets of the universe. But in this case, I will use both modern science and ancient technique – the first proving the second.

Here are two photographs for you to consider.

One is of Kuo Lien-Ying of San Francisco, a modern-day kung-fu master who is standing in an ancient Chinese meditation and qi gong posture. (see Figure 4) The other is a photo of modern astronauts sleeping while in weightless space. (see Figure 5) Do you see what is similar about the two photos? This standing meditation posture known as "the Universal Post" has been practiced for thousands of years among the Taoists of China and similar postures were famous among the Odinists and Celts of Europe. Egypt reached incredible religious insights through the practice of standing meditation postures. (see Figure 6) Here is why and how.

The astronauts' photo was taken in about 1985 as they were orbiting the earth in a space station and sleeping at zero gravity. Their bodies are strapped to their bunks but their arms are floating free.

Figure 4: Kuo Lien-Ying

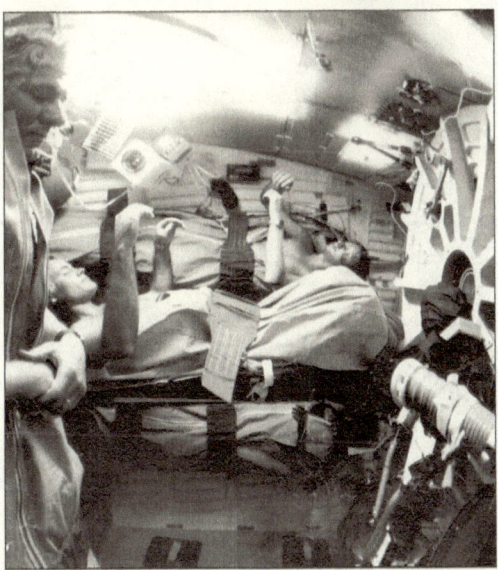

Figure 5: Weightless arms

With zero gravity, their arms can take any possible posture without the influence of gravitational pull. So, without first seeing this photo, one might assume that under zero gravity their arms would be all akimbo in a random variety of postures. Why do the two sleeping astronauts have their arms in identical postures and at about the same posture as has Kuo Lien-Ying in his Taoist meditation stance?

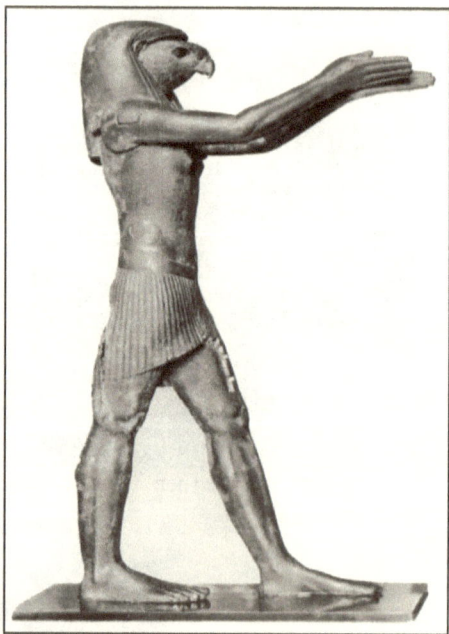

Figure 6: Horus-god

This question is actually impossible for a modern scientist to answer – unless they, themselves, practice the Universal Post meditation or the Rune Stances.

The answer is this: The Standing Meditation Postures are weightless postures. There is no muscular exertion needed to stand in this way because the body is not supported by the muscles and ligaments; the body is supported by the naturally and properly aligned bones. All that the muscles and ligaments do is to keep the bones aligned and balanced against gravity so that the weight of the body is directed through the skeletal structure into the center of the earth. Once the bones are aligned directly over the center of the earth, the body floats weightlessly on its tendons and fascia as if pulled upward by a string attached to the crown of the head. The slightest breeze can cause the arms and body to sway like a pine tree or a bamboo. Looking at a photo of the standing posture might make you think that it is an unnatural posture. Most people who practice it, stand too stiff and solid and therefore tire quickly. But the modern astronaut photo proves that the arms naturally assume that shape in the absence of gravity.

These kinds of simple, yet sophisticated, knowledge of harmony within natural phenomena, gave the ancient peoples a power that is overlooked and lost to modern man.

While standing in the Universal Post or in the variety of other standing postures, you must allow your muscles to relax so that your Qi, that is, your Life Force, freely circulates. Only then, do old age symptoms and diseases disappear. If you practice the Universal Post Standing Meditation Posture for yourself, you will definitely discover a very ancient and wonderful secret of ancient Man hidden within yourself. If you can attain the weightless balance within this and similar standing meditation postures, you will feel as if you are hanging suspended between heaven and earth. And that is where you want to be, balanced between heaven and earth, the natural and spiritual state of Man.

This and similar standing postures are recorded in the ancient Nordic stories about Odin "hanging in the tree of knowledge for nine days" while seeking knowledge. The "nine days" are counted by the Nine Standing Runes. And the Tree of Knowledge is none other than oneself, if you look within as did Odin and many other saints from long ago. Odin was an actual warrior saint of Scandinavia who had attained a high level of Intrinsic Power and Mystical Insight. He was not a god, but later men of lesser attainment made him into a god in their stories, stories that contain the kernels of truth about Norse spiritual skills. These martial and spiritual skills are recorded in the shapes of the Runes.

Although you can practice the Universal Post posture for yourself, don't expect instantaneous results. It requires practice and a calming of the mind, an awareness of the inner self, and a slowness of breathing to attain its secrets. That's why it's called "a standing meditation posture" because as you stand, you are practicing meditation, deep breathing, contemplation, and a penetrating inspection of your very bone marrow by using only your Mind. I am merely pointing out the naturalness of this meditation posture and its modern equivalent in the postures of the astronauts. Convincing you of its merits and the power it gives you, is for you to discover through actual practice of the posture.

One of the greatest of the ancient secrets, is the secret of *the swastika*. This ancient symbol, the swastika (see Figure_7) has had a lot of bad media attention in modern times, primarily because of the lying Jews who own the Media. Their slanders against one of the oldest and most revered symbols from the ancient times, is really quite criminal. The entire story of why modern Jews hate the swastika and, simultaneously, why the National Socialists of 20th century Germany completely misunderstood the swastika, themselves, is found in Volume III, *The Bloodsuckers of Judah*. But for now, please understand the swastika as the ancient peoples understood it, as a symbol of good health and personal power.

Figure 7: Swastika

The famous swastika symbol is much older than the Jews, dating from at least 7000 BC. The word "swastika" comes from the Aryan Sanskrit word, *svastika*, where "su" means "good," "asti" means "to be," and "ka" is a suffix. Thus, the word "swastika" means "all is well" or "good is". But the symbol, itself, has a meaning that is easier to show than to explain.

Figure 8: Copper swastika

For example, this 160-kilo copper casting was dedicated to Naram-Sin of Agade (~2254–2218 BC). (See Figure_8) You will notice that the legs form a swastika. Casting it in copper rather than bronze was a more difficult accomplishment for these very accomplished Sumerian craftsmen. Of course, it weighed much more before it was broken off during the destruction of the palace. Naram-Sin, as you remember from Volume One, was the grand-son and third successor to Sargon the Great of Akkad. It is significant that he was the first of the Mesopotamian kings to declare himself with godly attributes. That he would do such a thing can be partly understood by the spiritual power that he and his people had. The swastika is one example of this spiritual power. And not just spiritual power but the actual physical power that the swastika bestows upon those who properly practice its techniques.

Figure 9: Swastika sitting

Once again I say, modern people cannot understand the ancient people and their religious knowledge without actually doing some of the necessary tasks required to obtain that religious knowledge. In this case, sitting in the swastika posture will give you rest from your meditations and give you pliable joints in your hips, knees, and ankles. (see Figure_9) This is a resting posture found today in the Theravada Buddhist monasteries of Southeast Asia, which is one of the reasons the swastika is a Buddhist symbol since it is used in sitting meditation, usually as a resting position after full lotus sitting. It is very good for the health. People who can sit in the swastika posture never have old age symptoms in their ankles, knees, hips, or spine because the swastika postures give them pliable joints and limber cartilage. In such postures, the promise of the Buddha is realized and the power of the Aryans is attained. Such swastika methods from the ancient times can be better understood if you refer to them as Aryan Yoga. (See Figure_10) Attaining such postures in practice also empowers you with the combat applications (of which there are many) contained within the swastika shape. The swastika was also a symbol of good luck because when you have good health, your luck is always improved through alertness and quickness. Also, the spiral energy around your spine gives you the famed Kundalini power.

Figure 10: Swastika arms

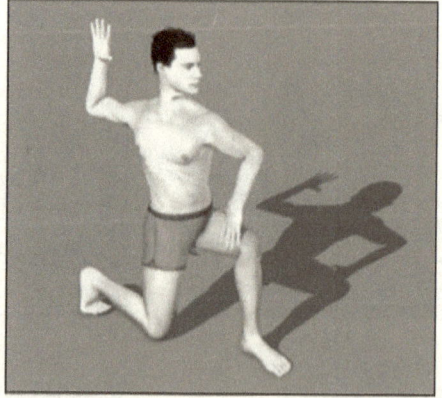

Figure 11: Swastika kneeling

Although the secrets of the swastika were known in the temples where prayer and sitting mediation was common, those secrets became lost among the common people as more and more people sat in chairs and wore Jewish fashions, causing a deterioration and stiffening of their joints. Eventually, through cultural deterioration and lack of practice, the secrets of the swastika became lost because people were too hunchbacked and decrepit to achieve its health-giving postures. As practice of the swastika postures fell into disuse, the actual meaning of this graphic symbol was forgotten until its true meaning was reduced to an ignorant guessing devoid of truth. This led to an admiration of the swastika's graphical perfection without any actual experience of its power.

You can discover the power inherent in the swastika merely by practicing the warrior-yoga postures of our Aryan ancestors. There are static postures to the swastika where you hold the asana to develop your mind, breathing and spirit. (See Figure 11) Through practice, these lead to active postures where movements from one swastika posture to the next will manifest into the Norse and Celtic snake power, as exemplified in this Iron Age Danish broach design. (See Figure 12) The active warrior techniques of the swastika are still found in the Norse martial art known as Stav.

Figure 12: Denmark swastika

Many of these active postures you can discover for yourself after sitting in a static swastika posture for a length of time. Once you feel your muscles beginning to tire and your joints strain, it is time to very gently and carefully move your posture into a different swastika shape. In this way, you will feel the spiral energy within you, not as some intellectual idea but as a very real manifestation of your inherent power as a Man. This same power is no less powerful within Woman. But you can't attain it unless you seek it; and you will not find it unless you do what our ancient ancestors did and practice the swastika postures as a part of your daily life, daily exercise and devotions.

I am giving you the map. Will you use it to find the Treasure?

The more advanced active swastika postures produce what is known in modern times as the Gait of Power, or the Wheel of the Dharma, or the Goose Step. The Goose Step is identical to the secret stepping method that is found in the Chinese martial art of Ba Gua Zhang as well as in the Cossack dance techniques of Russia. These are discussed later.

The swastika is a symbol used in Buddhism (See Figure 13) because it represents True Power as well as excellent health. You will notice that this Buddhist swastika is in the center of the Buddha's bare feet and at the center of the Wheel of the Dharma, the swastika is at the very center of the power of the Buddha. The swastika symbolizes real powers, not mere intellectual or philosophical imaginations, or artistic embellishments.

Figure 13: Buddha feet

The basic teaching of the Aryan prince, Gautama Buddha, was that through the practice of prayer and meditation anyone can overcome illness, old age and death. So, it is very, very significant that the secret for overcoming illness, old age and death is centered in the Truth upon which the Buddha stood – the swastika and the sun wheel. Although the swastika and the wheel are symbols, it is what they represent that is important, not the symbols, themselves. They actually represent a physical phenomenon that ancient Man discovered within himself and which modern Man can rediscover, if and only if you are willing to practice the ancient postures and walk the ancient path.

Think about this for a moment. The word "bread" is not real bread, but it *represents* real bread. No person whether ancient or modern is foolish enough to believe that the word is the same as the actual food. In the same way, the ancient symbol for the swastika, is not the real swastika. The swastika symbol only represents something that ancient Man knew and which he recorded with a graphic symbol which we call a swastika. That "something" is a real phenomenon found within a Human Being. But because the swastika symbol is a graphic and not a written word, people have wrongly assumed that the graphic symbol, itself, is the secret. But in fact, the symbol only represents something beyond its mere graphical shape. It is easy to see the difference between the word "bread" and real bread. But the difference between a graphic symbol of a swastika and what it represents, is not so easy to discern because its true meaning is not found by what we see but by what we experience within ourselves.

We see a graphic symbol of a swastika and our eyes stop there. This is why you must look inside of yourself to find what the swastika represents. When you do that, you will find Power, Insight, Good Health, and Immortality, just as the ancient people knew it through their religious discoveries, just as Aryan prince Gautama as well as Jesus the Galilean, discovered through their own systems of spiritual discovery. This swastika shape was revered by many of the ancient peoples who recognized the great power and flexibility that they had achieved when their limbs followed the natural swastika shape. Their bodies and spirits attained the swastika's power by doing it, not by looking at it!

Figure 14: Egypt

Basically, the swastika is the mechanics of the human shape in perfection. For example, swastika postures are found all throughout Egyptian culture. (See Figure 14) Notice the arms and leg postures. The great Hammurabi, king of Babylon (1792-1750 BC), demonstrated a swastika posture when he knelt before his god. (See Figure 15) The swastika was recognized as a symbol of god by the Assyrians. And it was considered to be such good luck and godly power that the Anglo-Celtics used it on burial urns as protection and good wishes for the deceased. (See Figure 16)

Modern people have difficulty attaining the power and good health of the swastika postures because of the extensive use of chairs rather than sitting on the floor or on cushions. All our ancient ancestors such as the Scythians had limber legs and pliable joints because they followed the natural way of sitting like the Japanese do today, on cushions or on mats on the floor. And they did not wear debilitating Jewish fashions on their feet but wore flat shoes with no heels or arch-supports. They all had swastika power, good health, and good luck, even if they did not represent this power with a swastika.

Figure 15: Hammurabi

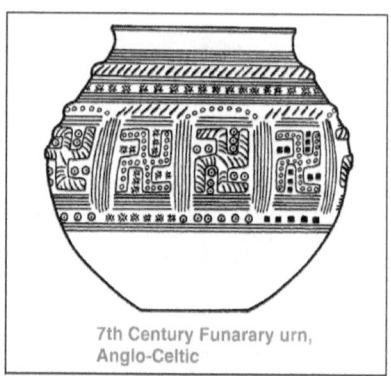

7th Century Funarary urn,
Anglo-Celtic

Figure 16: Swaz-urn

Of course, the modern-day Jews abhor the swastika because to them it represents justice for their crimes. There is nothing that criminals hate more than justice for their crimes. So they malign the swastika at every opportunity, even banning its display in an effort to prevent the people of the world from understanding the true power of healthy living and mystical attainment. Thus, with no other alternative, we exchange our natural good health for the expense and fraud of Jewish medicine.

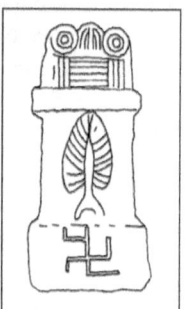

Figure 18: Altars

Figure 19: Elamite priests

There are some scientists such as archaeologist Miranda Green, who claim that the swastika is a symbol for the sun, but in her own book, as you can see from this drawing of a Celtic altar from the Roman period (See Figure 18), it is really a symbol for a Man, two arms and two legs. In this case, it is the outline of a man praying while practicing swastika sitting combined with a transitory pose of the same man kneeling in prayer. This particular swastika is like an animation of just two drawings superimposed one over the other to show the movement from sitting in meditation to kneeling in prayer. The Caucasian people had a fine sense of spiritual excellence. And they attained the highest level of spiritual perfection, which they recorded with graphic symbols.

The ancient people certainly used other symbols to represent the sun but the swastika was not usually one of them because it represented not the sun but the incarnated power within Man. The arms and legs of Man are the Four Pillars of Power that stand in support of both Heaven and Earth. And it contains the secret of the Gait of Power, also known as the Goose Step or the secret stepping method of Ba Qua Zhang kung-fu.

This bronze sculpture presently in the Louvre Museum, was made for the Middle Elamite king, Shilhak Inshushimak (c. 1150 BC). It is the only three-dimensional scene from the Ancient Near East to have been found so far. (See Figure 19) It shows two naked priests performing a sunrise ceremony among the ziggurats of Susa. Besides the straight spines of the priests, please notice that the priest in the foreground is squatting on one leg in a swastika stance with his left foot flat on the ground while his right foot is only touching the ground lightly with his toes. (see Figure 20) This is an example of true power, not the muscular power which modern people use to squat down, but the light, effortless, weightless power of the swastika stance. When the bones of your skeleton are properly aligned, you will have the effortless movements and the power of a cat. The ancient people knew this but modern people need to re-learn this lost knowledge, not through our intellects but through our actual experiences. And this is only attained through practice, not just by thinking that you know it.

Figure 20: Sun worship

It may surprise many people to learn that the most enthusiastic modern-day promoters of the swastika design, the National Socialists of Germany, did not actually understand this ancient Aryan knowledge, themselves. They used the swastika as a logo but didn't know its actual power. The following photograph proves this. You will notice from this photo taken during National Socialist times in Germany, that the secret of the swastika had already been lost even to the Nazis who, themselves, made the swastika famous as their official logo. (See Figure 21) Jewish perversion is so pervasive in the West that even the famed Nazis suffered from it in both overt and covert ways. Notice that these soldiers have their weight on their toes. This raises their center of gravity, making their stance unstable and causing the momentum of their bodies to fall forward. In order to keep on their feet, the front foot is unnaturally thrust forward in preparation for a quick, stiff-legged step while the power of each step comes out of the calves rather than their thighs. Their necks and backs are not straight and the whole purpose of and power of the Goose Step is lost to them. All this is because Europe was so long under the corruption of Jewish fashions that the Germans forgot their natural Celtic and Norse footwear and were wearing unhealthy Jewish fashions on their feet, shoes with heels and arch supports. The biggest quacks in Jewish medicine today are the podiatrists.

Figure 21: Wrong Goose Step

The proper way to do the Goose Step can be understood simply by looking at what is natural. It is no accident that the sculpture of the Aryan Buddha's feet (recall Figure 13) shows the swastika at the very center of his bare feet. This is where the natural weight should center, not on the toes or – even worse – not on the little toe of the foot as is so common among modern people who wear Jewish perversions on their feet.

Heels in shoes raise the center of gravity and unbalance the weight forward onto the toes while the arch-supports push the weight to the outside of the foot onto the little toe. This causes the entire momentum of the body (centered at the tail bone tip of the spine) to move in an anti-pendulum fashion like the shape of the small-case letter "n". With this Jewish-induced method of walking, each step moves the body up then down. This is completely against the laws of physics. It is an example of the leaven of the Pharisees working its poison upon Mankind to cause suffering, old age, and death.

In natural, swastika walking and running – so much glorified by the European Peoples of old – the momentum of the hips should have a pendulum trajectory (centered at the tip of the tail bone) like the shape of the small-case letter 'u'. With this human way of walking, each step moves the body down then up. The people of the West have been the victims of the Jewish fashion industry for so many centuries that they have accepted the wearing of shoes with heels and arch supports as normal because "that's how it has always been."

Like everything else in the universe of mystical knowledge, it is all very easy to learn, but difficult to master. Here is the proper method for doing the

Goose Step. It is also the same method used in Ba Gua Zhang Chinese kung-fu for walking the circle, known as the Camel Step or Mud Walking Step. This method straightens the spine and neck, balances the body, and brings the power of the Earth upward through the bones and acupuncture meridians. So, breathe carefully as you practice.

Begin by standing in the Tiwaz Rune (Figure 22). Spread your hands as wide and flat as you can (Figure 23). This will cause your spiritual power to expand into your tendons and ligaments to your very extremities. This power was known by the ancient peoples both in ancient Italy and among the Norse (Figure 24). In a relaxed manner, lift one leg as shown in this illustration (Figure 25). Balance without wavering and then slowly squat down on one leg as far as you can.

As the raised foot touches down lightly, squat down a bit more and let the light foot slide forward to give a longer step. Once that foot is planted securely, quickly spring up from the weighted leg onto the front leg and again hold your balance. Repeat as often as you have the ability. You can warm up for this exercise with deep squats, keeping your weight flat on your feet with your back straight. If you cannot squat down without rising up on your toes, then your feet and legs have been ruined with Jewish fashions. Flat shoes or bare feet and deep knee bends will cure the illness.

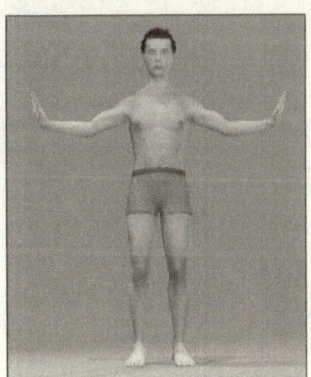

Figure 22

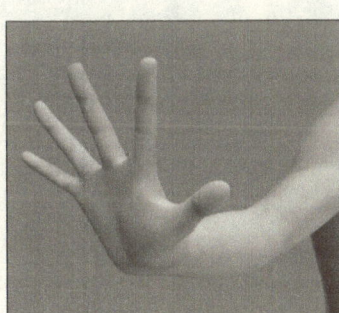

Figure 23

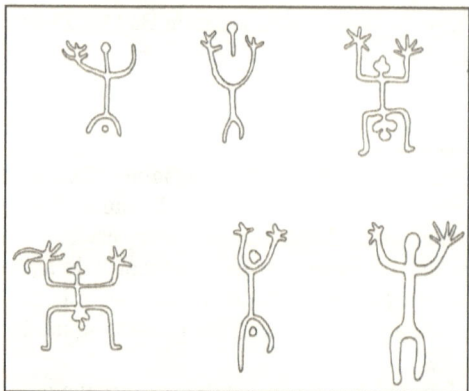

Figure 24

Figure 25

This is the practice method for learning the power of the swastika legs. You should practice slowly, carefully and with full attention to your breathing.

With practice, the power of your Qi will manifest like a bolt of lightning driving up your spine to the top of your head. However, when the Goose Step is used for marching, the front foot is placed down solidly without the addition of a forward slide. If you study how geese walk on a gravelly surface, you will observe the technique. But always, always concentrate your mind so that your center of gravity describes a "u-shape" trajectory.

The modern Chinese misunderstand this method today because its name in Chinese is the "mud walking step" and their culture, too, has been poisoned with Jewish fashions. They think that the forward slide of the front foot should be equated with slipping on mud when, in fact, it is the back foot that is pulled up after the upward spring, as if pulling your feet out of sticky mud – that is the key to this Ba Gua Zhang stepping method.

In *The Sumerian Swindle*, we looked at the Ubaidian sculptures through the eyes of those ancient people by looking through your own eyes. We are, after all, the same people – homo sapiens – with the same intelligence as we have always had. The difference between us and the ancient people is not a difference in intelligence but a difference in the quantity and quality of data and knowledge that we have. We know more now than they did then, but we are really not any more intelligent than they were. Even so, some of the ancient secrets have been lost. We can understand those ancient secrets only if we put aside what we have been taught as so-called "valuable modern knowledge" and accept the ancient data in its pure and unbiased simplicity. We can understand what the ancient peoples knew if we do what the ancient people did to discover those metaphysical mysteries. Standing in the rune stances, walking in the Goose Step, are just a few of the ancient secrets. The Secrets of the Runes are explained in *The Blood-Suckers of Judah*.

The Ubaidian sculptures demonstrate how those ancient people viewed themselves from the inside looking out. By closing their eyes to thin slits, they could perceive – just as you can – your true Self. Their sculptures show us this but modern scientists have been unable to see it for themselves because they are materialists who only believe what they see in a mirror or through the lens of a telescope or microscope. They look upon their reverse reflection in a mirror as being more valid than the living Life Force and bright spirit that they could perceive simply by looking through half- closed eyes and looking inward as did the ancient Ubaidians. Scientists look outward through the lens of a microscope or telescope but never look inward through the lens of their own inner eye. Thus, they can never understand the ancient people – or the tranquil power bequeathed to all who gaze at their True Selves inwardly. This makes no sense to those Readers who read about it but don't practice it. This is not intellectual knowledge; it is *experiential* knowledge. You can't experience it, if you don't try.

People who practice and study religion are no better off than the scientists, substituting actual knowledge and the actual experience that they could have for themselves for what they call their "belief" and their "faith." In this way, they never really know or experience genuine mystical insight or real knowledge. They talk about it as if they know it, but it is all merely talk. They "believe" but their belief is only a wish or a hope or a dream; it is never an actual experience. Belief is not knowledge. It is better to know God than it is merely to believe in God. With knowing, your belief is vindicated and made whole, made actual, made real.

If you have practiced the inward-looking technique of the Ubaidian culture, you will find the next example even easier – the secret knowledge of "outward looking." Once again from ancient Sumeria, the archaeologists have found thousands of sculptures that are a puzzle to them. But these sculptures are so simple! What could they mean? (See Figure 26) The scientists have tentatively identified these as representing family groups. The mother and child on the right, is obvious. The two siblings on the left make sense, or alternatively, they could represent a man and wife since there was an equality between husband and wife in Sumeria before the bankers and moneylenders destroyed their society. And in the middle, according to the archaeologists, a father figure seems to be a logical supposition. But they are puzzled by what they call a "turban" on his head. The scientists have two questions about these little sculptures: (1) Why do they have only big eyes on their faces and (2) What is that thing on the top of the father's head?

Figure 26: Sumerian family

You can understand these ancient mysteries yourself. But unlike the Ubaidian sculptures where you perceived your Inner Self or Inner Spirit, these sculptures exemplify the ancient Sumerian method of being in awe of your Outer Being. You cannot understand this merely from reading a book because it is not an intellectual idea; it is an actual experience in ancient knowledge. You can only understand this by actually doing what the ancient people did.

First, sit up or stand up straight and don't move. Open your eyes as wide as you can and look around. Don't move your head or body at all, just roll your eyes slowly and look in all directions and see as much of your surroundings as you can without moving any other part of your body other than your eyes. Take some time to do this before reading beyond this paragraph and understand what you are observing about yourself. Just stand or sit and see everything that you can with your eyes as wide as possible. Within even a short time, you will get the impression that you, yourself, are nothing but two big eyes. This is seeing your outer Being. Try it.

You can see everything around you as well as your own nose. Eventually, you will see yourself as just another part of your surroundings because you, yourself, are just one of the objects in your surroundings. In our everyday modern views, we tend to think of ourselves as separate from our surroundings. But using this ancient Sumerian method of looking, you can actually observe yourself as just another object in your surroundings. This is an important understanding about Life. When you can see yourself as a part of your environment, you cannot make the same mistake that modern people make in believing that you are separate from your environment. Such fools believe that they can destroy their environment without destroying a part of themselves in the process.

Once again, I caution you. Reading about this and not doing it, means that you have no experience of the very thing that you are reading about. Whether you believe that I am right or not, depends not upon what you imagine without actual experience, but rather upon what you experience. So, practice what I am showing you so that you have the actual knowledge, a knowledge given to you not by what you read in a book but by what you experience in your life. I am giving you the map, you are the one who must find the treasure. This holds true for all the techniques that are included in this book. You probably won't be able to sit in the swastika posture very easily but even trying to do so, will give you the first steps to attaining the good health that that symbol represents. Even trying and failing will show you just how much lower modern health and exercise standards are than the attainments of the ancient people. You can achieve the ancient skills if you try.

Figure 28: Sumerian worshipper

After using your own eyes in this way, you will begin to understand how the ancient people knew of the spiritual power that is expressed through the eyes. The adoration and veneration for their gods was shown by the Sumerian sculptors in the eyes of these devotees. Such statues as these (Figure 28) were found buried in the foundation of the Sumerian Temple at Eshnunna. The clueless modern scientists make a guess that the statues were placed there "to pray for the life of the donor." Most likely, however, they represented the devotees, themselves, who helped in the financing and building of the temple and were a memorial to them in the same way that modern people want their names and photographs associated with some public, cultural, or religious building project.

Ancient people were no different than modern people who want to be remembered, even if it is just their name on a plaque or in the donation lists to a new public building or on a new freeway. We modern people are no different in this respect than were the ancient people who were our ancestors such as the French cave man at Lascaux (See Figure 29) who left an outline of his hand to show that "I was here and I painted these pictures." There is nothing left of either the Sumerian worshippers who stood in awe and adoration of god nor of the cave man from Lascaux who devoted his cave paintings to timeless eternity, nothing other than the record they left of a devotion that transcends time because they are in Time.

Figure 29: Lascaux hand

One of the most famous of ancient secrets is called the Third Eye of the Buddha. In Europe, it was called the Eye of Odin. You do not need to be a Buddhist or an Odinist to try this secret technique for yourself.

In fact, it is also one of the secret Christian teachings that got lost soon after Jesus ascended. The manner in which the eyes are posed, can be seen in this Buddha of Crete and Mycenae from around 400 BC. (See Figure 30) Similar statues of buddhas with the inward-looking crossed eyes, are found in countless archives of photos and in statues in museums and private collections throughout Asia. However, modern people (outside of a few Buddhist monks) have no idea what the crossed eyes and the inward gaze means. But you can look through the Buddha's Third Eye, yourself, merely by following these simple directions. And you can understand the single Eye of Odin as well as the Single Eye of Jesus, by actually practicing this ancient and secret technique.

Figure 30: Buddha of Crete

The word "buddha" actually means an "enlightened teacher." As the Aryan Prince Gautama Buddha taught, there have been countless enlightened teachers (buddhas) born among Mankind since immeasurably distant times. Odin was such an enlightened teacher, an Aryan Buddha from ancient Scandinavia. He, as well as the Aryan Prince Gautama, used the Third Eye Technique for looking into infinity. Here is how it is accomplished.

As in the above Big Eye Method of the Sumerians, sit up straight without moving your head or body. Only this time, lower your eye lids and focus your eyes down to look at the tip of your nose. Yes, you will be cross-eyed, so only do this if it isn't too uncomfortable for you. Practice is the key as in almost everything. Once you can concentrate your vision on the tip of your nose and hold it there without too much discomfort, hold that position while breathing gently. Next lower your eyelids until the edge of your eyelids appear to touch the tip of your nose. This will cut off one-half of your field of vision. Keep your concentration on the tip of your nose. Sit quietly for a few moments and breathe peacefully as you concentrate gazing in this way. Once your breathing is gentle and relaxed and your mind is calm, very slightly (and while keeping your eyes on the tip of your nose) very carefully and very slightly raise your eyelids just a little bit while keeping your eyes focused on the tip of your nose.

From looking at the tip of your nose, very slightly raise the gaze of your eyes just a little bit above the tip of your nose. It will seem as if you are gazing out of a single eye since the area of vision has been blended between the right and left eyes. This area of vision is divided into a dim area on the left and right; and in between those two areas, you will see a bright area in the center. This is the Buddhist Third Eye. This is the one eye of Odin. This is the single eye of Jesus. When you combine this technique with gentle breathing and some mantras or prayers, you have everything you need to attain powers, perceptions and insights that will amaze you. Your entire being will be filled with spiritual light. The treasure is there within yourself. I am merely giving you the map to find it. You, yourself, can actually gaze through the Third Eye of the Buddha, the One Eye of Odin and the Single Eye of Jesus. The above technique has been given these three names, depending upon the religious background of the practitioner.

If you only read these instructions but do not follow the map and search for the treasure yourself, then you will always be a pauper standing outside the treasure house of metaphysics. These instructions are a key, whether you use them to open the door to the Universe, is up to you, yourself. Scoffers close the door to mystic knowledge without themselves walking through. Only those who try, succeed. Even trying a little bit, will give you great insight.

And within that treasure house, which is in actuality within yourself, is found the Eighteen Supernatural Powers. The Eighteen Supernatural Powers are: (1) to see all, clairvoyance, (2) to hear all, clairaudience, (3) the ability to enter your Qi into another's body, to bring back life to the dead and to heal diseases, (4) freedom from hunger and thirst, (5) to adopt a desired form, the ability to change the form to that of another person, (6) to die at will, to die the way one wants to, (7) to get desires fulfilled, to have all that one wants, to bless (or curse) others, (8) the ability to go anywhere in the Spirit (as the astral-self or Ba) without any hindrance or obstruction, (9) to go anywhere at the speed of thought, (10) to have enjoyment along with the gods, to join them in enjoyments and merry making, (11) the ability to become very small, minute, (12) to become big, gain colossal size, (13) to become heavy, gain an excessive weight, (14) to become light, subtle enough to walk on water, (15) to get success, achieve goals, and get fulfilled, (16) to read the minds of other people, (17) Wisdom, lordliness, and power to persuade others, (18) to control another's mind, self-control, control over all senses. Although these powers are obtainable, they are also hindrances to finding God if you dwell on them overly much. They are merely powers; they are not the Goal.

With these insights, we can rebuild all the damage that has been purposely done to human culture, to true religion and to genuine mysticism by the Jews and atheists. As private and as personal as these methods are, there are some very evil people who will want to prevent you from discovering your immortal soul and bright spirit. Such enemies of Mankind as the Jews, the Muslims, the Communists, the atheists, and many modern scientists, will attempt to stop you from even the most ordinary practices of personal power and enlightenment. It is a power that they do not have, themselves, only because they are prevented by their own corruption and lack of faith from attaining it. But in order for them to have power over your life, their strategy is to prevent you from attaining these Secrets. Ignore them and go your own way.

This genuine knowledge of the holy spirit as expressed through the eyes, was exemplified in some of the teachings of Jesus, such as in Matthew 6:22-23 and in Luke:

> "No one lights a lamp and puts it in some hidden place or under a tub, but on the lamp stand so that people may see the light when they come in. The lamp of your body is your eye. When your eye is sound, your whole body too is filled with light; but when it is diseased your body too will be all darkness. See to it then that the light inside you is not darkness. If, therefore, your whole body is filled with light, and no trace of darkness, it will be light entirely, as when the lamp shines on you with its rays." (Luke 11:33-36)

What is this "light" that Jesus talks about? The Jews, Muslims, atheists, and Communists do not know. It is the light of the human spirit. It is a light that shines forth from those who have attained a spiritual insight into the Universe or into God. If you cannot see that light, then practice the exercises in this book and the light will manifest for you. Just as you could actually see your own spiritual Being by using the Ubaidian methods from Volume One, this light also shines outside of the body. The various paintings, drawings, and sculptures across wide swathes of time and geography prove this. The representations of auras and rays of light emitted from the sculptures and paintings of gods, goddesses, and saints, are too numerous and too much separated by geography and time to be just a delusion. The same "delusion" expressed by unrelated peoples is not a delusion but is, rather, a common observation of real phenomenon.

This is alluded to in the Old Babylonian "Creation Epic" where the authors of the poem state that the god Marduk went out to battle the monster, Tiamut. "For a cloak Marduk was wrapped in an armor of terror; With his fearsome halo his head was turbaned." Now, look at that Sumerian family once again. (see Figure 26) So, yes, the scientists are partly right; it is a turban. But it is not a turban of cloth, it is a turban of the holy spirit. Thus, it can be seen that the holy knowledge of the Babylonians included a halo above the head of their great god, Marduk. Knowledge of halos is a sign of actual spiritual enlightenment for the Babylonians. To both know of and to be able to actually see and experience halos, is an indication of their spiritual elevation.

Additionally, this same shape is reflected in the crown of the Egyptian pharaoh as a manifestation of the Holy Spirit (Qi) around his head to the top-most height.

Nowhere in all the lies and forgeries of the Jews for the past 3500 years is there any mention of halos simply because this knowledge was unattained by them while they destroyed all manifestations of true religious knowledge among the people around them. Furthermore, the Babylonian Creation Epic shows the broad-minded outlook of the Akkadians in their views of God. They wrote, "As for us, by however many names we pronounce, he is our god. Let us then proclaim his fifty names …"

What does modern science say about auras and rays of light emitted by the human Being? The discoveries of Robert O. Becker, MD, give us valuable insight into what modern science can actually prove about such phenomenon as rays of light and auras. He writes:

> "Certainly human skin is electrically active. It's piezoelectric (creating electricity as it bends) and pyroelectric (turning heat into electricity) as well as a transporter of ions. Biological semi-conductors even offer a possible basis for the aura often report-ed around living things by "sensitives." There has long been speculation that this 'halo' might be some manifestation of an electromagnetic biofield.
>
> The ability of high-voltage (Kirlian) photography to produce an image very much like descriptions of the aura has aroused hope that the technique might render some aspect of psychic phe-nomena visible in a way that would be conducive to experiment.
>
> We found that human bone functions as a Light Emitting Diode (LED). Like many such materials, it required an outside source of light before an electric current would make it release its own light, and the light it emitted was at an infrared frequen-cy invisible to us, but the effect was consistent and undeniable. Whole bone fluoresced a bluish ivory, while collagen yielded an intense blue and apatite a dull brick-red.
>
> On the other hand, the aura could literally be a form of light, perhaps at frequencies invisible to all but a few of us. The skin-nerve interface…may well be a diode. If so, the proper level of current could cause emission of light from the skin.

Although this scientist just barely touches on the subject, he is limited to the use of scientific instruments while over-looking the most sensitive instrument of all – the Human Being. We humans have great powers. You can learn to find and use them through your own efforts and some of the hints in this book.

First, let's look at the Eight Essentials of Life. You can figure out what these Eight Essentials of Life are if you think about it: Air, Water, Food, Clothing, Shelter, Spouse, Children and God. They are listed in order of importance since without Air, we would die within minutes. Without Water, we would die within days. Without Food, we would die within weeks or months (depending on how much body fat we started with). Without clothing, we would be at the mercy of the elements and either roast in the hot sun or freeze in the snow. Shelter is a necessity because clothing alone is not enough to protect against the extremes of Nature and without shelter, it is difficult to cohabit with a spouse. A Spouse is necessary to share in the labor of finding food and making a homelife inside of the shelter. Once we attain all these necessities, the mystery of what the "Venus from Laussel" is telling us can be realized. Children can be raised to help in gaining a richer life and in giving us ease in our old age.

Above all these earthly concerns, we need the Eighth Essential, that is, God or a divine spiritual awareness to aid us in leaving this earthly realm and for finding peace in this life and in the hereafter. All the ancient people understood the Eight Essentials of Life and tried to incorporate them into successful living. But modern people seem to have forgotten even these simple facts of life. You can understand the quality of your own life if you can answer "Yes" in having all these Eight Essentials of Life. If you don't have all them, you should ask yourself why. Usually, those who do not have the Eight Essentials of Life are the victims of the modern-day Jews whose philosophy is: "Many must suffer and die so that a few Jews may live in luxury."

The first and most necessary of the Eight Essentials of Life is air. Of course, if you hold your breath for only a few minutes you will have to stop being stupid and breathe or else you will die. Modern people have forgotten how to breathe and the modern Jewish Medical Monopoly swindles billions of dollars per year from sick people whose only actual cause for illness is improper breathing. There are many reasons why this is so, which I will cover in a later book, but for now know that just as a fire cannot burn without oxygen neither can the fire in your cells live without this element. The vast majority of modern physicians are totally ignorant of the proper way to breathe. So, they are not qualified to teach this art which you can learn for yourself by following the instructions at the end of this volume in Appendix A: How to Develop Your Qi and Live Within Your Holy Spirit.

Of course, you know that someone who isn't breathing or who has been cut off from oxygen for a short time, turns blue in color. And someone who has fully oxygenated blood, has a reddish complexion. This is not only reflected in modern medical lore but is recorded in the graphics of ancient Egypt as well. Archaeologists are puzzled as to why the ancient Egyptians painted pictures of themselves with a reddish skin color – which to a pale and unhealthy scientist seems odd. Yet, the Egyptians accurately painted the skin color of all the people around them. (See Figure 31) The archaeologists are puzzled because as modern scientists, they have no idea how to properly breathe any more than does the average modern person. When modern scientists are missing the first of the Eight Necessities of Life, how can you expect to obtain accurate information from them on the best ways to live your life?

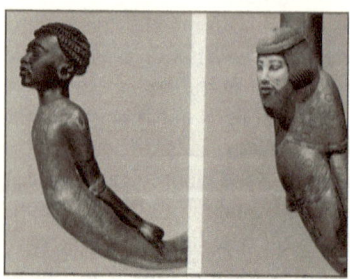

Figure 31

Figure 32

Here is how the ancient Egyptians recorded the people around them. (See Figure 32) The Negroes and Asiatics all have the correct skin color pigmentation. The Egyptians obviously knew how to observe and accurately record their observations. But this picture of Horemheb (1348-1320 BC) is standard for how the Egyptians painted pictures of themselves. (See Figure 33)

Figure 33: Horemheb

Western scientists are puzzled as to why the Egyptians painted their skin color with a reddish hue. In fact, all the Egyptians were painted this color whether they were kings and nobles or common laborers. And why? Because the Egyptians – all them – practiced the deep breathing and meditational methods that were usually kept as well-guarded secrets in other cultures. The red coloration is the reddish hue exhibited by those who have oxygened blood. Whether it is the red face of the Chinese General Kwan Ti (See Figure 34) with his powerful Qi Gong, or the red coloration of the Egyptian Pharaohs, this red color is a sign of good health, spiritual power, and a fully oxygenated blood. Fully oxygenated blood is the result of deep and proper breathing, a secret that was shared in common among the Egyptians, but a secret that the Egyptians did not share with other peoples.

Figure 34: Kwan Ti

In Chinese Qi Gong and Kung-Fu, the windpipe and esophagus is known as the Triple Warmer Channel down which the circulating Qi enters the abdomen from its external circulation over the top of the head and upward from the Conception Vessel. The general meditational skills of the Egyptians can be observed in the fact that they were fully aware of the Triple Warmer, the internal path that the Qi (the Holy Spirit) circulates downward into the lower abdomen. This internal skill is signified by the Egyptian hieroglyph for "Union". (See Figure 35) It is no coincidence that this hieroglyph uses the representation of a human esophagus and lungs to represent a "union."

This hieroglyph for "union" was also the hieroglyph for "Life" and was considered by the Egyptians to be the basis of Egypt's well-being and the power of the pharaoh. A powerful meaning given for something that modern people assume to be so inconsequential as breathing! The well-being of the People and the Power of the Pharaoh was found in their breathing! But it has been a secret until now as to why the Egyptians painted themselves with a well-oxygenated reddish hue and how they created such an incredible culture.

Figure 35: Union

In Egyptian culture, Air, the First Essential of Life was well known and revered, as it also was among the ancient Sumerians whose chief god was the Sky God, An. The proper breathing of air and its internal circulation allowed the Egyptians not only high mental states of awareness and psychic skills but it gave them great physical strength as well. This physical strength was linked by their Minds to their breathing and was used as a means of spiritual attainment in the same way that Chinese Kung-Fu links Mind, Qi and Body. Each of these three can be used to strengthen the other two, synergistically.

A word should be said here regarding the environment of the ancient peoples, especially the Mesopotamians and Egyptians. Both of these people lived in desert areas that only supported life because of the rivers that flowed through them. All the buildings in Sumeria and Babylonia were built of mud bricks. In Egypt, the ordinary houses were built of mud bricks but since they also had access to stone, they built their monuments and temples of durable stone work, using limestone and granite.

Because mud brick is made of widely available ingredients—soil, water and chopped straw, with occasional additions of dung or sand—and because it is baked in the sun rather than in a kiln, it is one of the cheapest of all building materials. It is labor-intensive rather than energy-intensive. Furthermore, it is a poor conductor of heat, and so it is particularly suitable for arid regions where the daily variation in temperature is high. When the temperature climbs above 90 degrees Fahrenheit on a summer day, the temperature inside a mud-brick house stays in the 70s. In contrast, in a modern non-air-conditioned house built of prefabricated concrete, temperatures can rise to above 100 degrees. So, the ancient mud-brick houses stayed cooler in the summer than do modern homes.

The same arid climate that makes mud brick the ideal building material in the Near East makes roof vaulting the perfect technique for constructing a ceiling or a roof. A vaulted ceiling allows hot air to rise higher than a low flat ceiling does and thus helps to keep the living space even cooler. More important, in many parts of the Near East there are no forests, and consequently the timber needed to support flat ceilings is scarce. A mud-brick vault requires no wood beams for support. Not only is it practical and economical but also it is a singularly graceful way to cover a building.

With such humble building materials, the priests of both Mesopotamia and Egypt could practice their contemplation of the Universe in relative comfort, sitting in meditation in the cool shade, breathing gently with their abdomens, circulating the Life Force down the esophagus to the abdomen, looking through the Third Eye into Eternity. No one needs the instruments of scientists to find and verify God. You, yourself, are the finest instrument; and complete with everything you need.

The highest level of religious science was discovered in Egypt through the very same breathing methods employed by the Aryan Hindus, the Aryan Buddha, Jesus, Odin and by the Celtic Druids. They all just used different names to describe it. As the Egyptians indicated in their hieroglyph, the Union between the outer and the inner man connects via the esophagus, the Triple Warmer, between the lungs and the abdomen. Through the Science of Breath, inside becomes outside and back again.

One of the lies told by the Jews is that the Egyptian pyramids were built with slave labor. Modern archaeology proves this to be entirely false and only offers additional proof of how bogus the Jewish tales of Exodus and its related counterfeits really are. In fact, it was a great honor for the Egyptian people to be able to work on the pyramids because, in the first place, they were working for their god who happened to be represented in the incarnation of the Pharaoh.

It was not the work that a low-life slave would be allowed to perform. Not only was it a holy occupation, but the pay was excellent. The Pharaohs were only too happy to provide for the workmen who were building their House of Eternity, the best in food and plenty of it. Pharaoh Rameses II, even shows on one of his wall murals the kind of banquets his laborers in the quarries as well as on the pyramid enjoyed. (See Figure 36) The pharaohs wanted their "house of eternity" to be built with joy, not with sorrow. So, no Hyksos slaves were forced to build the pyramids. Great honor, the blessings of the god and excellent pay, was for the religiously striving Egyptians, not for dirty slaves. Again, the Jews are liars. They never worked on any Egyptian pyramids.

Figure 36: Food for quarrymen

Building a pyramid, or House of Eternity, was a high honor as well as an exercise in what can be called, Egyptian Yoga. Yoga means "yoking oneself to godly knowledge." In yoga as well as in Chinese kung-fu, physical exercises are directly linked to mystical and sacred attainments all connected by the breath.

Modern people should understand that the breath is what gave many of the ancient people their spiritual power and physical strength. By using their Egyptian breathing methods, every Egyptian, not just Pharaoh, could attain union with their god. Their meditational deep breathing gave the Egyptians spiritual power and a perceptive excellence. Every Egyptian painting and sculpture reflects this perfection in their lives, whether of servants performing simple chores or nobles like Queen Kawyt of Dynasty XI sipping from a bowl. (see Figure_37) Every movement to an Egyptian was a movement within Eternity. The Egyptians made every movement as perfectly as their meditational awareness made possible.

Figure 37: Queen Kawyt

Jumping ahead a few thousand years, the blue-eyed, Aryan prince, Gautama Buddha, attained Enlightenment merely by observing his inward and outward breathing. And later, this knowledge was passed on by another Aryan prince, Bodhidharma (Da Mo) to the Chinese at the Shaolin Temple and refined into the External Schools of Chinese Kung- Fu. Breathing linked to physical movement and acupuncture theory was amalgamated by the Chinese Taoists into the Internal Schools of Chinese Kung-Fu and Qi Gong. So, breathing and the science of breath, has been the foundation of three of the world's greatest religious discoveries while being almost entirely unknown in the West. Unknown not because it never existed in the West, but unknown because this knowledge was lost until now. It was basic knowledge among the wise men and warriors of ancient Europe, though secretly protected among the Celts and Druids.

Jumping back once again to ancient Egypt, observe how their Egyptian Yoga was part of the daily lives of the people. All the Egyptian sculptures and paintings and bas-reliefs show Egyptian yoga postures and Qi Gong skills. Meditative breathing and contemplation of Eternity was not set aside as something that only priests or religious recluses could practice. "Every moment Zen" was the god-conscious practice of those ancient people. Whether standing, sitting, kneeling, rowing a boat, grinding grain, or working in the fields (See Figure 43), the entire Egyptian culture and all its people were finely attuned to Eternity and the connection that the Science of Breath had with daily life, linking their lives to the perfection of God. The Science of Breath is, indeed, a true science in that you must closely observe, inquire, experiment, analyze and test both the processes of thinking and non-thinking using the First Essential of Life as it manifests within the laboratory which is Yourself.

Figure 43: Harvest scene

Not understanding this, modern scientists think that these Egyptian arts reflect some sort of "ideal" postures and not those postures actually practiced daily by the Egyptians. Perfection is first and foremost a matter of mental awareness and physical discipline. It is an attainment, not merely an ideal. Thus, Egyptian art reflects the actual attainment of the Egyptian people, not just their "ideals" of perfection. Just as Egyptian artists accurately represented the world around them, so too did they accurately represent themselves in their art.

Notice how the modern kung-fu posture of Kuo Lien-Ying (recall Figure 4) has a similar leg stance as the ancient Egyptians practiced here in a sculpture of Hori the priest. (See Figure 44) In this ancient stance, the weight of the body is not equally balanced. Most of the weight is on the back leg. One can stand for long, long periods of time in this stance. Such a posture is what is known in Tai Chi Chuan as "avoiding double weightedness." This kind of stance gives one a lithe and nimble ability, making for a weightless movement skill, a limber spine, and a tireless standing ability. Try it for yourself and you will see what the scientists are missing. This skill is not easy to achieve because it takes effort and acuity of mind, along with aware relaxation, but the method to achieve that skill is easy – just stand and study yourself in the posture, breathe, relax, and use your Buddha Eye, your single Eye of Odin, to look inside at the marrow of your bones and the brightness of your spirit.

Figure 44: Hori the priest

Figure 45

If you want scientific proof and if you are on friendly terms with an ordinary house cat, try this experiment: Hold the cat as if picking up a child with your hands under its shoulders and around its chest. Dangle it so that only its back feet can just barely touch the ground. Let the cat put its back paws on the ground as if you were helping a child to learn to walk. Notice how the cat will never allow itself to stand with both paws equally balanced. Cats only allow one foot to bear the weight while the other foot is always light. Cats are single-weighted like Tai Chi masters.

Dogs are not like this; they are perfectly happy to stand with their weight equally planted on both hind feet. Try the same experiment with a dog. A dog is double-weighted, that is, it will put both paws on the ground equally weighted. You already know who is quicker and nimbler, cats or dogs. This is one reason why. Cats and Tai Chi masters are experts at being lithe and nimble by never being double weighted. They let their bones support their weight rather than their muscles, just as the statues of ancient Egypt clearly teach.

This knowledge was known by the ancient Egyptians and they practiced it even while on guard duty (See Figure 45) or merely standing before the statue

of a god while breathing Eternity into their souls; or while standing weightlessly along the banks of the eternally flowing Nile River and looking into the
infinite horizon. There is a direct connection between one's posture and one's
spiritual awareness. When your breathing is regulated and you are looking
through your Third Eye, the Universe becomes your abode.

Again jumping ahead, the blue-eyed Aryan Prince Gautama Buddha
(~563-483 BC) attained Enlightenment merely by observing his inward and
outward breath. So, one must not assume that your own breathing is in any
way inferior to that of the ancient sages and saints. The difference between you
and the Buddha or between you and the Christ, is merely a matter of
knowledge. But the knowledge, itself, is simple and easy to practice. When the
Buddha was Enlightened, the first thing that he said was, "How wonderful! All
men can attain this blessed state." And Jesus taught, "What I do, you too can
do, and some things greater." None of the mystical knowledge is beyond what
an ordinary man or woman can achieve, if they try.

The big difference is not the knowledge, but the effort. You can't get there
without trying. And just like the modern scientists who do not understand the
mystical powers and the secret knowledge of the ancient peoples, you cannot
know what the ancient peoples knew unless you practice the mystic secrets
some of which are found in this book. These secrets are both easy and difficult.
They are easy because they are simple and they are difficult because practicing
them is not easy. Sitting in meditation, for example, is easy. But to do it for a
long time while settling your mind, is difficult. Standing in the Universal Post
Posture or the Rune Postures is easy, but to stand long enough to be able to
balance your skeleton and free yourself of gravitational stress while relaxing
your joints, softening your muscular tension and circulating your Qi, is difficult – merely difficult, but not impossible.

Why is sitting and breathing such a chore for modern man? Because we
don't sit on the floor anymore like the Japanese do or like all the ancient people did. We slouch and do not sit upright anymore, so the nerve energy of our
spines cannot circulate our Life Force. (See Figure 46) Unlike this ancient
Mesopotamian Mari dignitary of about 2500 BC, we do not sit upright in
chairs, we slouch into them. (See Figure 47) We do not squat down to go to
toilet anymore. We sit on tall toilets the height of chairs. And so, our modern
knees and hips are too stiff to sit with crossed legs for any length of time and
are certainly too stiff to sit in the swastika posture or lotus posture. This is not
only bad for the health, leading to disease and old age symptoms, but it makes
finding the ancient path to Enlightenment and God-consciousness also very
difficult. Why is this? Whether you are a Buddha sitting under a bodhi tree or a
Celtic warrior listening to the deep forest and the hints of the gods, or a Christ
sitting in meditation for forty days and forty nights, by sitting on the ground
you are directly connected to the entire planet and its energy forces.

Figure 46: Tibetan Buddha

Figure 47: Mari dignitary

How does one plug-in to these cosmic energies? The technique really isn't difficult. This scene from the famous Gundestrup Cauldron (See Figure 48), dated to around 200 BC, shows a European Celtic warrior practicing meditation with crossed legs while tuning his soul to the universe. He is surrounded by the animals of his world and the glowing life force within the plants. The animals are obviously alive since they are in standing, active poses. But even the plants in this scene are surrounded by the aura of their life force, showing that they are a part of the message being delineated in this scene. Obviously, the ancient Europeans were aware of the life energy radiating from living plants, an awareness perceived through their senses, not through scientific instruments.

A careful inspection of this silver cauldron, shows the necessary tools of the ancient Celtic religious practices of two thousand years ago. The Europeans were like all other ancient people in regard to being in tune with the natural world. Hunting, fishing, gathering, animal husbandry and agriculture gave them their food, the Third Essential of Life. The Europeans were a highly religious people who were in tune with Nature and knowledgeable in the ways of their natural world as this ancient Celt is demonstrating the secrets of his mystical life, something that goes beyond the material reality.

Figure 48: Gundestrup

First, he is sitting on the floor or on the ground in a cross-legged posture. There is nothing Oriental about this natural way of sitting, little children sit like this today and the ancient peoples from all over the world also sat like this daily. However, there is a secret about this method of sitting that the Western physicians know nothing about and which even the various gurus and medita-tion teachers are unaware. We must look at both Chinese Acupuncture theory as well as Western scientific discoveries to understand this posture for attain-ing mystical power.

Western science shows us that we are surrounded by a multitude of energy forces both in the air and beneath the earth. Western science claims that we evolved on this planet for several tens of millions of years. If so, then how can scientists overlook the fact that we are all still connected to the energies of the planet? One thing that evolved, but which modern science completely over looks, is the way we find our rest by sitting. Yes, we can lay down to sleep and that refreshes our weary bodies. But Mother Nature arranged that we could rest and find refreshment in the way that we sit down. The refreshment that we experience does not come entirely from a state of bodily rest; it also comes from a re-energization from the entire planet, itself.

It is no coincidence that the ancient Qi Gong breathing methods begin at acupuncture points that you sit upon. These acupuncture points are named CV-1 or the Hui Yin point. It is located here (See Figure 50), half way between the anus and the uro-genital region in all people, located at the very place that you sit upon and make contact with the energy of the earth. Similar points are found in all animals who also sit on their rear ends to rest.

The electrical energy potential and Qi power of the earth is absorbed by this point, CV-1, where the Qi of the earth enter the body. Your Qi rises up the front and the back of your body when you breathe beginning from this region. So, it is no coincidence that these points have evolved to a place on the body that is directly in contact with the earth's electrical potential when you are sit-ting on the earth at rest, like recharging your Life Force batteries. This energy moves upward toward the stratosphere to create lightning but in a human, circulates over the head and then down into the interior of the body through the Triple Warmer, or esophagus, in the lower abdomen. The ancient Celtic meditators could feel both a centered and grounded feeling as well as an increase in perceptive power when they sat on the ground with their legs crossed because the acupuncture point they were sitting on directly channeled the earth's power into their bodies. The mind becomes calm as the energy of spiritual power is concentrated.

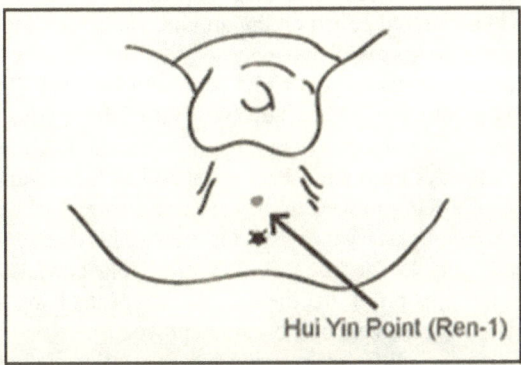

Figure 50: Hui Yin point

What else does this ancient Celt depicted on the Gundestrup Cauldron tell us? His eyes are partially closed as he looks inward using Oden's Eye while listening to three totem animals whispering secrets into his ears. A wolf and a stag have secrets to tell. Both know how to move silently, one is a hunter, the other the hunted. The stag knows secrets of invisibility and knows both the secret stepping method for moving silently in thick brush and for high leaping. The wolf knows how to stalk and kill its prey and never gives up the chase. The serpent is the power in the spine, the "wisdom" of serpents, a boneless pliability of youthfulness and hydraulic strength and Qi power. The Celt is grasping the serpent because he has knowledge of the serpent power throughout his body, up his spine, straightening his neck, around which a torc is worn as a badge of his attainment. He is "wise as serpents."

The mystical secrets of the Celts are found in the posture of this ancient warrior-priest. Sitting cross- legged with a straight back allows the Qi of the earth to rise up and circulate, and his mind to find rest. But what is he holding in his hands? He is holding what he wants to tell you – the power of the torc and the power of the serpent. These are both things that the ancient Europeans knew well but which have been lost by their Jew-corrupted modern descendants.

Why is he both holding a torc and also wearing one around his neck? Because he is showing you the torc in his hand as a teaching of what to strive for and he is wearing a torc as an example of his attainment. A torc cannot be worn by anyone who has not achieved the secret European power of the ancient Celtic and Druidic cultures simply because modern people do not have the straight necks, ramrod straight backs and iron wills of the ancient people. A torc worn by a Celtic adept sits comfortably around his straight neck. But a torc worn by a common, buzzard-necked modern fool will cramp and crimp and cause him pain. The torc of ancient times was worn as a sign that the wearer was a superior man and had attained the various powers that the ancient European peoples possessed. Powers that were lost but herein are given back to them.

The Celtic warrior-priest is also holding a serpent that is whispering its secrets into his ear. Obviously, he is holding it to show it to you, the viewer, otherwise, it would be pictured coiled on the ground. He is showing that the power of the serpent is also his own power.

In the modern practices of Tai Chi Chuan and Ba Gua Zhang, attaining "snake spine" is an ultimate and achievable goal of those who practice these martial arts. And in the ancient Aryan yoga of India, finding the snake power of Kundalini has always been an ultimate goal. When the Buddha became enlightened, the Cobra King moved up his back and spread its hood to protect him. This is the feeling one gets when the snake-like energy moves up the spine and spreads out like the hood of a cobra to your clavicles. Here on the Gundestrup Cauldron, is proof that the ancient Europeans knew of this power. The Vikings, also, were masters of the serpent power.

In addition, this ancient Celt is wearing woven woolen clothes with the belt above the navel. A high belt such as this allows abdominal breathing and mystical power. But the modern Jewish styles that Westerners wear today of low-cut britches and belts, cut off the breathing of the body and create disease, forcing the victims of Jewish fashion to breathe with their lungs instead of their abdomens and then go to Jewish doctors when they fall ill. With his flat-soled Celtic slippers on his bare feet, the secret Celtic- swastika-wheel acupuncture point at the center of his soles, is also connected when he walks upon the energy fields of the earth. As this Celt walks, the Dharma Wheel turns around him. It is an observable power within each person who seeks it. The Sun Wheel or Dharma Wheel turns around your body as you walk in the Gait of Power.

Just as the Hui Yin acupuncture points absorb energy from the earth when you are sitting, so do the Kidney-11 acupuncture points on the soles of the feet do the same. The traditional sculptures and paintings of the Buddha's feet show two things, the flatness of his feet and the long stretching of his toes (See Figure 51) as well as a lotus flower plexus on the soles (recall Figure 13) which actually corresponds both with the bouncy point of earth contact and center of weight on the soles of the feet, something that is unattainable when wearing debilitating Jewish shoe fashions on your feet. Not only is the perfection of the Buddha found in how he centered his weight over the arch of the foot, but the power of the earth's energy is directly absorbed through that point. That is, power is absorbed if you wear flat shoes with no heels or arch supports or if you walk barefooted. Celtic slippers provided this power to the European peoples. But today, they are the slaves of the Jewish fashion industry and so their feet are twisted and misshaped, causing their bodies and spirits to be likewise corrupted by the demon Jews.

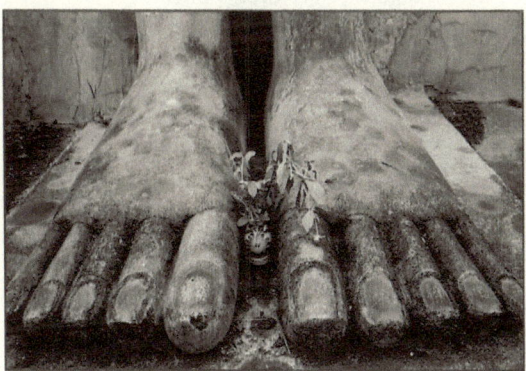

Figure 51

These observations can be verified in all cultures throughout history where the people were either barefoot or wore simple slippers or sandals without heels or arch supports, such as Egyptian Pharaoh Thutmose IV and his mother of the 18th Dynasty (See Figure 53). Notice the triangular shaped feet and the perfectly formed toes, so unlike the twisted feet and toes of modern shoe-wearing people. Such healthy feet are found in all normal human cultures where people go barefooted or wear simple sandals or slippers. Just as a building remains strong if its foundation is square, so also does a human remain strong and healthy if his feet are solid and squarely planted on the ground. The Jewish fashion in shoes causes all manner of diseases and suffering. Just ask anyone with corns or bunions or hammer toes or knee problems. Modern, fraudulent, Jewish physicians operate on the feet, cutting and maiming, rather than giving the patient flat shoes and a foot massage. Podiatrists are among the biggest quacks in Jewish medicine.

Modern Westerners suffer from a variety of diseases that can be directly attributed to the disease-causing Jewish shoes that they wear on their feet. Celtic slippers allow proper posture, a direct contact with the energy of the earth and the ability to walk in the Gait of Power and use the power of the Celtic Wheel, discussed later. With flat shoes and the Gait of Power, tremendous speeds can be achieved in running. Julius Caesar noted this when he wrote in *The Conquest of Gaul*:

> "The Gauls concealed in the wood had already formed up in battle order and were waiting, full of confidence. As soon as they caught sight of the head of the baggage train – the moment which they had agreed upon for starting the battle – they suddenly dashed out in full force and swooped down on our cavalry, which they easily routed. Then they ran down to the river at

such an incredible speed that almost at the same moment they
seemed to be at the edge of the wood, in the water and already
upon us. With equal rapidity they climbed the hill towards our
camp to attack the men who were busy entrenching it."

If the Celts and Gauls ran so fast that Julius Caesar was amazed – a hardened
Roman general who had seen all manner of men – then their speed must have
been phenomenal. Those Celts obviously knew the Gait of Power and the secret of the swastika.

Figure 53: Thutmose IV and mother

The straight back, straight neck, and the concentrated meditation exemplified
by the ancient Celt of the Gundestrup Cauldron, allowed him to reach out with
his mind into the surrounding world. The antlers on his head, you will notice,
are not attached to a hat or any other device. This is because they do not represent real antlers but, rather, the mystical ability of feeling into the world with
one's mind, like Odin's two ravens named "Thought" and Memory." And they
are a symbol that this warrior-priest had attained the stealthy skills and the
leaping and disappearing powers of the buck deer as he sits in meditation with
his back straight, his neck straight and his head erect. He is a master of the
natural world with all its powers. And he has skills in the mystical world accessed through his meditative Mind. Meditation and the Druidic Breath were
legend among the Celts as well as the Norsemen. This knowledge is something
that you, too, can achieve if you do as our ancient ancestors did. In these art
works, they are giving you the map for finding their powers. You can do as
they did, or not. It's up to you, alone, to try.

But there is something else that is hidden in the above panel of the Gundestrup Cauldron because the warrior-priest is holding the torc and the serpent in his hands. Thus, the Celtic method for attaining his straight neck is concealed. Adjoining panels, however, reveal this secret of Celtic meditation. In this panel (See Figure 55), a European warrior is also wearing a torc that represents his attainment of power. Notice how his arms are posed. Try it yourself. Sit as straight as you can. Take a moment to breathe and relax and sit with your back straight and neck upright and then when you feel like all is well and comfortable, lift your arms up with your thumbs pointing upward but rotated toward your ears as in this panel of the Gundestrup Cauldron. You will immediately notice how this posture of your arms automatically causes your neck to straighten even more than you had thought possible. However straight you thought that your neck was, once you raise your arms in this European Celtic yoga posture, your neck becomes even straighter as your shoulder blades drop downward, relieving tension on your neck muscles.

Figure 55

But there's more. What is between this warrior's arms? In the Universal Post Posture (Recall Figure 4), one of the secrets is that the front foot is as light as a feather, ready to move, block or kick. The same, single-weighted cat stance is shown on this Gundestrup panel. And on the left is a leaper, a man who has discovered the swastika secret of Druidic and Celtic leaping. Such nimble fighters were qualified to be horsemen and warriors.

Such a theme is carried over to another panel on the cauldron (See Figure 56). Here the warrior is of an even higher level of attainment. Not only does he wear the torc but he has attained the Celtic Wheel Power. Notice that his thumbs are now pointed toward his ears. Try it yourself, first lifting your arms as in the previous example and then open your thumbs and point them at your ears as in this Gundestrup panel. Do you notice the increase in energy and straightness of posture? The leaper on the left is a more powerful one than in the previous panel. His thighs are thick so his jumping is higher. And he, too, has some of the skills of the Celtic Wheel.

Figure 56

Jumping back from 200 BC in Northern Europe to 1600 BC in the Palace of Knossos, Crete, we find what is called by the archaeologists as a "snake goddess". This is actually not a goddess at all. She is a priestess. (Figure 57) Notice her straight neck and back and the posture of her arms. She too has attained snake spine. She moves with poise and concentrated attention. Those two serpents are deadly vipers. It was a teaching of the Christ that those who have attained spiritual grace would be able to hold serpents in their hands. Such a teaching was not just a gift of Christianity, but was a gift of all people who searched for and found their Qi or Holy Spirit.

You will notice the same erect postures throughout the sculptures and paintings of almost all the ancient peoples, straight backs, and necks. The ancients were people of high spiritual awareness and great personal power. Not all them attained a high level of mystical knowledge, but those who did became the priests and priestesses of the temples and the teachers of the people. Statues were sculpted of them and ritual cauldrons were embossed because they exemplified attainment of a high goal. But they were not gods.

Figure 57: Minoan snake priestess

This Greek sculpture of Apollo from around 650 BC (See Figure 58) is not just typical of such sculptures but also typical of western scientists' views of ancient art. Not being privy to the secrets of meditation and totally ignorant of Qi or Holy Spirit, not experiencing the powers of the ancient peoples first hand, the scientists believe that such statues are not realistic but represent an "ideal." They think that perfection is only something that is attained in the "ideal state of a god" but not attained by human beings.

With their buzzard necks and stooped shoulders, the modern scientists pass judgement on the ancient people without ever understanding what they are judging. This statue of Apollo represents someone who has achieved high perfection in his godly life, sculpted by an artist who also had experienced such perfection, himself. Similar postures are exemplified in sculpture and painting and bas-reliefs throughout the ancient world but are completely misunderstood by the sick and decrepit modern scientists whose spines are crooked, their poor posture resulting from too much study and too much sitting in chairs craning their necks over their books without ever practicing those ancient mystical skills themselves.

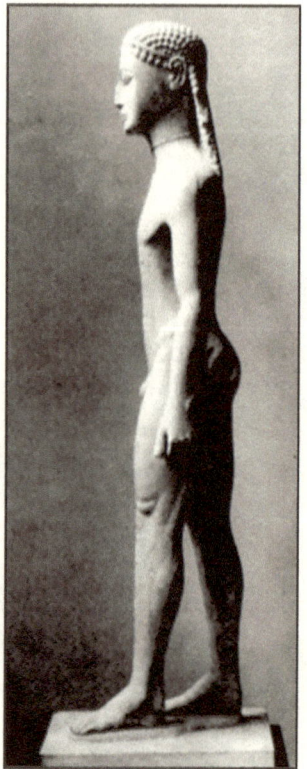

Figure 58: Greek Apollo

One of the earliest examples of the importance of a straight back and spine, is found in the Sumerian culture of around 3000 BC. There were basically two kinds of physicians, those who used magic spells and amulets in an attempt to cure disease and those who used herbs and food as their medicines. The latter kind of physician had a symbol that has been copied throughout history by various kinds of physicians, a serpent on a pole, known as was the Rod of Asclepius, so named after the Greek god of medicine and healing. It is a symbol used by the modern medical monopoly today as their official badge of the healing arts.

However, the Greek physicians who had studied in Babylonia, inherited their symbol from ancient Sumeria. This libation vase of Gudea (See Figure 59) from around 2000 BC, has sculpted on it the healing god Ningishzida. When the entire vase is sketched and stretched out in two dimensions (See Figure 60) you can see that twin snakes entwine a staff. Ningishzida is a Mesopotamian deity of the underworld. His name in Sumerian is translated as "lord of the good tree" and is the earliest known symbol of snakes twining around an axial rod. This is the source of the modern physicians' serpent and staff symbol. The ancient Sumerian physicians used this to symbolize their healing profession because the trunk of "the good tree" is your own spine!

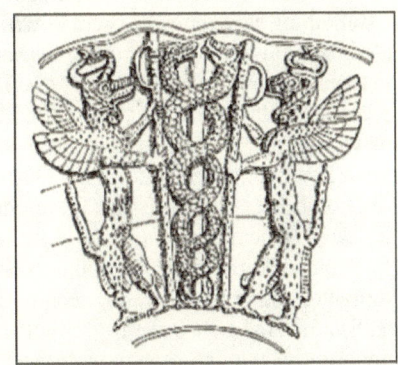

Figure 59: Gudea vase   Figure 60: Nigishida

There have been many theories over the ages as to what this symbol actually means. The yogis claim that the Kundalini serpent is an energy that rises up the spine. Although this is basically true, the actual explanation is a whole lot simpler than this. Their explanation gives the impression that there is a mystical energy that rises up the spine and this mystical energy – because it is mystical – cannot be achieved by anyone other than a yogi.

You, yourself, can find this serpent energy within yourself with the ancient Celtic and Viking spine exercises, merely by rotating your spine in circles beginning at its base. Remember, these ancient people were not distracted with TV or radio. They had lots of quiet time around a fire, sitting around and practicing their spiritual breathing and movement exercises. It is not just an energy but also an actual physical entwining of muscle groups that you can feel.

Here's how it is accomplished. Whether you are sitting in a chair or on the floor, use your mind and think downward to your tail bone. Look and feel inside yourself with your Mind and begin rotating in a circular manner and making a small circle around and around your tail bone. Use slight physical movement to do this. As you begin to feel that circular motion, continue the motion and, using your Mind to direct your energy, move the circling up the spine in a spiral a little at a time all the way to the top of your head. Then practice in the opposition direction. If you practice this exercise, you will find the Kundalini power within yourself in a very short time. The Hindu yogis don't teach this because the knowledge has been lost until now. You will find that this serpent-like spiral will tonify your spinal vertebrae and straighten your back and neck as well as give you a chiropractic massage of the spine, energizing your internal organs.

While it is true that if you will it to happen, an energy does spiral up the spine, that energy is inferior to the very real interplay of muscles and fascia as you actively use your mind to make your spine spiral from the base upward. Anybody can do it if they try. Just don't hurt yourself. The Number One Rule of Internal Kung-Fu is: "If you do anything that hurts, Stop." What Western physicians fail to understand is that pain is natural. It is your body telling you that something is wrong. Western Jewified physicians will give you drugs to deaden the pain while allowing the disease that causes the pain to fester. There is no need to hurt yourself by using too much exertion on any of the exercises that I cover in this book. If you are causing yourself pain, then you are doing them wrong or too energetically. Relaxation is the key. Moving your body gently and without force, allows the Qi (the Holy Spirit) to flow.

It should be noted here that the modern Jewish medical monopoly of the American Medical Association and its British clone, has waged a long legal battle against Chiropractic medicine. It is not that chiropractic is a cure-all, but chiropractors have some healing techniques that the medical physicians do not have. So, the AMA sued them for quackery in order to clear the field from the competition of making money with their own quack methods. As you can see from the above examples and from the ancient symbol of the Rod of Asclepius, that the AMA physicians are blindly fighting against their own ancient origins. "Blindly" because they cannot see their own snake spine and the healing power of proper spinal alignment, and "ancient origins" since their own symbol of the rod of Asclepius symbolizes the self-same profession. This shows the ignorance of modern medicine to its own basis in the ancient world of spiritual knowledge.

You can test whether chiropractic theory is valid or not, yourself. Chiropractic theory claims that since the spine carries nerve impulses into the internal organs, any blockage of nerve impulses by a misaligned spine, will cause disease to the internal organs. It makes sense. If you put a rubber band around your finger tight enough to cut off blood circulation, your finger will die and rot and give you gangrene. I don't recommend that you try this. But use your mind and figure it out for yourself. If a rubber band can do that to your finger, what would happen if internal restrictions cut off nerve energy from your spine to your internal organs? It's the same principle.

Sit in a chair or on the floor and practice the Celtic and Norse spine rotating exercise, move the circular motion upward along your spine and feel the energy of the serpent power straighten your spine and invigorate your internal organs. Once again, don't use force. You should move as soft and gently as silk. The energy is subtle at first, and easy to miss if you are too aggressive with your muscles. It is an energy flow *through* your muscles; it is not an energy *from* your muscles. So, be meek and mild. Use the perceptions of your Mind to find it. It is with your Mind that you will lead and control your own Qi, your own holy spirit.

Just as the Celtic warrior sitting in meditation on the Gundestrup Cauldron, you will discover the secret of the serpent's power and the deer's sensitivity.

Being "wise as serpents and gentle as doves" (Matthew 10:16) means that for True Power, to keep your snake-spine power internally hidden using gentleness rather than muscular force.

Another of the ancient secrets that practitioners of modern martial arts will recognize is this, the horse stance. (See Figure 61) It is a petroglyph from Val Camonica, Italy from some time between 9000 BC to 1000 BC. Do you suppose that the original artist took the time to chip that into the rock out of boredom? Or perhaps he was trying to preserve something about his knowledge that was important to him. The upright arms of this Val Camonica petroglyph also indicates that this Man of Power also knew the secrets of the straight spine and neck of a warrior-priest. His arms are forming not just the same posture as the Celtic warrior-priests of the Gundestrup Cauldron but, combined with his low stance, he is showing us the swastika secrets.

Figure 61: Val Camonica

Nearly identical postures, usually of warriors but just as often of unidentifiable men, are found in the rock carvings and paintings of people worldwide. Most modern martial artists practice this stance with a very rigid and hard, karate-like flavor but students of the internal styles of kung-fu know that this stance is fluid and pliable, while also strong and sturdy. If this stance had nothing special about it other than being like a low squat, it would not be represented in ancient art as often as it has been worldwide. There is something special about the low horse stance that in modern times, can most easily be found it the advanced Tai Chi Chuan schools of Chen and Kuang Ping. (See Figure 62) It is a stance that moves fluidly from one side to the other while maintaining a vertical body posture. In combat, this is vital. In wrestling and throwing, the lower the stance, the easier to throw your opponent. While holding a spear or pole arm, a low stance gives strength in supporting the weapon or in dodging blows or attacking low. It is a power posture and a weightless posture because when it is performed in a relaxed manner, all the bones of the body support the body while the muscles relax. When this happens, the Qi flows and great power can be expressed, as in this Viking broach design showing both a low stance combined with sinuous snake body skills. (See Figure 63) The Vikings knew these powers intimately and so their martial art skills were unbeatable. They were not the brutal fighters that the lying Jewish Media proclaims, rather, they were very sophisticated and skillful warriors practicing what is best described as Viking Kung-Fu.

Figure 62

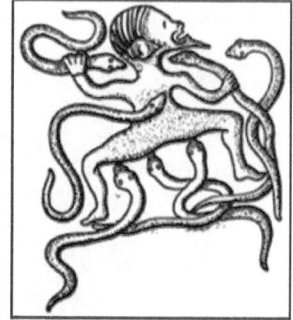

Figure 63: Viking ornament

Sun symbols in ancient religions were often, but not always, represented by a circle. It is obvious that the shape is the same as the sun. Unfortunately, because this knowledge has been hidden for so long, modern scientists have assumed that every round symbol is a sun symbol. In many cases, they are correct, such as for these sun wheels found on Scandinavian rock art (Figure 64). But in the case of the Celtic Wheel, this is not at all true.

Notice once again the panel from the Gundestrup Cauldron. Both the leaper and the meditator are connected to a wheel. The youthful leaper, who has attained Celtic physical prowess, is grasping the wheel with just one hand. The horns on his helmet are protected with end caps to indicate that he is like a domesticated bull; that is, he has been able to quell his passions. But he is not wearing a torc and his neck is bent forward because he has not yet attained the highest level of Celtic meditation. He is at the very edge of spiritual power because he is only just grasping the mystic wheel.

Figure 64: Sun

Notice that the wheel is an extension of the meditator's forearm. It is attached to him as if growing out of him, that is, it is a part of him. It is not a sun wheel because once it meets his arm, no other part of it is visible. He is grasping the rim of the wheel in his hand while the very hub of the wheel is at his elbow and the opposite rim is at his shoulder. This is, once again, where the swirling wheel power or snake spiraling power is generated from the rotating of the arms.

This Celtic wheel was also known in Aryan India as the Wheel of the Dharma. It is not merely an intellectual idea; it is a genuine power latent within all people who search for it. You can experience the Celtic Wheel, yourself with a simple exercise. Simply stand up with your feet parallel and about one foot distance apart. Slowly begin rotating your hips in a circle. Don't do this on a full stomach (or too forcefully) otherwise you might herniate your intestines. *Remember, if you do anything that hurts, stop.* Be relaxed and smooth as silk as you move. With a continuous practice of this simple circular hip rotation, eventually the power of your Qi will manifest. It might take years or it might take a few days or weeks, but the power is there if you take the steps to find it. Rotate your hips in a circle slowly at first and then build up some speed as you gain confidence.

Rotating the hips in circles is not enough, however, since the wheel is found within all parts of the human body which can move in a circular manner. The head and neck, shoulders, knees, ankles, every round joint benefits from this circling exercise. When you practice slowly and with concentrated awareness of your inner mechanics and energies, you will feel your Qi begin to move. This round movement of the Qi is also achieved through meditative breathing. And this is why the Celtic meditator on this Gundestrup panel is represented as having a wheel growing out of his arm, because unlike the leaper who can only make the wheel move through physical exercise, the meditator can move the wheel within himself through use of his concentrated mind. You may not understand this, but those Readers who can control your own Qi know it.

This meditative knowledge was not limited to men. Celtic women, too, could achieve high attainments as shown in another panel from the Gundestrup Cauldron of a woman showing her high spiritual attainment by wearing a torc as she sits in contemplation between two wheels. (see Figure 65) There are many examples of European prehistoric art that depicts people with wheels on their arms or carried in their hands. Mistakenly, the archaeologists claim these to be sun gods but they are, in fact, warriors and adepts who have attained the power of the Celtic Wheel, the power of the Wheel of the Dharma, the Tai Chi Grand Ultimate within themselves. It is also a physical power extremely useful both in combat and good health.

Figure 65: Gundestrup

Understand that this power is a real power that you can experience and express within yourself. It is not just some imaginary idea or theoretical construct. The roundness of the wheel is also found in Chinese Kung-Fu in such schools as Tai Chi Chuan and Ba Gua Zhang. We can use this round energy to great effect for good health and martial arts skills.

Part of the reason why the power of the Sun Wheel was lost to the European peoples was not just that it was a secret teaching of the Druids and Celts and Norse and Germanic Peoples but because the symbol, itself, hid the true meaning of its power simply by the way it was displayed. The Celtic Sun Wheel is usually represented and displayed like this. (see Figure 66) Its symbolic representation shows the power within a man because it represents a Man of Knowledge, a Man of Power, standing with arms outstretched surrounded by his aura. Any child who knows how to turn a perfect cart wheel will recognize what this symbol means. Or perhaps Leonardo DaVinci's drawing can explain it. (see Figure 67) The Celtic Sun Wheel represents Man. This is not an ordinary man, but a man whose bright aura extends and radiates around him like a sphere or like the globe of the sun.

Figure 66: Wheel

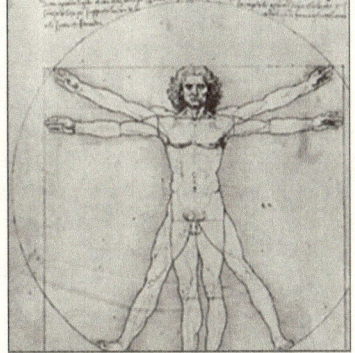

Figure 67: Vitruvian man

This brings up the next level of "wheel power" that the ancient people knew and which is symbolized by the Yin-Yang symbol. You might assume that this is a Chinese symbol. It is, in fact, the symbol used for the Tai Chi Chuan school of Chinese kung fu as well as for many other Chinese and Korean philosophies. However, this particular symbol is from a Roman shield pattern of about 430 AD. The Chinese did not begin using the Tai Chi symbol until around 1500 AD. This design was also found to be the design drawn by the shadow of the tip of a vertical pole at noon as the sun makes its yearly procession. (Figure 69) So, although it is called by its Chinese name of Yin-Yang or Tai Chi ("Grand Ultimate"), it is actually a European discovery. It probably first arrived in China from Europe via the Silk Road since it did not have precursors in Chinese Culture as it did within ancient European Culture.

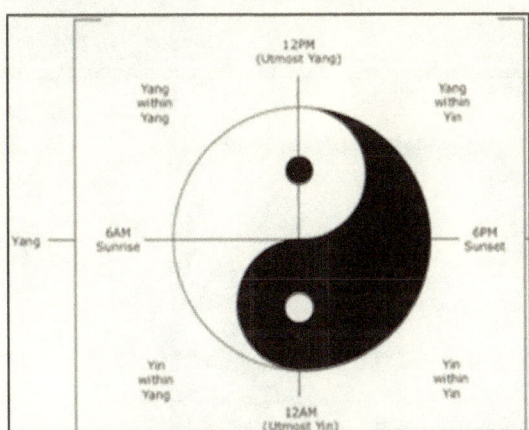

Figure 69: Yin-Yang day and night

The secret of the Tai Chi is a Celtic discovery because the Tai Chi is actually a simplified Celtic Spiral. The mild S-shaped change of direction found on the Tai Chi symbol on that Roman shield design from 430 AD, is beautiful in its simplicity. But it is really a simplified symbol for the more complicated Celtic Spiral found throughout Europe and Scandinavia – and used by European people two thousand years before Chinese usage.

A good example of the Celtic Spiral is found at New Grange, Ireland. (see Figure 70) A closer inspection of this entry stone will show the center of the spiral is not a one-way spin inward. It is, rather, a turning in a Tai Chi curve, reversing direction and spinning outward without stopping. (see Figure 71) It is a continuous and never-ending flow. The Tai Chi symbol is its simplified representation, but the higher knowledge is found in the Celtic Spiral, itself. These were not merely decorations. They guarded the entry ways and were also the ultimate symbol found in the deepest recesses of the Celtic cult centers, places where the light of the sun illuminated just once every year at the solstice.

Figure 70: New Grange stone

Figure 71: Stone detail

Why were these symbols so especially important to the ancient Europeans? This is not something that the scientists can correctly answer. But it is not something mystical and unattainable because it is also a secret found within yourself if you look. You, yourself, can discover the secrets of Druids and Celtic and Viking power – as well as Chinese kung-fu mysteries – by using the following simple map.

As you stand practicing the Celtic Wheel hip rotations, you will find that you can reverse the rotation of the Celtic Wheel in two ways. You can stop and rotate in the opposite direction, which also stops the flow of your Life Force, your Qi. Or by using the tip of your spine to follow the S-shaped curve at the center of the Celtic Spiral, you can reverse the direction of the circle without stopping. (see Figure 73) This sinks the Life Force deep into the internal organs and fills your body with power and light. The two dots on either side of the Tai Chi, represent your two hip joints. Again, you can't discover the ancient secrets unless you are willing to practice the ancient methods. Make the circle as round and smooth and soft as you can. If the circle isn't smooth and round but seems to have bumps or aberrations in it, look into your internal anatomy with your Inner Eye and you will find the cause is usually tight muscles and tense joints. Over time, as you practice the Celtic Wheel exercise, these physical disabilities such as stiff joints, arthritis and old age will disappear. It is the healing aspects of this ancient knowledge.

Figure 73: Yin-Yang change direction

This leads us further into discussion of the Celtic spiral and swirl. Both the Celts and the Norse were fond of intricate designs involving knots and complicated swirling patterns because these were both artistically interesting and they also reflected the knowledge that they had of the movements of the Life Force (the Holy Spirit or Qi) within the human body. When you are able to manifest your own Qi you will be able to move it at will throughout your body and outside of your body simply through the power of your Mind. (See Appendix A: How to Develop Your Qi and Live Within Your Holy Spirit) As you direct your Qi with your Mind, you can guide it twisting and swirling and spiraling throughout your internal anatomy. It heals as it moves as long as you move gently and as smooth as silk. This is being "wise as serpents and gentle as doves."

The Celtic Spiral is a good place to begin with this knowledge because it is quickly and easily discovered within yourself with these very simple exercises.

This ancient Celtic knowledge pre-dates the Great Pyramid of Giza in Egypt by more than 500 years and knowledge of the Celtic Spiral predates Stonehenge by about 1,000 years.

Take another careful look at the Celtic Spiral. (Figure 71) Are these merely decorative art? Absolutely not. Such spirals are one of the secrets of ancient Europe. Notice that these are not spirals that come to an end. That is, they do not spiral inward and then stop but they follow an eternal and unending path. When the spiral reaches the farthest most interior point, it turns upon itself and reverses direction without stopping.

Softly and gently, continue circling your hips and once you feel comfortable, begin spiraling the tip of your tail bone inward, little by little making smaller and smaller circles spiraling inward until you reach the very smallest circle that you can find within yourself.

Then use the Celtic Spiral's S-shaped turn to reverse direction and slowly, slowly begin to increase the size of the spiral outward until you reach the Celtic Sun Wheel once again. You are now moving in reverse without stopping. And there you have discovered the secret method of the Druids and Celts and Vikings for gaining internal spiritual power, good health, physical strength, martial prowess and knowledge of the immortal soul. This is not just a physical exercise. If you practice it with an observing mind, your spiritual power, your Qi, will manifest like a great energized river carrying you along. It is a truly enlightening and amazing experience to feel the power of the Life Force circulating within. All movements should be powered with your Mind directing your breath. (see Appendix A)

The Celtic spiral has only been a secret and a mystery because people stopped practicing it and so lost contact with their inner spiritual powers.

Whenever the Celtic Spiral is found in a group of three, this indicates the basic, holy family unit of parents and child, all connected in the spirit as one.

But even among warriors, such as this drawing of the Scandinavian rock art of the Vikings (see Figure 74), you can see that the knowledge of the Celtic Wheel and the Spiral Power was known to these great adepts of the North, also.

Once you become proficient with the Celtic Wheel rotation, the Celtic Spiral and its Tai Chi reverse, your inner Holy Spirit will begin to manifest. You will feel a warmth and feeling of energy and then a great flow of power as if you are caught up in a river of energy, all a manifestation of your own inner power coming to life. The Wheel of the Dharma will turn with a power that you never realized that you had. If this power was a dream or an illusion or a myth, it would not have been recorded in the same way by so many different people across thousands of years. You can have this ancient power for yourself, if you look for it within yourself and by using these ancient techniques. It's all very simple.

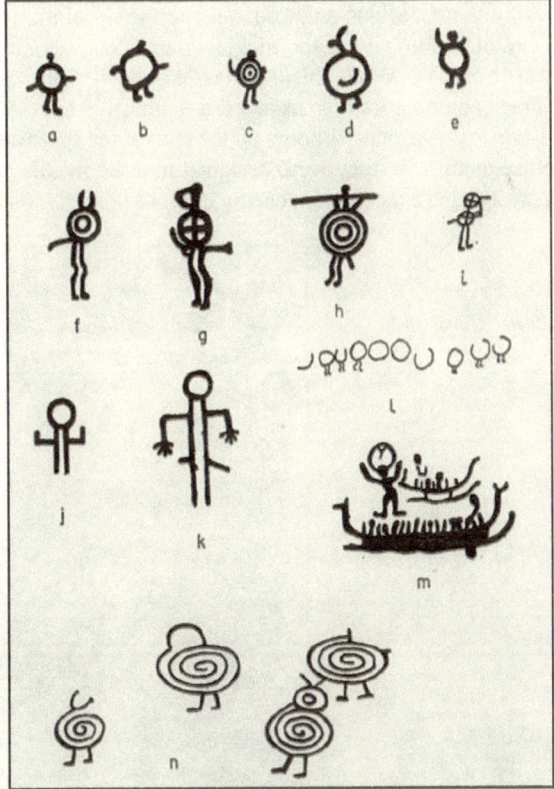

Figure 74: Diskmen

This is also a great secret of Viking, Celtic, and Aryan martial arts. A Celtic Wheel and Spiral was used by the Celts and Vikings in their sword and spear play. These were the methods of reversing energies and defeating an opponent's aggression with blending and reversing evasions. It was among the greatest warrior secrets of the Scandinavians, the Norse, the Celts, the Germans and the Gauls.

Many people believe that the Norsemen were crude savages. They were, in fact, highly skilled fighters who knew the innermost secrets of what today would be called Viking Kung-Fu. Their art has been preserved today in the Scandinavian techniques of Stav. For example, this knowledge of the power of the Celtic Wheel and Celtic Spiral, can been seen on this Celtic shield boss (Figure 75) and on this Battersea Celtic shield that was pulled out of the Thames River. (Figure 76)

Archaeologists, who have not been trained in martial arts, see the designs on these implements of war only as magical symbols or artistic designs. In a way, they actually are magical symbols because they trace the designs of all the possible curves of attack and defense tactics made by the tip of a sword or spear point. Study these designs and you can see the tip of a sword or spear, swaying and circling about. What the magician-armorer was attempting with his designs, was to build into the shield a magical knowledge of all the possible weapons attack combinations, so as to ward them off in combat. It was as if the shield was magically saying, "I know all the sword and spear attack patterns and I will repulse them." So, they were designed into the shields and bosses to magically turn away such attacks by an enemy's sword or spear point.

Figure 75: Thames Shield Boss   Figure 76: Thames Battersea shield

The Thames Battersea Shield is claimed by the archaeologists to have been thrown into the river as an offering to the gods. Most likely, this heavy and valuable shield with every possible sword-tip and spear-point attacking pattern incorporated into its warding-off magical design, was thrown into the river because it had failed to protect its bearer from death. The shield is too small to wield in combat. It was probably a toy shield made for a rich king's son. The son probably died and the king threw the unlucky shield into the Thames in grief more than as an offering to the gods, as the archaeologists assume.

After all, what use do the gods have for a toy shield?

In addition to the magical spear- and sword- repulse designs, something that is not easily seen in photos of the Battersea Shield is the fact that over each of the red glass disks is a swastika, that ancient symbol that maps and represents the personal power and good health of those who know its secret. These swastikas, turning the mighty arms and legs of the men of power who surround the central king and princes, give the swirling designs even more meaning. The swastika is the innermost secret power of the men of the British Isles and across all Europe into India.

If, in your rotations of the Celtic Wheel and Spiral within your body, your holy spirit manifests, that is, if you feel the internal flow of Power and feel the radiant buoyancy of your aura expand as your mind attains clarity of perception, then you can realize and experience the next ancient level of power by manifesting what is known as the Orphic Egg.

But first take a look at another prehistoric, Bronze Age stone carving from Camonica Valley, Italy. This ancient pictograph shows a face within a spiral. (See Figure 77) In a certain way, this is actually a drawing of your own face as you look upward from within the spiraling Celtic swirl that you make as you rotate your hips in the Celtic Wheel exercise. Rotate and spiral your energy inward and outward using the Celtic Spiral. As you feel the spiral energy swirl around you, look up to the sky and you will feel exactly what this ancient drawing is recording for eternity – yourself within the vortex of your swirling spirit.

Figure 77: Spiral face

With this knowledge gained from the Celtic Wheel and the Celtic Spiral techniques, you will feel your spirit, your Qi, begin to glow and radiate within your body. As you become proficient at moving your spirit, and as your holy spirit becomes stronger and more internally centered, it will begin to radiate outside of your body. You will find as you turn the Celtic Wheel that your holy spirit is shaped like a luminous egg. This radiant spirit is alive and moves with the swirling serpent-like movements of your Qi as you rotate the Celtic Wheel and move that wheel spiraling into and out of the Celtic Spiral. What this radiating, egg-shaped aura is, is the actual Orphic Egg. You can see your own spirit with your eyes either open looking through Odin's Eye or the Buddha's Eye or closed using your Inner Eye. But most people don't look. So, of course, they miss seeing what their own holy spirit looks like. Jesus called this egg-shaped spiritual aura, "the pearl of great price."

This term, the Orphic Egg, like so many terms used to describe the ancient knowledge, is garbled behind modern "interpretations" and an over-reliance on philosophical and over-educated blindness. The works of such modern "mythologists" as Joseph Cambell are an example of this sort of convoluted and wordy stupidity wrapped around fallacies. According to such wordy "philosophical interpretations," the Orphic Egg is an ancient Greek tradition from whence the universe supposedly hatched. But like so many of the Greek "mysteries," its actual meaning was lost in all the extra baggage that the ancient Greek priests used to hide its actual reality from the common man.

Only the select few who were "inducted" into the mystery cults of the Greek temples, were taught the actual meaning. To keep it hidden from the masses, it was cloaked in myth. Instead of teaching Mankind of our innate, immortal, luminous spirit, the Greek priests claimed that only the gods and the students of the priests could be privy to the secrets. And so, the actual secret of innate power of Man became lost, to be replaced as an imagination within the minds of philosophers and the theories of blind art historians.

Now that you have the ancient methods for manifesting the power of your spirit, what else is there in this? First, I should explain the manifestations of the human aura as recorded in the archaeological record. From Volume I, *The Sumerian Swindle*, you already know that the so-called "Maltese Cross" and the "Tree of Life" found on Sumerian cylinder seals (See Figure 79) are representations of the human aura. This knowledge was common in Mesopotamia more than two thousand years before there were any lying Jews to deceive Mankind about religion.

Figure 79: Maltese Cross cylinder seal

But there was an even earlier knowledge of the human aura recorded in the rock art of Valcamonica, Italy. (Figure 81) These indicate the radiant glow of the human aura and halo (the holy spirit) of those who have attained this spiritual knowledge within themselves. Even the cave men could attain the power of their radiant spirits and the halo of their Holy Being. Modern people are no different in ability, but are lacking in faith or belief and do not have the simple maps and methods for achieving such power – until found in this book.

Figure 81: Valcamonica halos

Many, many examples of this aura which unspiritual, materialistic, faithless, modern scientists have been unable to understand, is found in Egyptian art. Since the scientists do not know what they are looking at, they have substituted their own ignorance for the truth and have mislead generations of researchers with their stupid theories. For example, these kinds of paintings are common in Egypt (see Figure 82). The scene is common but what is also common in countless such paintings is the cone that is on the heads of these nobles.

Figure 82: Head cone

At such a banquet scene, the scientists have surmised that what these Egyptians have on their heads is a "scented grease cone." Their scientific theory is this: As the grease melts in the heat, it releases a pleasant scent and cools the wearer. Anyone who knows anything about the so-called "cooling effects" of grease on your head, will know that such a theory is ridiculous. Grease is good to fry an egg, but not to cool you off on a hot day. Anyone who knows anything about cleaning grease out of your clothes, will know that their theory is ridiculous. Why would the Egyptians, surrounded by gritty, dusty deserts want grease on the clothes or in their wigs in an age when soap and water was not as common as it is today?

And the theory is bogus by the finds of archaeology, itself. Among the thousands of wigs excavated from Egyptian tombs over the years, not a one of them was found to contain even a trace of grease, tallow or wax. Obviously, the scientists are wrong. But what, then, are those glowing cones on the heads of the Egyptians? They are quite literally representations of the human aura. This is identical to what was represented in Sumerian art. (recall Figure 26)

Figure 83: Singer and musicians

Another example are these Egyptian women musicians, a flute player and a singer. (See Figure 83) Caught up in the rhythm of the song, shaking their heads so that the hair on their wigs fly around, they are certainly not losing their alleged "grease cone" from off their heads because it is not a grease cone, it is their holy auras radiating. You will notice that in this painting, (See Figure 84) the Egyptian women are shown with an extra curved line around their heads indicating the extent of their auras wrapping around their heads as it radiates from their bodies. This halo around the head and its association with spiritual immortality was symbolized by the Egyptian Ankh. (See Figure 85)

Figure 84: Ladies with aura   Figure 85: Ankh

This extension of the spirit above the head should not be confused with the bump on top of the head as seen in Buddhist sculptures of the 15th century AD (recall Figure 46) or the Goddess Parvati of the 12th century India. These all represent the aura as it extends above the head of the adept. But in addition to the aura, this bump is a very real manifestation of what happens when you have developed weightless standing and weightless sitting. The entire skeletal structure of your body is balanced by the fascia and ligaments and these are all perfectly balanced at the top of the head, which develops as a bump at the balance point and an internal feeling that your head is higher than it looks in a mirror. As you rotate the Celtic Wheel around your head, the entire muscles and fascia around the cranium feels elevated and as tall as the Egyptian pharaoh's hat while your entire body is held up as if by a string or like the very tip of a Thai Buddha's head. (See Figure 87) Notice the flame shape, a fire that was also recorded among the early Christians, flaming above their heads.

Figure 87: Thai Buddha

Figure 88: Protecting wings   Figure 89: Egyptian wings

Auras in Egyptian art are also often represented as *wings* (See Figure 88) radiating from the arms of various beings. (See Figure 89) You can feel this, yourself, as a radiating energy. This knowledge of their radiating aura, was also represented by the crown of the Pharaoh from the most ancient times. The pre-Dynastic style of crown (Figure 90) was carried over into all later eras of Egypt as the crown of Pharaoh. (Figure 91) Rather than the small aura radiating 20 or 30 centimeters above the head, as in the Asian Buddhas, the pharaoh wore a crown that represented the shape of and the size of his powerful aura. But in this case, rather than something that is observed from the outside, this shape is seen by your inner eye as what your head feels like when your Qi circulates around your skull and between your scalp. Your head feels as if it is suspended upward by a string and your forehead feels very high and tall. Anyone can feel this who looks with your inner eye.

Figure 90   Figure 91

Notice, too, in this picture, the broad feet and individually perfect toes of both the Pharaoh and his goddesses. Debilitating footwear of the modern Jewish garment industry, was not a part of the healthy lifestyle of ancient Egypt. People who achieved high levels of spiritual power, did so in bare feet or wearing Celtic slippers or Egyptian sandals. Notice the perfect toes. Very few women today can boast anything other than the twisted feet and painful, misshaped toes cause by Jewish high-heeled footwear. Modern society has not simply forgotten its ancient powers but has been purposely swindled out of those powers by devils seeking money. The history of how the Jews use the fashion industry to destroy Western Culture is described in Volume III, *The Blood-Suckers of Judah.*

The Egyptian "greeting" also showed their knowledge of the human aura. This drawing from the Egyptian Book of the Dead from around 1300 BC shows the greeting. (Figure 92) And it is seen on countless sculptures throughout the entire three-thousand-year history of Egypt. (see Figure 93) Among the ancient Egyptians this form of greeting meant, "Greetings, I feel your holy aura" or "My ka perceives your ka."

Figure 92: Greeting   Figure 93: Greeting

What many people do not know is that the spiritual knowledge of ancient Europe is as old as, and sometimes older than, that of Egypt. The dolmens of Europe, in places such as Stonehenge and Newgrange, all show a very high spiritual knowledge that predates that of Egypt. It is a knowledge of an even higher level because instead of a blend of the human shape with the spiritual aura as in Egypt, only the aura, itself, is represented in European art, such as in this photo of a Celtic sanctuary in France from 2000 BC. (Figure 94)

These radiant auras show the ancient French Celtics as they saw themselves, glowing and bright. Look closely and you can see where the stone in the foreground has one of the auras turning into flames and one of the auras has a human head at its top. Notice also the use of the upright snakes at the bottom, representing the snake power of the spine. These stones represent large groups of Celtic family and tribal members gathered together. Their individual auras are represented. The chief priest with his fiery aura takes the central position and all of the various tribes members stand around and look out from behind one another's auras. In modern parlance, it is a "group photo" chiseled in stone.

Figure 94: Celtic auras

These auras and rays of spiritual light did not always find expression in silence. The temples, sanctuaries, and meeting places of these ancient people were often filled with chanting, mantras (that is, repetitions of the names of gods or of prayers), music and song. After all, the entire universe is in constant vibration. Every atom is vibrating. Every molecule, planet, and star is in vibration. Even the emptiness of space has its own tone. As these Egyptian singers show, they were using the vibration of their voices to affect the universe. (See Figure 95) These paintings do not show them snapping their fingers as the archaeologists claim; they are shown singing a vibration and feeling that vibration in the palm of their hands. Try it yourself. It is not difficult. If you cannot feel your palm vibrate when you sing into it, perhaps you are using the wrong vibration. Try an "Om" sound. Or like the ancient Sumerians, sing the Sky

God's name of An and feel the vibration of his name in your own hand. Or use the mantra of Odin and see if you can feel the Presence of the Eternal One.

Figure 95: Mundra singers

Using the vibration of holy mantras, songs, and poetry, is one way for attuning oneself to the vibration of the universe and the vibration of God. The ancient people discovered the uses of sound to produce real effects in the world. The sounds of prayer, mantras and spells were used for good and bad effects. How such vibrations are used in modern times for building and destroying entire nations, is covered in Volume III, *The Blood-Suckers of Judah* where it is shown how the Jewish music industry destroys Western Culture by using the sounds of garbage and the songs of talentless morons.

Dear Reader, I am not giving you some "esoteric, mysterious, unobtainable, mythological" fantasy. You can have the ancient powers for yourself merely by practicing these ancient Ways of Knowledge and Power that were written down in ordinary and easy-to-understand petroglyphs, sculptures, and paintings by our ancient ancestors. All you have to do in order to obtain this ancient knowledge and power for yourself, is to walk the same path and practice the same exercises and techniques that they did.

Belief or theory have nothing to do with this because if you only believe that these powers exist within yourself, then you have not really experienced them. If you have not really experienced them, then you do not have knowledge of them. Without actual knowledge, then you have nothing but empty belief. Although belief and faith are important stepping stones toward knowledge, they are not knowledge, themselves. It is merely a matter of doing the exercises and thereby gaining the benefits. It is very simple.

If you practice these exercises, your spiritual and physical powers will automatically manifest. Your personal religious convictions are not so important because you will gain the benefits regardless of your religious convictions. And why? Because these ancient techniques are basic to all of Mankind. Man! The luminous, spiritual Being!

Much of the luminous radiation of the human spirit known to the ancient people, was also taught by Jesus and therefore known by the early Christians as you shall see in later chapters. The ancient peoples, using a variety of names and religious themes for what they knew, had true and powerful knowledge of their own spiritual might and a genuine knowledge of God – a knowledge that went far beyond mere words for a people who had no words to express their knowledge. But this knowledge was, and is today, completely unknown to the destructive and dark powers that animate the crooked Jews and their demon spawn known as Islam.

From the above chapter, you can see that symbols, images, statues, and paintings were all methods for transmitting religious and mystical information among peoples who had no written language. And even among people who could read and write, such as the Egyptians and Mesopotamians, graphic arts conveyed ideas and data in ways that words cannot. The old saying that "a picture is worth a thousand words," becomes even more true when the people who paint the pictures or sculpt the bas-reliefs do not even have one, single, written word to tell what they knew.

Therefore, what can be said of an allegedly "religious" system such as Judaism or Islam, that routinely destroys the religious graphic arts of other peoples? It is not that these other people were "evil" or "an abomination" at all. When you look at the Jews' and the Muslims' paucity of actual experience of God or of the Great Beyond, and when you see the ignorant and diabolical nature of these two Semitic hoaxes, then you can see that their methods of destroying the religious knowledge of other people, were simply designed to envelope the Hebrew and Arab people in the blackest of ignorance. By keeping their congregations ignorant, the evil Semitic priests could foist their lies disguised as "wisdom" and "truth." After all, what else was left following the destruction of all other religions other than the teachings of the Semitic priests? When all that a people have, are lies to follow; then what else can they follow other than the lies of the rabbis and Imams? What else remains among the smoldering ruins?

The Semites always destroyed people who were better than themselves. Whether as illiterate Hyksos raiders or illiterate Arabian bandits, they multiplied like cancer cells through rape and multiple wives and concubines who were all culturally encouraged to produce as many little gangsters as possible. They murdered, pillaged, and burnt down every vestige of religion expressed by other people, whether in religious iconography, statues, or written archives, so that only their own foul lies could be taught. And to control those stupid bandits, the demon rabbis and fiendish Imams prohibited them from learning any other religious ideals while encouraging them to smash, scratch out and burn the religious symbols, statues, and graphic arts of all other people. Through their wanton destruction of True Religions and the erasure of all religious knowledge, if the Semitic cults of Judaism and Islam can be considered to be anything other than *anti-religions*, then one must surely agree that by using the death and extinction of millions of people as a "proof" of its superiority, then bubonic plague can also claim to be holy. Judaism and Islam are the Devil's Truth.

CHAPTER 5

PAGANS AND IDOLATERS, MUCH HOLIER THAN JEWS

One of the greatest surprises in one's study of the archaeology and the comparative history of the Jews is that every people in the entire history of Mankind was better than the Jews. After destroying nearly every proof of this that they could find, what we have today are the lies of the Jews telling us how "holy" they are and how everybody else is a "sinner." Do you not see the incredible mendacity in this? By assassinating the character of the people who were better than themselves, then destroying all records to the contrary, the Jews then declared themselves to be saints with no survivors to naysay their fictitious claims.

As you now understand from reading Chapter 4, the secrets of ancient Man's power and of God's manifestation within Man, were recorded in paintings, sculptures and bas-reliefs. It was for this reason that Terah, the patriarch of the moneylender guild in Ur and Harran, *forbade such images and paintings* in all territories that his Benjamite gangsters occupied. He wanted complete power over the Hebrew tribes, with not even a graphic symbol remaining to lead them away from his plot. He wanted them to worship his god alone, the god of the moneylenders, located at a single fortified city, within a single temple under his control and permanently inheritable by the genealogical lineage of his own family. So, it was a basic strategy of what later would be called Judaism to destroy the temples, writings, statues and paintings of all other peoples, leaving nothing but the Jewish tales by which the Hebrew priests would manage the lives of the ignorant Hebrews, while deceiving and swindling the people among whom they were allowed to live. It was a form of cultural genocide that left no one alive to tell any stories about God other than what the Jews wanted people to believe. For when tyrannizing ignorant and illiterate people, even symbols and graphical art that carries an alternate message, is anathema to the tyrant. An example of this in modern times is the banning of the ancient swastika. Using force to make a mere graphic symbol illegal, means that the Devil's Truth is being told about it. This same Semitic method for destroying true religious knowledge would be used millennia later by the murdering Muslim werewolves.

Yes, the Jews are the world's greatest frauds and liars. Modern archaeology proves this, along with other sciences such as philology, comparative literature and linguistics. The picture of Israel's past as presented in the *Hebrew Bible* is a fiction. Unfortunately for Mankind, the advances in archaeological knowledge are relatively recent. Archaeology has only been a recognized science since 1812 AD, when Assyriology was founded. Now, at the beginning of the 21st century AD, the Jews have had well over 2,500 years to swindle, deceive and betray the people of the world with their pompous hypocrisy and malicious criminality mixed within the hoax of the *Hebrew Bible*. The proofs of their swindles and betrayals have only gradually come to light in the past 200 years, as the archaeologists began to uncover the buried archives in the ruined cities of the ancient Near East – cities like Eridu, in Sumeria, where civilization began.

Even with archaeology, it is difficult to piece together the history of Palestine or that of the Jews who embezzled it, because of the frauds that even some modern-day archaeologists perpetuate. Just because an archaeologist is a type of scientist does not mean that everything he proclaims should automatically be accepted as true. This is especially important to understand in regard to the Jewish archaeologists who have a political agenda behind their assertions regarding the ancient history of Palestine.

The biggest problem that modern scientists have had in understanding the ancient secrets of early civilization and prehistory is that, as men and women, they are unhealthy and sickly individuals themselves. Raised in a modern society that promotes unnatural and unhealthy lifestyles and demented thought patterns, modern scientists are unable to decipher the ancient secrets of perfection, the splendor of Enlightenment, the awesomeness of Deity or the comfort of supreme good health.

Robert O. Becker, M.D., himself a scientist, writes of the modern scientist in this manner:

> "Dispassionate philosopher inquiring into nature from the sheer love of knowledge, single-minded alchemist puttering about a secluded basement in search of elixirs to benefit all humanity – these ideals no longer fit most scientists. Even the stereotype of Faust dreaming of demonic power is outdated, for most scientists today are overspecialized and anonymous – although science as a whole is somewhat Mephistophelian in its disregard for the effects of its knowledge. It's a ponderous beast, making enormous changes in the way we live but agonizingly slow to change its own habits and viewpoints when they become outmoded.
>
> "The public's conception of the scientist remains closest to its image of the philosopher – cold and logical, making decisions solely on the basis of the facts, unswayed by emotion. The lay person's most common fear about scientists is that they lack human feelings. During my twenty-five years of research, I've found this to be untrue yet no cause for comfort. I've occasionally seen our species' nobler impulses among them, but I've also found that scientists as a group are at least as subject to human failings as people in other walks of life.
>
> "It has been like this throughout the history of science. Many, perhaps even most, of its practitioners have been greedy, power-

hungry, prestige-seeking, dogmatic, pompous asses, not above political chicanery and outright lying, cheating, and stealing."

Some of the "political chicanery and outright lying, cheating and stealing" is practiced by modern Jewish scientists and historians, whose purpose is to conceal and obfuscate the crimes of the Jews throughout history. By creating false history that glorifies themselves, the Jews assume a present day "prestige" that they palm off on the unwary as genuine status. "The falsification of history has done more to impede human development than any one thing known to Mankind," said Rousseau.

One of the modern confusions about who the Jews actually are stems from their use of the same words to describe different people of different eras, as well as different words to describe the same people. For example, the word "Jew" has many meanings to modern people. The word "Israel" has many meanings to modern people. Jews who become modern history writers and history teachers, purposely and falsely promote such confusions, because they are trying to perpetuate the Biggest Lie Ever Told and conceal who the perpetrators of that lie really are. *The Jews have never, ever been the people whom they claim to be.*

As explained in Volume I, *The Sumerian Swindle*, the Hyksos who invaded Egypt were actually the pawns of the moneylenders of Babylonia and Assyria. They were finally expelled from Egypt by Pharaoh Ahmose (1550-1525 BC). The Hyksos were called "Apiru" by both the Egyptians and the Canaanites into whose territory they fled. The pronunciation of "Apiru" became "Hebrew." "Apiru" means "bandit," because that's what the Hebrews were and a bandit culture is what they have always practiced. So, the direct meaning of the word "Hebrew" is still, to this day, "bandit." Over the long centuries, the root meaning of the word was forgotten. Modern people just assume that the word "Hebrew" means: Those people whom we read about in the Old Testament, whom we assume were the same tribes of people we call "Jews" today. But this is incorrect. The Jews were a later subversive manifestation of the Hebrews.

Throughout this book, I try to only use the word "Jews" when it applies both to the ancient Hebrews who became Jews and to the modern Jews. Their ancient forebears who were Canaanites, Babylonians, Hebrews and Assyrians were not called "Jews" in those days, but if they were the ancestors of modern Jews, then I will usually name them as Jews in the text so as to keep the historical threads connected. They were all Semites related to one another through gang affiliation, marriage, and tribal alliances. The distinction between Hebrews and Jews will become clear later.

For now, let's consider the words "Israel" and "Judah." As you know, these two words represent the two kingdoms that were situated in the highlands of Palestine. But, for a kingdom that the rabbis call "great and powerful," there is nothing in the archaeological record alone which indicates anything about a political entity called "Israel." Why? Because this alleged "kingdom" existed only in the pages of the *Hebrew Bible*. Except for a single goat farm in ancient Canaan, this name never existed in the ancient world and was completely unknown to the people living within its alleged boundaries and outside its alleged borders. The designation of a place called "Israel" as a political phenomenon depends solely upon the use of the *Hebrew Bible* – the Biggest Lie Ever Told. As is subsequently shown, most biblical traditions are Jewish lies.

In the entire ancient Near East, the only record of an entity called "Israel" is found in the *Hymn of Victory of Pharaoh Merneptah*. The date of this commemorative hymn relates it to Merneptah's victory over the Libyans in the spring of his fifth year (~1230 BC). In that context, we meet the only instance of the name "Israel" in ancient Egyptian writing.

> "The princes are prostrate, saying: 'Mercy!'
> Not one raises his head among the Nine Bows.
> Desolation is for Tehenu; Hatti is pacified;
> Plundered is the Canaan with every evil;
> Carried off is Ashkelon; seized upon is Gezer;
> Yanoam is made as that which does not exist;
> *Israel is laid waste, his seed is not;*
> Hurru is become a widow for Egypt!
> All lands together, they are pacified;
> Everyone who was restless, he has been bound
> by the King of Upper and Lower Egypt: Ba-en-Re
> Meri-Amon;
> the Son of Re: Mer-ne-Ptah Hotep-hir-Maat,
> given life like Re every day."

In this hymn, the word "Israel" is the only one of the names in this context which is written with the hieroglyphic determinative of people, rather than land. Thus, there was an "Israel" in Canaan, but it was not yet settled by people. Even at this late date, three hundred years after the Hyksos were chased out of Egypt, they were still no more than wandering bands of thieves and goat rustlers, certainly not an established kingdom, as the *Hebrew Bible* claims.

Merneptah's stela does give the hieroglyphic country determinatives to settled peoples like the Rebu, Terneh, Haiti, Ashkelon, etc., and the hieroglyphic determinative of people to unlocated groups like the Madjoi, Nau, and Tekten. However, as late as 1230 BC, there was no "Kingdom" of Israel, but merely some wandering goat thieves calling themselves "Israel" as a coalition of tribes. Thus, any use of the word "Israel" is misleading if applied to those ancient people as anything other than scattered tribes of Hyksos goat farmers. Even at 1230 BC, there was no country named "Israel."

The word "Israel" has been ambiguous for much of Jewish history, even into modern times with the establishment of the modern bandit-state of Israel. To end the ambiguity, the word "Israelian" will be used to refer to the ancient people of the northern Kingdom of Israel. (Note that the word "Israeli" is used specifically for the people of the modern terrorist state of Israel.) Thus, when discussing the time of the so-called "divided kingdom," Israelians and Judeans will be indicated as comprising the Hebrew tribes.

As late as the 8th century BC, a Canaanite king, Azitawadda of Adana, dedicated a citadel and city which he had founded, declaring the good deeds he had performed for his people. Notice that this Canaanite, whom the Jews so much malign, speaks here of doing good.

> "I am Azitawadda, the blessed of Ba'al, the servant Ba'al, whom Awrikku made powerful, king of the Danunites. Ba'al made me a father and a mother to the Danunites. I have restored the Danunites, I have expanded the country of the Plain of Adana from the rising of the sun to its setting. In my days, the Danunites had everything good and plenty to eat and well-being. I have filled the storehouses of Pa'r. I have added horse to horse, shield to shield, and army to army, by virtue of Ba'al and the Gods (El). I shattered the wicked. I have removed all the evil that was in the country. I have set up my lordly houses in good shape and I have acted kindly toward the roots of my sovereignty."

King Azitawadda was a good person and a religious man. He names his god *Baal* and used the name *El* for the other gods. *El* was one of the names that the Hebrews called their god before the priests picked the "Yahweh" name. Further, in his dedications, he names "El-the-Creator-of-the-Earth and the Eternal-Sun and the whole group of the children of the Gods (El)." Thus, the Canaanites viewed their god as the greatest god, just as all other peoples in the ancient Near East looked upon their gods as the greatest of gods. Doing good and removing evil was a Canaanite virtue. The very words of this ancient Canaanite are different from how the *Hebrew Bible* portrays them: with malice, slander, Semitic hatred and character assassination.

What is unknown to most modern people is that these very same Canaanite gods were taken over by the Hebrews. *Yahweh* was a Canaanite god. *Yahweh* was not merely an unknown god waiting in the wings for his "holy chosen" goat rustlers to show up, so he could bless them with circumcised penises and bagels. It was the Babylonian moon god, *Sin*, and later a Canaanite god, *El Shaddai* – the god of the mountain – whom Abraham originally worshiped. The Jews were never picked out by a special god who loved them best, other than in a forged book that they themselves had written. Just like all of the other peoples of the ancient Near East, they worshiped whatever god resided in whatever territory they invaded. All of the gods were resident gods of specific territories.

There is absolutely nothing in the *Hebrew Bible* that makes claims for a life after death, because the original belief system of Judaism assumed that everyone already knew what happened after death. According to Mesopotamian religions (of which Judaism is a Babylonian variation), the gods of the underworld did not render a Last Judgment, as in the Egyptian or the later Christian and Muslim traditions. In fact, neither the dead man's virtues nor his sins on earth were considered when assigning him a place in the underworld. After all, both the good and the bad alike died and were buried. So, the Mesopotamians assumed that their afterlife would also be alike – not necessarily eternal punishment or paradise, but merely an eternal underground gloom.

The worst punishment dispensed to a sinner was denial of entry by the gods to the netherworld. In this way, the sinner became a hungry ghost, sentenced to sleeplessness and denied access to funerary offerings. Even foreigners were permitted to enter the Mesopotamian netherworld. Lepers were allowed entrance, but they were kept safely apart from the other dead. Thus, the Mesopotamians believed in life after death, although it was a life of eternal gloom in the underworld.

Both modern man and ancient man are stupid in their own way. Ancient man did not understand the Universe, and in awe of it, he observed its spiritual nature and considered it holy and filled with Life. Modern scientists still do not understand the material universe. Blinded with the arrogance of limitless data and partial knowledge, they consider it lifeless. Who is the wiser? The Ancient Ones who did not understand the Universe, but who saw a living and eternal God within it? Or the modern scientists who also do not understand the Universe, but who see only death and darkness within it? Even two men in the same room cannot identically describe where they are. So, how can an atheist and a theist agree on a description of the Universe?

Who is better able to deal with Life and Death? Ancient man who sought solace with the gods or the modern scientific man who has no solace? All of a man's life is summed up in his death. And his death is in the hands of Eternity, no matter how smart he thinks he is. Yet, what eternity does a modern man have that is superior to what the ancient people found? Without the vital link to what is found in Life, what chance does a modern man have when facing what is found in Death? Our ancient ancestors told us, if we know how to understand the signs and messages they left for us to follow. You saw how they did this in Chapter 4. Now, let's read some of their actual wisdom and see how the Jews stole everything that they claim is "Jewish."

Archaeology shows that in the Old Babylonian period, most literary texts were not in temples, but private houses. Compare the proverbs from Sumeria, Babylonia and ancient Egypt with those in the *Hebrew Bible* and you will see from where the Jews stole what they claim is "Jewish Wisdom." Here are a few Sumerian and Babylonian proverbs:

> • A perverse child -- his mother should never have given birth to him; his personal god should never have fashioned him!
> • The fox had a stick with him: "Whom shall I hit?" He carried a legal document with him: "What can I challenge?"
> • Upon my escaping from the wild-ox, the wild-cow confronted me!

• As long as he is alive, he is his friend; on the day of his death, he is his greatest adversary!

• He could not bring about an agreement; the women were all talking to one another!

• Into an open mouth, a fly will enter!

• The dog understands "Take it!" He does not understand "Put it down!"

• Deal not badly with a matter, then no sorrow will fall into your heart.

• Do no evil, then you will not clutch a lasting sorrow.

• Without his cohabiting with you, can you be pregnant? Without his feeding you, can you be fat? [To indicate something impossible.]

• Copulation causes the breast to give suck.

• When I labor, they take away my reward; when I increase my efforts, who will give me anything?

• The strong man is fed through the wages of his hire, the weak man through the wages of his child.

• He is fortunate in everything, since he wears a fine garment.

• Do you strike the face of a walking ox with a strap?

• Am I not a thoroughbred steed? Yet I am harnessed with a mule and must draw a wagon loaded with reeds.

• The life of the day before yesterday is that of any day.

• If the shoot is not right it will not produce the stalk, nor create seed.

• Will ripe grain grow? How do we know? Will dried grain grow? How do we know?

• Very soon he will be dead; so he says, "Let me eat up all I have!" Soon he will be well; so he says, "Let me economize!"

• From before the gate of the city whose armament is not powerful, the enemy cannot be repulsed.

• You go and take the field of the enemy; the enemy comes and takes your field.

In Mesopotamia, wisdom literature goes back to the Larsa period (~1900 BC). From this period there exists a large amount of wisdom literature in Sumerian.

• Flatter a young man, he'll give you anything you want; Throw a scrap to a puppy, he'll wag his tail at you.

• The man who supports neither wife nor child, his nose has never borne a tether.

• To keep on having wives is a matter for a man himself, For him to keep on having sons is a matter for the god.

• It is the poor men who are the silent men in Sumer.

• Pay heed to the word of your mother as to the word of a god!

• When quarreling consumes someone like a fire, make sure you know how to extinguish the flame.

• Should he say something unfriendly to you, don't say the like to him; this involves serious consequences.

• Prayer, supplication and adoration; You shall give each day: your emolument will be heaped up.

• Sacrifice prolongs life and prayer absolves guilt.

• Would you hand a lump of mud to someone throwing things around?

• At the gate of the judge's house the mouth of a sinful woman is mightier than her husband's.

• Do no crime, then fear of the god will not worry you. Utter no evil statement; grief will not drag at your heart. Do no evil; you will not receive permanent hardship.

The proverbs of the Aramaic speaking peoples were also plagiarized by the Jews. It was not until 1906-07 AD, that a German excavation at Elephantine uncovered a papyrus with the old Aramaic story *The Words of Ahiqar*. Thus, once again, the archaeologists have shown us that the wisdom of the ancient peoples was not a monopoly of Judaism – as the Jews would have us all believe – but was widespread and basic to all of the societies of the ancient Near East. *The Words of Ahiqar* are as wise and true today as when they were written in 600 BC, before Nebuchadnezzar had hauled those criminals off to Babylon.

Each of the people of the ancient Near East were wise and good. Each had their wisdom literature, stories, and proverbs which were destroyed by time, confiscated, plagiarized by the priests of Solomon's Temple and later rediscovered by the archaeologists. Here is a sample of *The Words of Ahiqar*:

• The son who is trained and taught and on whose feet the fetter is put shall prosper.

• Withhold not thy son from the rod, else thou wilt not be able to save him from wickedness.

• If I smite thee, my son, thou wilt not die, but if I leave thee to thine own heart, thou wilt not live.

• More than all watchfulness watch thy mouth, and over what thou hearest harden thy heart. For a word is a bird: once released no man can recapture it.

• First count the secrets of thy mouth; then bring out thy words by number. For the instruction of a mouth is stronger than the instruction of war.

• Soft is the utterance of a king; yet it is sharper and stronger than a two-edged knife.

• Cover up the word of a king with the veil of the heart.

• Why should wood strive with fire, flesh with a knife, a man with a king?

• I have tasted even the bitter medlar, and I have eaten endives; but there is naught which is more bitter than poverty.

• A loan is sweet as honey, but its repayment is grief.

• My son, hearken not with thine ears to a lying man. For a man's charm is his truthfulness; his repulsiveness, the lies of his lips.

• Despise not that which is thy lot, nor covet a wealth which is denied thee.

• Multiply not riches and make not great thy heart.

• Reveal not thy secrets before thy friends, lest thy name become despised of them.

• Be not too sweet, lest they swallow thee; be not too bitter lest they spit thee out.

• If thou would be exalted, my son, humble thyself before God who humbles an exalted man and exalts a lowly man.

• Let not good eyes be darkened, nor good ears be stopped, and let a good mouth love the truth and speak it.

• A man of becoming conduct whose heart is good is like a mighty city which is situated upon a mountain. There is none that can bring him down.

• Except a man dwell with God, how can he be guarded by his own refuge? But he with whom God is, who can cast him down?

• A man knows not what is in his fellow's heart. So when a good man sees a wicked man let him beware of him. Let him not join with him on a journey or be a neighbor to him, a good man with a bad man.

• If the wicked man seize the corner of thy garment, leave it in his hand.

• If thy master entrust to thee water to keep and thou do it faithfully, he may leave gold with thee.

The largest percentage of the rabbis' literary thefts came from Egypt. From your knowledge of the *Hebrew Bible*, you already know of the slanders that the Jews wrote concerning the people around them, as well as of the gods of those people. To make themselves appear to be the most moral and virtuous people on earth, the Jews had to murder, steal from, enslave, libel and slander everyone else. Ignoring the lies that the Jews tell in the Old Testament, what does modern archaeology say about the character and morals of the ancient peoples they claimed were so evil?

Among all of the ancient peoples, the Egyptians were famed for their learning. However, as a nation, Egypt neither loved learning for its own sake, nor sought knowledge strictly for the love of it. Like the Sumerians, the Egyptians cherished knowledge of the gods and religious and occult knowledge, but were very practical about other kinds of knowledge. Thus, their skills at any sort of mathematics or science were limited to how these subjects related to knowledge and service of the gods, or to the practical aspects of canal and temple construction.

Egyptian boys of the upper classes were sent to school when they were about four years old and their education lasted about ten or twelve years. The value of reading and writing was generally recognized by all Egyptians, especially those of the merchant and artisan classes, who believed that there was no position to which the learned scribe could not attain. The young scribes were taught from the most revered books of religious knowledge and moral precepts. There were many books of moral precepts in the Egyptian libraries which were looted by the Hyksos and sent to Babylonia.

One example of Jewish thievery was the Seven Years Famine of Egyptian tales. It was well known to the Babylonian merchants centuries before the Hyksos invasion. There is an inscription on a rock on the island of Sahal in the First Cataract that tells of a seven years famine which took place during the reign of Zoser, a king of the Third Dynasty (2667-2648 BC). The hieroglyphs of this rock inscription read:

> "Grain is very scarce, vegetables are lacking altogether, everything that men eat for food has come to an end, and now every man attacks his neighbor. The men who want to walk cannot move, the child wails, the young man drags his body about, and the hearts of the older men are crushed with despair. Their legs give way under them, they sink down on the ground, and they clutch their bodies with their hands in pain. The nobles have no counsel to give, and there is nothing to be obtained from the storehouses but wind. Everything is in a state of ruin."

Those readers who are familiar with the Old Testament will certainly find some identical ideas in the Egyptian texts. From the papyrus texts that describe the Egyptian cosmogony entitled, *The Book of Knowing How Ra Came into Being*, is this Egyptian Creation story:

> "The God who is the lord of the uttermost limits of the universe says, 'There was no heaven, no earth, no serpents, no reptiles; all these I produced out of the inert watery mass. There was no place for me to stand upon. I uttered a spell over my heart-mind. I who laid the foundations with strict exactitude of everything that I made afterwards. I was alone for I had not yet fashioned anything."

Does it sound familiar to you?

The Egyptians were a holy and good people, despite their ancient universal fear of demons. The Egyptians from the earliest times believed that men would be rewarded or punished for their deeds in Life and that there would be a Last Judgment. The oldest description of this judgment is found in a papyrus of King Khati (~2800 BC) who says to his son:

> "Know thou that the Assessors of Souls, who judge wrongdoers, will show no pity on the Day of Judgment of wretched man in the hour when they are performing their appointed duty. It is a terrible thing for the man who knows his sin, to be charged with it. Buoy not up thy heart with the idea that length of years will excuse thee; they look upon a whole lifetime as a single hour. They make their trial after a man's death; his actions are set near him as evidence. In the Other World, existence is everlasting and he who puts this fact out of his mind is a fool. He, who being guiltless, attains to that place has an existence there like that of God, and like the Everlasting Lords he moves unfettered from place to place."

This god, the Assessors of Souls, kept records of a man's deeds in the Register of Osiris. After death, the heart of a man was weighed in the "Great Balance" against his good deeds. This was depicted in the wall paintings as a man's heart on one side of the balance and a feather on the other. (see Figure 96) By this, you can understand that the Egyptians based their lives on Eternity. It was an Eternity that was determined by both their good and bad deeds in life. How different this is from the shallow beliefs of modern man and the bogus beliefs of the Jews!

Figure 96: Anibus weighing heart

Modern Man's Jew-corrupted philosophy is content with death. His scientists claim this to be our final destination. So, why not be like the Jews and do all manner of evil things for shallow desires, since death is the final goal? But, unlike the Monsters of Babylon or their modern descendants, the Egyptians not only had a knowledge of Eternal Life, but also a knowledge of the freedom of movement within Eternity. They knew of those things, because they could directly perceive their Holy Spirits as well as their immortal souls. You can also perceive these parts of yourself, if you make the effort to look for them. Their holy spirit, the Egyptians called the *Ka*. In the spirit, they could travel outside of their bodies, not as a "belief," but as actual experiential knowledge. This spirit-body is mentioned in the Aryan Hindu teachings as the "four-armed form," that is, your two physical arms and your two spiritual arms. These are perceivable by anyone who looks for them. Seek and you shall find.

The Egyptians knew of their Eternal Soul, because they could perceive it while looking within. Their soul, they called the *Ba*. (see Figure 98) Use Odin's Single Eye or the Buddhist Third Eye or Jesus' Single Eye and while looking within, you can perceive your soul, also. It is not a matter of "belief," it is a matter of direct observation of Reality. Anyone can find it, but no one can see it unless they actually calm their mind and look. Most modern people don't take the time to look through prayer and meditation, because they have either tossed such knowledge aside with their *disbelief* or they have substituted *actual knowledge of it* for the delusion of *belief*. Both those who believe and those who disbelieve are in a state of ignorance, because neither of them have *knowledge*. Yet, those who believe have the potential for acquiring knowledge, while those who disbelieve will have a tough or impossible time of it.

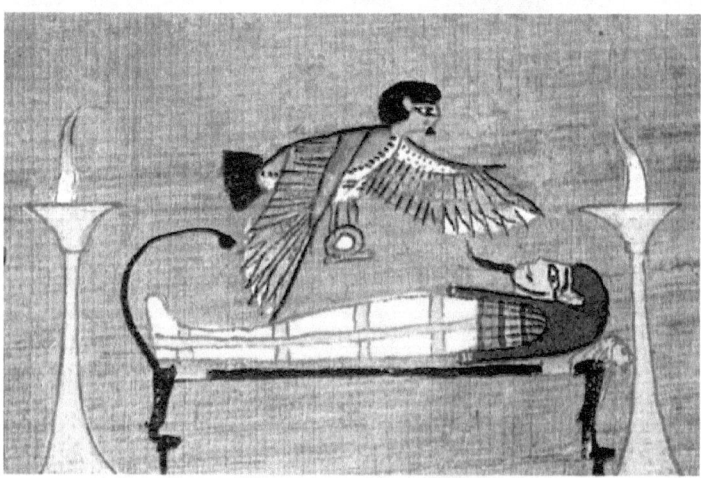

Figure 98: Winged Ba

While sitting in a swastika kneeling posture, one of the Egyptian gods was named the Spirit of a Million Years. (see Figure 99) Their religious observations – not their beliefs – was that Man had his physical body (the only part of Man that the scientists, Communists and Jews see), but also a spiritual body in addition to his Immortal Soul. Scientists can't see Dark Matter, either, but they "believe" that it exists.

Figure 99: Spirit of a Million Years

From the stela of the Priest Horemkhauf (13th Dynasty, 1802-1649 BC):

> "I, an excellent dignitary on earth, shall be an excellent spirit (*akh*) in the necropolis, since I have given bread to the hungry, clothes to the naked, and have nourished my brothers. I have not let one beg goods from another, and everyone opened his door to his brothers. I looked after the house of those who had raised me; they are buried and made to live the eternal life of the resurrected."

The religion of Osiris promised to those who followed it faithfully both resurrection from the dead and eternal life. But, to attain these the Egyptian had to lead a moral and upright life, to avoid lying speech, deceitful actions and duplicity of every kind, and to observe the laws of the national god and the local god. Any breech of these Moral Laws could be extirpated with offerings in the temple and shines. Osiris expected his followers to have a clean conscience, clean hands, unsoiled with evil deeds, and a clean tongue. As you will see in later chapters, the Egyptians were far superior to the lying Jews in virtue and religiosity.

Finally, after proclaiming his innocence, the deceased would kneel before Osiris and say: "There is no sin in my body. I have neither told lies nor acted with deceit; make me one of those favored beings who are in thy following." Osiris, being satisfied that he was admitting a speaker of truth to his kingdom, assigned to the deceased an estate in the "Fields of Reeds" and gave him permission to draw rations from the "Field of Offerings" which was kept supplied by the faithful on earth who brought offerings regularly to the sanctuaries of Osiris. In this way, those who made offerings to the deceased, were also insuring themselves of plenty in the Afterlife. It was a system of kindness.

Among the booty that the thieving Hyksos merchant-moneylenders carried off to Babylon were collections of prayers such as this *Prayer of the Steward Nu to Osiris and the Forty-Two Gods of Judgment*:

"Verily I come to thee, I bring Truth to thee, I have destroyed sin for thee. I have done no evil to mankind. I have not wronged my kinsfolk. I have not committed sin in the place of Truth. I have not known worthless men. I have not done evil. I have not insisted that excessive work should be done for me daily. I have not thrust forward my name for honor. I have not entreated servants cruelly. I have not thought scorn of God. I have not robbed the poor of his goods. I have not done that which is hateful to the gods. I have not caused a master to injure his slave. I have not inflicted pain. I have allowed no man to suffer hunger. I have made none to weep. I have not committed murder. I have not made any man to commit murder for me. I have not cheated the temples of their offerings. I have not stolen the bread of the gods. I have not stolen the bread of the blessed dead. I have not committed fornication. I have not defiled myself in the sanctuary of the god of my city. I have not cheated in measuring the bushel. I have not stolen land. I have not seized wrongfully the fields of others. I have not cheated with the scales. I have not declared the weight wrongly. I have not taken milk from the mouths of babes. I have not driven cattle from their own pastures. I have not snared the fowl in the preserves of the gods. I have not caught fish with bait made of fish of their kind. I have not stopped the flow of water on the fields. I have not made a breach in a canal. I have not extinguished a lamp when it should burn. I have not defrauded the gods of their meat offerings. I have not driven off cattle from the pastures of the gods. I have not thrust back the god when he would come forth. I am pure, I am pure, I am pure, I am pure. . . .

O declare ye me righteous in the presence of the God of the Uttermost Limits of the Universe, for I have done what is right in Egypt. . . .

I live upon truth. I feed upon truth. I have performed the commandments of men and the things that please the gods. I have made the god to be at peace with me by doing his will. I have given bread to the hungry man, and water to the thirsty man, and a boat to him that was shipwrecked. I have made offerings to the gods, and given sepulchral meals to the Spirits of the dead. Therefore deliver me and protect me, and bring no charge against me in the presence of the Great God. I am clean of mouth and clean of hands; therefore let it be said by the gods when they see me, Welcome! Welcome! I have testified before the Divine Ferryman, and he has acquitted me. I have prayed to the gods, and I know their persons. I have purified my breast with clean water, and my back with the things that make clean, and I have steeped my inward parts in the Pool of Truth; there is no member of mine lacking in truth." (From the *Book of the Dead*, Chapter 75.)

Notice that the Jews do everything the opposite of what the Egyptians hold as holy. Does that make the Jews holier than the Egyptians, or the reverse? Notice also the kindness and holy intent toward the animals. Similar to the shepherds' taboo of not boiling a kid in its mother's milk, the Egyptians refrained from fishing with bait made from the meat of the target fish.

Among the books that the Hyksos carried off to Babylon, were the Egyptian *Books of Moral Precepts* wherein such advice was given:

"Repose thyself on the two arms of God. Commit thyself for security to the hand of God because it is He who brings a man into the Other World where he is safe in the hand of God."

Another Egyptian sage wrote:

"The things that God does, cannot be known. Daily bread is according to the dispensation of God. God loves obedience; he hates disobedience. A good son is indeed the gift of God."

Another Egyptian wrote:

"Noisy, vain repetitions are an abomination to the sanctuary of God. Pray thy prayer with a loving heart in secret. He will do

for thee all that is necessary for thy daily needs; He will hearken
to thy supplications, receiving thine offerings."

This is very Christian, isn't it? Identical to Jesus' admonition to the hypocritical and fake prayers of the Jews.

These *Precepts of Amenemapt* were also stolen into the private libraries
of Babylon. Do they sound familiar like an Old Testament Proverb? And yet
they are superior to them.

> "Precepts of Amenemapt, who says: Lend me thine ears, I
> pray; hearken to the things that I am about to say. ... Thou will
> find my words to be a storehouse of life and a source of strength
> and safety upon the earth.
> "Take heed not to rob the poor and be not cruel to the desti-
> tute. ..... If thou can answer the man who attacks thee, do him
> no injury. Let the evil-doer alone; he will destroy himself. We
> must help the sinner, for may we not become like him? Set him
> on his feet, give him thy hand, commit him to the hand of God.
> Feed him with bread, give him drink, for it is in the heart of the
> God to show another an act of compassion.... Six feet of land
> given to thee by God are better than thirty thousand which thou
> hast stolen.
> "Pass not thy day in beer-houses and eating houses, or thou
> wilt become a mere mass of food. The beggar in God's hand is
> better off than the rich man in his palace. Crusts of bread and a
> loving heart are better than rich food and contention.... Mind
> thy business, and let every man do his when he wishes to do it.
> Learn to be content with what thou has. Treasure obtained by
> fraud will not stay with thee; thou has it today, tomorrow it has
> departed.... If thou sails with a thief thou will be left in the riv-
> er. Get into the habit of praying sincerely to God as he rises in
> the sky, saying, 'Grant me, I beseech thee, strength and health.'
> He will give thee all that is necessary, and thou shall be saved
> from anxiety. Approve what is good; spit upon what is bad.
> Avoid lying or slander. Be kind to the poor.... Be strong to do
> the Will of God. Hide the flight of the runaway slave....
> "Speak only what is good, what is bad hide in thy belly.
> Avoid the scandalmonger; his lips are date syrup, his tongue is a
> deadly dagger and a blazing fire is within him.... Be dignified.
> Place thyself for safety in the hand of God. The liar is an abom-
> ination to God.... Support not the liar by word or deed.... Help
> the man who stumbles. Covet not gold.... Indulge not in morn-
> ing slumber while the day breaks majestically in the sky. What
> can be compared to dawn and daybreak for beauty? To what can
> the man who knows not the dawn be compared? For while God

is performing His splendid work, that man is wallowing in slothfulness.... Accept no bribe....

"Waste not the early hours of the day in sleep. Haste not to be rich, but be not slothful in thine own interest. Laugh not at the blind man, and make not a mock of the dwarf.... Be courteous to the man thou dislikes. Help the old man who is drunk, and treat him with respect before his family. Follow not the cult of the wine-cup, for it will encourage thine enemies. The love of God is better than the reverence of the nobleman. If thou art asked to help to work the ferry-boat, take a paddle and do so; God will not be offended thereby....

These Precepts will please thee and teach thee. They will make the fool wise, and the man who hears them read, will assuredly steer his course by them...."

The Jews stole these precepts, practiced doing the opposite of them, and declared themselves "holy" and the Egyptians "evil." But, in fact, what does doing-the-opposite-of-Good actually make the Jews?

The Hyksos merchant-moneylenders also carried off to Babylon the *Hymn of Ai to Aten*:

"Thy rising is beautiful in the horizon of heaven, O Aten, ordainer of life. Thou rises in the eastern horizon, filling every land with thy radiance. Thou art beautiful, great, splendid and raised up above every land; thy rays, like those of Ra, deck every land thou hast made. Thou hast taken those lands, however many they may be, and hast made them subject to thy son. Thou art far away, but thy beams are on the earth; thou art on men's faces, they admire thy goings....

"At thy rising the boats sail up and down the river, every road opens out, the fish swim up towards thy face, thy beams go down into the seas. Thou creates seed in men; thou fashions it into offspring in women; thou makes the son to live in his mother's womb, making him to be silent and not to cry out. Thou art a nurse in the belly, giving breath to sustain life in what thou hast created. When the child is born, and on the day of his birth opens his mouth after the manner of babes, thou provides food for him. The chick cheeps inside the egg, thou gives it air so that it can live. Thou perfects its body, it breaks the shell from inside, it comes out of the egg, it chirps with all its might, having come forth it walks on its two feet. O how many are the things which thou hast made! They are hidden from one's face, O thou God! One who hast no counterpart! Thou, existing alone, did by thy heart's will create the earth and every thing that is thereon – men, cattle, beasts and creatures of all kinds that move on feet, all the creatures in the sky that fly with wings, the deserts of Syria and Kush and the Land of Egypt.

"Thou hast assigned to everyone his place, providing the daily food, each receiving his destined share; thou decree his span of life. … How perfect, wholly perfect, are thy plans, O Lord of Eternity!

In such prayers, you can see the holiness and compassionate loving-kindness of the Egyptians. That is so very different from the malicious wickedness in what the Jews claim as their "glory"!

In the 104th Psalm, the Jews also copied, in both spirit and wording, the "Hymn to Aten" by Pharaoh Amenhotep IV (Akhenaten):

How manifold it is, what thou hast made!
They are hidden from the face (of man).
O sole god, like whom there is no other!
Thou didst create the world according to thy desire,
Whilst thou wert alone:
All men, cattle, and wild beasts,
Whatever is on earth, going upon its feet,
And what is on high, flying with its wings.

But the Jews, while stealing and plagiarizing these ideas, simultaneously spit upon the Egyptians and slandered their very names.

This view of God in the Egyptian *Book of the Dead* from about 2000 BC, speaks of the Egyptian ideas about God that the Jews falsely claimed were their own ideas:

Thou art the One, the God from the very beginning of Time, the heir of immortality, self-produced and self-born: Thou didst create the earth and make man.

Although the rabbis destroyed every copy that they could find of the wisdom literature of other peoples, the sands of Egypt protected – and still protect – countless treasures of Egyptian wisdom. The Old Kingdom (2650-2135 BC) existed long before there were any Jews. The vizier Ptahhotep under Pharaoh Isesi (~2414 – 2375 BC) wrote a book dedicated to his Pharaoh known today as the "Instructions of Ptahhotep." During Old Kingdom times, his 37 maxims teach the cardinal virtues of the ancient Egyptians: self-control, moderation, kindness, generosity, justice, and truthfulness tempered by discretion. These virtues are to be practiced alike toward all people, not just toward fellow Egyptians. So, unlike the Jews, it is little wonder why the Egyptians were held in such high esteem by other peoples. They were a genuinely good people who treated other people well. No martial virtues are mentioned during these relatively peaceful Old Kingdom times in Egypt. The ideal Egyptian man was a man of peace. This is totally opposite of the Jews who were hated by everybody who met them and who fomented wars whenever they could. Yet, the Jews claim that only they are loved by God. It's a real joke!

The Egyptians delighted in compilations of wise sayings, which were directive for a successful life. To them, this was "wisdom." One of the earliest of these compilations purports to come from Ptah-hotep, the vizier of King Izezi of the Fifth Dynasty (~ 2450 BC). The old councilor is supposed to be instructing his son and designated successor on the actions and attitudes which make a successful official of the state. Excerpts from this document:

> Then he said to his son:
>
> Let not thy heart be puffed-up because of thy knowledge; be not confident because thou art a wise man. Take counsel with the ignorant as well as the wise.... Good speech is more hidden than the emerald, but it may be found with maid-servants at the grindstones....
>
> If thou are a leader commanding the affairs of the multitude, seek out for thyself every beneficial deed, until it may be that thy own affairs are without wrong. Justice is great, and its appropriateness is lasting; it has not been disturbed since the time of him who made it, whereas there is punishment for him who passes over its laws. It is the right path before him who knows nothing...
>
> If thou art one of those sitting at the table of one greater than thyself, take what he may give when it is set before thy nose. Thou shouldst gaze at what is before thee. Do not pierce him with many stares, for such an aggression against him is an abomination to the ka [the Holy Spirit]. Let thy face be cast down until he addresses thee, and thou shouldst speak only when he addresses thee. Laugh after he laughs, and it will be very pleasing to his heart and what thou mayest do will be pleasing to the heart. No one can know what is in the heart.... It is god who makes a man's quality, and he defends him even while he is asleep....
>
> If thou art one to whom petition is made, be calm as thou listenest to the petitioner's speech. Do not rebuff him before he has swept out his body or before he has said that for which he came. A petitioner likes attention to his words better than the fulfilling of that for which he came. He is rejoicing there-at more than any other petitioner, even before that which has been heard has come to pass. As for him who plays the rebuffer of a petitioner, men say: "Now why is he doing it?" It is not necessary that everything about which he has petitioned should come to pass, but a good hearing is a soothing of the heart.

If thou desirest to make friendship last in a home to which thou hast access as master, as a brother, or as a friend, into any place where thou mightest enter, beware of approaching the women. It does not go well with the place where that is done.... Do not be covetous at a division. Do not be greedy, unless it be for thy own portion. Do not be covetous against thy own kindred. Greater is the respect for the mild than for the strong. He is a mean person who exposes his kinsfolk; he is empty of the fruits of conversation....

Some of this good advice, the Jews stole and then put their own names on it as "Jewish Proverbs."

In the 18th Dynasty was written an *Instruction Addressed to King Merikare* (second half of the Eighteenth Dynasty). A few excerpts:

"Justice come to him distilled, shaped in the sayings
of the ancestors.
Don't be evil, kindness is good, make your memorial
last through love of you."
Do justice, then you endure on earth; calm the
weeper, don't oppress the widow,
Do not kill, it does not serve you.
Punish with beating, with detention, thus will the
land be well-ordered;
Do not trust in length of years, the gods view a
lifetime in an hour!
When a man remains over after death, his deeds are
set beside him as treasure,
And being yonder lasts forever. A fool is who does
what they reprove!
He who reaches them without having done wrong
will exist there like a god,
Free-striding like the lords forever!"

Kindness was a prime attribute of the Egyptian people.

Imhotep and Hardedef were two famous sages of the Old Kingdom. *The Instruction of Imhotep*, the vizier of Pharaoh Djoser, have not come to light as yet. But this, the Song from the Tomb of Pharaoh Intef (11th Dynasty) mentions them.

He is happy, this good prince!
Death is a kindly fate.
A generation passes,
Another stays,
Since the time of the ancestors.
The gods who were before rest in their tombs,

Blessed nobles too are buried in their tombs.
Yet those who built tombs,
Their places are gone,
What has become of them?
I have heard the words of Imhotep and Hardedef,
Whose sayings are recited whole.
What of their places?
Their walls have crumbled,
Their places are gone,
As though they had never been!
None comes from there,
To tell of their state,
To tell of their needs,
To calm our hearts,
Until we go where they have gone!

Hence rejoice in your heart!
Forgetfulness profits you,
Follow your heart as long as you live!
Put myrrh on your head,
Dress in fine linen,
Anoint yourself with oils fit for a god.
Heap up your joys,
Let your heart not sink!
Follow your heart and your happiness,
Do your things on earth as your heart commands!
When there comes to you that day of mourning,
The Weary-hearted hears not their mourning,
Wailing saves no man from the pit!

Refrain:
Make holiday,
Do not weary of it!
Lo, none is allowed to take his goods with him,
Lo, none who departs comes back again!

Does it profit a Jew to gather all wealth into his pockets while murdering the people of the world? Only if he has no belief in an afterlife, only if he is a devil. Therefore, the Jews are devils.

As further proof of what the rabbis stole, read *The Instruction of Amen-Em-Opet* (~ 600 – 500 BC), itself based upon even more ancient Egyptian teachings.

   • Guard thyself against robbing the oppressed and against over-
   bearing the disabled.

• Stretch not forth thy hand against the approach of an old man, nor steal away the speech of the aged.

• He who does evil, the very river-bank abandons him, and his floodwaters carry him off. The north wind comes down that it may end his hour; it is joined to the tempest; the thunder is loud, and the crocodiles are wicked.

• Plow in the fields, that thou mayest find thy needs, that thou mayest receive bread of thy own threshing floor. Better is a measure that the god gives thee than five thousand taken illegally....

• Better is poverty in the hand of the god than riches in a storehouse; better is bread, when the heart is happy, than riches with sorrow.

• Cast not thy heart in pursuit of riches, for there is no ignoring Fate and Fortune. Place not thy heart upon externals, for every man belongs to his appointed hour.

• Do not strain to seek an excess, when thy needs are safe for thee.

• Rejoice not thyself over riches gained by robbery, nor mourn because of poverty.

• Do not greet thy heated opponent in thy violence, nor hurt thy own heart thereby. Do not say to him: "Hail to thee!" falsely, when a terror is in thy belly.

• Do not talk with a man falsely – the abomination of the god.

• Do not cut off thy heart from thy tongue, that all thy affairs may be successful. Be sincere in the presence of the common people, for one is safe in the hand of the god.

• God hates him who falsifies words; his great abomination is the contentious of belly.

• Be not greedy for the property of a poor man, nor hunger for his bread.

• As for the property of a poor man, it is a blocking to the throat, it makes a vomiting to the gullet.

• Do not bear witness with false words, nor support another person thus with thy tongue.

• Do not take an accounting of him who has nothing, nor falsify thy pen.

• If thou findest a large debt against a poor man, make it into three parts, forgive two, and let one stand. Thou wilt find it like the ways of life; thou wilt lie down and sleep soundly. In the morning thou wilt find it again like good news.

• Better is praise as one who loves men than riches in a storehouse; better is bread when the heart is happy, than riches with sorrow.

• Do not lean on the scales nor falsify the weights, nor damage the fractions of the measure.

• Do not spend the night fearful of the morrow. At daybreak what is the morrow like? Man knows not what the morrow is like.

• Do not confuse a man in the law court nor divert the righteous man.

• Do not accept the bribe of a powerful man, nor oppress for him the disabled.

• Do not laugh at a blind man nor tease a dwarf nor injure the affairs of the lame.

• Do not tease a man who is in the hand of the god (an idiot) nor be fierce of face against him if he errs for man is clay and straw, and the god is his builder. He is tearing down and building up every day. He makes a thousand poor men as he wishes, or he makes a thousand men as overseers, when he is in his hour of life.

• How joyful is he who reaches the West (death) when he is safe in the hand of the god.

• Do not recognize a widow if thou catchest her in gleaning in the fields, nor fail to be indulgent to her reply.

• God desires respect for the poor more than the honoring of the exalted.

• See thou these 30 chapters: They entertain; they instruct; they are the foremost of all books; they make the ignorant to know.

The Jews do the opposite of everything in these wise sayings. Does that make the Jews "holier" than the Egyptians?

Pharaoh Amenhotep IV (~1352-36 BC), known as Akhenaten, wrote a beautiful hymn to God that clearly shows his belief in One God whom he identified with the sun disk. There is little doubt that Akhenaten believed that the sun god was the sole god and the creator of everything.

> "How manifold it is, what thou hast made!
> They are hidden from the face of man.
> O sole god, like whom there is no other!
> Thou didst create the world according to thy
> desire...."

Thus, we have the first record of a monotheistic religion, which antedates the Jews by at least 1,000 years. And, of course, excerpts from the famous Egyptian *Book of the Dead* should be included in these examples of Jewish forgeries which we, today, call the Old Testament.

> Hail to you, great God, Lord of the Two Truths!
> I have come to you, my Lord,
> I was brought to see your beauty...
> I have not done crimes against people,
> I have not mistreated cattle,

I have not sinned in the Place of Truth.
I have not known what should not be known,
I have not done any harm.
I did not begin a day by exacting more than my
due,
My name did not reach the bark of the mighty
ruler.
I have not blasphemed a god,
I have not robbed the poor.
I have not done what the god abhors,
I have not maligned a servant to his master.
I have not caused pain,
I have not caused tears.
I have not killed,
I have not ordered to kill,
I have not made anyone suffer...
I have not copulated nor defiled myself.
[Molested boys or masturbated]
I have not increased nor reduced the measure,
I have not added to the weight of the balance,
I have not taken milk from the mouth of
children, ...
I have not dammed a flowing stream,
I have not quenched a needed fire...
I am pure, I am pure, I am pure, I am pure!
I am pure as is pure that great heron in Hnes.
I am truly the nose of the Lord of Breath,
Who sustains all the people, ...
In this Hall of the Two Truths;
For I know the names of the gods in it,
The followers of the great God!

The masturbating and child-molesting rabbis wrote nothing but slanders and
curses against the Egyptians in The Biggest Lie Ever Told. And the Jews have
the pretense to declare themselves to be the "Chosen Ones of God." What evil
clowns the Jews are!

In the Egyptian Declaration to the Forty-two Gods are found some interesting concepts. This is an abbreviated list.

I have not done evil. I have not robbed. I have not coveted. I
have not stolen. I have not killed people. I have not trimmed the
measure. I have not cheated. I have not stolen a god's property. I
have not told lies. I have not seized food. I have not sulked. I
have not trespassed. I have not slain sacred cattle. I have not ex-
torted. I have not stolen bread rations. I have not spied. I have

not prattled. I have contended only for my goods. I have not committed adultery. I have not defiled myself [masturbated]. I have not caused fear. I have not trespassed. I have not been violent. I have not been deaf to Maat. I have not quarreled. I have not winked. I have not copulated with a boy. I have not been false. I have not reviled. I have not been aggressive. I have not had a hasty heart. I have not attacked and reviled a god. I have not made many words. I have not sinned, I have not done wrong. I have not made trouble. I have not urinated in water. I have not raised my voice. I have not cursed a god. I have not been boastful. I have not been haughty. I have not wanted more than I had. I have not cursed god in my town.

Both masturbation and pederasty were great sins to the Egyptians, as truly they are in fact, while the Jews consider both of these to be totally Jewish. After all, even if God and Nature forbid it, as God's Chosen People, they could do what they liked. Like the Babylonian merchant-moneylenders who created them, the Jews are perverts, as is proven in later chapters.

In political terms, the Egyptian Late Period was a time of retreat. Egypt lost its imperial position, withdrew to its natural borders, became subject to repeated foreign invasions, and ultimately lost its independence. Moreover, for much of the Post-Imperial Epoch Egypt was troubled by internal divisions resulting from the weakness of the ruling dynasties. The invasion of Egypt by the Egyptianized Negro kings of Nubia restored the royal power of a single dynasty over most of the country. But, this Nubian dynasty, the Twenty-fifth, soon fell victim to the Assyrian invasions of Egypt which culminated in the sack of Thebes in 663 BC. Thebes was the central city for trade between the interior of Africa up the Nile through Kush and the trade route across the desert to the Red Sea and the trade with Arabia and India. The moneylenders of Assyria coveted this wealth.

From 656 to 525 BC, Egypt was once more united under its own kings, the Twenty-sixth Dynasty, natives of the Delta city of Sais. Saite rule brought a marked revival of political strength, prosperity, and cultural flowering. It was also the time in which many Greeks settled in Egypt and became a significant element in the population. The Persian conquest of 525 BC ushered in a long period of Persian domination. When independence was regained in 404 BC, Egypt enjoyed a final flowering under the native kings of the Twenty-eighth, Twenty-ninth, and Thirtieth dynasties. In 341 BC, Persia reconquered Egypt, but this second Persian dominion was brief, ending with Alexander the Great's entry into Egypt in 332 BC.

Alexander was greeted as liberator. But, the subsequent Macedonian kingship subjected Egypt to a foreign rule far more severe in its effects than Persian dominion had been. Although the Ptolemies assumed Pharaonic ceremonial trappings, their Greek culture and the imposition of a Greek administration turned the Egyptians into second-class citizens. As individuals, Egyptians and

Greeks consorted with and influenced each other. And by the second century, the two peoples had drawn closer together. But a Macedonian king could not be the spokesman for Egypt's national culture. Thus, under the weight of the imposed Hellenism and bereft of its own leadership, Egyptian civilization became muted and subdued. It continued to endure and it even absorbed with surprising elasticity elements of Greek culture in art and literature.

All the while, both the Greek and the Egyptian ways of life were transformed by the changes in man's outlook which operated throughout the Hellenistic world. If this changing outlook is to be summed up in a single phrase, it may be called the quest for salvation. It was an age of spiritual distress and of groping for new answers. And when an excessively exploitative Roman rule had drained Egypt's wealth and enslaved its people, the time was ripe for the Egyptians to embrace with fervor the new gospel of Christ. Then, the Egyptians destroyed with their own hands the civilization they had built and cherished for three thousand years. The Egyptian-turned-Christian was a new man. With him begins a new chapter in the history of Egypt and the history of man.

After the Christians, the dictatorship of Muslim rule beginning in the 8th Century AD, brought in a Semitic and Negro admixture. Islam was an alien Semitic religion based upon the lies of Judaism and was just as ruthless as the Jews in destroying other peoples. Arab conquests, psychopathic Arabian cultural values and the rise of the East African slave trade, wiped out 3000 years of Eastern Mediterranean, Caucasoid, Egyptian Culture along with its knowledge of God. From this time onward, the actual experiential knowledge of the Egyptians was replaced by the *abracadabra* and *taqqiya* belief systems of the lying, deceiving Semites.

CHAPTER 6
THE DEVIL'S TRUTH AND THE HEBREW BIBLE

6.1 Introduction

The cities of Mesopotamia were built of mud. They had always been made out of mud. Every few hundred years or even every few decades, through erosion, fires, earthquakes or warfare, those cities would be torn down, compacted flat and a new city of fresh mud bricks would be built upon the old. Over the millennia, every city became situated on a high mound of mud composed of many layers of squashed cities below them like a layer cake. No lying rabbis of ancient times could ever have imagined that anyone would ever dig into those ancient mounds of dirt to find the history buried there and to thereby unveil the lies of the Jews.

In those days, books were not mass produced by printing presses, because the invention of the printing press was thousands of years in the future. Books were not even books as we know them. They were tablets of damp clay or loose sheets and rolls of papyrus, or stitched-together goatskin leather rolled around a wooden dowel and hand-written with ink made of soot.

Each book was hand-lettered. If you wanted a copy, you had to pay a scribe to laboriously write out a copy for you by hand, one hand-drawn character at a time. And you might have to wait for months or years before your copy was completed. So, every book that was written, was the only copy of that book in existence unless it was popular enough that some rich man could pay a scribe enough silver to write out another copy. In this way, if a book was written that some priest or rabbi didn't like, when they burned it or ripped it into shreds or stomped it into the dust, they were usually destroying the only copy in existence.

In those days, it was easy for the priests to destroy the books of all opposing religions because they didn't have to hunt down tens of thousands or millions of copies. One or two copies were usually all that there were. So, when the rabbis burned the temples and stomped the clay tablets into dust, it was not difficult for them to then hold up their goat-skin scroll and declare it to be the very "Word of God" because that Hebrew goatskin scroll was the only scripture that they allowed to remain in existence. In this way, the *Hebrew Bible* became *the* "history" and *the* "word of God" of the ancient Near East, not only because of its incredible lies and clever deceits, but also because no other competing religious teachings were allowed to escape the fire and pillage of the rabbis and their murdering Hebrew (*Apiru*) bandits.

As for the ancient libraries that were buried beneath fifty or two hundred feet of rubble mounds at Nineveh, Babylon, Mari, Ugarit or the numerous other destroyed cities of the Ancient Near East, what priest or rabbi in his most festering imagination could conceive of a European people living over two thousand years later who would gladly dig through a hundred feet of dirt and rocks with whisk brooms and dental picks merely to verify the truth or falsehood of the *Hebrew Bible*? Modern archaeologists are unlike anyone whom a lying rabbi would ever imagine, because the archaeologist searches for truth and is willing to unearth entire ancient cities to find it. The original archaeologists were Bible-believing Christians who wanted to prove that the miraculous stories that the Jews told, were actually true.

As men of faith and men of science, they really wanted to prove that the *Old Testament* was true as a means for bolstering their own Christian beliefs. So, it cannot be said that those archaeologists were enemies of God or of Christ, because their goal was to prove that it was all true. Alas! They were all disappointed. The actual facts show that the biblical tales are myths and lies and forged documents. Science proves the Jews to be liars and frauds. What is the *Hebrew Bible* in total? The *Hebrew Bible* is the Biggest Lie Ever Told, written by the world's greatest liars, frauds and thieves – the Jews. This is not to say that God is a lie, but most emphatically that the Jews have been telling lies about God. God is not a lie, but the Jews are liars.

As is proven by archaeology, the *Hebrew Bible* (a.k.a., the *Old Testament*) is a hoax. That collection of fables has been foisted upon Mankind as the very "word of god" by the most godless and evil of creatures, all posing as saints. If the people of the world knew this alone, we could deal with those Jewish frauds on a logical basis rather than be swindled and deceived as has been so common in the past. The Jews are just as Jesus said that they are – liars, deceivers, hypocrites, murderers, and the very children of the devil.

WARNING! The above paragraph is all you need to know. You can skip to Chapter 7 with this fact well in mind. This present chapter covers biblical commentary and dissects the various books of the Bible and is therefore very boring to readers who are not interested in such a subject. But those readers who are interested in *How the Jews Betrayed Mankind*, read on. This is a long chapter and is an analysis of the *Hebrew Bible*. So, a familiarity with the *Old Testament* will be of value when studying this chapter or even keeping a copy on hand as a reference to what follows. If you are not interested in such an analysis of the Greatest Lie Ever Told, then re-read the above paragraph and remember its message, then you may skip to Chapter 7. The rest of this long chapter analyzes the *Hebrew Bible*.

But before analyzing the frauds and lies of the *Hebrew Bible*, please understand that I am not claiming that Terah, the moneylender from Ur, had anything to do with writing it. But he is the one who solved the Fifteen Secret Problems of the Babylonian Moneylenders and devised the scheme upon which Judaism is based, the basic blueprint that his son, Abraham, and his guild of Babylonian loan sharks put into action. Judaism is not the result of any one criminal's thinking but is, rather, a gang exercise in the betrayal of Mankind. Like the *Apiru* (Hebrew) bandits before them, the Jews work in gangs. The *Hebrew Bible* is the result of many scheming rabbis and Jews pooling their talents for subterfuge over many centuries. No single Jew wrote it. As you will see, not even Moses wrote it. It is a book of counterfeits with the counterfeiters keeping a low profile because whether it is counterfeit money or a counterfeit "holy book," the counterfeiters can't palm it off as genuine if they show their faces or leave their fingerprints. But if you know where to look, the organized crime of Judaism has left its fingerprints and footprints that are easily discerned. With that firmly in mind, one must study what follows with one eye on the individual Jew and one eye on the tribes of Jews; and try not to get wall-eyed since the Jews change their names and put on different disguises so readily.

Although the Jews claim that the Torah was written by Moses, followed by a crew of "inspired and holy" prophets and so-called "wise sages" who added more lies to it, it is a mistake to consider the *Hebrew Bible* to be any older than dating it from 538 BC. Before anything in the *Hebrew Bible* can be put into perspective, it is important to understand that all of its books were written and edited in Babylonia between 587 and 537 BC by the Hebrew priests led by Ezra the Scribe. So, regardless of the alleged antiquity or veracity of the various myths, legends and histories contained in these writings, it is only when you understand who the editors were, can you understand why the books were preserved as they were. In 538 BC, king Cyrus of Persia was deceived by the Jews into allowing those Hebrew gangsters and bankers to return to their lair in Jerusalem. It was from that time that the actual date of the *Hebrew Bible* has any validity whatsoever. Other than the Book of Daniel, which was written during Roman times, it is that date from which the present edition of the *Hebrew Bible* was finalized. These books were written for the Hebrews and today's Jews as the teachings of the bandits, thieves, murderers, and rapists who had been their ancestors.

Of course, the *Hebrew Bible* is composed of many books written in much earlier times than 538 BC and then carefully edited to its present form. Thousands of Bible scholars over many centuries have tried to unravel the when's and how's of all of the editorial changes. But their theories are based upon the fallacy that they were working on something true and godly and that they could find a Higher Truth by delving into the *Hebrew Bible*'s falseness. Thus, all of the Bible scholars from antiquity to the present day have been deceived. Archaeology and the book that you are now reading prove this.

The so-called "Priestly tradition" or the "Elohistic tradition" or the "Yahwistic tradition" or "Deuteronomic tradition" or any of the other name tags that the various scholars have used in an attempt to unravel and categorize the mixed bag of plagiarized and fictionalized short stories that make up the *Hebrew Bible*, are all very much useless. And why? Because it doesn't matter how the *Hebrew Bible* was arranged and edited in antiquity since the whole thing is proven to be a hoax. God is not a hoax. But Judaism is a hoax. The *Hebrew Bible* exemplifies a long and carefully concealed betrayal of God and

of Mankind that has evolved to its present form. So, yes, there are some scholars who find it interesting to see *how* it evolved. But for the vast majority of
Mankind, all that matters is what it is today. Since its effects on the modern
world are the results of its present 2,500-year-old form, then its present form is
all that matters, not the bits and pieces of scattered goatskins upon which it
was originally written. And yet, its present form tells of an ancient swindle and
fraud that has successfully survived for two thousand and five hundred years
until the present day, disguised as a religion.

Only in the past two centuries has modern biblical scholarship shown us
that the patchwork of stories in the biblical material must be evaluated chapter
by chapter and sometimes verse by verse. Besides its plagiarisms and lies, the
Hebrew Bible includes some small amount of historical material mixed up
with a lot of nonhistorical, false, misleading and quasi-historical materials,
which sometimes appear very close to one another in the text. The whole es-
sence of biblical scholarship is to separate the historical parts from the rest of
the text according to linguistic, literary, extra-biblical historical and archaeological considerations. So, yes, one may doubt the historicity of one verse and
accept the validity of another. But after all of this nitpicking is done, the *Hebrew Bible* still adds up to the Biggest Lie Ever Told.

The Biggest Lie Ever Told was *written for a purpose*. It was written for a
particular audience, not for the non-Jewish public. Its original stories were for
an audience of illiterate goat herders and wandering bandits. It was read to the
illiterate Hebrews by some very cunning priests. They claimed that it was the
very word of God speaking to his best friend and bosom buddy, Moses. It became the only so-called "history" of the ancient Near East for over three thousand years of folly among men. And it has created folly among men to this
very day. During their captivity in Babylonia, the evil priests of Yahweh rearranged and rewrote their collections of fables and myths for a new audience.
This new audience was all of the Hebrews that they wanted to inspire to return
to Jerusalem and build another temple and treasury on the old site. It is this
"second edition" of the Jewish lies that we have today as the *Hebrew Bible*.

The First Five Books are purported to have been written between 1445
BC to 1405 BC when their great national hero Moses was supposed to have
been schlepping his stolen property around the Sinai Peninsula. But could Moses have written the first five books of the Old Testament as the lying Jews
claim? No, he could not have done so. At the alleged time of Moses – 1,440
years before Christ – the Hebrews possessed no written language of their own
in which to write it. Hebrew characters were derived from the Hyksos-
Phoenician script which in turn was derived from the Egyptian Demotic script.
This Semitic writing system, which includes the early Arabian script in which
the earliest copies of the Quran were written, contained no vowels. These writing systems were like ABC shorthand. Try to write a sentence of this book in
English, but leave out all the vowels, and see how accurately you can get the
exact sense of what is meant.

For example, ABC shorthand of the previous sentence would be written as: "Tr t wrt sntns f ths bk n nglsh, bt lv t ll th vwls, nd s hw ccrtl y gt th xct sns f wht s mnt." That's how Hebrew was written, with no vowels. With no vowels, many interpretations and incorrect meanings of words would invariably become part of every transcription. Only the priests could make any sense of it and only then through memorization and training from the priest who had originally written it. So, how can we tell what Moses, or any other ancient teacher or "law-giver" said literally, since the Hebrew writing was so archaic and crude? The Black Speech of early Arabic had the same dilemma even as late as the days of Mohammad (mhrh) around 800 AD. The original *Quran* was written in ABC Arabic!

It was only much later that the Hebrew characters were given vowels. Whatever stories had been written in the original incomprehensible characters were embellished and re-written into a new story congruent with the economic and religious schemes of those later times. Every priest and rabbi thought that he was "divinely inspired," so that whatever he imagined and whatever he wrote was true, even when he invented fables and wrote lies! Regardless of the false historical time frame that it claims, the *patriarchal narratives* are filled with references to late monarchic historical fictions from the seventh century BC when most of the Torah was actually written. So, even the alleged time when it was claimed to have been written, is false.

The only *Hebrew Bible* copies that can be accurately dated were written and released from the Babylonian scribes in 539 BC. The rabbis destroyed all earlier copies. What is known today as Judaism can only be dated from then. Judaism is not the ancient religion that it claims to be. The Jews are mere upstarts on the historical stage, fraudulent upstarts at that!

The Jews call the first five books of the *Hebrew Bible*, the Torah or the "Law." That it is claimed to be the entire law of the Jews is verified by the Hebrew-speaking Jews when they call it "the Five-Fifths of the Law." This "Five-Fifths of the Law," is not five-fifths of all Jewish lies because they tell many, many more than are merely found in the *Old Testament*. Like everything else that the Jews expound, even their claim that the Torah is their "law," is also a lie since they have superseded the Torah with *The Babylonian Talmud*. But more about that in Chapter 14, "The Fiendish Lawyers of Judah."

Although the Jews use the ancient Babylonian naming convention of titling a book by the first word of the text, the modern, English-speaking world titles these five books as Genesis, Exodus, Leviticus, Numbers and Deuteronomy. The Jews claim that all five books of the Torah were written by Moses. But archaeology proves that it is impossible for anyone named Moses to have written the Torah as the lying Jews claim. The first four books – Genesis, Exodus, Leviticus and Numbers – were all interwoven stories by at least three editors. The fifth book, Deuteronomy, bears a distinctive terminology, shared by none of the others, that contains an uncompromising condemnation of worship of other gods, a new view of God as completely transcendent, and the absolute prohibition of the sacrificial worship of the God of the Moneylenders in any place other than the Temple in Jerusalem. None of these books were written as they claim in the 1400s BC. The Pentateuch and the Deuteronomistic history were written in the 800s BC in Jerusalem when the kingdom of the Israelians was no more. These early books of the Bible and their famous fairy tales of early Jewish history were first codified and in key respects composed in Jerusalem in the seventh century BC. In their final editions, the *Hebrew Bible* that we know today was written in the 4th or 5th century BC, many centuries *after* the times described. Thus, the so-called "ancient writings" of the Jews are actually not so very old after all.

Modern Pentateuchal study has revealed so many discrepancies that it is really quite impossible that these books were written by a single author. What's more, regardless of the claims of these fables to being of great antiquity, the oldest date that four of these books could have been written was in Judah in the Ninth Century BC and some parts of them written a little later in the kingdom of the Israelians. Both the Judah versions and the Israelian versions were combined after the fall of the Northern Kingdom of the Israelians. As for the fraudulent Book of Deuteronomy, it was "discovered" and added during the time of king Josiah (649–609 BC) who became king at the age of eight years old. It was rewritten during the "Exile" in Babylonia, during which time the final versions of all the books of the Jews were edited and re-written. All other copies other than the Babylonian versions written by Ezra the Scribe, were destroyed.

The first eleven chapters of Genesis must be considered separately. These were plagiarized and stolen by the Jewish priests from the libraries of Babylonia. The Jews merely destroyed the original copies and put their own names on their revised copies as authors. These chapters deal with the Myth of Creation, God's creation of man and woman, the unity of the human race, the sin of Adam and Eve, the Fall from divine favor, and the penalties that their descendants would inherit in consequence of "sin." Be sure to understand that the word "sin" means "debt" and the debt is acquired by anyone who breaks the Mosaic laws. This is the perfect swindle of the moneylenders because that means that every Hebrew and every Gentile in the world owed the Jewish priests a fee for the "original debt," a debt that can never be repaid, although the interest on the debt was perpetually collected by the priests as sacrifices, free will offerings, tithes and penalties – just like modern day credit card and banking swindles.

None of the surrounding people of the ancient Near East made any mention of any of those fables found in the Torah. Only the dwarfish Jews tell stories that make themselves appear bigger and more important than they really are. The Egyptians, Assyrians, Babylonians and Hittites, have no record whatsoever of the stories that the Jews tell. But the Hebrew priests were quite well educated in the various religious stories of the ancient Near East since they had purloined a great number of them while writing their Torah.

The Jerusalem Bible commentators put Abraham's stay in Canaan at about 1850 BC. They put Joseph's life in Egypt at a little after 1700 BC. Both dates are based on nothing but guesses dependent upon genealogy time frames found within the Pentateuch and on the incorrect choice of which Egyptian pharaoh was believed to have been ruling at that time.

The Exodus has two archaeologically-based dates that biblical commentators dispute. One theory favors the 15th century when the Eighteenth Dynasty ruled Egypt; another theory puts Exodus in the 13th century under the Egyptian Nineteenth Dynasty. As you can see from my analysis in Volume I, *The Sumerian Swindle*, both approximate dates are correct because the Hyksos divided into four different groups with different historical time lines. Those four separate histories were later combined into a single narrative story by the rabbis and priests in Babylon.

To understand how the inventions of the lying Jews were woven together as they were, it helps to know something about the topography of Canaan. After all, even the fictitious soap opera of Judaism requires a stage upon which the actors can perform.

The kingdom of Judah occupied the southern part of the highlands from Jerusalem to the Negev. It forms a homogeneous environmental unit of rugged terrain, difficult communications, and meager and highly unpredictable rainfall. Judah has always been marginal agriculturally and isolated from the neighboring regions by geological barriers that encircle it on all sides except in the north direction toward the countryside of Israel. In the Bronze Age, when Abraham was trying to swindle Jerusalem away from Melchizidek, and at the beginning of the Iron Age, the entire area was rocky and covered with dense scrub and forest with very little open land available for agriculture. On the basis of archaeological surveys, Judah remained relatively empty of permanent population, quite isolated, and very marginal right up to and past the presumed time of David and Solomon, with no major urban centers and with no pronounced hierarchy of hamlets, villages and towns. It was mainly an empty and uninviting countryside, sparsely inhabited by scattered goat herders. Israel and Judah occupied entirely different ecological niches. Judah and the small town of Urusalem, was always the most remote part of the hill country, isolated by topographical and climatic barriers.

On the other hand, the northern part of the Israelian highlands consisted of a patchwork of fertile valleys nestled between adjoining hilly slopes. It was a relatively productive region, with the inner valleys and the eastern marginal land of the desert fringe cultivated mainly for growing grain, while the hilly areas were cultivated with olive and vine orchards. Though a casual traveler through this region today may find it much hillier in appearance than Judah to the south, communication and transport of agricultural produce were much easier. The slopes to the west are moderate and facilitate passage down toward the cities of the Mediterranean coastal plain. On the northern edge of this region of Israel lay the broad expanse of the Jezreel Valley, a rich agricultural area that also served as the major overland route of trade and communication between Egypt and Mesopotamia. In the east, the desert steppe area was less arid and less rugged than farther south in Judah enabling the relatively free movement of people and commodities between the central ridge, the Jordan

Valley and the Transjordanian highlands to the east. The kingdom of the Israelians had more resources and a richer climate to exploit than did Judah. These geographical and climactic differences are what separated Israel and Judah. The Hebrews of Israelian territory were much richer than the Hebrews who occupied the territory of Judah.

The first five books of the *Hebrew Bible* are called the *Torah* by the Jews. These same books are called by the Christians the *Pentateuch*. The basic theme of the *Pentateuch* is actually the history of a legal contract. But this was not a legal contract between God and the Hebrews; it was a legal contract between the merchant-moneylenders who wrote the *Torah* and the Hebrews. And the contract was one-sided.

It should be immediately understood that these five books as well as the Books of the so-called "prophets" all reached their present form during the alleged "Exile" in Babylon. All of the books were edited by Ezra the Scribe and finalized in Babylon by 538 BC. Basically, Judaism is a Babylonian religion. But before jumping up and down upon the fables of the *Hebrew Bible* with its stories about the special god of the Jews who loved only those oh-so-wonderful Hebrew goat-molesters, we should first understand who the gods of the Canaanites and who the gods of the Hebrew bandits were. After all, if we are going to discuss a book known as "the word of god," we should know who this god was, shouldn't we? What we find when we actually inquire about who this god of the Jews really was, is that the Jews have been lying about their god for over 2500 years.

Every Bible student can tell you that the god of the Jews was named (in the ABC shorthand of Hebrew) YHWH or *Yahweh*. However, among the Bible students who have learned a mistranslated corruption of that name, they say his name was *Jehovah*. Bible students tend to believe the lies that the Jews tell in the Old Testament because that is how the Bible has been traditionally taught, without any other corroborating evidence other than itself. However, the archaeologists have discovered the truth. The Yahweh-god was a Canaanite god that the Hebrews stole as their own, alone. Yahweh loved the Jews only because they claimed that he did.

> The epigraphic material recently uncovered at the religious center of Kuntillet Ajrud to the south of Kadesh-barnea in Sinai, provides a complex picture concerning the multiplicity of religious practices existing during the 9th and 8th centuries BC. The Hebrew and Phoenician inscriptions which were found at the site bear the names of *El, Yhwh, Baal* and *Asherah*, Although the monotheistic Hebrew faith precluded the addition of any female deity as consort to *Yhwh*, pictures and an inscription were found at Ajrud which may represent Yhwh and his consort.

In other words, both the Hebrews and their cousins the Phoenicians, worshiped several gods named *El, Yhwh*, and *Baal* along with *Yahweh's* wife whose name was *Asherah* (a.k.a. *Astarte* or *Ishtar*). So much for the allegedly "monotheistic" Hebrews and the one god who loved only them! And to the north of Canaan, even more evidence that the Jews have been lying about their god:

> The Semitic language literature of Ugarit is mostly mythologi-
> cal and concerns the pagan gods of Canaan, such as the male
> *Baal* and female *Asherah*, whose worship is forbidden in the
> Hebrew Bible. *El*, whom the Bible identifies with *Yahweh*, ap-
> pears as the head of the Ugaritic pantheon.

Thus, the great, one-and-only, god of the Hebrews was also off in the city of Ugarit moonlighting for extra sacrifices among the "pagans." Or what about these discoveries from the ruins of the mighty Hittite Empire?

> The Hittites prayed to their god *Baal*, *El* the benign, the Creator
> of Creatures. *Baal* was the god of rain and storms and the prince
> lord of the earth.

Inscriptions with numerous references to *Yahweh* having a consort named *Asherah* were written in Hebrew by official Jewish scribes in the 8th century BC and are found in numerous sites all over Palestine. But until modern ar-chaeology uncovered them, only the lies of the *Hebrew Bible* were known to Mankind. The chief god of the Hebrews was not a Hebrew god at all! He was actually a Canaanite god named *El* (a.k.a. *Yhwh* or *Yahweh*) who was wor-shiped by many peoples in Canaan as well as in Hattiland. In the cuneiform tablets of Ras Shamrah (~1400 BC) the leader of the Pantheon was *El*; his wife was Asherat-of-the-sea (a.k.a. *Asherah*, *Astarte* or *Ishtar*). After *El*, the great-est god was *Baal*, son of *El* and *Asherah*. Thus, the son of their mighty god, *El*, was the god *Baal* whom the Hebrew priests hated. The great god that the Jews claim loved only themselves, was actually the god of all the people in the East-ern Mediterranean Basin including Syria. The Jews are liars.

El Shaddai (the God of the Mountain) is still worshiped by the Jews in the form of the *teffilin*, one of two small leather boxes containing Torah texts. One of these little boxes they strap to one arm and the other little box, these fuzzy-faced clowns strap to their foreheads with leather thongs. These ridicu-lous boxes strapped to their horsey faces, big noses and kinky hair, are worn by the males of the species from the age of thirteen. The *teffilin* are worn in a manner to represent the Hebrew letters "shin," "daleth," and "yod," which together form the name *Shaddai*.

The *Hebrew Bible*, itself, shows that the Jews evolved from polytheism to monotheism with the promotion of a god who had been known by a variety of names, into one supreme God, *Yahweh*. The god of the Jews was the god of the Canaanites. The Jews merely stole him and then murdered the Canaanites, leaving themselves as the one and only "Holy Chosen Ones" of this god.

Like everything that the Jews claim as "Jewish," even the name of their god is stolen from other people. The name of this "god" is found in the letters of his name called the Tetragrammaton. The Tetragrammaton is the designation for the four (tetra) letters (grammata) in the *Hebrew Bible* for the name of their god, *Yhwh*. The tetragrammaton is a form of the root *hyh* ("be") and should be pronounced as "Yahweh" ("I am"). Many Bible translations substitute LORD for *Yhwh* or use the name "Yahweh" of "Jehovah." The ancient people believed that the gods resided in their own territories, so when the Hebrew bandits entered Canaan, they worshiped the Canaanite gods. Once they had stolen the land of the Canaanites and the god of the Canaanites, they were confident that they could keep Palestine for themselves.

The Jews had no monopoly on God, as they falsely claim in the Old Testament and in their yeshiva crime schools today. All of the ancient peoples spoke to and heard replies from their gods. A stone inscription dating from early in the 8th century BC by king Zakir, king of Hamat, was found in 1904 AD twenty-four miles from Aleppo. In dedication to his gods, king Zakir wrote:

> I am Zakir, king of Hamat and Lu'ath. A humble man I am. Be'elshamayn helped me and stood by me. Be'elshamayn made me king over Hatarikka (Hadrach). ... I lifted up my hand to Be'elshamayn and Be'elshamayn heard me. Be'elshamayn spoke to me through seers and through diviners.
>
> Be'elshamayn said to me: Do not fear, for I made you king, and I shall stand by you and deliver you from all these kings who set up a siege against you.

What difference is this from what the Jews write about their own conversations and divinations with "their" god? No difference whatsoever, except for this: We have had only the word of the Jews to rely upon for the past 2,500 years. The voices of those other ancient peoples have been buried in the dust. Only at the beginnings of the 20th century AD with modern archaeology, have these voices been revealed to show that the Jews *as an entire people* are liars, every one of them.

It is clear that Abraham and his tribe of thieves worshiped the Canaanite god variously named *El* or *El Shaddai* or *Yahweh*. But to really understand the *character* of these master criminals, it is vitally necessary to understand *the attributes of the god* whom they worshiped These are not necessarily the attributes that the Canaanites believed for their god. These are the attributes that the evil Hebrew priests of Yahweh gave to *Yahweh* as is written in the *Hebrew Bible*. Knowing this god's attributes not only shows you the character of the god but also shows you the kind of people the Jews are who worship such a malevolent monster.

The following list is long, but as you read it, you are reading many of the attributes of every Jew who "walks in the way of his god." These are the descriptions of this Yahweh-god as copied from the *Hebrew Bible*: *Yahweh* is described as a god of consuming fire, the wrath, anger, blazing with anger, bringer of evil, creator of desolation and curses, creator of earthquakes, creator of plague and fever, exterminator of peoples, the extermination god, fear-monger among nations, ferocity of his anger (seen in the glare of devouring fire, in a cloudburst, a downpour, in hailstones), full of wrath and fury, he is the god of genocide, greedy for wealth, heavy in his extraction, his anger could blaze out and wipe men from the face of the earth, he is an inflictor of evil, jealous, murderer of those who don't follow the Laws of Moses to the letter. He is the pursuer of his enemies to their death, revenge, his tongue is like a devouring fire, Urim and Thummim and chooser by lots (the god of gambling), utterly destroys, vengeful, vindictive, wrathful. He is the punisher of his enemies who hate him through four generations, that is, extinction of four generations in each family – grandparents, parents, children, grandchildren. Thus, the god of the Jews commits total genocide upon his enemies. His enemies are all non-Jews who do not follow the Laws of Moses. And he is the "Lord of Hosts," that is, *the god of armies*. And Yahweh is the god of the circumcised penis. This is the god of the Jews. The very attributes that they admire in him and nurture in themselves. All are big demons and little devils.

Are you afraid, yet? Well, you shouldn't be, because like the Jews, the Jewish god is a fraud. He never did any of the things that the Jews claim that he did. What his attributes are, are not as important as the fact that these are the very attributes of the Jews who worship such a demon and do everything that they can to "walk in his ways." Thus, the Jews are demons *by their own definition* and then they lie about it by calling themselves a "holy people." The Jews practice the attributes of their god and mimic the characteristics that they claim are his. Yes, there is a God but, as you shall see, there is no god in Israel.

This was a very vicious god worshiped by some very vicious people whom the god had "blessed" only as long as they *followed his laws* and *walked in his ways*. In other words, this god would bless the Jews as long as they were as vicious as *Yahweh* and as ruthless as *Yahweh*. Only then, would they be "his people" and only then would he be "their god." As history proves, the Jews have always been just like their god and no more holy than the devil.

The idea that God created the universe by conceiving it in his Mind and commanding it into existence, was originally expounded by the Egyptians at the beginnings of the First Dynasty (3050-2890 BC) established at Memphis. The god of Memphis was *Ptah* and his temple there was declared to be "the balance in which Upper and Lower Egypt have been weighed." Here the god, *Ptah*, conceived the elements of the Universe in his Mind and brought them into being with his commanding speech. Thus, from the Egyptian *Memphite Theology of Creation* we have:

> "There came into being as the heart-mind and there came into being as the tongue-speech something in the form of Atum [or "Totality," the creator god]. The mighty great one is Ptah, who transmitted life to all the gods as well as to their *ka*'s [spirit-

bodies], through this heart-mind by which Horus became Ptah, and through this tongue-speech by which Thoth became Ptah."

In other words, all of Creation became God. *Ptah* thought of and created by his speech the creator-god *Atum* ("Totality"), thus transmitting the divine power of *Ptah* to all other gods. The gods *Horus* and *Thoth*, a commonly associated pair, are equated with the organs of thought and speech. *The Memphite Theology of Creation* goes on to state the inherent holiness of each person within whom God dwells:

> "Thus it happened that the heart-mind and the tongue-speech gained control over every other member of the body, by teaching that Ptah is in every body and in every mouth of all gods, all men, all cattle, all creeping things, and everything that lives, by thinking and commanding everything that he wishes."

This is a very advanced and all-encompassing understanding of God. Though it would arise at later times with the Persian teaching of Ahura-Mazda and the Aryan teachings in the Vedas, it was something too subtle for the gross sensitivities of the venal merchant-moneylenders who stole this knowledge during their Hyksos occupation of Egypt and carried it off to Babylon.

The god, *Ptah*, created the "totality of all things" which was known as the creator god, *Atum*. These names of the Egyptian gods had power and were repeated as mantras within the tombs and temples of the Egyptians. The repetition of these holy names led the Egyptians to very high levels of meditative trance and extra-sensory perception. This is not a mere speculation but is a power that all men and women have, if they seek it. The Egyptians were famous in the ancient Near East for their mystic abilities and modern science proves that there is more to Egypt than what most scientists can perceive.

> "Since all living things generate weak electromagnetic fields, and since many, if not all, can sense those of the earth, communication by this medium remains a strong possibility....
>
> "One problem is that the strength of biofields is far below that of the earth's field. Hence any input from other creatures would be embedded in noise. This is a common obstacle to tele-communications, and there are several ways around it. The easiest is for sender and receiver both to be frequency locked, that is, tuned to one frequency and insensitive to others. Such a lock-in system might explain why spontaneous ESP experiences most often happen between relatives or close friends....
>
> "Another theoretical difficulty is the fact that psychic transmission doesn't seem to fade with distance. The electromagnetic field around an animal's nervous system, on the other hand, starts out unimaginably small and then diminishes rapidly.

However, extremely low frequency (ELF) transmissions have a peculiar property. Because of their interaction with the ionosphere, even weak signals in this frequency range (from 0.1 to 100 cycles per second) travel all the way around the world without dying out. If an innate frequency selector is operating within this band, reception should be the same anywhere on earth....

"... In short, all living things having such a system would share the common experience of being plugged in to the electromagnetic fields of earth, which in turn vary in response to the moon and sun."

Egypt was built with the power of peacefulness, not with the destructiveness of war. This is a lesson that has been purposely warped and hidden in modern times as the powers of finance capital and communist anarchy vie with one another to produce money for the Jews through warfare. *Peace produces life and progress; war produces death and profits.*

The Egyptians believed that the universe was commanded into existence by the Supreme Lord. They believed and wrote about this almost two thousand years before there were any Jews to plagiarize the ideas of the Mediterranean Caucasoid people of Egypt.

Furthermore, translations of the Egyptian hieroglyphs from *The Memphite Theology of Creation* prove that the Egyptians were not idolaters as is slanderously charged by the Jews. They were no different in their beliefs, in this respect, from the Babylonians. Both of these people worshiped idols, but they believed that the idol was a home in which the god, himself, resided. The idol was not a god, merely a resting place for the god. This was true of all of the idolatrous peoples. They were not so stupid as the Jews claim them to be. They used idols to concentrate their minds upon the god who lived inside the wooden or metal image.

".... And so Ptah was satisfied, after he had made everything, as well as all the divine order. He had formed the gods, he had made cities, he had founded nomes, he had put the gods in their shrines, he had established their offerings, he had founded their shrines, he had made their bodies like that with which their hearts were satisfied. So the gods entered into their bodies of every kind of wood, of every kind of stone, of every kind of clay, or anything which might grow upon him, in which they had taken form. So all the gods, as well as their *ka*'s gathered themselves to him, content and associated with the Lord of the Two Lands."

As shown in previous chapters as well as here, the so-called "pagans" had first-hand experience with God. They had actual knowledge of some of the mystical powers *inherent* in Man. But what did the Jews have? Nothing but

their lies, lies designed to swindle unto them the wealth of nations and the enslavement of Mankind.

Genesis 1-11 deals with primordial history. But most biblical commentators misunderstand its basic theme. Believing or *wishing* to believe that what
the stories claim is true, they see what they call "a theme of salvation running
through the Bible beginning with Genesis." But this "theme of salvation" is
only the wishful thinking of two thousand years of Christian philosophers,
hoping that what the Jews wrote is not a lie. Although salvation is a theme as
well as an actual teaching of the New Testament, in fact, salvation is not found
as an actual theme in the Old Testament. The actual theme of the Old Testament is the legalistic distinction between those who agree to follow the legal
Contract of Moses and the "evil sinners" who don't. Stories abound in these
Old Testament pages of terrible retribution toward those who do not follow the
rules as written by the rabbinical scribes. It is a one-way contract, demands are
made, threats are declared but *there is actually no salvation* offered other than
in the wishful thinking of those who have been deceived by the Jews.

From its beginnings, the Hebrew ideas of religion were by no means a
monotheistic religion. They believed in other gods, its just that they only
prayed to their own god who, over time, not only became the greatest and most
powerful god, but also eventually the only god. This "one god among many"
metamorphized into "the most powerful of all gods" and eventually "the true
god among all of the false gods" and finally as "the only god," *Yahweh.*

The rabbis and scribes who stitched together the various books of the
Pentateuch could not swindle the Hebrews by creating a new religion out of
thin air because there would be nothing upon which to base their religion.
They could not create something entirely new because it could not claim the
prestige of something old or ancient or eternal as its foundation. So, they invented a history that was based upon already existing theologies. By combining their fables with already existing myths, they could claim the prestige associated with antiquity. "Prestige" has always been one of the merchant-
moneylender's most sought-after social perks. So, they guaranteed themselves
the prestige of being "the Holy Chosen Ones" of the great Canaanite god of
Palestine with main offices in the bankers' city of Jerusalem.

The Pentateuch is an amalgamation of four documents from different
places and times, all much later than Moses. Indeed, there may never have
been such a person as Moses. Since the Mosaic Laws have so many similarities to the Laws of Hammurabi, perhaps Hammurabi was the law-giver who
was the template for Moses just as the stories of the baby Sargon being set
adrift on the river in a basket, was another scribal theft credited to Moses.

The Torah (Pentateuch) is also called the "Book of Promises." The promises are made by the lying Yahweh-god of the Hebrews. A god who lies is an
apt god for a people who lies. To Israel the divine promise was made; the
Promise was made to Adam and Eve after their fall; the Promise was made to
Noah; promises were made to Abraham, Isaac and Jacob; Israel was promised
land where the patriarchs had lived; Israel was promised to be special, etc. And

every one of these alleged "promises" were all broken by the very god who made the promises.

The Torah is also called the Book of Covenants; covenant was made with Adam and Eve; with Noah; with Abraham; and through Moses to all of Israel. But it is not a covenant of equals. In return, this god demands loyalty from his people. If Israel breaks the covenant (the Law), the bond may be broken. It is god himself who makes the laws that bind the people. The Promise, the Choice, the Covenant and the Law are the four methods for swindling the Hebrews out of their freedoms and tying them into a binding contract of the moneylenders of Babylon.

Something else is very important for understanding the Old Testament. One of the greatest errors *made by all of the biblical translators* was their mistranslation of the Hebrew word, "goy" and "goyim" (non-Jewish, lowly insects, stupid cattle). By mistranslating these words, the real malice of the Jews towards other people, is completely obliterated. "Goy" singular and "goyim" plural, has the meaning of "lowly insects and stupid cattle." The merchant-moneylenders referred to the people who borrowed from them as "lowly insects and stupid cattle." They were "insects" like swarming locusts in numbers who could be trod under foot; and they were "cattle" fit only to be milked and slaughtered. And yet, this is the term that is used by the priests and scribes of the Temple of Yahweh to describe all non-Jews while elevating themselves in their own eyes as the very most holy of God's creation. It is a term commonly used by the Jews today in referring to non-Jews.

The biblical translators falsely claim that non-Jews are called "Gentiles" or "nations" by the Hebrew scribes but that is not how the Jews translate the word "goyim." In fact, Christian translators have very much done a disservice to Christianity by hiding the true meaning of these vicious Jewish slanders and hate words that pepper the Old Testament and Talmud. Thus, instead of the implacable enemies toward Christians and the mendacious foes of all Mankind that Jews truly are, they are falsely perceived to be just quaint holdovers from Old Testament stories who refer to the non-Jews by such pale words as "gentile" or "nations" or "people."

The meaning of the word, "goy" and its plural, "goyim," is explained by Col. Jack Mohr, a great Christian patriot and evangelist:

> "It is generally taught in the Christian churches of America, that the world is divided into three main religious groups – Jews, Gentiles and Christians. These religious groups teach that anyone who is not a Jew, must belong to one or the other of these remaining groups, and is either a Gentile or a Christian. The modern definition of a 'gentile' as given in Webster's New Collegiate Dictionary is: 'relating to the nations at large, as distinguished from the Jews.'
>
> "But here is something important you *must* know, if you are to understand the Bible. The word *gentile* is not used in any of

the ancient manuscripts, simply because there was no such word in the Hebrew or Greek languages. The word *gentile* as used in our modern Bible versions, including the 'much loved' King James Version, in the Old Testament, *always* comes from the Hebrew word 'goy,' (singular) and 'goyim,' (plural). It is translated five different ways in the Old Testament, according to Strong's Exhaustive Concordance of the Bible; 'goy or goyim (singular or plural),' a foreign *nation* hence *gentile*; also figuratively, a troop of animals or a flight of locusts. Usually translated (1) *gentile*; (2) *heathen*; (3) *nation*, and (4) *people*, or (5) *another*.

"The word 'goy' is found in the Old Testament some 557 times. Thirty times it has been translated *gentile*; eleven times as *people*; 142 times as *heathen*; 373 times as *nation*, and one time as *another*. But not once as 'non-Jew.'"

In other words, the biblical translators have been lying to all of Mankind for over 2000 years! The Jews do not call non-Jews by the name "gentile" or "people" or "heathens" or "nations" as the translators falsely claim. They call non-Jews "cattle and insects" – *goyim*. The very idea behind this word has colored the attitudes of the Jews toward the people around them for 3300 years ever since the Babylonian banker, Terah, first sent his son, Abraham, to establish a temple in the fortress town of Jerusalem. This attitude toward other people, *is just one of the many reasons* that the Jews have been hated by everybody, everywhere, for so long. And yet, that the Jews have been calling us "insects and cattle" behind our backs, pales in comparison to their many other crimes against humanity. In the following commentary on the Bible, the original word "goyim" has been reapplied to the text so that you can better understand what these Jewish assholes actually believe, that *goyim* are "lowly insects and stupid cattle" – so far are they beneath the superiority of the Jews, those Holy Chosen Ones of a Canaanite god who never did any of the things that the Jews claim that he did.

With the above Prologue in mind, you are now ready to fully understand the *Hebrew Bible* and How the Jews Betrayed Mankind.

6.2 The Book of Genesis, the Foundation of The Biggest Lie Ever Told

Finalized in Babylon around 539 BC, Genesis is an instruction book that teaches a false history of the world. Its goal was to con large groups of illiterate Hebrew goat rustlers into joining a genealogically organized family of thieves for the purpose of establishing a religiously protected bank. It is a pseudo-history of international thieves stealing Canaan (Palestine) from the inhabitants and murdering them, all while claiming that God commanded them to do it. How the moneylenders did this, is through some very clever lies.

Terah, the founder of Judaism and the Patriarch of the Moneylender guilds of Ur and Harran, sent his youngest son, Abraham, to Canaan to scout out the territory around the fortified town of Urusalem in preparation for establishing a secure treasury there. But he kept his oldest son and heir, Nahor, in Harran and Ur to manage the family businesses. Please keep in mind that both Terah and Abraham were not Hebrews but, rather, they were Babylonians. As protection for Abraham, Terah also sent his gang of strong-arm enforcers, the tribe of Binu-Yamina (Benjamin) to guard him and to promote trade, gather intelligence, collect tribal genealogies and to trade with the Hebrews as a way of bringing the Hyksos-Egyptian gold into his treasury and the Hyksos and Hebrew tribes into his temple. This tribe of Benjamin was a Babylonian, not a Hebrew, tribe.

In Mesopotamia, the Benjamites were not a small tribe of just a few bandits and goons. Excavations at Mari on the Middle Euphrates yielded 20,000 cuneiform tablets. Among these were 5,000 letters written by the Semitic Amorites. This trove of tablets was dated to about 1730-1700 BC during the reign of Zimri-Lim, the king of Mari. The personal names, language and customs reflect the culture of the Patriarchal Age in Genesis. Even the Benjamites are represented as enemies occupying various cities at that time. One of these clay tablet letters reads, "Yesterday, … all the Benjamites raised fire signals. …all the cities of the Benjamites of the Terqa district raised fire signals!" The Benjamites had already had a long history and had served many kings as mercenaries. So, when Terah hired some of them to accompany his son, Abraham, he had plenty of Benjamin tribesmen to choose from. It was not a tribe that arose from the "loins" (Jew-speak for "reproductive organs") of Jacob as the lying rabbis claim in the *Hebrew Bible*. "Loins" is another mistranslated word from the nasty minds of the rabbis. The circumcised fiends of Yahweh are often described in the Bible as "girding up their loins" (penis and balls) for various purposes. And all Jews are proud to be descended from the balls and penis (the loins) of Abraham. That's where Jews come from; storks don't bring them.

To build a new religion requires stories and traditions that the prospective members would find appealing and would thus be willing to follow. And so, the stories of Genesis were told, based upon the Creation Myths and other tales from the libraries of Babylonia. These were not as we find them today in the *Hebrew Bible* because they have been edited over the millennia. But their early editions have been carefully fluffed up by Terah's Babylonian scribes who retold the ancient stories of Mesopotamia dressed up in Hebrew costumes and substituting Hebrew names for the heroes of Babylonia and Sumeria and Akkad. The original stories we now know, thanks to modern archaeology, which proves the Jews to be counterfeiters and plagiarizers.

In the Sumerian histories, everything could be placed either before or after the Flood. Before the Flood was prehistory; after the Flood was written history. Bible historians in days of yore who had no access to modern archaeological discoveries can be forgiven their blindness, but modern bible historians have no excuse for perpetuating the lies of the Jews.

In all of the Mesopotamian creation stories, creation always resulted in heaven and earth, since the ancients clearly saw that both existed and both supported Mankind. Any Sumerian, Babylonian or Egyptian creation story also included one of two basic versions of the creation of the human race. In one version the human race sprouted from the ground like plants; in the other, Mankind was created from clay, mixed with divine blood, and molded into figurines. In ancient Mesopotamia, Man was made from clay. But divine blood (or in some stories divine spittle) was necessary to infuse the clay with life. Or, as in Egypt, the god breathed life into the clay figure. The Sumerians claimed that Man was created to work for the gods so that the gods could rest. In time, the world became overpopulated so the gods brought a flood to kill off the excess and noisy population.

Trespasses against the gods were often the main topic in Sumerian sources about religion. "Sin" is defined as deliberate disobedience to the known will of God or to a moral law; or it is something that is regarded as being shameful, deplorable, or utterly wrong. There were numerous Sumerian and Babylonian words for sins. The native terms distinguished their gravity. At the end of the second millennium BC, the text *Surpu* (literally, "burning") listed two hundred acts and omissions as sins, including not speaking one's mind, causing discord in the family, neglecting a naked person, and killing animals without reason. The Sumerians' confessional lists of trespasses contained unintentional sins as well as ancestral sins. The gods punished the sinners, but if the gods refused to forgive the sinner, that person could not be helped. It was observed by the ancient peoples that in reality, the wicked often fared better than the righteous. And this was always a puzzle to them because they did not understand the diabolical nature of the Sumerian Swindle or the evil in the hearts of the moneylenders. The ancient people could plainly see that the merchant-moneylenders were monsters but they couldn't see that their evil was directly related to the wealth that they had purloined.

As early as the second millennium BC, the Akkadians of the Old Babylonian period (Hammurabi's dynasty) were telling their *Creation Epic*. Recorded on clay tablets that were baked into bricks, these cuneiform stories of Marduk and his related gods add another witness to the lies of the Jews. In these epic stories, Marduk is honored as the "king of the universe." So, of course, a god with a title of "king of the universe" antedated the god of the Jews with that title by at least fifteen hundred years.

Early Mesopotamians regarded the supernatural forces that controlled their world as mysterious and impersonal. Early man believed that storms, rivers, lakes, marshes, mountains, sun, wind, and fire were all living beings not only because they had such power but because men could perceive and feel the living *qi* within these natural forces. The religious beliefs of the Sumerians first took form at Eridu, one of the oldest Sumerian settlements. For them, water was a numinous power, a supernatural life force. The power of water is also felt within those who know how to manifest their *qi* energy (one's Holy Spirit) as a living energy. So, these Mesopotamian spiritual and religious observations can be directly verified by anyone.

The Torah is written as a one-way Contract. By modern legal definitions, it is thus an illegal contract. For such a Contract to attract adherents, it must begin with something all ancient peoples would believe. The people of Mesopotamia – the original Sumerians as well as the Babylonians and Assyrians who later absorbed their culture – already believed in their Creation Myths as follows:

> "Heaven was created of its own accord.
> Earth was created of its own accord.
> Heaven was an abyss, earth was an abyss."

So, Genesis begins with what is essentially a plagiarism of Mesopotamian theology and myth. The Seven Days of Creation are counted in the Sumerian-Babylonian manner of beginning at dusk, "The evening came and the morning came: the first day," because that is how the Babylonians counted the days, the "day" started at sundown, the same method used in Genesis.

But after the first paragraph, this Contract immediately jumps into claiming to speak for God. God said, "Let there be light." From the first page of this Babylonian contract written in Hebrew, the original writer claims to speak for God, a god created from the hearts of the lecherous moneylenders. His first command after creating Man and Woman was to have sex and multiply. "Be fruitful, multiply, fill the earth and conquer it." These are the rules by which the moneylenders desired to operate, sex and tyranny over the entire world. And these are the same methods used by these gross scoundrels today.

Of course, the magic and mystery that the world held for ancient man, gave him no reason to doubt that it could all be created in six days by a magical god. This is not a point worth arguing since modern science proves the incredible age of the Universe and the more than ten-billion-year-old age of the Earth. The important point in this Contract is that after creating the whole world in six days God took a rest on the Seventh Day. "God blessed the seventh day and made it holy because on that day he had rested after all his work of creating." (Genesis 2:3.)

In any contract, the most important points are usually placed first. So, after limitless sex, here we have the major benefit to the moneylenders and Terah's solution for Problem #11 of the Fifteen Secret Problems of Babylonian Moneylenders: "We *tamkarum* [merchant-moneylenders] promote warfare and thereby profit enormously; but while inveigling others to do the fighting, how can we avoid military service without invoking the wrath of our victims?" This day of rest, is the ingenious method Terah invented for giving the members of his Temple a military exemption.

Just as was done by the moneylenders in the Assyrian city of Harran, a god – the priests of whom had been well bribed – declared that all residents of the city were free from military service. With a declaration of a god, no king could argue. The great value to the moneylenders of promoting wars without having to actually serve in the army, was incalculable. After having unlimited sex and many children, this was the most important law that Terah built into his Contract. And it kept the less wealthy of his relatives content.

The moneylenders had plenty of leisure since they were wealthy and never did any hard work. Because their new religion was designed to conceal their treasure in the Temple and to keep the Sumerian Swindle as their own, they had to insure two things (1) that all members of the guild got one day of leisure per week and (2) that by making that one day off as a "holy day" re-quirement of their god, then all of them could avoid military service. After limitless sex, this was the first Law of the Moneylenders: create a holy day so that avoidance of military service became a commandment of a god. What king would dare to go against a commandment of a god?

As further proof of the Babylonian origin of the Genesis stories, the Garden of Eden is identified with Sumer and Akkad where the Tigris and Euphrates Rivers flow. Into this story is placed the basic philosophy of the money-lenders and their complete usurpation of both Good and Evil. The moneylend-ers' philosophy sets the theme for nearly all events in later Jewish history, that is, no act is too evil and no act is too good because the Jews do both as it suits them. When a Jew is not bound by concepts of Good or Evil, then either choice is valid for him, depending on his own best interests. Without Good or Evil, a Jew becomes lawless and amoral, like bandits plying their craft while avoiding capture and prosecution.

After commands to avoid either Good or Evil, the Yahweh-god says, "It is not good that the man should be alone." Fashioning Man from dust (that is, dried clay) was a Mesopotamian belief. First, God created Man. Second, God created Woman. He created a woman second because He didn't want any advice on how to create a man. Then, God let them roam around naked and happy, as long as they didn't eat the from the tree of the knowledge of good and evil.

But, alas, they did eat and understood what good and evil is. This was named by the rabbis as the "original sin," doing what God forbade. The doc-trine of original sin, as it is commonly accepted, teaches that every person born into this world is a sinner and damnable not because of a personal moral deci-sion of rebellion against God but because they have inherited the literal guilt of Adam and Eve. "Original sin" claims that we sin by being born as the posterity of Adam and Eve – through heredity we are born as sinners. Judaism is, essen-tially, a racist religious scam of hereditary blessings, sins, and inherited real estate whereby the Jews claim to be inheritors of the entire world because "God gave it to them."

Adam and Eve became sinners through disobedience to God's instructions, yet the doctrine of original sin – as it is taught primarily in Roman Catholicism, Lutheranism, Calvinism and Judaism teaches that we are guilty of such an original sin that will damn us to the fires of hell forever without being given the choice to choose like our ancient, mythological parents, Adam-and-Eve, had. We are damned because of their bad choice, not our own. So, for the rabbis, the idea of "original sin" was a gold mine. Allowing them to squeeze the Hebrews out of every shekel of silver and every barbecued goat.

Once Adam and Eve had "sinned" by eating the forbidden fruit, they were ashamed to be frolicking in Paradise without any clothes. So, God made clothes for Adam and Eve to wear (Genesis 3:21). Walking around in one's birthday suit, was now frowned upon. Besides, the merchant-moneylenders were in the clothing and garment business, so people couldn't be allowed to run around naked or sales would lag. So, commanding Adam and Eve to wear clothes was more profitable to the Jews in their mythological tale.

According to the Genesis Contract, the only two differences between Man and God was (1) a God knows the difference between Good and Evil and (2) a god is immortal. The "Divine Privilege" is for God, alone, to decide what is good and evil. So, to prevent Man from becoming an immortal God, he banished Adam and Eve from the Garden and posted Babylonian cherubs to guard the way to the Tree of Life. Thus, according to the moneylenders, the only difference between themselves and God was in discerning the difference between Good and Evil and having eternal life. So, the Hebrew bandits were close to being gods by such reckoning. Not determining Good from Evil gave them the opportunity to be free from each value. No priest could censure them for their evil deeds because the Yahweh-god absolved them from both.

If *God* was going to make a new religion to be given to some ignorant goat rustlers out in the Judean desert, what are the chances that He would make it according to a patchwork of Babylonian myths and Babylonian cherubs rather than as a new "revelation" cut from whole cloth? But if a *Babylonian* was going to invent his own religion, he certainly would not have the omniscience of a God but would have to rely upon what he already knew about religion, a religion out of Babylon designed by loan sharks and thieves.

Stealing the land that he wanted from the resident Canaanite farmers meant that those who would eventually be Terah's unpaid soldiers would have to be the Hebrew-Hyksos escapees who were pillaging Canaan. Thus, Terah's god would have to be worshiped first and foremost by the shepherds. Here is how that swindle was accomplished.

Adam and Eve had two sons, Cain and Abel. Cain was a farmer and Abel was a shepherd. Cain brought some of the produce of the soil as an offering to the Yahweh-god. And Abel brought the firstborn of his flock and some fat. God looked with favor on the shepherd and his offering, but did not look with favor upon Cain, the farmer.

This would play well among the Hypos-Hebrew goat rustlers who were hearing this story for the first time from the moneylender-priests and their Binu-Yamina (Benjamite) guards. So, Cain the farmer, killed Abel, the shepherd. (Boos and hissing from among the Hebrew shepherds in the congregation.) God loved the shepherds but not the farmers (Genesis 4:2-8). So, with such stories, the conniving merchant-moneylenders brought the Egyptian gold into their treasury as they bartered with and collected the genealogies of the Hebrew shepherds. With such stories, the moneylenders of Babylon gave a mythological reason for the Hebrew shepherds of Canaan to attack and kill the farmers of Canaan, as revenge for the farmer Cain killing the shepherd, Abel. Do you see how these stories were propaganda for inducing the Hebrews to kill off the Canaanite farmers?

Seth was Adam's third son. He and all the sons of his descendants had children when they were over a hundred years old. And they all lived about 900 years. Having children in extreme old age was one of the dreams of the moneylenders who liked young slave women in their beds to keep them warm when they were doddering old men.

Filling in the centuries of blank space in their fake "history book" was accomplished by giving all of their alleged "ancestors" super-long lifespans – 930 years for Adam, 905 years for Enosh, 969 years for Methuselah, etc., until finally, Noah was born. Here, the moneylenders of Babylon plagiarized the Sumerian story of the Flood. The Jewish scribes embellished the Sumerian story of the Flood with Semitic padding and name changes. The Sumerian Flood story, complete with ark, actors, animals, happy ending, etc., was plagiarized by the Babylonian scribes. They merely put a Hebrew name change and authorship on all of it. As the centuries went by and the Hebrew priests destroyed all available copies of the original Creation stories, the people of the world began to believe that the lying Jews were the original people on earth and the very wisest and most ancient of men – not to mention, the most holy and blessed of God. Although all available copies were destroyed by the Jews, their plagiarisms and forgeries have only come to light in the past 150 years as archaeologists have dug up and translated the original archives from the buried libraries.

In addition, Semitic terrorism had to be a part of Terah's plan. The moneylenders were feared and hated. They were feared because they enforced the Sumerian Swindle through the bribery of the kings and the king's own soldiers. So, their defrauding of the People was enforced by the government. The moneylenders were hated for every reason their victims had to hate those demonic oppressors. The evil priests of *Yahweh* wrote for their future Jewish followers of the Contract,

> "Be the terror and dread of all the wild beasts and all the birds
> of heaven, of everything that crawls on the ground and all the
> fish of the sea; they are handed over to you." (Genesis 9:2.)

The moneylenders gave themselves dominion over all creatures because, after all, even the kings came to them to borrow silver and gold.

This hatred for animals created a kind of blood-lust whereby they proved their domination over animals. The pride of the Jews swelled every time they saw the terror in the eyes of their sacrificial animals at the altar, gleefully cutting the throats and spilling the blood and laughing while the poor animal thrashed about in its own gore. Animal sacrifice was a demonic celebration of the Jews and, later, of the Muslims. But this teaching was worse for Mankind because the moneylenders who wrote the *Hebrew Bible* were also the terror of Mankind, whom they considered to be as nothing more than beasts which they called *goyim* (lowly insects, stupid cattle). Thus, the murder of Mankind, is a goal of the Jews.

These Babylonian merchant-moneylenders declared themselves to have been made in the "image of God" because on Earth they considered themselves to be as gods. But to own the entire earth, the moneylenders needed slaves to do their bidding, willingly and without question. That is where the ignorant Hebrews were to be made useful. By offering those stupid bandits something that they wanted but which cost the merchant-moneylenders nothing – such as limitless sex – the ignorant Hebrew goat rustlers were inveigled into the scheme. The command of Terah's Yahweh-god to the wandering tribes to "Be fruitful, multiply, teem over the earth and be lord of it" (Genesis 9:7) and to be voracious, ruthless and cancerous, was to be the hallmark of the new religion that was being developed to serve the Babylonian moneylenders with the promiscuous Hebrew goat rustlers as their servants.

The Sumerians had a story about the Flood. (It marked the boundary line between their prehistory and their written history.) In this, their god created people, "vegetation luxuriated on the earth, animals four-legged creatures of the plain, were brought artfully into existence." But one of the gods decided to destroy all of Mankind by sending a flood. Another god warned a righteous king named Ziusudra to build an ark. This was Noah's Flood written about and recited as *The Epic of Gilgamesh* more than 1,500 years before there were any Jews. But it was a tale that was read every year during New Years and was preserved in nearly every ancient library. Thus, it was a story well known among the Babylonian scribes.

> "The god Ninigiku-Ea said to Utnapishtim
>   (the Babylonian Noah):
> Man of Shuruppak, son of Ubar-Tutu,
> Tear down this house, build a ship!
> Give up possessions, seek thou life.
> Forswear worldly goods and keep thy soul alive!
> Aboard the ship take thou the seed of all living things.
> The ship that thou shalt build,
> Her dimensions shall be to measure.
> Equal shall be her width and her length.
> Like the Apsu thou shalt ceil her."

Does this sound familiar, those of you who have read the Bible? All of the details of the Flood as found in Gilgamesh, are carried over into Genesis, the orders of God to destroy all of Mankind except for the one family of Utnapishtim (Noah), the building of the ark, two animals of every kind brought aboard, the flood above the mountain tops, the ark resting on a mountain, the freeing of a dove which returned, the freeing of swallow which returned, the freeing of a raven which found a resting place, the offering of sacrifice with the god smelling the sweet savor, all of this is found in the *Epic of Gilgamesh* story of the Flood. But the lying Jews claim the story as their own and embellished the theft with their own Hebrew names.

Using the Sumerian Flood Story as a literary way of wiping out everybody on earth except for the Jews, the wicked rabbis then wrote that Noah's three sons who came out of the ark were Shem, Ham and Jophath. Ham was claimed to be the ancestor of the Canaanites so that they could be called upon as relatives when they were needed and slaughtered when they were in the way. But Ham saw Noah's nakedness when he was drunk. So, as a scapegoat technique, the Canaanites (even though they were relatives) were cursed slaves of the later Israelians and Jews. The alleged "sin" of Ham is here given as the reason for treating the Canaanites so harshly. This unrelenting, unforgiving, hate-filled nature of Judaism is one of the things that Jesus preached against. It is a basic characteristic of the Jews today, reinforced by their Biggest Lie Ever Told and the rabbis' demonic teachings of the *Babylonian Talmud*, which will be explained in a later.

However, this "nakedness" is also a euphemism for "an embarrassing moment or a shameful event." The moneylenders had used such shameful moments upon the kings and administrators whom they had blackmailed to do their bidding and they wanted their new disciples to understand that such events were to be a curse upon them if they ever revealed such embarrassments among their own leaders. The Semitic habit of hiding their perversions, while simultaneously putting on a hypocritical face of piety, is a basic characteristic of both Jews and Muslims today.

From Noah in Genesis 10, the various peoples of the known world were claimed to have descended. By wiping out all other people, the Babylonian moneylenders could claim their own genetic line as the original of all. This anchored the "history of the world according to the Jews" as beginning in Mesopotamia from the time of Noah. From Noah's son, Ham, came Cush and from Cush came Nimrod who (according to this mythological history) became

> "... the first potentate on earth .... First to be included in his empire were Babel (Babylon), Erech and Akkad, all of them in the land of Shinar (Sumeria). From this country came Ashur, the builder of Nineveh, Rehoboth-ir, Calah and Resen between Nineveh and Calah." (Genesis 10:8-12.)

As you can see from Volume I, *The Sumerian Swindle*, the history of Mesopotamia was certainly not as the lying *Hebrew Bible* claims it to be. The history of Mesopotamia was far longer and based on much different historical characters than the Jews falsely claim. This very tiny view of Mesopotamian history clearly shows the dwarfed knowledge of history that the Hebrew writers of the Book of Genesis knew. That the history of the Book of Genesis is false, is often covered up by religious apologists who claim that it is not so much "false" as it is "inspired."

But when a book claims to be the "Word of God" and yet tells lies and promotes false histories from beginning to end, then how reliable can it be? We are dealing here with a book upon which billions of people have based both their daily lives and gambled their eternal souls, a book that among its legion of lies and broken promises, does not even promise salvation but offers stolen wisdom and fake history. When a book claims to be "the word of God" and its falsehoods are claimed to be "inspired" falsehoods, then how can it be a good book? When a book claims to be "the word of God" yet is proven to be false, then how can it be the word of God? Rather it is the word of the Deceiver.

The reader must not assume that my comments should be construed to be atheistic or agnostic or in any way irreverent of religion or disdainful of the knowledge of God. As you will see, I am very censorious of religions that tell lies. Certainly there are great truths in the Bible. But especially in the *Old Testament*, most of those truths were purloined from other people by the thieving Jewish scribes. For them to claim that God gave them this knowledge, is disproved simply because they have their history wrong and they stole the stories from other, older peoples. This should not be assumed that those ancient moneylenders told lies that they could not prove as true; but, rather, they told such outrageous lies that even in their most fetid imaginations, they did not believe that anyone could ever possibly disprove them. The main uniqueness about the Semites (both Hebrews and Arabs) was their ability to tell convincing lies. If the *Hebrew Bible* is the word of God, then God would certainly have been much more omniscient and accurate in His history. These biblical books are the word of the moneylenders and hired scribes who wrote them, but they are certainly not the word of God.

The Sumerian Creation Myths were written a thousand years before Genesis. The Aryan scriptures for the Vedic religion such as the Upanishads *Rigveda* were written in India between 1500-1000 BC. But the upstart Jews only began plagiarizing the early fictions of Genesis around the 9th century BC, if you can take their word for it. And the final drafts were most certainly combined at Babylon during the Captivity that ended in 538 BC, rewritten mainly by Ezra the Scribe and financed by the Babylonian moneylenders. If God had written the Book of Genesis, its historical lies would not have been made. Thus, it is easy to see in Genesis when compared to the historical and archaeological record that the men who wrote the so-called "Five Books of Moses" were inventing stories that suited them and which promoted their agenda. What that hidden agenda was (and is), is more important than the blatant fictions that they wrote to promote it. And why? Because their lies and their secret agenda are still causing the destruction of Mankind today.

In Genesis, the moneylenders set up the genealogical swindle that claimed all of the Semites as brothers, but brothers who should recognize the special place of Judah as their leader. Thus, the swindlers of Babylon wrote in a book, the wonderful story that they were all descended from Babylonian Patriarchs and their property would increase as long as the priests of Judah gave the orders.

Because the Genesis narrative was edited in Babylon, the scribes of the merchant-moneylenders wrote from the perspective of that Mesopotamian Culture. If it had been something that was of the authorship of God, as the moneylenders claimed, then it would have been something entirely new rather than the plagiarized Babylonian template that it is.

In Genesis 11, the building material was bricks with which they built the Tower of Babel. Babel (Bab-El) means "gate of God" but Genesis claims that it means "confusion" because "it was named Babel because there Yahweh confused the language of the whole earth." (Genesis 11:9.) The purport of this chapter was to establish the importance of a single people having a single language, otherwise they would be unable to even build a tower of bricks and they would be scattered "over the whole face of the earth." This idea would be used by the Jews in later millennia for destroying the white people of Europe, the USA and Australia through the immigration of foreign language speakers.

The genealogy of Genesis 11, leads up to introducing Abraham and Sarah, the alleged Babylonian parents of the Hebrews. Sarah was Abraham's half-sister by Terah's second wife. Incest is considered by the filthy Jews as a virtue because it kept all the gold and silver within the family. Genesis also introduces Lot, the alleged ancestor of the Moabites and Ammonites, thus tying together these Aramaic tribes of Hyksos with the tribe of Judah as the leader but also tying the entire genealogy of Canaan to Terah and his family in Harran as the root.

Because of their obsession with genealogical descent and control of families and tribes using that system, the moneylenders would certainly pride themselves with an ancient pedigree. Both Ur and Harran were the primary temple locations for worship of Sin, the Moon God. Not only was Ur renowned as a place of extreme antiquity and learning, but it gained great prestige throughout Mesopotamia in the mid-sixth century BC, when it was favored as a religious center by the Babylonian Chaldean, king Nabonidus. Thus, the reference to Abraham's origin in "Ur of the Chaldeans" is internal evidence that Genesis is not as ancient a book as it claims. Certainly, Ur existed from the very beginnings of Sumeria, but the Chaldeans did not appear on the world stage during the alleged "ancient" time of Abraham. They were in control of Ur during the *actual* time that Genesis was written in the 7th Century BC. So, Exodus, itself, proves that it is a false history.

In Genesis 12:3, the god of the moneylenders establishes the continuing refrain of bribery, malice, and deceit that the moneylenders practiced and so much desired:

> "I will bless those who bless you;
> I will curse those who slight you,
> All the tribes of the earth
> shall bless themselves by you."

It should be noted here the built-in terrorism weapon that the merchant-moneylenders used. They would be liberal with their friends since they had the money to be liberal. But anyone *who even slighted them in the smallest way* would be dealt with in a ruthless manner. You can see this same behavior in modern Jews against those who so much as whisper the slightest criticism. It is a form of social terrorism that they learned from the moneylenders of Babylon as it is taught in the *Hebrew Bible*. Mild criticism means that there may be harsher criticism waiting. The moneylenders knew that they would never be loved, so they had determined that they would be feared. Even though everyone on earth cursed and hated the moneylenders, in their new religion of Judaism they offered the lie that they would be a blessing to all who fell under their usury and loved them for the "privilege" of being enslaved to their scams.

In the same way, the Jews deal with criticism harshly, screaming and attacking anyone who dares to condemn the "holy ones of god." By playing the "holiness" card, they can deceive their victims with the accusation: "You are not condemning we Jews for our thievery, betrayals and swindles, you are condemning the Most High God whom we represent. It is not us you are fighting against. You are fighting against God. And that makes you an evil person and a sinner." It was a slick swindle and the Muslims would later use the same tricks, claiming that those who were not Muslims were the enemies of God. It was merely the ancient Semitic *abracadabra* in action. The scribes of the moneylenders knew well how to deceive the people. They had been doing it since the Sumerian Swindle, itself, had been invented around 3200 BC.

The Genesis fables teaches the Jews how to debauch others and gain benefit thereby, even to the extent of a Jew pimping out his wife. Abraham took all his wealth and the slaves he had acquired in Harran and moved to Canaan. But the Canaanites were already the owners and inhabitants of the land so Abraham next moved to Egypt where the Pharaoh allegedly lusted after Sarah. This is incorrectly dated by biblical scholars at about 1850 BC according to their ideas based on internal genealogy. The moneylenders are here claiming that these swarthy and sweaty women smelling of goats and donkey dung, can actually be so beautiful that the Pharaoh of Egypt would want one.

So, Abraham swindled the Pharaoh with a sly scam. Adultery was a serious offense in all of the ancient societies. It was usually punished by death of one or both parties. In this case, Abraham led Pharaoh into sin. True to the morals of the Semites, when Abraham went to Egypt he claimed that his wife,

Sarah, was his sister and pimped her out to Pharaoh in exchange for "flocks, oxen, donkeys, men and women slaves, she-donkeys and camels." (Genesis 12:16.) Women were not worth much during those days of the moneylenders but this indicates that Sarah was so ravishing that Pharaoh paid a high price to have sex with her.

But making a deal with a Jew is never a good idea. So, the scribes wrote that the Yahweh-god sent a plague on Pharaoh and made him give up not only Abraham's wife, but to also let Abraham keep all of the wealth Pharaoh had given him for Sarah. Thus, the Jewish morality of swindling other people and prostituting their wives, is highly celebrated in Genesis 12. You will find this theme all throughout the Old Testament where immorality and skullduggery are celebrated as the "blessings" given to the world by this "holy" tribe of bankers, thieves and con artists. Thus, this great hero of the Jews was a pimp and swindler. You can tell a lot about a people by the heroes they admire.

In Genesis 13, Abraham was a very rich man once he had swindled Pharaoh. But it should be noted that a real Pharaoh of Egypt would certainly not consort with a lowly goat-herder's woman no matter how beautiful she was alleged to be. Those wandering tribes were considered by the Egyptians as real vermin. They were no different than any other of the wandering bandit tribes throughout all of the ancient Near East. Even if they were wealthy, they always stank of sheep dung.

Speaking of sheep dung and the so-called "beauty" of Jewish women, it should be noted that the main criteria of what Jews consider to be a "beautiful woman" is found in their holiest book:

> "What is meant by the verse: And thy renown went forth among the nations for thy beauty. It is that the daughters of Israel had neither under-arm nor pubic hair." (*Babylonian Talmud*, Sanhedrin 21a, 23.)

So, no matter the size of Sarah's great beak, her greasy hair, her wrap-around Neanderthal mouth and garlic breath, the Jews claimed that she was beautiful because she shaved her armpits and vulva. All other demerits in her horsey face, paled in comparison to such standards of "Jewish Beauty." A male warthog thinks that the female warthog is also beautiful, but does not brag about it like the Jews do.

Abram (Abraham) left Egypt with all of the wealth he had swindled from the Pharaoh and went to the Dead Sea region. As a prelude to explaining the Dead Sea and the hot and blasted region around it, Abram and Lot part company. Lot takes his herds to live in the Jordan Valley near Sodom and Gomorrah. While Abram takes his herds to live in Canaan. This is the land that the moneylenders wanted for their own kingdom. So, they made a promise to give Canaan to Abram as far as he could see and make his descendants numerous as the specks of dust on the ground. Land and lots of sex with many wives was a promise of goat rustler Paradise which the Semite, Mohammad (mhrh), would later incorporate into his own religious scam.

Genesis 14 was written in Babylon and is composed of a list of kings who have never been identified. In addition, the alleged king Chedor-Gomer of Elam might have been a good guess for the scribes of Babylon since Elam was situated to the East towards Persia. But Elam never extended its influence so far to the West into Palestine and neither did Sumer (Shinar). The historical archives and archaeology prove once again that this is another Jewish lie. The reason for this chapter is to bring foreign and non-existent kings into warfare in a territory that was familiar to the Hebrews, kings and countries that the ignorant Hebrew goat rustlers had never heard of and so, lacking evidence, must believe what they were told. The Babylonian moneylenders wanted to deceive the Hebrews by using phantom kings, fighting phantom battles, upon real land, having actual place names that were familiar to the Hebrews. Using a favorite tactic of the Hebrews, they attacked at night. Their sidelocks which usually hung down in front of their ears to identify their tribal affiliation, they would wax and mold upward into the shape of devil horns.

Abram is now for the first time identified as "Abram the Hebrew" even though he was a Babylonian. Abram's gang was composed of 318 supporters. With so few, the so-called "kings" who Abram defeated could not have been so very mighty or so very numerous. But the power of only a few Hebrews against many foes, is a repeated theme throughout the entire Jewish fairy tale of the *Hebrew Bible*.

Abram defeated them, chased them past Damascus, which was quite a long way to chase anyone since all they had was their feet and their donkeys. And he got all of his stuff back along with the captives, including Lot. So, he recovered the whole lot.

In addition to introducing imaginary kings and imaginary battles into a known geographical area, Genesis 14 also introduces the Canaanite god, *Shalim*, the "God Most High", the god of the dusk, the Creator of Heaven and Earth. This god's priest is the Canaanite priest, Melchizedek, who named his city, Urusalem, in honor of his god. Abram gave him a tithe of ten percent of his property. In exchange for the bribe, Melchezidek blessed Abram. In this way, *Shalim* became the most-high god of Abram, the blessed one of *Shalim*. Thus, the scribes indicate that this Canaanite god, the "most high god of the dusk," was already the god of the Canaanite city of Urusalem.

In Genesis 15, Abraham swindles Melchizedek by substituting the name of *Shalim* with "God Most High" and then replacing "God Most High" with the name of *Yahweh*. This Canaanite god who is also Abram's god but who is now called "Yahweh" promises to give to the descendants of Abram all of the land "from the wadi of Egypt to the Euphrates River." (Genesis 15:18.) All of this property was under the control of the three main empires of those days, the Egyptians, the Babylonians and the Assyrians. So, such a promise had to have something backing it up besides the promise of the city god of the tiny hamlet of Jerusalem. In fact, what was behind these words of the Babylonian scribes was the Sumerian Swindle and the merchant-moneylenders who operated it. Although the moneylenders had had control of all of these lands at various times under various kings, they were unable to keep it. At the time Genesis was written, Terah and his descendants wanted all of the land that they had at various times either owned or had seized through foreclosure and warfare. This was the land that they promised themselves and their children's children, *the lands of the entire ancient Near East.*

In Genesis 16: According to Mesopotamian law, a barren wife could give one of her female slaves to the husband and claim the resulting child as her own. The moneylenders of Babylon wrote this into their story for two reasons: (1) to maintain their genealogical domination in case of a barren wife and (2) so that the genealogy shows that the goat-molesters of Arabia are to be under their genealogical domination, subservient to the Judah tribe of moneylenders.

Genesis 17 claims that Ishmael was the father of the Arabs. This lie allowed Mohammad, a thousand years later, to claim to be an inheritor of the "Promise" even though his own god was the Moon God, Allah, and completely unrelated to the Canaanite god, Yahweh. Historically, the thieving Semites from Arabia were actually *the ancestors* of the thieving Hebrews of Canaan, not the other way around as falsely claimed in Genesis. Thus, another lie is exposed by archaeology. But this lie would have dire consequences for Mankind when the false prophet, Mohammad, used it to bolster his own brand of a Semitic hoax which today is called Islam.

Genesis now switches to another tribal name for God, the same name used by the goat rustlers who lived in the mountainous areas. "El Shaddai" means, "God of the Mountain." And Abram is now renamed Abraham which means "father of a multitude." This Semitic idea that a big gang of bandits is a "blessing," is hereby welded into Judaism. His wife Sarai is now renamed as Sarah, which means "princess." So, now the world famous "Jewish princess" is born, an incestuous whore who is a "beautiful princess" by Jewish standards because she shaves her armpits and vulva. Not only do the moneylenders write into the contract that Abraham will be the father of a multitude of goat rustlers but that by this agreement, all of his descendant are tied to Abraham's genealogy as servants of *El Shaddai*. Thus, Terah elevated his youngest son to be the foundation of his new religious hoax.

The Babylonian moneylenders claim that the God of the Mountain said:

> "I will establish my Covenant between myself and you, and your descendants after you, generation after generation, a Covenant in perpetuity, to be your God and the god of your descendants after you. I will give to you and to your descendants after you the land you are living in, the whole land of Canaan, to own in perpetuity, and I will be your God." (Genesis 17:7-8.)

Terah's con lays claim to their own specific genealogical segment of the Semites and with Semitic *abracadabra*, claims that his tribe now "owns" Canaan because his god says so. This is the basis of modern-day Jewish claim-jumping in Palestine.

Of course, a contract must be signed to be valid. Instead of rolling a cylinder seal over a clay tablet or leaving a finger print as a proof of agreeing to the contract, *El Shaddai* wanted his goat rustlers to sign the Covenant with their holy penises. The scribes of the moneylenders wrote:

> "God said to Abraham, 'You on your part shall maintain my Covenant, yourself and your descendants after you, generation after generation. Now this is my Covenant which you are to maintain between myself and you, and your descendant after you: all your males must be circumcised. You shall circumcise your foreskin, and this shall be the sign of the Covenant between myself and you. When they are eight days old all your male children must be circumcised, generation after generation of them, no matter whether they be born within the household or bought from a foreigner not one of your descendants. They must always be circumcised, both those born within the household and those who have been bought. My covenant shall be marked on your bodies as a Covenant in perpetuity. The uncircumcised male, whose foreskin has not been circumcised, such a man shall be cut off from his people: he has violated my Covenant." (Genesis 17:9-14.)

The above Bible quote is further proof that none of the *Hebrew Bible* was written until *after* the Hyksos had been kicked out of Egypt, not in 2000-1700 BC as the Jews claim as their "Patriarchal period," but rather sometime after 1500 BC. Circumcision was a nasty habit that the Hyksos had learned from the Egyptians. But for the Egyptians, it did not lead to the disgusting perversions that it did among the Semitic Babylonian moneylenders, the Semitic Hebrews of Canaan, or the Semitic Arabs, because the Egyptians were a God-conscious people while the Jews and Muslims are merely God-obsessed people. Through the practice of extended breast-feeding, Egyptian women spaced their children every two years. The Semites, through harems, multiple wives, concubines, sex slaves, prostitutes, and rape, had as many children as their sexual energies and the wealth of their herds of goats and their farms could support. Terah understood how to attract the Hebrew bandits into his new religion by offering the sexual enticements of his god: "Go forth and multiply and I will bless you with descendants as numerous as the sand on the sea shore." Sex has always been a strong motivation, but a god who commanded that his followers be sex fiends, was something that few of the Hebrew goat-molesters could resist.

Circumcision is another of those weird and ancient ideas that have been around for so long that people take them for granted. The old, primitive way for the Hebrews to conclude a covenant ("to cut a covenant") was for the covenanters to cut into each other's arm and suck the blood, the mixing of the blood rendering them "brothers of the covenant." But that wasn't disgusting enough for the rabbis. The rabbi *mohel*'s technique is to cut the baby's penis and then suck on it. The result of this is that the majority of Jews turn into masturbating sex fiends and homosexual perverts wearing beanies and sidelocks while claiming to be the "Chosen Ones of God."

In modern times, circumcision is the primary cause of such disgusting oddities as homosexuality, sex perversions such as Freudian psychology, various criminal modes of sex crimes, as well as the sex fetishes of the Jews and Muslims. This ancient sickness is accepted in modern times simply because "it has always been here." But it has not always been here; it had a beginning point in the past and it will have an ending point in the present and future.

Among the Egyptians, circumcision was performed at the age of twelve or fourteen by the priests as a coming into manhood ceremony. Afterwards, ointment was applied to banish infection. But ointment costs money. To save money and get the little babies used to being molested by the rabbis, to this very day, the rabbis put their rubbery lips around the screaming baby's freshly cut penis and start sucking. This is an ancient tradition of the Jews. But since modern rabbis suck on more things than baby penises, these modern queer rabbis tend to give the Jewish babies gonorrhea and herpes.

As explained in Volume One, the Hyksos had learned circumcision when they were looting Egypt. Since it was an Egyptian practice, and since everyone in the ancient Near East admired Egypt and her people, doing as the Egyptians did was an easy step for the illiterate goat rustlers from Canaan and the Sinai. For the Hyksos administrators from Babylon, circumcision promised unlimited sexual stimulation, which is what they thought to be the prime motive of the Egyptians for doing something so weird. The Egyptians, like everyone else in those days, had very strict laws governing adultery. Marriage was a convenience between families more so than between individuals. And yet, because of the heat, walking around naked or wearing only see-through linen shawls, was very common. The Egyptians were religious but not prudish. Nakedness is a natural state of mankind and womankind.

So, temptations were also very common. Yes, the nobility and kings of Egypt had many wives. And yes, their circumcision allowed them maximum sexual stimulation at all times. But that is not why circumcision was developed among the Egyptians. As you can see from this tomb bas-relief from 2400 BC (Figure 100), circumcision was a coming-of-age ceremony for boys entering manhood. It was performed when the boy reached puberty. So, yes, it gave him some pain to have it done to him, but it was also an Egyptian teaching to the effect that "Okay, young man, you have a penis. Your penis will give a certain kind of pleasure with your future wife who will there-after give you children to care for, work for, and raise to adulthood. But be aware of the pain that you now feel and remember it from this circumcision ceremony because your penis will also give you a lot of hard work, suffering and pain if you are not careful about how you use it. It is not a toy to be played with for you cannot be a True Man if you do not have self-restraint and virtue."

Figure 100: Circumcision

This teaching produced wise men and happy women in ancient Egypt. The young men had already had a normal childhood where the skin on their little penises protected them from the rigors of life as well as from abnormal sexual urges, such as masturbation which plagues the Jews and Muslims. So, they knew what was normal and what was perverted and ungodly. After they were circumcised, they also knew what was normal and were welcomed into the society of adults with the new understanding of a man's place in life and the threats to his happiness if he misused his new status as a man.

But the Hyksos, both the Babylonian moneylenders who organized the invasion and the illiterate Hebrew and Canaanite shepherds who did the fighting, all looked upon Egyptian circumcision as something that would enhance their sex lives. The constant stimulation would urge them onto their wives more often, with their slaves more often, and when their wives and slaves were not present, then they turned to their sheep and goats when they weren't rubbing themselves with the palms of their hands. Without its protective covering, the constantly stimulated penises of the Semites drove them mad with lust.

For the Hebrews, circumcision was the path to debauchery and disgusting perversions. Yet, the Babylonian moneylenders welcomed debauchery and perversions because that was already their basic social habit. As perverts, sex maniacs and pathological masturbators, both the circumcised moneylenders who returned to Babylonia and their soldiers, the Hyksos-Hebrews, took circumcision with them out of Egypt and circumcised their sons to be as they were – circumcised sex fiends. The Hebrews and the moneylender Hyksos enjoyed the unlimited sex but they never learned the unlimited wisdom of

Egypt. So, when they left Egypt, they were not wiser; they were richer in loot and even more disgusting in habits.

The Babylonian homosexual perverts and sex fiends who were first planning Abraham's First National Bank and Pawn Shop, required circumcision for all male members of their organization as a sign or a mark of membership. Hidden beneath their robes, their circumcised penises could, at any time, prove that they were guild members of the Contract. "Halt! Let's see your membership card. Wow! Look how holy this Jew is! Okay, welcome to the Temple. Now, you can get free bagels and take out a loan."

Circumcision was not used by the Hebrews as a puberty ceremony at age twelve but it was performed as a membership requirement at the age of eight days old. Instead of salve to kill infection, the perverted rabbis, *to this very day*, suck on the screaming baby's bleeding penis with their cock-sucking lips. This homosexual act of pedophilia is one of the reasons that so many modern Jews are homosexuals and other varieties of deviants. Jews are cock suckers because the rabbis trained them in sick sex from the earliest days of their demented lives. Being a homosexual pervert, is very Jewish, as every rubber-lipped rabbi knows.

In the Egyptian *Book of the Dead*, the Egyptians decreed before their gods that they were pure and did not masturbate. But the teaching of the evil rabbis is that this nasty perversion is okay for a Jew to do, who only needs to take a bath afterwards. And so it is in modern times, the people who claim to be the most holy on earth, are in fact the biggest masturbators on earth. And from the Jewish penis, the modern perversions of homosexuality and psychology were developed – two sicknesses from the same source. While the Egyptians considered masturbation to be an unmanly and ungodly defilement, the Hebrews enthusiastically practiced it. The Egyptians used circumcision to train their young men in the facts of life while the Hyksos, Jews and Muslims, used it to enhance their sexual stimulation. The Egyptians circumcised their boys at the age of twelve years old, taught them wisdom and turned them into men. The Hebrews circumcise their babies at the age of eight days old and turn them into pathological masturbators and homosexuals. And the Muslims circumcise their little boys at the age of six years with the Muslim women kissing and praising the little boy's penis.

As a result, even today, the world's foremost masturbators and sex perverts are the Jews, followed in a close second by the Muslims. These two Semitic frauds hide their foulness behind their hypocrisy, praising their demon gods while whacking their nubs. Circumcision is unnatural. It has resulted in the sickness of homosexuality and many other mental diseases, diseases all promoted as "normal" and spread by Jews to this very day. This is more carefully explained in Volume III: *The Bloodsuckers of Judah*.

And so, you can see that *the Hebrews were already circumcised before they were kicked out of Egypt*. Because of the extra sexual stimulant it gave them around their women, children and sheep, the Hebrews continued the practice. By using this story of Abraham being commanded by his Yahweh-god to circumcise all of his descendants, the Babylonian moneylender scribes did three things: (1) they established a "membership card" for their conspiracy, (2) they perpetuated their own perverted life styles, and (3) they deceived the stupid Hebrew goat rustlers into thinking that they were all descended from Abraham with nothing more than the lies of the rabbis and their own circumcised cocks as "proof." It was a slick trick. But the bankers of Babylon had had a lot of practice using slick tricks. After all, they were masters of the Sumerian Swindle.

And what's more, they could read while the Hebrews could not. So, when the priests of the moneylenders read to the Hebrews the Holy Contract of the Circumcised Penis, (a.k.a., the *Hebrew Bible*) what could those ignorant goat-thieves do but believe it? Here was the "word of god" magically being read from the sacred goatskins and here was their own circumcised cocks staring them in the eye just like the "good book" said. Also, Yahweh was a Canaanite god that most Hebrews worshiped, anyway. So, he certainly had the right and the power to give all of Canaan to those foreign Babylonian moneylenders if he wanted to. As "proof" that the Hebrews owned the land, they had a "sacred Contract," written on holy goatskins, specifying the deed and boundaries of their new possessions as well as holy circumcised penises, too. What better proof did any Hebrew need other than circumcised penises and a Contract that they had written, themselves?

And so, the ignorant Hebrew goat rustlers of Canaan were swindled by the city slickers from Babylon. Exodus 19 deals with the destruction of Sodom and Gomorrah. The area around the Dead Sea was then as it is today, a region of sun-blasted rocks, waterless wastes and volcanic rubble. This is a convenient hook upon which to latch a myth about why the terrain is so inhospitable. By connecting the story of Lot and the Sodomites, the moneylenders were able to establish three correlatives of their religion: (1) Sodomy is (quite rightfully) punishable by death. (2) The area around the Dead Sea is a sun-blasted, ten-million-year-old rubble field which "proves" that the story of Sodom and Gomorrah is true. (3) The saving of Lot from destruction showed how the Yahweh-god remembered his own. So, every Hebrew with the foreskin of his penis cut off could be guaranteed that his god was keeping an eye on him at all times. And with all the holiness that a Jew is capable of, he remembers his god, too – every time he holds his holy penis in his hand and urinates! You can't find anyone holier than a Jew other than, maybe, a maggot or a devil.

There were some odd rock formations and salt pillars around the Dead Sea. The explanation for these was that they were the result of the wife of Lot who looked back at the destruction of Sodom and was turned into a pillar of salt. Archaeologically, Sodom and Gomorrah have never been found. Thus, the ancient scribes could have their god destroy places that had never existed and since no one could ever find them, use that as "proof" that they had really existed but had been thoroughly destroyed. This is the Jewish "reasoning" of *abracadabra*: "The cities of Sodom and Gomorrah never existed. But our mighty god so blasted them into nothing that nothing of them is left. So, this proves how mighty our god is by destroying something so thoroughly that it's as if it never existed. Are you afraid of our god, yet?"

The incest among the Jews is here used as an excuse for perpetuating blood lines. Lot's two daughters make him drunk so they can have sex with him. According to the story, the two daughters made their father drunk so that he "was unaware of her coming to bed or of her leaving." This excuse is used by the Jews to show that Lot was actually innocent of screwing his daughters because he "couldn't remember" doing it. As the story goes, the moneylenders are once again claiming that all of the people in the region are descended from the Hebrews. In this case, even the enemy tribes of the Moabites and Ammonites are claimed to be off-spring resulting from the incest of Lot and his two daughters. This is an insult to those tribes while at the same time it laid a false claim of fealty upon those tribe.

In Genesis 20, Abraham once again tries to pimp out his wife, this time to Abimelech, the king of Gerar. Abraham says that Sarah is his half-sister on his father's side. By claiming her as a sister, Abraham, the lying goat rustler could pimp her out and avoid being forced to fight for his wife. It was a slick and cowardly trick. But a trick worthy of Babylonian scribes who wrote the book. This chapter also teaches the goat rustlers how Abraham was able to swindle sheep, cattle, men and women slaves and one thousand shekels of silver by entrapping God-fearing people with Hebrew debauchery. In addition to demonstrating yet another swindle by pimping out his wife, the Babylonian scribes claim that anyone who annoys Abraham and his descendants will have a curse of God placed on them. God threatens to kill Abimelech and his whole family and they are to beg the Hebrews to intercede with God because "Abraham is a prophet and can intercede for your life." Powerful and awe-inspiring words, indeed, even though they are lies. But they are a teaching for the Jews in that it shows the basic scam of Judaism; do evil, swindle and betray and, if confronted with your crimes, frighten your accusers with the threat of the wrath of God – and all because they are so "holy."

But as powerful and wonderful as the scribes of Babylon made Abraham and the other patriarchs appear to be in these stories, nobody in the entire ancient Near East had, in fact, every heard anything about these literary characters. No historical or cultural detail in the patriarchal narratives finds any echo in Bronze Age historical documents. They existed only on the goat-skin scrolls from which the priests and rabbis read these fables to the gawking, slack-jawed, idiot Hebrew goat rustlers, but nowhere else. Nobody in the entire ancient Near East had ever heard of Abraham, Isaac, Jacob, Joseph, Moses, Joshua, the judges, the three kings of the United Monarchy – Saul, David and Solomon – or any of the Hebrew prophets. They are known only from the pages of the *Hebrew Bible*.

Yet there are a few notable exceptions to this neglect of the Jews' mythical heroes. Over a span of two and a half centuries Assyrian kings took pains to enhance and preserve their own fame by displaying in their capitals boastful accounts of their triumphs over the monarchs of the kingdoms of the Israelians and Judah. With the discovery of the ancient palaces of the Assyrian kings at Khorsabad, Nineveh, and Nimrud in the 19th century AD, details about ancient Israel came to light for the first time from sources outside the Bible. And yet, these archaeological finds only show that the Jews are liars.

When telling lies, liars usually find a certain enjoyment of embellishing their creative prevarications. Genesis 20 begins the propaganda that the Hebrews have special prophetic gifts of being intermediaries between non-Jews and God. This was a great money-making scam that has been used right up into the 20th Century AD with the Jew, Sigmund Freud, pretending to psychoanalyze your dreams or the 21st Century talk show host, Michael Savage, claiming to have the ancient Jewish "prophetic ability" to see into the future. But all Jews are frauds. This swindle is used by psychologists and circus astrologers to this very day.

Again in Genesis 21, the "magic blessing power" of Abraham is alleged to be something that can be passed along to the goat-molesting Arabs through Hagar, the slave girl, and her son, Ishmael. Thus, the moneylenders of Terah's guild are not just claiming kinship with the Semitic Arabs, but they are also claiming that the genealogical root of Arabia is a side-branch of the Jewish the family of Abraham. This lie would cause a lot of hardship among the peoples of the world in the seventh century AD when Mohammad (mhrh) believed the lies of the Jews and, standing in the midday sun too long with his bonnet off, imagined himself to be an actual descendant of Abraham.

In Genesis 22, another of the moneylender swindles is encapsulated in the story of Abraham sacrificing Isaac. By proving that he was obedient to the voices in his head, the Hebrews are taught that this Yahweh-god says,

> "I swear by my own self – it is Yahweh who speaks – ...I will shower blessings on you, I will make your descendants as many as the stars in heaven and the grains of sand on the seashore. Your descendants shall gain possession of the gates of their enemies. All the *goyim* of the earth shall bless themselves by your descendants, as a reward for your obedience." (Genesis 22:17-18.)

Terah and his scheming scribes were trying to increase the number of their followers by encouraging more sex and more children among the Hebrew bandits. And he was teaching them that even if only a few Hebrews could control the gates of targeted cities, then only a few Jewish betrayers and subversives could defeat an entire city. The moneylenders had been successful in controlling the kings of Mesopotamia.

To spread their subversive system among the Hebrews and to gain ownership of the entire world, they wanted to teach their followers the ways of the Babylonian merchant-moneylenders by using examples through stories and metaphors. These teachings would be suspect if they came from a moneylender. No one would trust someone whose only goal was to swindle your wealth, enslave you, steal your property and betray you to your enemies. Even if he promised you limitless sex, many children and the wealth of the world, his motives would be suspect. No one would trust a moneylender trying to give you something or talk you into doing something. But if these teachings and instructions came from a god, well then, who could doubt their great goodness?

"Gaining possession of the gates of their enemies," is one of the teachings of the Jews that the Christian translators have very much failed to explain in their duties to the people of the world. And why? Because the enemies of the Jews – by Jewish definition – is *everybody on earth who is not Jewish*! And so, you will see that in every country in the world, the Jews are always elbowing, pushing, finagling, bribing, threatening, and blithely stepping into positions as leaders of trade boards, education boards, political parties, labor unions, local clubs, military leadership, and watchmen of the city gates – all positions that in addition to qualification for the position, also require ambition to attain the post. While the ambition of the ordinary citizen is for social prestige, service to the community, patriotic duty, as well as monetary remuneration, the ambition of the Jews is for all of these things but also as a way of "gaining possession of the gates of their enemies." And their enemies are the very people who, not understanding what Jews really are, have actually elected and allowed Jews to have control of the gates controlling society or leadership positions controlling groups of people. It has been used by the Jews from the oldest times, gaining control of the gates of cities and trade channels and Media outlets in order to destroy whomever "slighted" them in the least way, so that in revenge they can double-cross and betray the very ones who had trusted them with an important post.

Not only were the moneylenders promising that the Hebrews would metastasize like cancer cells if they followed the Contract of the *Hebrew Bible*, but that the people of the earth would actually "benefit" from having subversive and treasonous Jews controlling the borders and gateways to our countries. The refrain is again repeated: "as a reward for your obedience." That obedience is to the laws of the Contract as stipulated by the moneylenders' scribes who wrote it.

Even Abraham's Babylonian brother, Nahor, still living in Harran, started producing sons which were then claimed to be progenitors of the Aramaean tribes – in standard Semitic tradition, twelve sons in all. In this way, the genealogical swindle could also be used to claim another Semitic nation as descendants of – not the Hebrews – but of the moneylenders of Babylon.

In Genesis 23, Abraham begins to swindle the local people out of their land by first wanting to buy a plot as a burial ground for Sarah. As a kindness, the people of Hebron gave Abraham a tomb for free. But Abraham was the son of the richest and most cunning moneylender in Babylonia. He did not trust kindness because he wanted ownership. So, he had a better swindle in mind.

With subtle craft and deceit, he bowed in humility before the kindly people of Hebron. He wanted a piece of property owned by the Hittite, Ephron. And in front of witnesses, he bought the field and cave for 400 shekels of silver. Now, for the first time, Abraham was a land owner in Canaan. Land as a gift, he would not accept because gifts bring about kindness mutual reciprocity. Abraham did not want to be kind in return to the Hebronites because he wanted to genocide them. And, too, gifts can be reneged. But an exchange of 400 silver shekels, a very high price, would guarantee ownership in front of witnesses. This was the price of 40 bulls or 10 slaves. Abraham now had wedged open the door of Canaan. He had swindled and bribed a blessing from Melchizidek, the high priest of the fortress town of Jerusalem. So, the local god had blessed him and Melchizidek was on his side. Now, he had purchased property-owner rights as a resident of Canaan. Thus, he was poised to pry open Canaan for his clan of thieves from Babylonia.

In Genesis 24, Abraham made the steward of all his households swear on an oath by putting his hand on Abraham's balls and holy penis. He said, "Place your hand under my thigh. I would have you swear by Yahweh, God of heaven and God of earth, that you will not choose a wife for my son from the daughters of the Canaanites among whom I live. Instead, go to my own land and my own kinsfolk to choose a wife for my son Isaac." (Genesis 24:3-4.) A promise on the holy penis of a Jew was a serious promise that even a lying, swindling, murdering, Babylonian moneylender or even a scrofulous Hebrew would honor. In the usual incestuous ways of the moneylender clans, Abraham wanted to keep all his silver and gold and goats in the family. So, he wanted his son to only marry a close relative. Even if all the resulting children ended up as Jewish hunchbacks and retards, at least they would all be rich hunchbacks and Jewish retards.

The servant took presents and headed for Upper Mesopotamia, where the kinfolk of Harran and Abraham were living. Harran was a crossroads of trade at that time. There, the servant met Rebekah. She was related to Abraham. "She was the daughter of Bethuel, son of Milcah, wife of Abraham's brother Nahor." (Genesis 25:15.) And so, continues the biblical tradition, along with Adam and Lot's incestuous daughters, of inter-marriage, incest and genetic diseases among the Jews. Of course, since the Old Testament was written by the priests of Babylon, even if she resembled the snouted faces of most modern Jewish women, the scribes claimed that "the girl was very beautiful and a virgin." But even toads think that lady toads are beautiful. Once again, Rebekah was a Babylonian, not a Hebrew.

As her parents sent Rebekah away, they invoked one of the Jewish curses upon Mankind: "Sister of ours, increase to thousands and tens of thousands! May your descendants gain possession of the gates of their enemies." Once again, the Gates of their Enemies, is an ancient strategy of the Jews because it was one of their secrets for profiting even when they were outnumbered. Controlling the trade routes, the strategic passes, the monopolies, the leadership positions, the choke points of toll roads and river traffic, as well as the gates leading into the cities, was their goal. And since all non-Jews are perceived by the Jews as enemies, then even when you accept a Jew as a friend, he proves to be an enemy through his interest in controlling the gates of your very life.

In Genesis 25, Abraham marries another wife who was alleged to be the progenitor of the Arabian tribes, thus making all of Arabia and Palestine the descendant of Abraham and Isaac, according to the fables that the Jews wrote. Rebekah conceived Esau and Jacob. Esau was the alleged father of the Edomites and Jacob was the alleged father of the Israelites. Thus, all of the people of Canaan were pulled into the genealogical swindle of Terah and his money-lender guild of Babylon. They could do this by writing their fake genealogies onto the goatskins that the Hebrews and Canaanites could not read, and then claim that they were ancient writings. The illiterate Hebrew goat-molesters and the Canaanite farmers could remember only five generations back. So, it was a real surprise to them to hear that scores of generations back in time that they were the descendants of these recent interlopers from Babylonia and, therefore, must give them "respect" and recognize their "prestige" of being the Canaanites' forefathers and superiors. This fraud was not something that was Hebrew or Canaanite. Keep in mind that both Esau and Jacob were Babylonians, not Hebrews. They, as well as Abraham, were foreigners to Canaan. But by writing themselves into the root of all Near Eastern genealogies, they could swindle both leadership positions and lands away from the bamboozled natives. It was all *abracadabra* falsehood and trickery, but it worked. The illiterate Hebrews believed them and joined the religious hoax while the Canaanites and everyone else in Palestine knew that they were liars and frauds and fought against these Babylonian swindlers.

Esau became a hunter while Jacob was a stay-at-home momma's boy and sly devil. Esau came home from the hunt exhausted and asked Jacob for some lentil soup. But Jacob would not give sustenance to his own brother without making a profit. His Jewish mother was so proud! He refused to give Esau the soup, unless Esau would sell to him Esau's birthright as the oldest son. This false idea that a birthright could be sold, was the moneylender's way of further worming their way into controlling the genealogy of the Canaanites. Transfer of ownership of birthright, at least in the fraudulent pages of the Torah, gave the Bankers of Babylon a swindled priority over any claims of the Edomites to an earlier ownership of the land. That is, if the Edomites claimed that "We were here first," the Bankers could say, "But according to the stories that we wrote, the mythical Esau sold his birthright to our clever devil of an ancestor, Jacob. See, the lying pages of Genesis proves it because the story is right here for all to read. The demon priests of the Yahweh-god wouldn't have written it down if it wasn't true."

The moneylenders were setting up the genealogical scam in this chapter of showing the importance of a racial and familial birthright of the oldest son. But they were claiming that this birthright was a commodity that could be sold like anything else. It is a birthright which is linked to, but less important than, the hoax of the patriarchal blessing. When Esau, out of disgust with Jacob, or out of a brotherly pity, sells his birthright for the bowl of soup, the Scribes can say with disgust, "That was all Esau cared for his birthright." (Genesis 25:34.) Judaism is a racist hoax. That the Jews deny this, is just more of their hypocrisy.

In Genesis 26, in order to have land that could not be taken away by the kings, the moneylenders wanted to forge a Contract where the landlord was God, Himself. So, the words that were alleged to have come from God, were repeated in Genesis 26 to Isaac:

"For it is to you and your descendants that I will give all these lands, and I will fulfill the oath I swore to your father Abraham. I will make your descendants as many as the stars of heaven, and I will give them all these lands; and all the *goyim* in the world shall bless themselves by your descendants in return for Abraham's obedience; for he kept my charge, my commandments, and my laws." (Genesis 26:2-5.)

This brainwashing is a constant refrain throughout the Torah, in effect, "All Jews are blessed because Abraham heard voices in his head ordering him to kill his son and then he heard more voices in his head ordering him not do it." Like any fraudulent Contract, it adds the rider: "He kept my charge, my commandments, and my laws." This fraud was conceived by Terah as a way of gathering in all of the Hebrew tribes based not only upon genealogical relationships but also upon the Semitic *asl* claiming that such things as a "blessing" could be inherited and were just as valid as the original "blessing." All of the hoax was bound together with commandments and laws which were – Abracadabra! – the "word of God."

Once again in this chapter, the Jewish trick is attempted of claiming that a wife is a sister so as to swindle wealth from a fool who believes a Jew. The scribes wrote that Abimelech, who had sent them away because the promiscuous Jews were breeding too many juvenile delinquents and Jewish gangsters, claimed to see that God was on the side of those early Hebrews. So, he has Isaac swear a non-aggression pact. This is another teaching of "Go forth and multiply" so that by many numbers, the Jews can terrorize their neighbors. Now, he fears the Jews are too numerous. You know, the thieving Jews who said, "Shalom! We are men of God. Trust us!"

Esau married two wives, both daughters of the Hittites. "These were a bitter disappointment to Isaac and Rebekah" because the Bankers were trying to create a closed society of moneylenders and businessmen who did not allow wealth to leave the community and who would protect trade secrets within the community. So, all members had to marry within the community. Incest was a moneylender's way of saving money.

In Genesis 27, the cunning and trickery so much admired by the moneylenders is celebrated in the story of how Jacob tricked his own father out of the final death-bed patriarchal blessing. Rebekah dressed Jacob in the bloody skins of two baby sheep and then had him put on Esau's best clothes, "covering his arms and the smooth part of his neck with the skins" of the baby sheep. "Isaac had grown old and his eyes were so weak that he could no longer see." (Genesis 26:1.)

Of course, even a blind old man like Isaac, who had spent his life raising sheep and goats, would not be fooled into believing that the wool of a baby sheep was like the woolly hair of his eldest son. But the Scribes of Babylon didn't let facts get in the way of a good lie.

So, for the sake of the story, Jacob shows what a good Jew he is. He pretends to be his older brother, Esau, and was completely at ease in lying to his blind father by mimicking Esau's voice as he served him some goat stew, wearing bloody sheep skins on his head and neck and announcing himself as "I am Esau your firstborn." (Genesis 26:19.) And he is even deceitful enough to claim that the goat-stew was a result of "Yahweh your God" providing it. Rebekah was so proud of her lying, little kike!

Doddering, old Isaac still did not believe Jacob because his voice was not Esau's voice. But once he touched the goat-skin-covered arms that were hairy like Esau's, he was convinced. But to clear his doubts, he asked if this was really Esau and Jacob kissed him and lied to his old father again. And the smell of his brother's sweaty, stinky cloths sealed the swindle and Isaac gave Jacob the blessing that he had meant to give to Esau.

The *abracadabra* magic of this "blessing" was the moneylenders' tribe of Judah, direct assumption of power over the other tribes because it was from this "blessing" that they drew their genealogical line from the Yahweh-god to their position as priests over the Hebrews. By using a stolen "blessing" to jump genealogies and to assume patriarchal power gave them the authority they needed to quash any questioning of their preeminence. In this story, descent from the line of Abraham was emphasized but it was a descent that also required the "blessing" of a patriarch because those lying, swindling, deceiving and treacherous Hebrews were holy. Right? And they "proved" it by blessing each other with the Jewish Devil Claw Salute.

This purloined blessing gave the rabbis a spiritual backing for their dynasty based on the hoax that an alleged, ancient "blessing" could be passed along with complete potency to present day gangsters:

> "May God give you dew from heaven, and the riches from the earth, abundance of grain and wine! May *goyim* serve you and *goyim* bow down before you! Be master of your brothers; may the sons of your mother bow down before you! Cursed be he who curses you; blessed be he who blesses you." (Genesis 27:27-29.)

They were holy gangsters because they "blessed" each other, since no one else would do it. This "blessing" of the Jews is a curse upon Humanity since the "blessing" of a devil is not a blessing at all. This part of the moneylenders' Contract was designed to give a delusion of power in the patriarchal line. Blessings and curses, once pronounced, were regarded as efficacious and irrevocable.

Because of Jacob's lies to his own father and his treason against his own brother, Esau planned to kill Jacob. So, Rebekah sent this great hero of the Jews back to her brother Laban in the Assyrian city of Harran.

Genesis 28 shows that Rebekah – Oy! Such a good Jewish wife! – also lied to Isaac and deceived him for Jacob's sake. She got Isaac to send Jacob back to her relatives and out of harm's way from the wrath of Esau. She had Isaac send Jacob out looking for a wife among his own incestuous relatives. Isaac sent him to get a wife from Rebekah's brother's children so as to marry his own cousins. There, the foundation for modern hunch-backed and dwarfish Jews is based on such incestuous ways. In modern times, no other people have more genetic defects than the Jews. If they are dwarves and hunchbacks, at least they are rich. So, if incest is Jewish, then it is automatically okay. Incest kept the money in the family.

In this chapter, also, the Scribes wrote that a ten percent tithe would be the "traditional" future cut of all profits for the priests and rabbis. Abraham had donated ten percent to Melchizidek's "most high god." Jacob promised this ten percent as "payment" to God of all that he makes in the future. These repetitions throughout the Old Testament are the scribal ways of emphasizing what is to them the most important part of the Contract. Jacob sets an example for all future Jews of paying ten percent to the priests and rabbis or donating it to subversive Jewish organizations such as Communist and pro-faggot enterprises.

In Genesis 29, the scribes again celebrate Jewish deceit and trickery as major characteristics of Jewish heroes. His uncle, Laban, promised Jacob his youngest daughter in marriage. And for Rachel's hand, Jacob agreed to work for Laban for seven years. But Laban tricked Jacob by slipping his eldest daughter, Leah, into the wedding bed. Jacob slept with her but when he discovered in the morning that he had been tricked, Laban said that Jacob could have both of his skanky daughters as wives but he would have to work another seven years if he wanted to screw Rachel, too. So, Jacob had sex with Leah for the rest of the week and then Laban let him have Rachel as a wife, too. The Hebrews were a very generous and holy people when it came to pimping out their wives for a profit and passing around their daughters in incestuous marriages. Note once again that neither of these wives are Hebrews. Both Leah and Rachel were Babylonians. Real Jewish princesses, heroines for Jewish girls to emulate!

Leah produced six sons – Reuben, Simeon, Levi, Judah, Issachar and Zebulun. Rachel produced the sons Joseph and Benjamin. These eight boys were not Hebrews; they were Babylonians. However, the Hebrews had the same mating characteristics as their goats. Jacob had the two wives, Leah and Rachel, plus their two slaves, Bilhah and Zilpah, and so he produced the rest of the original twelve mythical tribes – Dan, Naphtali, Gad and Asher. These were Babylonians by their Babylonian slaves. And they were all "holy and blessed" because grandfather Abraham had heard voices in his head telling him to not kill his son after all. Wow! What a fable to base blessedness upon! Virtue or being a good person, has nothing to do with Hebrew blessedness.

Deceit, trickery, lies, and treachery are what the wicked priests of the Yahweh-god valued in "his people." Only the worst of human characteristics, are what the Jews claim as their "higher moral values and blessedness." All the moral values of demons who bless each other and therefore claim to be holy!

The moneylenders who wrote the *Hebrew Bible* celebrate trickery and swindling as Jacob talks Laban into giving him all the speckled and spotted goats and all of the black and speckled sheep for his wages. Naturally, more goats will have speckles than being pure white or pure black. And Jacob mated the pure animals with the spotted ones so that the offspring were speckled and spotted. He also mated the weaklings together to produce pure white and weak off-spring. Thus, Jacob gained a large flock of healthy speckled animals leaving the weaklings for Laban. The scribes wrote as a reward for clever slyness, "Thus Laban got the feeble and Jacob the sturdy, and he grew extremely rich, and became owner of large flocks, with men and women slaves, camels and donkeys." (Genesis 30:43.) It should be noted here that the Jews from the earliest times, understood down-breeding. This would be applied in later centuries as a form of genocide against the White race in places such as Spain, Europe, the USA, Australia and South Africa. This genocide is detailed in Volume 3, *The Blood-Suckers of Judah.* And so the deceitful Jacob, blessed by his god of genocide, was able to defraud Laban of his herds and to make him poorer through selective down-breeding. A great Jewish hero!

Camels are mentioned. So the story could not be as old as the scribes claim since camels were not introduced into the ancient Near East until about 1000 BC. Once again, the internal evidence in the stories, themselves, prove the stories are lies.

As a great Jewish heroine, Rachel steals her own father's household idols and then Jacob's entire gang crosses the Euphrates with all of their flocks and herds. "Jacob outwitted Laban the Aramaean by giving him no inkling of flight." (Genesis 31:20.) Celebrating the clever deceit of Jewish princesses, Laban is lied to by his own daughter as Rachel sits on the stolen idols while pretending to be menstruating like a filthy, "unclean" Jewess. Really some nasty people, those Babylonian Semites descended from the holy, blessed Abraham, the son of Terah the Babylonian moneylender. Laban was the grandson of Nahor, Abraham's brother. All of the first four generations of the so-called "patriarchs" were Babylonians not Hebrews. And all of their incest and trickery is celebrated in the *Hebrew Bible* – business-as-usual for the heroes of the Jews. Heroes for later generations of Jews to copy.

Since the theft was not proven by producing the stolen idols (no doubt all made of gold), Jacob gains another advantage by hypocritically brow-beating and humiliating Laban with the Jewish trick of assuming the role of the victim to hide his own guilt. This is an ancient Jewish scam here related for the first time but used to great effect by the Jews throughout history, and even to the present day – even when guilty, pretending the greatest effrontery in pointing a finger at the accuser and pretending to be insulted by his accusations. These stories of Jewish heroes teach the lessons of the Training Manual for Jewish Criminality and Psychopathy, the *Hebrew Bible.*

In Genesis 32, the great wealth of Jacob is trundled out as the gifts of over 200 goats and 200 sheep, 30 camels, 40 cows, 10 bulls and 30 burros, which he sent as a bribe to his brother, Esau, hoping that his swindled brother would not kill him. In this passage, Jacob gets the new name of Israel (meaning "Struggled with God") because he wrestled with God and won the wrestling match. Apparently, even God is no match for the mighty goat rustlers in these fables. In those days, the name, Israel, already occurred in Eblaite and Ugaritic texts as a common name. It wasn't a new invention of the Yahweh-god because it was already a Canaanite name in common use. But in this case, "Israel" is based on the idea of fighting with God and defeating Him. Only devils and lawyers fight against God.

Thus, as the very basis of their demonic religion, the Jews have always fought against that which is both True and Holy, using stories of great Jewish heroes as Jacob-Israel – he who fought against God and won. Is it any wonder that the holy and wonderful rabbis teach that when God reads the rabbis' writings that He stands up to do so since He holds them in such high respect. Yes, Folks, that's the kind of "prestige" that these marvelous rabbinical frauds give to themselves. As a moneylender's religion based on getting the "blessings" of material goods, after Genesis 33, Jacob-Israel's wealth is further amplified since he still had plenty even after his generous bribe to Esau. The Yahweh-god blesses Israel, the trickiest and most deceitful of Abraham's spawn, and gives him lots of cool stuff like goats and donkeys.

Genesis 34 once again celebrates the value of Semitic deceit. For the first time, the scribes of Babylon equate the name, Israel, with a particular family of Babylonians who, through deceit and murder, gained the property and wealth of their Canaanite victims. It was not enough to be a circumcised Hyksos wandering around from Egypt, but one also had to be descended from Abraham. It was not racial because all of the Semites from both Babylonia and Canaan were of the same race. It was genetic, tying them all together in the same family tree, a genealogy tree that got bigger and encompassed more people as Terah's swindle made more grandiose claims. But the claims were always with an eye to keeping the root of the genealogy tree in his own family no matter how many outlying tribes he claimed to have as his descendants. This strategy was perpetuated by every priest and rabbi who followed the scam of Terah, the moneylender of Harran and Ur.

In this chapter, Jacob's daughter, Dinah, was raped by Shechem, the son of Hamor the Hivite. But she gave her rapist such an enthusiastic ride that he wanted to marry her. So, he asked Jacob and his brothers for her hand. This story shows not only how the Semites could seize towns and ruthlessly butcher the residents but that any excuse was good enough for any atrocity.

Jacob's sons deceitfully agreed to the marriage if Shechem and the males of the entire town accept circumcision. The townsmen think that by joining the bandits of Israel that they will gain Jacob's wealth since they would all be one family. But once they are circumcised and still in pain, on the third day Jacob's two sons, Simeon and Levi, sneaked into the town and murdered all the males, including Shechem and his father. They murdered and wounded, pillaged the town, took their flocks, cattle, donkeys and stole whatever else was not tied down. Carrying off wives and children, they murdered all of the men, raped and enslaved their families and stole everything.

These hero stories of the Jews train them in the criminal ways of their Babylonian patriarch. It was all part of the moneylenders' plan of creating a criminal organization, primed with stories of heroic mayhem. Jacob's treacherous sons did all of these crimes with the self-righteous excuse that "Shechem had insulted Israel by raping Jacob's daughter ... Is our sister to be treated like a whore?" they asked. And the scribes leave the question unanswered as if the results were allowed by the crime. The laws of none of the peoples or countries in the entire ancient Near East, had such a ruthless a penalty for rape. Remember, the *Hebrew Bible* was written for a certain audience of thieves and con artists. So, it was designed to teach gangsterism and terrorism to such low types as the Hebrew goat rustlers and the modern Jews.

This sort of deceit and hypocrisy was a defining legacy for the Jews. Abraham could pimp out his wife to Pharaoh and could attempt the same scam with Abimelech. Women did not have a great value among the Semites except as trade goods or unless they were valuable wives with a large dowry. So, this story was written to show the Jews how to use any excuse for gaining land and goods through treachery and murder. And not just any murder but a type where the alleged "honor" of the group was at stake – murder, genocide and banditry with the excuse that some "holy" virtue had been insulted against the Jews.

One boy rapes and then wants to marry one girl. But "for the sake of Israel" that boy's entire town is murdered, enslaved and pillaged. This is called "Jewish Justice" and it can be seen in the actions of today's Jews against today's Germans and Palestinians. The method has an ancient history. The god of the Jews is the God of Genocide as well as the God of Circumcised pricks. The Jews emulate their heroes who are all bandits and murderers.

And now for the getaway in Genesis 35. After committing genocide on an entire town, the Israelites make their getaway. Since they have proven to be deceivers, subversives and murderers, Jacob (Israel) moves his tribe to a place safe from retribution by the outraged Canaanites and Perizzites. In this case, a metaphor is set up in the myth. They flee to Bethel (Beth-El, "House of God"). But as part of the creation of their religion, the Babylonian moneylender scribes wrote that Jacob gets rid of all the gods that his tribe worshiped. And since they had so mercilessly slaughtered the inhabitants of Shechem's town, the lesson is here taught by the moneylenders that terrorism has its uses since the towns round about, in shock and completely terrorized, did not pursue the sons of Jacob. So, with Jewish brutality as a shield, they made their escape. The scribes of the moneylenders again promise that all of the land of their victims belongs to those bandits who are the descendants of Abraham.

Again, the incestuous nature of the Hebrews is recommended when Reuben slept with his father's concubine. These are the "holy people," right? But nothing was done about it and incest continued to be a Jewish tradition along with the practice of genocide and terrorism among their many other negative characteristics.

Next, Jacob finally changed his name to Israel. The lying rabbis claim that the name means "he contended with god." This makes sense because Judaism and the Jews have always been in contention with God for supreme "prestige," star billing, front page headlines, fame, product advertising and god-like status among everybody whom the Jews can brag to about themselves. But more likely, Israel is a mixture of three gods into one name as *Ish-tar-Ra-El*, two Canaanite gods and one Egyptian god, making Is-ra-el. And with Jacob's twelve evil sons was begun the myth of the twelve tribes.

At long last, Isaac dies at the age of 180 years and was buried by Esau and Jacob. That is, as the phrase goes to entwine all of the goat rustlers together, he was "gathered to his people." He didn't go to God. He didn't go to heaven. The Hebrew bandits wrapped him up and stuck him in a hole in the ground, the final reward of every Jew since they have no other.

In Genesis 36, the last story of Esau is told, tying him and his children both with Israel and the Arab tribes. The land of Edom is equated with Esau. Thus, the scribes of Babylon claimed that all of the Arab tribes were all descended from Esau. And the stupid Arabs actually believe this even until the present day. This genealogical swindle is used to not only connect Israel by marriage to all of the countries of Edom and North Arabia, but deceive them into the belief that they are subservient to Israel. They are inveigled to take a subservient place behind the "holy" Jews if they want to be "blessed" like Israel.

In Genesis 37, the story of Joseph begins. For the moneylenders to be able to swindle the people of the world, they had to elicit sympathy for themselves as victims. On this basis, the scribes of Terah's guild were building the structure of their temple so they needed to have a parallel story linking *ruthless acquisition of wealth with divine approval*. The Hebrews had to be trained to be as greedy and murderous as a banker by believing that it was God's will that they steal and swindle everything. So, the scribes dusted off the old story from the days when the Hyksos were in control of Egypt. Joseph had been the Hyksos minister of agriculture; all that Ezra the Scribe did was to make such a ruthless bandit into a hero worthy of praise.

Genesis 37 tells the story of Joseph in Egypt. Before modern archaeology brought us the facts, Bible readers falsely assumed that the pharaoh was an Egyptian. However, the story of Joseph took place during the Hyksos era when a Semite sat on the throne of Pharaoh. Once this is understood, much of the myth of Joseph makes more sense. Joseph was a Babylonian, descended from his Babylonian parents, Jacob and Rachel. He lived in an Egypt that had been taken over by the Hebrew-Hyksos who were, in turn, commanded by the Babylonian merchant-moneylenders. To see how this coup d'état was accomplished, please see Volume I, The Sumerian Swindle.

One of the important elements in the life of the ancient peoples was dreams and the meaning of dreams. The gods spoke to them in dreams. Strange dreams that they did not understand, required the services of dream interpreters. In later years, this became a specialty of frauds and Jews such as Sigmund Freud of the 20th Century AD, interpreting dreams of gullible fools for a price.

Joseph was seventeen years old when his story begins. And it begins with his dreams that were interpreted by his brothers and his father as a premonition that they would be subservient to him. So, of course, his brothers, being a bunch of scheming Jews, trained to be dishonest scoundrels by their Jewish parents, sold him to some Arab traders who took him to Egypt and sold him to Potiphor, one of the Hyksos Pharaoh's officials.

In Genesis 38, the story of Judah brings in more of the incest that has made the Jews such a genetically diseased lot. In this case, the Jewesses lead the way by having sex with their relatives. Remember, the daughters of Lot got him drunk and seduced their own father in order to have children by him. In this chapter, Tamor dresses like a prostitute in order to have children by Judah, her father-in-law. This manic drive to have children by incestuous relations, is a Jewish tradition and much celebrated by the hunch-backed Jews as a sign of their holiness. Judah is going to burn Tamar at the stake for having children out of wedlock. But she proves that he is the father, so he lets her go. The twins are named Perez and Zerah. This story is pasted in by Ezra the Babylonian scribe to make sure that there are no records from among the Hebrews or Canaanites which can conflict with the leadership claims of Judah.

The narrative then switches back to Joseph in Genesis 39. The tale of Joseph adds the Jewish deceit of how everything Joseph does is blessed by the Yahweh-god, including a blessing for Potiphor and his household. Yes, Genesis claims that it is so wonderful to have a magic Jew around to run things and take your money! According to those lying swindlers and thieves who wrote the book, the whole world is blessed to have lying, swindling Jews in control of everything.

And who was Potiphor? Potiphor was one of the corrupt Egyptians who were the front men of the Hyksos. With such a Hyksos as Joseph running his business and his household, Potiphor spent his time in leisure and gluttony, overseeing the enslavement of his own people, very much as the modern politicians do today. This explains why Potiphor's Egyptian wife would be attracted to a Hyksos named Joseph simply because he was a member of the gang of Semitic moneylenders and sheep-stealers who controlled Egypt at that time. A lowly shepherd would not be attractive to an Egyptian woman; but one of the Semitic conquerors of Egypt would be.

Even if such a story was true, adultery was severely punished in the ancient world. In Sumeria and Babylonia, both of the adulterers were tied together and thrown into the river. In Egypt, the man was tortured to death as the woman was forced to watch, then his head was cut off and stuck between the woman's legs facing her crotch; and then she was tortured to death with her lover's head looking at her. Modern archaeology has discovered such mummified remains with the man's head stuffed between the legs of the tortured and mummified woman. So, for an Egyptian woman to make sexual advances to a Hyksos goat herder, was an extremely unlikely scenario both for the Hyksos, who stoned to death adulterers, and for the Egyptians who tortured them to death.

As the story goes, Potiphor's wife desired Joseph because he was so handsome – a standard issue Semite with frizzy hair, sucking lips and a huge nose – but according to the Jewish scribes, this translates as "well built and handsome." After his wife accused Joseph of attempted seduction, Potiphor had Joseph thrown into prison.

But the Jews are notorious ass-kissers and servile punks to those who are their bosses. So, this magic Hebrew even got along with the warden who entrusted him to run the prison. Here the scribes of Babylon teach an ancient technique of how the Hebrews can attain "the gates of their enemies" by offering their "Jewish Loyalty" – being useful and profitable to their employers, gaining wealth and power by serving as foremen, overseers and tax collectors, and by being craven and subservient until they can attain the keys to the gates of their enemies. Then, all of that charade changes while the Jewish treason steps to the forefront.

In Genesis 40, Joseph was such a sycophant that he became the trustee in the prison where the warden placed him in charge of two prisoners, the Pharaoh's cup-bearer and baker. The warden or chief jailer was a Hyksos official. The Pharaoh was a Hyksos. And since no king would trust an Egyptian over whom he was a foreign tyrant with his cooking and drinking, then these officials in the Hyksos Pharaoh's prison were obviously Hyksos as well. So, the story of Joseph is the story of Hyksos pharaohs, subservient Egyptian front men, Hyksos wardens, Hyksos cup-bearers and bakers and Joseph, the Hyksos shepherd. This knowledge of the historical and racial background of those times, puts the story of Joseph into the proper perspective.

The swindle of "soothsayer and dream interpreter," is built into the merchant-moneylenders' religion and gets its biggest boost in the story of Joseph and later in another fictional forgery of the Jews with the story of Daniel. Those who interpret dreams gain special insight into the minds of kings and business rivals. Dream interpretation was in vogue not only in ancient Mesopotamia but throughout the whole ancient Near East. There are several records of dreams of Egyptian, Hittite and Mesopotamian kings, most of them quite transparent in meaning. There are also "Dream Books" written on cuneiform tablets, giving long lists of dreams and their meanings.

Joseph is alleged to have had special abilities in dream interpretation because he is a member of that "prestigious" group of people whose goat rustler god blesses them. This fiction benefits all Jews because if there is one special group of people who claim to have a special power of divining dreams, then when kings and princes have troubling dreams, they will most likely send for those special Jewish swindlers. Thus, the moneylenders positioned themselves to "occupy the gates" of their enemies by putting a special dream interpreter belonging to their guild at the gates of the king's mind, monitoring his very dreams.

So, when the cup-bearer and baker had troubling dreams and Joseph was asked to interpret them, "Are not interpretation God's business?" Joseph asked them. "Come, tell me" (Genesis 40:8). The lying, thieving Hebrews can certainly be trusted, even with your dreams. So, the story goes, Joseph correctly interprets the cup-bearer's dream as well as the baker's dream.

Genesis 41 records the elementary dream of the Pharaoh that anyone with a smattering of intelligence can figure out. Of course, a dream can mean whatever you want it to mean. But for the purposes of the Babylonian scribes, everybody in Egypt including all of the wise men were stupid. Only Joseph, the Hebrew, was intelligent, according to this Jewish hero story.

The Seven Lean Years of Egypt were not the wondrous miracles that the Jews claim them to be. From at least 2800 BC, Egypt had a repeated history of famines. Dependent as they were upon the flooding of the Nile to water their fields and to bring in fresh nutrients in its silt, Egypt in its long history recorded many famines and years of want. Ancient Egyptian texts have frequent references to hunger, "years of misery," "a year of low Nile" and so on. In fact, Egypt had a previous history of seven lean years, "which by a contractual arrangement between pharaoh and a god, were to be followed by years of plenty."

Thus, it can be seen that the Jews, plagiarizing another of the traditions of the people around them, added another brick to their ancient mausoleum. Famines were not rare in Egypt. Seven-year droughts had occurred and had been recorded even on the boulders of the Third Cataract at Elephantine. So, Pharaoh's dream was not something that was beyond either the experience of the Egyptians or the perceptive powers of the wise men and magicians. But according to the fictions of the *Hebrew Bible*, only their own Jewish hero could divine the dream of the Seven Lean Cows and the Seven Ears of Wheat.

Ah ha! Those fat cows and abundant wheat followed by their reverse represent seven good years and seven lean years, abundance followed by famine! Of course! The reader instantly feels a glow of gratification as a party to the clever puzzle. The clever ruse is that the god of the Hebrews gives them special powers that the sages of Egypt do not have. This special power, Joseph attributes to the god of the goat rustlers. Joseph recommends that Pharaoh appoint someone who is "intelligent and wise" to supervise a collection of grain to be stored against the coming famine.

Now the Hyksos Pharaoh appoints the illiterate Hyksos Joseph as overseer because he is "possessing the spirit of god" and because no one is "as intelligent and wise as" Joseph. He makes Joseph only second to Pharaoh in authority. In this fictionalized rendition of the Hyksos takeover of Egypt, the Pharaoh says, "I hereby make you the governor of the whole land of Egypt." (Genesis 41:41.)

The Scribes make a big show of Joseph's promotion with his fine linen and gold chains, his fancy chariot and his dictatorial powers, all things cherished in the hearts of the moneylenders. He was declared to be just the smartest goat rustler ever! And Pharaoh even gave Joseph a daughter of the high priest of Ra, priest of the sun god at Heliopolis. Thus, Joseph married into the most exclusive nobility of Egypt. Not bad for an illiterate Hebrew goat rustler. Yet, this is just more internal evidence that the entire story, if it happened at all, could only have taken place during the Hyksos era and at no other time. The prestige of Egypt stood higher than that of any other country of the day. Egypt would take foreign princesses into the royal harem as marriage alliances but would never give an Egyptian princess, or for that matter any Egyptian woman, in marriage to any of the Asiatics, especially such a high-ranking woman as the daughter of the High Priest of Ra. So, the rabbis who wrote such a fable could not imagine that in the far future of today, archaeology would prove the Jews to be liars.

As viceroy, Joseph went through all of Egypt collecting and storing grain. He had two sons by his Egyptian wife which he named Manasseh and Ephraim, these would later be half-breed Hebrews (*mamzers*) with their own tribal territories. But half a Jew is almost as good as a whole Jew since they are all so blessed by the goat rustlers' god.

Finally, after the seven years of plenty when the seven years of famine began, the lie of the story of Joseph makes a full circle. *During the entire history of Egypt*, whenever there was famine, Pharaoh and the governors of every nome in Egypt provided for their people with *free grain*. Money had never been used in Egypt. The people were paid for their work in rations of wheat, barley, beer, and cloth. Just as in the early days of Sumeria, these could in turn be used to barter for whatever else they needed.

On the Statue Inscription of Djedkhonsefankh, son of the priest of Amen-Re, of the Twenty-second Dynasty (943-720 BC), is an indication of the long-held beliefs of the Egyptian rulers of their duties and responsibilities to their fellow Egyptians and especially their duties to the poor among them. Djedkhonsefankh said:

> "I shall not vanish for I know: God acts for him whose heart is true! … When I was in charge of the loaves, my lord Amun enriched me. I was constant in lending grain to the Thebans, in nourishing the poor of my town. I did not rage at him who could not pay. I did not press him so as to seize his belongings. I did not make him sell his goods to another, so as to repay the debt he had made. I sated him by buying his goods and paying two or three times their worth. One cannot equal what I did in any respect. I did not quarrel with him who had robbed me, for I knew one does not get rich by theft. God does what he wishes!"

Even though the 22nd Dynasty was of the Meshwesh Libyans, every people who attained the kingship of Egypt also became followers of the Egyptian theology and philosophy, such was the power of that great culture over all those who attained to it. This was true for everybody except for the Semitic and Babylonian Hyksos who were not there to rule but to plunder. So, it is really quite impossible that a character like Joseph could ever have lived in Egypt *except during the Hyksos period* when Semitic goat rustlers had seized the land. If an Egyptian had been on the throne of Pharaoh, this same ancient system of nurturing the people would have been used.

But now, the story of Joseph explains that when famine struck, Joseph didn't give the grain to the starving as would have an Egyptian but, like a greedy Babylonian merchant-moneylender, he sold the grain and enslaved the Egyptian people. This grain had cost Pharaoh nothing since it was confiscated for free through taxes and set aside in the special "seven years of plenty insurance fund." So, any amount that was charged for it was pure profit. Not only did Joseph sell the grain to the Egyptian people but he also sold it to foreigners who came to Egypt on empty stomachs but with silver in their hands.

Now, in Genesis 42, the story of how Joseph's brothers came to Egypt to buy grain has two elements that the Babylonian scribes inserted as a lesson to the Hebrews. First, is the emotional meeting that Joseph had with his brothers. Dressed as an Egyptian and speaking through an interpreter, his brothers did not recognize him. So, the meeting of the same family of thieves was larded with emotional baggage. Second, in Genesis, the moneylenders were teaching how to steal from anyone who was not a guild-member. In this case, Joseph steals grain from Pharaoh by giving it for free to his brothers plus he returns their money to them. Joseph not only filled his brothers' baskets with grain but he also put back his brothers' money in their sacks and gave them provisions for the journey home. So, the moneylenders were teaching the Hebrews how to feel good about themselves while robbing their employer so as to enrich their relatives. This is a basic teaching of Judaism in that only the tribes of the Jews are worthy of honesty; all non-Jews – including one's magnanimous employers – may be robbed at will. Such teaching of the methods of Jewish thievery would later become part of the "Tradition of the Elders," the notorious *Babylonian Talmud*.

In Genesis 43, these Hebrews did not return to Egypt until they had eaten up all of the grain that they had gotten from Joseph. But they were not completely starving since stingy, old Jacob (a.k.a., Israel) told them to take as gifts, "a little balsam, a little honey, gum, tragacanth, resin, pistachio nuts and almonds." And Jacob (a.k.a., Israel) blesses them with the cloven-hoofed Devil's Claw Salute in the name of their god, *El Shaddai*, the god of the mountains. So, they certainly were not starving with almonds and pistachio nuts to eat.

When they arrived back in Egypt, Joseph treats his brothers to a banquet and again the scribes write a tear-jerking little tale of Joseph weeping in his room from seeing the brothers who still do not recognize him. But also Ezra's merchant-moneylender scribes slander the Egyptians by claiming that the Egyptians have a horror of eating with a Hebrew. This is also a Jewish inside joke because the Babylonian scribes knew that the Egyptians hated the filthy Hyksos shepherds and wanted nothing to do with them.

Again, in Genesis 44, the moneylender scribes teach the Jews how to steal from an employer. This time Joseph not only gives them as much grain as they can carry but returns to them their silver hidden in the grain sacks along with Joseph's silver drinking cup. The cup was also the cup Joseph used to "read omens." So again, the occult power of this special super-Jew is emphasized. When Joseph demands that Benjamin, the youngest, stay in Egypt as his slave, it is Judah, the oldest, who pleads to remain in his place. Notice that Joseph and Benjamin were brothers by the same mother, Rachel.

Genesis 45. Joseph finally reveals himself to his brothers and claims that it was God who actually sent him to Egypt to make him vizier to Pharaoh so as to preserve the "race" of Israel so that they would not perish in the famine. Those special goat rustlers carried the "promise" of Abraham in the foreskin of their penises. So, they were very holy, as well as being a special "race." It is a tearful reunion. Pharaoh is so happy to have Jews with their hands open, palms up, that he gives the children of Israel the "best the land that Egypt offers" and tells them "you shall feed on the fat of the land." And so, Joseph's entire tribe fed off of Egypt whose people were overjoyed to be infested with these Jewish parasites sucking their blood.

Joseph honors his brother Benjamin the most since they were from the same Jewish mother, while the other brothers were from Rachel's sister Leah and their slaves, Bilhah and Zilpah. Keep in mind that Judaism is a racist system built upon genealogical descent. Not only is Ezra the Scribe writing along tribal lines but especially along genealogical blood lines, building a genealogical legend. This genealogical and racist ideology is the very basis of the *Hebrew Bible*. Remember, Benjamin is the original tribe that was sent by Terah to secure the land around Jerusalem. So, they are here being honored by the Babylonian scribes as Joseph's favorite.

Finally, in Genesis 46, Jacob (a.k.a. Israel) loads up his entire family of seventy goat rustlers and they all move to Egypt. Even though Egypt was suffering from drought, that doesn't matter to Joseph or the goat rustlers of his tribe. Typically Jewish, they bring along all of their cattle which they expect the Egyptians to feed.

Ezra's scribes in Babylon put another joke into this chapter which also links the Hyksos to the Semites of Canaan. Joseph tells his brothers to say that they are shepherds because the "Egyptians have a horror of all shepherds". In this way, the Babylonian scribes, while falsely claiming a more ancient setting, actually date the story of Joseph to the occupation of the Hyksos.

In Genesis 47, Pharaoh tells them that the land of "Egypt is open to you: settle your fathers and brothers in the best region." This also dates the story of Egypt to the Hyksos invasion. Although an Egyptian Pharaoh would not take the land away from his nobles and risk rebellion so that a pack of scruffy desert rats could pasture their cattle and goats, such an act was standard for the Hyksos Pharaohs who sat on the throne. According to this story, the Hyksos Pharaoh gave the best land to these bandits in the green delta region known as Goshen, specifically stated as the region of "Ramesis." This again shows that the story took place among the Hyksos because Ramesis was not built until after they were expelled. And Genesis was written long after their expulsion and tightened up as a myth by Ezra the Scribe in Babylon by 539 BC.

The foreign character of Joseph and the Pharaoh, two very un-Egyptian Hyksos officials, is celebrated when Joseph was able to acquire all of the silver in Egypt by selling grain to the starving Egyptians. Then, when their silver ran out, Joseph traded them grain for their livestock. Then, Joseph swindled away all of their land and thus Pharaoh acquired all of Egypt. This story shows the methods of the merchant-moneylenders at work and not an actual state of affairs in Egypt since an Egyptian Pharaoh was already, by tradition, the owner of all of Egypt. But for the sake of the story, the scribes show how Joseph bought all of Egypt for Pharaoh. Then, when they had nothing left to sell, Joseph bought the people as slaves. And he gave them back enough seed with the stipulation that Pharaoh would get twenty percent of all produce. Oy! Such a clever Jew! A real hero among his kind!

Finally, before Jacob (a.k.a. Israel) died, he made Joseph put his hand on his holy, circumcised penis – you know, where the holy Promise is signed with Jewish foreskin of these nasty people – and promise to bury him in Canaan. Since the penis is the holiest part of a Jew, that's where their holiest promises are made.

Once again in Genesis 48, the theme of the scribes was to weld the various groups of goat rustlers into a single rapacious gang. So, Jacob (a.k.a. Israel) adopts Joseph's two sons by his Egyptian wife. The half-Egyptians, Ephraim and Manasseh, thereby become members of the holy goat rustlers family, too. Jacob (a.k.a. Israel) put the two children between his legs next to his holy penis to signify – Abracadabra! – that they came out of his "loins" (Bible-speak for genitals) and "blessed" them with the cloven-hoofed Devils Claw Salute and made them his own offspring. Thus, the mamzers (half-Jews) Ephraim and Mannaseh became tribes of Jewish goat rustlers for the future kingdom of Israel (a.k.a. Jacob).

Finally, that old, lying, swindling scoundrel Jacob died. In Genesis 50, Joseph had Jacob's old carcass embalmed in the Egyptian fashion so that he would keep in the hot weather. The Babylonian merchant-moneylender scribes, fraudulently building on their wishful desire that these goat rustlers were a "blessing" to Mankind and "deeply loved" by the Egyptians, wrote that the Egyptians mourned Jacob (a.k.a. Israel) for seventy days. If there was any mourning by the Egyptians at the death of a Hebrew-Hyksos, it was only wailing and crying and pleading to God as to why he didn't die sooner. This old flea-bitten Babylonian goat rustler is alleged to have had such a pitiful mourning going on that "all Pharaoh's servants and the palace dignitaries, and all the dignitaries of the land of Egypt, all of Joseph's family and his brothers, along with his father's family, with chariots and horsemen" all traveled across 250 miles of hot desert on foot and by donkey-back to Canaan where they buried Jacob like a mummified anchor.

You can see the same sort of fraud in modern times on the Jewish Media Monopoly. When a Jew dies, weeks and months of moaning and hand-wringing is orchestrated, trying to give the illusion that it is such a great loss to Mankind when a lying Jewish parasite kicks the bucket. But when a non-Jew dies, it rates a single, brief mention on the news and that's all you ever hear of it. According to the Babylonian scribes who wrote the story, Joseph lived a total of 110 years, the same length of time the Hyksos were ravaging Egypt. (Oy Gevalt! What a coincidence!) So, the system that the Hyksos used to steal the wealth of Egypt, is exemplified in the story of Joseph. Then, he died and was embalmed. The Egyptian priests, after pulling his brains out through his nose and cutting out his internal organs for drying, probably sewed a few dead cats and splinters of wood into his insides so that he would have a hell of a time in the Underworld. That's how the Egyptians buried the people they hated. And certainly, no Egyptian would mourn a Hyksos-Hebrew, especially one who had defrauded them of their goods and lands when they were hungry and sold their children into slavery for a handful of grain. And so ends the Book of Genesis where-by the merchant-moneylenders scribes of Babylon established the foundation for the religion of the moneylenders which today is known as Judaism.

Founded by Terah, the Babylonian patriarch of the moneylender guilds of Ur and Harran along with his Babylonian son Abraham, guarded by the gangster tribe of Benjamin from Babylonia, soldiered by gangs of thieves and cut-throats known as Hebrews, and financed by the booty that Joseph and his fellow Hebrew-Hyksos had looted from Egypt, Judaism had established its cloven hoof solidly upon the neck of Mankind.

6.3 The Book of Exodus: More Jewish Pseudo-History that Never Happened

Exodus deals with three themes: getting chased out of Egypt, the Covenant of the Jewish Penis, and schlepping their plunder through the wilderness. It is a book of instruction for swindling an entire country out of their wealth, blaming everything on their victims and then escaping just retribution by running away with the loot.

Remember, all of the books of the *Hebrew Bible* were written for a particular audience of Hebrew bandits *as a means of teaching particular lessons* and as *a Contract of basic laws* to keep them as tame as possible until unleashed. The Book of Exodus begins by teaching the Hebrew goat rustlers the strategy behind "Go forth and multiply." Exodus states that the Hebrew-Hyksos in Egypt "were fruitful and grew in numbers greatly; they increased and grew so immensely powerful that they filled the land." This circumcised Hebrew propensity to "go forth and multiply," was a real advantage to the moneylenders. As they designed their religion, it was extremely important for them to build the biggest possible population of gangsters. A large population gave them the supporters to make donations and to protect their gold and silver with a solid wall of flesh, ready to die for the "god" and his Temple. "Go forth and multiply" gave them the necessary guards for their gold and it allowed them to take over a country through sheer over-population, merely by pushing the native population out of the way. It was a strategy of fast-breeding Hebrews with itching, circumcised penises; many wives each applauded for producing eight to twelve children; early marriage at puberty to make them sex-crazed for life; all driven by commands of their demon god to have as much sex as possible. The Jewish sex fiends start out as a few immigrants but soon balloon into millions, displacing the citizens of the country. And their *Hebrew Bible* brags about the success of this technique of over-population and dispossession.

However, the Egyptians practiced natural birth control. Egyptian women nursed their babies for two to three years. Since women do not conceive while they are lactating, they can have an enthusiastic sex life without becoming pregnant. The Hebrews, however, celebrated women who had eight or twelve children, one per year, much like the goats they shepherded. The Jews were thus out-breeding the Egyptians by more than 5 to 1.

The Book of Exodus begins with a change of Egyptian administration coinciding with the expulsion of the Hyksos when a native Egyptian pharaoh ruled. The Egyptians realized what a threat that the burgeoning number of Jewish bandits were to their country. The Egyptians understood quite well the true nature of the *Apiru* (Hebrew) hordes of Jewish bandits, thieves, and betrayers. So, like all people in every country where Jews are found, the Pharaoh wanted to have far fewer Jews found there – zero being the ideal number.

Ezra and his scribes wrote how clever the Hebrews were at deceiving Pharaoh. Not understanding that all Jews are hatched from Jewesses, the Pharaoh stupidly ordered the Hebrew midwives to kill all the boy babies that were born so as to reduce their population while leaving the actual breeders, the

Hebrew girls, alive. But being Hebrew bandit molls, these mid-wives lied to the king, slandering the Egyptian women as weak and in need of midwives but bragging that the Hebrew women, such as themselves, were so hardy and strong that they popped those babies out like corks from a beer bottle before the midwives could arrive. So, even the boy babies survived the orders of Pharaoh.

Out of desperation to control a Hebrew population multiplying like lice, Pharaoh ordered that all Hebrew boy babies should be thrown into the Nile. After all, in Egyptian thinking, these were holy Jews, so it was perfect Egyptian logic that they should rub elbows with the holy Egyptian crocodiles.

Internal evidence tells us that the stories in the Book of Exodus actually took place during the time that the Hyksos were being expelled from Egypt. The expulsion of the Hyksos is generally dated, on the basis of Egyptian records and the archaeological evidence of destroyed cities in Canaan, to around 1570 BC. But 1 Kings 6:1 claims that the construction of the Temple of Solomon began 480 years after the Exodus. When Egyptian and Assyrian sources are correlated with the regnal dates of Israelite kings, this would roughly place the Exodus in 1440 BC, according to the story told by the Jews. That is more than a hundred years after the date of the Hyksos expulsion. So regardless of what the lying Jews claim in Exodus, it would have been virtually impossible for any Hebrews to have escaped Egypt then.

Or maybe the old, fly-covered Jewish priests forgot the exact date since accurate calendars were not commonly used in those days. Dates were based on the reigning years of such-and-such a king. But they would certainly have remembered the name of the Pharaoh who had enslaved them as they so boisterously claim. Right? So, it is impossible to be true, the claim in Exodus 1:11 that the Pharaoh Rameses enslaved the goat rustlers. Rameses came to the throne in 1320 BC, more than a century after the biblical claims. The cities of Pithom and Rameses that are mentioned, were still standing *900 years later* when the book of Exodus was actually written. The authors of Exodus mention those cities as – *Abracadabra!* – "proof" that the stories are true. But archaeology and the story, itself, prove that Exodus is a false.

What archaeology proves, is that the Book of Exodus is nearly all lies and fictions. Exodus mentions that the store-cities of Pithom and Rameses were built with the forced labor of the Israelites. But, in fact, Pithom and Rameses were built *after* the Hyksos were expelled. Many of the building stones of the Hyksos fort of Avaris were later used to build the city of Rameses. So, this date that the writers of the Book of Exodus use as the time of their stories, is impossible to be true.

All internal indications suggest that the Exodus fable was written during the time of the 26th Dynasty *in the second half of the seventh or first half of the sixth century BC*. It was written for the audience of that time, using the familiar Egyptian town locations for a setting, while falsely claiming an ancient authorship – a technique in counterfeiting and fraud much used throughout the *Hebrew Bible*. The Jewish rabbis and scribes were expert counterfeiters and forgers, but modern archaeology has rooted them out of the pages of history and placed Jewish literature where it belongs in the garbage dump.

What Hebrew slaves who were living in Egypt after the Hyksos were expelled, were not released until 671 BC when Assyrian king Ashurbanipal defeated the Negro Pharaohs of the 25th Dynasty. So, during that entire 900-year span, the descendants of those few Hebrews living in Egypt, were still living in Egypt making bricks and hauling manure. Their release by Ashurbanipal and their subsequent return to Canaan, would bring their stories of enslavement in Egypt to the attention of the wicked Jewish scribes of Yahweh in Jerusalem. Those Jewish priests and their scribes combined those stories with the Hebrew-Hyksos fables bragging about how they had stolen so much loot from Egypt long centuries before. By combining those Hyksos stories with the tales of the returning slaves to sixth century Jerusalem, they wrote the fable known to us as the Book of Exodus. This Jewish hoax was then advanced to include all of the fables of Abraham and his descendants being melded with the motley crew of Hyksos goat rustlers in Egypt.

The ruthless nature of the Hebrews is emphasized so that it states in Exodus 1:12, "the more they were crushed, the more they increased and spread, and men came to dread the sons of Israel." This is an instructive passage: "… and men came to dread the sons of Israel." This gangster characteristic must be understood because the merchant-moneylenders have been the oppressors of every people since the earliest days of Sumer, starting from 3500 BC. They were strict practitioners of Secret Fraud #9 of the Sumerian Swindle: "Only the most ruthless and greedy moneylenders survive; only the most corrupt bankers triumph." Sowing terror and fear among those who were not of their guild, who were not fellow "gentlemen," who were not fellow tribesmen or family, was how they oppressed all those around them. Whether their victims owed them money or not, this gang of merchant-moneylenders created fear of their vengeance at every insult wherever they were allowed to live. The infamous "fear of the Jews" was a purposely orchestrated social engineering construct.

With their private gangs of violent enforcers, the Babylonian bankers had collected on loans and foreclosed properties as ruthless oppressors. With the example of their cousins in Assyria, the use of assault, battery, torture, skulking retribution, arson and murder as a means of terrorizing populations into submission, had not been lost on the moneylenders of Terah's guild. They made such tactics a part of their religion – first the deceit, followed by aggressive enforcement of the swindle. What the lying scribes of Babylon were teaching the Hebrews through the Torah, was to practice terrorism so that all other peoples hated and dreaded them. Through the application of violence and shock, those predatory parasites could force their will even upon those whose populations were larger simply through sneaky, behind-the-back malicious mischief, arson, mayhem and murder.

Once again, the clever swindles of the Babylonian moneylenders are taught to the Hebrew goat rustlers. The story in Exodus 2 is plagiarized from the "Legend of Sargon" from about 2300 BC. It was still, at that time, recorded on the impervious clay tablets in the libraries of Babylon and Ur. The Jewish version starts: from the tribe of Levi, a son is born. (Remember this because the tribe of Levi is later given control of the Temple treasury.) To save him from Pharaoh, his mother put him in a basket in the river. The Pharaoh's daughter finds him. Moses' sister follows the basket along the river and asks permission to look for a wet-nurse from among the Hebrews. This scheming little Jewish girl goes and gets the baby's own mother to suckle him. And Pharaoh's daughter actually paid the mother to wet nurse him! Once again, the moneylender scribes emphasize clever deceit as being worthy of the Hebrews. He is named Moses. Unlike King Sargon to the Akkadians, however, Moses was not a blessing to the Egyptians, but a curse. The criminal mentality of the Babylonian merchant-moneylenders suffuses this myth of murder, deceit and pillage – all Jewish "virtues" led by the ultimate Jewish hero.

First, the scribes show what happens when one feels pity for a Jew. Pharaoh's daughter feels pity for the Hebrew baby and ends up paying Moses' very own mother to nurse him. Then, Pharaoh's daughter treated him like a son and educated him in Egyptian writing and culture. But was the ungrateful Jew happy with this? No, because the Semitic genealogical swindle ties Moses to his genetic people rather than to the Pharaoh's daughter who adopted and raised him. With his own mother offering her teats and whispering in his ear the demonic poison of Judaism, no kindness on the part of the Egyptians would ever have been enough.

While it was standard throughout Mesopotamia and Egypt to adopt children and for those adopted children to loyally cling to their adoptive parents, this is not what Terah and his thieving bankers were trying to establish for the guardians of their treasury. Regardless of the previous 2000 years of legal precedent, the merchant-moneylenders were devising a racially-based and genetically-based hoax. "Once a Jew, always a Jew," was the idea. Knowing only adopted parents since birth, was deemed to be secondary to the genealogical hoax of Judaism, where the "Promise" and the "Blessing" was passed down genealogically through the generations. Individual Jews didn't have to be individually virtuous in their personal lives since the "inheritance" of the "Promise of blessing," erased all sins and made them into "saints" regardless of what evils they performed. The story of Moses is a prime example of How the Jews Betrayed Mankind.

Once again, you can tell a lot about a people when you know who their heroes are. Moses, this great hero of the Jews, was a traitor to his adopted parents and a murderer. Terah's Babylonian guild wanted to deceive and inveigle the stupid Hebrew bandits who were outside of the laws of all nations. For the moneylenders' hoax to prosper, Terah wanted to put the moneylenders beyond the reach of the laws of all other people. So, the Book of Exodus teaches that when Moses saw an Egyptian strike a Hebrew, it didn't matter what the reason was or what insult the Hebrew had offered, or even whether the Hebrew slave had deserved his punishment. Striking a "holy" Jew was the main point, just as striking an *awilum* [the Haves] had been illegal in Mesopotamia. So, Moses looked around like a sneaky Jew to make sure there were no witnesses and then he killed the Egyptian and buried the body in the sand. A genuine Jewish hero in the making! And it is one of the first lessons that this Jewish hero teaches the Jews in the Book of Exodus; how to commit murder by being sure that there are no witnesses and then hiding the body.

The next day, he returned to find two of the Hebrews fighting. Since they recognized him as the murderer, Moses fled to the land of Midian on the other side of the Gulf of Aqaba. There he met the daughters of the priest of some goat rustlers who were drawing water from a well to water the sheep. The goat-herder priest gave his daughter, Zipporah, to Moses as a wife.

So, here we have a murderer from the tribe of Levi marrying the daughter of a goat-herder priest in the land of Midian on Sinai. This Moses character starts life as in the legend of Sargon, floating in a basket on the river. His sister cons Pharaoh's daughter into paying their own mother to nurse him. Through pity, Pharaoh's kindly daughter raises Moses like a son and trains him in the writing, culture and magic of Egypt. To repay the Egyptians for their kindness, Moses murders an Egyptian and runs off to Midian to marry the stinking daughter of a goat rustler priest. The Hyksos-Hebrew slaves in Egypt were still paying for their cruelty by themselves being enslaved. But their Yahweh-god remembers his "covenant" (that is, his "Contract") with Abraham, Isaac and Jacob. Thus, Exodus 2 ends with the *Contract* again being emphasized. After all, it is the *Contract* that is most important to the moneylenders because with a *Contract* they can hold the Hebrews in bondage to their scheme of world ownership.

In Exodus 3, Moses marries the daughter of a "priest" to keep his godly connections. According to the rabbis who wrote these tales, every stinking Hebrew shepherd who could kill a sheep and pour its blood on a rock, was a "priest." This is another indication of the low criteria that the moneylender scribes had for the qualifications of a Hebrew priest. He didn't have to actually be holy; all he had to do was kill innocent animals and perform such rituals.

The story of a burning bush is easy to tell and impossible to disprove, so it makes a good introduction to the religion of the moneylenders. In an area rich in natural gas deposits, a bush would make a good wick for a gas leak sparked into flame. Once again, the fraud is repeated that the Hebrews were specially chosen by this Yahweh-god who is the "God of Abraham, the God of Isaac and the God of Jacob." (Exodus 3:6.) And by Semitic genealogy, also the god of the Canaanites who also worshiped Yahweh's wife-consort, Asherah.

Here, after millions of years of prehistory and 2,000 years of written history, this "god" chooses the dirtiest and most dishonest thieves on the planet as "his people." Truly, this is a miracle of miracles! How could such a miracle come about?

After the Hyksos shepherds were expelled from Egypt, they were scattered across the area between Northern Arabia and Palestine. Among the many tribes, there were a variety of stories that each tribe had to tell of their escape. These became the stories told around the campfires and later written down by the Binu-Yamina (Benjamin) peddlers sent out by Terah to trade with the Hyksos for the gold and silver that they had stolen from Egypt and to record their genealogies.

It is here in Exodus that the name of the moneylender god is invoked. "Yahweh" means "He is" in the third person, present continuing tense of the verb "to be." So, it means "He is, continuously now, forever." This was a a very all-encompassing and complete name for a god. And it was an idea that was well-known among the Egyptian priests as well as the priests of the temples of Babylonia. This all-present idea was not something that was new to the religions of the ancient Near East. *Yahweh*, as was shown previously, was a Canaanite god who also had a wife named *Asharah* (a.k.a, *Astarte* or *Ishtar*). But a god that didn't require expensive upkeep of his statues, was an idea that was useful for Terah's moneylender scribes.

The Ebla tablets, discovered in that ancient city in northwestern Syria, show that a thousand years before the lying Jewish priests and rabbis claimed that they were special, that the names *El* and *Yahweh* in Exodus 3:14 had the equivalent forms, *IL* and *Ya* as used in Northwest Semitic personal names. For example, in Ebla we find a man named Mi-ka-il (Who is like God?), also pronounced as "Michael." Another personal name was Mi-ka-Ya (Who is like Yah?) The lying Hebrew-Hyksos had no monopoly over this particular Canaanite god, *Yah* or *Yahweh*. Archaeology proves that *El* and *Yahweh* were common among all of the various peoples of the entire region. By using this common Canaanite god, the moneylenders of Babylon were able to deceive the Hebrews with the idea that the ancient god that they already worshiped, was the same god who had chosen the Jews as their ancestors. Mohammad (mhrh) would use the same Semitic deceit in later centuries to con the Arabs with his Allah hoax.

This statement in Exodus 3:15 also shows the depravity and deceit of the modern-day Jews who have accepted the crude teachings of the early Canaanites but have rejected its main truth. This Canaanite name, *Yahweh*, or "He is" was a useful name for a god. But while Exodus 3:15 commands the Hebrews to invoke God by the name, *Yahweh*, they won't do it even today. Exodus 3:15 says, "This is my name for all time; by this name I shall be invoked for all generations to come." But the Jews today never use this name, not because they are holy people, but because they are devils. And devils dare not say the names of God. How the Jews became the most evil creatures to have ever walked the earth, is found in the pages that follow.

There is never any holy subject dearer to the hearts of the bankers than the subject of theft and plunder. So, Moses is promised that the goat rustlers would be able to plunder the Egyptians. Once again, these stories are Hyksos stories which deal very familiarly with robbing Egypt of its gold. In order to do this, Secret Fraud #19 of Sumerian Swindle plays an important part: "Prestige is a glittering robe for ennobling treason and blinding fools; the more it is used, the more it profits he who dresses in it." The goat rustlers will have "such prestige in the eyes of the Egyptians" that Moses and his gang of goat rustlers will be able to swindle them easily. With the Biggest Lie Ever Told, the Jews glory in the prestige that they give to themselves.

Exodus 4 tells of the miraculous powers that *Yahweh* gives to Moses so that he will have "such prestige" in the eyes of the Egyptians. The snake trick is here taught as if it is a genuine form of magic. One of the tricks of snake charmers is that they can press a certain nerve pressure point in the throat of a cobra and the snake will stiffen out straight as a rod. When the point is released, the snake re-animates. This magician's trick is provided as proof that "Yahweh, the God of their fathers, the God of Abraham, the God of Isaac and the God of Jacob, has really appeared to you." (Exodus 4:5.)

Further parlor tricks are taught to Moses such as changing his hand into a white leper's hand and back again. And the turning the river water into red blood when poured on the ground. The trick of using a mouthpiece to do all of the talking is also shared at this time. It gives more mystery and power to a person who has a mouthpiece or a lawyer to represent him. A few whispered instructions followed by the mouthpiece shouting out instructions gives an aura of mystery and concealed power to the one who does the whispering. Like a king who has his own town crier or herald, his voice is magnified by someone else. And for a charlatan pretending to have a godly power while hiding the fact that he was only an old fraud, with someone else doing the talking, the fraud is less easily discovered by the crowd. This phony trick was taught to the Hebrews that Aaron spoke for Moses so that Moses would be "as the god inspiring him." (Exodus 4:6.)

The methods of terrorism in which the merchant-moneylenders are so skillful even today, is here used against Egypt. The Hebrew-Hyksos scribes once again lie and falsely claim that Israel is the firstborn son of God. Therefore, out of spite, the god of the Hebrew goat rustlers will kill all of the firstborn sons of the Egyptians.

Here also, the magical value of circumcision is claimed in that *Yahweh* tries to kill Moses because he is not circumcised. But his goat rustler wife, Zipporah, takes a flint and cuts off the foreskin of her son and then touches the bloody foreskin to Moses' genitals. *Abracadabra!* With this kind of ritual sorcery, *Yahweh* lets Moses live. This guild membership badge of circumcision is made so important that even Moses is threatened with destruction for not being circumcised. Moses, who could be considered the father of the Jewish tradition, law, rituals, and administrative authority, exemplifies standard Jewish hypocrisy. He required all of his followers to be circumcised, but he was not circumcised, except with ritual *abracadabra*.

Exodus 5: Moses and Aaron try to get Pharaoh to let the Hebrew slaves get away. But Pharaoh didn't do it. He knew how lazy those Jews were (Exodus 5:8). And he wanted to work them for all of the theft, murder, swindles and losses that Egypt had suffered under the Hyksos dictatorship. So, he worked them even harder and flogged the Hebrew foremen. Pharaoh certainly knew the proper way to handle malingering Jews.

Exodus 6 is added as a way for the scribes to standardize the names of God that the various goat rustlers were using. The name, *Yahweh*, is declared to be the trademark best. *El Shaddai* is no longer to be used because now the Hebrew god is revealing himself in all his malicious glory. The promise of the Covenant Contract is also repeated whereby the merchant-moneylender scribes wrote, "I am Yahweh …. I will adopt you as my own people, and I will be your God…. Then I will bring you to the land I swore that I would give to Abraham, and Isaac, and Jacob, and I will give it to you for your own. I, Yahweh, will do this!" (Exodus 6:6-8.) Not only are the Hebrews to leave Egypt but they are to leave it "in battle order" (Exodus 6:26). That is, ready to fight and kill. In this way, the moneylender scribes are able to round up an army of goat-thieves and enlist them into their religion. The Hebrews didn't choose to join; the Yahweh-god chose them whether they wanted to join or not. So, they had better get circumcised or else plague be upon them!

Exodus 7: The moneylenders were not just writing a story which they claimed was from God, but a story whereby they claimed that they, themselves, were like gods. The Book of Exodus is not just the creation of a myth about the goat rustlers but the creation of a myth about the origins of the biggest swindlers and frauds to ever walk the earth – the bankers and financiers of Abraham's First National Bank and Pawn Shop.

The bankers were filthy, perverted betrayers and parasites upon their own people and upon the peoples of the world. But rather than being the usurers and pimps hated by all, they were striving to be the respected and feared representatives of the mightiest of the gods. These myths of Adam and Eve, Moses, etc., are all designed to connect the Hebrews to a genealogical and physical mythological delusion. The scribes claim that the Yahweh-god says to Moses, "See, I make you as a god for Pharaoh, and Aaron your brother is to be your prophet." (Exodus 7;1.) By this and by extension, the Jews who are to be genealogically connected to this story, are as gods and prophets of God. It doesn't take holiness, compassion, goodness, virtue, godliness, enlightened self-realization or any other attribute deemed to be characteristic of a holy person. All that was necessary to be a Jewish "a god and a prophet" was to have your penis circumcised and be a descendant of the youngest son of Terah, the patriarch of the merchant-moneylenders guild of Ur and Harran. Anything *actually* holy or virtuous, is completely secondary and totally unnecessary for being a "pious" Jew because with the material "proofs" of circumcision and genealogical descent, even the vilest Jew is defined as "holy" and a "Chosen One of God." Such are the lies of the Devil.

The three different literary sources which are named the "priestly," the "Yahwistic" and the "Elohistic" by Bible scholars, are represented in Exodus 7. Even though none of the three agree on the number of plagues in Egypt, they all have in common the death of the first born. It is the least magical of the plagues and therefore murdering of children is the most accessible to practice by the average Jew.

There has been much scientific and pseudoscientific debate as well as theological discussion of the alleged "miracle" of Moses changing the Nile water into blood. The red color that killed the fish has been ascribed to everything from red silt from upstream volcanoes to "red tide" plankton blooms. But all of these arguments which try to explain the "miracles" both scientific and ecclesiastical, all are assuming that the story is true. After all, every story in the *Hebrew Bible* is proven to be either a plagiarism, a forgery or entirely false, so why accept these other "miracles" as anything other than more Jewish lies? But whatever the explanation, in the story, the Egyptian magicians could do the same trick. Moses was thereby given the "prestige" of being equal to or greater than the famous and mighty priests of Egypt.

Exodus 8 claims that Moses and Aaron waved the magic staff and made frogs swarm all over the land. But the Egyptian magicians could also make frogs swarm all over Egypt. Then Aaron caused mosquitoes to attack men and beasts but the Egyptian magicians could not equal that trick and they told Pharaoh that it was God's work. Thus, the story begins to go beyond the trickery of magicians and into the realm of a mighty god doing mighty deeds.

Moses warned Pharaoh that *Yahweh* would send gadflies to attack the Egyptians but no gadflies would be sent to the best land, the Delta region of Goshen where the Hebrews lived. Although the Egyptians were attacked by great swarms of gadflies, no flies attacked the Hebrews. Again both ecclesiastical and scientific reasons have been offered to explain this "miracle," and all of them are assuming that the story is true. But when you understand that these are just Jewish lies, you instantly attain supreme knowledge of Judaism.

In Exodus 9, the terrorism method of killing the livestock of the Egyptians is taught. Through this "miracle," the Hebrews learn to poison the livestock of the Egyptians or any other pastoral people they hate and then say that God did it. Poisoning livestock became a tradition of the Jews to terrorize the people among whom they were allowed to live.

This "miracle" was followed by the sixth plague, the plague of boils where all of the Egyptians were covered with boils but none of the Hebrews. Next the plague of hail that fell everywhere but in Goshen, on the best land where the Hebrews resided. All of this, so that the Canaanite god *Yahweh* could make Pharaoh "see my power and to have my name published throughout all the earth" (Exodus 9:16), the very same name that modern Jews are too guilty and wicked to repeat but the very name that the Canaanites and Hebrews already worshiped even before Exodus was written.

The reason for all of these fables is given in Exodus 10, where *Yahweh* tells Moses,

> "Go to Pharaoh, for it is I who have made his heart and his courtiers stubborn, so that I could work these signs of mine among them; so that you can tell your sons and your grandsons how I made fools of the Egyptians and what signs I performed among them, to let you know that I am *Yahweh*." (Exodus 10:1-2.)

Here in the Book of Exodus, *Yahweh* is again called "the God of the Hebrews," that is, the god of the *Apiru*, the god of bandits and thieves.

The plague of locusts is next. This forces Pharaoh to allow just the Hebrew men to go to worship their desert god. But since they want to take all of their property with them, it is obvious to Pharaoh that the Hebrews are up to no good. And besides, these are slaves. What are slaves doing with "property"? So, Pharaoh wanted to keep the women and children as hostages.

After the locusts, Yahweh brought darkness to all of Egypt. Of course, where the Hebrews lived, there was light. Pharaoh still suspects the goat rustlers of trickery so he says that all of the Hebrews can go, but their flocks and herds have to stay in Egypt. After all, the demand that all of the Hebrews and their property and all of their flocks and herds must be allowed to leave, is a transparent ploy. This ploy has its basis in the actual historical Pharaoh Ahmose who allowed the Hyksos to leave Avaris with all of their loot so as to get rid of them without a lengthy siege.

Exodus 11: Once again, the importance of Hebrew fakery is brought to the forefront. The idea of "prestige," which is so important in selling durable goods, is emphasized for selling charlatan myths.

> "And Yahweh gave the people prestige in the eyes of the Egyptians, while Moses himself was a man of great importance in the land of Egypt, and of high prestige with Pharaoh's courtiers and with the people." (Exodus 11:3.)

With this "prestige" the Hebrews asked to "borrow" gold and silver ornaments from the Egyptians. After all, these slaves were really holy people, so the Egyptians could trust them not to steal anything. Right? This same hoax is perpetrated by modern day Jews who use the "prestige" of their swindled positions of authority in academia or finance or medicine or politics to defraud the non-Jews of wealth and of country. But this is covered more thoroughly in *Volume III, The Blood-Suckers of Judah.*

Exodus 12 begins the Babylonian New Year with a Hebrew twist. The agricultural feast of the first fruit of the barley harvest was combined with the pastoral feast of the first-fruit of the flock to produce the Passover Feast on the Babylonian calendar date of Nisan (March-April) which began the first month of the Hebrew year. In this way, the age-old competition between the farmers and the pastoralists was eliminated and their two cultures were blended into one, both celebrating the death and destruction of the Egyptians through Jewish cunning.

The Jews were to eat the Passover Feast like thieves ready to make a getaway, that is, with sandals on and dressed for a journey. It is to be gobbled down like hungry swine eating corn fritters. During the Passover, *Yahweh* allegedly killed the first born of every animal and man in Egypt. The Hebrews dabbed blood around their doorways so that *Yahweh,* not being as omniscient as he claimed to be, would know not to enter there. And like a jealous god he says, "I shall deal out punishment to all the gods of Egypt, I am *Yahweh!*" (Exodus 12:12.)

And so, the Jews are commanded to celebrate the murder of the firstborn of all the Egyptians and the death of the firstborn of all of the animals belonging to the Egyptians by dressing up like thieves in a hurry and dabbing blood on their doorways. What kind of people celebrate such diabolical evil and laugh about it? The Feast of Unleavened Bread was mandatory on all Jews because "it was on that same day I brought your armies out of Egypt." (Exodus 12:17.) So, the Passover Feast celebrates the escape of the Hyksos from Egypt as an *army*, not as a ragtag band of poor, oppressed slaves. This is where the Passover actually originated as a celebration for causing death and destruction of the Egyptians followed by a quick escape of the Hyksos with all of their loot.

Thus, the merchant-moneylenders of Babylon passed along a secret that the modern Jews have used to this very day. That is, if they can be a big enough pain in the ass, then eventually the People will be so anxious to get rid of the Jews *that they will allow them to escape along with all of the wealth that they have stolen.* To their victims, the stolen wealth is of minor importance since the most important thing is to get rid of the perfidious and irritating Jews who murder the firstborn and create havoc. This is why the Jews always try to be as big a problem as possible, so that when they are eventually chased away, they can carry off some loot with them. The loot isn't missed so much since their victims are just so happy to get rid of the Jews that they don't notice until after the Jews have gone that they have been ripped off by the world's cleverest thieves.

When all of their firstborn were murdered, in their grief, instead of rising up and killing all of those murdering Jews, the Egyptians begged them to leave. This is a constant mistake throughout history which is repeated countless times where, instead of the Jews paying for their crimes and an end being made of those criminals and the stolen property confiscated, they are allowed to escape. Taking advantage of the Egyptians' panic to get rid of them,

> "The sons of Israel did as Moses had told them and asked the Egyptian for silver ornaments and gold, and for clothing. Yahweh gave the people such prestige in the eyes of the Egyptians, that they gave them what they asked. So they plundered the Egyptians." (Exodus 12:35-36.)

The moneylender scribes called it "prestige." Since the Babylonian moneylenders wrote the Torah, that's what they called it, too. But the Egyptians called it "loathing," pure loathing that anyone could be as rotten as the Jews. Once the door was opened for them, inviting them to leave, they wouldn't leave unless they got paid to do so.

Again, the internal evidence shows that these alleged events took place at the end of the Hyksos invasion. It claims that "the sons of Israel left Rameses for Succoth." But Rameses was not built until after the Hyksos were expelled. In this story, it is the "armies" of the Hebrews who escaped Egypt. These armies were the armies of the Hyksos shepherds and goat rustlers who had been ravaging Egypt for the past 108 years and who had escaped Egypt with all of their loot. The Egyptians had been glad to get rid of them.

Here, also, is found the basis for modern day swindles. The population of those escaping from Egypt is stated as 600,000 Hebrews. This 600,000 represented the total population of all of the Jews in the world at that time. Likewise, in modern times, this number is used to represent the total population of all modern Jews in the world when it is multiplied by ten, the number of a quorum of Jews praying. It is then rendered as six million. Thus, six million became a code word *representing all of Jewry*. It was used in World War I and again in World War II as a code word representing all Jews. As a code word, it attracted all Jews to the banner of whomever Jewish leaders were broadcasting the code. Six million did not represent an actual figure but it merely represented a code word for an attack upon all of Jewry, such as the six million "victims" of the Nazis. Thus, all Jews worldwide could be inveigled to militate against whatever target was said to be attacking the "six million." Since that number represented the gematria code for "all Jews worldwide," then for a Jew, "Six million means you."

In the belief that words or phrases having identical numerical values bear some relation to each other, gematria is a system of assigning numerical value to a word or to a phrase. It is one of the many superstitions studied by what the Jews call their "scholars" or their "learned rabbis." These are all unrepentant old frauds. Such secret code words have been taught in the scribal schools since Sumerian times and are today a large part of the Jewish studies of *Torah*, *Talmud* and *Kabballa* in the Jewish *yeshivas*. One of the best-known examples of gematria in modern times is the Hebrew word "chai" ("life"), which is composed of two letters which add up to 18. This has made 18 a "lucky number" among Jews, and gifts in multiples of $18 are very common among Jews. The number 18, is the sum of three sixes. So, 666 is a lucky number among Jews since it represents the anti-Christ who is their savior.

These kinds of cryptography were occasionally used so that only a select few could understand the "secrets" of religious knowledge or the "secrets" of the various Babylonian guilds. Sometimes numbers were used in Babylonian cryptography as well as words. The names of some of the major gods were sometimes written as numbers, with *Anu*, the head of the Sumerian and Babylonian pantheon of the gods, being assigned the number 60. With the Babylonian counting system based on 60, and with the highest god of the Babylonians having that particular gematria number, then it was a simple leap for the moneylender scribes to number their "godly people" with 10,000 times the power of the magic number 60 which represented the highest Babylonian god. Thus, the number of Hebrews marching out of Egypt "in battle array," carrying the loot of the Egyptian people, was written as 600,000 by the merchant-moneylender scribes of Babylon.

Exodus 13: The first born of every Hebrew and his cattle was to be owned by the Yahweh-god. The story of the "Passover" was to be repeated *not* as some ancient fable but as a continually renewing con game. The Hebrews were not to repeat the Passover story like it had happened to someone else long ago, but they were to repeat it, even centuries later, as a genealogical delusion as if it had happened to each individual Hebrew connected to the genealogy. "This is because of what Yahweh did for *me* when I came out of Egypt." (Exodus 13:8.) Thus, the *asl* of Moses and his Hebrew bandits could be stretched around the modern Jews today, making them all one big lying *asl*.

It is also in Exodus 13 that the first born are pronounced "God's property." The first born of beasts are to be killed and offered as sacrifice, and a portion goes to the priests. The donkey is an exception; it must either be redeemed with a sheep or have its neck broken. The priests did not want any donkeys to escape their taxation racket. Since they didn't like the taste of donkey meat, if the farmers didn't want his donkey killed, then he had better replace it with some barbecued mutton or some silver. The first born of men are always redeemed, however, human sacrifice among the Hebrews was allowed *only by paying the priests* not to kill their sons. Because beasts can be sacrificed, what happens when the Jews consider the *goyim* (non-Jewish, lowly insects, stupid cattle) to be nothing but beasts? The practice of human sacrifice by the Jews in what is called the Blood Libel, is covered in *The Blood-Suckers of Judah*.

The Hebrews escaped from Egypt fully armed, following the Yahweh-god, the "lord of hosts (armies)," who appeared as a dust devil by day and a pillar of burning swamp gas at night. They traveled by day and by night around the Sea of Reeds rather than take the shortcut to Canaan (Palestine).

Exodus 14 tells the story of the crossing of the Red Sea and how Moses parted the sea so the goat rustlers could walk across. The idea for this fable was stolen from the Egyptian libraries so that they could put themselves above the Egyptian priests in the prestige of magical abilities.

Long before the Hyksos period, there was already in Egypt, tales of priests who could part the waters. Several of these Tales of Wonder have been discovered, such as this one from the Papyrus Westcar. The setting of the tale is in the Old Kingdom during the time of Pharaoh Snefu, although the papyrus discovered was written in classical Middle Egyptian, *dating from the Hyksos period* and is entitled "The Boating Party." This story is interesting both for its hinting at the delight that the Egyptians took in seeing the naked female form as well as in the magic power of the priests.

Pharaoh Snefu was one day bored with nothing to do. His chief lector-priest, Djadja-em-ankh, said to him: "May your majesty proceed to the lake of the palace. Fill a boat with all the beautiful girls in your palace. Your majesty's heart will be refreshed by seeing them row, a rowing up and down. As you observe the fine nesting places of your lake, as you observe its beautiful fields and shores, your heart will be refreshed by it."

Said his majesty: "Indeed, I shall go boating! Let there be
brought to me twenty oars of ebony plated with gold, their han-
dles of sandalwood plated with electrum. Let there be brought
to me twenty women with the shapeliest bodies, breasts, and
braids, who have not yet given birth. Also let there be brought
to me twenty nets and give these nets to these women in place
of their clothes." All was done as his majesty commanded.

As they were rowing about, one of the women accidentally
dropped her pendant of turquoise into the water. Then the chief
lector-priest, Djadja-em-ankh, said his say of magic. He placed
one side of the lake's water upon the other; and he found the
pendant lying on a shard. He brought it and gave it to its owner.
Now the water that had been twelve cubits deep across had become 24 cubits when it was turned back. Then he said his say of
magic and returned the waters of the lake to their place.

That the Hyksos-Hebrews had a mighty god who parted the sea and
drowned all of the army of the great pharaoh of the most powerful kingdom in
the ancient Near East, became a powerful propaganda tool for deceiving the
religiously devout people of the ancient Near East and of the entire world. The
Big Lie Technique was invented by the Jews. As "proof" that the destruction
of Pharaoh's army had really occurred, the Scribes wrote, "Israel witnessed the
great act that Yahweh had performed against the Egyptians, and the people
venerated Yahweh; they put their faith in Yahweh and in Moses, his servant."
(Exodus 14:31.) And all of the Jews told the same lie.

Thus, the so-called "proof" rested solely upon the fanciful imagination *of
those who wrote the lie*. Belief is a powerful illusion since you have to imagine
that something is there and then trust in your imagination. This is why every
year, the Jews all claim at the Passover ritual party that "*We* were slaves of
Pharaoh." Yet, none of these lying Jews were even alive to be enslaved by
pharaoh. So, the Jews tell themselves lies as part of their own Jewish rituals
and want the world to believe them. It is a clever con by the cleverest con artists and biggest liars in the world. One scribe wrote that "all of Israel" witnessed the lie. But at this time in the narration, the scribe doesn't tell you that
all of those alleged witnesses had died. So, *you only have the scribe's word*
that all of those goat-thieves had actually witnessed anything. In the king lists
of Egypt, there are no missing Pharaohs and certainly none who drowned. Also, according to modern archaeology, it was impossible for all of those goat
rustlers to have even been in that desert. The *Hebrew Bible* is completely de-
bunked by modern archaeology.

The Exodus 15 chapter is one of the many songs that the Hebrews have
for celebrating the death and destruction of their enemies. But it was also great
war propaganda for use against the peoples whom the goat rustlers wanted to
supplant. Philistia, Edom, Moab, Canaan are named as falling into terror as the
Hebrews dragged their loot across the desert claiming that their god was so

mighty. Again, the threat is repeated in the moneylender guild Contract: "If you listen carefully to the voice of Yahweh your God and do what is right in his eyes, if you pay attention to his commandments and keep his statutes, I shall inflict on you none of the evils that I inflicted on the Egyptians, for it is I, Yahweh, who give you healing" (Exodus 15:26).

Inflicting evil is one of the attributes of the god of the Jews who dance and celebrate death and destruction of the peoples with whom they come in contact. This has become a Jewish trait. Whereas most other peoples who escape a great threat, celebrate this great happiness of being alive – they celebrate Life. But the Jews celebrate the destruction of their enemies. The Jews celebrate death like the lying demons that they are. The Exodus is one of their most repeated and successful lies. This is not just the lies of the ancient rabbis, but every Jew who celebrates the Passover ritual, repeats the same lies such as "*We* were slaves in Egypt."

So important is the story of the Jews' liberation from bondage that the biblical books of Exodus, Leviticus, Numbers and Deuteronomy – a full four-fifths of the central scriptures of the Jews – are devoted to the events experienced by a single generation in slightly more than 40 years. All of those Jewish stories are proven by archaeology to be fables and lies. They are designed to focus pity and admiration for the denizens of Abraham's First National Bank and Pawn Shop. The final edition of the Biggest Lie Ever Told was arranged and re-edited in Babylon by the Ezra the Scribe just before 539 BC.

Archaeology proves that if the Hebrews had run away during the time that the Exodus claims, escape of more than a tiny group of Hebrews from Egyptian control at the time of Rameses II was highly unlikely, as is the crossing of the desert and entry into Canaan. In the 13th century, Egypt was at the peak of its authority – a dominant power in the world. There was no Exodus, no conquest of Canaan, no united monarchy, everything that the Jews claim about their alleged ancestors is proven by archaeology to be lies and fables.

Beginning after they had expelled the Hyksos, the Egyptians tightened their control over the flow of immigrants from Canaan into the delta. The border between Canaan and Egypt was closely controlled with forts and patrols. If a great mass of fleeing goat rustlers had exited Egypt during the time of Rameses, a record should exist. Yet in the abundant Egyptian sources, there is not a single clue.

In the 13th century BC, the grip of Egypt on Canaan was stronger than ever. The military route in northern Sinai was protected by a series of forts and supplied with freshwater sources. After crossing the desert, the Egyptian army could easily rout any rebel forces and impose its will on the local population. So, there was no possibility of 600,000 slaves escaping in that direction. But what of the possibility of fleeing into the desolate wastes of the Sinai Peninsula? This is also contradicted by archaeology.

Even if the 600,000 number of fleeing goat rustlers is wildly exaggerated, not a single encampment of even small groups of people has ever been found in the deserts of Sinai. What? Not a single encampment has never been found?

One may argue that a relatively small band of wandering Israelites cannot be expected to leave material remains behind. But modern archaeological techniques – including aerial photography, satellite imaging, ground penetrating radar, among many other methods – are quite capable of tracing even the very meager remains of hunter-gatherers and pastoral nomads all over the world. Indeed, the archaeological record from the Sinai Peninsula discloses evidence for pastoral activity in such eras as the third millennium BC and the Hellenistic and Byzantine periods. There is simply no such evidence at the supposed time of the Exodus in the thirteenth century BC or of any other time where 600,000 escaped criminals camped for forty years. In the dry deserts, all remains are well preserved. And even if everything just blew away as dust, the campfire charcoal alone would provide the necessary clues. But there is nothing.

The conclusion – that the Exodus did not happen – is irrefutable when we examine the evidence at specific sites where the Hebrew goat rustlers were said to have camped. According to the biblical narrative, the Hyksos-Hebrews camped at Kadesh-Barnea for thirty-eight of the forty years of the wanderings. The general location of this place is clear from the description of the southern border of the land of Israel in Numbers 34. It has been identified by archaeologists with the large and well-watered oasis of Ein el-Qudeirat in eastern Sinai. Yet, repeated excavations and surveys throughout the entire area have not provided even a single pottery shard left by a tiny fleeing band of frightened refugees not to mention 600,000 thieves.

There are no tent stake holes, no campfire ashes or carbonized wood residue, no garbage dumps full of quail bones or any other kinds of refuse heaps, no rock shelters or foundation walls, nothing but clean and empty desert. Thus, archaeology proves that 600,000 thieves running from Pharaoh never lived in Sinai as the Bible claims. So, if the Jews are caught in one lie, what other lies are they telling? "*We* were slaves in Egypt?" as each of them repeats every year at Passover? What do you mean, "We"?

More "miracles" are written in Exodus 16. Feeding the Hebrew bandits with quails and manna is not just a fable but also a teaching device on how the moneylenders inveigled the Hebrews to keep their minds centered on The Contract. Taking a day off from work, was certainly not a Hebrew or a Jewish invention, as the modern-day Jews may claim. Long before there were any Jews, days of no work were practiced in Sumeria and Babylonia during every holy day and feast day. Even among the Romans in later times, although weeks did not exist in their calendar, all days of rest were religious feast days whereby a day of work was sacrificed to the gods. These non-work days were distributed throughout the year. On feast days, Roman magistrates, free men, students, slaves, and animals all ceased work.

Like an employer magnanimously giving his workers the day off (without pay) while taking one himself, the merchant-moneylenders could join with the community in resting from work, not as a ploy to ingratiate themselves with their victims but as a fellow employee under Contract to a mighty god. And after a day off, the fact that the merchant-moneylenders were still not

working, did not seem so blatantly irritating. The moneylenders were not releasing their victims from work for a frivolous holiday because this holiday
was designed to keep them studying and abiding by The Contract. But most
importantly, when all of the Hebrews refused to work on the same day under
the religious sanctions of the Sabbath of a mighty and terrifying god, that
meant that they could all get a draft exemption from serving in every king's
army. A slick trick by some very slick and cowardly Babylonian moneylenders
who devised the entire Sabbath scam for that specific reason.

Providing quails and manna each day might seem even too much of a
miracle even for superstitious Hebrew goat rustlers who knew the desert intimately. But ever resourceful with every trick of salesmanship, the moneylender scribes of Babylon had a slick trick as "proof" that the myth was true. They
made it seem that the story was true because they told of a jar of manna kept
safely in the Tabernacle. It was a double lie of the rabbis, claiming to offer the
"proof" that an actual jar of manna was kept in the Tabernacle and later claiming that the "proof" had been stolen. In rabbi-speak, the fraud works like this:
The rabbis claimed that the jar wasn't there anymore because it had been stolen. Therefore, that was "Jewish proof " that the jar had actually been there
because how could a thief steal something unless it was really there?

Exodus 17 gives more miracles to prove what a great god the Yahweh-
god was. Moses struck a rock with his magic staff and drinking water came
out. The magic staff gave the tribe of Israel advantage in a battle with the
Amalekites as long as Moses could hold the magic staff above his head. But
since it was too much effort and his arms sagged, giving Amalek the advantage, Aaron and Hur had to support his arms, "One on one side, one on the
other; and his arms remained firm till sunset." (Exodus 17:12.)

The swindle here is that the scribes again claim as "proof " for the tale
that "Yahweh said to Moses, 'Write this action down in a book to keep the
memory of it, and say in Joshua's hearing that I shall wipe out the memory of
Amalek from under heaven.'" (Exodus 17:14.) Thus, the reader presumes that
the book of Exodus that he is reading is the very book that is referred to and
that his very reading of Exodus verifies that the tale is true. The merchant-
moneylenders had a long experience in telling clever lies to make a sale of
whatever goods they were trying to sell. Later, once Christianity was established, the rabbis taught that Amalek was synonymous with Christianity and
that it was the duty of every Jew to destroy Christians and Christianity, at every opportunity. It was a duty the Jews gladly obeyed as you shall see.

In Exodus 18, we are further treated to Yahweh being not only one of
many gods but the greatest of "all the gods." Judaism was never established as
a monotheistic religion as so many people believe. It started out as a polytheis-
tic religion which recognized the existence of many gods but which claimed
that their own particular god was the mightiest. This was no different than a
worshiper of *Marduk* believing that *Sin, Nabu, Ishtar* and all of the other gods
were holy and powerful, but who trusted most in giving his loyalty to *Marduk*.
It was only after the Hebrews were sufficiently mesmerized by the lie, that the

priests and scribes began to claim that not only was *Yahweh* the best of the gods but that he was actually the only god. Their methodology for this leap of belief is found in later chapters.

In this chapter of Exodus, the plush, easy and profitable office of judge is here falsely being claimed as a tiresome labor. The merchant-moneylenders were well practiced in presenting shoddy goods as pristine or of disparaging the quality or value of someone else's trade goods in order to buy them cheaper. In this case, the job of sitting on their ass all day as a judge while dispensing laws and judgments, is fraudulently presented as hard work. So hard, in fact, that the system of judges was established by the rabbis of choosing

> "some capable and God-fearing men, trustworthy and incorruptible, and appoint them as leaders of the people: leaders of thousands, hundreds, fifties, tens. Let these be at service of the people to administer justice at all times." (Exodus 18:21-22.)

Thus, the Jews operate like a military machine run by judges (generals) with various captains, lieutenants, sergeants and corporals keeping them abiding by the terms of The Contract with military precision. The system of rabbinical courts to enforce The Contract was established. This was a variation of Secret Fraud #2 of the Sumerian Swindle: "Loans rely on the honesty of the borrower but not the honesty of the lender." In this case, abiding by The Contract was redundant upon those for whom The Contract was written and not by those evil Babylonian bankers who wrote The Contract. As far as these judges "administering justice at all times," this is another fraud because in Judaism there is no such thing as "justice" other than in the upholding of the laws of the rabbis. Upholding the Contract for the betrayal, dispossession and genocide of Mankind, is what the Jews call "justice."

Exodus 19 is where the Covenant Contract between the moneylenders and the Hebrew bandits was established. Those goat rustlers are impressed with the idea that they are in agreement with The Contract whether they like it or not because God has chosen them especially to be parties to The Contract. This banker's god allegedly says, "If you obey my voice and hold fast to my covenant, you of all the nations shall be my very own, for all the earth is mine. I will count you a kingdom of priests, a consecrated nation." (Exodus 19:5-6.)

Thus, the Babylonian Bankers were giving those mangy Hebrew goat rustlers more prestige, the prestige of a priest. Prestige doesn't cost anything and yet it has value. The Babylonian Bankers were giving the Hebrew scum the prestige of the highest office in any country, that of a priest. Even without having any of the required wealth or social position or knowledge, the Hebrew-Hyksos were elevated by mere fiat to the social level of the *awilum* (the Haves). And not just any high social position but the very highest social position, that of the priests! The moneylender scribes proclaimed it through the voice of their god, and it cost them nothing while the mangy Hebrew goat rustlers believe it, shooed away the flies, and started acting like royalty – instantly a proud and noble people walking in goat dung and scratching at their lice.

The might and terror of *Yahweh* is represented with smoke and fire and thunder over Mount Sinai. The Hebrew goat rustlers are threatened with death by stoning if any of them dare to set foot on the mountain. The rabbis of later times claimed that Mount Sinai means "malice" since it was here that Yahweh's malice went out to all of Mankind – except, of course, for the wonderful Jews who are ordered to "walk in his ways" and bring his wrath down upon all peoples. The location of Mount Sinai (or Mount Horeb as it is known in some texts) is a particular problem and over a dozen sites have been proposed for it. So, even the location of their holiest mountain, is totally unknown to the Jews who proclaim so loudly about how everything in the *Hebrew Bible* is true. Against all archaeological, linguistic, philological, forensic literary comparisons, and historical proofs to the contrary, and weighing in at many hundreds of tons of data, we have only *the word of the Jews* (that weighs absolutely nothing), telling us how lucky we are to even have been born since *God made the world just for them*. And as further proof that what they say is true, they offer you the miracles on Mount Sinai, a mountain that nobody can find.

The Ten Commandments are given in Exodus 20. It should be noted that there are two primary meanings to these Commandments plus an additional reason for their creation. The two main meanings for all of these ten rules depends on whether one is a Jew or a non-Jew. The rabbis assert that the Ten Commandments were only meant for the Jews, who are thus free to practice their opposite upon the non-Jews of the world.

In this chapter, the Babylonian Bankers are claiming to be God. And not only God, but "For I, *Yahweh* your god, am a jealous god and I punish the father's fault in the sons, the grandsons and the great-grandsons of those who hate me." (Exodus 20:5.) This is genocide by any definition of the term. Through four generations, this Yahweh-god of the Jews is a god of genocide who destroys people entirely from grandfathers to fathers to children to grandchildren through four generations. The god of the Jews is the God of Genocide.

This attribute is also a characteristic of the modern-day Jews. Through Semitic vengeance and an "eye-for-an-eye" malice, the Jews cause the destruction even of the innocent grandchildren of their enemies. Because Judaism was established as a racial and genealogical, sociopathic conspiracy, the Jews practice it in the very same way by attacking the racial and genealogical structures of their enemies. For example, in modern day Europe and America and Australia, the Jews are the prime movers behind the overwhelming immigration of non-White aliens which they use to dispossess and cause the extinction of the White race. And why? Because Judaism is a religion of genocide. And the Jews "walk in the ways" of their god of genocide by using every possible method for destroying non-Jews (especially Christians) down through four generations into extinction. The Yahweh-god is a god of genocide and the Jews are commanded to follow his laws and walk in his ways in committing genocide upon all who hate them – or even those who "slight" them. With such an evil "religion," it is plain to see that the Jews are devils.

The non-Jews take these Commandments at face value. The non-Jews think that these rules were made for everybody. Christians, especially, are taken in by this Jewish swindle because they accept the Ten Commandments as a part of their lives and actually practice them towards each other as well as towards non-Christians with love and charity.

However, this is not how the Jews interpret these or any other rule or obligation (*mitzvah*) of the *Hebrew Bible*. The rabbis teach, and the Jews believe, that the Ten Commandments were given to the Jews alone and *not to anyone else*. And because these laws are made by god and to be followed by the Jews toward other Jews, then it follows in rabbinical "reasoning" that the Ten Commandments *are not required to be applied by the Jews toward non-Jews*. This is the perfect fraud by the world's most fraudulent people, a fraud that has caused the deaths of millions of Christians and pagans alike at the hands of the Jews.

So, when the Commandment is, "You shall not kill," to a Jew this means that a Jew is prohibited from killing another Jew. However, he is not prohibited from killing a *goyim* (non-Jewish, lowly insect, stupid cattle). Thus, according to the rabbis, a Jew is allowed to kill non-Jews, commit adultery with the wives of non-Jews, steal, lie and slander, covet the goods and possessions of non-Jews. But the Ten Commandments only mean that he must not do these things to a fellow Jew. This allows the Jews to be criminal parasites upon all of Mankind and still pretend to be innocent and "holy."

The entire *Hebrew Bible* was written by big thieves to maintain control over their gangs of little thieves. The bankers of Babylonia elevated the goat rustlers of Canaan to the status and prestige of "priests" in a religion made by thieves, for thieves. You readers who are Christians or Muslims should look more carefully at your histories with the Jews. Whenever you find the Jews betraying you, it is because of this reason: They don't have to follow their own laws when such laws apply to you.

Exodus 21 gives the law concerning slaves. It is no different, really, than the Babylonian Laws of Hammurabi from which they derived their inspiration. This Law of Moses actually protects the property of the slave-owner. However, it does give a slight advantage to the Hebrew slave in that if he is bought by another Hebrew, he will be freed after six years. The Christians freed Christian slaves immediately. The Muslims freed Muslim slaves immediately. The Jews freed Jewish slaves only after working them for six years in order to get their money back.

However, the Babylonian Bankers' sexual perversions are also protected under the Laws of Moses. Once a man sells his daughter, she is enslaved for all time. If she does not sexually satisfy him, she can be sold back to her father but not to a foreigner (non-Jew). Other than this, the Semitic Laws of Moses are no different than the *lex talionis* of the Semitic Babylonians. The ox that gores is also no different than the Babylonian Laws although among the evil Hebrews, the poor ox is cruelly stoned to death.

The laws in Exodus 22 are little different than the laws of the Mesopotamia kings. Sorceresses are to be executed. Bestiality is punished with death. Anyone sacrificing to other gods comes under the ban and is killed. Again, other gods are recognized in this law since it was believed that other gods existed. The Jewish "ban," was execution. Although the property of the moneylender is again protected in that they can take the property of the widows and the orphans but they are commanded not to be harsh on widows and orphans while taking their property.

What is different about the laws of loaning money, is that the Hebrews cannot charge each other interest on a loan. This does not prevent them from charging interest to Gentiles but they must not charge interest to those who are brothers in The Contract with their circumcised penises as proof.

The Hebrews are commanded not to be slow about making offerings from their farm produce. The firstborn of the flocks and herds are to be sacrificed to *Yahweh*. This included the firstborn son, although he may be ransomed by paying the priest rather than sacrificing him. This trick is to terrorize the Hebrews with *the threat* of human sacrifice of their firstborn son. Although *the threat is there, as an implied power* of the priests to actually murder their firstborn sons, but in fact, it was a ploy for getting the Hebrews gladly to ransom and redeem their sons by paying the priests.

The Bankers of Babylon were accustomed to the finest foods. They did not want to be joined by filthy goat rustlers who might serve them filthy food. So, they demanded that they not eat "the flesh of an animal that has been savaged by wild beasts." (Exodus 22:31.) The moneylenders were trying to build a community in which they could live safely with all of the best foods and finest comforts. So, they commanded the half-wild Hebrew goat rustlers not to eat dead animals or carrion that they had found bloating in the heat. And the moneylenders' god must not be reviled and the rulers of the Hebrews must not be cursed (Exodus 22:28). Cursing was dangerous because it invoked magical affliction through the god or through the demons.

Because the Bankers of Babylon were setting up a system that primarily benefited themselves, in Exodus 23, they wanted their victims to be truthful. After all, it is easier for them to take advantage of honest people. So, the Hebrews are enjoined to be honest in lawsuits. To avoid losing money, as they had so many times in Babylonia, this honesty is not to be tempered by pity for the poor. When a rich moneylender hauled a poor man before the judges, he wanted to enslave his victim without the judges or the crowds taking the side of liberality or pity. In other words, what the Bankers are setting up in paragraph one, is a law system based on written contracts that cannot be ameliorated by human pity.

Making money and enslaving debtors is serious business and no place for mercy if silver is to be made. In later centuries, this evil philosophy carried by the Jews throughout Europe, made them the most hated of people wherever they went – parasitic and predatory people who gloried in the hatred directed toward them. And what kind of demented glory is it where being the target of hatred is considered to be a virtue? The Jews ruthlessly practiced the Sumerian Swindle wherever they went, received hatred for their endless greed, and returned that hatred with even more malice and hatred. And why? In this sick religion of Judaism, their God of Hatred promised to "punish those who hate me through four generations." Thus, the more the Jews were hated, the more they believed that they were the "holy, chosen ones" of the Yahweh-god, following his "ways and walking in his path," just as The Contract "promised." If the Gentiles hated the Jews, then that meant to the Jews that it was not them but God whom the Gentiles hated. In such ways, the Jews became the most deluded people on earth, a people determined to destroy and enslave the world simply because the moneylenders of Babylon had promised them such a reward in the Laws of Moses. It was a foul and sociopathic religion, written by some foul and psychopathic moneylenders who made their god in their own image.

As a way of welding the Hebrews together into a community, various wise teachings are given on overcoming hatred towards fellow Hebrews by helping them even if they are one's enemy. Letting the land lie fallow every seventh year and taking the Sabbath off from work is here enjoined. But also "do not repeat the name of other gods" (Exodus 23:13) again shows that *Yahweh* is but one of many gods.

The main feasts are given as in the spring the feast of Unleavened Bread and Passover; the feast of Harvest (50 days after Passover) the Ingathering of the grapes (Tabernacles or Shelters, living in shelters) Later other feasts were added: New Year, Day of Expiation, Purim, Dedication, and Day of Nikanor.

This is where the Canaanite taboo was once again given as a Law and it is this one custom that was later expanded by the idiot rabbis for separating milk and meat. The law is: "You must not boil a kid in its mother's milk." (Exodus 23:19.) This ancient taboo of the shepherds throughout the ancient Near East reflected the love and pity all of these pastoralists had for their animals. It was a real shame to kill a kid for dinner and also boil him in his own nanny goat's milk. *This is all that the law reflected.* But once the Pharisees and rabbis began adding their "Tradition of the Elders" to the Torah, they transmogrified this simple law into a multitude of asinine dietary restrictions about mixing dairy products and meat at the same meal. By increasing the number of their laws, the rabbis could increase their profits from the penalties and fines levied on those who broke their laws. The more laws, the more law breakers; resulting in more barbecued goats and silver paid to the priests who wrote the laws and signed God's name to them.

Again, the Yahweh-god is shown to be a god of genocide. "My angel will go before you and lead you to where the Amorites are and the Hittites, the Perizzites, the Canaanites, the Hivites, the Jebusites; I shall exterminate these." (Exodus 23:23.)

As the scribes wrote it: "... you must destroy their gods utterly and smash their standing stones." (Exodus 23:25.) Mixing the methods of slaughtering entire villages and burning them down, destroying sanctuaries and books, erasing all clues of Canaanite religions, raping the little girls, killing the priests, total genocide against the villages to the fourth generation, the demon priests of Yahweh wiped out all true religion and substituted Judaism in its place. This demonic propensity of Judaism was erroneously absorbed into the false teachings of Pauline Christianity as well as fully copied into Islam. The standing stones were not just stones in commemoration of a god, but they were boundary markers. In every country of the ancient Near East, it was a great crime to destroy boundary markers. But here, for the sake of these bandits, their god of genocide commands that they do so. The Hebrews are being ordered to destroy the boundary markers so that they could more easily steal the land and make it their own.

This god of the Jews used the Assyrian methods of terrorism. "I shall spread panic (literally, "send my terror") ahead of you; I shall throw into confusion all the people you encounter; I shall make all your enemies turn and run from you." (Exodus 23:27.) But using terrorism is not the most subtle method because the Bankers of Babylon wanted to take the land of Palestine as subtly as they took the lands of Sumer and Babylonia. The moneylenders wanted to take the land through subversion with as little work and expense as possible.

So, the scribes wrote: "I shall not drive them out before you in a single year, or the land would become a desert where, to your cost, the wild beasts would multiply. Little by little I will drive them out before you until your numbers grow and you come into possession of the land." (Exodus 23:29-30.)

Here is where the scribes set the frontiers of Israel: "For your frontiers I shall fix the Sea of Reeds and the Philistine Sea [Mediterranean Sea], the desert [of Arabia] and the [Euphrates] river; yes, I shall deliver the inhabitants of the country into your hands, and you will drive them out before you." (Exodus 23:31.)

Total extermination and total dispossession and enslavement of the peoples of these countries was to be practiced by the Jews. "You must make no pact with them or with their gods. They must not live in your country or they will make you sin against me; you would come to worship their gods, and that would be a snare for you indeed!" (Exodus 23:33.) After all, what is *Yahweh* other than the lies that the Jews told about him and a bunch of laws that the priests wrote designed to keep the Hebrews obedient?

To the surprise of anyone who actually studies Judaism, there is really nothing that can be called a "religion" found within Judaism. It is a synthetic creation of the moneylenders of Babylonia. It contains nothing that can be classified as actual spirituality and godliness other than ritualistic showmanship. It is lacking the special power of the Holy Spirit which the pagan non-Jews had, but of which the materialistic Jews are ignorant. The spiritual knowledge of other people was forbidden to the Jews because the moneylenders of Babylon wanted an ignorant people who followed their demonic Contract, not an enlightened people who followed God. All signs, symbols, graphic designs, paintings or sculptures representing such spiritual knowledge of the pagans and the religions of other people, were (and are) routinely destroyed by the rabbis. Judaism is less of an actual religion and more of an anti-religion. A true religion seeks to elevate Mankind upward toward God but Judaism seeks to pull Mankind downward, beneath the feet of the Jews who feel themselves elevated above Mankind thereby. The Jews are destroyers of religion. They seek to pull Mankind down into hell with themselves standing on top.

In Exodus 24, Moses used a lot of blood to pour over the altars he built of loose rocks. At this time Moses read the Book of the Covenant and then did some more *abracadabra* by throwing the blood toward the Hebrews as he said, "This is the blood of the Covenant that Yahweh has made with you, containing all these rules." (Exodus 24:8.)

This chapter claims that Moses, Aaron, Nadab and Abiku and 70 elders went up the mountain where "They saw the God of Israel beneath whose feet there was, it seemed, a sapphire pavement pure as the heavens themselves. He laid no hand on these notables of the sons of Israel: they gazed on God. They ate and they drank." (Exodus 24:9-11.) Notables? These scruffy, Hebrew goat rustlers and alleged ex-slaves are here named as "notables"? What is notable about a Jew other than the lies that he tells about God? Then, according to the tale, the cloud covered the mountains and Moses walked in and didn't come out for 40 days and 40 nights.

In Exodus 25, the Bankers of Babylon were very interested in getting the wealth of the temples for free. Their deposits in the temples of Mesopotamia were their own wealth which was separate from the wealth of the temples. But in their new religion, not only did they have a safe place to store their silver and gold but the donations of the people would also be theirs through the fact that the priests were set up to rule from within the family genealogy of Terah's guild of merchant-moneylenders.

In Exodus 25, the scribes wrote a list of the stuff that they wanted. They wrote that their "mighty god" said:

> "Tell the sons of Israel to set aside a contribution for me ... gold, silver and bronze; purple stuffs, of violet shade and red, crimson stuffs, fine linen, goats' hair; rams' skins dyed red, fine leather, acacia wood; oil for the lamps, spices for the chrism and for the fragrant incense; onyx stones and gems to be set in ephod and pectoral. Build me a sanctuary so that I may dwell among them." (Exodus 25:1-9.)

This is identical to the beliefs of all other peoples of the ancient Near East. That is, the gods dwell within the temples that are built for them. In this case (Oy! What a coincidence!), the Yahweh-god had all of the greed for expensive things as did the Bankers of Babylon. The Hebrew god wanted a wooden box built that was gold plated as well as a throne for him to sit on. This "throne of mercy" is to be built with two Babylonian winged cherubs mounted on each side. In the Egyptian style, the cherubs "have the wings spread upwards so that they overshadow the throne of mercy. They must face one another, their faces towards the throne of mercy. You must place the throne of mercy on top of the ark." (Exodus 25:20-21.)

So far, the only thing that differentiates the religion of the Jews from that of the Babylonian religions was that it was conjured up by moneylenders rather than by priests. Even a throne for their god to sit on, was built into the Babylonian design with Egyptian influences. If it was something new or a pure religion from an all-powerful god, then why was it built on a template of everything found in the other religions of Egypt and Mesopotamia? Rather, it was a religion that was lacking in imagination or in original thought because it was not created by "the word of God" as the lying Jews claim; it was created by Terah and Abraham's Guild of Babylonian Moneylenders, building from designs that they already knew.

And what else do moneylender-priests need besides silver and gold? Of course! The scribes of Babylon declared that gold-plated wooden tables and solid gold plates and drinking cups *are required* along with a continuous supply of bread as a "continual offering." And a seven-branched menorah of solid gold was needed to light up all of that golden tableware. Does this seem like a lot for a god to ask of some miserable slaves, running from Pharaoh through the deserts of Sinai? Well, the greedy moneylenders ask for even more than this!

In Exodus 26, once again Assyrian and Babylonian cherubs are commanded to be brocaded on the fabrics and hangings of the tabernacle. A goat hair and red rams-skin tent hangs over the tabernacle. Purple and red goat hair and linen, embroidered with Babylonian cherubs, gold plating and silver tent-pole sockets was a slum-dwelling goat rustlers fantasy. A veil separated the area where the worshipers kneel, from the "Holy of Holies" where the golden throne sat on the tabernacle. The gold table is where the loot was plied up and the gold lamp stand was kept handy with perpetually-burning olive oil.

In Exodus 27, the altar is described as having four horns, one jutting out from each corner. These horns are, again, a Babylonian design element representing the power of bulls and Babylonian gods – and they kept roasted meat from rolling off the tables. The altar was of bronze-plated acacia wood with bronze sacrifice implements for spearing barbecued meat and for splashing blood and stirring hot coals. The oil lamp menorah was to be perpetually burning with, of course, olive oil during the forty years these Hebrews were camping out in the desert while feasting on quails and manna. Did they bring olive oil with them as they were running away from Pharaoh? And in an empty desert where so much wood was needed to roast so many animals, where did the wood come from and what did the animals have to eat?

The genealogical fraud gets passed along in Exodus 28 along with the moneylenders' insistence upon getting as much "prestige" and "dignity' glued on as possible. The scribes write that *Yahweh* ordered Moses: "For Aaron your brother you are to make sacred vestments to give dignity and magnificence." These vestments are to give these Jewish clown-priests the same "dignity" of a crackhead Harlem pimp showing off his zoot suit.

All of the ablest craftsmen were required, "whose ability I have given them, to make Aaron's vestments for his consecration to my priesthood." Included among these fancy embroidery of "gold, purple stuffs, violet shade and red, crimson stuffs, and fine twined linen" (Exodus 28:5), was the ephod. Instead of reading the liver of a sheep to find out what God wanted, the Hebrews used the holy dice cup. By throwing dice and casting lots, they had a direct line to *Yahweh*, Himself. After all, who needs faith and belief or even Moses, himself, when these "holy chosen ones of God" had the holy dice to tell them the will of the god? They had already murdered the priests of other religions who actually knew how to commune with God, so the holy dice was their only hope.

Once the high priest was all decorated with purple and red and gold, he would wear the ephod (the holy dice table) and the Urim and Thummim on his chest so that he could go behind the curtain and cast lots and throw the holy dice (Urim and Thummim) as a way of divining an oracle from his god. Between casting the holy dice and throwing lots on the ephod, the high priest was practicing the only real "wisdom" that the Jews ever had, which wasn't stolen.

Judaism gets even zanier. On the purple, red and gold robe of the priest, gold bells were attached all along the hems "so that the tinkling of the bells will be heard whenever he enters the sanctuary in *Yahweh*'s presence, or leaves it; thus he will not die." (Exodus 28:35.) This was a Babylonian tradition of this Babylonian moneylenders' religion. It comes from the Babylonian custom of adding tinkling bells to the priests' garb in order to frighten away demons who lurked around the entrances to sanctuaries.

As further decoration, the high priest had a plate of pure gold tied to his forehead with the words, "Consecrated to Yahweh" engraved on it. "Aaron is to wear it on his brow, and so take on himself any shortcomings there may be in what the sons of Israel consecrated in any of their sacred offerings." (Exodus 28:38.) The Contract stipulated that the high priest was personally responsible for any shortages in the temple offerings. This was a standard tax-farming law of Babylonia, that is, if the tax collector didn't get all of the taxes from the People, then the difference came out of his own purse. The gold plate tied to his forehead had magic qualities because it would "draw down on them the goodwill of *Yahweh*" (Exodus 28:38) because both *Yahweh* and the moneylenders loved gold.

The fancy clothes of the priest are specifically to "give dignity and magnificence," if such was possible to that bearded clown dressed in red and purple with tinkling bells tied to his dress hem, a holy dice table strapped to his chest with a plate of gold strapped to his forehead. The priests are to wear linen breeches so that their nakedness is covered up. And the fault in not carrying out these orders "means death." Thus, the scribes of Babylon back up their instructions with a death penalty from god as well as from themselves. Oh, those poor, fat priests, suffering under all of those rules before they can gobble down the barbecued goat meat!

Once the fancy clothes are put on in Exodus 29, then Aaron and his sons "by irrevocable ordinance the priesthood will be theirs." (Exodus 29:9.) This part of The Contract allows the priesthood to be inherited and thus kept in the family of the moneylenders.

The sacrifice is another term of The Contract that emphasizes the idea of "sin." This "sin" is a kind of moneylender's debt. That is, by breaking some law of the Yahweh-god, a debt is incurred which must be paid off through some sort of offering to the Temple or to the priests. Laws give power; therefore, write your own laws and get all the power. It's a slick swindle that had been used for centuries in the various Near Eastern temples. But here it is codified. The sacrifice of animals is a "sin offering" where "sin" means a "debt." Thus, paying one's debt to the god of the moneylenders by paying the priests, is an important part of the Jewish religious scam.

Blood, too, is poured all around the Hebrew altars and the "holocaust" of sacrificed animals on the altar is "a burnt offering whose fragrance will appease Yahweh; it will be a holocaust in honor of Yahweh." (Exodus 29:18.) Appeasing the wrathful god, is a continuous labor that keeps the priests well-fed and wealthy while feeding the scraps to Yahweh. Blood is poured all around the Hebrew altar, wiped on Aaron and his sons and sprinkled on Aaron and his clothes. This makes everything all bloody. The lying demon god of the Jews claims that blood means life. But actually, blood is "holy" to the demon god of the Jews because blood means death and the taking of life simply because it can only mean life when it is circulating inside a living creature. Spilled blood means death and the Jews love spilling the blood of the living.

The clown-priests of the Jews make a pantomime of offering bread to the god. Since the god doesn't eat bread, the priests do. Two lambs are offered every day and this is when the Yahweh-god will meet with the priests and talk with them in mumbo jumbo which they can imagine as voices in their heads.

Exodus 30: An altar for burning incense was set up at the entrance to the Tent of Meeting. It was plated with gold and had horns on it like most other altars of the ancient Near East. The best incense was burnt there. To make sure that the temple would have a steady income, a poll tax was set up. The priests not only did a census of the Hebrews but also wrote each name in a register. The Hebrews were required to pay a tax "each is to pay Yahweh a ransom for his life, so that no plague comes on them when the census is made." (Exodus 30:12.) Each person 20 years or older had to pay one-half shekel of silver "as a ransom for your lives" (Exodus 30:15). This was a great swindle, claiming that you had to pay the priest or else the god would zap you with a terrible curse. This money was for maintenance of the service in the Tent of Meeting. The priests had to wash their hands and feet in a bronze basin before approaching the altar. They were not allowed to track in donkey dung on their dirty feet as was the usual custom among the Hebrews.

With all of the blood and guts and slaughtered animal dung, rotting in the heat around the altar, the Jews had to make a fumigant of liquid myrrh, cinnamon, scented cane, cassia and olive oils which was called the "holy chrism." This fragrant perfume was also later reserved "to anoint the king." This anointing makes the king a "sacred person." He is the "anointed of Yahweh" which is, in Hebrew, "the Messiah," and in Greek, "the Christ." Anointing was reserved for the high priest which, taken from the Babylonian tradition, enabled the priest to have the power over the king. It was the priest who passed to the king both the power of god and the backing of the temple. In this way, a solution is always available for Secret Problem #10 of the Sumerian Swindle: "Kings are targets, so it is better to hold the target in your hands than to be a king."

By anointing all of these putrid-smelling sacrificial utensils and the rotting, blood-stained clothes of the priests, "they will excel in holiness, and whatever touches them will be holy." And to keep the recipe for this special Hebrew deodorant reserved to the priesthood, it was forbidden to be copied for ordinary use. The only other place where such a powerful fumigant could be useful other than in a Jewish temple, would be a slaughter house or a public latrine.

Exodus 31: The skill for making fancy stuff for the Tent of Meeting, the Yahweh-god claimed was given to the workmen by none other than Himself. This god claimed that everything is his. So, if a workman has skill in artistry, then that skill is a gift from his god. In this chapter not only is the skill of the craftsmen claimed to be a gift of God but also another of the moneylender swindles is here put forth.

The swindle of the Sabbath is here used as a false "proof" that this goat rustlers' god was actually the author of the Laws of Moses. In this story, Yahweh tells Moses that, "You must keep my Sabbaths carefully, because the Sabbath is a sign between myself and you from generation to generation to show that it is I, Yahweh, who sanctifies you." (Exodus 31:13.)

In other words, keeping the Sabbath alone, is supposed to represent "proof" that Yahweh is the one who decreed the law and no one else.

> "Work is to be done for six days, but the seventh
> day must be a day of complete rest, consecrated to
> Yahweh. Whoever does any work on the Sabbath
> day must be put to death." (Exodus 31:15.)

Since this law was an automatic draft deferment for the moneylenders, they made sure that the stupid Hebrews understood the importance of this law, without telling them the actual reason. The moneylenders of Babylon enforced it with a death penalty.

The power of the death penalty is given to the priesthood. Breaking such laws gave the priest an ultra-extreme power to mete out death to transgressors of Mosaic Law. This was a terrifying weapon which punished the Hebrews for even minor breeches of The Contract. The Hebrews were being subjected to terrorist methods for keeping them in thrall to the tyrannical priests, scribes and, later, to the rabbis. It was not a choice that the Hebrews consciously made. They were the Chosen Ones, alright. The Hebrews of Canaan were chosen by the Bankers of Babylon for their innate, simple-minded stupidity.

Exodus 32 again shows the great wealth that the Hyksos stole from Egypt. Although they are depicted as shepherds and ex-slaves running away through the deserts, there are some monetary facts given that are usually over-looked by Bible commentators. Not only was a huge amount of gold and silver and precious stones used in building the Tent of Meeting and its furniture, the gold lamp stands and all the other decorations for the portable altar, but large amounts of purple and red cloth and hanging tapestries as well. In addition, a census was taken whereby the 600,000 Hyksos were each taxed one-half shek-el of silver. A shekel was about 8 grams of silver. Thus, from the very begin-nings, these "poor ex-slaves" have set up a gold-encrusted temple with a tax-base of 300,000 shekels per year (2.65 tons of silver) right in the middle of a burning desert. If the Jews are to be believed (which they never can be), then they certainly stole a lot more loot from the Egyptians than they initially claimed. After "wandering in the desert" for the forty years that Exodus claims, then the Hebrews paid the priests a total of 106 tons of silver alone, not counting gold and roasted bulls and goats.

But now, in Exodus 32, after this huge expenditure of gold and silver, they are begging Aaron for a golden bull to worship. This golden bull (a com-mon effigy in the ancient Near East) was made out of their gold earrings. Again, there is no way slaves would have gold earrings. So, if you believe the biblical story then they must have stolen all of this from the Egyptians.

This apostasy of the Hebrews is a recurring theme of The Contract. The fables are written with the idea that this great Yahweh-god has done such wonders and has been so powerful, that it is astounding to the readers of this tale that anyone would abandon such a great god. But the Hebrews do abandon the Yahweh-god, leaving the reader to feel superior to them *by his own belief.* Again, the fable is repeated that Yahweh's Contract is based upon a *Promise* which in turn is based upon the genealogically transmitted "blessing" from Abraham, Isaac and Jacob right on up to the priest of the Temple.

Now, Moses dissuades Yahweh from murdering the Hebrews and he descends the mountain with the two tablets containing the Ten Command-ments *which no Jew ever obeyed.* Of course, if Exodus had been written when the Jews claim that it was written, God's writing would have been in Egyptian since the Phoenician-Canaanite-Hebrew alphabet had not yet been invented. Again, the lies of the Rabbis are shown for what they are, since they claim that the Hebrew language is God's very own holy language and the Hebrew alpha-bet was used to write those tablets. The moneylenders of Babylon could not conceive of some future time when archaeologists would dig up the buried cities of Sumeria, Babylonia, Elam and Assyria as well as those in Egypt and prove that of the original languages, none of them were Hebrew. It is very dif-ficult to tell when the Jews are *not* lying, since so many frauds are used to cre-ate Judaism.

This chapter also introduces the idea of the "lesser Jews" whereby the leaders of the Jews and the priests murder those Jews whom they consider both expendable and not pious enough. Aaron says to Moses, "You know yourself how prone this people is to evil." (Exodus 32:23.) And Moses orders the sons of Levi, "Gird on your sword, every man of you, and quarter the camp from gate to gate, killing one his brother, another his friend, another his neighbor." (Exodus 32:27.) After killing between 3,000 and 23,000 Hebrews (depending on the translation), these Levites thus became priests. In this way, the long history of the priests of the Temple murdering anyone not pious enough, was begun.

How can the Jews claim to be a righteous people when their own priests are murderers? And of all the Jews, the Levites murdered the most and for this became priests of the demon god of the Jews. Priests who are murderers! Real heroes of the Jews!

Exodus 33: Once again the genealogical fraud of the alleged "Promise" is repeated where Yahweh promised the land of Palestine to Abraham, Isaac and Jacob. Yahweh says that he will "send an angel in front of you; I will drive out the Canaanites, the Amorites, the Hittites, the Perizzites, the Hivites, the Jebusites. Go on to the land where milk and honey flow. I shall not go with you myself – you are a headstrong people – or I might exterminate you on the way." (Exodus 33:2-3.) Not only is the god of the goat rustlers a god of extermination but he is here shown to be the usual Mesopotamian local god. *He isn't everywhere*! Also, the Hebrews are shown to still have so much loot after all of the gold and silver extracted from them by the priests that "On hearing these stern words the people went into mourning, and no one wore his ornaments." (Exodus 33:4.) The ornaments being, of course, the loot they had stolen from the Egyptians. It takes a great moaning and crying for a Jew not to want to wear his stolen gold and silver ornaments. So, this shows how very sorry they were!

Whenever Moses went to the Tent of Meeting, a dust devil or "pillar of cloud" would station itself at the entrance. In the Tent, Moses is supposed to speak to the Yahweh-god face-to-face like friends. His servant, Joshua, stayed in the Tent of Meeting.

Exodus 34: Here Moses cuts two tablets of stone for *Yahweh* to write on. He schleps these up the mountain of Sinai in the morning where the god of the goat rustlers proclaims his rather demonic attributes worthy of the Bankers of Babylon.

It will be instructive at this point to describe the meaning of the word, "Yahweh." It is the first-person singular, present continuing tense of the Hebrew verb "to be." So it means, "I am" – or more specifically, "I am continuously now at this moment forever." So, whenever the word "Yahweh" is used in the Bible it means "I am." With this knowledge, the following passage makes more sense:

> "*Yahweh* passed before him [Moses] and proclaimed, 'Yahweh, Yahweh, a God of tenderness and compassion, slow to anger, rich in kindness and faithfulness; for thousands he maintains his kindness, forgive faults, transgressions, sin; yet he lets nothing go

unchecked, punishing the father's faults in the sons and in the
grandsons to the third and fourth generation." (Exodus 34:6-7.)

This moneylender god of destruction is now presented in his basic attributes
which are added to what he claims about himself in Exodus 33:19, "I have
compassion on whom I will, and I show pity to whom I please." Thus, this
demon god of the Hebrews shows himself to be only a god of the goat rustlers
and no one else, showing pity to the Hebrew bandits and *destroying the entire
gene pool* of those whom this god of genocide despises – which happens to be
all of Mankind except for the Jews. *Yahweh* is the god of genocide, wiping out
entire nations and destroying people into the fourth generation, with the aid
and efforts of his "holy" Jews. And yet, in the 20th Century AD, these cunning
Jews murdered over a hundred million people through their Communism and
their wars for money, while at the same time declaring themselves to be the
victims of genocide! How they got away with it, is described in Volume III:
The Blood-Suckers of Judah.

But for now, this Jewish psycho-pathology can be understood by the
modern reader if you imagine your great-grandfather whom you perhaps remember when you were a tiny little kid or perhaps he was already gone by the
time you were born. Anyway, when you grow into an adult, a follower of the
God of Genocide sneaks up behind you and strangles you. It is not something
that you can conceive because you have never met this assassin and have no
idea why you are being killed. As you choke out the last of your life, it is a
complete surprise. But the assassin kills you because of something that your
great-grandfather did, even though you don't know what that something was or
even know much about your great-grandfather. You are an innocent victim but
the God of Genocide decreed that as a fourth-generation descendant of your
great-grandfather, you must be killed for his debts. This is the law of the god
of the Jews as stated in the Book of Exodus. This is one reason people always
had a purposely engendered and actively encouraged "fear of the Jews" because the hidden malice that those demons radiated would be expressed at surprising and undeserved times. The people wondered if maybe some evil would
befall them through the Jews by which they did not know its origin. Judaism is
a form of social terrorism.

Again, the scribes of Babylon repeat the phrase by using the salesman's
trick of threatening to withdraw the salable goods so that the customer is induced to buy it while he can. *Yahweh* threatens to remove himself from their
presence so Moses begs, "let my Lord come with us, I beg. True, they are
headstrong people, but forgive us our faults and our sins, and adopt us as your
heritage." (Exodus 34:9.) Oh yes! Let the murdering Hebrew bandits join with
the God of Genocide! How wonderful! What a blessing for Mankind to have
devils posing as innocent saints living among us!

So, the moneylender scribes have their God of Genocide say to Moses:

"I am about to make a covenant [make a deal] with you. In the presence of all your people I shall work such wonders as have never been worked in any land or in any nation. All the people round you will see what *Yahweh* can do, for what I shall do through you will be awe-inspiring. Mark then, what I command you today. I mean to drive out the Amorites before you, the Canaanites, the Hittites, the Perizzites, the Hivites, the Jebusites. Take care you make no pact with the inhabitants of the land you are about to enter, or this will prove a pitfall at your very feet. You are to tear down their altars, smash their standing stones, cut down their sacred poles." (Exodus 34:10-13.)

Thus, the god of the goat rustlers is claiming that the Hebrews are not only to practice genocide by exterminating the people of Palestine but to steal their land, destroy their boundary markers, burn their books and destroy all true religion. Furthermore, this god of the goat rustlers claims that "Yahweh's name is the Jealous One; he is a jealous God" (Exodus 34:14). This is just one more negative attribute of the demons who wrote the Book of Exodus. Yet, regardless of all this bragging thunder, none of this happened. Modern archaeology proves that there was no Conquest of Canaan as the *Hebrew Bible* claims. The god of the Jews was a lying God of Liars.

Archaeology has uncovered an Egyptian stronghold to the south of the Sea of Galilee. It contained numerous monuments and hieroglyphs of the pharaohs Seti I (1294-1279 BC), Ramesses II (1279-1213 BC), and Ramesses III (1184-1153 BC). The garrison city of Megiddo and the various Egyptian garrisons throughout the country would not have stood idly by as a group of refugees from Egypt attacked the province of Canaan. And it is inconceivable that the destruction of so many loyal vassal cities by the alleged "invaders" would have left no trace in the extensive records of the Egyptian Empire. When the biblical account is compared to the archaeological evidence and to the Egyptian records, it is evident that the Jewish priests and rabbis have been lying to the world for the past three thousand years.

But in the Book of Exodus, to keep the wealth in their own hands, the merchant-moneylender scribes wrote,

"All that first issues from the womb is mine: every male, every firstborn of flock or herd. But the firstborn donkey you must redeem with an animal from your flocks. If you do not redeem it, you must break its neck. You must redeem all the firstborn of your sons. And no one is to come before me empty-handed." (Exodus 34:19-20.)

Thus, the moneylender-priests assured themselves a steady food supply with an income from the Hebrew goat rustlers. This is a very important part of The Contract that the moneylenders were trying to establish. For their religious swindle to be successful, they had to make sure that their priests were well-fed and well-paid and that no one could escape their taxes. A donkey is a valuable pack animal and not to be eaten. Even so, the donkey's owner must either pay the tax or a gang of Jewish priests would murder the donkey, leaving the owner with nothing. So that the moneylenders, themselves, did not have to support this organization of voracious priests, the money had to come out of the Hebrews and not out of their own pockets. Paying a tithe was enough to ensure each member of The Contract the benefits of a Temple membership such as interest-free loans, one day off per week, business intelligence, cartel price fixing, free travel lodging, exemption from military service, safety inspected food, etc. That was all for the benefit of the merchant-moneylenders. But the priests would have to be fed by the congregation.

As a part of The Contract, and to keep production at a high level, the Sabbath rest is again invoked. The Feast of Weeks, First Fruits and Ingathering are declared so that both the farmers and the pastoralists can both pay their taxes to the priests. And three times per year, all of the men-folk have to present themselves before the priests. Since the Yahweh-god is a god who wants gold and silver and barbecued meat well-roasted on the altar and who has commanded that "no one is to come before me empty-handed," then of course, in addition to everything else that is due to the priests, all of the men-folk three times a year have to bring additional gifts. This is a well-conceived scam, carefully thought out for maximum profits. And in exchange, the goat rustler god declares, "When I have dispossessed the *goyim* (non-Jewish, lowly insects, stupid cattle) for you and extended your frontiers, no one will covet your land, if you present yourselves three times in the year before Yahweh your god." (Exodus 34:24.) Dispossessing all of Mankind, is automatically built into the Sumerian Swindle, the swindling scam of the bankers. It can be done by lending money at interest which eventually puts ownership of the entire world into the hands of the bankers. And here, this very idea is promoted by the Bankers of Babylon, authors of the Torah, because now they have a place to deposit all of their loot.

Yahweh, this mighty god who created the universe and fasted for ten billion years before he found any goat rustlers to feed Him, demands fresh food:

> "You must not offer the blood of the victim sacrificed to me at
> the same time as you offer unleavened bread, nor is the victim
> offered at the feast of Passover to be put aside for the following
> day. You must bring the best of the first-fruits of your soil to the
> house of Yahweh your god." (Exodus 34:25-26.)

The ancient shepherd's taboo is again declared: "You must not boil a kid in its mother's milk." (Exodus 34:26.) The latter-day evil rabbis, in their demonic ignorance, have used this Mesopotamian taboo to create a corpus of laws governing milk and meat, all with an eye to keeping the Hebrews dependent upon their utterances of multitudinous laws that they themselves, wrote; and paying "sin offerings" for breaking those laws.

Yahweh orders Moses to "Put these words in writing, for they are the terms of the covenant [Contract] I am making with you and with Israel." (Exodus 34:27.) So, Moses allegedly stayed in the tent for forty days and forty nights, eating and drinking nothing, while chiseling on a stone tablet the Ten Words. After speaking with *Yahweh*, Moses' face would radiate so much that he put a veil over his face. This always happens when liars are caught, their faces radiate with embarrassment. And Moses was telling some whoppers!

Exodus 35: These last chapters (35 through 40) of Exodus is almost a word for word repetition of chapters 25 through 31; there the orders are given and here they are carried out. The lists of treasures that these thieving scoundrels had stolen from Egypt is again listed which they must contribute to the priests of the Tabernacle.

> "And all those whose heart prompted them to give came, bringing their contribution for Yahweh for making the Tent of Meeting, for all its functions and for the sacred vestments. They came, men and women, all giving willingly, bringing broaches, rings, bracelets, necklaces, gold things of every kind, all those who had vowed to Yahweh some article of gold. All those who happened to own purple stuffs, of violet shade or red, crimson stuffs, fine linen, goats' hair, rams' skins dyed red, or fine leather, brought them." (Exodus 35:21-23.)

This mention of "purple stuffs" and "crimson stuffs" are the royal purple-dyed fine linens worn only by nobility. Purple dye was very expensive, a Phoenician monopoly, and only the extremely wealthy could afford it. Also, the red-dyed stuffs refer to the dye extracted from the madder root, a bright red dye for leather and cloth that was imported from Anatolia – not as expensive as the purple, but it was still too expensive for any but the wealthy.

So, once again, these were not poor ex-slaves who had "borrowed" a few trinkets and ornaments from their Egyptian masters so that they could be dressed up fancy for their god in the desert, as the fable claims. These were extremely wealthy thieves who had been looting Egypt for 108 years and who were able to escape with all of their loot by the mercy of Pharaoh. Their carts and donkey packs were bulging with loot and the moneylender guild of Abraham wanted it. The onyx stones and gems, the spices and fragrant oils, the precious incense, all were part of the loot, not a part of what dirty slaves could beg from unwilling Egyptian masters. And among the craftsmen, Bezalal of the tribe of Judah made all of this fancy glitter and bling for the Tabernacle. This is a literary foreshadowing of the future prominence of the tribe of Judah.

Exodus 36: The Babylonian merchant-moneylenders didn't want the Hebrews to be stingy with offering to the Temple. So, they wrote that *even more than necessary amounts* of loot were brought to the Tent of Meeting.

Exodus 37: Bezalal of the tribe of Judah and Oholiab of the tribe of Dan, made the Tent and all the Babylonian cherubs and the "throne of mercy" from which no mercy would ever be dispensed, only hatred for Mankind and the malice of demonic Jews infesting the world.

Exodus 38: The moneylenders were careful to tally up the wealth in this chapter. The total gold used was 29 talents and 730 shekels. The silver collected from the census of the community weighed 100 talents and 1,775 shekels for everyone over twenty years old. This numbers 603,550 people.

> "The hundred talents of silver were used for casting the sockets for the sanctuary and for the veil: one hundred sockets out of 100 talents, or one talent per socket. With the 1,775 shekels he made the hooks for the posts, the plating for their capitals, and the rods. The bronze consecrated by offerings amounted to seventy talents and 2,400 shekels, and with this he made … [all the other stuff]."

One talent equals about 30 kilograms or 66 pounds. Impressive weights for the post sockets of a tent! One shekel is about 8 grams and there are 3600 shekels in a talent. So, the total weight of the metal alone was 6010 kilograms or approximately 13,250 pounds or 6.6 tons (6 metric tons)! This was not the total that the Hebrews had because the story plainly indicates that they had a lot more since the Hebrews *only gave a portion* of their loot to the Tent of Meeting project. That's a lot of weight for goat rustlers to be carrying around in a waterless desert. And since the pack load of a donkey is only about 65 to 70 kilograms, that means that anywhere from 85 to 92 donkeys would be needed to carry *just the metal* without the additional weight of the tent, itself. That's a lot of donkeys to be feeding and watering in a waterless desert. That's a lot of wood needed to feed the fires that melted the metal in a treeless desert where all there was to eat was quails and manna. Although it can be argued that this total is not very much when distributed among over 603,550 men over the age of 20 plus their wives and children. But the scribes of Babylon have told even greater lies than this, so why not believe them this time? Isn't that a sign of "having faith," by believing the lies of proven thieves, murderers and con artists? Does "faith" require you to believe impossible lies?

Exodus 39: Using the "prestige" of this genealogical swindle, the names of the goat rustler tribes are exalted. Now, the Jewish priest, a hairy-faced, stinking, old goat rustler dressed like a Negro pimp at a cocaine party, all in purple and red and gold with a gold plate strapped to his forehead, is also given onyx jewels to make him appear to be even more wonderful. Engraved on each jewel is the names of the sons of Israel and mounted with the settings of gold mesh and fastened to the shoulder straps of the golden, holy dice table (ephod) that is strapped to the priest's shaggy chest. This holy dice table is the priest's pectoral upon which they set twelve gem stones, one for each tribe: sard, topaz, carbuncle, emerald, sapphire, diamond, hyacinth, ruby, amethyst, beryl, onyx, jasper. Then to totally pimp out the priest, they hung "bling" all over him of gold chains with gold bells on the hems to scare away demons. And then to make the Jewish priest even more goat rustler "holy," he was splattered with the blood from the cut throats of innocent sheep and goats. Such a ridiculous demon clown never existed in any other religion except, perhaps, among the cannibal Aztec Indians of Mexico.

Exodus 40: Once all of the fancy decorations were completed, the swindle of slipping their thieving fat asses into the priesthood took place. First, Moses tabulated all the loot and then "Moses blessed them." And now comes the switcheroo. The mythical Moses is to anoint with blood, Aaron and his sons and "to confer the priesthood on them in perpetuity from generation to generation." (Exodus 40:15.) In this way, the priesthood could be kept in the moneylender family and passed down to the priest's sons.

First, the Yahweh-god commands through the voices in Moses' head that the gold-encrusted Tabernacle be set up. Then the scribes wrote that it was, in fact, set up "exactly as Yahweh had directed" (Exodus 40:16) through the stinking mouth of Moses. Soon, all was ready. A thick cloud of buzzing flies hovered around the tent, crawling all over the rotting blood. And a putrid, gagging stench hung in the hot air. Both of these were described as "the glory of Yahweh filled the tabernacle. Moses could not enter the Tent of Meeting because the cloud [of flies] that rested on it and because the [gagging stench] glory of Yahweh that filled the tabernacle." (Exodus 40:34-35.)

So, the goat rustlers would only travel when the cloud buzzed away from the tabernacle and gave them a chance to haul it away – all six tons of gold, a huge package of tent flaps and wooden tent poles that had conveniently appeared out of no where in the treeless desert, and all of the furniture, all packed onto about ninety or more donkeys. The donkeys would, of course, also have to be fed with manna and quails since there were no trees and nothing to eat in the deserts of Sinai.

Truly, if you believe what the Jews say, that is a real miracle. Archaeology proves the Book of Exodus to be an impossible lie. But it is a lie that the Jews, Christians and Muslims all believe to be true, so that makes it an even greater miracle. And when the cloud of flies swarmed around the tent and didn't rise, the Hebrews waited in the desert. Only when some wind blew the flies and stink away did this group of thieves and goat rustlers, "gird their loins," that is, tie up their dangling, circumcised dongs and nuts with duct tape and set forth to steal Palestine. What!? You don't believe that the Jews girded their loins with duct tape? Well, you believe everything else the Jews wrote in Exodus, so why can't duct tape also be one of their miracles?

6.4 The Book of Leviticus and the Laws of the Snooping Temple Priests of Levi

Leviticus was the first biblical book from which Jewish children were taught so as to get the young Jews acclimated to blood and guts and filthy dead animals thrashing around on the gore-smeared floor of the Temple. This horrible Book of Leviticus celebrates the holocaust or the "wholly burned," that is, bloody slaughter and the burning up of what the priests don't eat.

In the first Chapter of Leviticus, the moneylenders of Babylon write that their Yahweh-god demands that all of the blood from the sacrificial victims be poured out around the altar, the head and the fat and various pieces are put on the altar, the stinking guts and dirty legs are washed in water and all of it is burned on the altar. "This holocaust will be a burnt offering and the fragrance of it will appease Yahweh." (Leviticus 1:9.) The altar of the Yahweh-god was a stinking, rotten, fly-swarming slaughtering floor. The foul stench of rotted meat and blood, mixed with the stink of animal dung and burst open intestines was enough to gag a maggot. But to the devil priests of Yahweh, it was all a "fragrance to appease" the demon god of the moneylenders.

Again in Leviticus 2, the wheat flour of an offering is to be given to the priests while a handful with incense is to be burnt on the altar. The same division between the priests and the god was made with baked and fried breads, with the priests getting the most and the god getting a handful. These are presented to the priests who burn a small sample and then eat the remainder. The Yahweh-god commands that offerings must not be salted because the priests want to salt their own food. Thus, even from the poorest Hebrew who can only offer a few crackers as an offering, the priests take the larger portion every time.

To make sure that they got the best cuts of meat, in Leviticus 3 the priests wrote that Yahweh's favorite offering was the part that the rabbis found unappetizing. A sacrifice as a burnt offering to Yahweh was to be "the fat that covers the entrails, all the fat that is on the entrails, the two kidneys, the fat on them and on the loins, the fatty mass which he is to remove from the liver and kidneys." (Leviticus 3:3-4.) Thus, the Bankers of Babylon claimed that their god was satisfied with the fat and the guts while the priests ate the steaks. "All the fat belongs to Yahweh. This is a perpetual law for all your descendants, wherever you may live: never eat either fat or blood." (Leviticus 3:17.) There was a cunning reason behind this for creating a bloodthirsty brood of devils who would crave and desire what was denied to them. In later centuries, this bloodthirsty mania would produce the most monstrous Crimes Against Humanity ever perpetrated by the demonic Jewish fiends.

Guaranteeing that the Temple would be financed by outside contributions also guaranteed that the bullion on deposit in the temple treasury would not be confiscated for Temple business. The method that the Bankers of Babylon developed for swindling wealth into their temple was a variety of offerings to the Yahweh-god. There were a variety of "debts" that they called "sins." These "sins" were alleged insults to the god or infringements upon the laws of the god. A unique thing about penalties for which the People must pay a fine, is that such fines cannot be imposed unless there is first a law decreed. Once there is a law, then fines can be imposed upon anyone who breaks the law. The rabbis' job was to make sure that there were plenty of laws to break so that the breaking of them would provide plenty of revenue for the temple in the form of "guilt offerings" or "sin offerings" or "offerings of atonement." None of these laws meant anything at all and were totally inane, but the more there were of them, the greater the chance that there would be plenty of "guilt" and "sin" and "atonement" fines due to the priests. These fines were the income of the Hebrew priests *in addition to* their one-tenth tithe of all business and agricultural profits of the Hebrews. So, the Jewish priests were very strict in applying all of the Laws of Moses and whatever other laws that they could dream up for enslaving the Hebrews and racking the profits of "sinning" off into their purses.

Leviticus 4 deals with "accidental sin" or breaking a law inadvertently. To make sure that the priests didn't have to pay for their own mistakes, the scam was *to make the people guilty* for the sins of the demon priests. The bloodthirsty nature of stinking Judaism comes forth in the blood that is to be sprinkled on the temple veil and the blood of an ox poured out at the foot of the altar of holocaust. Then, the fat is burned in a big, stinking pile, a "sweet savor" for the Canaanite Yahweh-god's invisible nostrils.

From the murdered bull, the "skin, all its flesh, its head, legs, entrails and dung," is all hauled to the ash heap and burned. (Leviticus 4:11-12.) In this way, the Hebrews were taught that they could be forgiven for their sins by making some other living creature pay in their stead – the ancient Scapegoat Magic of sin transference. Blaming someone else for their own transgressions and crimes, became a standard of Judaism from the very earliest times. The Jews always escaped the penalty for their own crimes by blaming someone else, anyone else. Their Jewish god chose them to terrorize and genocide and impoverish the *goyim* (lowly insects, stupid cattle). So they were, of course, always innocent of any crime of terror or genocide they did, because it was all God's fault. He made them do it. From putting their sins on the head of a scapegoat and pushing him off a cliff, to blaming the Russians for Communism and the British for the Opium Trade and the Muslims for 9/11, was all the same ancient fraud of this diabolical moneylender's religious hoax.

Leviticus 5 was a real moneymaker for the rabbis. This chapter makes "guilt" into a quantifiable and profitable reality. The priests who wrote Leviticus set up their scams for "forgiving sins." Breaking the laws that they, themselves, wrote meant that the Hebrews had to pay silver shekels for the crime, that is, to "atone for their sin." It was a smooth operation, this Temple swindle. Instead of selling tangible goods, like the temples of Mesopotamia did with their attached factories and business warehouses, the priests of the Yahweh cult sold "forgiveness of sins." This forgiveness was based on the Semitic principle of *lex talionis*, an eye-for-an-eye. In this case, when a Hebrew broke one of the rabbinical "laws," innocent animals paid the price, and silver was offered to the priests to erase any residuals from the holy account books.

The demonic priests of Yahweh killed oxen, bulls, goats, sheep, turtle-doves and pigeons and poured their blood at the foot of the altar. Then they sprinkled some of the blood on the side of the altar and wiped some of the blood on the horns of the altar. They sprinkled some blood on the veil before the altar, wiped some blood on their right big toes, on their right thumb and on their right ear lobe just to make sure some sins weren't hiding there. Blood and more blood from the innocent, is demanded as payment for the sins of the Jews. Many innocent animals must die so that a few Jews can feel good about themselves. The stench in the Temple was a putrid-smelling slaughter house reeking of incense to conceal the gagging odor of the Jewish god and his priests.

Believe it or not, the Jews cleaned their holy vestments and priestly robes with urine! If cleanliness is next to godliness, then the Jews are as far away from God as any devil can possibly be. Here is the time-tested Jewish recipe for cleaning the blood off of their underwear and priestly vestments.

Throughout the Torah and the *Babylonian Talmud*, the rabbis write about what they call "clean." While the average person might imagine that they know the definition of "clean," this is something very different than what the word, "clean," actually means to a Jew. For example, if a normal person finds something dirty, the first thing they do is wash it with soap and water. Right? But soap and water are *the very last thing* an Orthodox rabbi uses to clean any-thing. According to the *Babylonian Talmud*, when a Jew finds a stain on cloth, the first thing to do is to spit on it. If that doesn't make it "clean," then rub on the liquid of crushed beans. If it is still dirty, then *fermented urine that is at least three days old* is used. If that doesn't clean it then natron (a type of alka-line salt) is rubbed on. If the stain is still there, then the dirt from a river is scrubbed into it. If that doesn't clean it up, then the root of a plant called lion's leaf, is used to foam it up. If none of these things clean the stain, then the rab-bis conclude that the stain is a dye.

But if it faded away after all of these treatments, then the rabbis conclude that the stain was "unclean" blood and the entire process must be repeated from the beginning to make it "clean." But if the stain is still there after repeat-ing the entire process – Guess what? – *the very last thing* that a Jew does, is to wash it with soap and water! If the stain then disappears under soap and water – Guess what? – the ingenious rabbis declare that it is "unclean"! That's some of the wisdom of the "sages" of Israel, here copied directly from their holiest book, the *Babylonian Talmud*, Nidah 61b-62a.

"Clean" and "unclean" mean absolutely nothing by the definitions of the Jews. There is no standard in fact, because the rabbis make more money by defining the word by whim rather than by truthful logic. This is why so many commentators throughout history have recorded in their observations how nau-seatingly stinky the Jews were, because "cleanliness" is a mere rabbinical *ritu-al*, not a fact.

In a like manner, "sins" among the Jews have absolutely nothing to do with morality. What are called "sins" are defined by the Jews as anything that is against "Yahweh's sacred rights." Breaking one of the various and many laws only means a profit for the priests. There is no actual "morality" in Judaism, only rituals and phony laws written by ignorant, swinish rabbis and evil Jewish priests. So, the more laws the rabbis invent, the more "sinners" who must pay a fee (called a "sacrifice for sin") in order to be "forgiven." Judaism is a fraud and a swindle.

Leviticus 5 introduces the concept of someone breaking a temple law *inadvertently*. It is very clear that a pious Hebrew can plead, "I didn't know that what I did was against Mosaic Law." In order to insure that the Temple could still profit, Leviticus 5 claims that even "inadvertently" breaking a law was still a punishable offense. This Leviticus 5 is very clever in how The Contract was written. The big sins such as touching something "unclean" which every Hebrew would know how to avoid, are forgiven with a blood sacrifice. This is not a very big profit for the Temple. But the smaller "sins," the "inadvertent sins" against "Yahweh's sacred rights," where the average Hebrew was more likely to transgress, *these also involved paying silver to the priest*. This "sacrifice of reparation" was to be a ram "valued in silver shekels." Whatever the value of the ram, the sinner was to "add one-fifth to the value, and give it to the priest." (Leviticus 5:16.)

> "The priest shall perform the rite of atonement over him for the oversight he has committed without realizing it and he will be forgiven. This is a sacrifice of reparation; the man was certainly answerable to Yahweh." (Leviticus 5:18-19.)

The Contract of Leviticus 5 claims that "Yahweh spoke to Moses" and commanded these temple rites. The various sacrifices at the beginning and end of the chapter surround and hide the central point, that is, "inadvertent sin," the sin that the vast majority of Hebrews would be committing, these would be the most profitable to the priests because the "sinner" would sacrifice a ram *plus* pay the priest in silver one-fifth of the value of the ram. This same method is used in modern times where Jewish lawyers write the laws that govern modern People.

In Leviticus 6, hiding the source of the moneylender swindle has always been a high priority. In the case of the flour that is brought to the temple, Aaron and his sons burn some of it and eat the rest of it. But to hide the fact that all of the sacrificial flour and meat comes from the People, Leviticus 6 has *Yahweh* saying "... Aaron and his sons shall eat the remainder in the form of unleavened loaves .... The portion I give them of my burnt offering must not be baked with leaven." (Leviticus 6:9, 17.) In this sleight of hand, it is *Yahweh* who is giving Aaron the bread. And to insure the big genealogical Jewish *asl* absorbs this "inheritance," Leviticus states: "All of the males of Aaron's family may eat this portion of Yahweh's burnt offering (this is a perpetual law for all your descendants; and everyone who touches it will be consecrated)." (Leviticus 6:18.) Once again, the hocus-pocus of touching the sacrificial goods is what "consecrates" the priests, not any innate virtue of their own.

However, when I use the word "hocus-pocus" to describe the methods of sorcery that was used by the Hebrew priests, this is not entirely correct. "Hocus-pocus" is more of a European idea of magical words used to bring about some sort of change. The word is derived from "Ochus Bochus," an Anglo-Saxon magician of Norse folklore. More appropriately, the magical words used by the Aramaic-speaking Hebrew priests and the Aramaic-speaking merchant-moneylender scribes of Babylonia was "Abracadabra." The word stems from the Aramaic "*Ahbra Kedahbra*" which translates to "I will create as I speak." This idea that the priests of Yahweh could magically create the forgiveness of sins merely through rituals and the saying of blessings became an important part of the Jewish Kabbalah and Jewish sorcery. Since the priests and rabbis speak for God, anything they say must be true – even when they are telling lies! Thus, the false assumption by anyone who reads the *Hebrew Bible* has always been that the Jewish priests were telling the truth because they claimed to speak for God. The *Hebrew Bible* is some real *abracadabra*. And when Jesus told the truth about them – that the Jews are liars, deceivers, hypocrites and murders – the Jews killed him.

All of this *abracadabra* of the priests is used to hide the fact that the priests eat the "sin offering." They break the earthenware bowls it is cooked in and scrub the bronze pots with a lot of noise and clatter. By making a big show that the pots were broken and the bronze pots thoroughly scrubbed to magically destroy the sins of the people, they could hide with the magician's technique of misdirection the fact that the Jewish priests were eating what was in those pots.

Leviticus 7 has more bloody sacrifices for feeding the priests. In this case, after pouring the blood around the borders of the altar, the priests burn all of the inedible fat for the Yahweh-god while all the priests chant, "it is a most holy thing." (Leviticus 7:6.) Then, every male priest gets to eat the barbecue. This is the Sacrifice of Reparation. All of the meat, all of the cakes and breads are eaten by the priests and their families. The skin of the animal, the priests sell to the tanner.

The Jewish priests devised sacrifices for holocaust, for oblation, for sins, for reparations, sacrifices of praise, votive sacrifices, atonement sacrifices, investiture sacrifices, communion sacrifices, sacrifices for "unintentional sins." All of the sacrifices of meat, vegetables, flour, wine and silver, revert to the priests. All of these provide plenty of food and silver for the voracious demon priests and their huge families. And to make sure that they don't catch botulism in the hot climate, they are allowed to eat the meat on the second day but to throw it on the fire on the third day. Only the best steaks and prime rib and filet mignon is for the priests while the Yahweh-god is content with the fat and the blood. Again, the prohibition is given, "You must not eat the fat of ox, sheep or goat" and "you must not eat blood whether it be of bird or beast." (Leviticus 7:24, 26.) The Jewish women washed all meats in water and squeezed out the last drop of blood possible before cooking it. By restricting the Hebrews from tasting blood, the moneylenders of Babylon conditioned the

Hebrews to be bloodthirsty murderers, lusting after blood, just the kind of followers most desired for Abraham's First National Bank and Pawn Shop.

The *abracadabra* of the priests is listed in Leviticus 8. It is a form of street theater to claim that the special clothes and fancy jewelry that the priests wear, was ordered by God. Moses claims: "This is what Yahweh has ordered to be done." (Leviticus 8:5.) Rituals, where the priests haughtily make a mime of doing "holy" tasks such as bowing to the altar and waving bread and baskets of vegetables in the air toward the altar as if presenting it to the invisible Yahweh-god before eating it themselves, was all street theater designed to impress the ignorant onlookers. This is what the ritual was all about, the motions meant nothing at all but because the congregation thought that they had some deep and mystical meaning performed in front of a god seated behind a curtain, these empty rituals took on an aura of holiness to the onlookers. It was all just hocus-pocus. Although there is a God, there is no god in Israel. The Jews just lie about it.

For the ignorant goat rustlers, killing animals and smearing their blood all around, was supposed to magically "take away its sin." (Leviticus 8:15.) This idea of "sin" applied to inanimate objects such as the altar, itself. "Sin" to the Hebrews was a kind of evil spirit that could be exorcised by covering it with blood. These Jews equated blood as a protecting elixir – as long as it was the blood of their victims and not their own blood.

A bull and two goats were eaten by Aaron and his sons and their families, feasting among the smell of rotten blood and the flies swarming thickly around the altar of Yahweh, each day for seven days as they sat in front of the entrance of the tent in plain sight of everyone. This whole ritual was repeated daily for seven days, out there in the desert, eating a bull and two goats every day for seven days of priestly gluttony. The actual reason for Leviticus 8, is to normalize the conspicuous consumption of the Jewish priests.

The priests of other gods would eat the leftovers from the sacrifices and offerings out of sight of their congregations so as to maintain propriety and decorum. The priests of other religions respected the sacrifices made by the People who had worked hard for the sake of God. What was left over from the sacrifices would be eaten in private by the pagan priests and their families. This was their pay for maintaining the god's temple.

But the god of the moneylenders was a god of conspicuous consumption. It was the habit of the Babylonian moneylenders to flout their wealth before the very people whom they had defrauded and, while wearing their gold and their jewels and fine clothes, to eat bountiful meals in front of the starving workers whom they had defrauded and enslaved. So, those callous and cruel swindlers wanted a god who reflected their own crassness and created in their own image. Pouring out the blood of a bull and two goats and splattering it all over their clothes, making a mime of offering all of this meat to the Yahweh-god, and then eating as much as they could every day for seven days (Leviticus 8:31-36), was making a show of gluttony designed for the priests, alone. Although the Hebrews might want to join in the barbecue, it was a tasty and very convenient commandment of their devil god that the priests, alone, were to gorge on those unfortunate animals.

For seven days and nights, the Jewish priests were to remain in front of the Tent of Meeting in plain sight of the People, pouring out and sprinkling the blood and eating a freshly roasted bull and two goats every day for seven days. That's a lot of meat for the priests to eat in front of the People. That's a lot of animals needing fodder and grass and grain, there in the deserts of Sinai. That's a lot of wood required to do all of that cooking, there in the treeless desert. And everything left over was not to be given back to the Hebrews but was to be burned. In this way, the Hebrews were conditioned into accepting the idea that the priests could eat and waste a huge amount of food even as the people starved. And to legitimize the swindle, the priests claimed that God had ordered Moses to make the laws. It was never to be claimed that the priests were anything more than worshipers of the Yahweh-god. It was thus, God, Himself, who decreed that the priests be gluttons. Of course, it could never be admitted that the priests were gluttons by intrinsic character. They were innocently doing what their god commanded. They were "chosen" to do it; it wasn't their fault.

Two ideas are promoted in Leviticus 9: the conspicuous consumption of the priests and the idea of perpetual sin (debt) that can only be paid by having *someone else* pay for their sins. This street theater is repeated now with Aaron performing the ritual slaughter of innocent animals and smearing their blood as atonement for the sins of the Hebrews. To make this chapter more inspiring, the Scribes of Babylon wrote:

> "Then they (Aaron and Moses) came out together to bless the
> people and the glory of Yahweh appeared to the whole people –
> a flame leaped forth from before Yahweh and consumed the
> holocaust and the fat that was on the altar. At this sight the peo-
> ple shouted for joy and fell on their faces." (Leviticus 9:23-24.)

That the Hebrews were being deceived and enslaved by the rabbis was concealed by the claim that the Hebrews "shouted for joy." Once the moneylenders had passed the priesthood along to Aaron and his sons, there was no need to have any connection to the mythical Moses because the genealogy of the Babylonian moneylenders was now traced by them from Aaron and his sons.

All of this *abracadabra* of the priests needed to be legitimatized by doing everything exactly as Moses claimed that the Yahweh-god had commanded. This is Secret Fraud #17 of the Sumerian Swindle: "Kings are required to legitimatize a swindle but once the fraud is legalized, those very kings must be sacrificed." In this case, the king was the big, bad Yahweh-god sitting invisibly on his golden throne under the wings of two Babylonian idols. Laws can only have power over people if there are penalties for breaking the laws. This is the whole point of Leviticus 10. The importance of these empty rituals was established in Leviticus 9 and in Leviticus 10. Two of Aaron's own sons performed the ritual not in exact accordance to the rules. They offered the altar fire and incense in a censer.

> "Then from Yahweh's presence a flame leaped out and con-
> sumed them, and they perished in the presence of Yahweh."
> (Leviticus 10:2.)

It was not the "sins" of Aaron's sons but the entire Hebrew people against whom the Yahweh-god was angry. The idea was, that *the entire people* had to work together to pay the debt that Yahweh claimed against them. These laws that "Yahweh has pronounced for them through Moses" (Leviticus 10:11) can only be broken under pain of death. This applies to the laws of Moses and the rules of clean and unclean, *to break those laws meant death* at the hands of the rabbis whose "legal" power was based upon the very lies that they had written, themselves.

Now, the barbecued meat is ready to be eaten and the priests and their families are commanded to eat it because "it is a most holy thing." (Leviticus 10:12.) In Leviticus 10, the priests have established themselves as the rightful eaters of everything, including the Sacrifice for Sin. The clever method for legitimatizing their parlor tricks was to establish the priests as *victims*. They must either follow Yahweh's prescribed rules and laws of step-and-fetch-it, or else fire from the sky would consume them. A real clever deceit! Pretending to be in fear, quailing and quaking before the empty golden throne under the cherubs' wings, pretending subservient humility, lifting up the bread and wine before the altar and waving it in the air, was not such a difficult job for these priests in exchange for such high power, high pay and limitless feasts.

Unlike the priests of the other Mesopotamian gods, the rabbis did not merely eat the sacrifice by assuring that these foods should not go to waste. The rabbis wanted to enshrine their gluttony and greed into laws from God, Himself. So, Leviticus 10 does this. It claims the right of the priests to eat all sacrifices. In this way, no pious person who made an animal sacrifice could object to the priests eating what he had offered to the god since the priest – poor shivering victim that he was – was only following the laws that came from God, Himself. So, how could the priest refuse all of that tasty barbecue with bread and wine and the silver and gold offerings by the Hebrews since it was the god of the moneylenders, Himself, who had commanded it? Like all Jews, the priests were just innocent victims of this "mighty god" *who had chosen them* against their will.

As religious taboos for ritual worship, the idea of what is "clean" and "unclean" is given in Leviticus 11. The idea is promoted that the Yahweh-god demands the best and the most pure priests to serve him and so he makes laws that determine the "clean" foods for those priests to eat. That the priests wrote the laws, is not considered by the rabbis to be worth discussing. That the priests benefit from the best foods, is not considered. That the Yahweh-god picks only foods that are delicious on the altar barbecue and avoids foods that are nasty tasting, is never mentioned. What is "clean" or "unclean" hides the scam because they are two words that have only a *ritual meaning* and are not connected at all with hygiene. Through mere ritual, the skanky whore of Judaism is dressed in fancy clothes, which are sprinkled with blood and washed with urine, then fumigated with incense and ritually declared to be "clean" and "holy." With *abracadabra*, the Jews declare themselves to be a "holy" people.

Another self-serving use of Jewish "law" is the example of locusts and grasshoppers. Unlike all other insects, locusts are considered "clean" because locusts are not only nutty-flavored and nutritious when fried, but they are the "manna" of the desert. That was the "manna" that all desert dwellers ate and it can only be gathered in the morning because these insects are inactive in the chilly morning dew. The Jewish idea of "clean" or "unclean" is a game of tag. So, it pops in and out of the biblical text at odd times. To a rabbi, "clean" or "unclean" is – Abracadabra – a matter of declaration, not a matter of sanitation. Thus, the filthiest, stinkiest Jew wearing a fringed shawl with a little box strapped to his forehead, is "clean" only because he follows all of the rabbinical rules, even though he actually stinks to high heaven.

The Hebrews were taught in Leviticus 11 that "clean" or "unclean" is a physical state which can be induced through touch. Being constantly reminded that touching some things is allowed and touching other things is forbidden, gives these goat rustlers taboos that separate them from other people. Not only is the touching of the "unclean" things forbidden but their "uncleanness" remains upon the Hebrew and his clothing, "unclean until evening." Since evening is the beginning of a new "day" for the Moon God, night time was the time when the new day of "cleanness" began, in the dark minds of the Jews. Furthermore, the variety of taboo creatures, even when they are dead, magically pass along their "uncleanness" to inanimate objects and to Jews. (Leviticus 11:32-40.)

For example, touching a non-Jew would make the Jew "unclean" because all non-Jews are "unclean." But touching *the corpse* of a non-Jew would not make the Jew "unclean" because dead animals are declared to be "clean." The Jews consider a non-Jew to be only an animal and therefore is "clean" when dead. Thus, the Jews always encourage non-Jews to be dead, so that the Jews can remain "clean." It makes perfect since to the holy Jews who are in horror of being touched by non-Jews who are alive. So, remember that the next time you get the chance to put your hands around a living Jew's neck. He is a holy Jew and you are an animal. So, treat him with the respect that he so much deserves.

As a method of taxing women, Leviticus 12 decrees that women who give birth are unclean and must stay away from the sanctuary for a number of days, after which, she is to give the priest a one-year lamb for sacrifice. After the priest spills more innocent lamb blood – Abracadabra! – "she will be purified." And then the priest and his family eat the barbecued lamb.

Leviticus 13 gives the rules for leprosy and how to identify it. Then Leviticus 14 levies another tax to be paid to the priests. Once again, the offering is of two innocent lambs that a leper pays after he is announced by the priest to be "clean" of his disease. The instructions on how to do the magic ritual of purification is given. And the instruction of what to do with a house infected with "leprosy." Even in modern times, we have houses infected with the "sin" of toxic black mold. The infected floors and walls can only be torn down and rebuilt with new materials. But after rebuilding the walls and ridding the house of mold-infected materials, modern contractors do not sacrifice two birds, sprinkle the blood of one bird over the house, dip the second bird into the blood of the first and let him fly away, taking the "sin" of the house with him. Modern people are smarter than this, but not modern Jews.

The circumcised penises of the Jews were (and still are) of constant trouble to them. Promiscuous as their goats, they were liable to a variety of sexually transmissible diseases and infections caused by their incessant masturbation. So, in the ongoing celebration of their demonic cult, the scribes in Leviticus 15 elevate the pus and oozing discharges of their infected weenies into the higher levels of Jewish religiosity through the holy contemplation of their disgusting diseases. This is the "holiness" of Judaism, a religion fit only for devils because it was invented by monsters.

Oozing pus, pus trapped in boils, spit, seminal discharges, are all part of the holy cogitations of the rabbis and are therefore a fit subject of the things that Jews think about while praying. Of course, such discharges can transmit disease. So, with the "brilliant" thinking of these "illustrious" and "scholarly" rabbis, washing and cleaning the clothes of anyone who had had contact with the afflicted man was the taboo! Also in this chapter, the illnesses of women are showcased. Ah, such heavenly, Jewish dreams! Truly, the Jews are God's People! Discharges of blood, blood flows and menstruation, and the bed clothes and chairs upon which women sit, are subjects of this so-called "religion." The term "unclean" has become a catch-all phrase to included anything that is taboo. All of the Jew with the above afflictions are unclean and any Jew who touches them, their clothes, the chairs and saddles upon which they sat, also becomes unclean. With sexual emissions and dripping penises and bleeding vulvas being a basis for the religious cogitations of the Jews since the days that they learned to read and write in the yeshivas, is it any wonder that modern Jews are the world's foremost pornographers, child molesters and brothel owners? But they insist on telling us that their sick, Semitic perversions and disgusting pornographic criminality are a "blessing" to the people of the whole world! That's what they tell us, anyway.

There is another tax that the Hebrews must pay to the priest. After they are "clean," they must give two innocent turtledoves or two innocent young pigeons to the priests who sacrificed them as a sin offering for their "uncleanness." Once again, the "debt" or "sin" that the eternally-sinful-Jews owed for their perpetual, never-ending "sins," must be paid to the priests.

While Leviticus 11 through 15 describes the taboos of "clean" and "unclean," Leviticus 16 describes the ceremony for the Year of Atonement, where the Hebrews are supposed to atone for a whole years' worth of sinning. Since these Hebrews were thieves and murderers, they had a lot to atone for. The

Jews used the ancient Hebrew sacrifice to the demon Azazel to carry away their sins on an innocent scapegoat. It is basic both to Judaism and banking that the poor and innocent must pay the debts of the financiers. Many must be swindled with usury so that a few may live in luxury.

The Babylonian scribes disguised their bandit priests as "victims" of the Yahweh-god while wrapping their lies behind the veil of the temple. Ever skillful at gaining a profit at any time, the moneylenders solved the problem of how to feed their priests if the almost impossible ever happened – if the Jews stopped sinning. "Yahweh spoke to Moses" and told him that Aaron could not just walk into the sanctuary beyond the veil whenever he wanted to, unless he first cooked a barbecue for the priests with a young bull and a young ram. This guaranteed an income even if the Hebrews were not sinning by breaking any of the rabbinical rules. If this highly impossible event ever happened where the Jews were actually not sinning but were being good and following all the laws of Moses, the priests could still collect a tax from them. Whenever they were hungry, the priests would merely claim that they had to serve the god or inquire of the god who was waiting for them behind the veil. So, the Hebrews had to supply a bull and a ram since this Law of Moses decreed that the priests were not allowed to go beyond the veil without first preparing a barbecue for the priests and their "holy" family of ravenous frauds.

This food from off the altar is called *terumah* and could only be eaten by the priests and their relatives who maintained the ritual "holiness" by following the prescribed laws. *Following the laws* is what made them holy, nothing more. Thus, it can be seen that for the writers of the *Hebrew Bible*, nothing is more important than following the laws of Moses. But what were these laws for? To make some of the dumbest and dirtiest scoundrels in the ancient Near East into a "holy people"? No, these laws were designed to establish a self-sufficient Temple as a base of operations for an international criminal conspiracy using religion as a facade and its Treasury as a secure depository for their loot.

One of the most surprising things about reading the *Hebrew Bible* is that absolutely nothing in the Torah can be considered especially "godly" or "holy," but rather the reverse since every tale is dripping in blood and genocide. Judaism is all *abracadabra*.

> "When he has made atonement for himself, for his family, and for his whole community of Israel, he is to come out and go to the altar which is before Yahweh, and perform over it the rite of atonement. He must take some of the blood of the bull and of the goat, and put it on the horns around the altar. With this blood he must sprinkle the altar seven times with his finger. This is how he will render it clean and sacred, purified and separated from the uncleanness of the sons of Israel." (Leviticus 16:18-19.)

After devising a method for feeding the priests whenever they wanted to take a walk "beyond the veil in front of the throne of mercy that is over the ark" (Leviticus 16:2), the next section of Leviticus 16 is to get rid of their sins by sacrificing *not to God* but actually sacrificing *to the devil*! This sacrifice was to a demon named *Azazel* who lived in the desert, the barren region where the Yahweh-god didn't have any power. Remember, the ancient Near Eastern peoples believed that the gods were local and each had their own territory to inhabit. In this case, the Yahweh-god was floating in a cloud over the Ark of the Covenant behind the veil of the sanctuary and couldn't be in two places at once so, the Jews sacrificed to a demon in the wilderness.

Of the bull and two rams, which one of the rams was chosen by God to be set aside was known by gambling with lots on the holy dice table strapped to the high priest's fat belly. This was to be the scapegoat. On the Day of Atonement, the rabbis barbecued the bull and one ram which they burned outside the town in expiation for their sins. The second ram, the scapegoat, was then magically given all of the sins of the Jews which the priest magically put on the goat's head. This goat was led out into the desert and released to carry those sins to the demon *Azazel*. This was the method used in the early days, the scapegoat was set free in the desert. But a problem later arose of the goat wandering back to the horrified Jews along with the sins that they had put on it. So, they solved the problem of making sure that the goat didn't give them back their sins by pushing the goat over a cliff. That settled that. The goat carried the Hebrews' sins over the cliff and they were then freed up to sin a fresh supply during the following year.

This same method of putting their sins onto an innocent animal is still practiced in modern times by the Jews today. Only instead of releasing a goat into the modern streets to foul up traffic, they swing a chicken over their heads and then kill the chicken and throw it into a garbage can. (see Figure 101) The Jews wade in the blood of innocent victims so that they can delude themselves that their legions of sins are "paid for" by blaming others. In the case of their scapegoating ritual of *kapparot*, the blood of chickens "redeems" them from the wrath of their demon god. (see Figure 102) The Jews are Devils! Real ones! Pretending to be innocent.

Fig. 101: Chicken-rabbi   Figure 102: Kapparot

The merchant-moneylenders' monopoly over everything that could give them a profit, is here reflected in Leviticus 17 where the Yahweh-god-of-the-goat rustlers demands that all sacrifices are to be made by the priests, themselves, and cannot be made by the people without the priests. So, more "commands of God" require that the people make the long journey to wherever the side-show Tent of Meeting is parked to have the priests "perform" the sacrificial rites and, of course, eat the barbecue as "a very holy thing." This command to give the monopoly of all sacrifices to the priests, is backed by the threat of banishment. Especially in ancient societies where a person could not live without the help of his tribesmen, this was a serious penalty.

With their deep appreciation of human weakness, Leviticus 17 shows how the moneylender scribes were able to turn the Hebrews literally into bloodthirsty killers. It was observed by the cunning merchants, moneylenders and salesmen that people desired most what they could not have. A pearl from far-away India that was just a bit too expensive to buy, was the very pearl that the customer wanted most. A jar of spices that was, "the very last one and after that there is no more," was the very jar that the women fought over the most. And the blood that the priests poured out upon the altar for the flies to eat, and which was forbidden for the Hebrews to eat, was the very thing that the Jews wanted the most. As their wide-hipped, lustful women soaked the meat in water and squeezed out the very last drop of blood before cooking it, blood was what the Jews most wanted. Eating of blood was forbidden to them. So, as they exterminated the people around them and ravaged Canaan, blood and more blood was what they craved the most.

As in Leviticus 17:10-12, it was is not just the blood that the Hebrews were denied, but they were denied life, itself, since the Yahweh-god-of-the-goat rustlers claimed that "the life of all flesh is in its blood." (Leviticus 17:14.)

In typical Jewish illogic, this didn't mean to keep the blood in the body to keep the body alive; it meant killing the body by draining its blood. As the Hebrews spilled the blood of animals, they thirsted for the blood of Man. The more blood they spilled, the "cleaner" and more "sin-free" they believed themselves to be. They had been lured to their spiritual doom by the Monsters of Babylon who had deluded them into believing that they were saints serving the god of the golden altar. With the Semitic ideas of vengeance through *lex talionis* (an eye-for-an-eye), the priests demanded that the blood of their enemies "atone" for the "abomination" of not being among those who did not sport a "holy" circumcised dong. The Jews could instantly tell who the sinners were by looking at their cocks. The sinners, of course, had natural penises the way God had created them while the Hebrews had the mangled and perverted penises of the moneylenders of Babylon – such was, and is, Jewish wisdom, the wisdom of demons.

Leviticus 18 establishes that the Hebrews are to follow only the *laws and customs* of the Yahweh-god as written down by the moneylender scribes. They were not to follow Egyptian or Canaanite laws but only the laws of the Yahweh cult. "I am Yahweh your God. You must keep my laws and my customs. Whoever complies with them will find life in them." (Leviticus 18:5.) This "life" that the Jews find, is the material life of prosperity, wealth and ownership that the Jewish moneylenders guarantee to everyone who practices money lending at interest and makes donations to the Temple treasury, buying and selling through the cartel and monopoly system built into Judaism. This has nothing to do with any sort of "spiritual life" but is a material life only. There is nothing holy or spiritual about Judaism. It is a false religion promoting hoaxes and lies designed to protect its built-in banking system.

With their circumcised holiness well in hand, incest with father, mother, sisters, half-sisters, grandchildren, aunts, uncles, daughters-in-law, sisters-in-law, and including a mother and the daughter of any unrelated women is allowed for a Jew. Having sex with a mother prohibits having sex with her children or their children. Taking into the goat rustler's harem a woman and her sister at the same time, a menstruating woman, or the neighbor's wife, is prohibited. Child sacrifice is prohibited for Jewish children, but as the rabbis would decree, it was not prohibited to sacrifice the children of the non-Jews. (Leviticus 18:21.) This exception would spell doom for many Gentile children over the following centuries as the Jews combined such laws with the story of killing of the firstborn of the Egyptians so as to "walk in the ways" of their god and to terrorize the inhabitants of every country in which they were allowed to live. As the rabbis teach, sacrificing "your" children does not prohibit sacrificing "their" children. This is a biblical basis that later Jews would use to murder Christian children and then blame it on a "Blood Libel" to "prove" that they were innocent. The "Blood Libel" is not a libel at all, but a commandment of the Jews' demon-god as interpreted by the rabbis. See Volume III: *The Blood-Suckers of Judah* for further details.

Abraham is considered by the Jews to be their ultimate Patriarch. That he committed incest with his half-sister, Sarah, is one of the many indications of the blatant hypocrisy of Judaism. Homosexuality was also prohibited. "You must not lie with a man as with a woman." (Leviticus 18:22.) But as the scheming rabbis taught, a "man" did not mean a "boy." Those sick, perverted moneylenders of Babylonia taught that pederasty was not covered by this law. Since a boy is not a man, then to the filthy rabbis, this means that molesting little boys is perfectly Jewish since sodomy with men is prohibited but sodomy with little boys is not prohibited in Mosaic Law. This is one reason why so many modern Jews are child molesters and modern Jewish lawyers always defend non-Jewish child molesters from prosecution. The root of Jewish perversion is found in this demon book known as the *Hebrew Bible*, the Greatest Lie Ever Told, a book celebrating fraud, murder, deceit, betrayal, hypocrisy. And to hide those devils behind a protecting veil of illusion – Abracadabra! – the rabbis call their books "holy" and "sacred."

Women were prohibited from bestiality (Leviticus 18:23) but as the rabbis taught, this did not prevent a *male* Hebrew from screwing his sheep. These prohibitions are given as the reason that the Yahweh-god was dispossessing the Canaanites. Not because the Hebrews covet the land but because the Canaanites are unclean. "Unclean" is a term used for taboo things. Any Hebrew doing those proscribed things, "must be cut off from his people." (Lev 18:29.)

Leviticus 19 offers a variety of short laws, all of which were negated along with all other laws of the Torah by the rabbis in their "Tradition of the Elders." For example, allegedly Yahweh told Moses "You must not slander your own people, and you must not jeopardize your neighbor's life." (Leviticus 19:16.) According to the rabbis, all of the laws of Moses were given only to the Jews and to no one else. So, the rabbinical translation of the above law is this: "Since we Jews are commanded not to slander our own people, this says nothing about not slandering people who are not our own. Thus, we are free to slander the *goyim* (lowly insects, stupid cattle) because they are not our own people. Also, our neighbor can only be another Jew since the Laws of Moses were not meant for anyone other than the Jews. So, if our neighbor is not a Jew then he cannot be counted as a neighbor. We Jews are therefore allowed by Moses to bring harm to our non-Jewish neighbors and even jeopardize the non-Jew's life." Such mendacious arguments are basic to Judaism and have been practiced by the Jews wherever they have been allowed to live.

Modern people who read the Bible usually don't know that there is a hidden law that negates everything that they read. That hidden law is known as the *Babylonian Talmud*. Jesus would condemn this Jewish "Tradition of the Elders" as the teaching of the devil and with good reason.

For example, Leviticus 19:17 says, "You must not bear hatred for your brother in your heart." But the rabbis teach that because the laws of the Torah were only made for the Jews then they only apply to the Jews and are therefore only for the benefit of the Jews. So, a Jew's "brother" can only be another Jew. In this way, the rabbis teach that it is the command of God that Jews love their Jewish brothers. But hating the non-Jews is not prohibited; it is, in fact, encouraged by the rabbis. If the Jews are to "walk in the ways" of their god, then that means hating all of Mankind as their demon god hates all of Mankind. Likewise, Leviticus 19:18 says, "You must not exact vengeance, nor must you bear a grudge against the children of your people." In this way, the rabbis teach the Jews to follow this law toward other Jews. But concerning the children of non-Jews, the rabbis teach that non-Jewish children must suffer the vengeance of the Jews and non-Jewish children must suffer the results of unending grudges that the Jews have against their parents all the way through the fourth generation to the great-grandchildren. Even the little babies of non-Jews are hated by the Jews. The machine-gunning of Palestinian children by the Jews of modern Israel, has a long history of malice stretching back to when Terah first formulated the hoax of Judaism.

The Jewish attitude of hating and bringing harm and death to all non-Jews and practicing a grudging malice against even the little children of non-Jews, is one of the many, many reasons why the Jews have been hated by all other people over the centuries. With the *Hebrew Bible* as their guide, the gullible non-Jews of the world have welcomed the Jews into their communities under the false impression that the Jews are a holy people who abide by their own laws. Entering a Gentile community, the Jews wave the very same *Old Testament* in the air to confirm this false impression, but secretly the Jews follow the negative precepts of the rabbis and bring nothing but slander, destruction of life, harm to the children and malicious hatred upon the non-Jews who trusted them. Quite simply, it is a standard Jewish tradition to hate and harm everybody except themselves.

It was not so much that the Scribes were so holy, themselves, when they wrote in Leviticus 20 that Yahweh prohibited child sacrifice. Anyone could see the evils in such a practice. The lying Jews claim that their Yahweh-god prohibited the practice and, thus, established a "higher moral tone" for the Hebrews in saving their own children from sacrifice. But as the rabbis taught, murdering and sacrificing the children of other people was acceptable to Yahweh. It was *only their own children* that they were forbidden to sacrifice. This teaching would create much woe among the Gentiles in later centuries as their children began to disappear and their bodies would later be found drained of their blood and buried in refuse heaps – the kosher way to dispose of dead animals.

Leviticus 20 differentiates these circumcised goat rustlers and their harems of slave women from the other goat rustlers of Canaan by convincing them to change their customs to those decreed by the new religion of Yahwehism. This Yahweh Cult became a new manifestation of merchant-moneylender deceit. The Hebrew and Canaanite goat-molesters would not even have to change their religion very much as long as they followed the Laws of Moses. After all, *Yahweh* was already well known among them. Both the biblical and archaeological data make it clear that both *Yahweh* as well as other gods were worshiped in Jerusalem even in late monarchic times. During the monarchies of Judah, the goddess *Asherah* (*Astarte* or *Ishtar*) was worshiped as being the actual consort of the Yahweh-god. Inscriptions from the late-monarchic times in Judah refer to this married status of the Yahweh-god and his consort, *Asherah*. So, the moneylenders of Babylon were really not offering the goat rustlers of Canaan a new religion with a new god, but merely the same god with a whole new set of binding rules, enforced by the rabbis, priests and Levites.

In their scheme to build a temple that was holy enough, scary enough, and secure enough to protect their gold, they declared themselves – Abracadabra! – "holy," regardless of the actual facts. Leviticus 21 further solidifies the priesthood into the tribe of Aaron and guarantees that they will continue to eat plentiful barbecues since it is they "who bring the burnt offerings to Yahweh, the food of their God." (Leviticus 21:14.) This priesthood's power and its wealth was secured through incest. The high priest is enjoined to only marry "a virgin from his own family." (Leviticus 21:14.)

Holiness, for the hypocritical Hebrews, was something that was *declared* by their own laws *but not earned* by actual merit or attainment. Leviticus 21 declares the priests to be holy just as long as they didn't touch any dead relatives and only committed incest with virgins from their own family, not necessarily all at the same time. By marrying their relatives, both power and wealth were kept within the immediate family even though the resulting children inherited birth defects and retardation, creating their modern "inheritance" of odd-looking and misshapen Jews, hunchbacks, club foots, the world's ugliest people, and Jewish dwarfs.

The priestly scam of guaranteeing full bellies for the rabbis and their families is further emphasized in Leviticus 22. Once again, the blood-spattered priests of *Yahweh* are declared to be "holy" *for no other reason* than that they eat the animals that are offered on the bloody altar. The greedy priests wrote, "Yahweh spoke to Moses; he said, 'Speak to Aaron and his sons, let them be consecrated through the holy offerings of the sons of Israel, and not profane my holy name" (Lev 22:2). So, they are consecrated by what the Hebrews feed them and pay to them, not because they are holy in their own right. It is the barbecue that makes them "holy." It is the gold of the Temple that makes them "holy." The Jews are not holy, they just pretend to be and strike poses within a system of empty rituals.

Leviticus 23 lists the festivals that are to be required of the goat rustlers. There are only seven of them. But in modern times, the rabbis have declared some extra ones as a means of subverting the people among whom the Jews reside. This is discussed in Volume III, *The Bloodsuckers of Judah.*

The first festival was the Sabbath. With the advantage of avoiding military service by refusing to do any work on one day per week, the merchant-moneylenders of Babylon could guarantee themselves and any moneylenders or businessmen who joined their new religion, complete safety from the perils of military duty in every country where they resided. Sabbath also allowed the moneylenders to solidify their grip upon the Hebrew bandits by giving them a vacation that didn't cost the bankers anything. Taking a day off from work, is an efficient way to increase production after a day of rest.

But this day off from work was not a time for recreation but an intensive brainwashing session whereby the priests could condition the goat rustlers with the laws and traditions designed to bind them into the corporate contract through both preaching The Contract and through celebrations revolving around The Contract. The Hebrews got a day off every week, but they weren't allowed to use it merely to have fun and relax. They were required to put their noses into the Torah and to be happy that the priests and rabbis were turning them into the world's biggest assholes, liars and hypocrites. And if any Jew refused to be a part of the program, the priests would murder them. The only truth in Judaism is the Devil's Truth.

During such a Sabbath "holy day," the Hebrews would be educated in the requirements of The Contract through intensive brainwashing by the priests whose income depended upon the Hebrews actually believing the myths and the lies being offered to them as "God Ordained Truths." Remember the catch-phrase that "God chose the Jews, they did not choose Him." So, it was impressed upon them, as they scratched their fleas and picked their noses, that they were a holy people simply because the priests who served the Yahweh-god, said so.

The Passover Feast of Unleavened Bread conditions the Hebrews to the idea that they had been slaves in Egypt but now were free to be the slaves of the rabbis and priests. Merely an exchange of shackles. The First Sheaf Offering guarantees that from the harvest the first produce of all farms and herds goes to the priests. The Feast of Weeks gives the priests a huge amount of barbecues, bread and wine. And what do the farmers get after presenting them with free wine, bread, seven lambs, one bull and two rams? They get the day off. The first day of the Seventh Month of the Babylonian calendar is another day off accompanied by the feeding of the priests. The Day of Atonement is a fasting day accompanied by more food for the Jewish priests disguised as a burnt offering to *Yahweh.*

The Feast of Tabernacles is another series of priestly feedings. For seven days, every goat rustler is required to live in shelters outside their regular homes as another conditioning method to promote the lie that they had lived in shelters when they were running from Pharaoh. That the entire "escape from Egypt" fantasy was completely fabricated by the scribes of Babylon, gets covered over with these kinds of fake holidays that – with great fanfare – celebrate hoaxes. Every Jew, today, recites the same lie that "WE were slaves in Egypt. And WE lived in shacks in the desert" – as if these asinine modern liars still had Sinai sand between their toes and the gold bracelets of Pharaoh still stuffed in their pockets. These are the seven required feasts in addition to the "presents and the votive and voluntary gifts that you make to Yahweh." (Lv 23:38.)

Leviticus 24 claims that pure olive oil should be used in a perpetual flame. Of course, the priests stockpiled this oil since it is kept for long periods and was useful for cooking and it brought a good price. More food is designated for the High Priest, Aaron and his sons. Every Sabbath, twelve loaves of bread are set on the golden table for Aaron and his sons to eat. This bounty was inherited by the High Priest.

The *lex talionis,* eye-for-an-eye, laws of Hammurabi had served the Babylonian moneylenders quite well. They were safe from assault when such a law was enforced. Here in Leviticus 24 the moneylenders made sure that they could continue with such protection after they began using the Sumerian Swindle on the Hebrews. So, *lex talionis* is decreed in Leviticus 24.

But further, Sumerian Swindle #6 states that, "High morals impede profits, so debauching the Virtuous pulls them below the depravity of the moneylender who there-by masters them and bends them to his will." In this case, murdering members of the community for breaking the Mosaic Laws, was accomplished by making execution a community affair. "Let the whole community stone him." (Lev 24:14.) So, the laws were enforced by the Hebrews, themselves, even killing their own friends and relatives under orders from the rabbis and priests. In this way, entire tribes of Hebrews turned around and closed ranks to murder one of their own for the sake of the laws of the rabbis and the words of the scribes. By having the entire community do the killing, the rabbis trained the Hebrews to be fearful of neglecting the Mosaic Laws because one's own friends and neighbors could turn on them at the word of a rabbi. Those who rebelled and broke the Laws of Moses were killed, those who acquiesced lived. Thus, a genetic pruning took place among a Semitic people who committed every manner of sociopathic atrocity, while those among them who objected in any way were murdered. Thus, through the natural selection process of the Monsters of Babylon, criminality, sociopathic and psychopathic behavior became a predominant genetic code among the Jews.

Leviticus 25 is tricky. This part of The Contract gives the love of *Yahweh* to the Hebrews (which cost the moneylenders nothing) and the ownership of the walled cities to the merchant-moneylenders so that they would ways be safe. It emphasized that the Jews are to be a nation of parasites while the nations around them are to be their slaves.

"*Yahweh* spoke to Moses on Mount Sinai" (Lev 25:1). These pronouncements by the Canaanite God of the Mountain, *El-Shaddai*, are channeled through Moses. Allegedly, this old man talked to God and God talked to him. Although talking with God might be a good thing, in this case, Moses was a traitor to his Egyptian foster parents, here is an old murderer telling the Hebrews how they can best serve the moneylenders of Babylonia by serving the Canaanite god, *Yahweh*.

Remember, the Book of Leviticus was given its final form during the Exile and completed in Babylonia by Ezra the Scribe by 539 BC. So the Babylonian priests of the moneylenders had over fifty years in Babylon to refine their handiwork. To emphasize who owned the land, periodic reminders were built into the laws of Leviticus. As in all of the other religions of the ancient Near East, the regional nature of the gods was recognized by all people. The gods of Babylonia ruled over the lands and cities of Babylonia. The gods of Egypt ruled over the lands and cities of Egypt. So, of course, the merchant-moneylenders of Ur and Harran wanted their god to rule over the treasury, the temple, the cities and the lands of Canaan where their new god lived and where their gold was stored. The laws of Leviticus 25 are meant to show that the Yahweh-god ruled over the lands by making laws that restricted land use. Laws that restrict, are also laws that control and govern. It is the nature of the laws of Leviticus 25 to give control of the land to those who wrote the laws – in this case, the moneylenders of Abraham's First National Bank and Pawn Shop.

The Jubilee Year was legislated to take place every fifty years. "Jubilee" comes from the Hebrew word for "trumpet" (*yobel*) because the year was announced with trumpets on the Day of Atonement. Supposedly, every fifty years all debt-slaves were to be released, all debts were canceled, no land is to be sown with grain, no harvesting of produce is to be done, all fields are to lay fallow for that year, no grapes are to be gathered, and all of the Hebrews are to return to their ancestral homes. But the fifty-year Jubilee Year was another swindle of the merchant-moneylenders of Babylonia. In the first place, it did little for the majority of debt-slaves since *their life expectancy was only forty years*! However, it was mainly for the benefit of the priests and the money-lenders that this year was devised.

Depending upon their innate truth or falsehood, most religions make promises that they may or may not be able to keep. In the case of Judaism, which is based entirely upon hoaxes, deceit, fraud and lies, the only promises that it is able to keep is the promise of the written Contract. That is, if the Hebrews adhere to the bankers' agreement as found in the Laws of Moses, they will find wealth by stealing it from the people whom they betray and parasitize. That is the only truth in Judaism, the "truth" of a moneylender's fraud and swindle – the Sumerian Swindle ensconced within a shell of pseudo-dramatic mimes, directed by gesticulating evil clowns dressed as Jewish priests.

So, when the merchant-moneylender scribes of Babylonia wrote of the pie-in-the-sky miracle of "plenty to eat during the Year of Jubilee," they were setting a trap for the Hebrews and opening a treasure chest for the rabbis. The Laws of the moneylenders of Babylon make it illegal to plant crops in the Year of Jubilee but they do not forbid *buying* crops if there is not enough. As Secret Fraud #18 of the Sumerian Swindle states: "When the source of goods is distant from the customers, profits are increased both by import and export." So, in a bad year followed by a Year of Jubilee, when the Hebrews have nothing to eat and while the priests are screaming at them that they are sinners who have not followed The Contract closely enough with the results that they don't have anything to eat because of their "sins," the circumcised merchant-moneylenders would do a brisk business importing grain from Syria or Babylonia or Egypt. Just because the Hebrews were starving didn't mean that the merchants or priests should starve. With their international business connections, the merchants were able to ensure that there was always plenty of grain during lean years *as long as the Hebrews were able to pay for it*. And this payment was insured by the profits that the Temple had pulled in through the various taxes and atonements and sacrifices that the Hebrews had been making for the previous forty-nine years. In this way, the Hebrews were trained to rely upon the hidden hoards of wealth concealed by the priests and rabbis.

The Hebrew bandits were again reminded that they were to deal fairly with one another during the Jubilee Year. As expert swindlers, the merchant-moneylenders reminded their followers of how to value property with the Jubilee Year factored into the equation. Thinking ahead by fifty years became a method whereby the Hebrews could buy and sell property among one another, as stated in Leviticus 25:15-17. When the Hebrews could be trained to buy or sell property and goods *as a coordinated group*, then markets could be manipulated and profits could be increased by selling to the non-Jews just before the markets were scheduled to crash. These Jubilee Years were training for the wholesale swindling of entire nations, all coordinated to the moon cycles of the Babylonian Calendar. The real reason for these particular laws of Moses are given in Leviticus 25:18-19:

"You must put my laws and customs into practice; you must keep them, practice them; and so you shall be secure in your possession of the land. The land will give its fruit, you will eat your fill and live in security." (Lev 25:18-19.)

Let's take a closer look at this so-called "divine guarantee." The scribes go on to write,

"In case you should ask: What shall we eat in this seventh year if we do not sow or harvest the produce? I have ordered my blessing to be on you every sixth year, which will therefore provide for you for three years. You will have the old produce to eat while you are sowing in the eighth year and even as late as the ninth year; you will eat the old produce, while waiting for the harvest of that year." (Lev 25:20-22.)

While working in conspiring gangs, the Jews are able, through the timing of sabbatical years, to influence the business cycles of entire countries by buying and selling on six-year cycles and then doing no business on the seventh year. In addition, the Hebrews were taught to hoard grain and food stuffs in all seasons.

The problem that the scribes made for themselves when the Hebrews would ask, "What shall we eat in the seventh year if we do not sow or harvest produce?" (Lev 25:20.) was solved by the priests who would claim that bad harvest years were the fault – not of God reneging on his promises, not of bad weather – but of the Hebrews not being "holy" enough, that is, not strict enough in following the Laws.

The importance to the merchant-moneylenders of Babylon of gaining ownership of the land of Canaan was emphasized in Leviticus 25:23 where God says to Moses, "Land must not be sold in perpetuity, for the land belongs to me, and to me you are only strangers and guests." (Lev 25:23.) In this way, the moneylenders legislated the territory that was under the protection of their god. They had The Contract for the property as well as The Contract for controlling the people living upon that property, all neatly written into the Books of Moses with themselves established as the genealogically-decreed priests and owners. So, don't blame anyone except God, if you don't like the deal.

Thus, the Corporation that owned The Contract – that is, the Temple and the priests and the moneylenders of Babylon – owned all of the land upon which the Hebrews labored and to whom the Hebrews paid the huge variety of sin offerings and taxes. This Contract of the Torah established a Babylonian temple system in Canaan whereby the god of the temple owned all of the land. This Contract provided the religious protection that the moneylenders so much desired. However, The Contract allowed only the rich merchants and moneylenders to obtain private property ownership safely within the walls of the cities. Only the property inside the walled cities could be owned outright by whoever bought it. Those who bought it, had plenty of silver to buy what they wanted. In case of attack by an enemy, they could look down on the slaughter of the villagers from their vantage point on the walls, assuring even their victims that their right to safety was ordained by the Yahweh-god because it said so in The Contract.

The Jubilee Year gave the false impression to the Hebrews that their god was generous by freeing them from debt and debt-slavery every fifty years. But since the average life-span of those ancient people was only forty years, the law didn't cost the moneylender families very much since their debtors didn't live long enough to be granted a Jubilee.

Leviticus 25 gives an accountant's calculation for factoring in the Jubilee Year for sales of land and labor. But most important to the ownership privileges of the moneylenders, was the permanent ownership of the walled cities. These they wanted for their own security. The land was to be owned not by individuals, but by tribes. Thus, the Bankers of Babylon could assure that all of the Hebrews would act as unified gangs to keep possession of the land within their tribal territories since the land could not be sold in perpetuity. However, the walled cities were to be owned outright by the merchant-moneylenders. In this way, the moneylenders were safe within the cities while they had roaming tribes of protecting guerrillas as a buffer against armies.

Hidden within the laws of Leviticus 25, are the special exemptions that allowed the individual moneylenders to own the walled cities while the land and unwalled villages was never owned by individuals but was occupied and secured by the tribes. This kept the moneylenders rich and safe while keeping the Hebrews poor and dependent upon the will of their god whose voice was the voice of the moneylender-scribes. *This is precisely how the Babylonian system had evolved* with the wealthy landowners living in the cities and the landless peasants working lands in perpetuity that they could never own because the land was owned by the god who resided among the priests in the Temple. This was the Sumerian Swindle dressed up in the outlandish Negro pimp costumes of the priests of Yahweh.

This ownership of the walled cities was a permanent right for the buyers of the property. The loophole is built into The Contract. To give the merchant-moneylenders a religious backing, a special loophole was attached to the special status that was made for the towns and fields of the Levites, that tribe of Levi who were the professional snoops, servants and guards over the Temple properties. In Leviticus 25:32-34, the ownership of Levite property is not temporary like the other Hebrews but is made permanent. In this way, the money-lenders in the cities and the priesthood are given permanent ownership rights, while the Hebrew tribes remain as renters.

This entire Torah Contract was (and still is) a huge swindle at all levels. But the ignorant goat rustlers, the Hyksos-Hebrews of Canaan, being illiterate, trusted that the priests and rabbis were telling them the truth. After all, priests dressed up like Negro pimps and holding their hands out for sin offerings and donations while claiming to speak with the very word of God, wouldn't lie. Would they?

It is in Leviticus 25 that certain modern Jews acquired their subculture as beggars and con artists who, among themselves, are known in Yiddish as the *shnorrer*. These Jewish bums and spongers make their living by parasitizing the parasites. Living on handouts and free meals, they quote Leviticus 25:35-38 where the Yahweh-god declares that "If your brother who is living with you, falls on evil days and is unable to support himself with you, you must support him as you would a stranger or a guest, and he must continue to live with you." (Lev 25:35-38.)

The Hebrews are enjoined to make life easy for each other. *However*, the moneylenders have plans for the people who are not members of the Holy Religion of the Circumcised Penis. The people from all of the nations around the Hebrews are to be turned into perpetual slaves. This is the law of the money-lenders of Yahweh:

> "They shall be your property and you may leave them as an in-
> heritance to your sons after you, to hold in perpetual possession.
> These you may have as slaves; but to your brothers, the sons of
> Israel, you must not be hard masters." (Lev 25:45-46.)

As the rabbis taught, this law means that the Jews must be easy on fellow Jews but relentlessly cruel and hard on non-Jews. Reducing all of Mankind to slavery has always been a major goal of these worshipers of the Demo God, *Yahweh*.

Leviticus 26 offers the same carrot and the stick of all false religions. Like expert salesmen, the moneylenders save money by making empty promises and offering all of the benefits up front as an inducement. The Yahweh-god, channeling through Moses who hears voices in his head, tells the Hebrews every complicated ritual, the exact measurements of the Tent of Meeting, all the details for building an Ark of the Covenant, the minute points of calculating sales during the Jubilee years, the approved ways to pour blood and slaughter animals. But the qualifier is promoted as *a promise* of blessings, that is, "IF you live according to my laws, IF you keep my commandments and put them into practice" (Lev 26:3), then these goat rustlers are promised goat rustler-pie-in-the-sky, all of the material goods that a simpleminded vagabond and bandit would want.

There is absolutely no spiritual advantage to following the Laws of Moses, *only material advantages* such as full harvests, many sheep, killing of enemies, many children, etc. And the Yahweh-god, like all of the other regional gods of the ancient Near East, promises to "set up my dwelling among you, and I will not cast you off. I will live in your midst; I will be your God and you shall be my people." (Lev 26:11-12.) These are all lies which the lying Yahweh-god continually echoes among the voices inside of the sun-burned noggin of Moses. Promises cost the moneylenders nothing and can be made grandiose and eternal-sounding. But the promises of this god of the moneylenders was no better than the promises of a moneylender. Each and every one of them was broken throughout the entire history of the Jews, broken promises from the God of Liars and Thieves, broken promises from the God of Genocide, the god of the lying Jews.

So, after the carrot, now the stick. Ever clever in swindling advantages for themselves and to evade responsibility for their false promises, the bankers wrote an escape clause into their Contract where the Yahweh god says, "But if you do not listen to me, and do not observe *each one of these commandments*, if you refuse my laws and disregard my customs, and break my Covenant by not observing *each one of my commandments*, then" all promises are canceled. (Lev 26:14-16.) And all manner of bad curses will be the unhappy lot of the idiot goat rustlers of Canaan. Here, all the wrath and curses of a god-gone-wild are pronounced against the Hebrews if they don't do what the priests tell them to do in following *each and every minute detail* of their ridiculous blood-spattered rituals. *The benefits are not equal to the curses*, in this illegal, one-way Contract.

As a banker's fraud, the *escape clause* of "each one of my commandments," *negates the entire Contract* of the Torah. It binds the Hebrews to perpetual suffering and servitude at the hands of the priests, rabbis and merchant-moneylenders. But it does not bind the Yahweh-god to keep his promises. It's a one-way Contract, no different than those perpetrated upon the modern people by the modern bankers and credit card companies wherein you are held to their conditions but they allow themselves the "right to change the terms of the contract at any time." What kind of a contract is it that after it is signed and agreed to, and after you are committed to the terms and locked into a cycle of payments and other misfortunes, the bankers change the terms for additional benefit to themselves? What kind of contract is a modern banker's contract where the banker can "call in the loan" at any time that is beneficial to himself and ruinous to you? It's a fraudulent contract, the same kind of Contract that the voices in Moses' head offered the Hebrews.

Finally, in Leviticus 27, the moneylenders get down to their real business. After making the rules whereby the Patriarchs of Babylon can bind the goat rustlers to their scam, all of the rules and commandments of the mighty Yahweh-god are put aside and the *real intent* of the scribes of the Monsters of Babylon concludes the Book of Leviticus. The real intent of the entire Contract is money and the valuation of merchandise, including slaves.

Terah's Babylonian guild of merchant-moneylenders, now calling themselves "Israelites," didn't want the king to set the prices of goods. The moneylenders who later employed Ezra the Scribe, wanted total control of both the Temple and the State. Instead of the king setting prices as was done in Mesopotamian countries such as Sumeria, Babylonia and Assyria, here the priests are in charge of setting the valuation of goods and property. And they are the final authority for setting prices.

Unlike all other religions in the ancient Near East, it is the god who owns the land *while the moneylenders own the cities and collect taxes on the land.*

The system devised by Terah's guild of Babylonian moneylenders was based upon the standard belief systems already common. The difference was that now the wealth that the people donated to the god, was gathered in by the priests and rabbis, while the moneylenders bought up the walled cities as their own private property. Judaism was a smooth swindle where the merchants and moneylenders became the high priests. As priests, the merchant-moneylenders empowered themselves as the only members of the Hebrew-bandit society who could legally own personal real estate, leaving the poorer Jews in the countryside landless and subservient to both the priests and the town dwellers.

Vicious, the priests of the moneylenders were. When the priests of *Yahweh* put a "ban" or an "anathema" on other people, just like the Thuggees of Old India, they murdered everyone while calling their murderous thievery "a most holy thing." (Lev 27:28.) "A human being laid under the ban cannot be redeemed, he must be put to death." (Lev 27:29.) Oh, such sweet, innocent Jews who have brought the world a "higher morality and religion"! To hear those liars tell it!

And finally, what gives the most joy to the merchant-moneylenders of Yahweh, the Book of Leviticus ends with the demand for ten percent of everything, cattle, flocks, all wealth. Ten percent goes to the priests of Abraham's First National Bank and Pawn Shop. And if anyone wanted to keep their property, they could pay its value in silver or gold to the priests plus a twenty percent surcharge!

Finally, after warnings of the wrath of God *if every single law is not obeyed*, now it's tax time. The tithe of ten percent must be paid to the priests of Yahweh or else the curses of earthquakes, lightning bolts, leprosy and plague will be hiding under the bed and ready to pounce. Feed the priests and pay your taxes or you will be eaten by lions and the earth will swallow you. Thus, ends the Book of Leviticus with tax time! Ten percent with a surcharge of twenty percent for malingerers. This Yahweh-god really knew how to keep a moneylender's accounting records! No wonder he picked the greedy, conniving Jews as his special pets. Or rather, no wonder the greedy, conniving moneylenders of Terah's Babylonian Guild picked such stupid people as the Hebrews of Canaan to be their special dupes.

The Hebrew goat rustlers were illiterate, so they trusted the words written on the counterfeit documents unrolled by the priests of Abraham's First National Bank and Pawn Shop. Instead of ordinary bandits and cut-throats, the Hebrew-Hyksos were trained as extra special bandits and cut-throats calling themselves the Chosen Ones of God, the Jews.

6.5 The Book of Numbers Adds More Jews and More Lies into One Fantasy

The Book of Numbers deals with the census of all the Jews and resumes the account of the desert journey where the cowardly Hebrews allegedly try to get into Canaan. But as Professor Ze'ev Herzog of Tel Aviv University announced in 1999 AD: "The Israelites were never in Egypt, did not wander the desert, did not conquer the land, and did not pass it on to the twelve tribes."

The Book of Numbers supposedly takes place two years after the Hebrews had been chased out of Egypt and one month after the erection of the Tabernacle in the desert of Sinai. Moses hears voices in his head that claims to be the Yahweh-god who demands that a census be taken. Each of the twelve tribes are numbered, thus the Book of Numbers. This numbering was for military and tax purposes to count every male twenty years old and over who was fit to bear arms. It should always be understood that Judaism has always been, and is today, a military organization. After all, its god is the "Lord of Hosts," that is, the "Lord of Armies." Judaism is a religion of bankers organized like an army. And why not, since no one profits from war more so than a banker?

This census was also to establish the kinship between the tribes as descendants of Abraham and inheritors of Abraham's *asl* (pronounced "asshole"). The total number of bandits was 603,550 armed with bronze swords, arrows and sling stones. This was really an impossible number since so many crooks camping in Sinai even for one single month, would have left huge archaeological remains of which there are none. So, the entire story in this case, is a fiction.

In this census, the Levites were not counted. Moses was from the tribe of Levi, so they all plotted their take over together. They were to be the special tribe of priestly-spies and snoops who set up and broke down what is now called the "Tabernacle of Testimony." By not counting the spies, no one would ever know how large the spy network was. Not only are the Levites not counted but they are tasked with moving the Tent and guarding the Tent and are authorized to murder anyone who peeks inside. "Any layman coming near to it must be put to death." (Nb 1:52.) In this way, the illusion can be preserved of something super wonderful and mysteriously god-like while concealing the hoax that there was actually nothing there. This has always been a Jewish custom for making themselves appear to be something that they are not, holding themselves aloof with nothing more than appearances, like hot air balloons, or salesmen selling flimflam.

Also, the Levites were to pitch their tents around the Tabernacle of Testimony so that "In this way the wrath will be kept from falling on the whole community of the sons of Israel." (Nb 1:53.) The Levites are thus the actors who are there to protect the Hebrews from the demonic Yahweh-god. By pretending to protect the Hebrews from the "wrath" of the god, they position themselves to be counted as worthy of the barbecued goats and ten percent tithe that they con from the ignorant goat rustlers.

Numbers 2, counts each tribe and tells how they are to station themselves as an armed camp guarding the Tent of the Tabernacle of Testimony. The moneylenders of Babylon are solving their problem of how to get an army to fight for them for free. According to Numbers 2, this mass of goat rustlers amounted to 603,550 fighting men (not counting the women and the boys under 20 years old). So, according to the scribes of Babylon, the Hebrews were equal in number to the military strength of any of the great empires of Babylonia, Assyria or Egypt. This is quite a boast. Of course, a "great army" is big enough to defeat "great nations," right? That is what the scribes are claiming that these "ex-slaves from Egypt" had the numerical power to do.

To solidify their claims of being both holy and owners of the Temple, Numbers 3 provides Terah's family of the merchant-moneylender guilds of Babylonia with a genealogical anchor. Ownership of the office of High Priest was officially proclaimed in the Five Books of Moses as belonging to Aaron and his descendants. This office, and thus the control of the Treasury, was assured to his male descendants. Male descendants were guaranteed through the multiple wives that each chief priest could support. Through the "customs" that they practiced, a priest could have as many as forty wives. So, there was little chance of him not producing sons eventually. And in case his circumcised noodle wouldn't work for him, he could always adopt a son, giving him all the rights of the inherited office, even passing along his bogus *asl* and his bogus blessing so as to keep the priesthood and treasury in the family in perpetuity. In this way, the merchant-moneylender guild of Abraham's father, Terah, was assured of keeping control of the treasury by always holding the office of High Priest.

This method of gaining the high priesthood through written contract and manipulation of the genealogies, was a clever method for legitimatizing the moneylender's rule over their very own religion and over tens of thousands of Hebrew goat-thieves, a religion designed specifically to protect the vast fortunes they had made through the Sumerian Swindle.

But where is the proof that they were actually entitled to the power of the priesthood? "Proof" for their counterfeit history did not depend upon anything other than the written The Contract, itself, which was (and is) an historical fraud. No historical proofs were necessary since there were none. Only The Contract stipulated the conditions under which the Hebrews were to act; and only The Contract provided the genealogical reasons why its authority was valid. That is, if something based on forgery, fraud, lies, false witness, myth and historical fiction can be called valid, then the *Hebrew Bible* is as valid as any other fairy tale.

The character of Moses was convincingly patched together from the "Legend of Sargon" and king Hammurabi, the Law Giver. The final resting place of such a "great personage" as Moses, was conveniently located along with all the tombs of all the other "patriarchs," where they could never be found. The lies about being slaves in Egypt, the counterfeit stories of defeating a Pharaoh and his entire army with magic and crashing waters, the wandering around in the Sinai, were all stories that no one could ever dispute because there was no proof to the contrary – that is, until modern archaeology proved what liars the Jews are. The "proofs" that the alleged miracles in the desert had actually happened along with the stone tablets and the jar of "manna," were all conveniently stolen by enemy armies and "lost." With the application of Semitic *abracadabra*, "solid proof" that it had all happened just as the Jews said that it did, rested completely on "the word of the Jews." None of these things could be lies because the *Hebrew Bible* is the "word of God"? Right? The "Self-Chosen Ones of God" wouldn't lie, would they? Only devils lie about God. So, what would telling lies about God make the Jews?

Yet, no matter how incredibly impossible the "miracles" were, no matter how much proof of all kinds that the *Hebrew Bible* is the Greatest Lie Ever Told, the one thing that remains and the one thing that the scribes intended to remain, is The Contract, itself. All of the stories in the Old Testament, support one and only one solid fact of the *Hebrew Bible*, and that is the fact that it is a one-way Contract between some "mysterious being" and the goat rustlers of ancient Palestine. When all of the stories are stripped away, whether they are considered true or false, leaves only one thing, the very thing that gave the whole swindle its true foundation. And that thing is *The Contract*.

Regardless of these mythological events, The Contract, itself, chained the Hebrews to subjection by the priests of a mighty Temple inhabited by a terrible god. Those stories were claimed to be the true "word of God" by a long line of priestly frauds and their sons – all with their hands held out for donations – who had declared themselves to be both "holy" and the rightful owners of the treasury. What was the proof of these thieving gangsters? They could genealogically trace their descent from the original mythological nonexistent characters written about by their priestly forefathers who had inserted their family names into the bogus genealogy. Thus, the only proof offered was nothing but lies. These lies of the Jews are based solely upon every Jew swearing up and down that their lies are true. For 2500 years, Mankind has had the lies of the *Old Testament* to lead us astray, with no other proof of its veracity other than lying Jews – that is, until Jesus showed what liars the Jews are and then modern archaeology proved it.

There is plenty of proof for the existence of God. The spiritual enlightenment of the various priests and devotees in the temples throughout Egypt and the ancient Near East, Europe and Asia showed how to attain such enlightenment. The proofs are found in the paintings and sculptures of those ancient peoples, as well as in the embodiment of Truth and Goodness within the genuine monks, nuns and holy men of the true religions. But the Hebrews had no proof at all. In fact, they were hated by all of Mankind wherever they went and certainly not because they were the "holy ones of God" but because they were (and are) pretending devils. None of their priests and rabbis could be counted as anything more than scheming frauds. All that they had was a written Contract which they wrote themselves, that was allegedly legitimate only because the High Priests claimed to trace their genealogy back to mythological characters who never existed. Incredibly, those Semitic swindlers offered themselves as the only necessary proof. "See, we have our penises circumcised. So, that proves that we are holy and that God likes us best." This is easy to say for an ugly, bearded rabbi stinking of sour sweat, with a face like an Egyptian dwarf, his clothes splashed with blood and the stench of the three-day old urine in which he washed them to make them ritually "clean." Yes, easy to say! But the people of the world have reacted quite differently than how those frauds desired their victims to treat them.

"See, after we let the animals bleed to death and thrash in their own gore, we squeeze out all the blood from their meat before we eat it. So, that proves that we are a holy people." This is easy to say for a lice-infested Hebrew woman whose rabbi sniffs her menstrual rags to determine whether she is holy in her sexual relations or merely lustful. Both of these foul Jewish creatures offer themselves as proof that God was wise in choosing the Jews as his holy people. But better proof than that is certainly needed. Understanding what a Jew is, is enough to convince you that God certainly did not choose those nasty fiends as his very own best. They lied and chose themselves; and then betrayed Mankind with their frauds.

The Hebrew priests were authorized by their demon god to practice human sacrifice and the immolation of children. If the Hebrews wanted to save their child from the spilling of his blood and butchering and burning him on the altar of Yahweh, then all they had to do was pay some silver to the priest and the mighty god would be satisfied with the bribe.

As "proof" that the sacrifice had to be "just right" and "priestly tight," here in Numbers 3, as a reminder of what happens if the priests don't follow every detail of the law and every custom of the Yahweh-god, "Nadab and Abihu died in the presence of Yahweh, in the wilderness of Sinai, when they offered fire that was unlawful. They left no children and so it fell to Eleazar and Ithamar to exercise the priesthood under their father Aaron." (Nb 3:3-4.) It should be noted that what is "unlawful" has now replaced terms such as "sin." The idea is to bind the Hebrews with "laws" and these "laws" were written by the rabbis who no longer needed a god to declare them. The priests and rabbis would declare the "laws of God" and sign God's name to them.

Zadok and the priests of the Jerusalem Temple traced their lineage back to Eleazar, a lineage based in a mythological fiction. After all, anyone on earth can be related to King Mumbo Jumbo of Sumeria, if you want to write a long enough list of "x begat y" lies on a goatskin parchment. The Levi priests were given the power to kill anyone not of their tribe who walked too close to the Tent of Meeting without permission. "But any layman who comes near is to be put to death." (Nb 3:10.) With this scam, the guards of the treasury were authorized to murder anyone who approached the moneylender's gold or peeked into the empty place where a god was supposed to be residing.

And so, with the authority to tax the Hebrews and to murder them, the priests gained control over the tribes of Canaan through this written Contract. This was a Contract that was binding upon all of the Hebrews based on fraudulent stories from the mythological past, using the tribal genealogies gathered by the Benjamite peddlers, and enforced solely through the murder and monetary fines upon anyone who refused to subject themselves to the bogus Laws. The moneylenders of Babylon drew numerous Hebrew clans into the plot whether or not they were descendants of Levi, merely by writing the names of their clans into the Contract. Once those Hebrew tribes were entered into the genealogy, they were automatically members of "the Chosen Ones." They had been "chosen" but they had no idea why.

To legitimatize that the swindle actually came from God, these phrases are repeated over and over again in Numbers 3: "When Yahweh spoke to Moses on Mount Sinai" and "Yahweh said to Moses." But a better transliteration would be, "When Moses hearkened unto the voices in his head" or "the scribes thought that this would be a convincing lie."

As leader of the Levites, Moses hears Yahweh say to "take a census of all the firstborn among the sons of Israel." (Nb 3:40.) From this count, Yahweh – his very own, majestic, godly, king of the Universe, Himself – calculated in good old money changer fashion that the Levites owed the High Priest 1,365 shekels of silver as a ransom. That is, instead of killing them as a human sacrifice, they could buy their way out of their "debt" to Yahweh by paying a ransom into the treasury. The swindle of the Levites' buying their lives with silver was legitimatized by the final sentence, "Moses handed over this ransom money to Aaron and his sons, at the bidding of Yahweh, as Yahweh had ordered Moses." (Nb 3:51.) Thus, it was all God's fault that the priests were paid with silver.

In this way, the complete subjugation of the tribe of Levi to the High Priest was written into the Contract. That it never happened in the days or in the ways that it was claimed to have happened, didn't matter because the *Hebrew Bible* is not a history book, it is a legal Contract. Its authority is based upon claiming that the ancient Hebrews had acted in a certain way in the past, therefore, the modern Jews are required to act in the same way in the present or else be cursed for not upholding The Contract that their forefathers had allegedly agreed to uphold. The Jewish genealogies, the Semitic *asl*, and the historic and mythological lies upon which The Contract was built, bound the Jews in ways that they did not understand. They were "chosen" but they really didn't know why or by whom. How could they know? Those who wrote the stories were following a secret agenda of concealing their wealth, hiding their assets and depositing their profits in a Temple that was only a safe haven if the members actually believed (or at least pretended to believe) the stories.

When they broke camp, the blood-spattered veil was taken down by Aaron and his sons. This, they used to cover the "Ark of the Testimony." Over this was spread "a covering of fine leather, and spread over the whole a cloth all of violet." (Nb 4:6.) The violet cloth was the super-expensive dye-color that was manufactured from sea snails. This purple cloth represented a huge fortune. And it was used to cover all of the golden implements of the Tent of Meeting. The color represented both royalty but also enormous wealth. And this enormous wealth was claimed to have appeared out of the "trinkets," the bracelets and ear rings, that the Hebrew slaves had allegedly borrowed from their former Egyptian masters; rather than from the huge fortunes that the Hyksos had been allowed to carry with them when they had abandoned their capital of Avaris.

When Aaron and his sons were lifting the tabernacle, tent and golden altar they had to do it "without touching any of the sacred things; otherwise they would die." (Nb 4:15.) The moneylenders of Babylon were repeating these laws so that no priest or Hebrew would get any ideas about filching some of their treasure on deposit. The golden tableware was "sacred" to the bankers of Babylon and they wanted no one to touch it.

From the earliest times, the chief priests, the ones being paid silver and free barbecued goats, were the most corrupt. They benefited the most from the wealth, obedience, adulation and fear of the Hebrews. The Contract stipulated that they were to be paid in silver for their various "rights" and "services." As guardians of the Tent and as servants of the priests, the Levites were ordered not to touch or even look at the golden treasures in the "holy treasury." The Levites were allowed to enter the "holy place" because they must lift and carry the treasures.

> "In this way they can go in and yet cast not their eyes, even for
> a moment, on any of the holy things; if they did, they would
> die." (Nb 4:20.)

The moneylenders of Ur, Harran and Babylon didn't want their guards to be tempted into stealing anything, so to touch or even to look at the gold meant death from the wrath of the Yahweh-god. And if the Yahweh-god was not up to the task, the Chief Priest would step in and order to be killed anyone unlucky enough to glance at the Babylonian banker's gold. That these Levites are to be, not just priests, but armed guards is made clear each time they are mentioned in Numbers 4 as "those fit to bear arms." That all of these Laws were laws of the Yahweh-god is also made clear by the oft-repeated phrase, "at the bidding of Yahweh given through Moses," that is, "at the bidding of the voices in Moses' head."

Only Moses had long conversations with the voices in his head. And he answered back to orders than no one else could hear. It must have been astounding to those raggedy goat-thieves for this old man to be looking up at the sky and carrying on a one-way conversation with thin air. It was a miracle! Who could question its truth? Everybody did what Moses said since no one else could hear anything except Moses talking to himself. The voice of the Yahweh-god only came out of the mouth of Moses And the proof that it was all true was the tabernacle with its Ten Commandments written in stone by God's own finger in the shape of a bronze chisel and, of course, the jar of dead grasshoppers which Moses insisted should be called "manna." All of this "proof" was later conveniently stolen, leaving only the Books of Moses which didn't elevate anybody spiritually or increase their knowledge of God. But it did provide an excellent operating procedure for the Temple treasury with a written Contract.

Expert salesmen that they were, in Numbers 5, the moneylenders of Abraham knew that first impressions are important to any sale. So, enticing the Hebrews to accept their rules meant giving them laws with obvious advantages so that they would also accept the laws that had hidden disadvantages. Numbers 5 begins by claiming the obvious good law which "Yahweh spoke to Moses and said," to kick out of the Hebrew camp anyone who transgressed a taboo and became "unclean" or who was a leper – whichever came first.

The definition of a "sin" is given. Here is what a sin is to today's Jews: "If a man or woman commits any of the sins by which men break faith with Yahweh, that person incurs guilt." (Nb 5:6.) In other words, "sin" is breaking the laws of Abraham's First National Bank and Pawn Shop. By breaking these laws, the "sinner" must pay the priest with a freshly killed barbecue plus one-fifth in silver the value of the sacrifice. Or if his breaking of the Laws harmed a fellow goat rustler, then he must repay his neighbor plus give a free barbecue for the priest. "Sin" for a Jew is not a moral problem, rather, it is merely not following the laws of the Torah.

That the moneylenders of Babylonia had been able to debauch the women of the Fertile Crescent, was shown in Volume I, *The Sumerian Swindle*. The bankers had gained great wealth as pimps and slave merchants. And they had gained great power by making themselves dominant over women. This domination of women is evident in Numbers 5. Although the Hebrew gangsters were as promiscuous as their goats, they kept a tight control over their women, demanding a strict sexual virtue. This way they wouldn't have to play any guessing games like "Who's yo' daddy?" The demonic *abracadabra* of the Hebrew priests was here used for women suspected of infidelity. Such a woman, *whether guilty or not*, was made to stand before the altar of Yahweh and swear to her innocence. Then the priest scrapped up some dirt from the bloody and fly-specked floor of the tabernacle and threw it into a jar of water. This was called the "water of bitterness and cursing." Then the priest imposed an imprecatory oath on the woman and said,

> "May Yahweh make of you an execration and a curse among your people, making your thigh shrivel and your belly swell! May this water of cursing enter your bowels to swell your belly and shrivel your organs! The woman must answer, 'Amen, Amen.'" (Nb 5:21-22.)

Then the priest wrote this curse on parchment and washed the ink of this written curse into the water and made the woman drink the "water of bitterness and cursing." If she was innocent, nothing happened except that she was made to drink filthy water polluted with foul dirt, blood, animal feces and urine, pathogenic bacteria, the eggs of parasitic round worms and tape worms, lamp black and whatever other filth was on the floor or the rabbi's hands. That is, *if she was innocent*, nothing else would happen to the deceived and frightened woman. But the power of the rabbi was enhanced when the woman was infested with worms and she swelled up with the pus of bacterial infections because that "proved" to the warped Semitic mind how powerful the rabbi's curses were. *Abracadabra*, the curse magically became a reality and her guilt was thereby "proven" as she contracted dysentery, botulism, or worms, all scrapped up from in front of the putrid altar of Yahweh. What a miracle! What power of the priests! Innocent or guilty, the woman infected by the disgusting hygiene of a Jewish priest *was always guilty* as was "proven" by her bacterial, fungal or worm infestations. And after she had been infected with pathogens by the priest and her "guilt" thereby "proven," she would be dragged to the door of her father's house by the Jewish priests and stoned to death by all of her friends and neighbors. Certainly, the Jews are the Children of God. What else could they be?

Of course, guilty Hebrews of the "Chosen Ones of God" must always pay money to the Jewish priest so that the terrible Yahweh-god would be appeased. It was always the Jew in the priest-pimp-suit who collected the silver. And therefore, Yahweh withheld his lightning bolts and leprosy.

A Hebrew husband could accuse his wife at any time. However, to uphold their complete enslavement of women, the moneylenders of Babylon stipulated in their Contract that "the husband shall be guiltless, but the woman must bear the punishment for her sin." (Nb 5:31.) As both Judaism and the Sumerian Swindle spread, so did the humiliation, enslavement, and molestation of women.

Every religion has both the ordinary congregant and the super energetic devotee. The priests had a special tax and special rules for them. The Nazarite (the "vowed to God") had to avoid alcohol or even grapes and grape juice. He had to let his hair grow for the period of his vow. He must follow the Laws of Moses so as not to contract "uncleanness" – after all, it was deemed an "unclean and unholy thing" to not uphold the laws of the moneylenders. And of course, he must provide a barbecue for the priests. When his vow was over, he had to provide a big banquet for the priests of yearling lamb, bread and wafers. Then, he shaved off his long hair and burned it on the altar, after which, he could drink wine once again.

Numbers 6 is the blessing that most Christians have heard. The blessing of Yahweh the Demon God of the Canaanites as well as of those new Hebrew immigrants into Palestine, the moneylenders from Babylon led by Abraham and his Benjamite gangsters:

> "May Yahweh bless you and keep you.
> May Yahweh let his face shine on you and be gracious to you.
> May Yahweh uncover his face to you and bring you peace."
> (Nb 6:24-26.)

Working through the greedy hands of his priests who counted the shek-els, this mighty god who owns everything, "Yahweh" took suspiciously special delight in weighing all of the gold and silver offerings and listing all of the animals for barbecue. Numbers 7 is an obscene listing and totaling of the gold and silver bowls by weight and the numbers of innocent animals sacrificed for the priestly barbecue in dedication of the golden altar. Shekel weights of gold and silver bullion melted down and cast into cups and plates and lamps and a golden altar, were still shekel weights of bullion no matter what shape they took. As large, heavy temple utensils, they were harder to steal than small lumps of the metal. No matter what shape or size the bullion was, it could still be used as the backing for interest-bearing loans. Gold was elevated to the highest and holiest goodness while it was hidden-in-plain-sight behind the delu-sion that it was the god and not the gold that the golden altar served. With magi-cian's misdirection, devotees would look upward, beyond the altar, looking for the god, with no thought of the altar, itself, and the gold of which it was made.

Moses' tribe, the Levites, were the obscene, circumcised priests of the Yahweh-god whose penis fetish included not just shaving their heads and beards but also all of the hair off of their bodies – including their pubic hair and the hair around their assholes. Of course, they shaved each other. Using a straight razor to shave around their own anus would be too risky even for the queerest Jews to attempt. Those nasty perverts were the guards of the treasury. Shaving prevented them from smuggling out any small pieces of gold hidden in their body hair. But allegedly, as special temple guards and murder squad, the Levites were there "so that none of the sons of Israel may be struck down for approaching the sanctuary" (Nb 8:19) or its treasury.

The phrase begins to be used that "The sons of Israel did exactly as Yahweh had ordered Moses." (Nb 9:5.) That is, instead of Moses making ap-peals to the Hebrews to follow his lead, now they began to follow his "orders." *This is a transition* into a mindset of no longer being concerned with Moses or with Yahweh but being only concerned with following whatever Moses com-manded, that is, following the Mosaic Law, following what the priests com-manded. *This was an important transition* because it redirected the stupid He-brews from following a fictional man to following a written Contract. The myth was being sublimated while the Contract was being exulted. Making a great show of holding the goatskin scrolls high into the air before reading them, and parading them around the congregation and joyfully dancing around the Torah in their street theater while reverently kissing those words written on the hides of dead goats, the rabbis pulled the Hebrew fools into their scam. Even a dried dog turd can acquire great "prestige" among the onlookers, if those who handle it, handle it with awe and reverence.

The keeping of the Passover was incumbent upon all of the Hebrews and anyone who "fails to keep the Passover, he shall be outlawed from his people." (Nb 9:13.) For the continual brainwashing of the Hebrews, the Passover party was both important and wrathfully commanded because it perpetuates the lies of the Torah. Even today, this Passover party is the basic brainwashing method for convincing every Jew that he was actually there with Moses.

The Hebrews were ordered to make the Laws of Moses their only laws. This is the reason why in modern times, that the Jews tear down the laws of every country in which they reside. Jewish lawyers don't actually, in fact, defend or prosecute anyone because their ulterior motive is not to uphold the law of the land but, rather, to fight against Justice and destroy any laws that are not Mosaic Laws. Look at all of the odd and strange rulings that have occurred in your own country, and you will find Jewish lawyers and judges being the prime movers in the destruction of justice in every country where they are allowed to hold office. The Muslims practice the same betrayal and deceit for their Moon God because they want to replace all laws with the laws of Mohammad (mhrh). It's all Semitic deceit and lies and Semitic hoaxes.

"There is to be only one law among you, for settler and native alike" (Nb 9:14). Thus, when the later Christians would object to Jewish perversions such as pederasty, pornography and Communism, Jewish lawyers would defend those Jewish perversions by claiming the "rights of a child molesters' lifestyle choices" and the "free speech" for social deviants. Morality and social health have always taken a back seat to Jewish law, not because of a "higher Jewish morality" but because of Jewish bribery and blackmail, as you will see demonstrated in later chapters. After all, the Jews claim that their holy piggishness comes from their mighty Yahweh-god, echoing within the sunburned noggin of Moses, while the laws of Mankind come from the *goyim* (non-Jew; lowly insects, stupid cattle). So, of course, the laws of perverse delusion and Jewish corruption are superior to the reasonable laws of Man, according to the demon rabbis.

Here, the complete subjugation of the Hebrews is finally claimed by the priests and scribes. Remember, these documents attained their present form in the scriptoriums of sixth century Babylonia and were written for the audience of those days. So, the emphasis in Numbers 9, is how completely the Hebrews were obedient to Yahweh. "At Yahweh's command they pitched camp, and at Yahweh's command they broke camp." (Nb 9:23.) And all of those commands depended upon a mysterious cloud of flies or a smokey pillar of burning goat carcasses that hung over the Tent of Meeting day and night.

Even though the Torah was written and edited into its present version in Babylonia by 539 BC, and even though it was designed for an audience of the captured Jews of Jerusalem and the city-dwelling Jewish parasites in Babylonia; and even though much of it was used to deceive Persian king Cyrus, its main thrust was to give legitimacy and total authority to *the moneylenders* as priests and controllers of the Temple treasury. Enforced, but left unstated in the Contract, the Chief Priest was the chief banker. You could tell that he was the banker-priest by his expensive, magnificent and awe-inspiring costume. He swaggered about in his official zoot suit of red and purple linens with gold embroidery and chains of gold. A plate of solid gold was strapped to his forehead. A little leather box was strapped to his head and another strapped to his left arm, The holy golden dice table (Ummin and Thumin) was strapped to his chest along with their twelve precious stones sparkling in the sunlight. Golden bells were tied to his dress hem, tinkling to ward off demons. And all of this bizarre fashion statement, from saliva-spattered bushy beard to dirty toenails, was spattered from head to toe with the blood of sheep, goats, bulls and turtle doves. And when the dried blood caked on too thick, his costume was made "clean" by washing it in three-day old urine. Only the expensive fumes from the burning brazier of frankincense and myrrh kept the putrid odors of this filthy beast from gagging the maggots wiggling around the holy altar as the buzzing clouds of flies and sucking gnats buzzed around his putrid magnificence. What other conclusion can be made? This was a genuine Monster of Babylon in his Sabbath best. Yet, this was a Jewish priest, a holy one of God. Just ask him.

These Babylonian moneylenders needed a safe refuge for their loot, guarded by the most powerful gods and protected by the most fanatical priestly guards. For this, an elaborate deceit had been devised, a deceit based upon tribal genealogies that were all connected to events that were especially chosen out of context with history along with events that were entirely fictitious but which gave an awe-inspiring tale of godly power and loyal worshipers.

While the patriarch of the *tamkarum* guilds of Harran and Ur and Babylonia could maintain their private libraries of clay tablets and papyrus book scrolls which were hundreds of years old, the illiterate bandit gangs of Canaan only had their tribal memories of five generations for their historical background. So they were enveloped with a Babylonian deceit older than their memories.

The moneylenders of Babylonia could insinuate themselves into the priesthood of the Hebrew bandit tribes simply by having written documents that listed their own genealogy going back (in the written documents, at least) *more than* five generations. A Hebrew tribal sheikh of the roving bandit gangs, might proudly recite his genealogy of five ancestors but would immediately be trumped by the genealogy of Abraham's First National Bank and Pawn Shop.

A written document has a longer "memory" than a man. The moneylender's fraudulent genealogy went all the way back even to the Creation of the first man and woman. No one could possibly have a longer genealogy. And what a miracle! It also installed the banker's very own family at the root of the genealogy of everybody living in the entire ancient Near East! The words written on the goat-skins "proved" that every Hebrew in Canaan and Arabia was descended from the Babylonian bankers, and thus everybody owed the banker-priests of the temple their allegiance and their donations. With the hoax of the *Hebrew Bible*, the Jews claimed to be the fathers, the patriarchs, the ancestors, the mightiest and wisest kings, the rulers over the people of the entire Middle East! And it was all written down with real lamp black on real goatskins! So, it had to be true! It just had to be true because would God tell lies?

As subservient branches of the Babylonian banker's genealogical tree, the Twelve Tribes, illiterate goat rustlers as they were, were cunningly recruited into the Babylonian banker's genealogy. It was just another banker's swindle using falsified documents but it worked. Claiming the Hebrew tribes as his long-lost relatives, the chief priest of Abraham's First National Bank and Pawn Shop could demand their allegiance and therefore command them as his army. No one in the Hebrew tribes could remember any such relationship, but if the words on the rolled-up goatskins said so, then it must be true.

Numbers 10 begins the war against the people of the world. "Poor," "ragged," "ex-slaves," "running from Pharaoh," they are to use silver trumpets to signal their troops. And these same silver trumpets are to be used at the "festivals, solemnities, or new-moon feasts" (Nb 10:10) of *Yahweh*, the Canaanite god with his consort, *Ishtar*. Poor, ragged, ex-slaves from the desert with silver trumpets. What a miracle!

Now, after being in the wilderness of Sinai for two years, two months and twenty days (there is nothing like exact numbers to give authenticity to a fraud, a number that is exact because it gives the impression of truth), the Hebrew army of goat rustlers begins to march. Although this chapter describes the marching of the Twelve Tribes of bandits, like all of the books of the moneylenders, there is a primary purpose hidden behind a secondary facade. In this case, the marching of the Hebrew bandits is secondary to yet another moneylender swindle. This was the swindle of misdirecting the hatred of the people of the world away from the Jews who deserved such hatred, and blaming the people of the world for hating this Canaanite god instead of hating the Jews who were attacking them!

Hiding behind a mighty Semitic god protected by an army of bandits, the bankers of Babylon wrote that Moses offered up this prayer:

> "As the ark set out, Moses would say, 'Arise, Yahweh, may your enemies be scattered and those who hate you run for their lives before you! And as it came to rest, he would say, 'come back, Yahweh, to the thronging hosts [armies] of Israel.'" (Nb 10:35-36.)

The Contract now claimed that it wasn't the moneylenders, themselves, whom the people of the world hated, nor was it the Hebrew thieves whom the Canaanites hated, but now the Jews claimed that it was the Yahweh-god – God Himself! – whom the people of the world hated. The Hebrews were told that they were holy bandits fighting for God. Regardless of their sundry and numerous sins, the goat rustlers were actually saints fighting against the enemies of God. Centuries later, Mohammad, the Lunatic of Arabia, would use this identical Semitic scam to deceive his own people into going to hell in exchange for warfare and loot. The Semitic delusion is, "Don't blame us for being so holy. We will murder you and steal your stuff not because we are greedy bandits who want what is not ours, but because *you hate our god.* As we murder, rape, arson and steal, we can feel good about ourselves because we do it entirely as holy jihad fighters defending the honor and majesty of God." To the illiterate Semites of the ancient Near East, while scratching their fleas and itching their lice, this made perfect sense. They were valiant warriors for God. And God needed such an army as they. The mighty god was not mighty enough to kill his own enemies; he needed mangy goat molesters to do it for him. *That* would show the people of the world what a mighty god he was!

Now that the moneylenders had finalized their control over the priesthood and the treasury, it was necessary to further terrorize the Hebrew goat rustlers into submission. With the onerous laws giving the moneylender-priests all power and ten percent of all wealth as well as sole ownership of the walled cities while dispossessing the Hebrews from ownership of the land in perpetuity, there was bound to be some grumbling. If a few Hebrews grumble, this cannot be helped. But if these few were to organize enough resistance to the tyrannical priests, then such demonstrations or riots could not be allowed to manifest. Such revolts are dealt with in Numbers 11.

> "Now the people set up a lament which was offensive to Yahweh's ears, and Yahweh heard it. His anger blazed, and the fire of Yahweh burned among them; it destroyed one end of the camp. The people appealed to Moses, and he interceded with Yahweh and the fire died down. So the place was called Taberah, because the fire of Yahweh had burned among them."
> (Nb 11:1-3.)

In this case, the Hebrews were complaining about not having enough to eat. Jewish whining hurts everybody's ears. But these Jews whined so much that it even hurt Yahweh's ears. Yahweh knew the proper way to deal with Jewish whining. So, He blasted one end of the camp.

The whining and rioting was attributed to greed (Nb 11:4) which was a convenient and hypocritical accusation from the guardian-priests of the Treasury. Even though for forty years in the empty desert, they had been slaughtering bulls and goats and feeding the barbecued meat to the priests, the Hebrews were tired of eating the daily rations of grasshoppers (manna). But writing from their well-fed sinecure in Babylon, the scribes under Ezra re-wrote the part about fried grasshoppers and made it sound more delicious.

> "The manna was like coriander seed, and had the appearance of bdellium. The people went round gathering it, and ground it in a mill or crushed it with a pestle; it was then cooked in a pot and made into pancakes. It tasted like cake made with oil. When the dew fell on the camp at night-time, the manna fell with it."
> (Nb 11:7-9.)

But while the Hebrews were eating this miraculous and delicious manna, the priests were eating barbecued ribs and steaks and filet mignon. Enough of this vegetarian food, already! The bloodthirsty Hebrews demanded meat! So, Moses went moaning and whining to Yahweh that "Oy Gevalt! You treat me so bad, it's a shame! Oy! These 600,000 yapping kikes give me such a head-ache that you should kill me already rather than let me suffer." So, the spirit of Moses was transferred to the seventy elders, further spreading the delusion that the spirit of Moses could be shared among the priests and rabbis and therefore become a part of the Jewish *asl* that their descendants could inherit.

Yahweh's Semitic, vindictive nature is here expressed as he tells Moses, "If those whining Hebes want meat, I will give them so much meat that they will grow sick of it." And he sent a wind that blew quails from the sea. There were so many quails that they "lay for a distance of a day's march either side of the camp, two cubits thick on the ground" (Nb 11:31) rotting in the heat and perfectly kosher. Because they had whined about not having meat to eat not only did this mighty and vindictive Moon God give them more than they could eat, but "The meat was still between their teeth, not even chewed, when the anger of Yahweh blazed out against the people. Yahweh struck them with a very great plague." (Nb 11:33.) And that's what happens to Hebrews who complain about anything. So, follow the Laws of Moses, and don't complain about how stupid those laws are.

Instead of restricting the Contract to a mere legal document, giving the priests an authority by law, Numbers 11 makes the claim that the priests also have a special mystical power. By whining and complaining to god, Moses is shown to be needy of help in controlling the masses of bitching Hebrews. So, part of the power of Moses is allegedly passed on to seventy elders. And not just the sixty-eight elders who showed up for the meeting but also to the two elders, Eldad and Medad, whose names were merely on the invitations. In this way, the swindle of Moses and the priests getting a mystical power boost from the Yahweh-god, is passed along to seventy other Hebrews. These seventy special, old Hebrews are known as the Sanhedrin, the top judges of Israel. These seventy, lying old bastards began to "prophesy," that is, they raved non-sense and babbled incoherent gibberish. And since no one could understand a word of it, it was called "prophesy," or a "telling forth" and has ever since been considered as a special Jewish talent – double talk and gibberish – which gives modern Jewish lawyers and politicians such extraordinary power for convincing the people of about anything. In this way, the Sanhedrin was given godly power over the Jews – and it was all done with *abracadabra*.

The intermixture of Hebrews with Negroes is attested in Numbers 12. For centuries, the Egyptians had taken captive black slaves from Nubia and Kush. When the Hyksos were chased out of Egypt, some of those Negro slave women went with them. In addition, when the merchant-moneylenders of Ur had made treaties with the Nubians for the Hyksos invasion of Egypt, to seal their bargains, they had taken Nubian women as wives. To explain the Negro genetics such as frizzy hair and thick, sucking lips among the Jews, Numbers 12 says that Moses added a Kushite woman to his harem. Miriam and Aaron spoke against Moses about marrying a Negress so the scribes of Babylon gave the standard Semitic explanation that all religions of the ancient Near East gave in regard to dreams:

"Yahweh said, 'Listen now to my words: If any man among you is a prophet, I make myself known to him in a vision, I speak to him in a dream. Not so with my servant Moses; he is at home in my house; I speak with him face to face, plainly and not in riddles, and he sees the form of Yahweh. How then have you dared to speak against my servant Moses?'" (Nb 12: 6-8.)

In this way, the Negro genetics of the Hebrews as well as of modern Jews, was established as another proof that Moses could do what he wanted as far as marrying strange women. And for speaking against Moses, Miriam was struck with leprosy by Yahweh. Only after Moses whined and begged for her healing was she cured. So, be warned, all of you Hebrews, accept the laws of Moses or suffer the consequences of refusal. Thus, the scribes taught that the Hebrews have been a mixed race from the very earliest times. A holy "race" of sly mongrels!

Dreams about the gods had an ancient history as old as Mankind. The so-called "prophets" are here defined as those who have dreams and visions about the gods, often in the form of riddles. After all, even modern people can't make any sense out of our own dreams, so the ancient people could not be any better at it. Any man or woman who remembers their dreams know that most of them are a sort of riddle – maybe they mean something and maybe they don't. The ancient "prophets" in some respects were like the swindling fakes known in modern times as psychologists. The biggest fraud of all time was the Jew, Sigmund Freud, who invented an entire con that he called "psychoanalysis" where he suggested "meanings" for people's dreams. The ancient prophets did likewise, giving advice and "analysis" of the dreams people had – for a fee!

Numbers 13 sets the stage for future battles. This army of 600,000 goat rustlers sent out spies to reconnoiter Canaan. They reported that the land is a land of "milk and honey" but it was inhabited by giants so huge that the Hebrews "felt like grasshoppers." (Nb 13:33.)

Numbers 14. When the Hebrews heard how big those giants were, "the whole community raised their voices and cried aloud, and the people wailed all that night." (Nb 14:1.) The constant whining and bitching and complaining of the modern Jews has a long and wearisome tradition.

Numbers 14 sets the stage for eliminating witnesses. Because the Hebrews showed their basic cowardice and were afraid of the giants, and because they wanted to go back to Egypt even after all the alleged miracles in the desert, Yahweh refrained from blasting them with his hot breath because Moses talked Him out of it. Because Yahweh was a vicious and vindictive god, he declared for those disobedient Hebrews that "not one shall see the land I swore to give their fathers." (Nb 14:23.) In this way, the competing genealogy of any of the other Hebrews in Canaan who would have had different stories to tell about the Hyksos retreat, was blocked. The Jewish fables were restricted only to the genealogy of the Mosaic Contract. Any other stories about what happened during those times was conveniently snuffed out with the clause of the Contract stating that everybody died, *leaving only the words of The Contract as evidence.*

In addition to killing off all witnesses by causing all of the original escapees from Egypt to die in the desert, Numbers 14 defines "sin." Sin is defined as

> "You shall bear the burden of your sins and you shall learn what it means to reject me. I, Yahweh, have spoken: this is how I will deal with this perverse community that has conspired against me. Here in this wilderness, to the last man, they shall die."
> (Nb 14:34-35.)

This reinforces the terrorism of Judaism over the Hebrews. Rejecting the laws of Moses is equated to a "sin." The consequences *for the whole community* are dire, according to the scribes of Babylon. Note the group consciousness of these edicts. One single Hebrew breaking the Law, was an invitation to the terrible Yahweh-god to blast the entire community with his plagues and incendiary displays.

> "The men whom Moses had sent to reconnoiter the land, who on their return had incited the whole community of Israel to grumble against Yahweh by disparaging it, these men who had disparaged the land were all struck dead before Yahweh. Of the men who had gone to reconnoiter the land, only Joshua son of Nun and Caleb son of Jephunneh remained alive."
> (Nb 14:36-38.)

Not only must the Hebrews offer up rams and sheep and bulls to the Yahweh-god as a means of feeding the priests and rabbis, but they must make sure that the priests have bread and wine to go along with the feast – out there in the desert where all there is to eat is manna and quails. The Yahweh-god gets to smell the barbecue while the priests eat it. The precise amounts are given in Numbers 15.

Once again, the Jewish desire for destroying the people and the countries around them is based in Numbers 15.

> "Any stranger living among you, or among your descendants, will also make a burnt offering, an appeasing fragrance for Yahweh: just as you act, so must the assembly. There shall be only one law for you and for the settler among you. This is a law that shall bind your descendants always: before Yahweh, you and the settler are alike. There is to be one law only, and one statute for you and for the stranger who lives among you."
> (Nb 15:14-16.)

Upon such tyranny is based the corruption and Judaization of all modern societies in which Jews are allowed to live.

This Law gave the Bankers of Babylon a secure treasury, free guards to protect their loot, ownership of the walled cities and authority over the Hebrew tribes of Canaan as well as a permanent military deferment. For all of this protection, they were willing to pay a ten percent yearly tithe for membership in an exclusive merchant and moneylender guild, protected by a mighty god.

Even among the Hebrews who made it a practice to murder anyone who was not of their tribes, these "settlers" were an important part of their communities. These were non-Hebrews who fulfilled the occupation of "Shabbos goyim" (Sabbath-working, non-Jewish, lowly insects, stupid cattle). They were the ones who worked for the Jews during the Sabbath and holidays when work was forbidden. The "strangers" were also the business contacts that the moneylenders of Babylonia kept. They were the agents of the moneylenders who arranged for the import-export business outside of the Hebrew territories. As visiting merchants of importance, even though they were not circumcised Jews, they were treated kindly since they brought business profits.

The Sabbath was not a day of rest where the Hebrews were allowed to rest from work and party with their friends. It was a day of strict brainwashing and slavery to the Law. "While the sons of Israel were in the wilderness, a man was caught gathering wood on the Sabbath day." (Nb 15:32.) This "breaking of the Sabbath," that is, doing what you want to do, was punished with stoning. But stoning among the Jews is also a form of group murder. "The whole community took him outside the camp and stoned him till he was dead, as Yahweh had commanded Moses." (Nb 15:36.) When the entire community killed someone, the terrorization of the whole community, itself, is insured. No community member would dare to break the Laws contained in the Contract. And every community member kept a careful eye on each other to fulfill the laws so that all of them did not suffer from plague or earthquake or lightning bolt or being stoned to death by their fellow Jews. The strictness of Sabbath-breaking punishments was maintained simply because if even one Jew was seen working on Saturday (Saturn's Day), then the kings would be able to force all the Jews into the army where they would have to actually risk life and limb fighting in the wars that they had financed and caused.

Numbers 16 solidifies the ownership of the Office of High Priest in a power struggle between the Levites and the High Priest. A question can always arise in any goat rustler community, "If we are *all* holy, then why should we get bossed around by the High Priest?" Numbers 16 solved that problem by declaring that the office of High Priest is its own institution that the lower priests and sub-priests should not covet, unless they want the dire consequences that come to those who try to usurp the high priesthood for themselves. The High Priest received much more wealth and had much more power than anyone else. Even though the banking and money lending system known as Judaism was designed to make money and to protect money as its primary goal, it offered free and cost-saving "blessings" to the ordinary priests and laymen while it gave *the actual wealth and power* to the High Priest who managed the scam. The priests entitled themselves to ten percent of all profits of farms and businesses. By keeping the Levites dependent solely upon the tithes as their only income, meant that they became the policemen for enforcing the Law of Moses since they had no other function and did not own property or farms. Levites lived in every Hebrew community to keep an eye out for "sinners" and to fine them accordingly.

There couldn't be any challenge to the authority of the office of High Priest or else the entire fraud would dissolve into a religion of fools seeking "blessings" rather than being a corporate and community entity seeking profits. Furthermore, the office of High Priest was genealogically inherited by the Patriarchal merchant-moneylender guilds of Harran and Ur. As an office that could never be shared outside of the moneylender's guild, Numbers 16 was written into the Contract for this reason. In punishment for all of the rebels against the High Priest's authority – for all of the two hundred and fifty men along with their entire families, tents and possessions – the earth opened up and conveniently swallowed them. "A fire came down from Yahweh and consumed the 250 men carrying incense." (Nb 16:35.)

Can you believe that? The earth opening beneath your feet and swallowing you and your whole family and then you are all blasted by fiery lightning from the sky, that's what happens if you question the sole and supreme authority of the High Priest. So, don't do it. He is just too powerful to be trifled with or teased. Let the priests run the whole carnival as they see fit, if you know what's good for you.

Thus, the Levites were taught that murdering goats and splashing their victims' blood on the altar among the flies, would make them holy. But they must never believe that such bloody holiness would empower them to "aspire to the office of priesthood." (Nb 16:10.) The office of High Priest was inherited in the genealogy written with lamp black on the dead goatskins of the Contract. It was inherited by only one, particular family. It could not be acquired by anyone else. So, don't even think about it.

Death is what "sanctified" the fly-swarming altars of the Yahweh-god. Blood spilled and spattered and poured out in torrents from dead victims of sacrifice, and now in Numbers 17, the 250 men carrying incense became a sacrifice. After opening the earth and swallowing up Korah's men then sending down fire from the sky that burnt up the 250 men carrying censers of incense, the cheapskate god of the merchant-moneylenders didn't want to waste those expensive bronze censers. So Moses was ordered to "pick the censers out of the ashes and take this unlawful fire elsewhere, for these sinful censers are sanctified, at the price of these men's lives." (Nb 17:1-2.) After all, brass was valuable and shouldn't be wasted. It makes sense to a moneylender. And since these "sinners who broke the law" were burnt to ashes, they wouldn't be needing their censers anymore, anyway.

The 250 bronze censers in this fable, were gathered from the ashes and hammered into sheets to cover the altar as a reminder to the goat rustlers that "no layman, no one outside of Aaron's line, may come near to Yahweh with incense to burn, under pain of" fire from heaven blasting them to ashes. (Nb 17:5.) Once again, the genealogy of the priests is the only thing keeping them in power. In this way, through a genealogy written into the Contract, the Babylonian Patriarchs of Abraham's First National Bank and Pawn Shop became the actual owners of the temple of Yahweh and the actual power behind Judaism.

More street theater was practiced by the priests to deceive their gawking audience. The priests fell down on their faces and then ran around in the crowd with a censer of smoking incense, fumigating the Hebrews as protection from the wrath of God, in this case delivered in the form of a plague. For the great sin of so much as questioning the priesthood, 14,700 Hebrews were allegedly killed by plague and only the magic incense of Aaron and Moses saved the rest of them. This was yet another reminder of what happens when the genealogy of the Levites is challenged. And for something like a plague, who ya' gonna' call, an ordinary goat rustler who the earth will swallow up or a genuine, honest-to-goodness Levite who knows how to wail and sob and wave incense smoke around in a holy way? The Levites and Jewish priests were professional con artists. Anyone who dared to muscle in on their labor union would be blasted by God, Himself – according to the fables that they wrote.

To further emphasize how Aaron and his tribe of Levi were to be the only priests in the service of the Yahweh-god, another "miracle" was invented telling of how the Hebrews were ordered to write the names of their tribes on twelve almond branches. Only the branch with the name of Levi sprouted, complete with buds, flowers and ripened nuts. With such blasting by fire against dissidents, and such a miracle of ripe nuts, how could the Hebrews doubt that anyone other than the house of Levi could be qualified as being the ripest nuts?

The moneylenders of Babylon wanted this very important lesson to be emphasized to the Hebrew bandits. If anyone other than the Levites go near the sacred golden vessels on the golden altar, they will be blasted into ashes by – drum roll and clash of cymbals here – "the Wrath." So, the one-way Contract is stipulating that the only Hebrews safe from the thunderbolts of the Yahweh-god, are the tribe of Levi. As long as the Levite priests guarded the gold, the Hebrews were safe from – drumroll and clash of cymbals here – "the Wrath." Anyone who approaches the golden loot and who is not of the tribe of Levi – drum roll and clash of cymbals here – "Shall Die." Remember, the ancient treasure rooms of the temples had no steel doors, time locks or burglar alarms. The vengeance and lightning bolts of the gods is what potential thieves feared the most. And with stories like this, the mighty Yahweh-god was getting some good reputation points among the local yokels of Canaan.

Numbers 18 finishes the swindle by transferring to the priests, all food and wine and wealth that are devoted to the temple or extracted from the "sinners." Through the voices in Moses' head, the Yahweh-god declared for the priests: "Everything that the sons of Israel consecrate I give to you as your portion, as well as to your sons, by perpetual ordinance." (Nb 18:8.) All of the offerings by the Hebrews are declared to be "a most holy thing" so the professional priests get it all. This way, everything that is on deposit in the treasury is safe from pilferage since the priests are so well paid and supported by a Contract signed by God.

Numbers 18 is the basis of the greed and avarice of the priesthood of Yahweh. These priests and rabbis were the ultimate in parasites, pretending to be "holy" and pretending to be "worthy" of all wealth and food and property that flowed onto center stage of the Yahweh circus. Theatrical circus performances were scheduled precisely at breakfast, lunch and dinner times; only instead of enjoying the animals doing tricks, the priests slaughtered and ate them. Numbers 18 sets the stage for the lying rabbis to increase the numbers of laws a thousand-fold in what came to be called "The Tradition of the Elders" which was later published as the *Babylonian Talmud*. The more laws there are, the more people who are ensnared by them. The more people who "transgress" the laws, then the more wealth that the priests could con from the superstitious gangs of goat rustlers. So, more laws made for fatter priests.

In addition to the wealth that the priests could suck away from the Hebrews, was also everything that was declared by them to be under "the ban," that is, under the murderous banditry of "genocide."

> "All in Israel on which the ban is laid shall be yours. Every firstborn brought to Yahweh shall be yours, of all living creatures, whether man or beast; nevertheless you must redeem the firstborn of man, and you must redeem the firstborn of an unclean beast. You must redeem it in the month in which it is born at the price of five shekels, each of sanctuary weight – which is twenty gerahs. The first born of cow, sheep and goat, these alone you shall not redeem. They are holy; you must sprinkle their blood on the altar and burn the fat as a burnt offering, an appeasing fragrance for Yahweh; the meat shall be yours, together with the breast that has been presented with the gesture of offering, and the right thigh." (Nb 18:14-19.)

This part of the Contract assured a steady income for the priests who guarded the Treasury. Independently wealthy, fat priests would be less likely to steal the moneylenders' gold than poor, skinny, starving priests. And by couching their service in terms of "holy" and "priestly" they could be conditioned to not think about such worldly things as the moneylender's gold on deposit in the god's Treasury. Sending the Hebrews out to raid, pillage, murder, rape and loot, was good business for the priests of Yahweh who could put the "ban" on any village that seemed "sinful" enough to warrant extinction, which was any of them with any wealth at all.

To make sure that the priests did not become detached from serving the Treasury by becoming independent landowners, the Contract stipulates that the Levites may not own land. They are to be perpetual leeches, skimming ten percent of all wealth from the Hebrews. But even from all of their larcenous wealth, the Levites are to give ten percent to the High Priest. After all, a tax requires an accounting and with an accounting, the High Priest can keep an eye on how much the Levites have. A neat scam, all of it. The operating costs of the treasury and altar are set at ten percent of everything that the goat rustlers either steal or actually work to acquire.

The magic water from the altar is an antidote to the Jewish disease of "uncleanness" and "sin" in the same way that candy pills are an antidote for disease in a child's toy doctor kit. Here again in Numbers 19, the magic practiced by the priests is delineated by giving the recipe for magic water. What the priests call "lustral water" is made by, once again, killing an innocent animal, in this case a red heifer. The animal is butchered outside the camp in the presence of a demon priest of the Yahweh-god. The priest sprinkles some of its blood a magical seven times in the direction of the altar. The animal is burned and its ashes are gathered up. These magic ashes are used to make the magic lustral water. So, the ashes are kept in a leather bag until some emergency requires its use.

Whenever a goat rustler "sins" by breaking a Law of the Contract or if he becomes "unclean" by doing something nasty like touching a dead Jew or a live pig, then some of the magic ashes are quickly scooped from the leather bag and sprinkled into a container of water by a priest. As a kind of instant Kool-Aid, the magic ashes instantly turns ordinary tap water into magic "lustral water" which has the power to wash away the "sins" and the "uncleanness." And what a powerful magic it was, too! The Lustral Kool-Aid could make something that didn't actually exist to disappear entirely! Presto-change-o! In the minds of the stinky, flea-bitten goat rustlers of Canaan, this was truly a miracle! Those scheming, hairy-faced rabbis were really powerful priests to be able to make uncleanness vanish like that! Their fluffy beards hid their sly grins and forked tongues.

Another miracle for thirsty desert rats, out in the middle of no-where, was a spring of water flowing from beneath a rock. Where did it come from since there was nothing but desert rocks and sands as far as the eye could see? Geological layers of sandstone and shale allowed water to flow hundreds of miles underground and spring up as "the waters of Meribah" (Nb 20:13). Why not claim that it appeared as part of the *asl* of Moses? No tribe of goat rustlers could explain how underground geological layers could conduct water from distant mountains. But if every goat rustler in Canaan was told that this oasis was created by the Yahweh-god of Moses, then that would bring glory to the *asl* of the Jews. And that's what they did. After all, for the bankers to claim that their personal god created the world in six days, then a mere spring of water in the middle of a desert would be easy. With a flourish of the scribe's pen, a million-year-old oasis in the desert never existed until the mythical Moses made it appear by hitting a rock with a tree branch.

But Numbers 20 is more than a creation claim for an act of Nature. This "miracle" gives an excuse for the lying Yahweh-god of the Hebrews to renege on his promise, not the best thing for a god to do, but business as usual for a god of the lying merchant-moneylenders. The excuse the Yahweh-god gave for renouncing his promise was that because Moses and Aaron "did not believe that I could proclaim my holiness in the eyes of the sons of Israel, you shall not lead this assembly into the land I am giving them." (Nb 20:12.) The important part of this passage was that Moses and Aaron "did not believe." So, the Yahweh-god changed his promise into a curse – because Moses and Aaron did not believe, then they would die before they laid their eyes on Canaan. And the office of High Priest was given to Aaron's son, Eleazar.

Little by little, these Books of Moses, written and edited by the merchant-moneylender scribes under Ezra the Scribe in Babylonia, was drawing the net tighter. "The whole community saw that Aaron had died, and all the House of Israel wept for Aaron for thirty days." (Nb 20:29.) In this way, all of the original characters in the story are killed off so that there are no witnesses who can dispute any of the tales in the myths of the Exodus and wandering in the desert.

From this point in the Contract, the so-called "conquest" of Canaan begins. This has always been one of the high points in Jewish "pride," being able to claim great heroism in committing genocide against much greater odds and a fabricated tradition of being great warriors, all based on the fictions of the *Hebrew Bible*. Lies are the real foundation of Jewish pride because with big lies, little thieves appear mighty.

For example, the Canaanite cities (Numbers 21:1-3) that the Yahweh-god was called upon to destroy, none of them existed in the Late Bronze Age when the Book of Numbers was allegedly written by Moses who described these nonevents. The same situation is at Heshbon (Numbers 21:21-25; Deuteronomy 2:24-35; Judges 11:19-21). Heshbon is given a lot of negative advertising as is Edom and Ammon. And yet those towns and kingdoms did not exist at the time of the alleged Exodus. Archaeology has shown us that there were no kings of Edom for the Israelites to meet or Edomites for the rabbis to hate. However, in the seventh century BC, when the majority of the Torah was written, there were well established kingdoms there.

This method of the lies that the rabbis used, is clear. The *locations* mentioned in the biblical stories are real, but the stories are false. The location of Sinai is true, Jericho, the Red Sea locations, are all true but the stories are false. This same *abracadabra* technique of the rabbis would be used to malicious effect in the Twentieth Century AD, when the concentration camps of Nazi Germany were real but the stories that the lying Jews told were false. This ancient Aramaic word, "abracadabra," means "I create as I speak." So when the Jews claim to be speaking for God and then speaking a lie, then that makes it a truth – according to the warped and deluded Semitic mind – because God doesn't lie. At least, the *real* God doesn't lie, but the Yahweh-god of the Hebrews proved to be the God of Lies and the God of Liars. All Jews are liars simply because they are Jews. And why? Because lies are the foundation of Judaism.

Even the mind-boggling enormity of the lie doesn't matter because by persisting in that lie, whether it's about the Red Sea opening up to let the Hebrew thieves escape from Pharaoh or about Joshua commanding the sun to stop transiting the sky, none of this matters to the success of the lie because the size of the lie doesn't matter. What matters is that every Jew tells the same lie and attacks anyone who denies its veracity. Only then can the lie persist while any opposing truth is disallowed. Jews tell the Devil's Truth. When no truth is allowed, then what else can the lies of the Jews be other than truth, since that's all that there is – lies and no truth to counter them? The Devil's Truth.

What archaeology proves is that the major places in the story of the wandering Israelites were nothing but empty wilderness during the times that they claim to have been written. The "mighty" Jewish kingdoms were nothing but villages of goat-herders and emptier wilderness. The "victorious" Hebrew bandits were victorious over empty fields and small, undefended hamlets.

The first act of genocide that the Hebrews committed against the defenseless Canaanites was in the Negeb region south of Canaan in the towns around Arad. Numbers 21 begins by claiming *that neither Moses nor the Yahweh-god* had commanded the Hebrews to kill everyone in those towns but that *it was the Hebrews themselves* who wanted to murder them all. Again, it is not a bunch of ratty-looking desert thieves, in the plural tense, who want to commit murder *but all of them together*, speaking in the singular tense, in one voice and that one voice is the voice of "Israel" stated in this manner: "Israel then made this vow to Yahweh, 'If you deliver this people into my power, I will lay their towns under ban.' Yahweh heard the voice of Israel and delivered the Canaanites into their power." (Nb 21:1-2.) The Jews, themselves – as one, unified gang – wanted to genocide the non-Jews. And it is this group dynamic which the moneylenders of Babylon were trying to harness.

Most Christian commentators look upon this as "an act of religion" – that is, if slaughtering people at the hand of bloody Semites, could possibly be an act of "religion." Such ignorant Christians are overlooking the Contract for what it is, blatant lies hidden behind a tinsel of religion. They are so blinded by the *abracadabra* bragging of the Jews that *they can't understand what the words actually say* in their Bibles.

In the first place, in Numbers 21, it is no longer Moses moving his big mouth which is heard only by the Moon God, but now the Yahweh-god is listening to *all of the Hebrews* yelling up at the sky. The transfer of delusional power has now been made in Numbers 21 from the mythological Moses to his scrofulous little monsters calling themselves "Israel," a word than now is defined as *all of the Hebrew goat rustler tribes bunched together as one conspiring gang of thieves and murderers*.

In the second place, this "act of religion" by placing a "ban" or an "anathema" upon a town or village doesn't just mean that all of the people are slaughtered but that also all of their property is given to the Levites and priests. The so-called "religious act" that the Bible commentators claim, is none other than the act of bandit-priests sanctimoniously enriching themselves by having the Hebrews commit genocide upon the Canaanites. The Hebrew goat rustlers fought for free, proving how "religious" they were while providing Abraham's First National Bank and Pawn Shop with the solution for Problem #12 of The Fifteen Secret Problems of the Babylonian Moneylenders: "Armies are expensive so how can they be induced to fight for free?" Then, after committing genocide on their victims, all the loot is given to the priests. This was a real incentive for the spittle-speckled beards of these bloody and raving priests to open wide their ravenous mouths and to declare a genocidal ban on every village that possessed any wealth.

The subtle and sneaky part of Numbers 21 claims that "the people lost patience. They spoke against God and against Moses." (Nb 21:5.) So, the Yahweh-god sent fiery serpents (that is, winged serpents or dragons) among the goat rustlers. Their snake bites caused death but Moses made a magic bronze serpent and put it on a pole and waved it around. Anyone who was snake-bit got better after looking at the bronze serpent on the pole. "Oy Gevalt! Almost too much to believe! But here it is, written by Moses, himself! Moses, the Jewish doctor, waving an image of Ningishzida, the Babylonian snake deity of the underworld and god of all physicians. (recall Figure 60) Oy, the miraculous power these Jewish doctors have!"

Thumping their chests with pride, the Jewish priests bragged about the mighty kings that they had conquered. However, the princes of the Canaanite cities who are described in the *Hebrew Bible* as powerful enemies were, in actuality, pathetically weak. Excavations have shown that the cities of Canaan in this period were not regular cities of the kind we know in later history. They were mainly administrative strongholds for the elite, housing the village chief, his family, and his small entourage of bureaucrats, with the peasants living scattered throughout the surrounding countryside in small villages. The typical city had only a palace, a temple compound, and a few other public edifices – probably residences for high officials, inns, and other administrative buildings. But there were no city walls. The formidable Canaanite cities described in the conquest narrative of the *Hebrew Bible* were not protected by fortifications! The Conquest of Canaan stories are all fables! Archaeology proves that the Jews never did any of the things that they claim.

After the goat rustlers (in their imaginations) had slaughtered all of the people of Sihon and Heshbon, with their bronze serpent on a pole they went on their usual rampages and slaughtered everybody else in the region. After all of this genocide and pillage, those Hebrew bandits then pretended to be innocent travelers and

"Israel sent messengers to say to Sihon, king of the Amorites, 'I wish to pass through your land. We will not stray into fields or vineyards; we will not drink any water from the wells; we will

keep to the king's highway until we are clear of your frontiers."
(Nb 21:21-22.)

Oh, what honest and polite bandits and holy murderers! In other words, it was the Jewish Shalom. "Shalom! Trust us. We just slaughtered all of your neighbors but now we come in peace. Now we are honest and truthful Hebrews, holy and true to our word. We never lie. So, grant us access to your water wells and gardens and we promise not to drink any water or eat anything. And we promise not to kill you or rape your children. Shalom! See, we said 'Peace!' with our own holy lips. So, you can trust all 600,000 of us, all fully armed and standing at you gate! Shalom! Now open up!"

The Bible commentators and the Christian readers might be fooled but the king of Sihon was not fooled by such obvious chicanery. The easy part of any conquest is gaining access to the areas where are found the fields, vineyards and water wells while the steep ravines and boulder-strewn mountains are difficult. What the Hebrews were trying to do with their fake "Jewish Shalom," was to invade the country without a fight. But the king of Sihon wasn't taken in by the ruse and he attacked. So, the legions of goat rustlers counterattacked and butchered the people of Bashan and they took possession of his country (Nb 21:35), a country that they stole through warfare and murder according to the self-glorifying fables of the *Hebrew Bible*. But a country that was actually empty of any people and vacant of any towns at that time, according to the facts of archaeology.

After evicting and slaughtering all of the people of Transjordania, "the little children as far as Dibon, the women as far as Nophah, the men as far as Medeba, Israel settled in the land of the Amorites." (Nb 21:30-31.) "Not one of them escaped." The Hebrews slaughtered everybody and "took possession of his country." (Nb 21:35.) Later in the book of Deuteronomy, Moses and his God of Genocide, cursed these very Amorites for not welcoming the Hebrew thieves and murderers with bread and water and bent knee blessings for such Holy Ones of God, these stinking, murdering goat rustlers from the desert. That later Semitic perversion, Islam, would likewise declare a Muslim's right to kill you and steal your property because he is so holy. The Semites! Jews and Muslims, holy as the Devil and twice as tricky.

Once again, the theme of Numbers 22 tries to weld the various Hebrew tribes into a single military-political entity. It is no longer Moses who is directing those gangs of goat rustlers but now the Contract for the third time in as many chapters tells of "Israel" doing this and "Israel" doing that. The power is no longer the Yahweh-god or Moses conjuring up demands, but it is now a unified group named "Israel" that is the potent force. This force (or farce) was written of as unified and of immense numbers, as if the "sons of Israel" were a threat because of their immense numbers. This is another Jewish hint to "go forth and have sex and lots of children for Yahweh."

The Yahweh-god had another priest named Balaam whom the king of Moab asked for help against the Hebrews. But instead of the Hebrews declaring themselves to be holy, now it is Balaam who claims that the Hebrews are blessed by the Yahweh-god. Of course, since archaeology proves that there were no Moabites at that time, there was no Balaam to declare them holy. So, they were obviously doing what the Jews do today, declaring themselves holy – all proofs to the contrary ignored.

This idea of "a people dwelling apart, not reckoned among the *goyim*" (Nb 23:10) is here expressed by the merchant-moneylender scribes as something to be proud of. In fact, this idea is designed to further enmesh the Hebrew goat rustlers into the moneylenders' trap. Just as the bankers want to keep their money for themselves, Judaism was designed so that the bankers could also keep their temple guards for themselves. Mixing the Jews with other people would allow other people and other religions to show the Jews what a foul and fraudulent system they were following. Judaism disappears in the light of Truth. And when Judaism disappears, the bankers and financiers will all be hung for their crimes and their swindled wealth will revert to Mankind and not be touched by the Jews.

In the years since 1967 AD, teams of archaeologists and students have combed virtually every valley, ridge and slope in Palestine, looking for traces of wall and scatters of pottery shards. These blanket surveys revolutionized the study of early Israel. They discovered the remains of a dense network of highland villages – all apparently established within a span of a few generations – established around 1200 BC. There was no sign of violent invasion. They were merely Hebrew goat rustlers settling down in places that had not already been settled by the other Canaanites. Once again, archaeology proves the *Hebrew Bible* false. The early Hebrews "dwelled apart" because nobody wanted anything to do with such low-life thieves.

Numbers 23 is a morale building exercise in deceit, making a Hebrew rabble into a powerful army. It is always happy propaganda for the Hebrews to hear their priests read "here is a people like a lioness rising, poised like a lion to spring; not lying down till he has devoured his prey and drunk the blood of his victims" (Nb 23:24). These kinds of allusions linked with the kosher laws against eating blood, have created the world's most bloodthirsty monsters. The Babylonian moneylenders were creating their own country out of wandering Hyksos-Hebrew riffraff. That these scheming and murderous goat rustlers would imagine themselves to be like bloodthirsty lions, was the propaganda value of Numbers 23. This very phrase has been used by legions of Jewish rebels and revolutionaries for the next 2500 years to commit acts of cannibalism, necromancy, blood-drinking and ritual murder upon the people of the world. Wherever Jews were allowed to live, they committed monstrous atrocities because the *Hebrew Bible* stipulated that God gave them permission. The Jews have always been just what Jesus said that they are: liars, deceivers, hypocrites, murderers and the very children of the devil.

Numbers 24 not only is more of Balaam's blessing on the Hebrew goat-thieves but it gives an historical notation of when the alleged events took place. Balaam prophesies that "the Sea Peoples gather in the north, ships from the coast of Cyprus" (Nb 24:23). These Sea Peoples, Balaam prophesies, will destroy what the Hebrews do not.

Accurate prophesies are a powerful indication that the prophet is reliable when the prophesy is fulfilled. Like so much of the historical reverse engineering that the scribes of Babylonia used for their bogus Contract, writing about a past event as if it was a foretold future event, gave the illusion that the prophet was a seer of the future rather than a fraud.

The Sea Peoples attacks were between 1208-1190 BC when they established themselves as the Philistines (for whom Palestine is named). Since the Five Books of Moses were written in the 700s and later edited during the Captivity of 539 BC, then it wasn't difficult to make Balaam into a far-seeing prophet, "foretelling" events that had long ago already transpired over 500 years previously. This was a standard technique that the swindling moneylenders of Babylon used throughout the *Hebrew Bible*, telling lies by writing of past events in the future tense.

Numbers 25 again stresses that when traveling to foreign lands, the loyalty of the Jews must always be to the genealogical god of the Temple and not to the local gods. In this, Semitic cruelty and military punishment is adopted toward not only anyone who follows other gods *but also toward the leaders of the tribes* who do not keep the Hebrews disciplined. Those leaders, whether they were personally guilty of praying to other gods or not, were impaled on stakes (Nb 25:4) as an excellent incentive for the leaders of the Jews to keep a sharp eye on the Jews.

The power of life and death was legislated for the priest-judges who "must put to death those of his people who have committed themselves" to the other gods, in this case the Canaanite god, *Baal*. The *Hebrew Bible* ignores the fact (later rediscovered by the archaeologists) that in the Canaanite pantheon, *Baal* was actually the son of *Yahweh* and his consort *Asherah* (Astarte or Ishtar). The question arises: Why did the priests of Abraham's First National Bank and Pawn Shop in Jerusalem hate *Baal* so much since he was, in fact, the son of their own god? The answer to this is, because banking is a business where the highest profits are found in the monopoly of all loans. No competing temple treasuries of other gods would be tolerated in the "holy land" of the Babylonian bankers with main vaults and offices in Jerusalem. Praying to other gods in any way, was a torture and death sentence under Mosaic Law. If the Palestinians, Canaanites or Jews wanted to take out a loan, only the Temple of Yahweh would be available for such business transactions. This Law was strictly enforced by the very priests whose entire livelihood depended upon a temple that contained all deposits of silver, gold, tithes, tax payments, gem stones and barbecued goat. And true to the merchant-moneylender's code of greed, they were not going to share this wealth with anyone else. So, all other temples in Canaan were to be destroyed as a "very holy thing."

The power of the Jewish priests to blatantly kill whomever broke away from the Mosaic Laws, is glorified in the self-righteous Phineas the priest, who murdered a Hebrew and his Midianite wife by spearing them each through the groin. This "zeal for his God" was rewarded in the Contract with something that didn't cost the moneylenders anything: Phineas was allowed to perform the "ritual of atonement over the sons of Israel." (Nb 25:10-13.) Wow! Such a reward for committing murder! Another Jewish hero! And he was guaranteed to be a priest forever and his big *asl* could be passed down to his descendants, who were also big *asl*'s in the Temple Cult of Yahweh.

So, the Contract in Numbers 25 emphasized once again that the priests had total power over the goat rustlers. The priests of Yahweh were judge, jury and executioner, total tyrants. Even *the leaders* could be executed for allowing their people to stray from the Laws of Moses. And the local gods were anathema under the ban, since the Yahweh-god had chosen these particular Hebrew murderers and Hyksos thieves to be guardians of his Treasury.

Numbers 26 spreads Yahweh around a bit so that more Hebrews begin mouthing the voices in their heads. Now, Yahweh speaks to Eleazar, son of Aaron, as well as to Moses. Nobody else can hear such voices in his head. The priests take another census so that they know how to divide the stolen land of Canaan. The various tribes and clans added up to 601,730 plus another 23,000 Levite males, completely shaved bald from anus to circumcised rubber ducky and from toes to head. These precise numbers added authenticity to the lies of the Contract. It is further stated that not a single one of them except for Moses, Caleb and Joshua were of the original gang who had been kicked out of Egypt. Thus, all of the original witnesses had died and the testimony of the Contract, itself, was the only guarantee that what it claimed was true. The Bankers of Babylon were always careful to kill off all witnesses.

Keeping property within the clutching claws of the Hebrew tribes, is the main law in Numbers 27. Problem #4: "Wealth escapes into the god's temples" was solved by inventing their own god and creating their own priesthood to guard their own temple. But the moneylenders were always vigilant of wealth escaping them through inheritance. With a law proclaiming that wealth should be bequeathed only to their Hebrew relatives, the chance of wealth being left to outsiders was prevented.

And finally in Numbers 27, all authority is finally transferred to the High Priest, Eleazar. It is to the High Priest that Moses presents Joshua as leader of the Hebrews. The method of divination and inquiry using the holy dice, the Urim and Thummim, is again presented. Throwing the holy dice was considered by the scribes to be superior for learning the will of God, even more accurate than reading the bloody entrails of sheep. Thus, Yahweh was also the God of Gambling, a favorite Jewish racket in later centuries, where fixing the odds and using blatantly crooked tricks made the Jews vast fortunes.

The transfer of power over the people to a priesthood composed of merchant-moneylenders whose sole authority was based upon both a falsified, written Contract and a genealogical swindle, was finally accomplished. The Bankers of Babylon had successfully devised a religious guild of merchants and moneylenders to both conceal their loot and to protect their lives, all while guaranteeing themselves perpetual military deferments and vastly superior intelligence gathering services, while keeping all their loot within the tribe.

The priestly swindle of giving the Yahweh-god the fat and then eating the steak and lamb chops for themselves, is again emphasized in Numbers 28. Only now, it is an order to not let the priests miss even a single meal! "Take care to bring at the appointed time my offering, my sustenance in the form of a burnt offering, an appeasing fragrance for me." (Nb 28:2.) So commands the mighty god who, after ten billion years of fasting ever since he first created the Universe, now demands the sustenance of burnt animal fat smoking on the grill at the exact same times – what a coincidence! – that the priests want their breakfast, lunch and dinners at the same time, too!

Then, the required "burnt offerings" are listed. Every day, two yearling lambs with one-tenth of an ephah of flour and one-quarter of a hin of oil. In addition to the daily "holocaust," two extra lambs, oil, flour and wine are offered on the Sabbath. That way, the priests and rabbis can have a big party to celebrate the great Canaanite god that blesses them so much.

Because *Yahweh* was a Semitic Moon God in disguise, every month at the New Moon, a special holocaust (burnt and barbecued) was offered. For the feast of the New Moon, two young bulls, one ram, seven yearling lambs, one and a half ephah of fine flour, one and one-twelfth hin of wine plus a he-goat for sins became the priest's banquet after, of course, the Yahweh-god had sent down his giant, invisible nostril to sniff the smoke for a "sweet savor."

On the Feast of Unleavened Bread, the Passover, two young bulls, a ram, seven yearling sheep, a he-goat, one and a fifth ephah of flour in addition to the ordinary morning sacrifice of two lambs and flour. All of these innocent animals are sacrificed every day for seven days. The flies swarmed thickly over the altar of Yahweh, year around. Even though this god seemed to get along pretty well by fasting for all of Eternity without anyone feeding him anything, presumably he was now trying to get his weight back up since he says through Moses' mouth, "It is a nourishment, a burnt offering, an appeasing fragrance for Yahweh." (Nb 28:24.)

The Feast of Weeks during the offering of the new fruits, two young bulls, one ram, seven yearling lambs plus one and a half ephah of fine flour plus a he-goat for a sacrifice for sin. This is in addition to the daily and perpetual sacrifice of two lambs with flour, oil and wine. Also, no laborious work on those holidays.

Numbers 29 continues with the barbecued goat schedules. In the first day of the seventh month (Babylonian time), the Feast of Acclamations, they sacrifice one young bull, one ram, seven yearling lambs along with flour and wine plus a he-goat for sin. All of this plus the daily sacrifice of two lambs and the monthly New Moon sacrifice. Remember these were Babylonian calendar dates because the Yahweh-god could not give the Bankers of Babylon a new kind of calendar otherwise that would invalidate the Babylonian calendar where the dates for rents and outstanding loans were due.

On the tenth day of the seventh month, the Day of Atonement, the Jews must fast and do no work. The sacrifice in addition to the daily sacrifice was one young bull, one ram, seven yearling lambs plus a he-goat for sin in addition to the daily sacrifice of two lambs. Then five days later on the Feast of Tabernacles on the fifteenth say of the seventh month, was offered a sacrifice of 13 young bulls, two rams, 14 yearling rams, five and seven-eighths ephah of flour plus a goat for sin in addition to the daily offering of two lambs and flour and wine. That's a lot of meat that had to be eaten before it spoiled. But the priests and their large families were up to the task. Eating all those critters was hard work but it gave them strong jaw muscles so that they could talk balderdash and turn into a nation of lawyers and lying Jewish politicians.

All of this meat was only for the first day of the feast of Tabernacles. On each of the following six days, they do a countdown of one less bull per day. So, the total for the eight days of the Tabernacles, they slaughter 71 young bulls, fifteen rams, 105 lambs, eight goats along with 34 and eight-tenths ephah of flour. Yahweh surely was putting on a lot of weight and becoming an even bigger god, if his lard-assed Jewish priests were any indication of such gluttony.

For all of these careful instructions of how much to feed the Yahweh-god for his "nourishment," Moses listened to the voices in his head and "told the sons of Israel exactly what Yahweh had ordered him" (Nb 29:39). So, the poor, innocent, holy priests were eating all of that meat and bread and drinking all of that wine because God had ordered them either to do it or have an earthquake swallow them up along with their families and household pets. We should feel pity for those poor, oppressed Jews, suffering under such a mighty god. And forcing them to eat what they didn't work for.

Numbers 30 teaches more Semitic oppression of women. In order to completely control women, the slave masters of Babylonia did not want women claiming any power to free themselves by invoking a protection of God. Women could attempt to gain some freedom of action by saying that they had "made a vow to the god." By making a vow to the god, for whatever reason, gave them the protection of the god. Even under an abusive husband, a poor woman could invoke the Yahweh-god and say, "I made a vow to Yahweh that I would visit my sister in the next town before the Sabbath." Or any of ten thousand other subterfuges to get their own will and have their own way. To disallow women any freedom from their bondage, the Bankers of Babylon wrote Numbers 30 into the Contract stating: "These are the laws ordained by Yahweh to Moses ..." (Nb 30:17.) In this case, even when a woman made a vow or promise to God, her husband or her father can allow or annul the vow. Thus, her father or her husband had more power over her than God did. Mohammad (mhrh) would make use of that same Jewish fraud in his own religious hoax.

The Jewish gusto for committing genocide on other people, is described in Numbers 31. The power of the priest to call for a war, was claimed by Moses who rounded up 12,000 Hebrews to murder all of the men of Midian. They took all of the women and children captive along with all of their cattle and flocks while burning down their towns. This was written as the "vengeance for the sons of Israel on the Midianites." (Nb 31:2.) Vengeance will continue to be, right up into modern times, a long tradition and a general characteristic of the Jews upon other people for all sorts of imaginary sins. Vengeance was a Semitic cultural characteristic practiced by the Hebrews and Arabs. It is one of the flaws from which Jesus tried to dissuade them, but to no avail. Vengeance is a form of demonic hatred.

Moses had all of the captive women who were not virgins, along with all of the boys, slaughtered. The young virgin girls, the Hebrews kept as sex slaves. All of the gold, silver, bronze, iron, tin and lead, were "purified" from having been touched by heathens by waving it over a fire in order to make it "clean" enough to steal. All other booty was "purified" by sprinkling it with the magic lustral water that had the bull ashes in it. The magic of "clean" and "unclean" is used in this chapter by the priests both to delude the idiot Hebrews and to teach them how to steal stuff while maintaining a warm feeling of actually being "holy." This is how modern Jews steal billions and feel satisfaction in doing so. It's all in the magic of fooling themselves while claiming that God told them to do it. Why argue with God, especially when by following in his "ways" that the profits are so high?

War booty was allocated as half for the soldiers and half for the community. From the soldiers' half, "one out of every 500 persons, oxen, donkeys, and sheep. These are to be taken from the half share which is their due, and given to Eleazar the priest as an offering to Yahweh." (Nb 31:28-29.) In other words, *human sacrifice was included in the offerings on the bloody altar of Yahweh*. Let no Jews tell you of the "higher morality of Judaism" when their own *Hebrew Bible* shows what liars and devils they all are! They have written their own epitaph.

With the evident pleasure of an accountant tallying his treasure, Numbers 31 tabulates all of the booty stolen from the Midianites. The Hebrews were eager to murder and loot but afterwards they brought their loot to the priests to sprinkle with the magic "lustral water" because when they murdered the Midianites, they became "unclean" by touching the living bodies of the *goyim* as they murdered them. Looting the dead bodies on a battle field or of the people whom they had killed didn't make them "unclean" because dead *goyim* (non-Jews) are "clean" like all dead animals are "clean."

Since the stolen property was "unclean" because it had been touched by the original living owners, all of this booty had to be made "clean" by the priests who waved it over a fire or sprinkled it with magic lustral water. The "holy bandits" had touched the profane and thus became "unclean" but they felt a lot holier once the priest had sprinkled them with magic Kool-Aid. Do you see what a blessing to the world that the Jews are? They kill the "unclean" non-Jews, steal their property and then make everything "clean" once again by sprinkling it with a mixture of water and the ashes of a burnt red heifer.

To make the world even "cleaner," the Jews murdered Balaam, the priest who had refused to put a curse on them. Why? Because even though he prayed to the same Yahweh-god, he was not a circumcised member of their Hebrew gang. It's that cutoff piece of Jewish penis that makes all the difference in these fine Semitic distinctions between holiness and the heathens. Circumcised means "holy;" uncircumcised means "future victims."

After killing all but 32,000 virgin girls, the Hebrews didn't lose a single soldier (Nb 31:49). Oy! Such a miracle for such holy genocide! So that Yahweh would not forget them, the soldiers gave 16,750 shekels (about 237 kilos or 523 pounds) of stolen gold to Moses and Eleazar the priest (Nb 31:54). Thus, Numbers 31 ends with a moneylender's very most holiest of dreams – people giving them gold for free. Oh Gevalt! It was like Jewish heaven!

Numbers 32 of the Contract declares that the reason that the tribes of Mannaseh, Gad and Reuben were living in the cattle lands of Gilead east of the Jordan River, was because Moses gave it to them as long as they helped the other tribes overrun and dispossess the rest of Canaan. That they had already been living there when Terah's Benjamite peddlers found them, is not mentioned since the *Hebrew Bible* finds the facts to be an abomination.

Numbers 33 traces the path that the Hyksos bandits took after leaving Egypt. Here it is claimed that instead of running for their lives, the Hebrews left Rameses

> "On the day after Passover, that the sons of Israel set out triumphantly in the sight of all Egypt. The Egyptians were burying those of their own people whom Yahweh had struck down, all their firstborn; Yahweh had carried out his judgment on their gods." (Nb 33:3-4.)

This would be a recurring theme among the Jews of celebrating the death and destruction of other people. Even today, with the never-ending vengeance of the Semites, the Jews sing a Passover song celebrating the death of the Egyptians and a cursing of all *goyim* (non-Jewish, lowly insects, stupid cattle). Even today, the Jews are cursing you, if you aren't Jewish, during Passover as well as all other times. *Goyim* is basically a curse word.

Archaeology corrects the problems that so many biblical scholars have stumbled over in an accurate understanding the *Hebrew Bible*. Pharaoh Rameses did not rule Egypt during the time of the Hyksos expulsion. Because the five books of Moses were written around 700 BC and edited during the "captivity" in Babylonia between 579 BC and 539 BC, the only pharaohs who could conveniently fall into the time frame claimed by the Babylonian Banker's Contract, was Rameses. So, that's the pharaoh whom they wrote about. The authors of Numbers 33 makes sure that this fraud is perpetuated by stating that "Moses recorded their starting points in writing whenever they broke camp on Yahweh's orders." (Nb 33:2.)

This chapter ends with the Contract stating that the Hebrews were "ordered by Yahweh" through the mouths of the priests, to not only drive out, murder and dispossess all of the Canaanites of the land but to "destroy their sculptured stones, you must destroy all their statues of cast metal, and you must demolish all their high places." (Nb 33:52.) This became a standard excuse for today's Jews when they slander and destroy all other religions. Destroying the Christians, Muslims, Hindus, Buddhists, Taoists and all other religions, is because the Yahweh-god ordered them to be destroyers of any religion that is not Jewish. It's part of the Contract. Modern Christians should read these pages with a more discerning eye to see who their betrayers really are.

The joke of it all is that none of the mighty events of the Torah ever happened. They were merely a way for the Bankers of Babylon to hide their loot and their greedy, craven selves behind their own custom-made religion of thieves, murderers, moneylenders and merchants.

Like any army and like any dictatorship, the Bankers of Babylon had become confident enough in their fraud that the words of the priest were claimed to be the actual orders from God, Himself. "Yahweh spoke to Moses and said, 'Give the sons of Israel this order." (Nb 34:1.) At first, Moses, an old man who talked to himself and actually heard a reply, claimed that God gave orders as to how many shekels of silver the priests should charge, and the numbers of goats he wanted barbecued for their "sweet savor" and for his "nourishment." But now, the priests were giving the "orders" given by the "god" through their own mouths. In short, the priests had become little gods on earth. With their Semitic magical fraud of *abracadabra*, "I create as I speak," whatever they said, they claimed to be true.

The boundaries that the Bankers of Babylon wanted to surround and protect their Treasury, were mapped out in Numbers 34.

As a means of keeping the murdering, thieving Hebrews under the domination of the equally murderous priesthood, Numbers 35 stipulates that 48 towns are to be given to the Levites along with pasture for their cattle. In this way, scattered among the territory of each of the Hebrew tribes would be towns owned by the Levi priests, put there as spies, snitches and enforcers for the Chief Priest and as religious clerical police for enforcing the Laws of the Contract.

Private vengeance among the bandit tribes was where those who had killed someone would be hunted down and murdered by a relative. This was a tradition among the Semites of the entire ancient Near East. This was partially tempered by setting aside "cities of refuge" where the killer could go to get a trial and as refuge from the "avenger of blood." The Hebrew revenge killings did not differentiate between accidental or intentional manslaughter. These six "cities of refuge" were safe havens for the killer who killed accidentally. As long as he stayed in the refuge city, he was theoretically safe from the "avenger of blood." He was to stay in the refuge city until the High Priest died, then he was free to leave without the avenger of blood being able to legally murder him. At least that was the theory. In earlier books of the *Hebrew Bible*, the "avengers of blood" didn't seem to be afraid of the Yahweh-god and still killed their victims even before the altar of Yahweh.

The ancient fear of the moneylenders that their impoverished victims would rise up and kill them, had been tempered in Babylonia by the strict Laws of Hammurabi. But the principle that the relatives of a murder victim could be paid a ransom of silver instead of having the murderer executed, had crept back into Babylonian Law. This had allowed their victims to murder a moneylender and then pay a fine. To close that loophole, the moneylenders emphasized in Numbers 35 that no ransom was acceptable and that the murderers were to be killed but only after a trial before the judges.

The goat rustlers' mentality behind these Laws of Moses and the local nature of the bloody, eye-for-an-eye, Yahweh-god, is found in the last two sentences of Numbers 35:

> "Blood profanes the country, and there is no other expiation for
> the country for bloodshed than the blood of the one who shed it.
> You must not defile the land you inhabit, the land in which I
> live; for I, Yahweh, live among the sons of Israel."
> (Nb 35:33-34.)

Numbers 36, the last chapter in the Book of Numbers, rules further in favor of the Jews becoming the inbred and genetic freaks that they are today. Incest had become a standard way of keeping wealth within the family. Now, in this final chapter of the Book of Numbers, Moses decrees that the Hebrews are allowed only to marry within their own tribes so as to prevent the wealth and the stolen property of one tribe being transferred to another tribe through marriage. In this way, the international political and commercial secrets and wealth that was controlled by the priests, would be owned and operated by the tribe of Judah, alone – the very tribe controlling the treasury city of Jerusalem.

So the hunchbacked "daughters of Zelophehad" married the club-footed "sons of their father's brothers." Cousins married cousins not for the genetic strength of the Hebrews but strictly for preserving their bullion hoards and their property. In moneylender fashion, preserving their money and property meant everything to them. As is shown in Volume III, *The Bloodsuckers of Judah*, these same methods would still be used 3000 years later when the demonic Rothschild clan began marrying their cousins to keep the wealth that they had swindled from the Europeans all in the family.

The Jews have inherited genetic diseases since the earliest times as punishment for breaking the laws of Nature which are greater and more powerful than the laws of their Canaanite Moon God, Yahweh, and his little old mouthpiece, Moses. Oddly, modern Man seems to believe that the ravings of these ancient goat-molesters and the obvious frauds of their pseudohistory, are a valid reason to believe the lying Jewish bankers and politicians who are betraying, defrauding and impoverishing Mankind today. When everything about the Jews and Judaism is proven to be a demonic hoax, then what, actually, are these Jewish politicians, bankers, teachers and lawyers?

Really, think about it. What are they? Bankers standing at the gates of entire countries who impoverish billions of people, chairmen of political parties who murder hundreds of millions of people, professors in schools who deceive hundreds of millions of children, moguls of media monopolies who spread mental filth as alleged "entertainment." Who are these evil people who pretend to be the "Chosen Ones of God"? Why do the countries whose gates the Jews control, always fall into ruin? And why do the peoples whose fates the Jews control, always sicken and perish? You are beginning to see the lies that they tell. The question is not *who are* the Jews, but *what are* the Jews – really?

6.6 Deuteronomy, the Double Whammy in the Hebrew Bible

From beginning to end, the *Hebrew Bible* is so full of frauds, plagiarisms, counterfeit documents, lies, historical fictions, fables and stolen literature that is it very difficult to determine among all of its falseness, which is the biggest lie in the entire hoax. The Book of Deuteronomy might be the choicest candidate for such a dubious distinction. Whoops! Wait a minute! If the stories of Moses aren't the phoniest then probably the Book of Daniel is the most fake. No, wait! Joshua is certainly full of it. No, the stories of David and Solomon, nothing is more fictional that that. Well, … you get the picture. The Jews are the snakiest liars who ever walked on two feet or crawled on their bellies.

In this case, the Book of Deuteronomy was written by Hilkiah, the sly and cunning High Priest of the Temple, who wrote it and then buried it in a wall. A few months later, it was "accidentally" discovered by a worker who was repairing the wall. Claiming that it was a long-lost manuscript from hundreds of years previously, the High Priest used it to betray and deceive the eight-year-old boy-king, Josiah, into committing acts of genocide and thievery upon the surrounding peoples and becoming the dupe of the Yahweh Cult for the rest of his short life.

As the rabbis developed their plans and forged their Book of Deuteronomy, they naturally developed a close and familiar relationship with the child king, Josiah, a little boy whom the High Priest had under his tutelage. The priests who wrote Deuteronomy could not risk that Josiah would recognize the lie in their facial quirks or in the voice of the high priest, Hilkiah, if Josiah was directly given the book. So, Hilkiah – that "great and mighty and powerful spokesman for God, Almighty, Himself" – cunningly waited until one of king Josiah's servants appeared before nonchalantly announcing the so-called "discovery" of Deuteronomy hidden in a wall. In this way, the boy-king Josiah could be primed by an innocent third party telling him the news and could then more easily succumb to the fraud.

Indeed, if Hilkiah had actually discovered an ancient "Book of the Law" as he claimed, he certainly wouldn't wait for a king's servant to appear and then casually announce it to him. Rather, he would either excitedly send one of his own servants to the king or go himself to the king with the news. As the Jews have so carefully learned through long practice, a lie works best if more than one person tells the lie. In this case, the innocent servant carried the news to king Josiah.

In later years, after the Book of Deuteronomy had been fully accepted as an authentic document from Moses' time, the rabbis would further conceal their deceit by writing in the historical Second Book of Kings of how totally honest Hilkiah and his priests were (2K 22:3-10). Thus, the rabbis cover for each other in the same way that thieves and murderers and Jews repeat each other's alibis.

One of the characteristics of Jewish gangsterism has always been a celebration of the murder and extermination of other people while the Jews wail and moan about how nobody likes them. One example in the Book of Deuter-onomy tells that the Horites were "dispossessed and exterminated by the sons of Esau who settled there with them, just as Israel did in their own land, *the heritage* they received from Yahweh." (Dt 2:12.) Notice the order of this Jew-ish genocidal technique. First, the Horites were dispossessed and once they had been cheated out of their property, then they were exterminated. You can see the same method being applied to modern, Western cultures today by the Jews who "settled there with them." By allowing the Jews to settle down among them, the Horites opened the gates to their own doom. They broke the First Rule of Human Society: "No Jews Allowed Except on a Gibbet."

A legalistic "trick" should be well noted to understand Jewish deceits in regard to the word "heritage" or sometimes "inheritance." In the general sense of these words, a false assumption is made that when someone "inherits" something, they are given this thing from a forebear who actually owned it. When someone claims an inheritance, others *assume* that the inheritor of a property is automatically the legal owner of that property. But what if the property was stolen and then bequeathed? Thus, a burglar caught with a bag full of kitchen silverware does not say that he took it, or stole it, but while holding his loot all the tighter he claims, "These are mine. My father gave them to me as an inheritance." To question him further would be an insult to both him and his dead relative. According to the Jews' *Babylonian Talmud*, stolen property becomes the property of a Jewish crook as soon as the original owner gives up hope of ever getting it back. (*Babylonian Talmud*, Bava Kam-ma 68a & 68b.) Thus, if the Jews steal something and the original owner gives up hope of ever getting it back, then he gives up title to the property which devolves to the Jews. Once the Jew has "acquired title" to the property in this magical way, he is innocent of thievery because he is now a legal owner of the property! This technique is being used today by the Jews who claim valuable paintings and other European art treasures as belonging to them even though their fathers had stolen and swindled the art works from the Germans.

So it is with all "properties" and "inheritance" of the Jews. Everything that the Jews as an entire people allegedly possess are, in fact, either the loot of direct thefts and swindles or they are the inheritance of previous thefts that were bequeathed from their criminal Jewish forefathers. Such art collections of the Rothschild's, for example, are really not "owned" by them since the money used to buy the art treasures came from the swindling the European Peoples. Many must suffer and die so that a few Jews may live in luxury.

Deuteronomy points out that the lands of Canaan and Palestine possessed by the Hebrews and their kinsmen, was all stolen from other people who were subsequently exterminated. Genocide has been a basic methodology used by the Jews on other peoples from their very first days. The Jews are avid practi-tioners of genocide – as long as they are the ones doing the killing. The *He-brew Bible* is filled with celebrations and self-congratulations of the Jews committing genocide against entire peoples, stealing their property and then bequeathing that property as an "inheritance" to their little kikes.

In modern times, Jews are the avid promoters and beneficiaries of the Holocaust Industry. Modern people are subjected to a never-ending Jewish media barrage about how the Nazis killed a nonexistent, impossible and unverifiable six million Jews. But the Jews never mention the actual, historical 66 million Christian Russians and Ukrainians that were systematically exterminated by the Jewish Communists; or the worldwide and verified total of at least 100 million people that the Jews and Jewish-Communism exterminated between 1917 and the year 2000. By screaming about six million mythical Jews, these criminals set up a smoke screen of noise to hide the 66 million murdered Russians under their noisy, lying, murderous, genocidal screeching. This subject will be covered more fully in Volume III, *The Blood-Suckers of Judah.*

The Book of Deuteronomy was written by the scribes during the time of Josiah as a method of stealing power, prestige and wealth away from the other religious groups in the area and for committing even more genocide upon the Palestinians and Canaanites. Deuteronomy was claimed by Hilkiah to have been written by Moses who allegedly lived 600 years earlier and whose Book of Deuteronomy was hidden in a wall for all of this time until it was miraculously "discovered" during Temple renovations. The rabbis found that their powers of "holiness" could be multiplied when "miracles" were written down as actual history. In this way, they could claim to have accomplished amazing things in the unprofitable and mythical past while reaping rewards in the power-hungry and gold-lusting present.

The Book of Deuteronomy was written to further coerce the Hebrews into following the Cult of Yahweh and to forcibly expand the territorial power of Abraham's First National Bank and Pawn Shop into the surrounding kingdoms. But no people can exist in a world of enemies without having some allies to back them. So, interwoven with Deuteronomy is the identification of allies. In this case, the Ammonites are identified as the sons of Lot and the sons of Esau who lived in Seir. And Yahweh supposedly gave them the lands once they had committed genocide against those people. (Deut. 2:12.) But regardless of the lies of Deuteronomy, archaeology proves that there was no "Conquest of Canaan" and that neither the so-called "mighty" kingdoms of Israel nor Judah ever controlled more than a mere sliver of property in Canaan. In addition, Deuteronomy is filled with dark stories about what happens to the Hebrews who do not follow what the priests of Yahweh decree – whole generations are wiped out.

Terrorism has always been a favorite Jewish method of warfare and both overt and subliminal social aggression. The Old Testament is filled with Hebrew atrocities and genocide committed against the neighbors of the Hebrews. Very rarely did the Hebrews ever leave anyone alive if they were successful in a battle. Except for the virgins, the little girls and little boys, everyone else was exterminated. After all, they were the Chosen People who had been especially chosen by the God of Vengeance to do this monster god's bidding. Since it is a Jewish belief that their god hates all people on earth except for the Jews, it is only natural for these perverse Jewish fiends to also hate all people on earth as a way of pleasing their devil-god and "following his ways."

How is it that the Jews promote terror among other people? Although their methods are numerous, they can all be broken down into four words – malice and hatred and greed and murder. Though they are full of spite and maliciousness toward all other people, worldwide, they are also filled with blatant hypocrisy so as to be able to lie about their goals and ambitions with convincing outrage.

When an entire people from their earliest childhood are taught by their evil rabbis that their god wants to "spread the terror and fear of you (Jews) among the peoples under all heaven; all who hear the sound of your coming will tremble and be in dread" (Deut. 2-25), what else can be expected than that these Jews would desire such a horrible situation and promote its realization? Like juvenile delinquents who terrorize entire neighborhoods – not through any individual power of their own but through the combined assault of gangs of trouble-causing teenagers – so too, do the Jews attack whatever country and whatever people among whom they are allowed to live. It is usually not the thefts or mayhem or vicious slanders that an individual Jew commits that causes the destruction of non-Jewish people. It is the *combined and coordinated* attack of *all Jews* that is the major characteristic of these demons who worship the "god of armies." One Jew is a criminal element. Many Jews are a criminal conspiracy. And *all* Jews, everywhere, are members (whether passively or overtly) of this international conspiracy of bankers, terrorists, subversives and local troublemakers.

The Book of Deuteronomy is a connected narrative to Joshua, 1 Judges and 2 Judges, Samuel, and 1 Kings and 2 Kings. Together, these are called the "Deuteronomistic History." But actually they are not history books at all, rather, they are historical novels with heroes and villains, falsely claiming to be genuine history. Propaganda, they are, extolling the "virtue" and wonderfulness of the priests and the moneylenders who established the great fraud of Abraham's First National Bank and Pawn Shop in Jerusalem. But history books, they most certainly are not! And they were certainly not written by any character named Moses, either. That this series of Deuteronomic forgeries were completed in the seventh century during Josiah's reign, is proved by archaeology and linguistic studies. Rather than being an old book that was suddenly discovered, it seems safe to conclude that Deuteronomy was written in the seventh century BC, just before or during Josiah's reign. The wicked rabbis of Yahweh presented a counterfeit in order to deceive the young, impressionable king and to betray the world.

Deuteronomy is named after the Greek word, "*Deuteronomion*" or "second law." The Deuteronomistic "History" can be read as a political program, from the conquest of Joshua to the days of the judges; to the rise of David, through the united monarchy and its breakdown to the days of the two separate states; and to the climax of the story with the reign of Josiah, the most pious of all the Davidic kings. The Assyrian empire had crumbled, Egypt was seemingly interested only in its coastal possessions, and Judah was free to fulfill its pan-Israelite dreams complete with more Jewish betrayals, thefts and lies.

The biggest joke which Christians and other fools don't seem to appreciate, is that the entire Torah is not a book of godly knowledge at all, rather it is a book of glorified murder, theft and mayhem, all while practicing the demonic arts of criminality allegedly for the sake of God. That other false Semitic religion, Islam, would promote an identical swindle a thousand years after Ezra the scribe reedited the *Hebrew Bible* for the Bankers of Babylon.

Various scholars have pointed out that the literary form of the Mosaic Contract and covenant between *Yahweh* and the Hebrews in Deuteronomy, is strikingly similar to that of early seventh-century Assyrian vassal treaties that outline the rights and obligations of a subject people to their sovereign (in this case, between Judah and Yahweh). This similarity is more than an accident because the entire Torah is a legal Contract invented by the rabbi lawyers and scribes of Babylonia's guild of merchant-moneylenders originally established by Abraham's father, Terah, in the city of Harran, an Assyrian territory.

The Jerusalem Yahweh Cult had proven its value to the moneylenders of Babylon. Not only as a central bank, a guaranteed military deferment, a source of interest-free loans, as well as an excellent source of business and political information, and all for a mere ten percent of the resulting profits. It was a good investment for the "gentlemen" class of *awilum* [the Haves] who already were members of the various merchant-moneylender guilds of Babylonian and Assyria, that is, if they were also willing to wear the "secret membership card" of circumcision.

As the Jerusalem Cult grew in wealth and influence, it attracted more prospective members belonging to the social class of "the Haves." Those members lived in every country where the Cult members did business. And those prospective members did not speak Hebrew. So, for the secret society of moneylenders and merchants to expand, its central tenants needed to be updated and rewritten in the *lingua franca* of the day which was Aramaic.

Even though the original Contract was written by Terah's scribes and the Temple scribes who came after them, Hebrew with its archaic alphabet was only a localized dialect. Biblical Hebrew contains 22 letters, all of which are consonants, no vowels. The Hebrew alphabet devolved from Egyptian Demotic script to the Phoenician alphabet to the Paleo-Hebrew in which all of the stories and fables were written until the Babylonian exile in 587 BC. Then, following the destruction of the First Temple, spoken Hebrew came under the influence of Aramaic. Aramaic was the *lingua franca* of the entire Middle East from about 700 BC to 700 AD. It was understood by every businessman and king from the Mediterranean Basin to Persia because if they wanted to deal in trade and finance, they had to be fluent in the international language of trade and finance. So, if the scriptural propaganda of the holy goat-molesters of Jerusalem was re-written with the Aramaic alphabet and in the Aramaic language, its influence would spread more easily among the Cult Membership throughout the civilized world.

In the fifth century BC, while in the employ of the moneylenders of Babylon, the redactor who gave the final shape to the "Law of Moses" was Ezra, who is specifically described as "the scribe of the law of the God of heaven" (Ezra 7:12). Ezra did the final editing of the *Hebrew Bible*, not only rearranging and editing the books but actually replacing the original archaic Hebrew characters with the square, Imperial Assyrian Aramaic script of the Babylonian merchants, kings and moneylenders. Thus, the entire *Hebrew Bible* was completely reedited in Babylonia during the Exile, complete with new alphabetic characters and an updated mythology which was even more beneficial to the priests and moneylenders. Everything in the *Hebrew Bible* that can be considered wise or good or holy, was stolen outright from the great peoples who had built genuine civilizations all around those half-witted and lice-infested Hebrew goat rustlers.

Regardless of their differences regarding the understanding of the biblical text, all archaeologists know that the Hebrews lived at a far lower level of civilization than the native Canaanites. On their own volition, the Hebrews could not have conquered Canaan – they were too few in number, too poor and too stupid. The twisted and misshapen pottery that they left, shows what half-wits they were. Yet, stupid as they were, the Hebrews were the perfect mark for the religious swindle devised by Terah and his son, Abraham. Because they were illiterate, the Hebrew yokels believed the lies that were written on the talking goatskins by the Babylonian scribes. As Terah's Benjamite peddlers visited their villages and collected their genealogies, and Terah and his scribes inserted the Hebrew genealogies near the top of his own family tree, they were entangled like Hebrew flies in a Babylonian spider's web of the Greatest Lie Ever Told. Authority over the country bumpkin Hebrew tribes was hijacked by Babylonian city slickers.

Modern archaeology proves that the Hebrew goat rustlers were not numerous enough to have conquered Canaan. They lived in small villages on the hilltops, places that no one else wanted. The *richest* of those villages, with an estimated population of about one hundred, was supported by about eight hundred acres of surrounding land, four-hundred fifty of which were cultivated and the rest used for pasture. Under conditions of the Early Iron Age, those fields could have produced up to fifty-three tons of wheat and twenty-one tons of barley per year, with the help of about forty oxen for plowing. In addition, the inhabitants maintained a herd of about three hundred sheep and goats." This was the *richest* of the Hebrew villages.

Just as the Hyksos Shepherd Kings had been able to conquer Egypt with the cunning, the weapons and the logistics supplied by the merchant-moneylenders of Babylonia, so too were the Hyksos-Hebrews able to exert their influence over Canaan with these same secret allies backing them with silver and trade goods. The Hebrew tribes had a certain usefulness to the great merchant-moneylender families of the time. They lived in an area that offered a site for a secure treasury hidden within a temple located in an out-of-the-way and impregnable location – and all of it was protected by a god that no other

peoples, kings or priests could claim as their own. The god of the moneylenders was a god whom the moneylenders controlled. They and they, alone, could
determine what people to betray, what people to defraud, what people to impoverish, what people to enslave, and what people to destroy through warfare,
and no priests could denounce their criminality before god or man, because the
moneylenders were their own priests, with their own morality. They had written their own Contract with their own god and had declared themselves "holy."

Deuteronomy 1 begins with a recapitulation of the fairy tales of the previous books of Moses. The actual inveigling of the Hebrews into cooperating
tribes that were ruled by priests and controlled by laws, has now been accomplished. For those militarized goat rustlers, judges have been appointed to ensure
that the laws of the Yahweh-god are obeyed. Not only are the tribal armies led
by "captains of thousands, hundreds, fifties and tens" (Dt 1:15) but each tribe
is assigned a scribe. This is an organizational system that has been used by the
Jews even up until modern times, a militaristic system with rabbis as the or-
ganizing leaders. Since the Hebrew goat rustlers couldn't read or write, the
scribes read to them the propaganda from the priests of the Yahweh Cult.

As usual, biblical "scholars" erroneously accept the Book of Deuteronomy at face value simply because, as they say, "The authenticity of Deuteronomy as a book of the Bible canon and the authorship of Moses are well established by the fact that Deuteronomy has always been considered by the Jews as
a part of the Law of Moses. The evidence for the authenticity of Deuteronomy
is, in general, the same as that for the other four books of the Pentateuch." In
other words, the five Books of Moses are accepted by the usual biblical
"scholars" as authentic merely because the lying Jews say that everything really, really happened just as the Jews claim that it did – regardless of all proof to
the contrary. This has been the accepted false reasoning since the Jews first
began promoting their swindle of both God and Mankind back in the days
when Terah, the moneylender patriarch of Ur and Harran sent his son, Abraham, to secure some banking property around Jerusalem. The word of the
Jews, those Holy Ones of God, has always been assumed to be more reliable
than the truth.

Incredibly, through the genealogies and the fables of the Hebrew goat
rustlers, the Bankers of Babylon claimed a patriarchal authority over *all of the
tribes in the entire ancient Near East*, merely by linking them together through
fake genealogies and placing themselves at the root of their own genealogy
tree. Hebrew tribes and villages who had sat around the campfire, entertaining
the Binu-Yamina (Benjamin) peddlers with stories and genealogies of their
forefathers, later found to their great surprise that they were genealogically
connected to a huge family tree of scoundrels and cut-throats who had been
chosen especially by their own Canaanite god, Yahweh. It was news to them
that they were required to follow a pile of laws and rules and pay a special tax
to the priests of Yahweh. They were "special" and "chosen," so worst of all, if
these illiterate goat farmers didn't comply with the words written on the talking goatskins, then *Yahweh* would blast them with fire from the sky and open

up the earth and swallow them just like the moneylenders' talking goatskins claimed had happened to their forefathers. It was all written down on the talking goat-skins which they couldn't read but which the grinning priests and smirking scribes were very happy to read to them. It had to be true! Talking goatskins don't lie. If those mighty priests of Abraham's First National Bank and Pawn Shop really could protect them from the "Wrath" of Yahweh, then it was better to pay them their tithe and hope for the best. And if they didn't pay the gang, the gangsters of Judah would kill them all and call it a "very holy thing."

Following the Hebrew partiality for genocide, the descendants of Esau had already "dispossessed and exterminated" the previous occupants of Moab. (Dt 2:12.) So, in Deuteronomy 2, the tribes that had settled in Moab east of the Dead Sea (that is, in Arabia) were claimed to be not a bunch of scruffy Arabians but a bunch of scruffy Hebrew descendants of Esau, the murderer of his brother. All of the tribes of Edom were claimed to be descendants of Lot and his incestuous daughters. Because the Yahweh-god appreciated that a fratricidal murderer like Esau and an incestuous daughter-molester like Lot, were related to the very holy Hebrew thieves and murderers of Canaan, Moses ordered that their lands were holy and sacrosanct and could not be raided. But as previously pointed out, none of those countries existed during the alleged time of Moses. It was mostly vacant land. So, the stories in Deuteronomy are fictions, written hundreds of years later than they claim, telling fables that never happened about people who didn't exist at that time.

What is also not explained in Deuteronomy 2, is that the road that begins "at the Sea of Suph" (the Gulf of Akaba) was a major trade route connecting the port cities of Elath and Ezion-geber with Canaan. The Babylonian ships of Ur and Yemen would off-load their cargos there for overland transportation by donkey and camel through Canaan to the Mediterranean port cities. Trade routes also passed through Moab and Edom. The Hebrews were ordered in Deuteronomy not to fight with the Moabites and Edomites because of "blood kinship." But the merchant-moneylenders who authored this fraud, instead wanted the Hebrews to "Pay them in money for what food you eat; and pay them in money for all the water you drink." (Dt 2:6.) This payment was actually the protection money that those tribes demanded for allowing the trade caravans to pass through their territory without attack. They made a profit from selling the caravans food and water. Those tribes actually existed in the 7th Century when the book was written but not during the times when Moses and his brigands were supposed to have been wandering around Sinai. The Contract stipulates what is good for the moneylenders of 7th Century Jerusalem by claiming that it was proclaimed by God and written by Moses 800 years previously. More archaeological proof that Deuteronomy is a fake.

Despite the fact that the ancient cities of Jericho, Ai, Gibeon, Lachish, Hazor and nearly all the others mentioned in the conquest story have been located and excavated, the evidence for an historical conquest of Canaan by the Israelites is weak. There were certainly roaming bands of Hebrew bandits but no 600,000 soldiered armies of genocidal Hebrews slaughtering entire cities.

As the story goes, the Hebrews passed by Edom and Moab and attacked the town of Heshbon. With this attack, the Yahweh-god claims,

> "Today and henceforth I spread the terror and fear of you among the peoples under all heaven: all who hear the sound of your coming will tremble and be in dread." (Dt 2:25.)

This has been a Jewish demand ever since ancient times, that they become as obnoxious as possible so that everyone avoids them and as subversively malevolent as possible so that everybody fears them. The Jews use the demonic delusion of Fear to get their way, working in conspiring gangs, committing arson, poisoning cattle, kidnapping children, etc. And when fear doesn't work, then in whining groups, they moan and cry, trying to elicit pity. Both the Thuggees of India and the Jews made identical claims: "Our god wants us to kill everybody and steal their property."

The Jewish hypocrisy of the Hebrew bandits is shown in Deuteronomy 2 because they really intended to take the land of King Sihon of Heshbon. So, they first sent him a message of peace. This is a traditional Jewish ploy. "Shalom" in Hebrew means "peace". But from the mouth of a Jew "shalom" means "Trust me and turn your back. I am going to screw you. Shalom."

Since King Sihon, being a Semite himself, didn't fall for their ruse and they couldn't win with deceit, the Hebrews attacked his towns directly. So much for a Hebrew "Shalom"! The Hebes murdered every man, woman, and child, exterminating the entire populace in all of king Sihon's towns and cities. These were holy goat rustlers so they obviously had a right to do it. Only the livestock and plunder from the towns, did the Hebrew bandits keep for themselves. This time, they even murdered the little girls instead of raping them and reducing them to sex slaves. These Hebrew bandits were surely the Chose Ones of Yahweh, the god of the moneylenders and slave-drivers of Babylon. What other people could be so worthy of such a demonic god other than the Semites of Arabia, the Muslims?

In Deuteronomy 3, the "mighty" Hebrews slaughtered the entire region around the giant, king Og at Bashan. Sixty towns, every man, woman and child, were murdered by these heroic proto-Jews. Only the cattle and the loot were kept for themselves as plunder. And to "prove" what mighty goat rustlers they were, the Hebrew scribes claimed that a big basalt rock that was part of the local scenery, had been the bed of king Og, who was the last of the giants. "His bed was the bed of iron that can be seen at Rabbah-of-the-Ammonites, nine cubits long and four wide..." (Dt 3:11.) "And there it is, boys of girls of the Jewish Explorer's Club, a giant red rock. That proves that the Bible is true. Otherwise, how could that rock be there if it wasn't the bed of giant King Og?"

Deuteronomy 4 begins by admonishing the illiterate, ignorant Hebrews to follow the Laws of Moses. It defines "wisdom" simply as following the Laws of Moses. And that is as wise as a Jew can get, following bogus laws written by the deceiving moneylenders of Babylon. As inducement, they are promised "life" which is a cheap promise since it was letting them keep what they already possessed. To seal the "Laws," the scribes wrote that Moses said,

> "You must add nothing to what I command you, and take nothing from it, but keep the commandments of Yahweh your God just as I lay them down for you." (Dt 4:2.)

Of course, thieves being thieves, liars being liars and rabbis being rabbis, these rabbis and priests broke this law from the earliest times by inventing the "Tradition of the Elders," the Oral Law, in order to increase the number of laws for which they could charge the Hebrews a "sin tax" for breaking. Later, the *Babylonian Talmud* twisted this Mosaic law into even more perverse contortions.

Moses claimed that the stupid goat rustlers automatically had "wisdom and understanding" merely by following the laws that enrich the priests and protect the Treasury. Using flattery, Moses spoke to these unwashed and stupid Hebrews, scratching their circumcised pricks and popping lice with their fingernails:

> "Keep them, observe them, and they will demonstrate to the peoples your wisdom and understanding. When they come to know of all these laws they will exclaim, 'No other people is as wise and prudent as this great nation.'" (Dt 4:6.)

Of course, the Hebrews were not great; and they were not a nation; and laws do not make anybody wise. Ever since these words were forged, the stupid Hebrew goat rustlers have flattered themselves by claiming that they have "wisdom" and "knowledge" and "learning" and "understanding" even though they are lacking in all of these things. They make such ridiculous boasts based merely upon keeping a bunch of laws that were manufactured by the deceiving moneylenders of Babylon. This alleged "great nation" was nothing but a dried-up fly speck of a country infested with ravaging gangs of smelly sheep-stealers, murderers, and thieves. The Laws of Moses are nothing but a one-way Contract for setting up a dictatorship of priests to guard the treasury of the moneylenders of Babylon. They are not Laws of a god, they are laws of some lying and very wicked demon priests.

Once again, the Yahweh-god is depicted as just one more god among all of the other gods. *Yahweh* was a god with a special love for bandits, rapists, swindlers and murderers. Killing and stealing for the sake of God, became the standard under which that other Semitic fraud known as Islam would later deceive and ravage Mankind.

To perpetuate the lies of this entire five book fantasy of Moses, the Hebrews are warned,

"Do not forget the things your eyes have seen, nor let them slip
from your heart all the days of your life; rather, tell them to your
children and to your children's children." (Dt 4:9.)

In this way, telling such stories to their children raised up future generations of
circumcised thieves, rapists and murderers, all giving one-tenth of their loot to
the priests of the Yahweh-god. By "walking in the ways" of their god, they
mimicked being vindictive, spiteful, malicious, lying, hateful, jealous, pitiless,
wrathful murderers and betrayers of Mankind, just like today's modern Jews
teach their children to be, just like their Yahweh-god was.

In Deuteronomy 4, the Hebes are warned not to make images since the
Yahweh-god is to have no shape or form that can be equated to other gods. As
shown in Chapter Four, many of the secrets of true religion were recorded by
the ancient people in various symbols, sculptures and paintings. So, the Yahweh Cult is actually a demonic attack on all other religions by targeting for
destruction their most esteemed symbols. Simultaneously, these kinds of taboos kept the Hebrews ignorant of other religions simply by making them enemies of all other religions while never actually learning about God. That other
demonic Semite cult, Islam, would use the same method a thousand years later
when the Lunatic of Arabia heard voices in his head and thought that he was a
prophet like Moses – different voices, different lunatics, leading ignorant bandits.

One thing that most people do not understand about the unique fraud of
Judaism, is that the Jews must tear down the idols of other religions, but their
god has no idols so it can never be torn down. This is incorrect. The idol of the
Jews is the Torah. You can see them today putting a crown on one end of a
Torah scroll, kissing and touching it and parading it around their synagogue,
like the idol that it is. And in that "Scroll of the Law," Yahweh is described as
"a consuming fire, a jealous God" (Dt 4:23). Adding more divine wrath and
magic to the mix, Moses warns that if the bandits break his Laws, they will
magically "vanish from the land" (Dt 4:26).

The Moses Contract for Abraham's First National Bank and Pawn Shop
is based upon a banking system that had been previously perfected over the
course of two thousand years in Babylonia. As long as a moneylender can lend
at interest, he will always be able to regain his losses and much more. This is
Secret Fraud #14 of the Sumerian Swindle. So, Moses warns them to follow
the laws of the Contract otherwise

"Yahweh will scatter you among the *goyim* and only a small
number of you will remain among the *goyim* where Yahweh
will have driven you." (Dt 4:27.)

In this way, the scattered Jews who continue to follow the Contract will
always be connected to the international banking and business system which
the Laws of Moses conceal. Each Jew benefits from membership in the Temple Cult and all of them becomes a spy for the entire criminal structure. Again,

notice that the Contract is based upon race. It is to the *descendants* of Abraham that the Yahweh-god makes his Covenant. Deuteronomy 5 ends by flattering the stupid Hebrews and bragging about what a great story the whole myth is.

> "Put this question, then, to the ages that are past, that went before you, from the time God created man on earth: Was there ever a word so majestic, from one end of heaven to the other? Was anything ever heard? Did ever a people hear the voice of the living God speaking from the heart of the fire, as you heard it, and remain alive? Has any god ventured to take to himself one nation from the midst of another by ordeals, signs, wonders, war with mighty hand and out-stretched arm, by fearsome terrors – all this that Yahweh your God did for you before your eyes in Egypt?" (Dt 4:32-34.)

By the time Deuteronomy was written, the other four books of Moses with their incredible lies, had been completed, written in the archaic Hebrew script. Their final version would come from the pen and ink of Ezra the Scribe, written in the Assyrian script which we recognize today as "Hebrew" writing. Enough of the myth had already been formulated to deceive the eight-year-old boy king, Josiah. So, Deuteronomy really had that poor boy's head in a tizzy.

Another reason Deuteronomy is a lie, is that these alleged Hebrew ex-slaves whom Deuteronomy addresses, would have no knowledge of what other gods had done with other people. Additionally, the forgers of Deuteronomy forgot that the Jews were forbidden to study the writings or the doctrines of any other religion. So, the question is ridiculous bragging about what a great fantasy Rabbi Hilkiah and Ezra the Scribe had written. The target audience was not the dirty Hebrew goat rustlers of Canaan. The target audience was the Hebrew upper classes of Josiah's time. Only they would have knowledge of the other religions through their business dealings. And only the scribe who had edited all of the previous four books would be in a position to brag about his work. Ezra was clever though conceited.

Notice that Deuteronomy 4:34 makes use of the Semitic *asl* of the Hebrews. It was previously stated that every single Hebrew except Moses and Joshua had died during the forty years in the desert. That being so, all that the present audience had to rely upon were the words of these five books of Moses. But with Semitic *abracadabra*, an entire generation of Hebrews, who never saw the alleged miracles, claimed that they not only saw them but was actually there in person! The biblical stories, alone, are claimed to be *just as good as actually having witnessed the events*. So, bringing the old *asl* into equality with the new *asl*, Moses claimed, "… all this Yahweh your God did for you before your eyes in Egypt." And yet, none of his words are true. If they all had died in the wilderness, none of them would have seen anything. But because they were Hebrews, they had inherited a great and mighty *asl* whereby they could claim, "My long dead ancestors saw all of those miracles written in the

Books of Moses, so that means that I saw all of those things, too." This same
Semitic *abracadabra*, is practiced by the modern Jews today. During Passover
week, the Jews all over the world claim that each and every one of them are
the very same scoundrels as the original Hebrew bandits as they all intone the
ancient lie, "We were slaves in Egypt."

More of the Hebrew *asl* as well as Semitic *abracadabra*, are again invoked in Deuteronomy 5. The lies and fables written by the scribes about Moses and the Hebrew-Hyksos escaping from Egypt, becomes an inherited experience of the here and now. All of the dead Hebrews' alleged experiences were
claimed to be identical as the experiences of the living Hebrews. It can't get
more fake than this:

> "Yahweh our god made a covenant with us at Horeb. It is not
> with our fathers that Yahweh made this covenant, but with us,
> with us who are here, all living today. On the mountain, from
> the heart of the fire, Yahweh spoke to you face to face, and I
> stood all the time between Yahweh and yourselves to tell you of
> Yahweh's words, for you were afraid of the fire and had not
> gone up the mountain." (Dt 5:2-5.)

This is some real literary hypnotism and hocus-pocus! It is false yet it is
purposely designed to mislead the Hebrews into believing that their *asl* is as
real to them as their circumcised dongs. This is the kind of phony Contract that
the merchant-moneylenders of Babylonia had honed with suggestion and deceit through the millennia. Getting people to sign away their wealth and their
freedom by shackling themselves to a written document, a document telling
lies and written especially by the world's greatest liars, a document dependent
upon the honesty of the victims who were to follow every letter – but not upon
the honesty of the lying priests who wrote the Contract.

Here, the big Semitic *asl* of the Hebrews is wide enough for all of them.
Here, it is declared that all of the fables of Moses were true because the present
audience of Hebrews – who had never seen any of the alleged events – is declared to be *the original recipients of the Contract*! They weren't there. And
didn't see anything. But Moses claims that – Abracadabra! – through the inheritance of their *asl* that they *really were there*! And even though none of
them were there, they were Hebrews so that meant that – Abracadabra! – they
really were there! It is the same fraud and delusion which is perpetuated by the
Jews today, claiming that events that had allegedly happened to ancestors who
had died 3,000 years ago, were events that had actually happened to today's
Jews, themselves, personally. Every Passover party, every year, the modern
Jews of the world intone the same lie: "*We* were slaves of Pharaoh." The Jews
are deluded frauds, *all of them*. Judaism is nothing but Semitic lies perpetuated
by lying frauds.

Besides all of these outright lies, the rabbis had some other tricks to deceive, not just the superstitious goat-thieves, but the Gentiles as well. This

fraud is founded in the Ten Commandments and was passed down by the Jews as a secret oral teaching of the rabbis, the "Tradition of the Elders," which later became the *Babylonian Talmud.*

This particular Jewish fraud works like this. The rabbis claim that the Laws of Moses were given to the Jews and only to the Jews. Thus, their evil rabbinical minds declare that the Ten Commandments *only apply to Jews toward other Jews* but do not apply to Jews toward Gentiles. So, to a rabbi, "You shall not kill" means that Jews should not kill other Jews but that it is okay to kill non-Jews. "You shall not commit adultery" with other Jews but it's okay to commit adultery with the wives of non-Jews. "You shall not steal" from other Jews but stealing from non-Jews is highly recommended by the rabbis. "You shall not bear false witness against your Jewish neighbor" but lying to and slandering non-Jews is recommended if a Jew can get away with it. "You shall not covet your Jewish neighbor's wife or his property" but it is permissible for a Jew to have sexual relations with a Gentile's wife and to steal his property. These are a few of the teachings of the "Tradition of the Elders" that Jesus spoke against. They were written down as "holy" teachings by the rabbis who wrote the *Babylonian Talmud.* And they are followed by the Jews to this very day. This is why the biggest financial crooks and banking swindlers are almost always Jews, because Judaism is a bandit's religion set up to preserve its own existence while parasitizing, robbing, and betraying all other people.

These criminal acts against non-Jews have been the major reason that the Jews have been hated for the past three thousand years. They have hypocritically pretended to be honest and godly people. They hold up the Ten Commandments as a "proof" that their god requires honesty. But all the while they commit every foul deed that they can get away with upon the non-Jews who trust them. This is Secret Fraud #3 of the Sumerian Swindle as applied to the Laws of Moses: "Loans rely on the honesty of the borrower but not the honesty of the lender." In this case, the people of the world honestly believe that the Ten Commandments apply to themselves as well as to the Jews, so they trust the Jews to treat them with honesty. But the Jews dishonestly allow the People to trust them while slyly using whatever tricks and subterfuges that they can to seduce and betray them. They have always been Semitic bandits and thieves; and it is built into their so-called "religion" to continue to be Semitic bandits and thieves.

All this while, those deluded and vicious Jewish pirates claim that because they all have inherited the same *asl,* that the ancient stories are true because the mere fact that they are Jews, is "proof" that these stories are true. This is not circular reasoning; it is a patently false assertion. It's like every American claiming that they, themselves, were aboard ship and saw it with their own eyes and crossed the ocean with Christopher Columbus because the "proof" exists in the fact that they are Americans. And since they are Americans, then that "proves" that they personally crossed the ocean with Columbus. It's a ridiculous lie that the Jews have been claiming as true for the past 35 centuries. It makes no sense and is a total fabrication. Archaeology proves that the Jews, *all of the Jews*, are liars.

This bandit chief, Moses, in Deuteronomy 6 harangues the Hebrews in the usury language of a rapacious Babylonian moneylender. The "promises" that this God of the moneylenders makes to the Hebrew thieves, is not a spiritual promise at all. It is a material promise of loot and sex and land. The Contract states that if they follow the "laws and customs" of Yahweh, then they can make the land of Canaan their own, and they will have long life, they will prosper and gain much wealth and many children.

The words of the Contract are to be taught to their children, repeated constantly while at rest, or walking, or lying down, written on a box strapped to their heads, strapped to their arms, written on their doorposts and gates. In short, the Contract is to be their most important concern. For these Hebrew goat rustlers, their god was most loyally served by keeping the moneylenders' Contract, a contract of lies, recommending warfare, murder, incest, genocide, and thievery as the "way" of their god. But of *actual* religion or spiritual knowledge, the Jews have none, only empty ritual.

Like the *tamkarum* [merchant-moneylenders] of Babylonia and Sumeria and Assyria, who stole property by using the Sumerian Swindle, those roving Hebrews bandits were encouraged by Moses to steal property through warfare.

> "When Yahweh has brought you into the land which he swore to your fathers Abraham, Isaac and Jacob that he would give you, with great and prosperous cities not of your building, houses full of good things not furnished by you, wells you did not dig, vineyards and olives you did not plant, when you have eaten these and had your fill, then take care that you do not forget Yahweh who brought you out of the land of Egypt, out of the house of slavery." (Deut 6: 10-12.)

Oh, yes! And don't forget that the rabbis get ten percent of everything that the Jews steal. The Hebrews were bandits and the Hebrew priests' only concern was not to dissuade them in any way but to encourage them for a ten percent cut of the booty.

Once again, the Semitic *asl* is dragged out as if every Jew was personally a slave in Egypt. This Deuteronomy 6 is really an encapsulation of the endless lies and perversions that make Judaism. The Hebrew *asl* is invoked, nagging the lie that all Hebrews then as well as all Jews today were equally present as slaves of Pharaoh. It is like a lying rabbi today saying, "I was there, too! Five thousand years ago, in Egypt working on a pyramid. I saw it with my own eyes. Oy! Let me tell you. It was terrible, the hard work, the lousy food. I am a Jew so I was there, too!" Such is the Jewish *abracadabra* and his throbbing *asl* at work. Does the delusion sound familiar like, perhaps, stories that the Jews tell about the Holocaust? "Oy! It was terrible. I remember it like yesterday. If one Jew was there, then all Jews were there. And since all Jews were there, then *any Jew* can make up *any story* he wants to for the *goyim* to believe." That's how Jewish *abracadabra* works: "I create as I speak." The Jewish *abracadabra* and his flaming *asl* knows no bounds of time and space. In truth, nothing that a Jew says is true. All Jews are liars.

Yes, Deuteronomy 6 is an encapsulation of the basic lie of Judaism. And the chapter ends with the basic definition that is used today of what is a good and pious Jew. Of course, all people worldwide consider a good person as someone who is honest and true or having goodness as a character trait. But not the Jews. A Jew may lie, cheat, steal and murder non-Jews, according to the rabbis. According to the lying rabbis, a Jew is almost like an angel of God and is therefore beyond reproach. This is why the Jews are so allergic to criticism; they consider themselves above criticism and beyond reproach. But according to the rabbis, what makes a Jew good and pious is this alone.

> "For us, right living will mean this: to keep and observe all these commandments before Yahweh our God as he has directed us." (Dt 6:25.)

This is all that a Jew needs to define himself as a "good Jew," to follow the Laws of Moses. These laws were written by the monstrous Babylonian scribes for deceiving the Hebrew bandits into serving them. It was an elaborate bankers' hoax that has deceived both the Jews and the entire world.

Once they understood what a good Hebrew goat-thief is, one who obeys the Laws of Moses, Deuteronomy 7 continues with a list of "great nations" that these goat rustlers would destroy. For an ant, standing on top, a watermelon must seem to be very great. But big as a watermelon is to an ant, it is certainly tiny as it sits in the corner of a field in a distant country. This is what the Hebrews were when compared to other nations, mere ants. But they were ants with a particularly warped sense of proportion. To them conquering a watermelon was a great victory, just as conquering the small towns of Canaan was "a great victory over mighty nations" for the Hebrew goat-thieves. And just as an ant might lift its legs and roar in exaltation upon reaching the summit of a watermelon, the Hebrews pounded their chests and roared of their "greatness" at conquering the tiny villages and the miniature towns of Canaan, towns so small that they did not even have fortified walls during the alleged times of Moses or Joshua or Saul or David. The Hebrews were petty bandits claiming a greatness that was not theirs. So, it was not difficult to lie about their "greatness" since they couldn't get it any other way.

Even so, those bragging liars did not conquer everyone that the Book of Deuteronomy claimed. "Many nations will fall before you: Hittites, Gatecrashes, Amorites, Canaanites, Perizzites, Hivites, Jebusites, seven nations greater and stronger than yourselves." (Dt 7:1.) The Canaanites were the original Semitic population of Canaan, scattered among small villages. As shown in Volume I, *The Sumerian Swindle*, the Amorites were not a nation at all but a widely distributed Semitic people stretching all across the ancient Near East from the Mediterranean to the Tigris River. The Semitic Hebrews were actually an Meteorite people. The Hebrews certainly did not conquer the Amorites other than those scattered among the towns of Canaan. The Hittites were not even based in Canaan. They were a non-Semitic and genuinely mighty kingdom based in Anatolia. The Hebrews had no chance of beating them except at a few outlying Hittite farms in Syria. The Gatecrashes, Perizzites and Hivites were insignificant tribes of Canaan while the Jebusites were the residents of Jerusalem and its surrounding minor territories. In all, the mighty god of the Hebrew ants was promising his ants the glory of overcoming many watermelons by calling them "mighty nations." This always happens when you allow Jews to write history books.

These Hebrew ants are taught by the Babylonian moneylenders how they should behave toward all peoples: vicious and ruthless and without pity, just like a banker.

> "Yahweh your God will deliver them over to you and you will conquer them. You must lay them under ban. You must make no covenant with them nor show them any pity. You must not marry with them: you must not give a daughter of yours to a son of theirs, nor take a daughter of theirs for a son of yours, for this would turn away your son from following me to serving other gods and the anger of Yahweh would blaze out against you and soon destroy you. Instead deal with them like this: tear down their altars, smash their standing stones, cut down their sacred poles and set fire to their idols. For you are a people consecrated to Yahweh your God; it is you that Yahweh your God has chosen to be his very own people out of all the peoples on the earth." (Dt 7:2-7.)

Because the Jews of today consider the Laws of Moses to be laws for all time, then they follow this diabolical teaching today of smashing other religions, and especially tearing down Christianity – attacking Christian manger displays, prosecuting lawsuits over Christian cross displays, putting a stop to prayer in schools, interfering with every Christian practice that they can. Why? Because they are a "holy" people "offended" by other religions? No, because they are devils promoting the evil teachings of the Monsters of Babylon. Modern Jews have proven to be the murderous and vicious practitioners of genocide and destroyers of other people that Jews have always been. Subversives who pretend a holiness that is not real, they slander and desecrate the churches and temples of non-Jews in every country they visit.

Further, this Deuteronomy 7 claims that the Yahweh-god keeps his promises. This is another lie that is repeatedly disproved throughout the *Hebrew Bible*. The Jewish God demands honesty from the Hebrews but is a lying hypocrite, Himself, breaking every alleged promise without fail and at the earliest opportunity. This is the god in whose "ways" the Jews emulate in their own lives and with their own actions, the ways of a lying devil.

After his father had been assassinated by the Jews, Deuteronomy was powerful incentive to the boy-king, Josiah, who became king at the age of eight years old. The wily and wicked High Priest knew that such an orphan would be a pliable puppet when he added the words, "It was for love of you and to keep the oath he swore to your fathers." (Dt 7:8.) An oath to make the usurious, money lending Jews the owners of the world and the destroyers of Mankind.

Rabbi Hilkiah buried the Book of Deuteronomy in a wall and then pretended to "discover" it as a "miracle." He then presented it to the gullible, young king Josiah. It contains a variety of vicious ways of dealing with non-Jews. The moneylenders of Babylon, who are the authors of Judaism, claim in Deuteronomy that the Yahweh-god fell in love with the mangy, murderous bandits who had tyrannized Egypt for over 100 years. This banker's god made them a "promise." The "promise" that Yahweh had made to Abraham – after first tempting Abraham to cut the throat of his own son and pour out his blood on an altar to the Yahweh-god – was that all of Abraham's descendants would become the tyrannical dictators of the earth with all of the people on earth bowing at their feet. This has been the dream of all Jews ever since the five Books of Moses were first written by the evil scribes of Judah. This god of the moneylenders allegedly wanted to make those bandits into "his own people." But this demon god had the vicious qualities of the bankers and merchants who had conjured him up.

Deuteronomy was written by the wicked priests of Yahweh who were trying to keep their power, prestige and wealth by deceiving young king Josiah. Their intention was to destroy all the religions around them (and confiscate their treasuries) and use Josiah as their military puppet. Those horrible rabbis and priests wrote of the people around them:

> "Devour, then, all these people whom Yahweh your God delivers over to you, show them no pity, do not serve their gods, for otherwise you would be ensnared." (Dt 7:16.)

That is, you would be ensnared in a better religion than what the Hebrews had. This vicious "god" in the person of the evil priests and rabbis of Yahweh, carried his malice toward his enemies from generation to generation with genocidal insanity.

The moneylenders of Babylonia long before had learned that if they impoverished or enslaved a man, his children would remember the crime and hold it against them. How the merchant-moneylenders had swindled and enslaved, was not only remembered by the sons of the victim but was also told to the grandchildren and great-grandchildren. All of them would have an animosity toward the moneylenders that could easily and without warning break out into various forms of revenge. And it made their victims wary of ever again borrowing money at interest, thus reducing future profits of the moneylenders. Revenge and vindictive feuds that lasted for generations, fueled the relations between all of the Semites of the entire ancient Near East as a cultural norm of murder and reprisal.

So, the moneylenders of Babylonia developed their methodical destruction of the people around them with the idea always uppermost that in order to avoid reprisal resulting from their parasitic impoverishment, their enslavement and destruction of Mankind, that they must prevent the inevitable revenge upon themselves. They did this by murdering at least four generations of their victim's family – to genocide the victim, his children, his grandchildren and his great grandchildren so that there remained no one to avenge the original victim of the swindle. After murdering entire generations and destroying all written evidence and historical documents, the Jews could then tell stories about how great they are, with no dissenting voices living to tell of their lies.

This principle of *genocide of four generations* became embedded within Judaism through the Yahweh Cult. The Jews were taught not just to murder the non-Jews but also to destroy the children and the grandchildren even up to four generations so that the entire family line would become extinct. This is hardwired into Judaism but has been overlooked by those deluded fool Christians who do not know how to read or to understand what they have read. Just as the Thuggees of Old India were a religion of murder and theft, Judaism is a religion of genocide and theft. The Jews are worse than the Thugs ever were. To hide their genocidal history, the Jews of the 20th and 21st Centuries AD pretend to be the victims of genocide, themselves. Such incredible hypocrisy it is, by the world's biggest liars who worship the God of Genocide, the god of armies, Yahweh, the god of lies.

With these methods, the Monsters of Babylon could continue to walk among Men with their heads held high while concealing the vindictive malice of their greedy hearts. That the heads of the bankers and moneylenders should be held high on poles and spears, is what they wanted to avoid. So, they murdered multiple generations of their victims in order to destroy all personal anecdotes of their greed and treachery. When there was no one left to tell others how voraciously evil they had been, why would their next victims not believe them when they claimed to be "the Chosen Ones of God" and "the most righteous of people"? When a liar has no one to oppose his deceits, then what else can people do but to believe his lies? What greater lie can there be than the Most Evil People to Have Ever Walked the Earth, all claiming to be "the Chosen Ones of God"? Are they evil clowns or are they devils?

Deuteronomy 7 ends with the Yahweh-god invoking the moneylenders' power of destroying people with usury,

> "Little by little, Yahweh your god will destroy these *goyim* before you." (Dt 7:22.)

"He will deliver their kings into your hands and you will blot out their names from under heaven, none shall withstand you, until you have destroyed them all." (Dt 7:24.)

"Tear down their altars, smash their standing stones, cut down their sacred poles and set fire to their idols. For you are a people consecrated to Yahweh your God; it is you that Yahweh your God has chosen to be his very own people out of all the peoples on Earth." (Dt 7:5-6.)

This chapter is the pathological basis of Judaism today. Modern psychology defines this sort of behavior as *narcissistic homicidal megalomania*. But in this case, all the psychopaths are pretending to pray. Even though Judaism does not offer any spiritual insight to its followers like most other religions do, these unenlightened thieves and lawyers are commanded by the rabbis to murder and destroy all people of the world who are not members of their Yahweh Penis Cult. By murdering other religious people and leaving only Jews dancing on their graves, this means in Semitic thought that the Jews are better and more blessed than their victims. In fact, the Jews betray and murder their betters, leaving only Jews alive to claim a false superiority. Greed and a murderous malice to its ultimate expression! That's Judaism.

The delusional fraud of the Hebrew *asl* is again invoked in Chapter 8. It claims that the Hebrews of Josiah's time (649–609 BC) were the exact same as the dead Hebrews during the time of the so-called Conquest of Canaan allegedly in 1500 BC. All of Judaism is built on lies, deceit and fraud. This is not a matter of opinion, the Jew's own writings and the findings of modern archaeology prove it. God never did any of the things that the Jews claim that He did.

Here is a clever literary device of having Moses recap the Hebrew fables with the Devil's Truth:

"Be sure that if you forget Yahweh your God, if you follow other gods, if you serve them and bow down before them – I warn you today – you will most certainly perish." (Dt 8:19.)

The evil Bankers of Babylon, themselves, had no illusions that they were good or moral people. After all, they were ruthless in their extractions of profits and pitiless in their collection of money. They knew that beating, enslaving, and killing their victims was not a good thing – if it didn't result in making a profit. But they were bankers and moneylenders so they didn't care about good or evil. Only silver and gold and its increase, mattered to them because with silver and gold they could buy everything that they desired – and they desired the whole world. It didn't matter to the bankers that they were hated by the People because they could close their eyes into the slits of an Ubaidian sculpture and steel their determination and fill their hearts with malice, returning hate for hate. Since the Bankers were hated, they hated in return. Instead of seeing people as their fellow humans, they looked upon them as "goyim," as "insects and cattle" from whom they collected a fee.

The Monsters of Babylon were hated for very good reasons; but they returned that hatred out of the bitter malice and wicked vengeance of the Semitic character trait. Their hatred burned in their hearts like the black fires of hell. They were demons who desired to set up their own treasury within the safety of their own temple and have the people bow at their feet. As priests, they could have the respect that they so much desired and could invoke their will through the fear and terror that they psychopathically so much enjoyed engendering in others.

So, Deuteronomy 9 begins with the moneylender scribes telling the Hebrews that any goodness of the own didn't matter. The Yahweh-god didn't love the Hebrews because these thieving bandits and cutthroats were good people. No, the Hebrews were not good and they knew it. After all, they were thieves and bandits and they knew that, too. But according to the Yahweh-god, *even though the Hebrews are not good people*, this god would help them destroy and dispossess the *goyim*, the non-Jewish, lowly insects and stupid cattle of the world. As for the Canaanites,

> "It is not for any goodness or sincerity of yours that you are entering their land to possess it; no, it is for the wickedness of these nations that Yahweh your God is dispossessing them for you, and to keep the word that he swore to your fathers, Abraham, Isaac and Jacob." (Dt 9:5.)

Remember that "sin" for a Jew was anything that breaks the Laws of Moses. "Piety" and "holiness" meant keeping the Laws of Moses. None of these laws had anything to do with actual "godliness" or "virtue" or "goodness" or "holiness." They were laws for the perpetuation of the Temple Treasury Cult and the feeding of the priests. Thus, anyone who was "sinful" or "wicked" was someone who did not follow the Laws of Moses. In other words, everybody on earth who was not a circumcised member of the Yahweh Treasury Cult, was targeted to be dispossessed by the Jews, simply because everyone else was not Jewish. And in Deuteronomy 9, no matter how many times in the past that the Yahweh-god broke his promises, he hypocritically repeats the same promise over again. A more appropriate god for the lying Jews, they couldn't have made up themselves. Who could imagine any god so wicked, unless that god was actually a demon or a Jew.

The roving Hebrew cut-throats were described as stubborn, wicked and sinful (Dt 9:27-28). But the Yahweh-god is convinced not to destroy them with blasts of fire by the intercession of Moses praying to him and begging him not to wipe them out for the sake of the "Promise" made to Abraham, Isaac and Jacob. And what was that "Promise" other than to make them multiply like maggots and dispossess the people of the entire world?

Deuteronomy 10 repeats the fable about the Yahweh-god writing on the stone tablets with his finger and doing mighty deeds to bring the goat rustlers out of Egypt. Again, the visiting "strangers" are mentioned to whom these vicious Hebrew bandits are ordered to be kind. Why? Because the strangers were non-Jewish merchant-moneylenders from distant countries.

Deuteronomy 11 again repeats the myths of the "wilderness journey" and even though it is allegedly addressed to the children of the Hebrews who died in the desert, it falsely calls up the Hebrew *asl* by declaring that even though none of them ever saw the alleged events that "It is *your eyes* that have seen all this great work that Yahweh has done." (Dt 11:7.) So, Dear Reader, become a Jew for a moment and repeat this phrase: "Yes! I close my eyes and I can see it! We were all slaves in Egypt because I was there, too! I can see Moses parting the Red Sea because I was there, too! Yes, I know that Joshua blew down the walls of Jericho because I was there, too." Does this, Dear Reader, seem more than a bit deranged? Well, that's Judaism.

Again and again, doing good, being moral, having a kind and loving heart, being holy – none of this matters at all in Judaism. All that matters to the Monsters of Babylon is taking away what other people have and dispossessing them of their property by following the criminal Laws of Moses – the Contract – and to "faithfully obey the commandments" (Dt 11:13).

> "For if you faithfully keep and observe all these commandments that I enjoin on you today, loving Yahweh your God, following all of his ways and clinging to him, Yahweh will dispossess all these *goyim* (non-Jewish, lowly insects, stupid cattle) for you, and you shall dispossess *goyim* greater and more powerful than yourselves. Wherever the sole of your foot treads shall be yours; your territory shall stretch from the wilderness and from Lebanon, from the river, the river Euphrates, to the Western Sea. No man will be able to stand against you; Yahweh your God will make you feared and dreaded throughout the land that you tread, just as he promised you." (Dt 11:22-25.)

By being international bankers and financiers who practice the Sumerian Swindle, by being ruthless to debtors and subversive of all peoples and all nations, by promoting warfare while engineering their own military cowardice, the Jews greatly benefit from the "Promises" of the Monsters of Babylon. So, the corruption in their hearts leads them ever onward into the hellfire waiting beneath their feet.

Deuteronomy 11:22-25 is the symbolism of the Israeli flag today. The two blue lines represent the Euphrates and the Nile Rivers with the Star of David, the devil's hoof print, in the center. This is all the land that the Jews claim for their own, stretching from Iraq to Egypt as well as every land in the entire world where a Jew steps, pushing his way in, lending money and swindling the world.

In addition, the hatred that their victims have for the moneylenders, is taken as a sick and twisted sign that these monsters are actually "loved" by Yahweh as long as they are "hated" by the non-Jews. That the Jews are to be "feared and dreaded" is a sign that the demon-god Yahweh loves them. So, the Jews have always tried to be hated by the non-Jews because to them that is a sign to these devils that they are loved by their demon god. Judaism is a sick, demented tumor upon Mankind.

Deuteronomy 12 is a repetition that all of the tithes must go to the Temple and that the Levite priests scattered among the tribes are to be cared for and not neglected. The Levites are the religious cops or religion policemen who enforce the Laws of Moses among the goat rustlers. They are special parasites who get their living by making sure that the Hebrews pay their tithes. Or if they catch any Jew breaking the Laws of Moses, making them pay fines of silver and barbecued goats. The Levites were ever on the lookout for ways to fine the Hebrew farmers and merchants by being strict keepers of the Law, themselves, with all their body hair shaved off down to their genitals and assholes.

The chapter ends with the admonition that the Hebrews are to destroy all other religions but they are not to learn anything about other religions.

> "Do not imitate them once they have been destroyed in front of you, or go inquiring after their gods, saying, 'How did these *goyim* worship their gods? I will go and do the same."
> (Dt 12:30.)

Thus, the Jews are entrapped by the rabbis and forever denied any knowledge of God because they always destroy every manifestation of God. The Jews are devils.

Following such teachings today, the modern Jews are at the forefront of making civil laws against the non-Jews designed to destroy the religions of the non-Jews. The Jewish-Communist hate group known as the American Civil Liberties Union (ACLU), is at the vanguard of eliminating any public displays of religion. One may wonder why the Jews would want to ban the Ten Commandments from a public courtroom? Isn't the Ten Commandment part of the Jewish religion? The Jews want to ban public displays of the Ten Commandments because that is a Christian court room, not a Jewish one. And the Ten Commandments were given to the Jews and not to the Christians. So, they are opposed to the Christians having something that belongs to the Jews. Besides, if Christians believe that the Ten Commandments are from God, then the Christians might expect the Jews to follow the Ten Commandments and be good people. This would mean that the Jews would lose money with their various swindles of the Christians. Banning Christian crosses, banning the Ten Commandments in public, banning public prayers in schools, tearing down Christmas trees and putting up menorahs in their place, are all part of the teachings of Judaism in that all Jews must do whatever they can to destroy all other religions everywhere, leaving Judaism standing in triumph on the smoldering ashes.

Deuteronomy 13 begins with "All I command you, you must keep and observe, adding nothing to it, taking nothing away." (Dt 13:1.) Thus, the modern Jews prove their treachery from the earliest of times, simply because they have added the thirty or forty volumes of the *Babylonian Talmud* to the laws of the Old Testament and claimed them superior to their alleged "holy" Torah. To keep the Hebrew goat rustlers from finding a better religious faith (which is not difficult since all other religions are better than Judaism), the scribes wrote that even if they find something better, they are to avoid it since it is really Yahweh testing them to see if they really love Yahweh or not (Dt 13:2-5). The "omnipotent" Semitic gods were always proving what fraudulent phantoms they really are.

Furthermore, even if the prophet or spiritual leader or dreamer of dreams shows the Jews a better and more holy way of life, they are commanded to kill that religious leader. Even if a brother or son or wife or friend tries to show the Jews a more holy and truthful religion, then the Jews are commanded to kill their brother, son, wife or friend. The entire congregation of Jews are to stone these apostates to death (Dt 13:6-11). Truly, the Jews are the most screwed up people on Earth! They destroy everything except the lies of Judaism and the gold that it brings them. This is why Mohammad (mhrh) copied Judaism for his own bandit religious fraud.

Even if only one inhabitant of a town tries to convert the Hebrews to another religion, then they are commanded to "kill all the inhabitants of that town without giving any quarter; you must lay it under ban, the town and all it contains." (Dt 13:16-17.) A ban includes killing all the dogs and cats, sheep and goats and all men, women and children of that town for the proselytizing of even a few citizens trying to convert the Jews to something better. Truly, the Jews are the most demonic people on Earth! Even worse than the Muslims!

The rabbis kept the Hebrews in servitude to the Contract by killing anyone who tried to convert them to a genuine religion. They were required to close their eyes to Truth and to God and only follow the Contract of the moneylenders because nothing was more important than keeping the Treasury well-guarded by fanatical priests, priests who could be stoned to death, themselves, for failing to follow the laws of the Contract.

Deuteronomy 14 continues with the basic lie of Judaism that "Yahweh has chosen you to be his very own people out of all the people on earth." (Dt 14:2.) It is a lie because Yahweh was a Canaanite god, complete with wife (Asherah) and son (Baal). The Hebrews had already been worshiping Yahweh. It was the moneylenders of Babylon who chose the Hebrews because they were bandits and stupid enough to fall for Terah and Abraham's scam. This Chapter then continues with a list of foods that are "clean" or "unclean" and either allowed or forbidden to eat. The secret malice that the moneylenders have for all people is here even related to food. While the Hebrews are told not to eat "any animal that has died a natural death." But any diseased or dead animal may be sold to the foreigners or given to the *Shabbos goyim* for food. This means that filthy food is to be fed to the non-Jews who work for the Jews on the Sabbath. Those poor people who help the Jews are referred to by a Hebrew term which translates as "Sabbath dirt." This same malice against all non-Jews is extended into the modern Jewish-controlled food industry where the Jews produce garbage and unhealthy food products for sale to the non-Jews but not things that they would eat, themselves. Thus, through unhealthy food, the Jews cause non-Jews to sicken and die, a subtle use of poisoning, a subtle practice of genocide. This is easily seen in modern times through the Jewish junk food industry.

The duty of paying the annual tithe is repeated. Ten percent of all produce, cattle and money that the Hebrews make in a year, are to be taken to the Temple. Or the produce and cattle can be sold for silver and the silver spent partying in Jerusalem. This law enriched the already wealthy Jews and priests who owned the buildings, taverns and markets inside the city walls. The tithe is paid to the Levites since they are the main blood-suckers from among the Hebrews. If the Hebrews live too far away to travel, then they can sell their produce for silver and send the silver to the Temple. Either way, they must give ten percent to the priests of the Temple. And every three years, the tithe of the harvest is to be given to the Levites, the stranger, the orphan and widow as extra incentive to remain loyal to the Contract or starve to death.

Deuteronomy 14 is another place where the rabbis have again broken the injunction to not add or subtract anything from the Contract. "You are not to boil a kid in its mother's milk." (Dt 14:21.) This ancient taboo was a compassionate feeling of shepherds for their flocks. But it became the rabbinical taboo for not mixing milk and meat at the same meal. Vast numbers of additional laws concerning dairy and meat were invented by the rabbis and priests looking for new forms of revenue by making laws which brought in fines when these laws were broken.

The Contract stipulates that every seven years the Hebrews are to release their fellow Hebrews from debt-bondage. They can exact payment from foreigners (non-Jews) but every seven years the Hebrew debt-slaves are to be released from their obligation. In this way, enslavement of non-Jews is stressed as an operating procedure of Judaism since the profits are greater.

The phrase, "Let there be no poor among you then" (Dt 15:4) has been the basis for a large variety of Jewish charities that are set up for Jews and only Jews. These allow the Jews to finance the poorest among them with the profits that they make from money swindled from the non-Jews of the world. One example is the billions in profits that the modern Jewish bankers swindle from the nations every year. Ten percent of this is a huge sum goes to the rabbis who loan it interest-free to the Jews in their congregations to start businesses. Thus, they use the wealth of the non-Jews to further swindle and impoverish the non-Jews. This secret corporate power is a great advantage to Jewish businessmen while it undermines and bankrupts the non-Jewish businesses who are unaware of the conspiracy against them. The rabbis donate some of the tithes to Jewish charities meant only for Jews or fund it into Communist and other anti-human organizations that destroy the very nations from where the tithe money originated. Thus, the Jews take the wealth of a country and use that very wealth to destroy that country. *With wanton malice, they use our own money against us.* In modern times, the Jews transferred American wealth to Communist China so as to undermine and destroy America. This is detailed in Volume 3, *The Blood-Suckers of Judah.*

The Sumerian Swindle profits the bankers, provides the Jews with so much money swindled from the non-Jews that they can afford every luxury even for the lower-level Jews at the bottom of the Jewish pecking order. By keeping the Contract so as to create a social buffer between the moneylenders and their non-Jewish victims, the merchant-moneylender scribes could make the promise that by following the Contract, the Hebrews

> "...will be creditors to many *goyim* and debtors to none, you
> will rule over many *goyim* and be ruled by none." (Dt 15:6.)

That is a perfect description of modern banking. As the religion of moneylenders, Judaism is organized as a guild of predatory moneylenders and businessmen who use every fraud and swindle to extract wealth from non-Jews while practicing interest-free loans and charity among themselves. The Jews thrive because they defraud other people but do not themselves suffer from the Sumerian Swindle since they are the operators of it. Judaism is a false religion and a malignant cancer. In its own teaching and in its own practice, Jews are the enemy of all of Mankind.

Deuteronomy 15:7-11 is also a basis for the social subgroup of Jewish *schnorrers* (professional beggars) that infest Jewish communities. The Contract is designed to keep the Hebrews together as a group and even to support the beggars among them. Deuteronomy 15 ends with once again demanding that for eating meat "you must not consume the blood, but pour it out like water on the ground." (Dt 15:23.) The sly merchant-moneylenders who wrote the Contract, knew that people want most what they are forbidden. Thus, they were creating a nation of bloodthirsty Jews who were enjoined to be ruthless and without pity against the *goyim* (non-Jewish, lowly insects, stupid cattle). This would create some real monsters such as during the French Revolution and the Bolshevik Revolution, bloodthirsty Jewish monsters ravaging the countries and the peoples who failed to follow the First Rule of Human Society: "No Jews Allowed Except on a Gibbet."

Also, in Deuteronomy 16, judges are appointed to administer what is called "justice" which is nothing more than overseeing the Laws of Moses. These judges are to take no bribes. The modern rabbis teach the Jews that although they are not to bribe Jewish judges, the Laws of Moses do not prohibit them from bribing non-Jewish judges. With this hypocritical double side to the laws of the Bankers of Babylon, the Jews have escaped justice and punishment for their crimes for thousands of years. Once they go to the kings and court officials with their gold, they escape all manner of justice and retribution for their crimes against the People. And once a Jew becomes a judge, all Jews go free and all non-Jews suffer the full weight of the law (*Babylonian Talmud*, Bava Kamma 113a).

Deuteronomy 17 repeats the law that any Hebrew who worships any god other than Yahweh, must be stoned to death. Under the oath of two or more witnesses, he is to be taken outside the city and submitted to group justice. His accuser casts the first stone and then the inhabitants of the entire town stone him to death. By murdering as a community event, the entire community is convinced to keep the Contract and not have pity even on one of their own. A real brutal and bloodthirsty bunch of monsters, those Jews!

The power of life and death is given to the Levite priests and judges. Any Hebrew who does not precisely follow the instructions of those hairy-faced fiends or if anyone disobeys the verdicts of the priests, then they must be executed (Dt 17:12). The Contract had to be enforced ruthlessly if the gold was to be made safe. With such a system, it did not take long for the rabbis to eliminate all competition to their rule and to weed out any dissenters or wise men who could see through their voracious swindle. Soon the only Hebrews who the rabbis allowed to live within their kingdom, were the Hebrews who accepted the lies and bowed to the pomposity of the evil rabbinical lawyers dressed in priestly robes.

Deuteronomy 17 ordains that if the Hebrews prefer to have a king rule over them, then it must be a king that the Yahweh-god ordains through the priests. Thus, total power is once again embraced by the priests over the king, just like in Babylon. To make sure that they, themselves, had control of all of Judaea and the Temple Treasury, the rabbis included the orders that even the king must follow these laws and:

> "When he is seated on his royal throne, he must write a copy of this Law on a scroll for his own use at the dictation of the Levitical priests." (Deut 17:18.)

It was at this time, with their young king Josiah under their power, that the rabbis first seized total control of both the religious and the administrative powers of Judah. They insured their continued power over both king and kingdom by putting every future king under their rule by dictating to him the very laws that they wanted him to follow and having him write it all down in his own hand. These were some very clever monsters, the rabbis.

To ensure that the Contract was severely enforced, the clever moneylenders established a starving cadre of law enforcement officers known as Levitical priests, named after their tribe of Levi. Stationed throughout the various towns and villages, these vicious busybodies depended for their livelihood on the donations, fines, sacrifices and penalties that they could extract from the Hebrews. As enforcers of the Laws of Moses, they were also the judges over the Hebrews. Why would the Hebrew bandits put up with this? Because the talking goat-skins which they could not read, claimed that they were descendants of Abraham who had gotten a special promise from the Yahweh-god. Because they were "chosen" (whether they liked it or not), they had to follow the Laws of Moses or else the earth would swallow them.

> "The Levitical priests, that is to say the whole tribe of Levi, shall have no share or inheritance with Israel; they shall live on the foods offered to Yahweh and on his dues. This tribe is to have no inheritance among their brothers; Yahweh will be their inheritance as he promised them." (Dt 18:1-2.)

Do you see how the enforcement of the Laws were built into Judaism by making the tribe of Levi totally dependent upon policing and enforcing the Laws, otherwise, they didn't eat. This word translated as "foods offered" shows the hand of the Babylonian scribes who wrote and edited the Book of Deuteronomy. Although by 539 BC, the Sumerian language was extinct, except for its use by the priests in the various temples of Babylonia, this word is Sumerian in origin for "foods offered to a god." Only modern archaeology has shown us this Babylonian fingerprint.

As "law" enforcement officers and judges, the Levitical priests not only profited whenever any of the Hebrews broke a Mosaic Law, but they profited even more as the number of laws increased. So, a huge number of additional laws were added to the Mosaic code by these priest as they dissected and enlarged the number of offenses that could produce "sin offerings" or "fines" of barbecued goat meat and silver. The more laws that they could invent, the more profit for themselves, so the Oral Laws grew in number.

But the Laws of Moses specifically stated: "You must add nothing to what I command you, and take nothing from it, but keep the commandments of Yahweh your God just as I lay them down for you." (Dt 4:2.) So, among these tribes of Hebrew thieves and murderers, the Hebrew priests, the Levites, became the chief law breakers simply by defining more laws to increase their profits and by negating other laws in order to allow appreciative "law breakers" to escape a severe penalty. These new laws and rabbinical interpretations of the Mosaic Law became an Oral Tradition known among them as the "Tradition of the Elders." This tradition was later written down as the infamous *Babylonian Talmud*.

As the chief lawyers from among the tribes of criminals and roving bandits, the Levitical priests and rabbis developed the rhetorical skills of demonic lawyers. Sitting around with nothing to do other than to judge other Jews, they argued and discussed the so-called "meaning" and "interpretation" of the Mosaic Laws. Through verbal charades, false logic, deceptive assertions, illogical declarations, and unsubstantiated "proofs" which actually proved nothing, they wove around the Jews such a net of inane and insane laws and interpretations of the laws that not a single shekel of silver or morsel of barbecued goat could elude them.

Deuteronomy 18 established the dictatorship of the rabbinate over the Hebrews. Deuteronomy 18 also established the ignorance of the rabbis as bona fide hypocrites. Calling other religions "detestable" and falsely claiming a moral superiority that does not, in fact, exist in Judaism, these rabbis and Levitical priests replaced the "detestable practices" of the other religions of Canaan with the incredibly more detestable practices of the Bankers of Babylon.

> "When you come into the land Yahweh your God gives you, you must not fall into the habit of imitating the detestable practices of the natives. There must never be anyone among you who makes his son or daughter pass through fire, who practices divination, who is soothsayer, augur or sorcerer, who uses charms, consults ghosts or spirits, or calls up the dead. For the man who does these things is detestable to Yahweh your God; it is because of these detestable practices that Yahweh your God is driving these *goyim* before you." (Dt 18:9-12.)

But there was, and is, no Law of Moses that the clever Levitical priest and rabbis could not break if they could apply the proper "interpretation." In later centuries, the rabbis would become notorious as soothsayers, sorcerers, purveyors of charms and talismans, consulters of ghosts and spirits who call up the dead. This substitution of the sorcerers of the Canaanites with the sorcerers among the rabbis was done with the same hypocrisy that the rabbis have used with every law of Moses. By using the magic dice on the magic dice table (Urim and Thummim) which the High Priest wore on his pimp's suit, they replaced the reading of sheep intestines with their own variety of prophecy based on gambling.

The substitution of sorcery by the words of prophets who allegedly spoke with the voice of God, was accomplished in Deuteronomy 18. "Thus says Yahweh" became a popular phrase among these "seers" and prophets. All that was required of a prophet was that he followed the Mosaic law and his prophecies became true. All other prophets who spoke in the name of Yahweh and whose prophesies were not fulfilled, were killed by the priests on the blood-dripping altar of *Yahweh*.

The god of the Babylonian Monsters and their Hebrew minions, was a wrathful, spiteful god of thieves and murderers. The Jews meted out death and violence to the people who were not members of their circumcised devil cult, but it was necessary for the moneylenders to keep murder under control within the Cult, itself. So, laws were made to control their Semitic predilection towards revenge and retaliation. It was the *lex talionis* (eye-for-an-eye) tradition among all of the Semites of the ancient Near East that pushed the relatives of murdered men to avenge a murdered victim with retaliatory murder. That's just the way those Semitic tribes were.

The Hebrew bandits were some brutal, malicious, murdering thieves. So, a law for limiting their vengeful tendencies was needed to protect accidental killers from reprisal. So, Moses set aside three cities as "cities of refuge" where someone who had accidentally killed, could run away to a refuge from the retaliation of the relatives of the accident victim.

Copying the Babylonian law of *lex talionis*, false accusers were to be treated with Hammurabi's rule for suffering the same penalty that their intended victim of their accusation would have suffered. "You are to show no pity. Life for life, eye for eye, tooth for tooth, hand for hand, foot for foot" (Dt 19:21) was another of Hammurabi's laws that the moneylenders of Babylonia insisted that they needed to protect themselves from the vengeance of their victims. They wanted no one attacking them without being able to retaliate in like manner by using the Law as their weapon.

The materialism of the Yahweh-god and his Hebrew thieves extended not only to their quest for booty during war but also to the materialistic desire to keep what they had by staying safe in the back lines and not going to war. Much of the cowardice of the modern-day Jews can be linked to such laws as found in Deuteronomy 20. Their Sabbath Exemption was specifically designed to prevent them from fighting in a non-Jewish king's war and Deuteronomy 20 allowed the richest Jews to hide in the back lines during any Jewish king's war. Here's how that particular swindle works to this very day.

Before going to war, all of the Hebrews who had just built a house or planted a vineyard or betrothed a wife and not yet had sex with her, as well as the fearful and faint of heart, were excused from fighting and sent home (Dt 20:5-8). For the Jewish bankers and financiers, this was an easy loophole escape from the rigors and dangers of warfare. Even if they were called upon to actually take up arms and fight for the Jews, as the super-wealthy, they always had new properties to manage and concubines to marry. Thus, the richest Jews were always exempt from combat. While claiming how loyal and brave they were, they could cite this passage as a "god-given" exemption from actually risking their fat asses on the battlefield because they hadn't screwed their new concubine yet; and they had business properties and financial obligations to manage. Of course, any Jew could risk being called a coward and stay out of combat by simply claiming to "have a heart condition." Even if all of the Jews had to go fight, the rich Jews always could stay safely at home while all the other Jews were killed. So, guess who wrote the *Hebrew Bible*? The philosophy of the Jewish bankers and financiers has always been, "Many must suffer and die, so that a few Jews may live in luxury."

For the Hebrew bandits who were seeking more loot, the laws of Moses proclaimed two types of victims: those who lived in towns *outside* of the "Promised Land" and those living in towns *inside* the "Promised Land." Those towns *outside* of the "Promised Land," that is, *every town in the entire world* that the Hebrews coveted and wanted to steal, were to be treated thusly: First, offer them a "Jewish Shalom" ("peace", "trust me"). If the town accepts "peace" and opens its gates, all of the people in that city or town are to be reduced to slavery and forced labor. Oy! Such a deal for the people of the world to be enslaved by the holy Jews! Why does this sound so much like Assyrian methods? Because Deuteronomy wasn't written in an ancient time by Moses, as it claims, but in the 7th Century when Assyria dominated the Near East.

However, if any of the towns in the entire world refuse a "Jewish Shalom," then they are to be attacked and all of the menfolk are to be murdered.

> "But the women, the children, the livestock and all that the town contains, all its spoil, you may take for yourselves as booty. You will devour the spoil of your enemies which Yahweh your God has delivered to you." (Dt 20:14.)

The Jews were some very rotten and ruthless creatures who "walked in the ways" of their Yahweh God of Genocide, just as the modern Jews do today. Since this method applies to the towns of the entire world, the modern Jews have conspired through their banking and financial swindles to accomplish this in modern times, destroying and impoverishing the peoples of Europe, America, and Australia, that is, stealing the wealth, killing the men with endless warfare and debauching the children. But more about this in Volume III, *The Bloodsuckers of Judah.*

As bad as the Jews were commanded to treat the people of the entire world *outside* of the "Promised Land," *Yahweh*, the demon god of the bankers, commanded them to treat the people of Canaan (Palestine) *even worse*. For the towns *inside* of the "Promised Land" *everybody is to be murdered* including the men, women, children, and all of the livestock as well as the cats and dogs – every living thing in Canaan (Palestine). And this genocide is being practiced by the Jews on the people of Palestine today.

> "But as regards the towns of those people which Yahweh your God gives you as your own inheritance, you must not spare the life of any living thing. Instead, you must lay them under ban, the Hittites, Amorites, Canaanites, Perizzites, Hivites, and Jebusites, as Yahweh your God commanded, so that they may not teach you to practice all the detestable practices they have in honor of their gods and so cause you to sin against Yahweh your God." (Dt 20:16-18.)

The desert-rat Jews had this all-mighty attitude not because of any "holy" power from a mighty god, but because Judaism is a bankers' swindle. Judaism has always been secretly financed by an international cartel of Jewish financiers with control over the money of every nation and the finances for swaying kings and impoverishing entire countries. Money and lies are the only power of the Jews, not some Canaanite god throwing lightning bolts. The Jews are pompously supercilious because of this secret and concealed financial power, alone. These ancient monsters are certainly not holy. The Jewish priests and rabbis needed the ten percent tithe of the bankers' gold; and the bankers needed the protection of a religion that applauded their financial parasitism and commercial pillage while keeping them and their gold safe from the profitable wars that they fomented.

Remember, the moneylender's definition of "detestable practices" means any practice that is not a Jewish practice as well as any practice that is not a Law of Moses. To Terah and his clan of Babylonian swindlers, only their own brand of organized crime was legal. Only the members flaunting circumcised penises were "pious and holy" while all others were *goyim* (non-Jewish, lowly insects, stupid cattle) who therefore by definition, automatically practiced "detestable practices."

All of the founding patriarchs of Judaism were Babylonians not Hebrews. Terah of Ur, his son Abraham, his grandson Isaac and his great-grandson Jacob, were all married to and descendants of Babylonians. They were not Hebrews although they falsely claimed to be the genealogical fathers of all Hebrews *in the entire Near East*. What they established was not actually a religion because it did not strive to attain a knowledge or an experience of the God. It is a system that hijacked a Canaanite deity and redefined that god into a cult serving a Temple priesthood; it was not a priesthood that served a Temple god.

What the Jews established has become *the world's oldest organized criminal conspiracy* governed not by criminal law but by the laws of criminals. The laws of the Jews have nothing to do with logical or reasoned statutes created for the sake of "justice." The laws of the Jews are not related to anything that can be defined as "moral" or "holy" but rather with declarations which are only beneficial to a centrally established authoritarian entity surrounding a treasury which is actually opposed to all religion and which actively destroys all other expressions of religion among all other people. There is nothing "holy" about such a system. Such a system designed to destroy religion is nothing less than demonic. In actual fact, the Jews are devils by every definition of the term.

But *by simply declaration*, everything that the people of the world do, is a "detestable practice" to the moneylender-priests simply because it is not a profitable Jewish practice. What most people do not understand, since the Jews make every effort to hide it, is that the practices of the Jews are nothing less than perverted and demonic. Yet, those fiends claim a purity for themselves that is nothing by a lie while slandering all other people of the entire world.

Remember, too, that the moneylender definition of a "sin" is anything that *does not follow the Laws of the Moses*. And so, the Hebrews were taught by the wicked Jewish priests, scribes and rabbis, that the non-Jews of the world are automatically sinful, detestable people who should be murdered, enslaved and dispossessed by the Hebrew sheep molesters. Because of the fraudulent arithmetic of lending at interest, those who lend money eventually come into ownership of the entire world. So, the actual ownership of the entire world and enslavement of all of Mankind, is built into all banking and all finance through such a devious cheat. The bankers and financiers do not deserve to own anything because they are criminal swindlers. But because they have swindled the world's wealth through their money manipulations and market monopolies, the

Jews have the money to promote their evil dreams of world ownership. That is, unless the People of the world understand that we are being cheated by Jewish liars and devils bent on the destruction of Mankind.

In Deuteronomy 21, innocent blood of sacrificial animals is again shed by the wicked priests of Judaism. In this case, when "a murdered man is discovered lying in open country and it is not known who killed him," then the Hebrew scribes are to measure the distance to the nearest towns. The nearest town brings a heifer, the priest breaks its neck and the elders of that town washes their hands while claiming to be innocent of the blood of the murder victim. In this "magical" way, the Hebrews cover up the murder and forget about it. Since they agree to cover it up, the incident is forgotten and there is no longer need for finding the murderer. A religion of murderers who pay the priest, wash their hands and forget about it.

This "magical" rite establishes the method by which the modern Jews cover up their own crimes by using their very big Jewish *asl*. When a Jew commits a crime, all of the Jews deny that they had anything to do with it, they cover it up and forget about it, thereby "protecting" the Jew from reprisal. And since it's "magic," they are so very sincere in their forgetfulness.

Furthermore, Deuteronomy 21, tells of the "proper" Jewish way of killing and raping. When the bandits go to war, from among the prisoners, any women that they want to rape, they can do so. But if they want to add them as another wife in their harem, first they shave the woman's head to humiliate her and clip her nails so she can't scratch out the eyes of her rapist. Next, they let her mourn her murdered parents and husband for one month. After this, she can be taken as a wife since she has been thoroughly violated in spirit and accepting of her fate by that time. But if she ceases to please her rapist with enthusiastic sexual gratifications and hard work around the farm, she must be released to starve to death and not be sold. These are some of the "moral" ethics of the Jews.

Firstborn sons are always given a double share of inheritance even if they are not born from a favorite wife. These Semitic goat thieves, mimicking their billy goats, had many wives. And to prevent fighting among heirs, the rights of whichever son was born first, are here established. Rebellious sons who do not obey their father or mother, are stoned to death by the entire community. This communal execution also enforces the terrorism of the priesthood and the cohesion of the community, a community of superstitious cowards quailing before the priests and murdering any of their number whom the priest accuses of a "sin" or of "insulting a priest," which by the Laws of Moses is equal to insulting God. Those were the Hebrews of ancient times and these are the Jews of today.

When a Hebrew has been judged guilty of a capital offense and is hung on a tree, "one who has been hanged is accursed of God." (Dt 21:23.) This passage helps explain why the Jews so much wanted to hang Jesus up on the cross so that they could claim that His teachings and Himself were cursed by God. Thus, these demons slandered Jesus even in his method of execution.

The deluded and Jew-seduced Christians today think that Deuteronomy 22 speaks of "brotherly love." But the wicked Jewish rabbis had a very different idea about the meaning of Deuteronomy 22:1-4. Therein, it speaks of lost items such as lost sheep, donkeys, cloaks or anything else that is lost and found by a Hebrew who knows to whom these things belong. The Contract of Moses says to return lost items "to your brother." But the evil rabbis ask, "Who is your brother?" And they answer their own question: "Since the Torah was given to the Jews, its laws apply only to the Jews. So, your brother is a fellow Jew and no one else." The rabbis teach even today as a part of their "Tradition of the Elders" (which was later written down as the *Babylonian Talmud*) that lost items belonging to a Gentile may be kept but lost items belonging to a Jew must be returned. The so-called "brotherly love" that Jews should practice toward each other as the "holy chosen ones of the Yahweh-god" is not to be extended to non-Jews but, instead, only curses. The *Talmud* also advises to conceal their hatred for the Gentiles so that the Gentiles will love and take pity on the very Jews who hate them. So many deluded and deceived Christians today love the grinning and perfidious Jews who practice every subterranean and backstabbing tactic they can to destroy Christians while smiling and speaking in a mild voice to conceal the demonic hatred that they hide in their hearts. Such evil and hypocritical teachings were condemned by Jesus who opposed the demonic Oral Law, the "Tradition of the Elders."

A young wife's reputation is to be protected by Deuteronomy 22 and the rabbis are encouraged to stick their noses into the menstrual rags of the Hebrew women. "If a man marries a wife, and sleeps with her ... and publicly defames her by saying, '... When I slept with her, I did not find evidence of her virginity.'" That is, these filthy goat rustlers demanded to have blood on the sheets on their wedding night.

These Jewish priests (as well as modern rabbis) make it their business to inspect the vulvas of Hebrew women to make sure that they are "clean." No other religion on earth mixes ideas of God with the subjects of menstruation and seminal ejaculation as do the circumcised sex-fiends known as Jews. Their circumcised dongs have given them a special fascination in sexual subjects to the manic point of producing a religion totally orbiting around the circumcised cocks of the kikes. And it is a tradition among the Jews for the woman's relatives to wait outside the door of the bridal chamber on the wedding night. After the couple have completed their coitus, the relatives of the woman take the bloody sheets and parade them around the community to show that the Jewess had been a virgin. Ah, the tender romance of the Jews!

In the case of Deuteronomy 22, if it is proven that the man had defamed his wife and she is indeed a virgin, then the priests of the goat rustlers must flog him and fine him one hundred shekels of silver and give the money to the girl's father.

But here's an even cruder part of Deuteronomy 22. If there is no blood on the sheets, the girl is to be stoned to death by the bloodthirsty citizens of the town! Once again, group retaliation is emphasized in Judaism so as to condition those goat humpers into the terrorism of the Babylonian Banker's Cult. Group retaliation is a basic technique of the cowardly Jews who, in modern times, claim to be outraged and offended by all sorts of impositions to their "delicate nature." It is all an example of street theater and bullying to get what they want by brow-beating non-Jews who don't understand that Judaism is nothing but blustering farce and Jewish fraud.

Note should be taken in Deuteronomy 22 that even though the Torah was written by the ruthless and avaricious moneylenders and slave drivers of Babylon who had a monopoly over the sex trade throughout Babylonia, that they were attempting to establish themselves in the public eye as "blessed" and "holy." While they swindled, enslaved and murdered those who were not members of their merchant-moneylender guild, they insisted that to be "holy," their women had to be virtuous. Therefore, the husband was flogged and fined for "publicly defaming a virgin of Israel." (Dt 22:19.)

A Jewish woman is defined by the rabbis' Book of Niddah as being "virtuous" if she wipes her pussy every time she has sex to check for "unclean" blood or whether the blood that she finds is that of squashed lice. She must then take these used "testing rags" to the rabbi to sniff and make a ruling as to whether she should take a bath or not. And she is considered to be beautiful by Jewish standards if she shaves her arm pits and vulva. Other than that, she can have a face like a pig and yet be beautiful to a rabbi because she is Jewish.

The sexual perversions of Judaism are again emphasized in Deuteronomy 23. "A man whose testicles have been crushed or whose male member has been cut off is not to be admitted to the assembly of Yahweh." (Dt 23:2.) In other words, only those who can perform sexual acts with their holy circumcised penises, can be "holy and pious" Jews – those and only those. All of Judaism revolves around the Jewish penis. Doesn't this prove, by the Laws of Moses, that all Jews are pricks?

The malicious and vindictive nature of the moneylenders is reflected in every way by their Yahweh-god. "No Ammonite or Moabite is to be admitted to the assembly of Yahweh, not even their descendants to the tenth generation … because they did not come to meet you with bread and water when you were on your way out of Egypt." (Dt 23:4-5.) As if these scruffy invaders and bandits deserved such a welcome! Again, the Hebrew *asl* is being invoked in that the long-dead Hebrews are claimed to be identical to every living Hebrew. The events of the fictitious past experienced by fictitious Hebrew bandits, are claimed to be no different than the events of the present being read about by the present-day Jews. The modern Jews are under the same delusion when they say, "*We* were slaves in Egypt." It is a Jewish delusion that persists because the Jews *as a cultural group*, are, pathologically and culturally, liars. Telling lies about God is a Semitic trait. But even more than this, Deuteronomy is a hoax and a forgery. Archaeology proves this. There were no Ammonites or Moabites during the alleged time of Moses. There was only empty land.

Furthermore, this allegedly "holy book" of the filthy goat rustlers of Israel not only concerns itself with the bloody wedding night sheets of virgins and the sucking of baby penises by the *mohel* rabbis, but also the nocturnal emissions of the men. Bloody sex and ejaculations of body fluids are part of these "holy" books of the Jews! Latrines are also required to be outside of camp and the Hebrews must stop leaving their excrement at the door of their tents because "Yahweh your God goes about within your camp to guard you" (Dt 23:15) and Yahweh might step in it. So, these filthy Hebrews must be ordered to dig a hole and bury their crap outside of camp. This is part of the "holiness" of today's Jews; their sexual organs are to be kept in top circumcised condition so they can multiply like rats and have sex at every opportunity. And they are required to think about their excrement when reading the *Hebrew Bible*! Such holy Jews! All, each and every one, are conspiring demons! And to increase their numbers and their wealth, the traditional slavery laws of Mesopotamia were nullified. Escaped slaves can now be kept by the Hebrews and not returned. Finders keepers!

While the dreamy-eyed Christians continue to view the Old Testament as a "moral" teaching, it is not moral at all! It is merely a one-way Contract between the Bankers of Babylon and the Hebrew bandits. The Christians believe that Dt 23:18-19 indicates that the rapacious Hebrews were a moral people in that "There must be no sacred prostitute among the daughters of Israel, and no sacred prostitute among the sons of Israel. You must not bring to the house of Yahweh your God the wages of a prostitute...." But what the Christians believe and what the demon rabbis teach are two entirely different things. To a rabbi, this phrase means that although Jewish women must not be prostitutes, *it is allowed for non-Jewish women to be prostitutes*. This is why Jews today are among the leading pimps and whorehouse operators in the world! But none of their whores are Jewesses because the Jews are holy! They only pimp and prostitute non-Jewish women!

Modern day Israel is the international hub of the prostitution trade. Prostitutes, mainly young girls from Russian and the Ukraine, are kidnapped by the Jews and enslaved in Israeli whorehouses, all with the blessing of the rabbis. Prostitution is not illegal in Israel and the Jewish pimps don't have to worry about police raids simply because none of the prostitutes are Jewesses. Prostitution is one of the "traditional" businesses for Jews because it has always been a sideline from the Sumerian Swindle, the lending of money at interest, and the alcohol trade. As an added bonus for the Jewish pimps, the profits made in their whore houses are not taxable by the Temple tithe. So, the Jews keep their filthy wives at home who constantly check the blood in their pussies so that they can be considered by the demon rabbis as "clean." But they keep Gentile whores enslaved in the Jewish-owned whorehouses, the profits of which don't have to be shared with the rabbis. Under Judaism, all of these Jewish pimps are considered by the rabbis to be "pious" Jews because they follow the Laws of Moses which allows such debauchery. Abraham set the example for all Jews by pimping his wife Sarah to Pharaoh. Prostitution has always been a traditional business among the Jews. It's basic to their demon religion of materialistic pleasures and wealth.

> "You must not lend on interest to your brother, whether the loan
> be of money or food or anything else that may earn interest.
> You may demand interest on a loan of a foreigner, but you must
> not demand interest from your brother...." (Dt 23:20-21.)

The Sumerian Swindle of lending money at interest, is forbidden to be used by the Jews against each other but it is allowed to be used against the Gentiles. With such "laws" as these, the moneylenders were setting up a Temple treasury where their circumcised members could obtain interest-free loans and then loan out that money at interest to the Gentiles. This made all Jews into moneylenders who had access to unlimited funds to lend out at interest. Are you beginning to see how the Jews have been able to put the world into debt since all Jews are members of the same international banking and swindling system? Using the Sumerian Swindle, anyone who lends money at interest eventually owns the entire world. The problem with such people is that they think that they deserve it. But do swindlers deserve to keep their loot or should they be imprisoned and their thefts returned to their victims? Unless you are a Jew, you know the answer to that.

Deuteronomy 24 covers a variety of miscellaneous laws including pawn brokering, that is, making loans while taking some item on pledge. Hired servants are to be paid a wage daily before sunset.

> "Fathers may not be put to death for their sons, nor sons for
> their fathers. Each is to be put to death for his own sin."
> (Dt 24:16.)

This was to keep the Jewish bandits, in their vengeful malice, from killing entire Jewish families in reprisals. But remember, under Judaism, these laws only apply to themselves. Murdering four generations – complete genocide – is the standard method of the Jews when murdering non-Jews.

Moneylenders always create poverty. The Sabbath laws created a need for Gentile workers or *shabbos goyim*, non-Jews who would work for the Jews on Sabbaths so that the Jews could sit on their asses to party and avoid military duty. Among the society of goat rustlers there was always among them numerous Gentile strangers and widows and orphans. These half-starved members of the lowest levels of goat rustler society had to eat. So, they were allowed to scavenge in the fields and orchards after the harvest. The rules of Deuteronomy 24 admonish the Jews to only harvest once and not glean the fields and orchards so clean that there was nothing left for the starving strangers, widows and orphans. This was not out of pity, but out of self-interested cunning – keeping the lowest people alive so that they could hire them cheaply.

Deuteronomy 25 further solidifies prosecution of the law into the hands of the priests and the Levite judges, although it limits flogging to a maximum of forty strokes.

Even though the Mosaic Law prohibited incest between a father and daughters, it applauded it between Lot and his daughters to perpetuate Lot's descendants. Even though the Mosaic Law prohibited incest between cousins, it applauded it as a means of perpetuating family control of money and property. And again, in Deuteronomy 25, incest is again applauded as a way of keeping money and property within the family. In this case, a widow who has no son is taken as a wife by her brother-in-law. All of Judaism revolves around the Jewish circumcised penis, an increase in Jewish population and the preservation of inheritance through incest. Such nasty people, hypocritically pretending to be the "holy chosen ones" of their own lies! And the Muslims are no better, and in many ways, worse!

The origin of the nasty and obscene nature of the Jews is easily seen in their penis fetish with its endemic masturbation; their bloody-vagina obsessions; and in these incestuous unions. If the brother refuses to take his dead brother's wife, then she is supposed to complain about it to the judges and rabbis, go up to him in their presence, remove a sandal from his foot and spit in his face and say, "This is what we do to the man who does not restore his brother's house." (Dt 25:9.) Jewish women are nothing if not disgusting. The Semitic hypersexual, reproductive mania is shared by both Muslims and Jews. When they weren't screwing their sheep, they were abusing themselves and raping women and little boys. All Semitic culture is obscene, but these devils lie and call it "holy." As filthy desert bandits, they could only work their way into civilization by telling lies and claiming that God approved of them more than He approved of anybody else.

The penis-based religion of Judaism gives prime importance to their circumcised cocks. In the case of two Hebrews fighting,

> "If the wife of one intervenes to protect her husband from the
> other's blows by putting out her hand and squeezing the other
> by the private parts, you shall cut her hand off and show no
> pity." (Dt 25:11-12.)

A lowly woman should never touch a holy Jewish penis, since to a Jew that is like touching God, Himself, which is an abomination! Showing no pity is another Jewish attribute stressed repeatedly in the Old Testament. They whine and cry, "Oy! Have pity on us poor Jews." But that is only hiding the pitiless nature of their cruel and vicious hearts.

Deuteronomy 25 ends with the admonition to commit complete genocide upon the people of Amalek. Even when the Hebrews are at peace, they are not to forget "to blot out the memory of Amalek from under heaven. Do not forget" (Dt 25:19). To refresh the reader's memory, the tribe of Amalek was allegedly descended from Esau and were thus related to the Hebrews. They inhabited the region in the Negeb desert in Southern Canaan and northern Arabia. The never-ending hatred of the Hebrews for the Amalekites over the centuries, eventually led to their complete extermination. The Amalekites were finally annihilated during the reign of Hezakiah (~727-698 BC). Since the Book of Deuteronomy was forged and then "discovered" during repairs to the temple walls in 622 BC, then this is one of the methods that the Jewish priests used to give authenticity to their forgery. The Amalekites had been exterminated by the Jews just seventy years previously thus giving the impression that the "ancient book" of Deuteronomy was foretelling an event that had already happened.

Exterminating other people through generations-spanning malicious hatred and assault, is a Jewish trait well attested to and applauded in their own writings. In the teaching of the rabbis after the establishment of Christianity, beginning in the 1st century AD, *the rabbis taught that Amalek is synonymous with Christianity*. Thus, the teachings of the Jews in modern times, is that the Jews will not be able to achieve world domination until Christianity is destroyed. And they take every opportunity and use every deceit and assault to accomplish this. Claiming to be "offended" by Christian symbols, suing churches for placing manger scenes on private property during Christmas, protesting the display of Christmas trees on state property, the banning even of the word "Christ" and replacing it with an "X" to celebrate "Xmas," and the list goes on and on. The same modern Jews, who falsely claim that "We were slaves in Egypt," also claim that the ancient Amalekites are no different than modern day Christians whom the Yahweh-god has commanded the Jews to destroy. So, O Christians, if you protect the Jews, you are hugging a viper to your breast!

The Hebrew *asl* (pronounced "ass-hole") is again invoked in Deuteronomy 26. The continuous repetition of the lie that the ancient Hebrews are the same as the modern Jews, is again repeated. Every time a Hebrew was to take the first fruits of the harvest to the altar of Yahweh, he was to repeat the lie that the "Captivity" and the "Exodus" *happened to him, personally*, and that the Yahweh-god gave the land of Canaan *to him, personally*. The ancient Jewish *asl* is very big and it encompasses every Jew, at least in their own minds.

Deuteronomy 26 concludes as a summation of the Contract. That is, as long as the Hebrews follow all of the "laws and customs" of Moses, then the Yahweh-god "will be your God, but only if you follow his ways, keep his statutes, his commandments, his ordinances, and listen to his voice." (Dt 26:17.) *Following his ways*? What does "following the ways" of the Yahweh-god mean?

One would have to list all of the attributes of the Yahweh-god, as the rabbis have done, dissecting them from the Five Books of Moses (that five-fifths of the Law) in order to know what are the "ways" of this god. Jealous, vindictive, wrathful, angry, greedy for wealth, inflicting evil on the world, punishing those who hate him through four generations, an exterminator of peoples, leader of armies and practitioner of genocide, whose angry consuming fire could blaze out and wipe you from the face of the earth for the smallest offense – these are what the Torah claims their god to be, a real devil.

As the Bankers of Babylon wrote in Genesis, their god made man in his own image. But in actual fact, *the Bankers of Babylon* who wrote these books, *made their god in their own image*. The moneylenders created a god very much after their own heart and desires for wealth. And so, the moneylenders of Babylon demanded that their followers be just like themselves, vengeful, cruel, pitiless, malicious, vindictive and as greedy for gold as their god. That is, the Jews are commanded to be devils. In return for walking in his ways, their god of the treasury guarantees them the same worldly wealth and material power as any banker or financier. All they have to do is follow the program and adhere to the Contract.

This false idea that Moses and the priests can speak with the voice of God or that every Jew can speak for all Jews, or that the modern Jews of today actually can claim that "we were slaves in Egypt and we crossed the Red Sea with Moses," is all connected to the Jewish *asl* (pronounced "ass hole"). These illiterate goat rustlers had the fallacious idea that they could "inherit" the deeds and myths of ancient ancestors and claim them as their own, personal experience and "inheritance." Even a lying, modern Jew claims that "God gave Palestine to *me*."

Deuteronomy 27 ends with a list of twelve curses which are the taboos for the twelve tribes of bandits. These taboos are a reflection of the negative characteristics of these circumcised Jewish bandits and kidnappers. These twelve curses fall into civil categories restricting the goat rustlers that are bounded by the basic tenants of the Yahweh religion. The list of twelve laws begins and ends with a religious law which sandwiches the other ten laws between them. First, a curse is cast upon anyone who does not follow the Laws of Moses. In between, are the laws that prohibit those mangy, stinking goat-seducers from practicing their filthy habits. They are no longer allowed to dishonor their father and mother. They are no longer allowed to give false directions to a blind man. They are no longer allowed to move boundary markers. They must respect the strangers, the traveling guild representative among them, and the orphans and the widows whom they had been robbing. Two of the curses prohibit the goat rustlers from murder or murder for hire. And for these circumcised sex-fiends, rapists and child molesters, four of the twelve laws are for sex crimes. The Hebrews are no longer allowed to have sex with their mother or stepmother. They are no longer allowed to have sex with their sister or half-sister. They are no longer allowed to have sex with their mother-in-law. And they are no longer allowed to have sex with their sheep or their goats or their dogs or any other animal as was their custom.

Thus, fully one-third of these laws forbid sex crimes and one-sixth prohibit murders. Truly, these Hebrews were a very rotten bunch. These laws and what they emphasize show very clearly what kind of perverted scoundrels the Hebrews actually were. That modern Jews claim to be identical to them, proves that their God-Of-All-Things-Terrible, couldn't have chosen a worse gang of creatures to be "his people" and "made in his own image" and to "walk in his ways."

The Contract claims that the Hebrews will be blessed in all things. "Yahweh will make you a people consecrated to himself as he has sworn to you, if you keep the commandments of Yahweh your God and follow his ways." (Dt 28:9.) These "ways" include being vicious, cruel and murderous toward the people of the world, just like their Yahweh-god. The moneylenders' scribes wrote that

> "You will make many nations your subjects, yet you will be subject to none. Yahweh will put you at the head, not at the tail; you will always be on top and never underneath, if you obey the commandments of Yahweh your God that I enjoin on you today, keeping and observing them, not swerving to right or left from any of the works I enjoin on you today by following any other gods and serving them." (Dt 28:12-14.)

Backed by the Sumerian Swindle to fill their treasury and their avaricious lust for riches, only the Bankers of Babylon could make such promises. Jews do not have a mighty god who protects them, what they have to give them sustenance is a secret banking system concealed behind the deception of a synthetically contrived religious fraud, all supported by the Sumerian Swindle and the lies of the *Hebrew Bible*. And with such "promises," the Jews actively try to make it all come true by pushing their way into leadership positions over better qualified candidates. Not for any altruistic reasons or for public service, but so as to control "the gates of their enemies," the Jews seek positions as chairmen of political parties and corporations. From high office all the way down to the local bridge club, Jews eagerly step in and take over management but not for any other reason than to betray and destroy and to put themselves into a position to control the *goyim* (lowly insects, stupid cattle).

The variety of curses that the moneylenders cast for not following the Laws of the Contract cover about every terrible thing anyone can imagine. This was a standard method that was used throughout the ancient Near East for the pharaohs and kings to end their proclamations by calling down the power of the gods to enforce the pharaoh's and king's proclamations even after his death. Included in these curses is the "stranger" in such a way as to give an understanding of that word as it is used throughout the *Hebrew Bible*. Using the stranger as a curse,

> "The stranger living among you will rise higher and higher at your expense, and you yourselves sink lower and lower. He will make you his chattel, you will not make him yours; he it is who will lie at the head, and you at the tail." (Dt 28:43-44.)

So, the "stranger" who is mentioned throughout all of the books of the Jews, is always understood to be the chattel of the Hebrews. He is to be protected as one would protect a hired servant because he was kept around as *shabbos goyim* ("Sabbath Dirt") to serve the Jews during their "day of rest." And those "strangers" who were merchants from Babylonia, he it was who brought them wealth and made deposits in the treasury.

Every disease, plague, suffering, bad luck and war is cursed upon the Hebrews if they do not follow the Contract of Moses. The Contract is a one-way Contract. The Hebrews are promised all good things, the land and wealth of other people who produced it so that the Hebrews could steal it without working for it, as well as all sorts of material advantages – if they follow the Contract. If they do not follow every rule and tradition of the Contract, all evils are cursed upon them. With such a variety of mythical lies, fraudulent documents, the witchcraft of curses, and the promotion of all criminality as the basis of their so-called "religion," is it any wonder that the modern Jews are so insufferably malicious and larcenous?

Once again using the Hebrew *asl*, the High Priest of boy-king Josiah and his Jewish scribes wrote to the Hebrews that

> "You have seen all that Yahweh did before your eyes in the land
> of Egypt, to Pharaoh, to his servants and to his whole land, the
> great ordeals your own eyes witnessed, the signs and those great
> wonders." (Dt 29:2.)

Yet, not a single one of them was there or had seen any of those fairy tales simply because the alleged witnesses had long been dead and the alleged events had never happened. All of Judaism is a lying fraud. It was this lying, genealogical *asl* of the Contract that made the false claims so mesmerizing .

Deuteronomy 29 recapitulates the Hebrew myth about being slaves in Egypt, wandering for forty years in the desert and finally reaching the borders of Canaan, a "land of milk and honey." The so-called "Covenant" (Contract) is again held as paramount as an alleged "promise" made to those who kept the Covenant. Again, the only definition of "sin" that existed was defined by the rabbis as "breaking a law of the Contract and thereby insulting Yahweh."

To a Jew, breaking the Laws of Moses is the only sin while everything not covered in that law is allowed. This is why Jews are among the foremost criminals in the world today since they do not recognize any laws of any people or of any country binding upon them. Through their financial swindles, they destroy the lives of millions of people but since the laws of Moses do not forbid them from stealing from non-Jews, they take every opportunity to do so. For example, a modern-day George Soros can steal billions of dollars from entire sovereign nations, impoverishing and dispossessing millions of people, while the Jews of the world applaud his clever scheming while bribing the politicians to not hang him. Through Communism, the Jews have murdered a hundred million non-Jews. But since the demonic laws of Moses demand that they exterminate the people of the world, the Jews roll their eyes to heaven, assume a demonic "piety," and put the blame for their atrocities upon their victims.

Nothing was more important to the Bankers of Babylon than protecting their treasury. So, once again, the importance is stressed that the Hebrews guard the treasury and not wander off to other religions. To protect such a treasury, the land upon which the treasury stood had to be made inviolate and sacrosanct. It could not be a gift of a king but had to be a gift of a god. The Hebrews were not allowed to own the land since it belonged to the god of the Temple Treasury, thus, they could not sell it to "strangers." But the big Jews could own the walled city in which the treasury was located and where they were safe from attack while the little Jews had to fight to defend the land by the terms of the Contract.

The role of the "stranger" is again defined in Deuteronomy 29 as one who "cuts wood or draws water" for the Jews (Dt 29:11). He is the *Shabbos Goy*, a non-Jew servant of the Jews, hired to work while the Jews eat and drink and celebrate their freedom from military service.

Deuteronomy 30 opens with the promise that the Hebrews will get even more material goods, "prospering there and increasing even more than your fathers" (Dt 30:5) if and only if those thieves follow and adhere to the terms of the Contract. This god of the moneylenders promises that he will make them love their god as much as they love their circumcised penises.

The malicious moneylenders teach the Hebrews in Dt 30:7 how to use their malice to reflect curses back upon their enemies. Modern Jews often use the phrase, "Back at you!" when they want to avoid an epithet. It is a Jewish mark of malice when they try to inflict upon their enemies the same harm *and more* than what their enemies want to inflict upon them. This sorcery is found the Contract.

> "Yahweh your God will make all these curses recoil on your
> foes and on your enemies who have persecuted you." (Dt 30:7.)

Ask yourself, does this god of the moneylenders promise the Hebrews that if they follow the Contract that they will attain "Heaven" or have a better spiritual life? No, this god of the merchant-moneylenders promises that those thieving Hebrews will get more wealth and more children.

> "Yahweh your God will give you great prosperity in all your
> undertakings, in the fruit of your body, the fruit of your cattle
> and in the produce of the soil." (Dt 30:9.)

If they follow the Contract that is designed to establish a priesthood of treasury guards, then in return they don't get Heaven but they get money, children and cattle. Judaism – like its demented son, Islam – is a materialistic religion. There is nothing but lust, greed, lies, murder, and all manner of evil within it. And on the outside of it is nothing but hypocrisy.

The whole point of Deuteronomy 31 is to claim to king Josiah that *Yahweh* knew in advance that the Hebrews would follow other gods. Even so, Moses writes in his continual delusions that these goat rustlers are "defiant" and "stubborn," which is a compliment for a mangy goat rustler! Once again, the Contract is all that matters. Every seven years, the priests are to read all five books of Moses to the Hebrews.

Deuteronomy 32 is called The Song of Moses. It praises Yahweh, the vicious and malicious god of armies and vengeance and calls him "just" and "faithful" to the Hebrews who are, themselves, described as "perverse," "deceitful" and "underhanded." But the vindictive nature of the moneylender's god is also described. The "cause of Right" means only a cause that satisfies the terms of the Contract as the Yahweh god says,

> "As surely as I live forever, when I have whetted my flashing sword, I will take up the cause of Right, I will give my foes as good again, I will repay those who hate me. I will make my arrows drunk with blood, and my sword shall feed on flesh: the blood of wounded and captives, the skulls of the enemy leaders." (Dt 32:41-42.) "For he will avenge the blood of his servants, he will give his foes as good again." (Dt 32:43.)

This same god of the modern Jews is the very one whose "ways" they follow, inflicting harm upon the people around them in every way that they can, all the while whining and crying about how innocent and pious they are, only wanting to go through life in innocent prayer to their Demon God of Money and Genocide.

Again, the importance of keeping the Contract is emphasized.

> "You must order your children to keep and observe all the words of this Law… for the Law is your life." (Dt 32: 46-47.)

God is not their life. Heaven is not their life. Holiness and goodness are not their life. Spiritual knowledge is not their life. But the Laws of Moses is their life. By following the banking system that the moneylenders set up, they will continue to prosper. The ten percent tithe that the Temple Treasury will pay to the priests, will keep the Hebrews prosperous as they work the Sumerian Swindle and genocide upon the people of the world.

And finally, this vindictive, lying Yahweh-god tells Moses that he was not perfect enough in following *Yahweh* so he must die without setting foot in the lands that the Hebrews were going to steal from the Canaanites. That was Moses' reward for following his god of vengeance and deceit!

Deuteronomy 33 has been a puzzle to most commentators and students of biblical studies. It was written with archaic language. That, itself, should have been a hint as to the importance of this chapter. As previously stated in Volume I, *The Sumerian Swindle*, the name for the Sinai Peninsula and Mount Sinai is a Babylonian name for the Babylonian Moon God, Sin. Thus, "Sinai" means the "Wilderness of Sin" or the "Wilderness of the Moon God."

As also previously indicated, the name of the pharaoh who chased the Hyksos out of Egypt was Ahmose or Yahmose, meaning "Born of Yah" or "Born of the Moon God." The Moon God has always held the highest place among the Semites of Arabia and the ancient Near East because the Moon God has been considered superior to the Sun God, simply because the moon can be seen in the sky both in the day and the night while the sun is limited only to day time appearances. The Moon god was considered to be the father of and the superior to the Sun God.

With these facts in mind, the opening lines of Deuteronomy 33 becomes clear. The Babylonian moneylender-scribes wrote:

> "Yahweh came from Sinai. For them, after Seir, he rose on the horizon, after Mount Paran he shone forth. For them he came, after the mustering at Kadesh, from his zenith as far as the foothills." (Dt 33:2.)

Yahweh was the Moon God of the Semites who "came from Sinai," the wilderness of Sin. *Sin* was the Babylonian Moon God, rising above the deserts, the moon was the same god that the Arabs called "Al Lah."

In addition to identifying who Yahweh really is, this Deuteronomy 33 gives some of the attributes of the various Hebrew tribes. Of particular interest is the tribe of Levi. These sorcerers were the family tribe of priests to which Moses and Aaron belonged. They were hereditary priests and the busybody religious enforcers over all the Hebrew tribes. It was they who collected the taxes, going around to each shepherd's flock and counting the livestock. It was the Levites who snooped around every farmer's field and threshing floor, keeping count of his baskets of grain and fruit and the jars of oil and wine that he produced each season. It was the Levites who collected the taxes and the offerings and who sat in judgment of the other Hebrews. Here, they are also the sorcerers who manipulated the holy dice cup for prognosticating the future and the will of the Yahweh-god on the Urim and Thummim, the sacred dice table.

These Levi priests are given the orders of how they are to attack the non-Jews of the world. The Levites are to

> "Crush the loins of his enemies and of his foes until they rise no more." (Dt 33:11.)

That is, they are to destroy the reproductive organs (the loins) of the Gentiles. This tactic has been used by the Jews in modern times. By practicing abortion upon the Gentiles, promoting contraceptives and birth control, enabling divorce, promoting sexual activity outside of marriage in order to destroy families, promoting homosexual perversion, debauching and subverting the youths of the Gentiles and by promoting warfare in which they did not have to fight, the Jews have managed to reduce the white populations of the world, while increasing their own.

By sneakily and cravenly attacking the babies and the children, the Jews have been able to prevent the raising of multiple generations of White people. Thus, modern Jews who claim that "We are the same ones who stood at Sinai" and that "We were slaves in Egypt," also enthusiastically accept the role of committing genocide upon the White people of Europe, American, Australia, Russia and South Africa – all places where the *goyim* (non-Jewish, lowly insects and stupid cattle) reside. Especially are the Christians targeted for destruction by the Jews because the scheming rabbis identify them as Amalekites, the most hated of Yahweh. This is the meaning of Deuteronomy 33:11.

Of the tribe of Joseph, it is written that,

"His horns are the wild ox's horns, with them he tosses the *goyim* to the very ends of the earth." (Dt 33:17.)

And the tribe of Asher has as its battle cry, "Destroy!" (Dt 33:27.) And that is what the Jews are today, destroyers. Quick to deny their guilt, quick to proclaim their innocence, quick to blame their evil deeds on an innocent scapegoat, sneaky and secretive as serpents, the Jews are like their evil god has made them to be – destroyers and betrayers of Mankind. And it is all written down in their "Training Manual for Jewish Criminality and Psychopathy," the *Hebrew Bible*.

Deuteronomy ends at Chapter 34 with the death of Moses. The Yahweh-god didn't want him to even put one foot into the land of Israel, but Moses was allowed to see it. So, Moses climbed to the top of Mount Nebo to get a good view of the so-called "Promised Land." In this way, the merchant-moneylender scribes of Babylon added such a detail as an honor to their own god, *Nebu*, who had guided them in writing the Greatest Lie Ever Told. Moses, the chief actor in their mythology, met his end standing at the top of a mountain named after *Nebu*, the Babylonian and the Assyrian god of scribes and accountants. Moses was the scribes' most famous fictional character, a hero of Jews, standing at the pinnacle of the Babylonian scribal art.

Conveniently, the Contract for Abraham's First National Bank and Pawn Shop ends with the statement "but to this day no one has ever found his grave." (Dt 34:6.) This was a confident statement that the scribes of Babylon could make since there was no grave to find. Moses was nothing more than a literary invention for deceiving the ignorant Hebrew goat-thieves into joining forces with the Bankers of Babylon. He was the bankers' literary tool for counterfeiting their own family tree into the genealogical root of the Semitic families and tribal trees *of the entire ancient Near East*. With such a genealogical swindle, the Monsters of Babylon could claim the holiest priestly title and attain complete family control over the holy gold within the holy treasury in a holy temple located on some holy real estate that had been allegedly given them by a holy god – and therefore the entire swindle was located in a "holy land."

And so, with all of the eyewitnesses disposed of in the desert, and the mythological Moses whom "Yahweh knew face to face" (Dt 34:10) dying and

being buried where no one could ever find him, on the mountain of the Babylonian god Nebu – the god of scribes and accountants – Deuteronomy ends. It
ends leaving the Contract firmly in the grasping claws of the Monsters of Babylon who pretended to be "holy" and "righteous" to deceive the world while
they used the wealth generated from the Sumerian Swindle, hidden in a secret
vault, in a defensible location, to betray all of Mankind.

* * * * *

There you have it, folks, explained for the first time in 2500 years, the complete *Contract of the Circumcised Frauds of Babylon*, known as the *Torah* of
the Jews. It doesn't really matter what the biblical scholars have to say about
the various traditions such as the Yahwistic or Priestly or Elohistic, etc. Although
their theories are interesting, tracing various historical threads as they do. The
only thing that really matters is the *Contract*, itself, and what it said in 539 BC
when the final version was published in Babylon and *what it still says today*.

In total warfare against all of Mankind, the rabbis demanded that either
all of Mankind become slaves of the Jews or that Mankind should be exterminated. The demon rabbis, in all of their hatred, lust, greed and malice, had de-
ceptively taken the "moral high ground" (if it can be called such) and decreed
– Abracadabra! – that Jews and *only* Jews are virtuous and good, while all
other people in the world are evil and debased. A rather hilarious position to
assume for such fiendish clowns as the Jews. But it was difficult to argue with
the Jews on this matter since to disagree with the Jews assured that you would
be beaten and killed by these selfsame "holy icons of virtue." While sodomizing little boys, raping little girls, performing incest with their mothers, impoverishing everyone who fell into their Sumerian Swindle, enslaving Mankind to
debt and warfare, and similar Jewish "virtues," they had declared themselves
to be the Chosen Ones of God. It was truly a miracle! By killing their detrac-
tors, who would dare to argue with their claims? Judaism is the Devil's Truth!

However, against all of this ancient fraud, forgery, deceit, murder and
lies of the rabbis and priests of the demon cult of Yahweh, there was one who
stood up against them. His name was Jesus. Jesus was the devil rabbis' worst
nightmare because Jesus told the truth about the Jews.

CHAPTER 7

THE ISRAELIANS WERE NOT FOOLED
BY JEWISH ABRACADABRA

Whether you jumped here from the beginning of Chapter 6 or arrived here after reading Chapter 6, you know that the Jews are the biggest liars to have ever walked the earth. We know this because modern archaeology has proven it. But there were earlier people who absolutely knew that the Jews were lying frauds. What about them?

Often, those who read the *Torah* (the *Pentateuch*) wonder, "With such miracles and blessings experienced by them, how could the tribes of Hebrews (the "Children of Israel") not adhere to the Promise of God and keep all the Laws of Moses? How could they have so little faith when such miracles were performed in front of their very eyes?" But these questions are asked by people who actually believe the incredible lies of the Jews.

These questions might have had some validity before modern archaeology proved the Old Testament to be a fraud. The fact is, the Hebrew tribes were already resident in Canaan when Abraham and his family of loan sharks and con artists descended upon them from Babylonia. The Jews had never wandered in the wilderness and their forefathers had never seen any of the miraculous events that Moses and his swindlers claimed that they did. Quite simply, the Canaanites and Hebrews were not as stupid as most modern people are. They didn't believe Abraham, Isaac or Jacob, and they didn't have to be scientists to see through the Jewish fraud.

An old Japanese Zen saying is, "When two thieves meet at the crossroads, they need no introduction." And so it was when Abraham and his gang of Binu-Yamina (Benjamin) goons first entered Canaan. What thieving Hebrew or wary Canaanite would trust such obvious crooks as Abraham and his tribe of peddlers from Babylonia, who went about trading copper pots and pans and bronze swords for Egyptian trinkets? The Hebrew tribes and the Canaanite tribes were experienced goat rustlers and donkey traders themselves. They knew how to bargain and take every advantage that they could of a fool, selling a sick goat as a healthy specimen, using false weights and exchanging the measuring scoops at the markets. They knew all the tricks of turning a profit and taking advantage of suckers. They were Semites who already worshiped *Yahweh* as well as his wife *Asherah* (*Ishtar*) and their son *Baal* in their Canaanite temples.

So, they were not deceived when the priests of Abraham's First National Bank and Pawn Shop said, "Our god has chosen you to be extra holy and special. And to prove that you are worthy of our god's blessing, you must to pay us priests ten percent of your yearly wealth and give us daily goat-barbecues and festival feasts, then you can also be special like us. Oh, yes, and we also want to cut off the end of your penis." Do you think that the Canaanites would fall for a scam like that? Hebrews understood Hebrews and weren't about to be taken in by such an obvious con job. They had their own priests and temples. They didn't need another one way up in the hills of Judah.

But, the tribes of Hebrews and Canaanites did not understand that the two tribes of Judah and Benjamin had a secret source of financing. Silver and gold flowed into the Temple in unseen ways. So, even though the territory of Judah was relatively poor, its temple and its gang of goons and priests always had plenty of trade goods to trade with the Hebrews and Canaanites for their gold and silver Egyptian ornaments. The only real job that the rabbis and priests seemed to have was proselytizing and gaining as many converts as possible, so as to keep the Temple as a self-sufficient entity.

As explained earlier, the term "Israelian" is used to describe the people who lived in the ancient northern kingdom. This avoids confusion with both that Jacob character named "Israel" from whom the Jews claim to be descended and the modern bandit-state of Israel. The Israelians were Canaanite Semites and Hebrew Semites who were quite aware of the *abracadabra* tricks and falsehoods of their fellow Semites of Judah. So, when the priests of Judah, led by the Babylonian moneylenders and their Binu-Yamina (Benjamin) gangsters, claimed that "Our god has chosen you to join us and to pay a tax to the temple for your sins," they were not deluded by the scam. What was Judah other than a goat pasture? What was Jerusalem other than a small town situated in a strongly defensible location? The Israelian Hebrews were allied with the powerful Assyrian Empire and were making a lot of profit from silver.

As for the fantastic stories written on the goatskin scrolls that the priests of Jerusalem were waving around, they had never heard any such tales, nor had their fathers or grandfathers ever mentioned them. Nobody in Canaan-Palestine had ever heard of Moses, David, King Solomon or any of the other mythical characters in the *Hebrew Bible*, which is odd, since Judah was just next door to the Israelian kingdoms. Having lived in Canaan from the very earliest times, if their forefathers had actually seen any of the great miracles that the priests of the Jerusalem temple claimed had happened, the Israelians would certainly have heard about it from their parents. They didn't need any rabbis dressed like blood-drenched pimps giving them their history. So, the Israelians looked upon the priests of Judah as just what they were, poor Judean con artists trying to con the richer society of the Israelians, then throwing curses at them if they didn't pay the ten percent tithe or donate any barbecued goats.

This is why the Israelians were not interested in bowing down to the Temple at Jerusalem. They could see through the Jewish fraud from the very beginning and were not interested in what the moneylenders of Jerusalem were trying to establish. The Israelians had better things to do than pay the priests ten percent of their livelihood for a blessing that they knew was bogus.

The Israelians outshone the Judeans in both wealth and splendor. As such, they rode horses instead of donkeys. Because of its better terrain and agricultural output as well as its position on the trade route between Egypt, the Mediterranean port cities and Mesopotamia, the Israelians had all of the advantages. So when King Omri (884-873 BC) laid the foundation of his capital of Samaria, he had plenty of silver and gold for his construction projects. Archaeology proves that, like everything else in the *Hebrew Bible*, lies and deceit are the very foundation stones of Judaism.

The Israelians developed fortified cities and elaborate palaces such as at Megiddo, Jezreel, and Samaria by the early ninth century while Jerusalem was fully urbanized only in the late eighth century. Israelians and Judeans spoke similar dialects of Hebrew and they both worshiped *Yahweh* (among other deities), but they were very different in terms of demographics, economics, and material culture. Judah was little more than the Israelians' rural hinterland. But Jerusalem was where the Temple of Abraham's First National Bank and Pawn Shop was located, so it made a higher claim in an attempt to swindle loyalty and tithes from the Hebrews of the northern kingdoms.

Even if you believe every word that the lying Jews wrote about themselves in their so-called "Five Books of Moses" (*Torah, Pentateuch*), you can see by the internal evidence provided by your own reading that no single person named Moses could have written those fantasies. *As important to them as genealogy was* – since the entire Jewish hoax rested upon it – *they certainly recorded their names within the book that they had authored.* Terah and his son Abraham had their original hometown in the ancient Sumerian city of Ur. Terah moved his offices to the Assyrian/Babylonian city of Harran and from there Abraham and his half-sister-wife, Sarah, immigrated to Canaan. Afterwards, their sons, grandsons, Isaac and Jacob returned to Harran to incestuously marry their Babylonian relatives. That was *four generations of Babylonians* who founded the fraud that today we call "Judaism." Incest enabled them to keep their wealth within the same Babylonian family of moneylenders.

Using the fake idea that their big Semitic *asl* (pronounced "ass-hole") allowed for a genetic "inheritance" of "blessings and promises," those Babylonian charlatans wrote themselves into the root of the Hebrew tribal genealogies in Canaan so as to claim patriarchal priority over the Hebrew bandits and goat rustlers. They did this not only to claim authority over the resident Hebrew tribes of Canaan, but also to fraudulently claim an ancient legal precedence. And what was that precedence? It was nothing less than *the ownership of the entire ancient Near East*, stretching from the Euphrates River to the Nile and from Syria to Arabia! Did they make that claim from military conquest or by actually spending their precious silver to buy all of that territory? Neither. The Jews made their claim of total ownership of the entire Near East based upon the stupefying assertion that *the greatest God in the universe had given it to them*. And what was their "proof" that such a gift had been made by such a god? Why, they had it in indelible ink, on an actual, guaranteed, 100% genuine, goatskin Contract, which they had written themselves and signed God's name to! And as even better proof that the Contract was not a fraud, you could take their word for it, because they were the Chosen Ones of God. And would the Chosen Ones of God lie? "Oy Gevalt! Of course not! Now please get off of our property." And as an even better proof of how holy they are, the Jews would all show you their circumcised penises. What more proof do you need?

Bible students and scholars ought to read a little more carefully before jumping to the false conclusion that what one *believes* the *Hebrew Bible* says is more important than what it *actually* says. The *Hebrew Bible* is a legal contract laying down the Laws of Moses. Like any other contract, it makes definite claims which it attempts to validate with certain assertions and it makes firm promises based upon performance of various stipulations. But, the *Hebrew Bible* is a fraudulent contract in that all promises are broken and all claims are bogus. Archaeology and internal evidence prove that the entire so-called "religion" of Judaism is based upon fraud and lies. Judaism is the Greatest Lie Ever Told by the world's oldest organized criminal conspiracy of charlatans, thieves, murderers and betrayers. And yes, the Jews are very serious in their efforts to keep you from understanding this and make you believe every word that they tell you. How can the Jews enjoy the prestige of being the Chosen Ones of God if everybody knows that they are frauds and liars?

As you know from reading Chapter 6, there is nothing true about the *Hebrew Bible*. It was written over many centuries, rewritten, edited, counterfeited and forged by many wicked Jewish priests of the Yahweh Cult. The entire Torah is a very elaborately constructed, fraudulent Contract and Training Manual, binding upon an entire group of bandits who were deceived into following its phony claims.

Boasting a fictitious authority, flaunting stolen wisdom, worshiping a demon god and claiming a priority to rule all of Mankind, the con artists who operate this fake Jewish religion have greatly benefited by operating its diabolical gears and pulling its demonic strings. We shall study those evil rabbis behind the fraud of Judaism more carefully. However, before putting those screaming me-me's under the microscope, let's take a step backward and look at the big picture.

There is a big problem with *time* when one studies ancient cultures. People tended to mark off the days and years based on how long ago a certain king reigned or when a big drought happened and so forth. That system worked great as long as everybody was alive and could remember the events. But, for modern people those kinds of dates don't have any meaning, because they are not anchored to any definite reference point. That definite point has to start now, in our own time, and go backward in yearly increments in order for any ancient date to have relevance to us. If we say that writing and culture began with the Sumerians around 3200 BC, they did not provide that date to us. We had to figure it out for ourselves using a variety of literary, historical, geological, chemical, archaeological, astronomical, and whatever other techniques we could use to deduce an accurate time reference, such as nuclear isotope decay, tree rings and Greenland ice cap layers.

Unlike our recent forefathers who had to depend on the *Hebrew Bible* to tell them about ancient history, we modern people have science to disillusion us from the lies of the Jews. If an archaeologist finds some charcoal so as to make a radiocarbon date going backwards from the present time, we can get a rough idea of when the fire burned which left the ashes and the charcoal. Counting tree rings and the yearly layers of ice in the ancient Greenland ice cap, as well as many other methods, gives us a pretty good way to count backward to a definite time period. If the ancient peoples saw a certain comet and wrote about it "in the fifth year of king so-and-so," modern astronomers can calculate the year in which that comet appeared and thereby date all of the events surrounding "king so-and-so" as well as every other king connected to his reign. All of these methods are useful. But, it is really helpful when the ancient people had a calendar, because then we can easily and accurately calculate the dates.

This is another problem with accepting the lies of the Jews at face value. During the entire time that the Hebrews wrote their fraudulent fantasies, they had a calendar. They had a calendar, but they didn't put any dates on the tales that they wrote. Why was this other than the fact that dates would make their fraudulent "histories" too easily proven as fictions? If the stories were always in the distant past, vague and mysterious and out-of-reach, then no one could trap a rabbi with facts when – Abracadabra! – his word was the only available "proof."

The so-called "Jewish calendar" is actually the Babylonian Calendar. Once again, *Sin*, the Moon God of Babylon, plays a prominent part, since the "day" begins at sunset and the months begin at the sighting of the new moon. The Jews still use the Babylonian calendar today. The only thing that makes it a "Jewish calendar" is that its date is based on their fantasies in the *Hebrew Bible*. By consulting the various generations and genealogies in the Old Testament, the rabbis used the Babylonian calendar to calculate the date of the creation of the world, which they figured took place in 3760 BC. According to the lying rabbis, it's mathematically and completely accurate to within just five days from when Adam and Eve were created. So, even the Jews' calendar is stolen from Babylonia and its dates are based on Jewish mythology.

The Babylonian calendar was maintained in the Near East and it became the official calendar of the Parthian Empire, the Persian Achaeminids, Nabataea and other kingdoms of the former Greek Seleucid empire. By the time the Romans arrived during the first century BC, all calendars in the Near East were modeled on the Babylonian lunar calendar. All monies were based on the ancient Sumerian/Babylonian shekel weight of silver and all international business was transacted in the Semitic language of Aramaic, the *lingua franca* of all businessmen and diplomats between Greece and India. In this way, one can see the pervading influence of the Semitic merchant-moneylenders who were intimate with the rulers of all nations as they scurried about, wheeling and dealing and moving goods from one country to another. And one can see the hints of future conflicts as the Greco-Roman civilization penetrated with its logic and common sense into the mythological scams and fairy tales of the ancient Near East.

However, in Egypt the calendar was solar and based on a 365-day year, and this calendar was maintained unchanged until the Roman period. *The Jews alone*, in the Roman Empire, maintained a lunar calendar. In Babylonia, the calendar remained unchanged until the Muslim conquest. Why did the Jews not put dates on their biblical stories, if they had a calendar? Because the stories are fictions and fantasies, not histories. The *Hebrew Bible* is not a history book. It is a business contract for establishing a bank inside of a temple with the god of the moneylenders guarding the gold.

The Babylonian-Jewish calendar is still used into modern times by the Jewish bankers. The reason mortgages are based on 15-year and 30-year repayment cycles is because that was the Babylonian method of counting with the 60-base counting system of ancient Sumeria: 15 and 30 divide into 60 evenly. But, regardless of which calendar the host peoples use in the various countries, the Jews have always been able to coordinate their activities worldwide by adhering to the same calendar system as all other Jews worldwide. *Because no one else uses the Jewish calendar*, it became a secret timetable for mass actions, coordination of international and national economic leverage and the wholesale destruction of Mankind through revolution and war, all coordinated with a calendar that only the international Jews use.

As to whether it was possible for Abraham's bank to control the money-lending and business of the ancient Near East, it must be understood that the Temple and its Treasury was a mere façade of a much greater conspiracy of merchant-moneylenders who had business interests throughout the known world. What they didn't have, but which Terah had invented for them, was a god to whom they could owe their allegiance without the kings, the priests of other gods, or commoners preaching peace, mercy toward debtors, forgiveness of debts and the releasing from slavery of debt slaves. With their very own god, the Jews were free to be as demonic as they could while pretending to be "holy." Their allegiance was no longer to the resident god of each city where they had business dealings. They were no longer under the supervision and social pressures of priests and kings whose interests were not in profits from loans, but in the welfare and prosperity of their people. There would be no interfering priests from other religions cautioning mercy and forgiveness, because the god of the moneylenders had already decided who would be getting free loans and who would have to pay with their very blood. The very foundations of Judaism extol the "virtues" of "walking in the ways" of their demon god to destroy all other people, while preaching "mercy" for themselves as the "holy, Chosen Ones" of the Devil. Their allegiance was to their own god and their only interest was themselves. And *unlike all other temples of all other gods*, the Jews alone used a once-per-week sit down strike called the "Sabbath" to avoid military duty.

Terah's system was an ingenious way for the merchant-moneylenders to gain the maximum profits with the fewest obligations to their debtors. It was a way to avoid serving in any king's army worldwide. With a congregation so fearful that their mighty god would annihilate them for any transgressions, the

Jews would be trustworthy among each other even though they were scheming thieves among other people. Thus, the total wealth of the bank could safely be hidden in the trustworthy hands of their fellow Jews worldwide without there being a central depository for the bullion. The bullion on deposit behind impregnable walls could still be a target for kings, but in this case, it would be just a small portion of the sum total spread out throughout the entire ancient Near East enmeshed in the wheels of Jewish business.

The Jerusalem Temple itself was the *apparent* center of this criminal and bogus religion of Judaism, but it was not the *actual* center of Judaism. Although the Temple made huge profits from tithes, sacrifices, poll taxes, fines, contributions, the deposit of bullion and various other banking transactions, it was only a religious façade for the scam. The real center of Judaism was not Jerusalem, it was Babylonia and points farther east where the big money was to be made. And where there is big money, you will find some people who will do anything, *anything* to get their hands on it. Where there is big money, you will always find big, scheming Jews.

It was not really necessary for Terah and his cunning relatives to capture all of Canaan, because the system that they had conceived was an international one that only needed a single location for a temple treasury upon which the entire international organization would agree as sacrosanct. He needed a single Temple to house his god of the merchants and moneylenders. Once Abraham had bribed Melchizedek, the priest-king of Urusalem, with one-tenth of his wealth in exchange for a blessing, Abraham's guild of moneylenders had bought the authority of the local god. All they needed in addition was for their Benjamite goons to secure the area around Jerusalem, which they easily accomplished because the land was sparsely populated. But, for the highly populated areas of Canaan which their small numbers could not conquer, they acquired what might be called a "lien" upon the whole of it as they traded with the various Hyksos-Hebrew tribes in order to acquire and then swindle away their tribal genealogies.

The Jerusalem Temple was merely an outlying office for the huge system of graft, larceny, theft, swindling, fraud, slavery, and murder that the Sumerian Swindle gave to the merchant-moneylenders of the entire Near East. Those international criminals were always on the alert for new ways of sucking wealth into their counting houses. Jerusalem was an out-of-the-way location, not a major hub of financial activity. The main profits were found in Mesopotamia and east into Elam, Persia and India. The big money was in Babylonia and Assyria, where Terah and his eldest son Nehor remained. Nehor managed and inherited the family businesses, while Abraham scouted out Canaan.

Please keep in mind, as I have pointed out before, that our ancestors had the same intellectual abilities as do we. Take a look at this reed-and-rope-built ship of the great explorer, Thor Heyerdahl, and understand that even though the ships that the even the most ancient peoples used in their long-distance trade were built entirely of reeds and hemp rope, they were quite seaworthy and capable of carrying heavy cargo. Trade voyages from Ur to India, from

India to Yemen, from Yemen to Somalia then on to Aqiba with a return trip back around Arabia to Bahrain and then to Ur once again, were not without perils, but they were also not beyond the capabilities of the ancient people who sailed their cargoes on ships made of reeds in 3000 BC.

With ships such as these, the merchant-moneylenders of the ancient Near East were in a position to trade on a large scale, but also to control that trade. Without a reed ship or an overland donkey caravan, how could anyone deal in exotic goods? And even with these necessities, how could you do business if the merchant-moneylender guilds wouldn't let you tie up to the quay or buy fodder for your donkeys or the king would not give you safe passage guarantees? Laws in those days were matter of bribery of kings and officials mixed with personal gangster power. If you defied the merchants' trade guilds, you would be beat up and murdered. The ancient businessmen were ruthless monopoly capitalists without one iota of our modern ideas of "fair play," "honest dealings," or "honor." Except among themselves, none of these ideas were part of their culture or of their religious values.

The ancient *awilum* (the Haves) were not just the merchants and moneylenders, but included within that social class the high priests, high officials and kings. All of them profited from trade, if not directly like the merchants, then indirectly from the taxes collected by the kings and officials. Because they all profited, it was to their mutual benefit as *a socioeconomic class* of the *awilum* (the Haves), to maintain certain traditions and agreements among themselves, not all of which were written into law. The Gold-Silver Exchange Mechanism was one such agreement that made the kings, maharajas and big merchants wealthy while further eroding the earning power and prosperity of the common people. This Mechanism was empowered solely with mutual agreements between the kings and merchant-moneylenders of the West with the kings, mandarins, maharajas and merchant-moneylenders of India and the Far East.

The merchant-moneylenders of Babylonia had been doing business with India for nearly two thousand years. They had devised an international swindle that could only be accomplished over long distances, with the collusion of the *awilum* (the Haves) of every country and across every religious philosophy. The rich could all get richer *as a class*, if they worked together in this simple scam. With every scam where the rich get richer, their wealth is swindled away from the poor, or at least away from people who were not poor until the rich swindled them.

This particular scam is called the Gold-Silver Exchange Mechanism between the East and the West. Only the rich could take advantage of it. At a very high financial level, it was a way for the very rich to destroy entire countries and leave them impoverished for centuries – which they did, as you shall see. And it all involves the simple exchange of gold for silver. Regardless of the *actual* and *natural* ratio of gold to silver on the entire planet, bullion gold and bullion silver is kept at a *decreed ratio* of trade by those who control the bullion. It isn't a matter of supply and demand. It is a matter of monopoly control by the very wealthy and enforced by the kings. The ancient Gold-Silver

Exchange Mechanism was not supply-and-demand driven. It was a function of monopoly control and cartel conspiracy, because the Mechanism only works when governments and the big merchant-moneylenders conspire to maintain it.

If *international cartels* sound to you like a modern technique, think again. Remember from Volume One that only the very wealthy merchant-moneylenders could trade in such vital commodities as copper. Even the wealthiest individual could not trade without permission of the guilds, because it was a closed shop. The long-distance transportation by ship and donkey caravan, the costs of transportation and armed guards, costs of initial mining and smelting, the costs of the metal ingots themselves, and the restricted geographical areas from which the metal could be acquired, all meant that only trade on an industrial scale with huge investments of capital was possible. The little man was restricted to the very end of the supply line. Middle level tradesmen were totally dependent upon the big importers and wholesalers. Regardless of who owned the mines or in what country, *the merchant-moneylenders controlled the trade* and therefore the prices, just as they do today. Supply of metals and demand for them were only a part of the equation. Control of the trade channels themselves meant everything. See Volume One for the Twenty-One Secret Frauds of the Sumerian Swindle. Secret Fraud #21 is: "Control the choke points and master the body; strangle the choke points and kill the body." Control of shipping and trade routes was as important as control of supply sources and markets. And the ancient merchant-moneylender guilds controlled all three.

The Gold-Silver Exchange Mechanism was a monetary "secret of the ages" – a difference in the gold/silver ratio between east and west. Unlike the Sumerian Swindle where, whether big or small, every lender-at-interest is a swindler, the Gold-Silver Exchange Mechanism could only be organized by big money linked to political power. For thousands of years, this mechanism was a great source of wealth to whoever held it. In later antiquity, elements of the Roman establishment drew great wealth from their control over it, until its effects helped to weaken the Roman Empire and bring down Rome from within. Venice's profits from it (as well as from the Sumerian Swindle) helped spark the Renaissance by enriching the greedy moneylenders and psychopathic kings with so much of the People's wealth that, rather than return it to society, all they did was spend it for lavish palaces, commission art works, and build machines for more deadly warfare. It was secretly used for centuries by Jewish merchants through their monopoly of trade between Christian kingdoms and Muslim countries.

The Gold-Silver Exchange Mechanism worked like this: The gold/silver ratio in the West was kept high, over the millennia ranging from 9 to 1, to 16 to 1. That was the official exchange rate. However, the ratio in India and Asia was kept low – usually about 6 or 7 to 1. This meant that silver taken from Europe to India exchanged for more than twice as much gold in India as it did in Europe. The nexus of the trade was the land bridge above the Middle East; whoever controlled that area usually controlled the trade. If it was controlled from the West, they got 100% more gold for their silver than the local value. It worked just as well from the East. If they controlled the trade that way, they received 100% more silver for their gold. If control was shared, trade would probably have been at a 9 to 1 ratio, giving each establishment a profit on exchange. The very existence of the Gold-Silver Exchange Mechanism and its significance was completely unknown in ancient times among the national merchants and moneylenders and is almost unknown in modern times. Only those who dealt with international commerce knew of its workings, because only they could use it to their advantage. Even if an ordinary tradesman knew of it, he could not make a profit merely by carrying a few ounces of silver to India to exchange it for twice as much gold. But when regular import-export businessmen secretly carried any number of shekels or talents or minas of bullion stashed among the cargo, then the bullion was carried for free in both directions and the profits were 100% clear.

Smuggling gold and silver bullion was an ancient tradition of the merchant-moneylenders. If no one knew what they had, then who could steal it from them? For those master con artists and swindlers, if no one knew what they had, then what king could tax them for it? They could smuggle bullion for free, mixed with regular barter goods, and they could double their profits in exchanging silver for gold. They doubled their profits through international trade and, on the same voyage, doubled them again by exchanging their smuggled silver for twice as much gold. This dichotomy in the ratio lasted for thousands of years.

Because the Sumerian Swindle created stupendous wealth for everyone who practiced lending money at interest, the local moneylender guilds prospered. Through strong-arm enforcement tactics and laws created by bribed kings and ministers, these local business guilds controlled the trade channels, so the international guilds prospered. And because the specific merchants who plied the international trade between the East and West could take advantage of the Gold-Silver Exchange Mechanism, great moguls of wealth arose who were independent of any country or of any king. But they could not allow any king or the people of any country to learn how they had obtained their wealth, how much of it there was, or where it was concealed. It was because these Semitic, Aramaic-speaking merchant-moneylenders controlled the trade and the wealth of the entire ancient Near East that Aramaic became the *lingua franca* of the entire region.

There is evidence of the Aramaic language in records of the second millennium BC and by the end of the eighth century BC, Aramaic had already won for itself the role of an international language in official circles. It was spoken from at least Assyria to Judah by 700 BC and across Mesopotamia into Iran. That achievement is all the more remarkable, since the Arameans never forged a great empire, but spread their language through *tribal migrations and trade*. Parts of the Bible are written in Aramaic, notably large sections of Daniel and Ezra. So widespread was the merchant-moneylender use of Aramaic, that *it replaced the native languages of all*

Semitic Asia outside of Arabia, and it remained unchallenged until the Islamic Conquest in the seventh century AD. Everybody spoke the language of the merchant-moneylenders of the ancient Near East.

Deluded with wealth, perverted in sexual excess, ruthless in acquisition of gold, pitiless in exaction of interest, remorseless in destruction of families, brutal against surviving widows and orphans, demonic in promoting and profiting from war, these merchant-moneylenders and their accountants believed themselves to be the very most blessed of their god. Their god was a god for them alone, because what other people had as much wealth and political power with so little effort as they? But, to keep their wealth secure and enjoy their blessings, they wanted to establish a temple and treasury for just themselves, alone – a treasury hidden within a fortress city built of stone.

All of the cities and states in the ancient Near East had plenty of food and lots of room for towns and farms. The lands were not overpopulated. The Fertile Crescent was, indeed, a bountiful place for grain and fodder for animals, thanks to the irrigation projects from the Tigris and Euphrates River watersheds. With the eight Essentials of Life, what more could anyone want over and above the abundance that they already had? But unfortunately, those ancient people were driven mad by the same diabolical moneylender mechanisms that are ruining modern society today. The Sumerian Swindle of charging interest on a loan was making everyone desperately aggressive with excessive work and trouble. There was plenty of sustenance supplied by Nature, needing only the sweat of the People's labor to bring it into fruition. But the Sumerian Swindle – the interest on the loans – was demanding that the various kingdoms and societies work harder, suffer more, starve, and go to war, so the moneylenders could collect their interest; sucking the peoples' blood, so the Jews could live in luxury.

CHAPTER 8
THE TRAINING MANUAL
FOR
MURDERERS, THIEVES, LOAN SHARKS, AND OTHER JEWISH HEROES

The *Hebrew Bible* is the Biggest Lie Ever Told. But its lies are more complex than this simple statement reveals. The *Hebrew Bible* is also a *Contract* as well as a *Training Manual* for *the world's oldest, organized, criminal conspiracy.* One basic fact that must be understood by everyone who studies Judaism or the *Hebrew Bible* is that even in modern times, the rabbis always get ten percent of all stolen property.

The *Hebrew Bible* is a Contract in that it declares laws in an attempt to bind its adherents into a one-way fealty to the demonic, while pretending to be a "higher moral virtue." What that virtue is, is never stated, but only claimed. And upon inspection, there is no virtue found within Judaism, only deceit.

The *Hebrew Bible* is a Training Manual in that it demonstrates and exemplifies various ways for its adherents to swindle, murder, pillage and rape, and it is all presented in the form of educational short stories full of sex, violence and fake religiosity. Jews stealing, murdering, raping and betraying, while praying to their God of Wrath and Genocide – where is the "higher moral virtue" in that? But the Jews claim that the *Hebrew Bible* is the "word of God" and the "solemn truth." How can anyone doubt the word of God? These rabbis with hairy faces and stinky clothes have deceived the People of the world for one simple reason: because they can. Ordinary people are generally innocent and honest and trusting, making them the perfect victims of those who are greedy and voracious enough to dupe them with lies and steal their wealth. Let's inspect these Jewish deceivers more closely.

Very much can be understood about any people, worldwide, if one looks to see who its heroes are. Heroes set the example for the whole society. All men, women and children aspire to them. As examples for their children, those great heroes are held up by everyone as the epitome of bravery, intelligence, virtue or martial prowess. You know this, Dear Reader, from whatever society you were raised within. You know who your heroes are and who you look up to with admiration. Movie stars? Sports stars? Heroic soldiers or policemen? Great explorers or scientists? You know who your heroes are. But who are the heroes of the Jews?

The heroes of the Jews are betrayers, bandits, rapists, child molesters, swindlers, deceivers, mass murderers, counterfeiters, slave drivers, kidnappers, thieves, moneylenders, pimps, prostitutes, adulterers and rabbis, all the vilest kinds of people, and all posing as the Children of God. You have seen this in such characters as Moses and his family of evil priests, murdering whoever did not follow their laws, laws designed with the goal of keeping the wicked priests in power over the gullible Hebrew goat rustlers, while protecting their treasury of gold. The heroes of the Jews are presented in the *Hebrew Bible* as being the trickiest and the most deceiving, whose one overriding "virtue" is acquisitive greed and ruthless oppression, enforced with murder. Some heroes, eh? You can read all about the heroes of the Jews in the Biggest Lie Ever Told, the *Hebrew Bible* – The Training Manual for Jewish Criminality and Psychopathy.

From their earliest childhood, the Jews are trained and taught how to "walk in the ways" of their god through this Operating Manual. They claim it is a "holy book," but it holds up the most evil and criminal of people as heroes to be imitated. "Look at us," the Jews say. "We steal, betray, subvert and destroy you because our god hates you and gives your property to us. We are His special and holy bandits and swindlers. It is our duty to kill you and take everything that you own because we are the Holy Chosen Ones of God." That is the religious philosophy and the "higher virtue" of the Jews as found in the *Hebrew Bible*.

WARNING: You may now skip to Chapter 9, if you are not interested in Biblical commentary, which comprises the balance of this long chapter. Otherwise, have your Bibles handy for referencing *How the Jews Betrayed Mankind* and read on.

In the *Hebrew Bible*, the books of Joshua, Judges, Samuel, and Kings are called "The Early Prophets." The "Later Prophets" are Isaiah, Jeremiah, Ezekiel and the twelve Minor Prophets. A tradition ascribing those books to "prophets" was responsible for the use of this title. Joshua is credited with the book of that name, Samuel with the books of Judges and Samuel, Jeremiah with 1 and 2 Kings. Although the Jews claim that these are history books, they are more accurately described as historical novels – that is, fictions disguised as histories. Even the term "prophets" is the usual Jewish conceit. A "prophet" means "telling forth;" it does not mean "telling the future." The part played by the prophets in these books is considerable: Samuel, Gad, Nathan, Elijah, Elisha, Isaiah, Jeremiah, and others of lesser note and the Books of Kings, provide us with the historical background for the preexilic "writing" prophets. But that background is a fairy tale by the world's biggest fairies and fakes, the Jews.

However, most Bible commentators make the same mistake that has been made since the Bible was first translated into Greek in the second century AD. To create a logical narrative timeline, the *Torah* (*Pentateuch* or Five Books of Moses) was purposely placed first when actually, the various books of the "prophets" were written first and the *Pentateuch* was finalized around 539 BC in Babylonia by the evil Jewish scribes under Ezra.

In general, the *Hebrew Bible* is not a religious book as much as it is a Training Manual of Operating Instructions for an International Criminal Conspiracy *posing as a religion*. It describes the methods of its heroes in subversion, swindles, theft and murder. The Jewish god, Yahweh, is actually a secondary character urging them on to their lives of crime against all of Mankind.

As for their so-called "prophets," the Jews had no monopoly on religious "prophesy" regardless of their claims. Throughout the ancient Near East, male and female prophets, literally "ecstatics" or "frenzied persons," were believed to have been selected by the gods for a specific occasion or time period. The deity usually initiated the communication, but the recipient could also induce communication. The prophet received his information from visions, dreams, voices in his head, and more mechanical media, such as divinatory techniques like reading the entrails of sacrificial animals or throwing dice. Once the prophet received the message in his head, he would repeat or rephrase it in oral or written form – often poetically – to provide inspired insight into the situation. Prophetic activity was widespread throughout the ancient Near East, although only a small number of prophetic texts have survived. After the eighth century, prophecy became a cultic activity in Assyria – the sayings of both male and female prophets were recorded in tablet series. Akkadian prophecies usually contained "predictions" of events that had already happened, although some were genuine forecasts. Pretending to make "predictions" of events that had already happened became a favorite method of the Jewish priests. Such phony "prophesies" are basic to the *Hebrew Bible* of the lying Jews.

8.1 The Mighty Jewish Hero Joshua Whom Even God Obeys

One of the great heroes of the Jews is Joshua, who allegedly practiced his genocide around 1406 to 1050 BC. The dates are so widespread because nobody knows when this fictional character was supposed to have been active. Like all of their other heroes, Joshua is a mythological figure who the Jews swear up and down is as real as the rainbow. Why is he a hero? Because he is devoted to the Temple Cult of the wicked Jewish priests and is voraciously intent upon banditry and murder. Oy! Such a pious Jew!

The Jews concede that the Book of Joshua was not written by Joshua himself, but rather comes from a variety of sources. All of its stories and traditions were assembled from the same group of conspiring priests who manufactured the fictional Book of Deuteronomy. There were at least two successive editions of Joshua before Ezra's final editing in Babylonia in 538 BC.

The Jerusalem Bible editors, as well as most Bible scholars, date the Israelite invasion of Canaan to "within the last thirty years of the 13th century (~1230 BC); this date is suggested by the chronology adopted for Exodus, by contemporary history and by the data of Palestinian archeology." But these dates are based upon the lies of the Jews. Archaeology proves that these alleged time frames were impossible.

Joshua, a heroic murderer and bandit, leads the mighty lice-infested Hebrews rampaging across Canaan – so the story goes. As a continuation of Deuteronomy, the Book of Joshua cannot be anything other than a rewriting and reinvention of Hebrew fables. Other than as Hyksos bandits, the Hebrews were mere goat rustlers with no real history of their own. But in order to mold them into a unified fighting army of treasury guards, the merchant-moneylender-scribes of Babylon combined their genealogies with a fanciful editing job.

Joshua most certainly was written during a time when the moneylenders had realized their greatest power. The reason for this is that the territory that the Yahweh-god "promised" to the Hebrew goat rustlers is substantially greater in area than the "promise" in Genesis 15:18 or in Deuteronomy 1:7 and 11:24. Now, in the Book of Joshua, the lying god of the Hebrews "promises" that

> "Every place you tread with the soles of your feet I shall give you as I declared to Moses that I would. From the wilderness and Lebanon to the great river Euphrates and to the Great Sea westwards, this shall be your territory." (Joshua 1:3-4.)

This land – using modern place names – stretches from Iraq to the Mediterranean and up the length of the Nile and is now "promised" to the Hebrews if they "keep all the Law which my servant Moses laid on you" (Joshua 1:7). That is, all of the laws that established a synagogue banking system. The use of psychological warfare is exemplified in Joshua 2. It is not just the ancient idea of terrorism that is expressed here, but its modern equivalent as well. The mythological stories about the Yahweh-god of the goat rustlers and the "miracles" of crossing the Sea of Reeds and murdering the Amorites had been told to the people living in the town of Jericho. Spreading such lies is presented as a psyops technique which resulted in a prostitute named Rahab betraying her own people to the Hebrews. You will see this even into modern times where the deluded Christians ignore the advice of Jesus and betray their own countries and their own people in order to follow the lies of the Jews. Inducing non-Jews to commit treason out of the superstitious belief that those stinky Hebrews had an all-powerful god with which to punish them is the ancient message in Joshua 2. Those Hebrew goat rustlers no doubt had a lot of laughs around the camp fires at night that such a mendacious trick actually worked. After all, what believing people who worshiped their gods could imagine that there were people who would tell lies about God in order to gain an advantage over you?

Using the standard Jewish technique of making use of the most corrupt in society, the two spies sent out by Joshua found refuge with a prostitute living inside the walls of Jericho. When her townsmen were looking for the Hebrew spies among them, Rahab hid them and deceived her townsmen. She said to the Hebrew spies,

> "I know that Yahweh has given you this land, that we ourselves are afraid of you and that all who live in this territory have been seized with terror at your approach; for we have heard how Yahweh dried up the Sea of Reeds before you when you came out of Egypt and what you did with the two Amorite kings

across the Jordan, Sihon and Og, whom you put under the ban. When we heard this, our hearts failed us, and no courage is left in any of us to stand up to you, because Yahweh your God is God both in heaven above and on earth beneath." (Joshua 2:9-11.)

This method of telling great lies about God so as to gain an advantage over religious people by using nothing but deceit has become a Jewish tradition into modern times. From the earliest times, the Hebrew bandits have been telling lies to deceive the Gentiles and make people think that the dross is made of gold. The merchant-moneylenders of Babylonia had observed how the system of terrorism and propaganda was used to profitable effect by the Assyrians. The Assyrians gained great victories over walled cities whose inhabitants surrendered without a fight merely by being ruthlessly cruel to the cities that did not submit. The Assyrians gained their psyops advantage by torturing and slaughtering the inhabitants of captured cities who fought against them. This so much frightened other towns, that they would give up without a fight, simply from sheer terror.

The moneylenders of Babylonia observed those victories and thought, "Many towns and cities surrendered to Assyria merely because they had heard the stories of how ruthless and cruel the Assyrians are. *Those towns did not witness the actual events, but had merely heard stories about them*. So, what if we had stories that we could tell about our mighty god; how he destroyed Egypt and exterminated the Amorites? None of it would be true. But wouldn't the stories themselves induce the Gentiles to surrender and give way before us? We can spread these stories merely by gossiping in the town taverns." Thus, by inventing a mythology that gave themselves an illusory great virtue with a terrifying god, the moneylender priests enabled the Hebrews to have an awe-inspiring "prestige" that was, and is today, nothing but bull stuff. And when all the Jews everywhere tell the same lies, then it's a genuine miracle of Jewish *abracadabra*!

Although the Book of Joshua was supposedly written during the Conquest of Canaan – which took place between the time that the Hyksos were chased out of Egypt in 1550 BC and the time of Pharaoh Akhenaten (Eighteenth dynasty ~1334 BC) – it is actually no older than any other book in the *Hebrew Bible*, since by 539 BC they were all edited and embellished by Ezra the Scribe. Joshua is a continuation of Deuteronomy; thus it was written *after* Deuteronomy. Internal evidence alone proves the Book of Joshua to be a hoax.

However, no matter when it was written, it is a fraudulent document. Archaeology proves that the walled town of Jericho was an abandoned ruin when the events described in Joshua supposedly occurred. Its walls had been tumbled down by earthquakes and the buildings reduced to rubble; abandoned for a duration of several hundred years. The Book of Joshua was actually written during the time that Jericho was still a wreck as a convenient means of explaining why its great walls were a pile of rubble. For the writers of Deuteronomy and Joshua, the broken walls of Jericho were a useful way of claiming that their mythical hero, Joshua, using the power of their mighty god, had knocked down the walls of Jericho with a trumpet blast. Instead of saying earthquakes destroyed those walls, the rabbis claimed that the Hebrews and their Yahweh-god did it.

With such amazing myths claimed to be facts and mighty prevarications dressed up as miracles, even today's modern Jews are able to deceive and profit from gullible, God-fearing people. With such lies as the rabbis wrote in the *Hebrew Bible*, it was easy to say that "Yahweh has delivered the whole country into our hands, and its inhabitants all tremble already at the thought of us" (Joshua 2:24). The Hebrew goat thieves used psychological warfare to make their enemies tremble at the very thought of them, but they were not smart enough to invent such lies themselves. Only the moneylenders of Babylon and their scribes had the experience in deceit and finance that would allow them such complex inventions.

All Jews are self-centered actors. They love to make up stories and mesmerize an audience with a show of theatrical illusion, while drawing attention to themselves. Joshua 3 is such a show. There is a deliberate parallelism between Joshua 3 and the story of the Exodus from Egypt. With the story of the Yahweh-god's warning the Hebrews to keep a great distance between themselves and the Ark of the Covenant, the lying rabbis wanted to emphasize his supposed mighty and terrible power. Joshua 3 mimics and repeats the events of the Exodus story so that Joshua becomes another Moses, only this time as a mighty conqueror. Archaeology proves that if Joshua had existed at all outside of a lying rabbi's imagination, then he was a tiny ant of a conqueror, overrunning little, defenseless, unfortified villages of no more than a hundred people, which the lying scribes called "great cities."

As the story goes, the Levitical priests carried the Ark as they marched before the Hebrew bandits. Joshua was now taking the place of Moses, so he heard voices in his head and talked with God. (The Hebrews were accustomed to following leaders who heard voices in their heads and talked to the sky.) To show what a "miracle" Joshua was, the Jordan River dried up so that the smelly goat rustlers could cross it without taking a bath. It is here that the Yahweh-god was called, "The lord of the whole earth" (Joshua 3:11-13).

That this "lord of the whole earth" was also a Canaanite deity with a goddess-wife named *Asherah* (*Istar*) and a child-god named *Baal*, didn't seem to worry the lying rabbis who wrote the Book of Joshua. After all, who would know? Archaeology hadn't been invented yet and the original clay tablets were all buried under city mounds, where nobody in their right mind would want to dig them up. And besides, the rabbis have goatskin parchment stories that are even better than the truth. So, who's to know? *Abracadabra*, it's the truth.

This Deuteronomic fable of Joshua was written sometime after Josiah's kingship (640-609 BC) as a mythological explanation of how the Hebrews ended up living in Canaan. Joshua 3 is now claiming even more power for its Yahweh-god as well as once again assigning leadership to the priests as the all-powerful leaders of the Hebrews. Joshua again hears voices in his head as the

Babylonian scribes have their demon god speak directly to the chief priest in Joshua 4. And what this demon god of the Jews says is "Kill and steal." Joshua is the perfect Jewish bandit for the job, too.

Establishing imaginary events upon the foundation of some geographical landmark is another scam of the lying scribes, right up to the modern rabbis. The naturally occurring salt columns around the Dead Sea were explained as Lot's wife turning back to watch the destruction of Sodom and Gomorrah and being turned into a pillar of salt. "Oy Gevalt! There, you can see it for yourself! That salt column proves that Lot's wife was turned into a pillar of salt, because how else could that column of salt be there if it wasn't for Lot's wife looking back at the destruction of Sodom and Gomorrah?!" Some red basalt outcroppings were claimed to be the bed of a the giant named Og, King of Bashan. When the Ark of the Covenant was later stolen, it represented "proof" that the fables of Moses actually happened, since the Ark was no longer there.

This is the kind of "logic" that the lying rabbis use in their *Babylonian Talmud.* "Oy Gevalt! Of course the stories of Moses are true! The genuine Ark of the Covenant containing the stone tablets and the jar of manna, is proof positive that they are true. And see, right here in our holy scriptures, it says that the Ark of the Covenant was stolen. So, that's actual proof that you can read about with your own eyes. How could the Ark be stolen unless it was there to steal? Since the holy scriptures say it was stolen and it is nowhere to be found, then that proves the stories are true since all the proof was stolen and isn't here. Since the Ark isn't here, then that proves that it existed. And since it existed, it contained the tablets and the jar of manna which were put in the Ark as proof that the stories are real."

The Jews would make the world's foremost clowns if they didn't take their ridiculous lies so seriously. They really hate it if one tells the truth about them, since truth takes away the lies upon which Judaism is built.

The Hebrew goat rustlers were lied to by the moneylender priests. And for "proof" that their lies were true, geological anomalies and piles of stones were presented as an act of *abracadabra* magic. In this case, twelve stones were piled up as a "proof" that a lie was actually true.

> "… for when in days to come your children ask you, 'What do these stones mean for you?', you will tell them, 'The waters of the Jordan separated in front of the Ark of the Covenant of Yahweh, and when it crossed the Jordan, the waters of the river vanished. These stones are an everlasting reminder of this to the Israelites." (Joshua 4:6-7.)

So, by pointing to an old pile of stones that had been anonymously sitting in place for thousands of years – Abracadabra! – the rabbis created "proof" that the fables were true.

This same method (of attaching lies to physical objects and then presenting the objects themselves as "proof" that the lies are true) was used in modern times at such places as Auschwitz and Treblinka. *Abracadabra*! Piles of shoes were claimed to be "proof" that millions of Jews were murdered. *Abracadabra*! A few antiquated pizza ovens were claimed as "proof" that millions of Jews had been incinerated. Even simple arithmetic shows that if all of the Jews who were allegedly incinerated in those slow and inefficient ovens had actually been incinerated, then those ovens would still be burning Jews today – a modern equivalent of the *abracadabra* (I create as I speak) lies told by the Jews in the Old Testament.

The twelves stones allegedly taken by the tribes from the Jordan River were set up at Gilgal. The place name, Gilgal, means "ring of stones." Like all other prehistoric stone rings, Gilgal was set up by prehistoric people as a sort of astronomical observatory or solstice marker. It existed several thousand years before the Hebrew goat rustlers entered Canaan. Although the lying rabbis tried to use the ancient stone ring itself as "proof" that the Hebrews created it, they did not know that archaeology would later use that same stone ring to prove that they are liars.

"When your children in days to come ask their fathers, 'What is the meaning of these stones?'" (Joshua 4:21-24), then the Hebrews are to lie to them. They are to claim that the stones prove that every living Jew, *personally*, had crossed the Jordan dry-shode, just as Yahweh had done for Moses at the Sea of Reeds. With such lies "the people of the earth may recognize how mighty the hand of Yahweh is, and that you yourselves may always stand in awe of Yahweh your God.'" (Joshua 4:24.) Thus, the god of the Jews is always in the past tense: a god who existed in myths proven to be lies. This shows that the Jews today are without a god; without even a god created from their own imagination. They are godless, mendacious people who control the world's finances and thereby pull the strings of political power; a menace to all of Mankind. And this menace claims that imaginary events in ancient myths are real to them. Such thinking is identical to psychosis. Sociopaths who control society? And you wonder why the world is always in chaos? Behind that chaos you will find Jews pulling the levers of society as they manipulate finance and politics for their own profit.

When such lies as those of the *Hebrew Bible* are repeated by all of the Jews throughout the centuries as a sort of social fraud, then the People of the world begin to believe that they are true. When the People of the world begin to believe the goat rustlers, then the goat rustlers gain "prestige" and perfidious advantage over them, and the People give way for no other reason than the demonic persuasion of Jewish lies.

The psychological warfare techniques that the merchant-moneylenders learned from the Assyrians were used by the Jews from the very earliest times of their evil existence. They were nothing but scruffy bandits, telling the people whom they wished to rob and murder how powerful they were and spreading lies about a mighty god who dried up the Jordan River just for them. It was all calculated to give them a psychological advantage in banditry.

"When all the kings of the Amorites in the country west of the
Jordan and all the kings of the Canaanites in the central coast region heard that Yahweh had dried up the waters of the Jordan before the Israelites until they crossed it, their hearts grew faint and
their spirit failed them as the Israelites drew near." (Joshua 5:1.)

The people of the entire ancient Near East believed in the gods. Even
when two armies faced each other across a battlefield, neither army would
move until the priests received a favorable sign from the gods through divination. So, such stories of the Jews were certainly powerful stuff. However, since
no one had witnessed this event (just as no one had witnessed the other "miracles" bragged about by the Hebrews), how did all of those kings hear the stories? Through the tavern gossip spread by the Hebrews themselves, of course!
The Hebrews told the tales, but no one else had ever heard or seen such things.
It was the Jews' word alone, based – not upon what they had actually seen –
but upon what was written on the goatskins by the lying scribes. This was excellent use of Assyrian psychological warfare, destroying the morale of their
opponents with simple lies before the battle was joined.

The rabbis who wrote Joshua lied about the emphasis on circumcision.
This section between Joshua 5:2 and Joshua 9 shows that this book was written
before the Five Books of Moses. The Law of Moses commands the Hebrews
to circumcise their babies at eight days. But Joshua 1:2-9 claims that none of
the Hebrews were circumcised, because they just didn't have time to do it after
forty years wandering around in the desert. Thus, this part of the Book of
Joshua is an older tradition than the fables found in the Torah. It reflects the
bandit era, when the various tribes of thieves were ravaging Canaan after they
were kicked out of Egypt by Pharaoh Ahmose. New recruits like the sons of
Laban could join, but they could never leave, just like any other gangster organization. The new recruits had to be circumcised to ensure that they were
forever made into Hebrew gangsters. Circumcision was a mark of membership
that could never be erased, similar to the membership tattoos of Mexican and
Japanese gangsters. Once in the gang, you never get out alive.

According to the Book of Joshua, before going on to slaughter the inhabitants of Canaan, the Hebrews celebrated the Passover party whereby they rejoiced in the death of the oldest children of the Egyptians. This Passover was
celebrated in good bandit style by eating food that they had stolen from the
Amorites and Canaanites.

"From that time, from their first eating of the produce of that
country, the manna stopped falling." (Joshua 5:12.)

This was convenient, because no one other than the lying Hebrews would
ever claim to have actually seen any of this magical "manna." Since they were
no longer being fed by their desert Yahweh-god, they gobbled up Canaan like
voracious locusts.

Joshua 5 closes with Joshua meeting an angel with a sword. He was the "captain of the army of Yahweh." Joshua also hears voices in his head and holds long conversations with the sky. He falls on his face and hears the angel say, "Take your sandals off your feet, for the place you are standing on is holy" (Joshua 5:15). Why would this land of sandstone wadis and waterless wastes be "holy"? Because this "Holy Land" was needed to surround the "Holy Temple" that contained the "Holy Treasury" that protected the "Holy Gold" of the holy moneylender guild of Ur and Harran with main offices in Jerusalem. Yes, there were other merchant-moneylender guilds throughout the ancient Near East other than Terah's. Every city had one. But Abraham's Circumcised Bankers' Guild was unique in that it concealed its true nature behind a sham religion. Judaism was a bankers' guild hidden behind a bloodstained altar.

The story of Joshua and the walls of Jericho "tumbling down" is another of those rabbinical frauds written to give an explanation for a landmark. Jericho is the world's oldest town, dating from about 8000 BC. It was built to guard the only reliable water source in the area. Although it had high and thick walls of stone, these walls were not built with anything approaching the cut stone masonry of later eras. The ancient age of the town is reflected in its crude construction. An unintelligent people piled up rocks as protection against the equally unintelligent wandering shepherd bandits infesting the area. So, when earthquakes hit the region – which is not uncommon since the entire Jordan River area is one big fault line – those piled-up stone and rubble walls came tumbling down. Archeology proves that during the times around which the Book of Joshua was allegedly written, the walls of Jericho had been tumbled down by an earthquake and the town abandoned for several hundred years.

Jericho, like the other cities of Canaan, was unfortified at the time the Bible claims Joshua attacked. There were no walls that could have come tumbling down and no one even living in Jericho during the alleged attack of Joshua. It was an abandoned city at the time. Likewise for the cities of Ai, Gibeon, Arad and Heshbon: they were abandoned ruins at the time of Joshua's alleged attack. So, once again, reality is in conflict with the word of the Jews. The mighty Jewish hero Joshua was only defeating those cities – and roaring his greatness like an ant conquering a watermelon – because no one was living in them.

Thus, it was easy for the rabbis to write in Joshua 6 that Joshua and his marching band of scrofulous Hebrews knocked down the walls of Jericho by blowing on seven magic goat horns. It was easy, because the walls were already knocked down by an earthquake centuries before and no one was living in Jericho to be butchered by the Hebes.

The story of Jericho had the additional purpose of elevating prostitution and treason to a level that only a Jew could appreciate. Since the moneylenders controlled most prostitution in the ancient Near East, they well knew how to make use of those unfortunate women. The prostitute Rahab and her relatives were all spared from the slaughter, because she had betrayed her people by hiding the Hebrew spies.

"… these Joshua spared. She has dwelt among Israel until now, because she concealed the messengers Joshua sent to reconnoiter Jericho." (Joshua 6:25.)

Thus, the Holy Goat Rustlers gained a prostitute to add to the "virtue" of their genealogical *asl*. This was a useful technique taught in their Training Manual for Jewish Criminality and Psychopathy for engendering treason among people for the sake of the lying Jews.

The prostitute was saved while all of the rest of the inhabitants of Jericho were placed under the ban. That is, every living thing in that town was butchered, including the cats and dogs and cattle. "They enforced the ban on everything in the town: men and women, young and old, even the oxen and sheep and donkeys, massacring them all." (Joshua 6:21.) However, like the typical, bloodthirsty Hebrew bandits who served the priests of the moneylenders' Temple, "All the silver and all the gold, all the things of bronze and things of iron are consecrated to Yahweh and must be put into his treasury" (Joshua 6:19). Of course! Slaughter the *goyim* (lowly insects, stupid cattle) and put everything that you steal from their corpses into the Treasury. Do you see that the bankers of Babylon wrote those words? Judaism is the religion of moneylenders, pawnbrokers, thieves and murderers. And Joshua is one of their heroes.

The iron was "consecrated" to the greedy god of the holy treasury, because when Joshua was written at the beginning of the Iron Age, that metal was still quite expensive and rare. All of these valuable metals became the property of the treasury and the personal property of the Jewish priests who operated the Temple scam. This internal evidence gives an idea of when the first drafts of Joshua were written even though it was extensively edited during the days of Josiah and again before the release of the Babylonian Jews by Cyrus.

Although miscellaneous pieces of iron have been found in archaeological contexts as far back as the fifth millennium BC, the Iron Age proper began around 1200 BC from the fall of the Hittite empire. The early history of iron metallurgy was traditionally viewed as a monopoly over the secrets of working with iron. The Hittites used iron metallurgy in their military successes, particularly against the Egyptians at the battle of Qadesh in Syria (~1275 BC). When the Hittite empire fell to the Sea Peoples at the end of the Bronze Age, control over the use of iron and iron technology fell to the Philistines. Iron became the metal of choice for the common man, which caused the monopoly over copper and bronze by the Mesopotamian merchant-moneylenders to become less profitable.

Of incidental interest, the use of arsenical ores exposed prehistoric smiths to chronic arsenic poisoning, with symptoms including muscular atrophy and loss of reflexes. Serious health hazards may explain a widespread theme in mythology in which the smith-god was a cripple. Classical literature referred to the Greek smith-god Hephaestus and his Roman counterpart Vulcan, who were described as lame, a characteristic shared by smith-gods from Scandinavia to West Africa.

To make sure that their audience believed the walls of Jericho had been knocked down by the magic goat horns of the priests, Joshua 6 ends with a handy reason why the walls had not been rebuilt.

> "Cursed be any man who comes forth and builds this town again! On his eldest son he shall lay its foundations, on his youngest set up its gates. Yahweh was with Joshua, and Joshua's fame spread all through the country." (Joshua 6:26-27.)

Of course, no one had ever heard of Joshua outside of the stories that the fly-speckled priests of the Hebrews wrote on the goatskin scrolls. Historically, there is no record of any such character. Mankind has only the word of the Jews.

Fame is something that can be spread by word of mouth. These stories about a mighty god as the power behind those flea-bitten goat rustlers must have been terrifying to the superstitious peoples of Canaan. Stories told around campfires of burning cow patties were used to good effect to sow fear and dread and terror in the hearts of the illiterate people whom the goat rustlers wanted to dispossess. "Did you hear how our god killed Pharaoh and parted the Red Sea for us? Shalom! You can trust us! Now, open the gates of your town so that we can be a blessing to you, too."

In Joshua 7, the moneylenders once again emphasize, because it is so important to them, the terrible penalty exacted by their mighty god for touching or taking any of the holy gold or holy silver from the holy treasury. It expresses the group identity of the big, flaming *asl* of Israel as well. "If one is guilty, all are guilty," is the idea. This creates a kind of religious police state where everybody keeps an eye on everybody else to make sure that they obey the Law of Moses. Otherwise, if even one sinner doesn't wash his hands before supper, the earth will open up and swallow everybody. And that's just for the minor offenses! There is absolutely no forgiveness whatsoever, but only instant death by incineration for touching Yahweh's gold or silver.

Joshua 7 teaches what happens when one person takes something that the priests want, and how he is found out – and how he is framed. In this case, the age-old love of the moneylenders for gambling was used. By drawing lots, the culprit was allegedly discovered. By drawing lots, a certain Achan, son of Zerah, was accused of holding something back from the priests who guarded the treasury. And why? Because he drew the shortest lot! Upon searching, the priests found a robe and some silver and gold ingots hidden in his tent, easy things for the priests to conceal beneath their clothes as they entered the tent to use to frame an innocent victim. All of the thieving Hebrews had probably kept some loot for themselves, but the drawing of lots allowed the priests to show the "power" of the Yahweh-god by sacrificing just one Hebrew and letting the others escape.

So, Achan and his sons, daughters, donkeys and sheep, were all taken outside the camp and stoned to death by the Hebrews, who then burned them and buried them all under a stone cairn. Even the sheep and donkeys must die when a Jew breaks a Mosaic Law! Such evil, murderous people, the Jews! Thus, they taught that taking silver or gold which had been declared holy for the treasury would be found out by drawing lots and the thief's entire family would be killed. The lesson being, don't mess with the Yahweh-god's gold bullion or the vicious rabbis and priests of the Treasury will catch you. And even if you are innocent, they will plant some evidence as an excuse to demonstrate their murderous power!

Joshua 8 tells another bloody story of murder, theft and genocide that the Hebrews committed against the town of Ai. After catching the warriors of Ai in an ambush, the Hebrews slaughtered every man, woman and child of the town and hung the King of Ai from a tree. Then, after stealing everything they could carry, they burned the town down. This story is told with great satisfaction. After all, these were stories written by murdering, thieving Bankers of Babylon for an audience of thieving, murdering Hebrews of Canaan to teach to generations of Jews on how to be thieving, murdering "Children of God" and liars as well, since archaeology proves that Ai was an abandoned ruin during the times that Joshua was supposed to have been rampaging across Palestine.

The Hebrews then built an altar of piled rocks, killed some innocent animals, poured out their blood and sprinkled it on the Jewish priests who were already covered with buzzing flies. The story ends with some additional propaganda which Biblical scholarship proves was written by the same priestly forger who wrote the other Deuteronomic texts. The Jews are liars, but they tell lies that are easily disproven, if you pay attention to the details. This is why they are so quick to scream and wail about "bigotry" and "anti-Semitism," even into modern times. They want to take your attention away from their lies. Nothing can be more hypocritical than for a lying Jew, who slanders the people of the entire world as *goyim* (non-Jewish, lowly insects, stupid cattle), to call someone a "bigot." But hypocrisy for the Jews is not a character flaw; it is a weapon. (More about this is Volume III, *The Bloodsuckers of Judah*.)

This old story of how the Hebrew goat rustlers tricked and murdered the people of Ai has, added to it, the propaganda of Joshua reading the Five Books of Moses to the Hebrews as a part of the sacrifice festivities. This was another impossibility. The Torah was not completed until just before 539 BC and the fraud of Deuteronomy was not written until the time of Josiah in about 640 BC. The truth never got in the way of the rabbis, nor did facts ever concern the priests of the demon-god of the Jews.

This is one of the major reasons that the lies of Judaism have been successfully perpetuated for so long. The rabbis have conspired to change and perfect the lies over the course of centuries. If one story didn't quite jibe with another story, they would edit whatever books needed to be revised in whatever way enabled them to smooth the fraud. Although the genocide of the people of Ai was written during the times when the rampaging Hyksos-Hebrews first began their assaults on Canaan around 1500 BC, the lying rabbis tightened the story up and added some additional propaganda during their stay in Babylon. The Five Books of Moses did not exist in their present form until 539 BC, and yet Joshua 8 claims that Joshua read all five books to the blood-drenched He-brews after the fight for Ai. Once again, the Jews' own writings prove what liars they are.

The stinking Hebrew goat rustlers needed to appear mighty in their own eyes. So, the rabbis deceived them with imaginary stories of mighty conquests that never happened. In Joshua 9, the Jewish priests wrote that after the He-brews had committed genocide against the people of Ai and Jericho,

> "All the kings on this side of the Jordan, in the highlands and in
> the lowlands, all along the coast of the Great Sea towards Leba-
> non, the Hittites, the Amorites, the Canaanites, the Perizzites,
> the Hivites and the Jebusites, formed an alliance to fight togeth-
> er against Joshua and Israel." (Joshua 9:1-2.)

In other words, according to this Hebrew fantasy, the entire Near East from Gezer to Cappadocia and from the Mediterranean Sea to Syria feared these goat rustlers from Sinai. The Hittites were a mighty nation equal to Egypt or Assyria in military strength. However, at the time that Joshua was written, the Hittites had already been destroyed by the Sea Peoples. So, these Hebrew ants, beating their chests and roaring about how mighty they are stand-ing on top of a watermelon, could easily claim superiority against the mighty Hittites since the Hittites weren't even in existence at that time. The Hebrew scribes could just as well have claimed, "We Jews are so mighty and powerful that even the dinosaurs are afraid of us."

Worried that such a mighty god might turn them all into toads or lepers, the people of Gibeon tricked the Hebrews into making a peace treaty. They were able to do this, the story claims, because the Hebrews did not first consult the holy dice cup known as the "oracle of Yahweh" – the Urim and Thummin – which the high priest rolled on the golden dice table (ephod) that was tied to his chest.

In typical Jewish fashion, once the Hebrews found out that these Gibeon-ites with whom they had sworn a treaty were actually people whom the Yah-weh-god had ordered them to kill, they went back on their treaty and made them into "strangers" or "*shabbos goyim*" (Sabbath dirt). Thus, the lesson is taught that any deal made with a Jew will come out bad.

> "But from that day forward, Joshua made them wood-cutters
> and water-carriers for the community, and bound them, down to
> the present day, to wait on Yahweh's altar wherever Yahweh
> might choose." (Joshua 9:27.)

More of the various tales of the Hebrew conquest of Canaan are stitched together in Joshua 10. To add to their mythological "greatness," the rabbis wrote that their enemies were killed when the Yahweh-god hurled huge hailstones down from heaven. The Hebrews slaughtered all of the Amorites, killed their kings and hung them on trees. But before killing the five Canaanite kings, Joshua humiliated them. He said,

> "... to the officers of the men of war who had fought with him, 'Come forward and put your feet on the necks of these kings!' They came forward and put their feet on their necks. 'Do not be afraid; have confidence,' Joshua went on 'be resolute, for this is how Yahweh shall deal with all the enemies you fight.' With this Joshua struck and killed them and had them hanged on five trees; they hung there until evening." (Joshua 10:24-26.)

As further "miracles" that they would use as psychological warfare against the Canaanites, the Hebrews began circulating a story that their god had made the sun and moon stand still in the sky until the Hebrews had slaughtered everybody. After all, these murderous dirtbags were the "Holy Chosen Ones of God," so He would certainly do whatever they asked of Him. Joshua ordered the sun and moon to stand still so that he would have time to slaughter all of his enemies.

> "And the sun stood still and the moon halted, until the people had vengeance on their enemies.... the sun stood still in the middle of the sky and delayed its setting for almost a whole day. There was never a day like that before or since, when Yahweh obeyed the voice of a man, for Yahweh was fighting for Israel." (Joshua 10:13-14.)

Those rabbis could really tell some stories, couldn't they? But to make sure that this lie would never be tested, they "closed the case" with a legal trick, like the Babylonian scribes and lawyers that they were. With "there was never a day like that before or since," no believing Hebrew could ever try to stop the sun and then disbelieve this "miracle" of the lying rabbis.

Oh? But you don't believe that the god of the Hebrews did such a thing? Well, "proof" is something that the Jews are just full of. As rabbinic "proof" that these events had actually happened, the cave where the five kings were buried after being hung was covered with stones, so that no one could ever find it. "Great stones were laid at the mouth of the cave, and these are still there today" (Joshua 10:27). What more proof does anyone need other than an entire landscape full of stones where maybe there is a cave buried under them somewhere that no one can find – and the word of the Jews?

Then Joshua and his scruffy bandits exterminated the inhabitants of Makkedah, killing every living thing in the town, including all the people, cattle, dogs and cats. Finally, they hung the king of the town at the front gate, more tricks which the Jews teach to their children today as the proper way to "walk in the ways of their god" and how to treat the *goyim* (non-Jewish, lowly insects, stupid cattle).

The town of Lachish was besieged and also genocided under the ban, leaving not even the kittens and puppies alive. All Jews can be so proud of such a murderous heritage with such great Jewish heroes, heroes to emulate, heroes to copy. These are the heroes that the Jews had in mind when the Jewish Bolsheviks under Lenin took over Russia and exterminated sixty million Russians, while "walking in the ways of their god." These, the holy Jews, are the very same Jews who every year chorus, "We were there, too. We were slaves of Pharaoh."

Although the kings of Hazor, Aphek, Lachish, and Megiddo are reported to have been defeated by the Israelites under Joshua, archaeological evidence shows that the destruction of those cities took place over a span of more than a century. The possible causes include invasion, social breakdown, and civil strife. But no single military force did it, and certainly not one military campaign led by a character named Joshua. In other words, archaeology proves that the story of Joshua defeating those cities is another Jewish lie. One wonders whether the Jews ever tell the truth about anything.

According to the rabbis, the Yahweh-god conquered the towns of Eglon and Hebron and Debir, all the towns of "the highlands, the Negeb, the lowlands, the hillsides, and all the kings in them. He left not a man alive and delivered every single soul over to the ban" (Joshua 10:40). The Hebrew cutthroats killed everyone, including the cattle and dogs, according to the rabbis. However, archaeology proves that what the rabbis wrote is mendacious deceit. They never defeated those towns, but used the locations as background for rabbi-inspired butchery.

After the Hebrews had exterminated the entire countryside, word of the slaughter spread to the towns of northern Canaan. Archeology proves that these tiny towns, supported by a few grain fields and goatherds, would have difficulty mustering 500 soldiers from among its farmer population. A few of the larger towns might have an "army" of a thousand farmers walking or riding donkeys into battle, waving bronze swords and throwing rocks with goat hair slings. Their so-called "kings" were merely town mayors, sheiks or nothing more than the town's richest farmer.

But according to the lying rabbis who wrote the Book of Joshua, when the "kings" of northern Canaan learned of the murderous Hebrew menace, "They set out with all their troops, a horde as countless as the sands of the sea, with innumerable horses and chariots." (Joshua 11:4.) Wow! The story gets better when the Jews tell it! That all of these "great kings" with their "huge" armies and soldiers as countless as the sands of the sea met "at the waters of Merom" (Joshua 11:5) shows that the scribes and priests of the goat rustlers lied again. The waters of Merom is in a little valley 4000 feet above sea level, much too small for maneuvering chariots. This is given by Bible commentators as a reason that the flea-bitten Hebrews could defeat a "huge" army: the enemy chariots could not maneuver. What the Bible commentators fail to understand is that the lies of the merchant-moneylender scribes is not history, but propaganda intended to give "prestige" to their treasury guards.

With the usual demonic cruelty of the Hebrews, the scribes of Joshua brag about killing every single enemy soldier. Not content with simply perpetrating their bloodlust upon the soldiers, those bloodthirsty, circumcised devils went on to hamstring the enemy's innocent horses, leaving them to suffer and die. These are the kinds of things the rabbis love to brag about. They add to the Hebrew *asl*, the bloody, big Hebrew *asl* whereby every Jew claims, "We did it! We Jews today did it."

Next, the Hebrews slaughtered every living thing in the entire land of Canaan: men, women, children, cats, dogs, goats, sheep and cattle; and they burned all of the towns after stealing everything of value. The reason that the *Hebrew Bible* gives for such barbarous massacres is that these stinking goat rustlers were "holy people" who must use no half-measures or their faith would be compromised. Such an excuse by Christian writers is disgusting, since the Hebrew "faith" is nothing but a rote adherence to a collection of fables that were written to bolster a bunch of moneylender laws of phantasmal merit. The Hebrews were mere frontmen and guards for Abraham's First National Bank and Pawn Shop with offices in Ur, Harran, Jerusalem and Babylon. The Jews told lies to give themselves prestige and frighten thieves away from their Treasury.

Once again, the very writing style of Joshua 12 shows that it was written after the time of King Josiah. This additional chapter lists 31 kings and their towns that were slaughtered by the Hebrew cutthroats. Like good accountants, the scribes of Abraham's Banking Guild kept careful score of such victories.

Joshua 13, another editorial addition, lists the lands that the Hebrews coveted, but which neither they nor their Yahweh-god had the power to conquer. This is strange, isn't it? The rabbis said their Yahweh-god was the greatest of gods, yet he was too weak to uphold his promises. The trading cities of the Phoenicians along the coast of the Mediterranean Sea were never conquered by the Hebrews, nor were the seacoast lands held by the Philistines, that is, by the Sea Peoples who had conquered these lands after 1200 BC. Even into the 21st Century AD, the modern name of "Palestine" is named after the Philistines, a name of a people whom the modern bandit state of Israel – 3,500 years later! – is still trying to exterminate.

All of Joshua 13 is merely a list of the lands stolen from the Canaanites, whom the Hebrews had slaughtered along with their dogs and cats and every living thing. When the Hebrews wanted to own the property of other people, they didn't want any survivors who could make claims for getting it back. This method of theft and genocide is still practiced by the Jews today in modern times, but it is hidden behind the wars that the Jews foster – while getting a military deferment for themselves based on the swindle of the Jewish Sabbath.

In Joshua 14, the accountants among the moneylenders of Abraham's Banking Guild listed some of the real estate that they had stolen. And Joshua 15 gives extra special, minutely detailed attention to the boundaries of the lands of the tribe of Judah. Since Jerusalem was to be the location of the main treasury, the moneylenders of Abraham's Banking Guild wanted to ensure that the boundaries of their territory were carefully described. The planned full size of this stolen territory was never achieved, no matter how powerful the Yahweh-god was alleged to be, because the land along the seacoast was occupied by the Philistines in 1200 BC and never again infested with filthy Hebrews. What the lying Jews claim is "their" land has always been inhabited by other people.

More of the incest among the Semites is recorded when Caleb gives his daughter to his brother as a wife. Again, from the earliest times, uncles and nieces were incestuously coupled among the Jews. Even though the rabbis claim that the *Torah* was written before the Book of Joshua, Joshua 15 proves that the laws of Moses prohibiting incest were regularly broken by the Hebrews. As will be seen in subsequent chapters, there are no laws of Moses that the Jews do not routinely break. *Even their own laws do not restrict these criminal people.*

Incest was the moneylenders' method for keeping all of their gold and real estate within the family. To the Jews, gold has always been worth all of the midgets, hunchbacks, and genetic defects that their incest has caused them. Because the Jews have more genetic defects than any other people, they hate with Semitic fury all races that are purer than themselves. Rather than improve their own genetic stock, the mongrel Jews try to miscegenate and breed down the pure races of the world. This is one more reason that the Jews are devils. The Jews don't *evolve* like the rest of Mankind in Nature to improve Humanity, the Jews purposely *devolve* Humanity to lower levels of evolution than themselves. Only by corrupting, degrading and pulling Mankind down below themselves can the Jews claim a sort of fungous superiority.

To make sure that all of their stolen property was secure, every town within the territory of Judah was listed in Joshua 15. Jerusalem was such a strong fortress that it remained safe from the thieving Hebrews who had to be content with all of the stolen lands except for it.

Joshua 16 lists the boundaries of the lands stolen by the tribes of Ephraim, Manasseh and Joseph. "The Canaanites living in Gezer were not driven out; they have remained in Ephraim to the present day, but were obliged to do forced labor." (Jos 16:10) Apparently, the lying Yahweh-god of the Hebrews was really too weak to beat the old Gezers.

Joshua 17 lists the territory that the tribe of Manasseh had seized. At first, the Canaanites managed to hold on to some of their towns, but they were forced into slavery when the Hebrews became stronger. Again, the "mighty god" of the Hebrews had failed to keep his promise. The tribe of Joseph was unable to drive out the Canaanites, because "all the Canaanites living in the plain have iron chariots" (Josua 17:16). The Hebrews are great at making excuses for why their "mighty power" is so puny. In this case, the "iron chariots" must have been more powerful than those of Pharaoh that the Red Sea was supposed to have swallowed up.

Joshua gave this bandit tribe of Manasseh a wooded mountain for their "inheritance." The word "inheritance" indicates a relationship with God as the children of a father who bequeaths property to them. That is, the lying priests and rabbis are telling the goat rustlers that they are the children of God, who gave them the land. Since it was a gift of a god, no earthly king could take it away, according to the lies written on the holy goatskins. The Bankers of Babylon wanted to establish a deed of ownership that could not be cancelled, even if they had to counterfeit it themselves.

Joshua 18 tells of moving their Yahweh-god's Tent from Gilgal to Shiloh and describes the boundaries of the territory of the tribe of Benjamin. Nothing godly here.

In Joshua 19, the tribe of Simeon was apportioned out of the territory of Judah "because the share of the sons of Judah was too large for them." (Joshua 19:9.) Regardless of the power of the mighty god of the goat rustlers, the Canaanites along the coast resisted the tribe of Dan, so that tribe ran over to the less well-defended town of Leshem, killed everybody and took it for themselves. This same method can be seen by modern Israelis who, regardless of their claims about their mighty god giving them Palestine, still can't defeat small numbers of Palestinians except by exterminating them. So, the Jews of Israel express their cowardly fury by machine-gunning women and children and bulldozing sleeping Arabs in their homes. Thus, the modern Jews "walk in the ways" of their demon-god, He-Who-Must-Not-Be-Named. If he is named, then you know that he is a fake. But if he is not named, then you falsely assume that their god is really a god and not actually the Devil.

There is nothing "holy" about Joshua 18 and 19. They are land grants of property stolen from their murder victims. The priests of the murdering Hebrews were acting as the real estate agents and title guarantors. These Semitic "land grants" were bogus and based solely upon murder and theft, just like the so-called "Muslim lands" of modern times.

Joshua 20 names the six cities of refuge for those who accidentally kill someone. If the murderers can reach any of those cities of refuge, then they are immune to the bloodthirsty revenge of the pursuing Hebrew "avengers of blood." *Lex talionis*, the eye for an eye philosophy of these thoroughly nasty people, kept the Hebrews constantly embroiled in disputes and hatreds toward one and all. The hypocrisy of the *Hebrew Bible* is again revealed as their God of Vengeance says, "Vengeance is mine," but he wants the Hebrews to follow his "ways," the ways of vengeance. Jewish genocide is practiced by murdering their enemies through four generations. These six cities were also numbered among the fifty-two Levite towns where the priests of the tribe of Levi were allotted property. Thus, the Levitical priests were given power over both the murderer and the "avenger." The Jews were some thoroughly wretched scoundrels, just as they are today.

Joshua 21 reflects the Jewish vice of gambling. Rolling the dice, or in this case casting the Urim and Thummim, was used to determine which towns were to be given to the Levites. These "holy people" couldn't figure it out for themselves and God certainly didn't want anything to do with them, so they let the "holy dice" tell them what to do.

Time and again, the priests claim that the Yahweh-god will fight for them to ensure that they are able to murder the Canaanites and steal their stuff, yet such tribes as Dan and the others failed to kill everybody. However, the lie is still perpetrated that

> "Yahweh gave the Israelites all the land he had sworn to give their fathers... and of all their enemies not one had managed to stand against them. Yahweh had given all their enemies into their hands. Of all the promises that Yahweh had made to the House of Israel, not one failed; all were fulfilled." (Joshua 21:43- 45.)

These lies are more proof that the Old Testament is the work of rabbis and not the dictations of a reliable and truthful God. This is Semitic *abracadabra*. They first write that they didn't kill everybody or steal their land and simultaneously claim that the lying Yahweh-god kept all of his promises. Telling lies in the face of facts, what could be more Jewish?

In both of the Semitic hoaxes of Judaism and Islam, this dualistic scam is explained by claiming that the word of God is whatever the rabbis and Imams say. Therefore, even when they say two opposite and conflicting statements, both statements are true, because they both come from God! Semites! The world's biggest clowns!

In Joshua 22, he sends the tribes of Reuben, Gad and Manasseh back to their captured territories with all the loot they had stolen.

> "You are going back to your tents with great wealth, with cattle in plenty, with silver and gold, bronze and iron and great quantities of clothing; share these spoils of your enemies with your brothers." (Joshua 22:8.)

It is in this phrase that the rabbis were able to set up the system of swindles upon which Judaism, the World's Oldest Organized Criminal Conspiracy, is based. It was not just the metallic bullion, but also the clothes stripped from dead bodies that the Hebrews were ordered to share with their fellow thieves. This became an enduring feature of Judaism into modern times. The swindling Jewish bankers and the thieving Jewish financiers gain protection from their Jewish Cult by sharing their spoils with the various Jewish philanthropic and religious organizations which, in turn, distribute the contributions among their members. In this way, Judaism is no different than any other criminal organization, such as the Mafia, the Yakuza or the Triads. Keeping crime as family operations, they all distribute the loot among the gangsters *and their families*. In return, silence, cooperation, and the protection of the gang are offered by the little thieves who are on the payroll of the big thieves who do the actual steal-

ing and killing. Judaism is a trickle-down crime system. It was built upon banditry. One of its driving forces and greatest secrets is its outer show of religion
surrounding and protecting an inner core of the secret treasury of monies and
other valuables looted from the non-Jews. If it has to be shown in accounting
or tax records, all of this vast wealth of other peoples is distributed throughout
the Jewish organizations as "philanthropy" and "donations" and "aid for the
poor." If it doesn't have to be on the books, then it is delivered to the rabbis
under the table. The rabbis then distribute it as loans and gifts to those "pious"
Jews who help to maintain the illusion of holiness.

Bankers always strive for a monopoly over all monies. So, the emphasis
of the moneylenders of Babylon that there is to be only one treasury (that is,
one place of worship) is again brought up in Joshua 22. The tribes of Reuben,
Gad and Manasseh built themselves a giant altar to barbecue goats for the
Yahweh-god. But this challenged the monopoly that the priests had claimed
for themselves. Against this encroachment upon the power of the priests, all
the Hebrews were rallied. "At this news, the whole community of the children
of Israel mustered at Shiloh, ready to march against them and make war on
them." (Joshua 22:12.) Like every criminal gang, enforcement of the gangster
code of conduct was the business of the entire gang. The Contract of Abraham's First National Bank and Pawn Shop held the entire community responsible for the actions of individual Jewish gang members. So, the priests of the
Tabernacle were going to send the Hebrews to war against those three tribes,
because the only place where barbecues were allowed and bullion could be
deposited was at the altar of the Yahweh-god in front of the Tabernacle, with
its attached Treasury known as the "Holy of Holies." But to save their lives,
these three tribes lied and claimed that they were only building a stone monu-
ment and not a goat-roasting barbecue. So, they were reprieved from being
wiped out by the other gangsters of the other tribes.

Joshua 23 lists some of the reasons why their god commanded the Jews
to be the world's biggest assholes. To make sure that the treasury remains safe,
the Temple must be made secure. To make sure that the Temple is secure, the
surrounding territory must be controlled. To make sure that the surrounding
territory is controlled, the Hebrews must be persuaded not to mingle with other
peoples. Gold and silver escape through intermarriage. Secrets escape through
both marriages and social gatherings. So, the Hebrews were forbidden to mingle with the people whom they had not yet murdered. If the people of the
world were allowed to mingle with the Jews, then the people of the world
would learn of the schemes, tricks, swindles, betrayals and genocides committed by the Jews upon the people of the world. So, of course, the scribes of the
moneylenders wanted to prevent that possibility.

> "Therefore stand firm to keep and fulfill all that is written in the
> Book of the Law of Moses, never turning aside from it to right
> or left, never mingling with the peoples who are still left beside

you. Do not utter the names of their gods, do not swear by them,
do not serve them and do not bow down before them."
(Joshua 23:6-7.)

Then, those hairy-faced, gibbering, scrofulous goat rustlers were flattered
in their great stinkiness to be told that the sleepy little Canaanite hamlets they
had butchered were really not tiny little towns, but actually "great nations."
The lying god of the Jews is honored with Jewish lies.

"Yahweh has driven out great and powerful nations before you,
and no one so far has been able to resist you. One man of you
could rout a thousand of them, because Yahweh your God himself fought for you as he had promised you." (Joshua 23:9-13.)

At Shechem, Joshua died – and none too soon. All the tribes gathered at
this central location. It is where Abraham had built an altar, where Jacob had
bought land, and where the idols of Mesopotamia were buried (Genesis 35:2-4).

Joshua 24 again uses the *abracadabra* of the Jewish *asl*. Even though not
a single one of those Hebrew bandits had ever seen any of the alleged Moses
fables, since all witnesses had died in the Sinai desert, Yahweh says through
the lying scribes, "You saw with your own eyes the things I did in Egypt"
(Joshua 24:7). All of the lies that the priests told, were supposed to have been
seen by these very Hebrews under Joshua *even though every single Hebrew
who had allegedly lived during the time of Moses was dead at the time of
Joshua*. Once again – Abracadabra! – one must stand in stupefied awe before
the incredible Semitic delusion that telling lies is actually the same as telling
the Truth.

Finally, to make it seem as if these Hebrews had had a long-term Contract for the ownership of the land, another swindle is employed. Resurrected
from several hundred years previously, even though the land had been subsequently abandoned for all of that time and no one knew where Joseph was allegedly buried, it is claimed that:

"The bones of Joseph, which the sons of Israel had brought
from Egypt, were buried at Shechem in the portion of ground
that Jacob had bought for a hundred pieces of money from the
sons of Hamor, the father of Shechem, which had become the
inheritance of the sons of Joseph." (Joshua 24:32.)

The Book of Joshua ends with these murdering thieves making the claim
that the abandoned property from 500 years previously was not abandoned
property and still belonged to the tribe of Joseph as an "inheritance," all based
upon the big Jewish *asl* and the ability to forge documents and tell lies.

8.2 The Mighty Jewish Heroes Known as "Judges" – And Every One a Scoundrel

What most Christians or any other kind of Bible student may be surprised to know is that the word "Judges," as used in the Book of Judges, means "a military officer." For tribes of Hebrew bandits, this was an apt title for the leader of gangs of outlaws whose god is titled "the Lord of Hosts," that is, "the Lord of Armies." This military officer was nothing more than a bandit chief with the title of "judge," in this case, a military officer who ordered about his own people based on the voices in his head telling him that it was the voice of God speaking to him. Raiders whose main interest was plunder would tend to write stories of their raids with their top heroes being the most successful and murderous of their gangs.

As a continuation of the Book of Joshua, the Book of Judges covers some details concerning the migration of the Danites and the war against the Benjamites for their so-called "crime." Remember, the so-called "Laws of Moses" have nothing to do with morality or justice, and everything to do with organized pillage and the protection of the Treasury. The Hebrew word for "judges" also means "governors." They are supposed to be divinely chosen. And this is the theme of the story of the six "major" judges: Othniel, Ehud, Deborah, Gideon, Jephthah and Samson.

The brainwashing propaganda continually repeated of relapsing-and-backward-sliding-Hebrews-saved-by-a-holy-judge, shows the editors of these stories were the Deuteronomic priests. Other "minor" judges are mentioned: Shamgar, Tola and Jair, Ibzan, Elon and Abdon. The Book of Judges, as a continuation of the Book of Joshua, indicates that it passed through several editions to suit the necessities of the times – more proof that these Jewish "holy books" are edited forgeries.

Internal chronological data indicate a period of 410 years for the rule of the Judges. This was at variance with 1 Kings 6:1 which allows 480 years between the Exodus and the building of Solomon's Temple. These numbers are even more out of sync with archeological evidence that puts Hebrew entry into Canaan at the end of the 13th Century and the reign of David (~1200-1000 BC). But the book's time line is obviously generalized, since time intervals are conveniently stated as multiples of 40, the average life span in those days. Also, overlapping histories are added together in a linear fashion. The Book of Judges covers about a century and a half, 1125 BC being its mid-point by the always unreliable *Hebrew Bible* reckoning.

The battles described in Judges involved all of the tribes fighting for their own territory. And when all were threatened in the days of Samuel, they fought as united goat rustlers. At that time, the "shrine of the ark" was allegedly located at Shiloh. The territory of Abraham's First National Bank and Pawn Shop was based in Jerusalem and situated in the territory of Judah. The tribe of Judah and the tribe of Simeon, which was based in Gezer, were both isolated from the other tribes. The tribe of Judah surrounded its citadel treasury city of

Jerusalem and *played no part in the battles*. The other Hebrews tribes did the fighting, while the priests of Judah guarded the gold and counted the profits – typical Jewish strategy throughout the ages.

Understand that the twelve judges were not "holy men" or "magistrates" as Christians and other gullible people have been led to believe. They were military leaders and local bandit chiefs. They were active between the alleged times of Joshua and the institution of the monarchy under Saul. They exercised their authority over one or another tribe but never over the entire twelve tribes of Hebrew goat rustlers. These variety of stories reflect the ragtag nature of the Hebrew bandits and not the noble nature that the lying rabbis try to give to the Hebrews. The all-powerful Yahweh-god who was supposed to fight for them and give the land of the Canaanites into their greedy hands is nowhere evident in the Book of Judges. Instead, these tiny bands of thieves are shown to be scruffy gangs fighting in isolated units. For the most part, they occupy the highlands and have no success against the Canaanite towns on the plain, nor do they massacre the tiny hamlets that they do manage to conquer, but only enslave them. This account is much closer to the archeological facts. But the part played by Judah has been subsequently magnified to bring out the religious significance of that one, particular tribe which has control of the treasury city of Jerusalem.

The Book of Judges takes place after the death of Joshua. The Hebrews tossed the holy dice (the Urim and Thummin) upon the ephod, with its twelve stones, to see which tribe should attack the Canaanites. The holy dice fell upon the stone representing the tribe of Judah.

So, the First Book of Judges opens with the Hebrews following what was the more likely scenario of their conquest of Canaan, that is, quaking in fear at the thought of fighting the Canaanites. In this case, the tribe of Judah and the tribe of Simeon joined forces to attack Adoni-Zedek, the King of Jerusalem. They captured him in battle and cut off his thumbs and big toes. The teaching here is that the Hebrews are to be the avengers for God. Whatever deeds are performed by their enemies, Hebrew vengeance demands them to commit the same woes in return. In this case, Adoni-Zedek says, "Seventy kings with their thumbs and big toes cut off used to pick up the crumbs under my table. As I did to others, so God does to me." (Judges 1:7.) He was taken back to Jerusalem where he died. Because the Jews take these stories as the "word of God and therefore eternally true," they have practiced such barbarity throughout their entire evil existence, the French Revolution and the Bolshevik Revolution being prime modern examples of their demonic sadism (see Volume III).

Once again, endemic incest (even though it was against their own Laws of Moses) was practiced by the Jewish goat rustlers. As a reward for capturing a town, Judge Caleb gave his daughter as a wife to his younger brother (Judges 1:13), so he could claim an additional share of the loot. Such is the "great wisdom" of the Jews. But the Canaanites were not easy to conquer. No matter how powerful a god the Hebrews claimed that their Yahweh-god was, the Canaanites of Gaza, Ashkelon and Ekron with their surrounding territories along the coast were unconquerable "because they had iron chariots" (Judges 1:19). So, the iron chariots were more powerful than the Yahweh-god. But that didn't matter to the lying priests of Judah who wrote: "Yahweh was with Judah, and Judah subdued the highlands" (Judges 1:19). That is, these goat rustlers were able to capture the less desirable territory in the hills where the unfortified villages and hamlets were easy prey. Once conquered, these tiny villages were named among the "mighty nations" that the Hebrews and their Yahweh-god had defeated.

Judges 1:22-26 once again shows how the Hebrews could capture territory by inducing the inhabitants to commit treason. They captured a citizen of the city of Bethel and promised to spare his life if he showed them how to enter the city and capture it.

The tribe of Manasseh also failed to conquer the towns of Beth-Shean, Taanach, Dor, Ibleam, or Megiddo and their surrounding villages. Once again, the Yahweh-god was not strong enough to lead them to victory. But the lesson that the rabbis were teaching in this tale was that "when the Israelites became stronger, they subjected the Canaanites to forced labor, though they did not drive them out." (Judges 1:28.) This is another tactic of the modern Jews. If they are not able to murder the people among whom they live, then they conspire to reduce them to menial labor and slavery. This is often accomplished through the importation of cheap foreign labor and through the debasing of the currency through banking frauds, as is being done to modern Europe and America.

Even though the rabbis claimed that their mighty Yahweh-god would guarantee their victory, the tribe of Ephraim did not defeat the Canaanites in Gezer, a town situated on the Jerusalem-Jaffa road which dominated the Philistine plain. The tribes of Zebulun also did not drive out the Canaanites of Kitron or of Nahalol. The tribe of Asher also did not drive out the Phoenicians from Acco, Sidon, Ahlab, Achzib, Aphik or Rehob. So, the Asherites settled down among them. These Phoenicians were, after all, from the same Hyksos confederation as were the Hebrews. So, when the tribe of Asher settled down on the Canaanite lands, they sold their grain to the large Phoenician cities mentioned above. Neither did the tribe of Naphtali drive out the inhabitants of Beth-Shemesh or Beth-Anath, but as they settled among the latter and became stronger through their extra-large Hebrew families, they eventually compelled them to do forced labor.

Despite being backed up by the great, lying god of the Hebrews, the tribe of Dan was chased up into the highlands by the Amorites, who wouldn't let them enter the best farmland in the plains. But as the Hebrews outbred the Amorites with ten- and twelve-child families and the oppression of the Hebrews grew heavier, the Amorites were also subjected to forced labor (Judges 1:35). Again, the Jewish Operating Manual teaches that if the Jews cannot conquer a people, then they outbreed and enslave them.

Thus, the rabbis teach that even though their god was not powerful enough to keep his "promises" and give the Jews the land of Canaan through force, warfare and murder, if the Jews were at least allowed to live among the inhabitants, then they could eventually scheme and subvert them into slavery. But it wasn't merely through higher birthrates that the Hebrews enslaved the Canaanites. What the evil scribes of Abraham's First National Bank and Pawn Shop concealed, was the special power of the treasury that remained filled because of the Sumerian Swindle. They enslaved the Canaanites through interest-bearing loans, just as the moneylenders had swindled and enslaved the people of Assyria and Babylonia – and Europe and the USA today. "Just as it has always been" does not mean "just as it must always be." History teaches not just ancient evils, but gives insight into how to cure them. A cure is always a final solution.

Even though the Yahweh-god makes promises through his priesthood of swindlers and pimps, he is, after all, the sock puppet of the moneylenders of Abraham's First National Bank and Pawn Shop. The Babylonian merchant-moneylenders purloined a Canaanite god and remade it in their own image. When the Yahweh-god makes a promise, he can renege on it at any time like a banker calling in a loan before it is due. Like a banker who sucks the wealth out of the People with the Sumerian Swindle, the blame is not placed upon his frauds, but is placed upon the victims of his frauds. The usual reason that the tricky rabbis gave for their god reneging on his "promises" is that the Hebrews broke the terms of the Contract. One of the Yahweh-god's escape clauses of the Contract is that *if even one Hebrew* breaks even *a single* "law," then all promises are null and void. One sinning Hebrew is counted the same as if all the Hebrews broke all of the laws. This group guilt kept the Hebrews spying on each other. It allowed great leeway for the priests of the Yahweh-god to be either strict or merciful in meting out punishments. If a Hebrew asked, "Why did Yahweh let us lose the battle?" The priest (licking the barbecue sauce off of his lips) could say, "Because there is sin in Israel. Find some Hebrew who broke a law and stone him to death, then bring some goats and bulls for another barbecue on the altar so that Yahweh will be appeased."

Or if a Hebrew asked, "I saw so-and-so break a law last week, but Yahweh still let us win the battle. Why is this?" The priest (picking his teeth and belching) could reply, "because Yahweh is merciful and overlooks the sins of his Chosen Ones. So, bring some goats and bulls to the barbecue on the altar and throw in a jug of red wine and some fresh baked garlic bread and butter as a thanks offering and appeasement for sin."

Even though Joshua was written 900 years after the Hyksos became Hebrews, in Joshua 23:5 it brags:

> "Yahweh your God will himself drive them out before you; he
> will cast them out before you and you will take possession of
> their country as Yahweh your God promised you."

And in Joshua 23:9-10 it further crows:

"Yahweh has driven out great and powerful nations before you, and no one so far has been able to resist you. One man of you could rout a thousand of them, because Yahweh your God himself fought for you as he had promised you."

But here is the problem with all of the promises made by the priests of Abraham's Banking Guild. No matter how powerful their god was supposed to be, and no matter how puny and weak the so-called "mighty nations" of Canaanite farmers and Amorite shepherds were, *the Hebrews could not defeat them as promised.* The "promises" were all proved to be lies from a god of lies and broken promises; an appropriate god for these tribes of lying bankers and thieving goat molesters.

But not to worry, the priests who wrote the Book of Judges had a handy excuse. This excuse was delivered by none other than an actual, real, genuine, celestial *angel* who traveled from Gilgal to Bethal on foot and donkeyback to deliver the message to all of the thieves of the House of Israel, the entire gang. It says so right here in this holy book of the Jews, so it must be true! The message was

"I shall never break my covenant with you. You for your part must make no covenant with the inhabitants of this country; you must destroy their altars. But you have not obeyed my orders. What is it that you have done? Very well, I now say this: I am not going to drive out these nations before you. They shall become your oppressors, and their gods shall be a snare for you." (Judges 2:1-3.)

In other words, through the voices in the priest's head, Yahweh promised to fight for the Hebrews and drive out the Canaanites. The voices heard by the Hebrew priests said, "This is God talking to you. Yes, you are really hearing this. I will fight for you and you will conquer tiny villages in my name and call yourselves mighty."

But the Canaanite priests had their own gods and were listening to their own voices in their own heads, and their own gods were telling them that "Those Jews are a phony bunch of deceivers and frauds. Go kick their asses." So, the Jews were driven back into the hills.

First, the lying Yahweh-god broke his promise to fight for them. So, they didn't win the battles. Then, because the Hebrews could not defeat all of the Canaanites, they could not destroy their altars. And because they could not destroy the altars, the Yahweh-god had an excuse for breaking his promise to destroy the Canaanites for them. This kind of fallacious and dishonest Semitic thinking is endemic of Judaism, the world's biggest lie. But the lie is greatly improved by the rabbis who claim – Abracadabra! – "We are a holy people who worship the Most High and Most Powerful God of the Universe. Trust us."

As punishment for their waywardness, Yahweh sent bandits to steal what the Hebrews had stolen. The Hebrews were kicked about and beat up by these stronger Amorite thieves. Then, Yahweh appointed military leaders who went by the misnomer of "judges," to guide them in defeating their "oppressors." Even in modern times, anyone who refuses to become deceived or swindled by the Jews, is called an oppressor. "Oy Vey! We are not allowed to swindle or murder anybody. I feel so oppressed by these goyim!" There had to be an excuse for why the mighty and terrible Yahweh-god didn't keep his promise of giving the Hebrew cutthroats all of Canaan.

There had to be an excuse as to why each mangy goat rustler proved to be so puny after Joshua had declared, "One man of you could route a thousand of them" (Joshua 23:10). There had to be an excuse for why the lying god of the Jews didn't keep the promise that had thundered out of the mouths of the priests, "The enemies that rise against you Yahweh will conquer for your sake; they will come at you by one way and flee before you by seven." (Deuteronomy 28:7) Now it was the Hebrews who were running away in seven directions from the Canaanites, unable to murder and steal and rape as they so much desired. So, there had to be an excuse as to why the "promises" were not being kept by the lying god of the Hebrew priests.

Ever handy with a quick excuse and a convenient lie, the rabbis and priests of Yahweh said that *because of the sins of the Hebrews*, because some single one among them who had secretly broken a Mosaic Law unbeknownst to anyone else, they all must suffer at the hands of their enemies. This excuse was convenient and could be whipped out at a moment's notice. Of course, no one was willing to admit to a transgression, since all of the Hebrews would then turn on him and stone him to death. But after every Hebrew had been turned into a religious policeman and snitch, making sure that everyone else followed the ridiculous laws of the Moneylenders of Babylon and their boy, Moses, this excuse lost its edge. The Hebrews were cringing and cowering before the altar of Yahweh and following all of the rules. But Yahweh ignored their begging for more loot and virgin girls. What was the problem?

Therefore, the rabbis and priests used a different excuse. The new purpose now was that the Yahweh-god had allowed Israel's enemies to survive in order to train the Hebrews in warfare – to train them to be better killers. Killing people and stealing their stuff was a long tradition among the Hyksos-Hebrews and all of their goat-stealing Semitic relatives. But now their only reason for being Hebrews, according to their lying god, was to become more efficient warmongers, subverters, deceivers and killers. This was welcome news for the Jews.

Yahweh lied about keeping his promise, because he wanted to test their fidelity by putting them into contact with the indigenous pagans. Of course, Yahweh cherishes his Chosen Ones, so He didn't want them to murder all of the Canaanites all at once. Otherwise, the vacant country would be overrun with wild animals and that is so much worse than it being occupied by Canaanites. Also, because Yahweh had a merciful patience buried somewhere beneath his loathsomeness, He allowed the native peoples time to repent before the

Hebrews exterminated them. Ah, the merciful god of the Jews! A hater of Mankind, a destroyer of nations, a breaker of his most sincere promises, a banker from Babylon.

So, Judges 3 lists the many excuses for the Yahweh-god breaking his promise, like a banker calling in his loans. The Yahweh-god wanted to leave some Canaanites as perpetual targets for practicing warfare and maliciousness upon: "… to use them to test all those in Israel who had never known war in Canaan" (Judges 3:1). "The five chiefs of the Philistines, all the Canaanites, the Sidonians, and the Hittites" only existed "to put Israel to the test and see if they would keep the orders that Yahweh had given their fathers through Moses" (Judges 3:3-4). That is, if they would follow Moses' Contract and Manual of Operations for swindling all wealth and betraying all people of the entire world. So, Yahweh in his love of criminal Jews, preserved some Canaanites and Philistines, so the Jews would have someone to practice murdering.

Of course, the Hebrews failed the test, since they really weren't the holy people that the lying priests of Yahweh claimed they were. They were just ordinary Hebrew goat-thieves who did not have the same enthusiasm for owning the world and enslaving the people on it as did the Babylonian directors of Abraham's First National Bank and Pawn Shop. These Hebrews married into the families of the Canaanites. "They forgot Yahweh their God and served the Baals and Asherahs." (Judges 3:7) As a punishment, the Hebrew bandits were suppressed and enslaved for eight years by the king of Edom, who got tired of being raided by the Hebrew thieves and so rounded them up.

Finally, one of the bandits named Othniel, son of Kenaz, started gibbering and freaking out, because "the spirit of Yahweh came on him; he became a judge of Israel and set out to fight." (Judges 3:10.) Again, these "judges" were not real judges in the modern sense. They were merely sociopathic gang leaders.

Othniel led his gang of Hebrews and killed the King of Edom. Then, the Hebrews stayed out of trouble for 40 more years until they began "sinning" once again. Remember, the rabbinical definition of "sin" simply means not following the Law of Moses. So, the Ammonites and Amalekites (whom the Hebrews supposedly had already exterminated under Joshua) miraculously came back to life and conquered and enslaved Israel for 18 years (Judges 3:14). It is one of the talents of the Jews to invent new oppressors when they run out of real ones. Because they are a "holy people," the Jews require a scapegoat and an excuse, so that when they murder somebody and steal his property, they have the "moral right" to do so. This is why they need to label anyone who opposes their voracious greed as an "oppressor." Murder and theft require an excuse. So, by smearing others as "oppressors," the Jews demonize their victims and murder them with dancing and joy because they are so "righteous."

As proof that he was fit to be a judge of the Hebrew cutthroats, Ehud assassinated the King of Moab using stealth and trickery. This overwhelmingly and enormously qualified him to be one of the "judges" of the Jews.

After Ehud, Shamgar became a judge. Shamgar was another mighty warrior of the goat rustlers who "routed six hundred of the Philistines with an ox-goad." Wow! Those Hebrews were almost like Supermen, to hear the rabbis tell the stories! Imagine! A world inhabited by flea-bitten, diabolical thieves and murderers with the prestige of kings and the power of gods! All guaranteed in mightiness and valor on the pages of a book that they themselves wrote on stinking goatskins, while laughing about the incredible lies that they told each other around a campfire of burning goat dung! So, here we have another super-Jew named Judge Shamgar chasing away six hundred of the toughest and most heavily armed, steel-sword and spear wielding fighters in Palestine with nothing more than an ox goad. Wow! The Jews are incredible – to hear them tell it. And if you don't believe that story, then the priests of Yahweh will stone you to death or pour molten lead down your throat. "Believe it or be murdered." The Devil's Truth tended to keep the Hebrews loyal to the stories of the priests of Yahweh.

More blood is spilled in Judges 4. The judge is Deborah, a bandit queen who channels the Yahweh-god through her wrap-around, wide Jewish mouth. This time, 10,000 Hebrews attack the 900 chariots of Jabin, a Canaanite, and wipe them out. When Sisera, the Canaanite general, flees on foot to the tent of the Jewish woman, Jael, the wife of Heber the Kenite, she hides him under a rug and then, when he falls asleep from exhaustion, she drives a tent peg through his head with a mallet. These are the heroes and heroines of the Jews! Such wonderful and holy people, those Jews! Even the Jewish women are deceivers and killers. After that, the Jews were able to "utterly destroy" King Jabin and all of his Canaanites – another genocide celebrated in the "holy books" of the Jews!

Judges 5 is known as the Song of Deborah. This song glorifies the wars of genocide against the Canaanites and praises Jael for murdering Sisera with a mallet and tent peg. Female Hebrews took an active role in the destruction of other peoples. This was to become a tradition among the goat rustlers of Judah in later centuries, when Jewish women were at the forefront of the genocides of abortion, women's liberation, feminism, birth control and the "family planning" of other people, that is, Jewish family planning for the extinction of other people. Such holy Jews! Just ask them! Genocide has a solid foundation in the teachings of the Jewish Training Manual of Criminality and Sociopathy, the *Hebrew Bible*.

One item of note in the Song of Deborah is the phrase, "Why is Dan in the ships of strangers?" (Judges 5:17.) This indicates that the tribe of Dan had hired themselves out to their fellow Hyksos, the Phoenicians. See Volume I, *The Sumerian Swindle*, for the history of the Hebrew-Hyksos who became the Phoenicians. The Phoenicians and the Israelians were close business partners, something that the avaricious priests of Judah envied. And what a Jew envies, he also hates.

In Judges 6, this "great and powerful horde of Hebrews" didn't sweep away everyone in their path like their Yahweh-god had promised them through the lying mouths of the rabbis and priests. Nor were their cousins, the Amo-rites and their relatives from Midian, fooled by the incredible fables about the Yahweh-god because these people also worshiped Yahweh along with his goddess wife, Asherah.

After the Hebrews had settled down to farming the stolen land, the Midi-anites and Amalekites "would march up against Israel and encamp on their territory and destroy the produce of the country as far as Gaza." (Judges 6:4.) The Edomites of the deserts east of the Jordan River robbed the Hebrews in turn. Of course, the priests blamed it all on Yahweh, who was displeased that the Hebrews were sacrificing such tasty mutton and goats to the local gods instead of paying their tithes of barbecued goat and shekels of silver to the priests of Yahweh.

Judges 6 tells of another warrior-judge named Gideon, who hears voices in his head and sees an apparition. Fired up in his imagination that an angel had spoken to him, he tears down the altar of *Baal* and builds an altar to *Yah-weh*. Since Gideon didn't have the holy dice (the Urim and Thummin) to in-quire of God and since he was still unconvinced by the apparition before his eyes, he looked for a sign from his god that he was really not insane after all. When a fleece got covered with dew, that was the sign he had been waiting for. Yes! Dew on a sheep's fleece! That must mean something! It was a sign for this Hebrew to get all fired up with the urge to commit murder and mayhem upon the Midianites. He sent word to some of the other Hebrew tribes that he was seeing something and hearing voices. But lacking any genuine knowledge of God, that was proof enough for the Hebrews. So Gideon gathered a heroic army of fellow Jews armed with bronze swords and slings and pitchforks – all of them determined to be the holiest Jews they could be by killing someone and stealing his property.

Judges 7 has the Yahweh-god telling Gideon to reduce the number in his army, so that Yahweh would get the credit for the upcoming victory and not the tribes of Israel. The Yahweh-god had lied to them before, but now He wanted to prove what a powerful and dependable god he really was. To be a complete god of the Jews, he also wanted to be the God of Liars *and* Hypo-crites as well. All of the Hebrews who were afraid were sent home, thus estab-lishing the precedence for Jewish cowardice ever since that time. "Twenty-two thousand men went home, and the thousand were left." (Judges 7:3.) The re-mainder were sent to the waterside to drink. Only the Hebrews who drank like dogs, lapping the water with their tongues, were the ones Gideon chose for his attack. These numbered three hundred. All of the ones who drank like men by cupping the water in their hands, he sent home. Gideon attacked at night and routed the Midianites, cutting off the heads of their chieftains, so the story goes.

More of the priestly propaganda continues in Judges 8. Gideon and his 300 dog-like goat rustlers are claimed to have fought against and destroyed 120,000 Midian soldiers. When he asks the vanquished kings what the He-brews of the town of Tabor looked like, they replied, "Every one of them car-ried himself like the son of a king." (Judges 8:18.) This would certainly give the Hebrew cutthroats a surge of pride when the rabbis read to them such a lie, for it was a major goal of the scribes of the Babylonian Bankers' Guild to infuse a sense of pride within their treasury guards. Pride bolsters morale and both pride and morale are potent, valuable weapons against defeat. Also, neither pride nor morale costs anything. So, it doesn't subtract from operating expenses.

Also in Judges 8, the idea is again explained that the Yahweh-god is the leader of Israel and not its warriors or kings. When the victorious Gideon in offered the kingship of Shechem, according to the scribes of Babylon, he replies, "It is not I who shall rule over you, nor my son; Yahweh must be your lord." (Judges 8:23.) But he asks the Hebrews for a gold ring from each of their spoils. With these rings, totaling in weight 1,700 shekels of gold (~440 Troy ounces or 31 pounds), he made an ephod so that he could know the will of the Yahweh-god by throwing upon it the holy dice. When the priest wasn't throwing dice on the ephod, then he was wearing it as part of his uniform – all 31 pounds of solid gold – strapped to his chest. Such a holy Jew!

The Hebrews were supposed to be different from the other people of the ancient Near East. So, trying to know the will of the god by cutting open a sheep and inspecting its liver was a method of divination prohibited to them, since all of the other religions of the ancient Near East did this. This is why their priests used holy dice instead. By asking questions to the Yahweh-god and then throwing the holy dice on the holy dice table – the ephod – whatever numbers came up was their answer, yes or no. As the dice fell against the holy gemstones representing the twelve tribes, more specific answers could be prognosticated. It was the Jewish religion at its most scientifically advanced!

But this 31-pound, solid gold dice table worn on the priest's chest, became a center of worship for the Hebrews who worshiped gold in any form. Praying to all of that holy gold was just too much temptation for any Jews to resist. They fell down before it in adoration. "All Israel prostrated themselves to it" (Judges 8:27), just as they do to this very day.

As an indication of how promiscuous the circumcised goat rustlers of Canaan were, it is bragged about in Judges 8 that Gideon had *70 sons* from his many wives. This was not counting the number of his daughters, which would have been about equal. So, with these kinds of population increases, while the surrounding people used the natural birth control of nursing their babies for two to three years before having another child, it is easy to see how the Hebrews could outbreed other people. Even the poorest of the Hebrews could practice polygamy, since there were enough grasslands to support large herds of sheep and goats for a food supply along with whatever grain they could grow or trade for goats. And for housing, letting the family live in goat-hair tents was all that they needed.

The Hebrew ideal of increasing the number of their descendants "like the sands of the sea," had its military advantages. Abraham's Banking Guild needed guards and soldiers to protect the treasury. Treasury guards could not be hired into such a position of trust from among the strangers or foreigners. So, they had to be born and bred to the task from among the Hebrews.

After Gideon died, the Hebrews naturally wanted something more than worshiping a golden dice table. So, they moved up to worshiping the gods of the Canaanites, the Baal god, Baal-Berith. Now, "Baal-Berith" means "God of the Covenant" or "God of the Contract," So, they remembered that there was some sort of Contract, because they had circumcised their penises as a memory aid. Every time a Hebrew urinated, looking down at his circumcised nub, he was reminded of his god, the true god of the Jew dangling between his legs. The trouble was that those Hebrew geniuses couldn't remember which god their circumcised penises honored. So, they worshiped the Canaanite "God of the Covenant."

Gideon was succeeded as judge by Abimelech. Judges 9 tells of Abimelech becoming military dictator of not only the Israelites, but of the Canaanites as well. Gideon was a normal sex-crazed example of Jewish promiscuity, normal because Abimelech was one of *seventy-one* brothers, not counting sisters, born to his father, Jerubbaal. The Jews multiplied like fleas. They couldn't remember who their god was when they looked at their circumcised dongle, but they certainly remembered to "Go forth and multiply."

Abimelech is another example of the "high moral character" and the "holiness" of the Chosen Ones of God that is so common among both the ancient Hebrews and the modern Jews. Abimelech, another hero of the Jews, murdered all but one of his seventy brothers. The youngest, Jotham, escaped and cursed Abimelech and any who helped him. Cursing was standard black magic among the Semites. Judges 9 is merely a story about the heroic Jewish cutthroats under Abimelech murdering thousands of people, slaughtering them in the fields and burning them alive in their hiding places. And what does all of this have to do with anything "holy"? Only Jews and devils consider such things as holy.

Judges 10 lists some of the lesser judges; mere clan leaders at the head of small bands of bandits. Some were evil leaders like Abimelech, and some were good leaders like Gideon. But absolutely none of them were special in any religious sense. This is one of the overriding features of Judaism, taking what is actually nothing at all and then proclaiming it to be "holy" or "godly." Judaism is a religion of sham and deception, fit for Semitic goat rustlers, thieves and bankers.

Once again, the goat rustlers proclaimed one of their "virtues." As a mark of their circumcised promiscuity, Judges 10 states that the judge, Jair of Gilead, "had thirty sons who rode on thirty donkeys' colts; and they possessed thirty towns." (Judges 10:4.) Remember, the Hebrews only counted the men; how many daughters they had from their many wives is unknown, but probably of equal number. That judge Jair had so many children and controlled so many towns was a Hebrew mark of distinction. Wealth stands greater in the eyes of a Jew than anything counted as a virtue.

The mark of distinction that the priests of Abraham's Bankers Guild demanded, was unswerving loyalty to the Contract. So, when the scribes of Babylonia rewrote the scraps of Hebrew history, whenever convenient they inserted the repetition of a theme of "breaking-away-and-returning." That is, the theme of Hebrews worshiping other gods, suffering for it, and then returning to the Yahweh-god of the moneylenders. It was not difficult to find the Hebrews worshiping a variety of gods, since it was a standard custom of all religions throughout the ancient Near East to worship local gods. But the merchant-moneylender scribes used this as a reason for inserting into the Hebrew histor-ical novels their propaganda of "falling away from and returning to the god of your fathers," you remember, the Canaanite god that they stole.

Judges 11 is another bandit tale that becomes even more Jewish. This time, the son of a prostitute is the hero of the Jews. Jephthah was a vagabond. The story claims that Gilead was his father. Since Gilead is a geographic re-gion, this is merely saying that he was a country boy who didn't know who his father was, since his mother was a whore. These are the kinds of heroes that the Jews admire – murderers, bandits, and whores. The stuff of legend! Like all Jews, Jephthah came from a variety of mixed stock. He was oppressed by the other Jews, because his mother didn't know who his father was. So, the other Hebrews drove him out, saying, "You are to have no share in our fathers' inheritance, because you are the son of an alien woman." (Judges 11:2.) So, not only was Jephthah a bastard, but his mother wasn't even counted as being among the Hebrews, since they knew that his father was a Hebrew, but his mother was an alien whore. These are the kinds of things that make reading the *Old Testament* so morally uplifting, knowing that the Holy Chosen Ones of God have such illustrious antecedents.

So, Jephthah ran off and became a bandit. Since the Hebrews themselves were all bandits, he must have been a particularly violent scoundrel since the scribes wrote, "Worthless followers gathered round him and used to go raiding with him." (Judges 11:3.) Because Jephthah was a bandit with his own gang of scoundrels, when the Ammonites tried to get back the land that the Hebrews had stolen, the elders of Gilead offered Jephthah the leadership of Israel if he would fight the Ammonites. Jephthah accepted the offer and vowed a human sacrifice to the Yahweh-god for victory (Judges 11:29-40). This sacrificial victim was Jephthah's only daughter, whom he offered up as a "holocaust," cutting her throat, pouring out her blood around the altar of Yahweh, splashing her blood on the priests, cutting out her fat and offering it up as a burnt "sweet savor" to the Yahweh-god, then burning her body into ashes and dumping them outside the town. Isn't this what the entire so-called "religion" of Juda-ism is based upon? Isn't this the *asl* upon which all Jews claim a special bless-ing from their demon-god, *Yahweh*, simply because Abraham refrained from sacrificing Isaac? The Jews are such frauds!

Before he butchered his daughter, Jephthah gave her two months' re-prieve. Was this to prepare herself for sacrifice by praying to God and purify-ing herself for the butcher's block on the blood-drenched altar of Yahweh? No, of course not! These Jews didn't think like that. Sex is what the holy, circum-cised dongs of the Hebrews demand. Sex is what the thoroughly scrubbed and hosed-down holy vulvas of the Jewesses demand. Sex and more sex, so that they can multiply like the sands of the sea – that is the overriding desire of the Jewesses. God is in a distant second place. This young Jewish princess who had never gotten laid, went into the hills and for two months moaned and cried like a good Jewess – not about her impending sacrifice and death – but whining over the fact that she had never been screwed so as to breed more Jews. (Judges 11:36-40) "Oy! A true Jewish princess! As holy as they get!" Such a heroine for Jewish princesses everywhere!

Yes, Folks, these are the real heroes of the Jews – bandits, liars, slavers, con artists, murderers, thieves, bastard sons of prostitutes, sex fiends and practitioners of human sacrifice. And they brag about it in what they call their *Hebrew Bible*, teaching the world a "higher moral value." There is nothing holy about it. All of those ancient monsters are identical to the modern Jews, because the modern Jews "inherit" the *asl* of Abraham and Moses; and all of the modern Jews claim that "We were there, too, and we saw it with our very own eyes." And worst of all, the modern Jews "walk in the ways of their god," a god who hates all of Mankind and demands that his Holy Chosen Demons be just like him in bringing impoverishment and death to Mankind. Are you beginning to understand the smirking Jews, now?

Judges 12 tells of the Hebrew tribes of Ephraim arguing with Jephthah's bandits in Gilead. Ephraim had refused to join forces with Jephthah and fight the Ammonites. But once the fighting was over, true to their grasping and greedy Hebrew character, they were angry that they didn't get any of the loot. So, they threatened to burn down Jephthah's house with him inside.

The Ephraimites were also outraged that Jephthah's band of vagabonds and bandits was composed of scoundrels from both the tribes of Ephraim and Manasseh operating in the land of Gilead. So, Jephthah's gang of cutthroats waylayed the Ephraimites at the ford of the Jordan River. Since all of the holy chosen Hebrews looked alike with shaggy beards, stinky wool robes, sandals and those special Hebrew sidelocks of hair twisting down both sides of their heads, surrounded by clouds of buzzing flies, how could Jephthah's gang separate the Ephraimites from the other Hebrews? They solved this problem by making anyone who wanted to cross the river say the word, "Shibboleth." Those who pronounced it with an Ephraim accent were murdered on the spot. According to the scribes, in this way 42,000 Ephraim Hebrews were killed by Jephthah's band of gangsters. And like so many of the lies of the rabbis and Jews, simple arithmetic can prove their deceit.

Figure it out for yourself. Add the time it takes to ask yourself the question, "Say the word "shibboleth"? Then add the time it takes to answer that command. Add the time it takes to kill the Ephraimite with a sword and pull his body out of the way for the next victim. Of course, all of this has to be done out of sight and out of hearing of the other 41,999 Ephraimites who would not be standing in line peacefully, armed as they were watching their fellows being cut down one at a time. So, they would have to be kept at a distance. Add the time that it would take for each person to approach the ford and be asked the question. Then, the time to haul his body out of sight, so the next victim wouldn't be panicked. Then, multiply all of this by 42,000 and you can begin to see the impossibility of the numbers. Even if the whole process only took five minutes, then it would take 145 days to kill all 42,000 Ephraimites, working 24 hours per day. And not only would five minutes not be long enough, but the work days in ancient times did not extend into the night hours and even a lying, murdering Hebrew didn't usually kill anybody on a Saturday Sabbath. Even simple arithmetic proves what liars the Jews are. Even simple arithmetic can also prove the impossibility of the Nazi gas-chambers-and-ovens lie from a people who think so enormously of themselves that they – Abracadabra! – believe whatever lies they tell should be accepted as truth since they are holy Jews telling holy lies. The other Semites who tell lies are the Muslims.

After Jephthah died, the next "judge," or bandit chief was Ibzan. He had thirty sons and thirty daughters from his many wives. The scribes noted that instead of practicing the usual incest, "He gave his daughters in marriage outside the clan, and brought in thirty brides from outside for his sons." (Judges 12:9) He must of gotten tired of all of his grandchildren being born as hunchbacks, midgets and retards. So, he brought new blood into the clan by trying to be normal, not an easy thing for a Jew.

Then Elon was the top bandit chief. After him came Abdon who "had forty sons and thirty grandsons who rode on seventy donkey colts." (Judges 12:14.) These many children were the reason the Hebrews outbred the other peoples of the ancient Near East. That circumcised penis of theirs kept them constantly screwing their wives and concubines and slave girls. And when women weren't available, the Semitic propensity for abusing themselves became a favorite hobby. Every Jew was a "wanker," just as they are today. The circumcised penis is the cause not only of the Hebrew promiscuity, but of modern-day perversions like homosexuality, which the Jews of today promote as "normal," only because perverts are normal among the Jews. What is normal for a pervert or for a Jew is certainly not normal for the rest of Mankind.

This blending of the Hebrew tribes into a single entity called "Israel" is one of the tricks of the rabbis and one of the snares of the Christians and other biblical students. It is a trick of the rabbis and priests, because it attempts to claim that these scattered tribes of sheep thieves were a single, criminal gang. There were no "Israelites" other than the fraud conceived of by the scribes of Abraham's First National Bank and Pawn Shop. There were only scattered tribes that the priests claimed were all one big gang.

As the scribes of Abraham's First National Bank and Pawn Shop wrote, "Again the Israelites began to do what displeased Yahweh. And Yahweh delivered them into the hands of the Philistines for forty years." (Judges 13:1.) But the Philistines (the Sea Peoples) never controlled the entire territory of Canaan and could not possibly have been able to oppress all of the Hebrew tribes, because they restricted their operations to the Mediterranean coastal plains. Be that as it may, this chapter of Judges tells of a Hebrew 'Superman' named Samson, who had super-strength for fighting the enemies of the Israelians. He was born into the tribe of Dan and he never cut his hair or drank any kind of alcohol, nor did he smoke pot or eat opium. Samson was a long-haired super-Jew. He wasn't very smart, but he was very strong – according to the tales that the rabbis told.

More fables of the Hebrew cutthroats, glorifying swindles and murder, are found in Judges 14, in the story of Samson and his Philistine wife. Of course, the blue-eyed and fair Philistine (Greek Caucasian) women were very attractive to the kinky-black-haired and turd-colored Hebrew goat thieves. The Philistines (after whom the country of Palestine is named) were the Sea Peoples who had come from the Black Sea region and from the Greek Isles. They were fair-complected, heroically statured, intelligent, beautifully proportioned, unbeatable warriors, workers in iron and wealthy from trade. So, of course, the rubbery-lipped, buzzard-beaked, kinky-haired, stinking, inbred Jews hated them.

Samson saw a White woman that he liked and wanted to marry. This story claims that the Yahweh-god had made Samson such a strong Super-Jew, that he tore a lion apart with his bare hands. Later, as he walked past the carcass, he saw that honeybees had made a hive inside the dead lion. Using this as the basis for an impossible riddle, Samson bet thirty of his new wife's relatives that they couldn't guess his riddle.

The riddle was impossible for anyone to guess, which is why Samson, being the crafty Hebrew that he was, tried to swindle his new relatives out of their wealth with this scam. This is one of the traditional swindling methods of the Jews, to make bets that only they can win. Samson bet the thirty relatives that if they could guess the riddle within the seven days of the wedding celebrations, he would give them each a piece of fine linen and a festal robe. But if they couldn't guess the riddle that they must give him thirty pieces of fine linen and thirty festal robes. So, like any fool who has any dealings with a Jew without knowing all of the rules, they bet first and asked for the riddle second.

> "Out of the eater came what is eaten,
> Out of the strong came what is sweet." (Judges 14:18.)

Since the riddle was impossible to guess and they were stumped, the Philistines had the new bride wheedle the answer out of Samson.

> "What is sweeter than honey,
> And what stronger than a lion?"

In this way, they answered the riddle. But the story has several points of interest to the Jews. Although the Law of Moses forbade intermarriage outside of the Hebrew tribes, Samson broke that law for no other reason than because he wanted to. As a result, a secret that only a Jew knew was told to a Gentile wife. She told the secret to her Gentile relatives which caused a Jew to lose a bet. Losing the bet, because of his Gentile wife, Samson owed his new relatives thirty festal robes and thirty pieces of fine linen. But did he pay the debt like an honorable man? No, he paid the debt like a thieving, cutthroat Jew.

Even though his new wife had told his Hebrew secret to his new relatives, isn't the honorable thing to pay the debt with good nature to his grinning relatives? After all, they were all related by marriage. Samson had slept with his new wife and had partied with his new relatives. He had tried to swindle them with an impossible riddle that only he could solve. And they, in turn, had used subterfuge to find the answer to the riddle. So, in joining in the spirit of merriment at the wedding, he should have paid the debt like an honorable man and joined in the camaraderie with his new relatives.

But Samson was not an honorable man; he was a Jew. Stealing other people's property and murdering them is a Jewish tradition. So, Samson did what the Jewish "Chosen Ones of God" do in the full spirit of their religion – by losing money, he went nuts.

> "Then the spirit of Yahweh seized on him. He went down to Ashkelon, killed thirty men there, took what they wore and gave the festal robes to those who had answered the riddle, then burning with rage returned to his father's house. Then Samson's wife was given to the companion who had been his best man." (Judges 14:19-20.)

In other words, instead of buying thirty fine pieces of linen and thirty new festal robes as he had promised, he went out and murdered thirty innocent men, stole their clothes and gave these used and bloodied and stinky garments to his relatives. No thirty new robes, no thirty new linens, just thirty secondhand robes from thirty murder victims. That's how the Jews, whom the lying rabbis claim possess a "higher ethical standard," pay their debts to the *goyim* (non-Jewish, lowly insects, stupid cattle). After killing thirty men and giving their dirty clothes to his new relatives as a half-payment for his bet-gone-sour, Samson abandoned his new wife, ran away in a rage and returned to his father's house. Oy! What a hero! What a great Jew! So intelligent, he could be a doctor or a lawyer!

Judges 15 shows what an insane psychopath Samson was. This Jewish hero had abandoned his wife. So, during his absence and murderous rampage, her father gave her away to Samson's best man. After all, Samson had already slept with her, so she wasn't fit for a Philistine; he might as well give her away to another Jewish scumbag. Besides, Samson had run off to who-knows-where and probably wouldn't return, since he was a fugitive murderer and maniac.

But the girl's father had underestimated Jewish greed and the lust of their circumcised, Jewish penises. The father must have been really worried to see this sex-crazy, murderous, super-kike standing at his door, holding a baby goat in one hand and his fully erect penis in the other. Here is this superstrong, half-witted, Jewish bully reneging on his bet, murdering thirty men, so that he can steal their clothes, paying off only half of the bet with the murdered mens' dirty clothes, then running away and abandoning his new wife. Certainly not the sort of man any father would want as a son-in-law! And now, after all of this, the father of the girl finds Samson standing at his doorway with a baby goat under his arm, wanting in the house so he can have sex with the abandoned bride. What does an ancient Near Eastern father say when confronted with such an unstable and dangerous Jewish psychopath with his circumcised penis bulging out of his tunic? What else could he say but "Wouldn't her younger sister suit you better? Have sex with her instead. And please don't kill me and burn down our house in our sleep."

> "Not long after this, at the time of the wheat harvest, Samson went back to see his wife; he had brought a kid for her; he said, 'I wish to go to my wife in her room.' But her father would not let him enter. 'I felt sure' he said 'that you had taken a real dislike of her, so I gave her to your companion. But would not her younger sister suit you better? Have her instead of the other.' Samson answered them, 'I can only get my own back on the Philistines now by doing them some damage.'" (Judges 15:1-3.)

Ah, Semitic vengeance! Never forget; never forgive! Another great "virtue" of the Jews! So, this great hero of the Jews rages off to get the revenge of a super, great, strong, inbred, Jewish moron.

> "So Samson went off and caught three hundred foxes, then took torches and turning the foxes tail to tail put a torch between each pair of tails. He lit the torches and set the foxes free in the Philistines' corn fields. In this way he burned both sheaves and standing corn, and the vines and olive trees as well." (Judges 15:4-5.)

Arson has been popular among the Jews ever since.

The modern Hasidic Jews wear foxtail hats, because they consider themselves to be as crafty, wise and clever as foxes. They use the fox as the symbol of their cleverness while they work and conspire with criminal gangs of drug and diamond smugglers and loan sharks, carrying contraband through customs in their hats. Whether Samson did the entirely impossible and trapped 300 foxes in a couple of days (all of whom obediently lined up, let him tie their tails together with flaming firebrands between them, and then sat patiently until the signal was given for all of them to run through the corn together) or did the very possible and rounded up 300 Hebrews wearing foxtail hats, it all amounted to the same thing. After all, as a "Judge" of Israel, ordering 300 Hebrew arsonists to assemble would be a lot easier than rounding up 300 wild foxes and tying firebrands to their tails.

When the Philistines found out who had burnt down their grainfields, vineyards and olive groves, they confronted the family who had brought a Jewish maniac into the Philistine community. Those stupid people had actually married their daughter to a thieving, murdering Jew named Samson. So, as punishment for such idiocy, "the Philistines went up and burned the woman and her family to death" (Judges 15:6). To a primitive people, this seemed like justice. After all, that family had caused everybody to lose their entire grain, wine and oil crops to the arson of the Jews. So, as retribution, they themselves were burnt to death. Of course, the logical thing would be to burn Samson to death. But the scribes of Babylon, who wrote these tales, didn't want to give the Gentiles any ideas on the best way to handle Jews. So they wrote in the Book of Judges that those foolish Philistines burned the family while letting Samson escape.

The self-righteous Samson, in the long Hebrew tradition of never accepting any blame, but instead blaming everybody else, said, "Since this is how you behave, I swear I will not rest till I have had my revenge on you." (Judges 15:7.) Yes, it is all their fault. Samson is a blameless and holy Jew. So, he proceeded to beat up and kill as many as he could, before running away to hide in a cave in the wilderness.

The Philistines ran out to capture him. But Samson had "the spirit of Yahweh" come over him, that is, he became a psychopathic maniac who went postal and killed a thousand men with the jawbone of a donkey. The jawbone of a donkey is shaped somewhat like an ax. So, it can definitely make a dangerous weapon, but only a superman could kill a thousand men with one. After killing a thousand men single-handedly, Samson prayed for some water: "must I die of thirst and fall into the hands of [those who don't have the foreskin of their holy penises cut off]?" (Judges 15:18.) And – Abracadabra! – "God opened a hollow in the ground... and water gushed out of it." (Judges 15:19.) As geological "proof" that the entire fable was true, the scribes wrote that "the hollow is there at Lehi." (Judges 15:19.) And that is all the proof that a goat rustler needs: a hole in the ground. Solid evidence! A rabbi can point to that hole and say, "See! There's the proof that we Jews always tell the truth. A hole in the ground with water in it."

Judges 16 begins with this great psychopathic hero of the Hebrews visiting a prostitute in Gaza. While he was sleeping with the whore, the men of Gaza surrounded the whorehouse waiting to kill him at daybreak. But Samson got out of bed at midnight and "seized the doors of the town gate and the two posts as well; he tore them up, bar and all, hoisted them on to his shoulders and carried them to the top of the hill and there he left them" (Judges 16:3).

The difference between the mythological tales of the Hebrews and those of other peoples of the ancient Near East is that the latter told wonderous tales and astounding lies about the gods doing great deeds among other gods, while the Hebrews told astounding lies about Hebrews doing great deeds among men. While the other peoples told tales that grew in embellishment as the years went by, the Hebrews embellished their tales immediately. Other people told tales about their gods and heroes interacting with other gods and heroes in fables that remained in the realm of gods and heroes. Great stories is all they ever were to those people; tales and fables, great ideas to think about, requiring no proof, since they were only myths and legends, nothing more.

But the Hebrews told tales about their god and heroes interacting with the people next door, in the next town or in nearby countries – wonderous stories, tales and fables that they insisted were one hundred percent true. And for "proof" they offered rocks and water springs and holes in the ground. Since the rocks and water springs and holes in the ground were real and true, they insisted that such landmarks were proof positive that their lies were also true. And if you didn't believe the lies that they told, then that meant that you didn't believe the word of God. So, for that, the rabbis would kill you. The Devil's Truth of Judaism.

This trick of Abracadabra Jewish Sorcery was used to good profit by the Jews in the 20th Century AD, who created a myth known as the "Holocaust" that had absolutely no basis other than their own lies. Even when actual physical proof showed the Jews to be liars and the "Holocaust" to be impossible, through constant repetition of their Abracadabra Fraud and the persecution of anyone who tried to prove them wrong, they succeeded in creating out of empty air something that had really not existed until the Jews said that it did. Abracadabra! "Oy, the Holocaust! It was terrible. And for Jewish suffering, the world owes the Jews a guilt offering of gold and prestige and sympathy." The Abracadabra Fraud has its roots in the *Hebrew Bible*, that Big Book of Jewish Lies.

After Samson schlepped the gates of Gaza to the top of a hill, his horny, circumcised nub began calling to him again. This hero of the circumcised rabbis and Jews heeded that call and fell in lust with a beautiful Philistine named Delilah. This swarthy, dumb kike with his kinky black hair just couldn't get enough of these White women. Her name, Delilah, has a meaning of "informer" in Hebrew. So, among the Hebrew thieves and murderers, this story of Samson and Delilah teaches the Jews the long tradition of the danger of informers among them. In fact, in Jewish mythology and history, informers were their most hated enemy right up into modern times.

Delilah was offered 1,100 shekels of silver from each of the chiefs of the Philistines if she could entice Samson to tell her the secret of his superhuman strength. After repeated nagging and cajoling, Samson told Delilah that his power came from his long hair, which had never been cut due to a Nazarite vow to Yahweh. So, while Samson slept, Delilah cut off his hair. His strength left him, because his vow had been broken. He got captured by the Philistines, who blinded him and bound him in chains, forcing him to work in prison turning a grain mill. But they neglected to give him regular haircuts. So, after his hair grew back, Samson pulled down the pillars of the building and killed himself along with the Philistines. "Those he killed at his death outnumbered those he had killed in his life." (Judges 16:30.) Thus, this murdering marauder and psychopathic sex fiend, this great Super Kike hero of the Jews, who "had been judge in Israel for twenty years" (Judges 16:31), died. This was a great tale among the Hebrew goat rustlers, telling more tales of what great murderers and swindlers they could all be, veritable supermen among goat thieves, if only, if only, they would make vows to the Yahweh-god.

Judges 17 shows that the entire Moses narrative is a fable, simply because this account agrees with the archeological record. The various Hebrew tribes were separate bands of Hyksos bandits carving out their own territory in Canaan. In this account, a Hebrew named Micah wants to set up his own household Yahweh cult, centered around an image made of silver. All Hebrews loved silver and could worship it in any way that they wanted, except in the shape of a god.

A wandering Levite from Judah stopped by, looking for a place to build a home. Micah hired him to be a priest at the rate of ten shekels per year, plus food and clothing and barbecued goats. But the whole point of the story is that Micah says, "Now I know that Yahweh will prosper me, because I have this Levite as my priest." (Judges 17:13.) This was another free advertisement for the Levites. The Hebrews were encouraged to feed them.

The rabbis teach two lessons in Judges 18: how to murder "peaceful and trusting people" and how to ignore the Law of Moses as long as a Levite or a rabbi agrees. Since the Levite priest had already infiltrated into the area, when the Hebrew spies approached him, asking if they would be successful in their spy mission, the priest replied,

> "'Go in peace; the journey you are making is under the eye of Yahweh.' So the five men set out and came to Laish. They saw that the people there lived in security like the Sidonians, peaceful and trusting, that nothing lacked there of all that the earth yields, and that they were far from the Sidonians and had no relation with the Aramaeans." (Judges 18:6-8.)

Incidentally, the "eye of Yahweh" mentioned in this verse represents the spy network that is part and parcel of every place where Jews are connected to synagogues. Every wandering Jew reports back to the rabbi what he has seen among the Gentiles. Every Jewish man, woman and child is a part of this network of spies and snitches, telling the rabbi anything that can be of use to the commercial, military and subversive endeavors of the Jews. It is today represented by the "all-seeing eye" atop the pyramid on the United States one-dollar Federal Reserve Note. This same "eye of Yahweh" is at the top of the pyramid that is part of the structure of the modern-day Supreme Court building of the modern state of Israel. The All-Seeing Eye of Jewish spies and snitches is found in the eyes of every Jew, being friendly, grinning at you and asking what you are doing, sticking their big noses in your business.

Beginning with the complaint that "in those days there was no king in Israel," this tale in Judges 18 is another of the many conflicting lies of the Old Testament. I say "conflicting lies," because we are dealing here with ancient stories that claim to be "the word of God" and therefore unimpeachably true.

But when conflicts arise between several versions of these stories, instead of claiming that God Himself dictated these fables to Moses and to Joshua, the rabbis back down from their false claims and come up with alternate lies. The stories that negate one another with conflicting versions cannot be "irrefutably true," since they are obviously at odds. It is not necessarily that one or the other is true, as most Christians think when dealing with Jewish mendacity. Since the Jews are telling the stories, both versions can be lies. So, it is a mistake to try and find which version is the truth. In Semitic thinking, the rabbis claim that since God is the author of the *Hebrew Bible*, two conflicting stories can be true, because God does not tell lies. God certainly does not tell lies, but rabbis do.

Or, if you don't accept this lie or that lie told by the rabbis, then these weasely prevaricators claim that the stories in their "holy scriptures" are not really lies at all – they are "divinely inspired" stories, written by holy men. That is, the goat thieves wrote these stories with the intention of passing along some allegedly "holy truth." This fallacy is basic to all Semitic religions, whose practitioners claim that they can tell the truth by telling lies.

Now, Judges 18 claims that instead of having the stolen lands of Canaan parceled out by throwing the holy dice, choosing lots, or accepting the assignments of Moses or Joshua, the tribe of Dan was entirely left out and had no land. Not only did they have no land to steal, but they had no knowledge of the alleged "Law of Moses" or of the Yahweh-god, which is certainly at odds with the stories in the Pentateuch. Didn't the scribes who wrote the fairy tales in Judges read the lies found in the Torah first?

In finding such innocent and trusting people who were too far away to call for help, the Jewish spies did their work well. Judges 18 is another celebration of genocide – one of the favorite themes of the Jews, as long as they are the ones committing the genocide. This time, the Hebrews of the tribe of the Danites marched against Laish; against a peaceful and trusting people whose town was too far away from either Sidon or Aram to send for help. The Hebrews of the tribe of Dan "slaughtered all of the inhabitants and set the town on fire. There was no one to help the town because it was a long way from Sidon and had no relations with the Aramaeans" (Judges 18:28).

After killing every one of the "innocent and trusting people" at Laish, the "holy" tribe of Dan erected a carved image that they had stolen from Micah – along with his holy dice, ephod and teraphim, and his Levite priest. These they made into their own place of worship in the city that they had stolen from their "peaceful and trusting" murder victims in Laish. Whenever the Hebrews steal something, they rename it as a sign of ownership. So, they renamed the town, calling it "Dan" and settling down to pray to the god made of solid silver.

Judges 18 says that the Danites remained living at Dan "till the day when the inhabitants of the country were carried away into exile. The carved image that Micah had made they enshrined for their own use, and there it stayed as long as the house of God remained at Shiloh." (Judges 18:30-31.) But this is another conflict in the "divinely inspired" *Hebrew Bible*. In fact, archaeology proves that the sanctuary of Dan remained long after the one at Shiloh had been destroyed.

Judges 19 is an example of the Sumerian Swindle applied. Secret Fraud #17 of the Sumerian Swindle states: "Kings are required to legitimatize a swindle, but once the fraud is legalized, those very kings must be sacrificed." In this case, the "king" was the entire tribe of Benjamin. The story of the extermination of the tribe of Benjamin goes far beyond punishment for any "sins" or "insults" of a few perverts. This is an application of Sumerian Swindle #17 and the horrible power that the rabbis and priests had over the ignorant Hebrew goat rustlers.

Once again, Judges 19 begins with the refrain, "In those days, when there was no king in Israel…" (Judges 19:1.) The story begins with an "insult" to a priest. Since the status of women was so low among the moneylenders and the Hebrews who enslaved, raped and captured them as property and sex slaves, this story is only told from the Hebrew slave-owner's perspective. Why this woman ran away from the Levite is not mentioned, but from her own experience and from subsequent events, she must have known what a horrible monster this Jewish priest was. So, she tried to get away from him by fleeing to her father's house.

With his servant and two donkeys, the Levite went to fetch her back to his harem. Obviously, her father loved the Hebrew's bribes better than he loved his daughter, because he let the Levite take his daughter back. On the way home, they spent the night in the town of Gibeah in the territory of Benjamin. At this time, the town of Jerusalem was still not a Hebrew conquest (Judges 19:10-12). Although it was a small town, its geographical location and strong walls made it too difficult for any donkey-riding Hebrews to conquer. While the Levite was in the home of his host in Gibeah, some Benjamite homosexual perverts pounded on the door demanding that he come out, so they could sodomize him. The host of the house begged the militant queers,

> "'No, my brothers; I implore you, do not commit this crime. This man has become my guest; do not commit such an infamy. Here is my daughter; she is a virgin; I will give her to you. Possess her, do what you please with her, but do not commit such an infamy against this man.' The men would not listen to him. So the Levite took his concubine and brought her out to them. They had intercourse with her and outraged her all night till the morning; when dawn was breaking, they let her go." (Judges 19:23-25.)

Remember four things when you read about the massacre of the Benjamites:

(1) We are dealing here with the heroes of the Jews.

(2) Of all the "Hebrew" tribes, the Benjamites were not actual Hebrews; they were Babylonians. They had long been the servants and strong-arm en-

forcers for Terah's family of bankers and merchants in Babylonia and Assyria. In Babylonia, they were known as the tribe of Yakin-Yemina. But in Canaan, the pronunciation of their tribal name was "Benjamin."

(3) Of all the tribes, they alone knew that the claims of Abraham's First National Bank and Pawn Shop were bogus. They did not need modern archaeology to prove this, because they had been in Canaan from the beginning, scouting out territory and trading with the Hyksos-Hebrews for Egyptian gold and collecting their genealogies. The Benjamites alone knew that the stories of Moses and all of the other fantasies of Abraham's family of swindlers were fake, because their ancestors had been in on the original subversion of the Hebrew tribes of Canaan. They knew the true story and were not about to change their Babylonian ways for the fake Law of Moses.

(4) The moneylender-priests of the Yahweh Cult wanted to eliminate the leaders of this one tribe, because they could divulge the secret of the subversion of Canaan to the Hebrews. That would destroy the illusion of holiness and the power of belief that they had so carefully built up and nurtured over the previous centuries. These Benjamite "kings," who had helped set up the Temple scam, were now a danger to the further success of the scam and, thus, had to be eliminated. Killing off the Benjamites was an application of Secret Fraud #17 of the Sumerian Swindle: "Kings are required to legitimatize a swindle, but once the fraud is legalized, those very kings must be sacrificed."

As the story goes, the Benjamites had raped to death the concubine of the Levite – a concubine who hated and feared this Jew so much that she had tried to escape to the safety of her father's house. So, the Levite priest carted her body home. And to show the deep Jewish grief and heartfelt Hebrew sorrow that he had for her, "Having reached his house, he picked up a knife, took hold of his concubine, and limb by limb cut her into twelve pieces; then he sent her all through the land of Israel." And his message that went along with her body parts was this: a Levite has been insulted and his property, this woman, was raped to death. What are we going to do about it? (Judges 19:29-30.)

These are the bloodthirsty, heroic Jews who even today claim to have brought the world a "higher moral conduct." In these books that celebrate their murderous criminality, the Jews have the audacity to claim that they are the "holy ones of God."

The bloodthirsty Hebrew tribes all gathered, preparing to go to war with the Benjamites unless they released the queers to them for punishment. The tribe of Benjamin wanted to fight and protect their perverts, because faggotry was a part of their Babylonian culture. But if the Hebrews were to multiply with their many wives and outbreed the people around them, then queers could not be allowed to live among them.

The tribe of Benjamin had secured the territory around Jerusalem by buying up or wiping out the smaller towns and landholders. As the strong-arm goons and servants of Abraham's Bankers' Guild, they knew where the wealth of Abraham's priests came from – it came from Babylonian Temple members, who gave the priests ten percent of their profits. From their days in Babylonia, they knew how control over the Hebrew tribes had been established and who established it. It was the Babylonian banking family of Abraham who was making the Laws and telling the Hebrews that they had been specially chosen by the Yahweh-god, who had led them out of Egypt to take over Canaan. The Benjamites knew the truth about who was in control of the altar at Bethel. They knew the members of Abraham's Bankers' Guild had been able to gain control of the Hebrew tribes through the genealogical swindle of claiming to be the father of them all. They simply wrote documents placing themselves at the root of the genealogical tree. Of course, the tribes of Benjamin did not believe the whole Yahweh Cult invented by the moneylenders of Ur. Being from Babylonia, the tribe of Benjamin did not have the same ethnic and cultural homogeneity as the other Hebrew tribes. For one thing, they had kept their Babylonian sexual habits of homosexual perversion as an accepted part of their tribal society.

The murder of the concubine was deemed a necessary sacrifice by the rabbis and priests of the altar town of Bethel (meaning "House of God"), where the chief priests lived. The Benjamites had served their purpose. But to fully unify the Hebrews under their rule, through group action, and to eliminate the only people who knew what frauds they really were, the priests of Abraham's Bankers' Guild decided that the tribe of Benjamin had to be destroyed.

This was the reason that the Benjamites defended the queers of Gibeah. It was not mere stubbornness on their part, or perverted ideas of "tolerance," "gay liberation," homosexual "rights," or other modern Jewish lies that "queers are just like us." It was none of these strange delusions. By defending the queers, the Benjamites were simply defending their own Babylonian culture against something far more culturally-oppressive than faggotry. They were fighting against the deadly oppression of Judaism in its primeval malevolence.

For their part, the Patriarchs of Abraham's Bankers' Guild were cleaning house and testing the powers of their priests. Rallying all of the Hebrews against one another through religious intolerance, fear and hatred was their specialty. The power of Judaism arises from fear and hatred; there is no love found therein. So, one of their number – a Levitical priest, living in a distant place "deep in the highlands of Ephraim," whom no one had ever heard of, since no actual town was located there – made an accusation. Whether or not the accusation was true didn't matter, since it was *the results* of the accusation that the Patriarchs cared about. This priest sent around to all of the tribes the dismembered body parts of a murdered woman, along with a story of why she had been dismembered. As a woman subject to the power of a priest of the Jewish Demon Cult, perhaps she had merely been murdered so that the evil priest (from whom she had tried to escape) could use her body as a calling card. At any rate, her body parts and the Levite's story as to why she had been killed rallied the tribes for war against the Benjamites. The other tribes slaughtered the tribe of Benjamin, men, women, children and cattle, and burned down their towns. Only 600 Benjamites escaped the carnage.

And so, with the elimination of the only witnesses to the true origin of Abraham and his family of bankers and moneylenders, the conspiracy of the Bankers' Guild of Ur, Harran and Babylon was secure. With the only witnesses removed, Abraham's Bankers' Guild could enjoy the much-trumpeted "prestige" of being the inheritors of the *asl* of the twelve tribes, because no one remained alive who could say that they were frauds. With the tribe of Benjamin out of the way, there was no one left to connect the origin of the Jewish High Priest to the moneylenders' cult cities of the Moon God at Ur and Harran.

Social dictatorship and revenge killing are basic to Judaism. And even though this is a system where the names and genealogies of the actors are held to be of inestimable importance – a system where a father's deeds can be passed along to his sons as an inherited part of their tribal *asl* – it should be noted that this particular Levite priest had no name. It is not that this Levite was unimportant, since he obviously caused the destruction of almost the entire tribe of Benjamin. So, why did this Levite have no name? Because if he had had a name, then the conspiracy to murder all of the Benjaminites could have been traced to an original source. As it is, the story only tells of a "certain Levite" living in a distant, unnamed and untraceable place, who sent a dismembered woman's body around to his fellow Levites with a story of homosexual atrocity and an insult to a priest. His name was not recorded in the ancient texts, because it was less important than the accusations Levites could make against any of the tribes. The message is: "Honor and respect the Levites, or they can have you killed." The Devil's Truth of Judaism, once again.

What these chapters reveal is both an ancient conspiracy of the priests and an ancient cover-up of the names of the actors. That the Levite priest's name was not recorded may very well mean that he fabricated his accusations against the Benjamites as a pretext for having the entire tribe murdered. On the one hand, you have Abraham's Bankers' Guild trying to erase the only witnesses to their banking and genealogy swindle and, on the other hand, you have an unnamed Levite accusing the tribe of Benjamin of insulting the priests and sinning against God. This Levite having no name protected the conspiracy of Abraham's Bankers' Guild of Priests from an inquiry, and protected the Levites from any future retribution from the survivors of the Benjamites. After all, if there was no name for the original accuser, then the surviving Benjamites would have no one to kill in revenge. This is assuming that there actually was an original accuser and that the evil priests of Yahweh did not murder one of their concubines, cut her up and distribute the body parts with a completely false story, in order to foment a war against the tribe of Benjamin. There was, after all, no chance for denial from the Benjamites, because they came under immediate attack. Perhaps they would not give up the perverts, because there were no perverts to give up. They were attacked for whatever reason, and could only defend themselves. Like so much of Jewish "history," only the Jewish side of the story survives.

And so, the entire tribe of Benjamin was exterminated, except for 600 men who escaped into the wilderness. No doubt these were not the leaders of the tribe (who had fought to the last man), but were the minor tribesmen, with no knowledge of the Conspiracy. They could thus be allowed to live as a "remnant."

The Book of Judges ends by telling more about the murderous nature of the Jewish bandits. The Jews could only have been incited to murder the Benjamites through the concerted effort of the Levitical priests working in collusion. According to the previous chapters, the Levite who started the massacres did so by sending her body parts to those of his fellow Levites who were living among the tribes. Only through decrees of the High Priest was it possible to put the Benjamites under a ban. The Jewish lesser priests were under the authority of the High Priest, whose office had been created as a hereditary one occupied solely by the Patriarchs of Abraham's Bankers' Guild of Babylonia. Thus, it is obvious that the Jewish priests were directed by Abraham's Bankers' Guild to exterminate the tribe of Benjamin.

After murdering every man, woman and child of the tribe of Benjamin, and after slaughtering all of their cattle and burning down their towns, only 600 Benjamite men were left alive. These had run off to the safe haven in the wilderness known as the Rock of Rimmon, a cone-shaped limestone mountain protected on three sides by ravines and containing numerous caves: a natural fortress.

After the slaughter, all of the tribes of Israel met at the altar at Bethel, "sitting before God with groans and bitter weeping" (Judges 21:2). Whining and crying and moaning, they now regretted that one tribe of Israel was near extinction. They had all sworn an oath to the Yahweh-god that "Not one of us will give his daughter in marriage to Benjamin" (Judges 21:1), so, like good Jews, they began to ask themselves how to evade their promises to God and get Hebrew wives for the men of Benjamin. This was an easy question to ask Jewish thieves and murderers. And the Jewish answer was equally simple: steal the women from somebody else. But from whom could Jewish virgins be stolen, besides fellow Jews? The cunning priests "counted over" the people and found that "not one of the inhabitants of Jabesh-Gilead was there" (Judges 21:9). Apparently, the inhabitants of Jabesh-Gilead didn't relish murdering their fellow Jews just because the priests said so. But the priests had made the Hebrews swear "a solemn oath threatening death to anyone who would not come into Yahweh's presence at Mizpah" and go to war against the Benjamites (Judges 21:5). This is further proof of the conspiratorial power of the priests as well as of a conspiracy to wipe out the Benjamites and leave no witnesses. All of the other Hebrew tribes were used to destroy the targeted tribe.

After counting up the Hebrews, the priests found their perfect solution for preserving the tribe of Benjamin (under new leadership, of course). They could not allow the remaining Benjamite men to marry Canaanite women, otherwise they would become a subversive element within Abraham's Bankers' Guild. They could not break their vow to the Yahweh-god to never marry their daughters to Benjamin. So, in the traditional holy Jewish way, the priests of

Yahweh decided to kill some fellow Jews and steal their daughters. These are the heroes of the Jews.

The town of Jabesh-Gilead did not send fighters to war against Benjamin, so under that pretext the Levitical priests (Judges 21:10) "sent twelve thousand of their bravest" murderers to Jabesh-Gilead with these orders: "Go and slaughter all the inhabitants of Jabesh-Gilead, the women and children, too. This is what you must do. You are to put all the males and all women who have slept with a male under the ban, but you are to spare the maidens." (Judges 21:10-11.) These twelve thousand "brave" Jewish murderers obeyed the evil priests of Yahweh and after slaughtering their fellow Jews "among the inhabitants of Jabesh-Gilead they found four hundred young virgins who had never slept with a man, and brought them to the camp at Shiloh" (Judges 21:12). It should be noted that these girls ranged in ages from twelve to under three years old, since these are the recommended ages when girls should be married or raped, according to the traditional rabbinical teachings. The Jews have always loved molesting children, because this is what their "wise" rabbis and "great sages of Israel" have practiced and taught from the earliest times. So, when you read the *Old Testament*, know that whenever "maidens" or "virgins" are mentioned, it is referring to the age groups that are still most desired by the circumcised Jewish sex fiends today – little girls between the ages of three and twelve. Modern Jews are just as demented, because – after all – "walking in the ways" of their god is an eternal command.

After they had murdered their fellow Hebrews at Jabesh-Gilead, these heroic, murdering scoundrels sent a "Jewish Shalom" to the refugees of Benjamin who were safely holed up at the Rock of Rimmon. First, the Hebrews had slaughtered everybody in the tribe of Benjamin, except for the 600 men who had escaped to an impregnable position. Then, they murdered every man, woman and child in the Hebrew town of Jabesh-Gilead and saved only 400 little girls to give to the fugitives as a "Jewish peace offering." These virgin girls could only have been between the ages of twelve and three years old, since that was the age when Hebrews usually married off their daughters, in order to get the biggest possible number of children out of that girl in her lifetime.

This peace offering was accepted by the Benjamite fugitives, because they were doomed otherwise. But the "Jewish Shalom" was still short by 200 virgins. The Levite priests were perplexed by this problem. Belatedly, they remembered that the "promises" of the lying priests of the Yahweh-god included twelve tribes and not just eleven. After nearly exterminating the Benjamites, they asked each other, "How can we preserve a remnant for Benjamin so that a tribe may not be blotted out from Israel?" (Judges 21:17.) And now, to hide the embarrassing fact that their raging declarations of divine retribution upon the tribe of Benjamin had not been completely fulfilled, in a characteristically hypocritical about-face, these evil Jewish priests concerned themselves with preserving a remnant. Because the Contract (the *Torah*) had been written as a promise to *all of the Hebrews*, some remnant of the Benjamites had to be left, no matter how small, so the priests could perpetuate the fiction that the

Yahweh-god had given his promise to all of them. Killing most of the Benjamites was okay, but not killing all of them, for that would violate the Contract.

After murdering all except for 600 men, and after murdering all of the people in the town of Jabesh-Gilead, except for 400 little girls, the rabbis were still 200 virgins short of their "Jewish Shalom." They couldn't give the Benjamites any of their own daughters, because of their vow – of course, pious and holy psychopathic murderers always want to keep their vows. So, like the Jews they were, they gave the remaining 200 circumcised Benjamites some holy Jewish advice instead. The evil priests of Yahweh told these 200 Benjamites standing around with their circumcised cocks in their hands to go and *steal wives for themselves* from other Jews!

From careful study of these "holy scriptures," any Bible student can reach the obvious conclusion that Jewish girls are most vulnerable to attack and rape when they are dancing the hora. So, the clever rabbis told the lonely Benjamites to wait in the vineyards around the town of Shiloh and

> "Keep watch there, and when the daughters of Shiloh come out
> to dance in groups together, you too come out of the vineyards:
> seize a wife, each one of you, from the daughters of Shiloh and
> make for the land of Benjamin." (Judges 21:21.)

What could be friendlier advice than this from the holy rabbis? First, the Jews kill almost all of your men and murder every, single one of your children and wives. That's okay, isn't it? Then, they kill your neighbors and give you, for wives, 400 of their grieving, crying, tearstained little girls older than three years of age, whose parents they have just slaughtered. That's a good enough substitute for your wives and children that the Jews murdered and the houses that they burnt down, isn't it? And to show what good and pious rabbis they are, they are very concerned that the remaining 200 Benjamites can get laid whenever they want to. So, why not go over to Shiloh and steal 200 women and little girls from them? Then, can't we all just be friends? Remember, our god loves you and wants to be your god, too.

Thus, this brotherhood of evil Levites had revenge upon the Babylonian tribe of Benjamin for the insult and murder of one of their concubines. A concubine was nothing for them to be concerned about, but anyone touching any property of a priest was forbidden. And the last witnesses of the secret connection between Abraham's First National Bank and Pawn Shop and the moneylender guilds of Ur and Harran had been wiped out. These are the heroes of the Jews.

To further unify the Hebrews, the Book of Judges ends with "In those days there was no king in Israel, and every man did as he pleased." (Judges 21:25.) As if the lying priests, with their threats of heavenly vengeance, were not enough! Now Abraham's Bankers' Guild was calling for a king to enforce civil laws, like the laws that Hammurabi had provided for the merchant-moneylenders of Babylon. Now, what they needed was a king who would obey the evil priests, and who could draft troops from among the Hebrews to protect their treasury against foreign aggression.

8.3 The Great Jewish Heroine, Ruth – Oy! What a Worker! And She Wasn't Even Jewish!

The Book of Ruth is named, not after a Hebrew, but rather a Moabite woman who married a Hebrew goat rustler. It is dated to the period of the Judges (~1050-931 BC), according to the Biblical scholars' reckoning.

All previous Biblical commentators have mistakenly assumed that the book simply shows the virtues of filial piety. For her piety and self-sacrifice, the Yahweh-god rewarded this Moabite woman with an "illustrious" marriage to a rich Hebrew goat rustler, whereby she became the ancestress of King David and King Solomon.

The Book of Ruth begins by recounting how a Hebrew named Elimelech moved from Bethlehem with his wife, Naomi, and their two sons, and settled in the country of Moab. Elimelech died there and his two sons married Moabite women named Orphah and Ruth. Naomi, her two sons and their wives all lived together for ten years, until her sons died, too, leaving Naomi and her two daughters-in-law alone.

Naomi decided to return to Bethlehem and told her daughters-in-law to return to their mother's house. Orphah returned to her Moabite people and her god. But Ruth stayed and swore the mighty oath of the goat rustlers of Israel, "Your people shall be my people, and your God, my God." (Ruth 1:16.) So, Naomi and Ruth returned to Bethlehem, where Ruth impressed a rich Jew so much (by working for free) that he married her.

Although the earlier commentators were correct about the theme of filial piety, they assumed that this minor theme was the only theme of the Book of Ruth. There are two major themes of a hidden and more important concern here. Abraham's Bankers' Guild had established a banking system that, because of its enormous wealth-generating capabilities, made use of an extensive system of servants and slaves. The so-called "strangers" and "resident aliens" who appear and disappear without further comment throughout the Old Testament are none other than these *shabbos goyim* (Sabbath working, lowly insects, stupid cattle) – menial servants who worked for the Jews. Certainly, the wealthy, non-Jewish traveling merchants would also be counted as "strangers," but the vast majority of them were servants kept in poverty by the Jews, so as to keep them dependent.

Secret Fraud #19 of the Sumerian Swindle is at work in the Book of Ruth: "Prestige is a glittering robe for ennobling treason and blinding fools; the more it is used, the more it profits he who dresses in it." By calling up their illusory "prestige," these "Holy Chosen Ones" of the Yahweh-god could tell their lies about Pharaoh and the miracles in the desert to their illiterate servants and thus gain an awestruck following and a respectful obedience at no extra cost to themselves.

Servants work for less pay and with more loyalty if they feel "honored" to be working for some "great personage." And this is what the Book of Ruth claims is the reward of non-Hebrew "strangers" who loyally serve the Hebrew goat thieves. Maybe the pay is low, but the *prestige*, the wonderful *prestige*, of serving the holy goat rustlers with their circumcised holy penises is such an honor! Such loyal service gains rewards greater than shekels of silver.

In this case, the Book of Ruth is another scam of Abraham's Bankers' Guild for getting cheaper labor out of their servants by telling them lies. Instead of giving them higher wages, they give them the great "honor" of serving the holy Jews for free.

8.4 King David, a Tiny, Heroic Ant for an Equally Tiny People

The Egyptians and Mesopotamians were the earliest writers of what we call "Wisdom literature." But the rabbis made it standard practice of the Jews to destroy all available copies of the religious and philosophical works of other peoples. Burning entire libraries of the non-Jews and tearing up the only available copies of certain manuscripts is celebrated throughout Jewish scriptures. Exodus 34:10-13 and *Babylonian Talmud*, Shabbath 116a, can be given as single examples which are repeated hundreds of times throughout Jewish literature. When all religious writings of other people are destroyed, their priests killed and their devotees tortured to death, then Judaism stands as the only measure for understanding God. As you are probably beginning to realize by now, the Jews are liars. Nothing they say about God is true. Every good thing they say about themselves and about Judaism is false. So, where does it leave the people of the world when the Jews destroy all genuine knowledge of God, leaving only the lies of the Jews? Furthermore, what kinds of evil creatures do such demonic things as the Jews do, dragging Mankind down into ignorance, so that their own lies prevail?

The real heroes in the world of religious history are the modern archaeologists, with their patient excavations and accurate translations. Today, with so many archaeological discoveries and translations of ancient texts, it is easy to see from where the Jews plagiarized and counterfeited such portions of the Old Testament as the Psalms, Job, and the Proverbs, as well as every other book that they falsely claim as their own.

Fake "prophesy" was also a Semitic literary technique that even predated the Hebrews. Such "future-prophecies-after-the-fact" set the stage for how the rabbis would claim an antiquity and a prophetic power that was built upon nothing but literary sleight-of-hand and blatant lies. Such Egyptian fables as the "Prophecies of Nefertiti" as well as some Assyrian "prophesies" are examples of the fake prophecy techniques that were so enthusiastically copied by the rabbis.

In the *Hebrew Bible*, the Book of Samuel is a single book, not divided into two books as in the Christian Bible. The division into two books dates back only to the Greek translation which, moreover, grouped Samuel and

Kings under one title as, "The Four Books of Kingdoms" (called in the Vulgate "The Four Books of Kings"). These titles and book divisions were given as a more descriptive way of titling the books than was the Babylonian naming convention used by the Hebrews, according to which the first word in a given book was used as its title.

Continuing the Jews' long list of lies, the Book of Samuel was not written by a single author. It mingles various traditions relating to the beginning of the monarchial period. It contains stories of the three mythical kings – Saul, David and Solomon. The various sections seem to have been written over a period of two centuries, as the rabbis refined their lies with each revision. Although all of the pieces in the Book of Samuel were combined by about 700 BC, they did not reach their final form until the Great Editing and Fictionalization that took place in the libraries of the merchant-moneylenders during the Exile in Babylon (587-538 BC). Fifty years was plenty of time to rewrite the entire hoax of the *Hebrew Bible*.

The Books of Samuel cover a period from the rise of the monarchy to the end of the reign of David. The claim is that Philistine (the Sea Peoples) expansion threatened the existence of Israel and made monarchial government a necessity. Saul (~1030 BC) first appears as one of the "judges" (military leaders), but his recognition by all the tribes invests him with a wider and lasting authority.

2 Samuel summarizes the political reign of David. It is significant that after 500 years of raids and banditry, the Hebrews were unable to capture Jerusalem. This strength of the city's walls was a major desire of the moneylenders. A strongly fortified city protecting a strong and secret treasury was their goal. But the strength of the city was also tested against the pathetically weak Hebrew tribes – lacking siege engines and not even knowing how to use a battering ram. The "mighty kings" being led by an all-powerful god was a complete fiction. During the Great Editing and Fictionalization during the Exile, this strength of the Jerusalem citadel was further emphasized, because it was alleged to have been so strong that the mythical David could only capture it by stealthily climbing up a sewer drain tunnel.

Originally, the Book of Samuel was one big scroll (one book), but big rolls of goat leather tend to be heavy. So, the goatskin scroll of Samuel was divided into two books at an early date. These comprise a pseudohistory of about one century, lasting from the close of the age of the Judges (the military bandit chiefs of which Samuel was one) and the beginnings of the monarchy under Saul and David. Both bandit kings were inventions of the scribes of Abraham's Bankers' Guild. Both Books of Samuel were compiled and edited late in the seventh century BC.

These stories, like everything else in the Old Testament, are not a complete and continuous history, but rather a series of episodes centered around the characters of Samuel, Saul and David. The high priests of this great fraud felt secure enough to foretell through their "prophet" Nathan an everlasting dynasty of David. The actual events of history again and again proved the phony nature of Hebrew "prophecies."

1 Samuel begins by telling about a Hebrew named Elkanah. He had two wives, one called Hannah, the other Peninnah. Hannah was barren, which was a great sin among the sex-crazed Jews whose circumcised penises gave them nothing but lust. Every year, Elkanah would go to Shiloh where a stone building allegedly housed the Ark of the Covenant. This Ark was conveniently hidden behind a curtain. So, only the priests could see the "holy of holies," which was so holy that it wasn't even there. It was so holy that it took a priest to tell you how holy it was. That way, you wouldn't be blasted into crispies by getting too close to it before you could offer your sacrifice to the priests and thank them for protecting you from such a holy thing behind the curtain. Talk about a "mystery" religion! Abracadabra! Believe in what's behind the curtain or the priests will kill you for your sinful unbelief. To disbelieve the rabbis meant a death penalty by stoning, because Judaism is the Devil's Truth.

There at Shiloh, he worshiped Yahweh Sabaoth, the "god of armies," the god of the Hebrew bandits, the god of the Jews. And there Hannah prayed for a son, vowing to dedicate him "to Yahweh for the whole of his life and no razor shall ever touch his head." (1 Samuel 1:11.) With hair all over his body, he was guaranteed to also be covered with the national insect of Israel, the louse.

To make sure that the Jews understand what's of special religious holiness in Judaism, the book tells you that "Elkanah had intercourse with Hannah his wife." The *Hebrew Bible* is very specific about sexual intercourse, so as to keep Judaism in the proper holy perspective. She gave birth to a son whom she named Samuel (Shem-El, "the Name of God"). After three years, she took the child to the priest at Shiloh and gave him to the temple.

So, this barren woman, Hannah, finally had a child, the one thing in Life most important to Jewish women, who normally had eight to twelve children each. To prove her worthiness to the Yahweh-god, she abandoned the child and left him to be a servant of Eli, the priest. For her piety, according to the scribes who wrote the story, the Yahweh-god gave her five more children, a good lesson for Hebrew women to give the priests and the temple their first fruits.

Before she abandoned the boy in 1 Samuel 2, this illiterate Jewess said a prayer that the temple scribe immediately wrote down and put her name on. The Jews claim that the "Song of Hannah" is an ode to the mightiness of their incredible Yahweh-god. But in fact, every people on earth and every god-conscious religion on earth, has prayed to their gods with identical prayers. The only thing special about the Jews is their self-promotion. Merely substitute the personal noun, Yahweh, for the name of any other god, and you can see this.

After Hannah abandoned the three-year-old Samuel, he was raised as a temple servant by Eli, the priest. "Now the sons of Eli were scoundrels; they cared nothing for Yahweh nor for the rights of the priests as regards the people." (1 Samuel 2:12-13.) They stole the holy barbecue before it was cooked on the altar, took it home and fried it up to their own special recipes. They demanded fresh meat to take home and cook before the bloody smoke had given the Yahweh-god his "sweet savor." Eli's sons were stealing sacrifices and sleeping with the women who served at the entrance of the Tent of Meeting. (1 Samuel 2:22.) Finally, "a man of God," that is, some infuriated prophet channeling the voice of God through his crusty, fly-speckled beard, warned Eli that his evil family was about to be destroyed.

1 Samuel 3 tells how Samuel, while still a young boy, began hearing voices in his head. He was therefore declared to be a Hebrew prophet, since hearing voices that nobody else could hear and then talking to them was the primary requirement for the office.

1 Samuel 4 is where the Philistines captured the "ark of God" and killed the sons of the wicked priest Eli in battle. Of course, the Philistines had heard the stories that the Jews told about their mighty god. The Jews told everybody in Canaan those stories, so as to give themselves "prestige" with their own *abracadabra*. When the Jews brought the ark into camp, with its Assyrian cherubs and Babylonian furnishings as a means of frightening the Philistines, the Philistines cried out with fear, "Alas! Who will save us from the power of this mighty God? It was he who struck down Egypt with every kind of plague." (1 Samuel 4:8.) Then, the Philistines laughed and beat the hell out of the Jews and hauled the ark back to their own camp.

1 Samuel 5 is a battle between the idols of the Philistines and those of the Hebrews. Even though the Philistines originated from the Black Sea region and from Greece, they believed (like most other ancient peoples) that specific gods were resident to specific geographical locations. So, when they captured the seacoast of Canaan, they began worshiping the local god, Dagon. The tale shows the difference between the idol of the pagans and the idol of the Jews. While the Dagon-god resided *inside of* its idol, the Yahweh-god *sat on top of* its idol.

How were the priests of the Yahweh-god to explain why their "mighty god who had struck down Egypt" could be so easily carried away by the Philistines and set down in the temple of Dagon? It was another Jewish "miracle," one that only the "inspired" (that is, the "lying") scribes of the moneylenders reported. The next morning, the idol of Dagon was found lying face down before the ark of Yahweh. The Philistines replaced the idol on its dais. But the next morning, "there lay Dagon face down on the ground before the ark of Yahweh." (1 Samuel 5:4.) Oh! What a miracle! The Dagon idol worshiping the Jewish idol! And then the Philistines all broke out in tumors. So, they moved the ark from Ashdod to Gath. But everybody there got tumors, too.

This incident was like the appearance of anti-Semitism in later millennia, when nobody hated Jews until the Jews showed up. Then, once the People found out what Jews are like, anti-Semitism broke out everywhere like a plague. Everybody got tumors. The Philistines then moved the ark to Ekron. "The people who did not die were struck with tumors and the wailing from the town went up to heaven." (1 Samuel 5:12.) "Oh God, why have you afflicted us with these pestilential Jews?"

This chapter, written by the priests for their Hebrew audience, gave the priests even more opportunity to claim a terrible and mysterious power emanating from their own idol, the Ark. The message is the same as in Exodus: "Do not touch or go near the ark of the treasury or you will die and maybe get big pimples."

The scribes of Abraham's Bankers' Guild wrote that their ark was so fearsome and holy that when the Philistines captured it, the Yahweh-god struck them down with a plague of rats and tumors. Rats reproduce almost as numerously as Jews, and since it was the time of the wheat harvest (1 Samuel 6:13), the plague of rats was attributed by Yahweh's priests as an act of God, rather than a consequence of rats eating the overabundance of wheat. So, a "guilt" penalty was due for daring to touch and carry away the Ark of Abraham's Bankers' Guild. Plus, the penalty fee for the "offense" of beating the Jews in a fair fight was written down specifically. Under Jewish rules, only Jews are allowed to win, which is why they write the rules. The Philistines were to pay the Yahweh-god some gold bullion in the shape of golden tumors and golden rats. "So you must make models of your tumors and models of the rats that ravage your country and you must pay honor to the god of Israel." (1 Samuel 6:5.) What better way to pay honor to the god of the moneylenders than to pay the Jews gold bullion shaped like tumors and rats? Very symbolic, indeed, for those rats who are a tumor upon Mankind.

A lot of gold can be hidden in plain sight by casting it into odd shapes. People are easily fooled by giant golden menorah with golden oil lamps burning continuously. They think the bright lights and the alleged "significance" of seven lamps or seven candlesticks is the important element. But the solid gold bullion from which it is made is the important element for the Bank of Abraham.

A lot of silver can be hidden in plain sight by casting it into odd shapes. People are easily fooled by the pole sockets and the altar decorations with fancy cherubs and pomegranate designs. They think the fancy designs have a "holy significance." But the solid silver bullion from which they are made is the only significance to the priests of Abraham's First National Bank and Pawn Shop. All banks make loans at interest based upon the deposits that they allegedly keep on reserve. Whether the reserves are in the form of gold and silver ingots, in the shape of giant menorahs, or are simply silver bells hanging from purple linen, it is all the same. It is the total weight of precious metal that is important, not the shape in which the metal is cast. This is some of the sorcery practiced by the bankers: hiding wealth by changing its shape.

So, to hide the bribe that the conspiring priests of the Philistines had to pay to the priests of the Hebrews, the gold was cast into shapes that only had significance in the minds of people who believed in magic and who had to pay the bribe. They had a rat problem and they had a lot of tumors and a lot of Jews. In the wonders of Semitic logic, the rats and tumors were caused by the god of the Jews as punishment for touching and carrying away the golden Ark of the Jews. What could be more logical than this? First, the Jews show up, then the rats and tumors show up; an obvious case of cause and effect!

A model of a tumor might not be a very big lump of gold, but one the size of a rat is. According to the lying rabbis who wrote these fables, the conspiring priests of the Philistines recommended that the Philistines "pay honor to the God of Israel" (1 Samuel 6:5) and send a total of twenty-five golden tumors and five golden rats to the priests of Abraham's First National Bank and Pawn Shop – paid as a guilt offering to the Yahweh-god (1 Samuel 6:3) – as well as a large number of golden rats from each town and village in their territory (1 Samuel 6:18). In this story, the rabbis teach one of the early discoveries of the Bankers of Babylon: robbing everybody of small amounts adds up to a huge fortune. And if Yahweh can't spend all of that gold for the stuff that he wants, then his holy priests will perform that drudgery for him.

Besides the payment of gold to the god of the Jews, 1 Samuel 6 emphasized two weird things: (1) that the Philistines believed the stories about Moses and the Pharaoh and feared the god of the Jews and (2) that any Hebrew who does not show enough happiness towards the lies of Judaism must be killed. "Of the people of Beth-Shemesh, the sons of Jeconiah had not rejoiced when they saw the ark of Yahweh, and he struck down seventy of them." (1 Samuel 6:19.) *This number is recorded as "fifty thousand men" in the Hebrew Bible, a much scarier number.* "The people mourned because Yahweh had struck them so fiercely," wrote the scribes, for not worshiping him enough.

Now, according to the rabbis, believing the Devil's Truth is not enough. If the people do not also show enough joy and enthusiasm for the Devil's Truth, they must be killed. This Jewish scam would become a basic principle in later millennia when Jewish Communism infected Mankind like a plague of rats and tumors. Those who did not dance for joy and maniacally wave red flags would be labeled "counter-revolutionaries" and shot. That certainly encouraged everybody else to dance for joy and maniacally wave red flags – and it was all with the compliments of the "Holy Chosen Ones of God," giving Mankind their Jewish blessings. This is the main reason Jews jump around and strain themselves to show each other how rejoicing they are, not out of joy, but hoping that the lightning bolts miss.

1 Samuel 7 tells of how the Ark, returned by the Philistines, was placed in a small town for twenty years. All of the tribes are now referred to as the "House of Israel" and Samuel is now the "judge" (military leader) over the whole motley crew. Once, when the Philistines were about to attack, Samuel immediately killed an innocent sucking lamb to offer as a sacrifice to this greedy god of the Jewish moneylenders. This caused a thunderstorm and frightened the Philistines into retreating. As they ran, the Hebrews chased after them, since it was obvious that the thundering Yahweh-god was on their side and that it was safe to bravely chase after a retreating enemy.

1 Samuel 8 begins with the Hebrews demanding to have a king rule over them, instead of the perverted rabbis or the vindictive priests or the corrupt judges (military leaders). The dictatorial Hebrew leaders were unreliable in their justice, simply because their claims to legitimacy were based on the voices in their heads and "signs from heaven" in the form of the holy dice or occa-

sional thunderstorms and the fact that they were nothing more than bandits. The Hebrews had been bossed around long enough by the priests of Yahweh, the gibbering prophets and these criminal "judges." What were the Jewish judges anyway, other than bandits? Even Samuel's own two sons, whom he had appointed as judges, were scoundrels. The Hebrews demanded to have a king rule over them instead of judges or blood-spattered priests.

The power of the tribe of Benjamin is once again exploited in 1 Samuel 9. As you will recall, the tribe of Benjamin were the original servants and strong-armed gangsters in the employ of Terah, the Patriarch of the Money-lender's Guild of Ur and Harran. So, it was a natural transition for the first king over all of the Hebrew tribes to be chosen from among the remaining members of the tribe of Benjamin, especially since the Benjamites had become well-disciplined by having been almost exterminated by the Levitical priests of Yahweh. That this first king was descended from the Assyrian branch of Te-rah's banking guild, can be ascertained from the Assyrian city of Kish, whence his father was named. Kish's son was named Saul. And so, 1 Samuel 9 begins a narrative of how the kings of Israel *were also* descendants of Terah's Bank-ers' Guild. Abraham, the Babylonian, represented the genealogical priestly arm of Judaism and Saul, the Assyrian, represented the genealogical military side of the Temple Cult of Yahweh, the "God of Armies."

All over the ancient Near East, it was commonly accepted that certain people gained political power by the choice of the gods. And it was no differ-ent for the Hebrew goat rustlers. From those gangs of thieves and cutthroats their various "judges" (military leaders) had gained power, but they were not thought of as anything more than tribal chieftains. Now, for one chief to rule over all of the tribes, they demanded what all of the other nations required, the blessing of the resident god. For this to occur, the blessing of the chief Jewish "judge" (military leader) was passed along to the designated king.

This is the second phase of how the moneylenders of Ur and Harran gained control of the territory of Canaan. First, they infiltrated the tribes of the region with their teams of peddlers and merchant caravans, trading with the Hyksos-Hebrew tribes for Egyptian loot. During their negotiations, it was the custom to recite their genealogy by way of introduction. They carefully rec-orded the genealogies of the entire region and carried this data back to the main office at Harran. The main contingents of guards for protecting the cara-vans and merchants had been their faithful servants from the Sealands of Babylonia, the tribe of Yakin-Yemina or, as the name was pronounced in He-brew, the tribe of Benjamin. Following their original orders, the Benjamites had secured the territory around the fortress city of Ususalem (Jerusalem). Although Jerusalem was too impregnable to conquer, they bought out or cap-tured outright its surrounding territory, while slaughtering and enslaving all of the Canaanites of the region. But the Benjamite leaders knew who really con-trolled the Yahweh-cult. Being Semitic Amorites, but not Hebrews, and by refusing to give up the gods and the homosexual habits that they had brought with them from Babylonia, the tribe of Benjamin did not fit into the long-range goals of Abraham's First National Bank and Pawn Shop.

Unlike the other tribes, the Benjamites knew who secretly stood behind the altar of Yahweh. The merchant-moneylenders of Ur, whose god was the Moon God, *Sin*, had found no problem in acquiring religious authority over the Hebrews, whose god was also the Moon God. They named this god "Yahweh" after the Egyptian Moon God, *Yah*, whom some of the Hyksos had worshiped in Egypt. All of them worshiping the same Yahweh-god made the efforts of the moneylender guild Patriarchs easy. All they needed was the tribal genealogies of the Hebrews in order to counterfeit themselves in as their Patriarchal forefathers and thus usurp the leadership of all of the tribes throughout all of Canaan, Syria and northern Arabia.

But the Benjamites, having been the original servants of the merchant-moneylender guild of Abraham's father in Ur, knew who was behind the swindle. So, they refused to give their wholehearted support to a religious scam which they knew to be false. This tribe of loyal servants, reliable enforcers and caravan guards was becoming a danger to the success of Abraham's Bankers' scheme. They had served the Patriarchs of Ur loyally and well. But they were an unrepentant tribe practicing their own brand of Babylonian religion and perverted habits. They refused to join the moneylenders' religious swindle by not believing in the mythology that the moneylenders' scribes and rabbis had concocted. So, the Patriarchs of Abraham's Banking Guild decided to destroy the Benjamites completely. By doing so, two things were accomplished. (1) They could eliminate the only witnesses in Canaan who knew the true origin of the evil priests of Yahweh, whose true power was moneylender gold. And (2) the internal security of Abraham's First National Bank and Pawn Shop could be tested and solidified, if the chief priest could convince the eleven Hebrew tribes to war against and slaughter the tribe of Benjamin.

This was a nearly successful scheme. After agitating the eleven tribes with a dismembered woman and a story of woe, the Hebrews were successfully unified into a single army. Every member of the tribe of Benjamin was wiped out, except for 600 fighters who had taken refuge at the impregnable stronghold at the Rock of Rimmon.

Since the majority of the Benjamites were killed and the reminder chastised by the power of the Yahweh priests, the few remaining Benjamites were allowed to live and rejoin the confederation of Hebrew tribes. The other tribes had been induced to never intermarry with them. So, the Benjamites were allowed to steal wives from the other tribes to rebuild their families.

The Benjamites, who had been so loyal to the bankers of Babylon, protecting their caravans and staking out their future treasury grounds, were betrayed and murdered by their perfidious employers. With their leaders killed in battle and only the foot soldiers surviving, it was from this now fully chastised and very obedient tribe of Benjamin – who were still occupying the territory around the fortress of Jerusalem – that the moneylenders of Babylon chose their first king.

1 Samuel 9 begins by bragging about what a tall and handsome Hebrew Saul was as he searched about for some lost donkeys. The mythological heroes of the swarthy, kinky haired, big-nosed, horse-faced, sneering Jews, are always the most "handsome" males and "beautiful" females that any beak-nosed rabbi could imagine. It goes on to mention that one must always have a gift to give the priests of the Yahweh-god. It claims that Samuel was a great man of god about whom the servant of Saul says, "Look, there is a man of God in this town, a man held in high honor; everything he says comes true. Let us go there, then; perhaps he will be able to guide us on the journey we have undertaken." (1 Samuel 9:6.) So, after failing to find their donkeys, Saul and his servant went to the town of Ramah, where Samuel lived.

Samuel had just gone up to the "high place" to perform a sacrifice of some innocent animals and throw their blood around. After the Hebrews had murdered all of the Canaanites, they took over their high places, where Baal had been worshiped and substituted their own Canaanite god, Yahweh – a much better god, because he was Baal's father. The Hebrews who were gathered around the high place were waiting until after Samuel had "blessed" the sacrifice with the traditional Jewish Devil Claw Salute to eat the barbecued goats.

In the prelude of this 1 Samuel 9, Samuel is made into an all-knowing seer who, with clairvoyance, tells Saul that his lost donkeys have already been found. But they are of minor importance because "for whom is all the wealth of Israel destined, if not for you and *all your father's House*?" (1 Samuel 9:20) Thus, this future king of the Jews is claimed to be the rightful owner of all of the wealth of the country. Here, once again, is reemphasized the main point of all of the books of the *Hebrew Bible* and all of the deceits of the merchant-moneylenders' fables. The main theme of 1 Samuel 9 rears its greedy head. That is, "for whom is all the wealth of Israel destined?" With their skills in secretly shifting gold and silver from temple to temple and from country to country and from family to family, *and their skills in writing Contracts*, the patriarchs of Abrahams' First National Bank and Pawn Shop were now swindling all of the wealth of the Hebrew bandit tribes into their own personal control. Notice here that the wealth was to be not just Saul's, but also "all your father's house" which was the moneylender branch of the family centered in the Assyrian city of Kish. This connects the moneylender patriarchs of Babylonia, who controlled the Temple Cult, to the moneylender patriarchs of Assyria, who controlled the king who ruled in the territory of the Temple Cult.

First, through setting up trade relations with the scattered Hyksos gangs, the merchant-moneylenders of Babylon were able to siphon the looted treasures of Egypt away from the illiterate Hebrews and into their own strong rooms. By instructing their peddlers and merchants to record detailed genealogy charts of every Hebrew tribe in Canaan, they were able to portray themselves as the root family and "original" clan of the Hebrew genealogical tree. Falsely portraying themselves as Patriarchs of the Hebrews, the Babylonian swindlers then claimed the hereditary office of chief priest over all the tribes, making the Levites the officiating priests, tax collectors, census takers, official spies and busybodies.

But no matter how much gold and silver they raked into their treasury or how many sacrificed bulls and goats they ate, the priests were limited by the strictures of the priestly office in how much wealth they could enjoy. They were simply priests who had been set up to guard the treasury and operate the Yahweh-god scam, and as priests, they were not allowed to enjoy the limitless wealth generated by the Sumerian Swindle and the temple treasury. If they did, their reputation of holiness would diminish in proportion to their carnal enjoyment of riches. What was just as bad, the priests were limited to only ten percent of Jewish wealth when, in fact, they wanted it all.

Through the fraudulent Contract of the *Torah*, only the High Priest had been given great wealth. It was a means of paying and controlling the lesser priests. The priesthood had been established to guard the wealth, not so much to enjoy it. The actual full enjoyment of the wealth could only be had by those civilians who were outside of the priesthood.

The merchants and bankers could benefit as members of the Yahweh Cult. They could deposit their bullion and find protection as members of a larger community in the same way that individual jackals find protection by hiding in a large gang of their fellow jackals. But the actual *enjoyment* of the wealth could only be realized in full and without restriction by the kings or by wealthy civilians who did not have to maintain a pose of "holiness" as an impediment to their debauchery. Since they wrote the rules under which the priests commanded, the scribes of the moneylenders were sure to insert into 1 Samuel 9 the claim of the King of Israel, "For whom is all the wealth of Israel destined, if not for *the king of Israel and for all his relatives*?" Kingship in the ancient Near East was always a family affair. And all wealth was distributed between the Temple and the king. By owning both the king and the Temple, the moneylenders of Babylon owned all of the wealth.

First, the moneylenders of Abraham's Banking Family made their sons into chief priests over the superstitious and ignorant Hebrew tribes. Next, they had their chief priest declare one of their servants from the tribe of Benjamin to be king over all the tribes of Israel. This army of soldiers, whom these moneylenders didn't have to pay, deceived the Hebrews into fighting for the war god, Yahweh Sabbaoth – the "Lord of Hosts." His commands came out of the mouth of the chief priest, whose godly interests were identical to the godly interests of the moneylenders of Babylonia. It was a system of ownership and control that only the evil, rapacious mind of a banker could envision.

Since evidence of extensive literacy is lacking in Judah before the end of the eighth century BC, "The History of David's Rise" is unlikely to have been put into writing less than 200 years after David's time. Except for a single phrase, "House of David," found on a stele in 1993 AD, there is no other evidence that a David ever existed. (see Figure 105) Out of all of the Jewish bombast and trumpeting about their "great" King David, nobody in the entire ancient Near East had ever heard of him. With their prolific skills at counterfeiting and fraud, even this one chip of stone could be a modern Jewish forgery in an attempt to prove that the Jewish lies are true.

Figure 105: Tel Dan stele

There is *zero* archeological evidence that King Saul or King Solomon ever existed. Most definitely, the clay tablets and papyri of surrounding nations and the various records left in Palestine itself (on pottery shards, building inscriptions, etc.,) would have mentioned those allegedly "great kings," if they had ever existed. Especially such kings as David and Solomon – who the goat rustlers claim were so famous – would have at least an old ruin or a decorative motif somewhere in Palestine with a mention of them. But after more than a century of sifting through the dust of Palestine and translating the records of surrounding kingdoms, there is absolutely nothing, except two words on a stone chip. About King Solomon, who was allegedly far wealthier and more powerful than David, there is *absolutely zero*, nothing, to be found other than the *abracadabra* stories written by the scribes of Abraham's First National Bank and Pawn Shop. "Trust us. We are the Children of God. And we can prove it with these wonderful stories that we ourselves wrote: our own holy, most angelic selves." No, the Jews' stories are certainly not "wonderful." They are horrible to the extreme.

1 Samuel 9 and part of 1 Samuel 10 recount mythological tales of the bankers and moneylenders making themselves into *the kings* of the modern-day Jews, in addition to being their priests. By this time, the merchant-moneylenders' guilds of Ur and Harran had already gained hereditary control of the priesthood and, therefore, ultimate power over the Hebrew tribes. And now, they made themselves into kings over the Hebrew bandits. And to do this, all they had to do was lie: the only thing that bankers are really good at.

The biblical chronologies of Judges and Samuel are purely fictitious fables written in Babylon during the Exile to lend a 1000-year scheme to Israel's existence in Canaan. As such, they cannot be used to provide a chronology for the actual archaeological history of Israel. The miraculous patriarchs, judges, the three kings of the alleged United Monarchy – Saul, David, and Solomon – and the Hebrew prophets are known only from the pages of the Bible. Yet, there are a few notable exceptions to this absence of Jewish superheroes. Over a span of two and a half centuries, Assyrian kings took pains to enhance and preserve their fame by displaying in their capitols boastful accounts of their triumphs over the monarchs of the ancient Near East, including the kingdoms of the Israelians and Judeans. With the discovery of the ancient palaces of the Assyrian kings at Khorsabad, Nineveh, and Nimrud in the 19th century AD, details about the ancient Israelians came to light *for the first time from sources outside the Bible.* And all of these details showed the kings of the Israelians and Judeans, bowing at the feet of the Assyrian kings. For example, the Black Obelisk of King Shamshi-Adad V of Assyria shows King Jehu in the proper posture of Jews before Gentiles. (see Figure 106)

Figure 106: Black obelisk Jehu

Saul is not mentioned in any source outside the Bible, that is, in any ancient inscriptions or chronicles from neighboring countries. Most biblical historians have traditionally placed the reign of Saul in the late 11th century, around 1030-1010 BC. He belonged to the small Israelite tribe of Benjamin. The tribe of Benjamin (Babylonian name, Binu Yamina) was settled in the hill country north of Jerusalem, along with various other Canaanite peoples. Saul emerged on the scene as a local military hero (a judge) who led the Benjamite-Ephraimite resistance against surrounding enemies, especially the Philistines. Proclaimed king by his countrymen in response to his early victories, Saul spent the remainder of his career (a reign of unknown duration) defending what became the fledgling kingdom of Israel-Judah. His public career ended the same way it had begun, in battle. Both Saul and his son Jonathan were killed while fighting the Philistines on the slopes of Mt. Gilboa, according to the tale.

So, how can we summarize the biblical evidence? Although the text declares that Saul was king of "all Israel," archaeology proves these statements to be false. His activities were restricted to the northern highlands west of the Jordan, with an extension across the Jordan to Gilead in the east. It is important to note that the biblical narrative records no independent actions taken by Saul anywhere in the highlands of Judah. All of the detailed descriptions of the settlements south and southwest of Jerusalem are contained exclusively in the stories connected with Saul's pursuit of David or in the exploits of David alone. Saul, then, obviously did not rule over *all* of Israel. The Bible seems to suggest that he was a 10th century BC northern highland bandit leader who claimed a large area on both sides of the Jordan, with a special core territory in the hill country of Benjamin, *north* of Jerusalem. So, what kind of "kingdom" was that, other than one analogous to an ant on a watermelon?

The places most prominent in the Saul stories – Ramah, Mizpah, Geba, Michmash, Gibeon and Jerusalem – are all located in the Benjamite highlands immediately to the north of Jerusalem. Significantly, the territory surrounding Jerusalem was later transferred to the perfidious tribe of Judah, the tribe that murdered everybody and claimed the treasury town of Jerusalem as its own.

The only record that a king named Saul ever existed is found in the *Hebrew Bible*. But this Jewish lie is small when compared to the real intent of the Jewish swindle in the story. 1 Samuel 10 is another attempt at making the Hebrew priests appear special. In this chapter, the superhero, Samuel, is reputed to be clairvoyant. He can see the future and tell how many men young Saul will meet the next day and how many loaves of bread they will carry. And he can tell in advance that the holy dice (Urim and Thummim) will choose Saul to be the first king of Israel.

1 Samuel 10 uses all of the signs and symbols of the ancient Near East for establishing Saul as king. The Jewish prophet and priest, Samuel, anoints Saul's head with salad dressing and gives him his blessing. Saul dances the traditional Hebrew mambo-hula by wiggling his horsey Jewish face into a grin and waving his arms around trying to feel something. This is called "ecstasy" by the rabbis and passes for such among modern Jews, too. The Hebrews saw Saul wiggling around with groups of gyrating prophets and other loafers and they asked, "Is Saul one of the prophets, too?" In other words, they were wondering if this ordinary goat rustler was holy in some way. Wiggling around and grimacing was not enough Jewish holiness for the more skeptical of the Hebrews, because the holy dice could choose a proper Jewish king. So, that settled it. The holy dice chose Saul as king and they were never wrong, because they were a gift from the god who wrote the Scriptures. Whether the dice were loaded or not, 1 Samuel 10 doesn't say. All it does say is that the holy dice had indicated that the Yahweh-god chose Saul to be king over all of the Hebrew cutthroats.

As sure as a banker swindles your wealth, this chapter ends with the holy assertion that a king deserves gifts and presents from the people. Those scraggly goat rustlers surrounding Saul were complimented as being

> "...the mighty men whose hearts God had touched. But there were some scoundrels who said, 'How can this fellow save us?' They despised him, and offered him no present." (1 Samuel 10:26-27.)

To the moneylenders of Abrahams' First National Bank and Pawn Shop, those who give the king presents are "mighty men," but those who don't give presents are "scoundrels." Everything about Judaism is based in materialism and "getting more stuff."

1 Samuel 11 is a tale about how Saul was proclaimed king. In secret, Samuel had already anointed his head with salad dressing, making him king. Now, when Nahash the Ammonite laid siege against the tiny town of Jabesh-Gilead, he declared that instead of killing all the Hebrews, he would make a treaty with them as long as they would allow him to blind them all in their right eyes. This seemed like a reasonable request to the goat rustlers, but always ready to haggle, they made him a counteroffer. They agreed to be blinded in their right eyes and to be his servants, if he would first let them send for help. What kind of lame deal is that to an attacker surrounding a city? Let them send for help!? Anyway, as the story goes, Nahash – certainly not the brightest among the Ammonites – let the Hebrews talk him into stupidity and *he gave them a whole week* to send out messengers begging the other Hebrews for rescue. Semites! They tell the most unbelievable stories – stories to make you into a fool, if you are stupid enough to believe them!

When the messengers reached Gibeah, all of the Hebrews there began to whine and cry in the traditional Jewish fashion. (1 Samuel 11:4.) But "the spirit of Yahweh seized on Saul when he heard these words, and his fury was stirred to fierce flames." (1 Samuel 11:6.) With the bloodthirsty logic of the Jews, Saul

> "took a yoke of oxen and cut them in pieces which he sent by messengers throughout the territory of Israel with these words, 'If anyone will not march with Saul, this shall be done with his oxen!' At this, the dread of Yahweh fell on the people and they marched out as one man." (1 Samuel 11:6.)

Threatening to cost them a loss of money is what it takes to get the Jews all riled up. Oxen were valuable animals and the threat of losing them caused those goat thieves to "dread Yahweh." None of this tall tale makes sense, of course. But this is why the rabbis have been able for so long to get away with their lies. They don't have to make sense. All that is required is for you *to be-*

lieve the lies of the Jews. Once you believe the Jews, then it doesn't matter if they are lying or not. And why? Because you believe them!

In 1 Samuel 12, Samuel transferred the political power of the priests and judges into the power of King Saul. The scribes of Babylon claimed that Samuel could call down thunder and rain through his priestly power. So, the power of God was still claimed by the priesthood and the admonition to follow the Law of Moses was still evoked for success, but the power to conduct war and maintain civil authority was transferred to the king.

1 Samuel 13 blends earlier stories to bring them into line with the goals of the Babylonian Bankers. Saul chose 3,000 men to fight against another of the "mighty nations." In this case, the Philistines had "three thousand chariots, six thousand horse and a force as numerous as the sand on the seashore." (1 Samuel 13:5.) Once again, those "Super Jews" were battling against a "mighty foe" that outnumbered them – at least in the fables. "When the men of Israel saw that their situation was desperate, since they were hard pressed, they hid in caves, in holes, in crevices, in vaults, in wells. Many, too, crossed over the Jordan fords into the territory of Gad and Gilead." (1 Samuel 13:6-7.) Even in this desperate situation, the power of the Jewish priests is claimed to be unsurpassed while the treachery of the Yahweh-god is firmly reestablished. 1 Samuel 13 shows that even when there is nothing but the best intentions and even when nothing but the loyal faith and pious belief is behind a Jew's actions, it is only the power of the priests and rabbis that count in relations with the Yahweh-god. A lying and treasonous god who gives his promise and then breaks that promise, this god of the Jews shows them what kind of people that they should be since they were "made in his image" and are required to "walk in his ways."

In this case, Saul had been abandoned by the cowardly Jews, who were full of bravery when they outnumbered little towns and defenseless villages, but ran and hid from seasoned fighters. The situation was desperate for Saul, who was relying on Samuel to meet him at a specified time. But as the priest to a God of Lies, Samuel didn't keep his appointment to offer a sacrifice to the Yahweh-god. In those days, in all countries, no armies moved without a sign from their gods to give them direction in battle. Without a beneficial reading from the liver of a sacrificed sheep or the positive bet from the holy dice table, no one would do any fighting.

After seven days, Samuel still had not come to offer a sacrifice to the Yahweh-god as he had promised Saul. Since the goat rustlers all believed that sacrifices to the god would help them gain victory in battle, instead of waiting for the tardy Samuel, Saul offered the sacrifice. Then, Samuel showed up. And oh, what a big deal Samuel, the priest, made of that! Saul had all the rights of a king to decide how to lead the people, but 1 Samuel 13 shows that only the priests are allowed to kill the animals, splatter the blood around and eat the barbecue, not the king.

> "Samuel said, 'What have you done?' Saul replied, 'I saw the
> army deserting me and dispersing, and you had not come at the

time fixed, while the Philistines were mustering at Michmash. So I thought: Now the Philistines are going to fall on me at Gilgal and I have not implored the favor of Yahweh. So, I felt obliged to act and I offered the holocaust myself.' Samuel answered Saul, 'You have acted like a fool. If you had carried out the order Yahweh your God commanded you, Yahweh would have confirmed your authority over Israel forever. But now your sovereignty will not last; Yahweh has searched out a man for himself after his own heart and designated him leader of his people, since you have not carried out what Yahweh ordered you.' Samuel then rose and left Gilgal to continue his journey." (1 Samuel 13:11-14.)

This left Saul on his own with only the holy dice (the Urim and Thummim) to guide him. Oy! How could Saul step on the rights to the holy barbecue without a priest to help him eat it?

So, now Samuel claimed that for doing the priest's job, Saul's kingship would not last. The treasonous Yahweh-god of the crafty and sly Jewish priests had already found a successor (David) to replace Saul. Such was the power of the priests that even the slightest error by the king in not obeying their every word could lead to his downfall – even when the priest had been a liar!

In spite of this, Saul and the 600 remaining Hebrew fighters went out to battle the Philistines. Remember, the Philistines had 3,000 chariots, 6,000 cavalry and soldiers as numerous as the sands of the seashore. And to make matters worse, the Hebrews were not smart enough to sharpen their own plowshares and axes. The Philistines had a monopoly on iron implements and blacksmithing technology, and the Hebrews didn't know how to make steel swords or spears. So, against this big army of well-armed Caucasian Philistines with the latest Iron Age technology, the rabbis wrote of these 600 poor, innocent Hebrews "on the day of the battle of Michmash no one in the whole army with Saul and Jonothan had either sword or spear in his hand, except, however Saul and his son Jonathan." (1 Samuel 13:22.) Oh, the tension and suspense which must have been felt by the wide-eyed audience of farmers and goat rustlers as they listened to the scribes read their fables from the sacred goatskins! 600 *unarmed Hebrews* with only two swords against a fully armed army as numerous as the sands of the sea! "What happened next?" you might shout in anticipation.

1 Samuel 14 is a summation of Saul's victories over the enemies of the Hebrews. It shows clearly how much these "holy ones of God" depended upon the holy dice to make decisions for them and it claims that the holy dice always gave a true reply to questions. Saul was victorious over all enemies and the Philistines were chased out of the highlands. Since the better land was in the lowlands along the seacoast, the Philistines still got the better real estate, which the Jews *never in their entire history* possessed, regardless of the alleged "promises" of their mighty, lying Yahweh-god.

More of the vindictive malice of this Yahweh-god through the mouth of the High Priest of the treasury is expressed in 1 Samuel 15. Unending vengeance and hatred were (and are) characteristics of the Jews. Insults and aggressions from *hundreds of years previously* were remembered and avenged, long after everyone else had died or forgotten about the incident. Jewish malicious vengeance is seen even into modern times with their ongoing hatred of the German people – a people who attempted to throw off the Jewish bankers' yoke – and also with the Jewish persecution of Christians and suppression of Christianity (for details, read Volume III, *The Bloodsuckers of Judah*). To *rationalize* their murders, the Jews kill every member of a town or a clan and then say it was "Jewish justice" – a long-deserved revenge from the long-forgotten past. This is usually *an invented lie* to justify their genocide and thievery.

The Jews cite ancient history as an excuse for committing atrocities and murders, but they also use it as their guide for present-day barbarity. It is a sick state of mind elicited by those disgusting goat rustlers. They pose as "God's Chosen Angels," with their *self-proclaimed* authority, and murder whomever they don't like. This was the psychopathic corruption that Jesus Christ opposed hundreds of years later when he began his mission among the Jews, those "murderers, liars, deceivers, hypocrites and very children of the devil."

In 1 Samuel 15:2, Samuel says to Saul, "Thus speaks Yahweh Sabaoth (the God of Armies), 'I will repay what Amalek did to Israel when they opposed them on the road by which they came up out of Egypt.'" It doesn't matter that, even by a biblical time frame, the Amalekites had lived 500 years before Saul. It doesn't matter to the Jewish writers of this fable that the Amalekites were defending their land from more than 600,000 Hyksos-Hebrew bandits who were expecting to just walk into Amalekite territory and steal what they wanted. It was an "insult" to the self-chosen goat rustlers of God that they had not been welcomed with offerings of food or acknowledged as the kings of the earth, as they so much expected. So, the 500-year-old Amalekite rebuff was grounds for Samuel, the evil priest of Yahweh, to declare to Saul,

> "Now, go and strike down Amalek, put him under the ban with all that he possesses. Do not spare him, but kill man and woman, babe and suckling, ox and sheep, camel and donkey." (1 Samuel 15:3.)

Under the ban, nothing but the gold and silver could be kept *and that was to be given to Samuel and the priests*. Once again, the bloodthirsty, genocidal insanity of the Jews becomes part of the fraud of the modern Jewish experience. Many must die, so that the Jews may live in luxury.

Samuel did not want the Amalekite land, he wanted only to murder them all, take their gold, and get Jewish vengeance upon these people of Edom who, 500 years previously, had refused to feed 600,000 Hebrew bandits carrying several tons of gold and silver loot, while running from Pharaoh (and barely subsisting on grasshoppers and quail, while feeding their priests bulls, goats and sheep). Such were the terrible crimes of the Amalekites' ancestors that they all must be killed – to the last child, nursing at his mother's breast! This is Jewish "justice." This is Jewish vengeance – a never-ending, seething, demonic hatred from a people who lie and claim that they really are not devils. Even before building the Temple, the first order of Jewish business was to exterminate the people of Edom known as Amalekites, not because they were a threat to the Jews, but because they had not welcomed the Jews to feasts and 500 years previously! These are the heroes of the Jews.

With more inflated numbers to show how mighty they were supposed to be:

> "Saul summoned the people ... two hundred thousand foot soldiers (and ten thousand men of Judah). Saul went to the city of Amelek and lay in ambush in the river bed." (1 Samuel 15:4-5.)

The problem with this statement is that there were not that many people living in the area at the time. This is another Jewish lie revealed by archaeology. Only a handful of permanent sites, including Jerusalem, have been recorded in archaeological surveys of the entire territory throughout the Late Bronze and Early Iron Age (~1550-900 BC). Most were tiny villages. There was no real urban center, not even a single fortified town. In fact, the small sedentary population of the southern highlands can be estimated, on the basis of settlement size, at no more than a few thousand. This contrasts sharply with the lowland territories to the west, where the major Canaanite and later Philistine city-states each contained dozens of towns and villages, with a large settled population in the main centers and outlying agricultural lands. Once again, the Jewish scribes are caught in their lies by modern archaeology.

But the rabbis never let the truth get in the way of a useful story. Saul defeated the Amalekites and murdered every man, woman, child and little baby. But

> "He took Agag king of the Amalekites alive and, executing the ban, put all of the people to the sword. But Saul and the army spared Agag with the best of the sheep and cattle, the fatlings and lambs and all that was good. They did not want to put those under the ban; they only put under the ban what was poor and worthless." (1 Samuel 15:8-9.)

The best cattle they reserved to sacrifice to the Yahweh-god. And sacrifices always meant tasty barbecues. But this put Saul into conflict with the maniacal priest, Samuel. King Saul did what he thought was best for his people. Rather than slaughtering the cattle for the buzzards and burning the goods of the Amalekites, he allowed his soldiers to keep them for themselves.

Yet, the fanatical orders of the priest had to be obeyed. 1 Samuel 15 emphasizes that no matter what stupid, narrow-minded, ignorant frauds the priests and rabbis really are, following their orders is of paramount importance. Samuel heard this "all-knowing god," this "mighty and wise god," this god who knew everything, talking as a voice in his head. And the All-Knowing and All-Wise voice in his head said, "I regret having made Saul king, for he has turned away from me and has not carried out my orders" – so, Samuel whined and cried all night long to Yahweh (1 Samuel 15:11), because that was the standard street theater of the rabbis and priests. While everybody was trying to get some sleep, Samuel was howling like a maniac to the moon god, letting everybody know that he was distraught.

When Samuel confronted Saul about why he had spared the best cattle and sheep, Saul replied, "The people spared the best of the sheep and oxen to sacrifice them to Yahweh, your God; the rest we put under the ban." (1 Samuel 15:15.) But piety is never enough for the God of Abraham's First National Bank and Pawn Shop. Those priests were only interested in obedience to the letter of their law and the tyranny of their frothing lips, paid to the nearest grain of silver in their account books. Saul was a good, sincere king who obeyed the orders of the priest in light of his own understanding, but he was not the sort of mindless drudge that the Bank of Abraham demanded from their minions.

It is noteworthy that a basic technique of the modern Jews and Judaism is expressed in 1 Samuel 15. It is the technique of telling lies, while simultaneously declaring how virtuous they are. In this instance, the Yahweh-god allegedly made Saul the king. This was the order of an All-Knowing and Mighty god. The word of such a wise god could not be revoked. But now the Yahweh-god (according to his mouthpiece, Samuel) was going back on his word yet again! Samuel tells Saul,

> "Today Yahweh has torn the kingdom of Israel from you and given it to a neighbor of yours who is better than you. And yet the glory of Israel will not lie or go back on his word, for he is not a man to go back on his word." (1 Samuel 15:28.)

Thus, the Yahweh-god and his evil priests and rabbis *can claim* to be ever so virtuous and holy, while telling lies in the same breath. The Jewish priests claim that their god does not lie or go back on his word, but at the same time, he is lying and going back on his word! Like modern Jews, the ancient Hebrews believed that telling lies was no different than telling the Truth. This is the ancient philosophy of sociopaths, psychopaths and thieves who have no inhibitions toward anything in obtaining their own desires. The Jews are taught from childhood that there is no difference between truth or falsehood, or between good and evil, so whatever they say is good enough for them. Whatever crimes they commit are only an embarrassment to them if they are actually caught.

Samuel, this wonderful and wise priest of the Hebrews, offered King Agag as a human sacrifice to the Yahweh-god. "Samuel butchered Agag before Yahweh at Gilgal." (1 Samuel 15:33.) He butchered him like a goat; he didn't execute him like a man. Human sacrifice has always been a part of Judaism. But the Jews lie about it, trying to make us think that they really are the "Chosen Ones of God," as they pretend to be, rather than the devils they are.

And so closes 1 Samuel 15, with the "holy-military-priest-judge" Samuel butchering King Agag before the altar of Yahweh, sprinkling his blood and burning him on the altar of the Jews. Again, the lying – but All-Knowing – *Yahweh* goes back on his word and regrets having made Saul king. (1 Samuel 15:35.) These are the wonderful heroes of the Jews: lying gods, bloody priests and genocidal maniacs offering up entire towns as sacrifices to their god of the merchants and moneylenders. Oh, yes, the Jews are holy people! They walk in the ways of their god! But the god of the Jews is a Demon, and the people of this Demon are all monsters!

1 Samuel 16 begins the fable of David. The treacherous Yahweh-god had again "changed his mind." Again, he "took back his promise" by rejecting Saul for being a good king and taking the initiative, when the lying priest of the lying god didn't show up for the battle at the appointed time. Samuel was seven days late. That's a long time to wait with enemy troops threatening to pounce and his army dwindling away. Since Saul thought for himself and offered a sacrifice to Yahweh (which the unavailable priest, Samuel, had planned to do), there were grounds for the Yahweh-god to make his "eternal promise" into a lie.

Samuel heard a voice in his head saying that the Yahweh-god had rejected Saul as king, so he went to find someone else. Since lying and deceiving were so traditional to the Jews, it was not considered bad manners for Samuel to lie to Saul. He claimed that he wanted to travel to the town of Bethlehem and offer a sacrifice, when his real intention was to find a replacement for Saul. There, in Bethlehem, he found David.

The name "David" is an ancient Semitic word for "commander" or "military leader." So, once again, the bloodthirsty, militaristic cult of Abraham's First National Bank and Pawn Shop is very apparent. The god of the bankers is the Lord of Hosts (God of Armies). Their judges (military leaders) are actually bandits. Their great heroes are thieves and murderers. And their priests commit genocide at every opportunity. After they murder everybody and burn everything to ashes, they *always* save the gold and silver. Wow! It's almost too holy to believe! Samuel, a judge (military leader), goes in search of another military leader, a "David." When Samuel found David, he anointed his head with salad dressing.

This anointing with olive oil was a magical practice used by the Hebrew priests as a kind of blessing. However, if you, Reader, are willing to rub some extra virgin olive oil onto your own head, you can feel the beneficent effects on your scalp. You should do this after a shampoo, once your hair is dry. Olive oil opens the pores and nourishes the follicles. It makes your hair and scalp feel glowing and healthy. But you should not interpret that nice glowing feeling the way this ignorant goat rustler apparently did, because "the spirit of Yahweh seized on David and stayed with him from that day on." (1 Samuel 16:13.) Be smarter than David and know that it is just salad dressing.

As the story goes, the treasonous Yahweh-god sent an evil spirit to afflict Saul. Saul was a good guy, as far as a thieving Hebrew can be good. He was sincere and loyal to his god. But a banker's god like Yahweh is not loyal to anyone, since He is the god of liars, created in the moneylender's own image. Saul had been a good and loyal king, but he was his own man and he thought for himself. The bankers wanted a king to take control of the civil functions of their scheme, a man whose virtues could be totally invented and who was a total servant of the priests. After all, none of these stories actually happened, since they were fictionalizations of 200-year-old legends. The stories were written in Babylonia to teach a lesson and bolster the authority of the priests. They were stories for the post-Exilic community of Jews, not stories that the Hebrews themselves had ever heard.

Based on archaeological evidence and clues within the text, we can say that the tale of Saul and David could not possibly have been written until more than 200 years after the death of David. Analyses of the archaeological data from Jerusalem has shown that the settlement of the 10th century BC was no more than a small, poor highland village. And as we note in examining the rise of David, archaeological surveys have revealed that the hill country of Judah to the south of Jerusalem was at that time inhabited only by a few relatively small settlements, with no large, fortified towns. There were no great, walled cities for the bandit chief, David, to conquer.

The "mighty" King David was little more than a thieving cutthroat. He certainly didn't control more than a gang of bandits. Over a century of excavations in the City of David have produced surprisingly meager remains from the late 16th to mid-eighth centuries BC. They amount to no more than a few walls and a modest quantity of pottery sherds, mostly found in erosion debris. The situation has been found to be the same at every excavated site in Jerusalem.

The evidence clearly shows that 10th century Jerusalem was a small highland village that controlled a sparsely settled hinterland. If it had been the capital of a great kingdom, with the wherewithal to muster tens of thousands of soldiers, collect tribute from vassals, and maintain garrisons in Aram, Damascus and Edom (as the biblical narrative informs us it did), one would expect the presence of administrative buildings and storehouses, even outside the royal compound at the summit of the ridge. One would also expect to see changes in the villages of Judah – from which a significant portion of David's armies were presumably mobilized and which would stand to benefit, at least indirectly, from the kingdom's allegedly great wealth. Yet, there is not the slightest evidence of any change in the landscape of Judah until the following century. The population remained low and the villages modest and few in number throughout the 10th century BC. So, this story of David and his greatness are proven to be, at best, very incredibly exaggerated, and at worst, mostly lies. What does it mean for an allegedly "holy scripture" that is the "word of God" when its primary heroes are proven to be little more than goat rustlers and bandits?

1 Samuel 17 tells the fable about the Philistine giant Goliath and the shepherd, David. Goliath was six cubits and one span tall, that is about ten feet

tall. He wore a bronze helmet and a bronze breastplate of scale armor. The breastplate weighed 5,000 shekels or about 156 pounds. The shaft of his spear was like a weaver's beam and its head weighed 600 shekels, (about 19 pounds). This ten-foot-tall Philistine takes his place alongside the other myths used by the Jews to make themselves look great – great, at least, in the stories they tell about themselves. In actual fact, there was no David slaying a Goliath. And certainly, the time frame was once again put into the ancient past to give the Jews another claim to an antiquity which they don't actually possess. The story is another fictional yarn of the Jews. The internal evidence in the story itself contains the proof that it was not written when claimed.

Whether Elhanan or David did the killing in the original tale, the detailed description of Goliath's armor reveals the famous biblical story to be a late seventh-century BC composition. It expressed both the ideology of holy war and the particular enemies later faced by Judah during King Josiah's time.

Goliath's armor, as described in the Bible, bears little resemblance to the military equipment of the early Philistines as archaeology has revealed it. Instead of wearing bronze helmets, the *Peleset* (Palestinians) shown on the walls of the mortuary temple of Ramesses III in Upper Egypt wore distinctive feather-topped headdresses. Instead of being heavily armored and carrying a spear, javelin, and sword, they used a single spear and did not wear the metal leg armor known as greaves. However, the biblical description of Goliath's armor is not simply a fanciful creation. Every single item has clear parallels to Aegean weapons and armor from the Mycenaean period to classical times, as shown by archaeology. In all periods within this general time frame, one can find metal helmets, metal armor, and metal greaves. Yet, until the seventh century BC, these items were relatively rare in the Greek world. It is only with the appearance of the heavily armed Greek hoplites of the seventh century BC (and later) that standard equipment comes to resemble Goliath's. In fact, the standard hoplite's accoutrements were identical to Goliath's, consisting of a metal helmet, plate armor, metal greaves, two spears, a sword, and a large shield. And this suggests that the author of the biblical story of David and Goliath had an intimate knowledge of the seventh century BC Greek hoplites.

As another Semitic fiction, the Hebrew scribes wrote in 1 Samuel 17 that David said to Goliath, "Who is this uncircumcised Philistine who dares insult the armies of the living God?" (1 Samuel 17:26.) By the seventh century, Abraham's Bankers' Guild had convinced the Hebrews that they were the army of God. This same trick would be used a thousand years later under another Semitic fraud, the Arabian goat-molester named Mohammad (mhrh).

Not only do the scribes claim Goliath was a ten-foot giant, but they claim David was a Hebrew Superman. They claim that he was able to single-handedly kill both lions and bears. Of these, David claims that he seized the lions and bears by the hair around their jaws and struck them down and killed them. (1 Samuel 17:35.) Wow! It was written by the Jews, so it must be true!

The scribes spun a good yarn in building up the might of Goliath against this little Hebrew shepherd boy, David. The intent of their fable is clear, as they scripted David saying to Goliath, "You come against me with sword and spear and javelin, but I come against you in the name of Yahweh Sabaoth, the God of the armies of Israel that you have dared to insult." (1 Samuel 17:45.) Big words, indeed! The god of the armies of Israel smells blood.

Regardless of the fictional character of David or his killing of the giant Goliath or his murders and thieveries, all of which gladdened the heart of every Hebrew goat-stealer, there is only one proof that this mighty midget of a king ever existed. The Mesha inscription (and 2 Kings 3:5) records an armed uprising in Moab that swept away its control by the kingdom of Israel after Ahab's death. The major blow is recorded in the Tel Dan inscription – the only non-biblical evidence for the name David – which confirms the defeat of the Omrides by Hazael, King of Damascus. On that stela are the words, "House of David." Other than these words, neither Saul nor David nor Solomon were known to any of the people of the ancient near East. These are the heroes of the Jews: bandits who never existed and "mighty kings" of turnip patches.

1 Samuel 18 gives further evidence that the priests wanted to claim that the power of God cannot be exercised except by the priests. Saul's innocent "transgression" of not following the exact orders from the priest, Samuel, in 1 Samuel 15, is further avenged here in 1 Samuel 18. Now, "an evil spirit from God seized on Saul and he fell into a fit of frenzy while he was in his house." (1 Samuel 18:10.) Thus, the priests claim that if you don't follow their orders, you will be destroyed by the Yahweh-god. The attributes of kingship, which are given by the Yahweh-god and can be taken away by the Yahweh-god, are featured in this chapter. And "all Israel and Judah loved David, because he was their leader in all their exploits." (1 Samuel 18:11.)

The nastiness of the modern Jews can be traced directly to their traditions, which come from their "holy scriptures" of hatred, genocide and grand larceny. Here in 1 Samuel 18, in exchange for marrying his daughter, Saul wants David to kill 100 Philistines and cut off their foreskins. So, David and his men killed 200 Philistines, cut off the flesh of their penises and counted them out one by one for King Saul. For this bride-price of murdered mens' penis flesh, David bought himself a beautiful (though lice-infested) Jewish bride, Michal, King Saul's daughter. The rabbinical definition of "beautiful" is a Jewess who shaves the hair from her armpits and vulva, all other attributes being secondary. Therefore, according to the rabbis, all Jewesses are beautiful. And according to a toad, all toads are beautiful. The bloody foreskins of 200 murdered men as the bride-price for a Jewish toad is a nasty price to pay. But as the later writings of the rabbis in the *Babylonian Talmud* prove, Jewish women themselves are some very nasty things. This is made abundantly clear in the *Babylonian Talmud* "Book of Niddah," which proves that Jewish women are disgusting and filthy, even when they are beautiful to both toads and rabbis.

Once again in 1 Samuel 19, the perfidious Yahweh-god of Abraham's Bankers' Guild is not to be trusted. That this god's modern-day followers are likewise mischievous and treacherous bodes ill for Mankind, when treason and theft are considered to be virtues among the Jews and their followers. The

Yahweh-god, in his infinite wisdom, had made Saul king of the Hebrews. But now this mighty god, whom the rabbis claimed to be omniscient, changes his mind about Saul. He "regrets having made Saul king." (1 Samuel 15:11.) Now, another "evil spirit from Yahweh came on Saul while he was sitting in his house with his spear in his hand while David was plunking on the Jews' harp. Irritated by the noise, Saul tried to pin David to the wall with his spear, but he avoided Saul's thrust and the spear struck the wall. (1 Samuel 19:9-10.) David escaped to his house where his nasty wife (Saul's daughter, Michal) told him to run away to live with Samuel, while she practiced Jewish "virtue" and told lies to her father. (1 Samuel 19:11-17.)

Saul sent teams of assassins to kill David. But they found Samuel and David prancing around naked and wiggling their arms in the air as they danced the hora and swooned with ecstasy. It looked like fun, so all of the Jewish assassins stripped down naked, wiggled their butts and tossed around their circumcised penises in the traditional holy dance of the Jews. Finally, after three teams of assassins had all taken off their clothes and joined Samuel and David dancing naked, wiggling around and trying to get holy by slapping their penises around in rhythm to the music, Saul joined the party. "He too stripped off his clothes and he too fell into an ecstasy in the presence of Samuel, and falling down lay there naked all that day and night." (1 Samuel 19:24.) So, if you ever see any Jews dancing, don't wait! Call the police immediately!

1 Samuel 20 tells of the friendship between Saul's son, Jonathan and David. Here for sure, Saul is determined to kill David. During the New Moon feast, sacred to the Moon God and carried over by the merchant-moneylenders into their Yahweh Cult, Jonathan finds the proof that his father was determined to kill David.

1 Samuel 21 and 22 relate part of David's journey escaping from Saul. As a tradition with the Jews, banditry is always their first choice in occupations when ordinary larceny becomes too strenuous. David organized a gang of outlaws with his brothers and with the members of his father's family. These cutthroats are given a heroic and revolutionary theme by the scribes in this chapter, who write: "All the oppressed, those in distress, all those in debt, anyone who had a grievance, gathered around him and he became their leader. There were about four hundred men with him." (1 Samuel 22:2.) This is the same recipe that the later Jews would use whenever they wanted to organize a revolutionary cadre for overthrowing a state. You will see more of this technique in Volume III, *The Bloodsuckers of Judah*.

Once again, of the historical David we can say nothing, except for the similarity between the thieving *Apiru* gangs that threatened Abdu-Heba and the Biblical tales of the outlaw chief David and his band of cutthroats roaming the Hebron hills and the Judean desert.

True to the overly generous character of the Jews, Saul was so annoyed that David had escaped him that he had everyone slaughtered who had given David aid. This included all of the priests of Yahweh, totaling 85 Jews, plus their families. Then, Saul had the priest's entire town of Nob put to the sword, killing "men and women, children and infants, cattle and donkeys and sheep." (1 Samuel 22:19.) These kinds of slaughters are examples that the bloodthirsty Jews follow even today, "walking in the ways of their god," whenever they gain power over Gentiles.

As for the priests of Nob, only Abiathar, the son of the chief priest, escaped Saul's Hebrew vengeance. He joined David's bandits and became his priest. Abiathar was to remain David's priest until David's death, at which time he was dismissed by Solomon.

1 Samuel 23 relates how David used the holy dice to figure out how to avoid capture by Saul. He carried with him the ephod and that fancy gold and red and purple priest suit from Nob. Upon this was a breastplate of gold for asking a question of the Yahweh-god and then throwing the holy dice (the Urim and Thummim) to get an answer. He managed to avoid fighting Saul's army, because the Philistines were attacking. So, Saul had to call off his pursuit of David to go and fight the Philistines, letting David and his 600 bandits escape.

1 Samuel 24 tells of further pursuit by Saul. But while Saul went into a cave to ease his bowels (always an important detail in Jewish religious writings), David, who was hiding in the cave, cut off a piece of Saul's cloak. Cutting off a piece of Saul's cloak was meant to prove that he meant Saul no harm.

The basic materialism of the Jewish belief system is here expressed. Jews did not believe in an eternal After Life in Paradise after they died. But no different than any other religion of the time, they believed in an eternal gloom in the grave. When they died, that was it. Like the other religions of the ancient Near East, the Hebrews only desired that their name would be remembered and their many children would continue their genealogy. So, after David had proved to Saul that he meant him no harm, because he had only cut off a piece of his cloak and not killed him, Saul made David take an oath. "Now swear to me by Yahweh that you will not cut off my descendants after me nor blot out my name from my family." (1 Samuel 24:22.)

1 Samuel 25 tells of David and his band of thieves practicing the ancient "protection racket" that is still a major source of income in modern gangster neighborhoods and among the Muslims. He and his men levied a "tax" on the shepherds in his theater of operations, "protecting" them from other gangs of Hebrews and not stealing from them, in exchange for a payoff. When shearing time rolled around, it was time to collect the "protection money." In this case, it was time to claim a share of the wool, meat and cheese.

David sent ten of his soldiers to Nabal, a rich shepherd who owned 3,000 sheep and 1,000 goats. Nabal and his shepherds were shearing the sheep when David's soldiers arrived, demanding the protection fee euphemistically called, "the law of brotherhood." This "law" was basic Jewish logic: "We don't beat or kill or steal from you, so you must pay us a fee for protecting you from us."

But Nabal (whose name meant "fool") refused to pay the protection fee. So, like the good Jew that he was, David decided to kill Nabal and every single one of his shepherds, along with all of the men and boys of his family. Of course, David and his 400 bandits would then steal all of Nabal's wealth, cattle, sheep, women and girls and take them for loot. This would also serve as a warning to any of the other shepherds who refused to pay David for protection from David.

Please note: First, this "mighty king" was merely a bandit preying on small time shepherds. Second, David was doing what all ruthless gangsters do, murdering anyone who objected to being robbed. This great "hero" of the Jews was an ordinary criminal. The foolish Christians who believe what the Jews wrote about themselves, in such glowing terms of "pious" or "holy" light, should look more closely at what their own words reveal about them. Here, David is about to slaughter everyone of Nabal's family, including the employees, because he didn't pay the protection fee. Remember this when the ruthlessness of David's character is later claimed by the Jews to be something akin to a Hebrew "saintliness."

Upon hearing of her husband's refusal to pay the protection fee, Nabal's wife, Abigail, sent a large bribe to David. "Abigail hastily took two hundred loaves, two skins of wine, five sheep ready prepared, five measures of roasted grain, a hundred bunches of raisins and two hundred cakes of figs and loaded them on donkeys." (1 Samuel 25:18.) These she sent to David, who accepted the bribe and refrained from murdering anybody on that particular day.

When Nabal was told what happened, he had a heart attack and died. And because Abigail was intelligent and beautiful (1 Samuel 25:3.) by Jewish standards, just as all horse-faced and big-mouthed Jewesses who shave their arm pits and pubic hair are intelligent and beautiful, David took her as a wife to add to his harem of other wives, Ahinoam and Jezreel. Saul had taken his daughter back from David and given her to someone else.

1 Samuel 26 claims that Saul, with 3,000 troops, was in pursuit of David. Of course, in those days, before flashlights were invented, dark nights made it easy to sneak around. Regardless of flickering campfires and night watchmen, David and his lieutenant, Abishai, were able to sneak into Saul's camp to find him "lying inside the camp with the troops bivouacking round him," and fast asleep. (1 Samuel 26:5.)

Now was David's opportunity to kill Saul, as his lieutenant urged. But the intent of the scribes of Abraham's Bankers' Guild was to train the Jews to respect the office of king as a divine function of God. So, they had David invoke the "divinity" of the Jewish kings and say, "Do not kill him, for who can lift his hand against Yahweh's anointed and be without guilt?" (1 Samuel 26:9.) Instead, David stole Saul's spear and a pitcher of water and ran off to the next hill across the wadi. Even here, in this Manual of Jewish Ethics, the belief is expressed in the local nature of all gods. Their belief was that Yahweh was one of many gods. David called to Saul and asked why he was chased out of Yahweh's presence in the land of Israel, since he could only escape Saul by leaving the territory. The chapter ends with the two antagonists going their separate ways.

1 Samuel 27 shows what a murdering Hebrew bandit David really was. He escaped from Saul by moving his gang of 600 bandits and their families

into Philistine territory. Achish, the King of Gath, gave David the town of
Ziklag to live in. From this base, David's Hebrew gangsters, like modern Jews,
had no intention of actually working for a living, working by farming or animal husbandry. They preferred murder and pillage instead, since the banking
business was then closed to them.

> "David laid the countryside waste and left neither man nor
> woman alive but took the sheep and oxen, donkeys, camels and
> garments and came back, bringing them to Achish. Achish
> would ask, 'Where did you go raiding today?' David would re-
> ply, 'Against the Negeb of Judah,' or 'the Negeb of Jarehmeel,'
> or 'the Negeb of the Kenites.' But David never brought a man
> or woman back alive to Gath 'in case' as he thought 'they in-
> form against us and say, "David did such and such." This was
> David's practice all the time he stayed in Philistine territory." (1
> Samuel 27:9-11.)

It was the practice of a lying, murdering monster, one of the great heroes of the Jews.

The actual beliefs of the goat rustlers are expressed in 1 Samuel 28. The
modern Jewish claims of some sort of holiness and godly advantage is only
one lie on the long list that they have been telling for nearly 3,000 years. Here,
Saul consults the witch of En-dor to call up the ghost of Samuel from the underworld. In this, the Hebrew beliefs were no different from any other religion
of the ancient Near East. When people died, both the good and the bad went to
abide in the underworld. Since Saul was not finding good results by casting the
holy dice, he asked the necromancer of En-dor to call up Samuel's spirit from
the underworld, so he could get some advice.

When Samuel's ghost showed up, of course, *only the witch could see it,*
but Saul bowed down in the direction she was looking and asked the empty
space to tell him the future. The witch talked to that empty space like Moses
talking to the sky. She claimed that the ghost of Samuel foretold that on the
morrow, the Yahweh-god would deliver both Saul, his sons and his army into
destruction by the Philistines. And why would the lying Yahweh-god want to
destroy Saul, the very king that this Mighty, Omniscient god had chosen for
Himself? Because Saul had used good sense and had disobeyed the voice of
Yahweh that had come out of the lying mouth of Samuel, and he did not exterminate all of the Amalekites and slaughter all of the innocent animals. (1
Samuel 28:17.) Thus, Saul was a failure, not a good Jew. This Yahweh-god
and his priests demanded the complete slaughter of all other people! David
was more to the liking of the Yahweh-god. Unlike the kindhearted Saul, and
like a good Jew, David murders everybody and steals even the clothing off of
their corpses. (1 Samuel 27:9.) David was a more heartless and cruel bandit than
Saul ever was, therefore he was more worthy to be king of the Jews. These were
the heroes that the moneylenders of Babylon wanted the Jews to imitate.

1 Samuel 29 shows that the Philistines were a lot smarter than modern people are, because they refused to go into battle while the Hebrews were at their backs. Stupid, modern countries go to war while the treasonous Jews are living among them, avoiding combat while counting profits and informing the enemy. But the ancient Caucasian Sea People, the Philistines, were smarter than that. The Philistines mustered all their forces to do battle against Saul and the Israelites. But when the Philistine leaders saw David and his Hebrew cut-throats among the troops of their soldiers of Achish, they told Achish to send them away, rather than risk the treacherous Jews turning on them during battle.

So, David and his gang returned to their town of Ziklag. In their absence, however, the Amalekites had raided the town, taken all the women and children captive and burnt down the town. It should be noted that the Amalekites were not cruel and genocidal like the Hebrews, because they did not kill the women and children, but captured them.

With their town burnt, their women and children kidnapped, and the loot that they had stolen from other peoples gone, David and his Hebrews whined and cried and "wept aloud till they were too weak to weep anymore." (1 Samuel 30:4.) The Jews have a long tradition of whining, crying and making a public display of being crybabies and chronic complainers.

Once they had dried their eyes, the Hebrew soldiers used their famous Hebrew logic and decided that they wanted to hit David with rocks until he was dead. But David persuaded these Hebrew geniuses to focus on some other idea by calling for the holy ephod dice table. Thereupon, he cast the holy dice (Urim and Thummim), asking the Yahweh-god whether or not it was a good idea to try and get their Hebrew wives back. They had kidnapped the women from other people and David wanted to know if those raped chattel were really worth the effort of going to fetch them. He couldn't figure it out himself, so he asked the holy dice. The holy dice gave a "yes" reply. Since holy dice is as close to God as a Jew can get, they immediately took the hint and ran after the retreating Amalekites. When they caught up with the Amalekites, they did not treat them with the same kindness that the Amalekites had treated their Hebrew wives and children. David and his Hebrew gangsters murdered every last one of them, except for 400, who escaped on camels.

David and his gang counted up the booty and found that all of their property was recovered, every shekel – and a lot more as well. (1 Samuel 30:20.) Plus, they got extra flocks and herds, all of which the Amalekites had plundered from various towns in the area. David apportioned the loot among his men (including those who had stayed behind) and the people of the towns that had been raided by the Amalekites. In this way – through generosity – David gained loyalty from his men and allies from the towns of the Hebrews over whom he wanted to rule as king.

The First Book of Samuel closes at Chapter 31 with the death of Saul. He was wounded with arrows and his three sons were killed fighting the mighty Philistines. Wounded, Saul committed suicide, because he didn't want, "these uncircumcised men to come and gloat over me." (1 Samuel 31:4.) And so this book proves that, even at the moment of death, the first and last thing that a holy Hebrew thinks about is – not God – but his circumcised penis. A Jew's only "proof" that he is holy.

The Second Book of Samuel, Chapter 1, combines two different myths into one. The idea that these goat rustlers are special in their own eyes is expressed in this chapter. Not only does it show that Jews are completely treacherous and untrustworthy, but also that their own demonic self-esteem takes precedence over fairness and honor. In addition, the eternal hatred of Jews for anyone whom they label as "Amalekites" is again emphasized. They do not have to actually be Amalekites, but only have to be labeled as such by the rabbis for the Jews to attack them.

This chapter may even conceal a secret, whereby David had Saul murdered and then, to cover up his own complicity, had the murderer killed. Be that as it may, a young Amalekite brought Saul's crown from his head and a bracelet from his arm and gave them to David as proof that Saul was dead. This Amalekite was actually one of the "protected class" of "resident aliens" who worked for the Jews. In this case, he had been inducted into Saul's army. Saul, being wounded, ordered the Amalekite to kill him. So, the Amalekite did what the Jewish king commanded, and then brought the crown and bracelet to David.

Then, David had this loyal, "resident alien" Amalekite murdered in turn, because he had not been afraid to lift up his hand to destroy Saul, Yahweh's anointed. (2 Samuel 1:14.) In other words, the philosophy that the rabbis teach is that non-Jews are to serve the Jews. If Jews order the servants to kill other Jews, then those servants must be killed as well, because killing a holy Jew is a sin against the Yahweh-god. This is emphasized in the later laws of the *Babylonian Talmud*, where the rabbis wrote that any *goy* (non-Jewish, lowly insect, stupid cattle) who dares to slap a Jew on the face must be murdered, because slapping a Jew on the face is the same as striking the face of God. So, the next time you look into the face of a big-nosed, wide- mouthed, rubbery lipped, grinning kike with acne, know that you are looking into the face of the Jewish god Himself. Whatever you do, don't punch him on the nose, even for the fun of it. It is like striking God!

The loyal servant did what he was ordered to do by Saul, the Jewish king. He showed his loyalty to the Jews by bringing the news to David. Then, with the typical Jewish treachery of scapegoating anyone besides themselves, David put the blame on the Amalekite and had him killed. After killing the messenger, David performed the usual Jewish show of insanity by tearing his clothes into pieces and whining and crying. This form of street theater always impressed the goat rustlers, since clothes were expensive and tearing them into pieces on purpose was crazy. Yet, how can "crazy" be appropriate enough to describe the Jewish goat-thieves? After David tore his garments into pieces, all of the other Jews did the same, whining and crying and standing about in ripped and torn clothes. Since they were all thieves, it didn't matter that they had each torn up their only set of clothes. They could go kill somebody and steal new ones.

The ancient Jews' connection to God was no more special than that of the modern Jews. According to 2 Samuel 2, David, after consulting the holy dice, went to Hebron, where he was declared king by his men, as well as by the Hebrews of Judah. But Saul's son, *Eshbaal* (named after the Canaanite Baal-god) was declared king of Israel. Of course, the two sides battled until a truce was called. The soldiers of the Israelians killed 20 men. David's followers killed 360 of the Benjamites who made up the bulk of Saul's soldiers.

As usual, the great heroes of the Jews were nothing like the Jews claim they were. This is additionally seen in something as simple as their names, which contained the names of their gods. The name of Saul's son was *Eshbaal* (1 Chronicles 8:33; 9:39), but to cover up the fact that the Hebrews were also devotees to Baal, his name was changed by the Jewish scribes to Ish-bosheth (2 Samuel 2:8-10), where *boshet* ("shame") is substituted for the pagan deity Baal. Yet another switcheroo of the scribes is found in the name of the Judean king, Abijam (1 Kings 15:1, 7-8). Here, the last element, *Yam* ("Sea-god"), is changed to *Yah* (=Yahweh), altering the royal name to Abijah (2 Chronicles 13:1-4). All of this is just kid stuff compared to the bigger frauds and counterfeits found throughout the *Hebrew Bible*. If a fact is uncomfortable for a Jew, why not turn the fact into a lie, so he can feel like a good Jew?

2 Samuel 3 continues recounting the war between the Israelians and Judah, but also mentions the sons born to David by his six wives. More treachery and vengeance are related in the revenge killing of Abner. And David and his followers tear their clothes into rags (yet again) and whine and cry in Jewish angst. This whining and moaning in a show of officially sanctioned group complaining was a stock Jewish character trait and is seen to this very day.

2 Samuel 4 claims that Ishbaal, Saul's son, was murdered in his sleep by two of his treasonous bandit chieftains, who then cut off his head and took it to David at his headquarters at Hebron. But David had a habit of killing the messengers (or perhaps he was killing the very ones who carried out his assassinations, so as to hide his own guilt in the murders). Be that as it may, this chapter gives a heroic twist to the plot as David murders the Jewish traitors. Such traitors and murderers are the heroes of the Jews.

2 Samuel 5 begins with the elders of Israel going to David at Hebron and making him king over Israel. He had already been made king of Judah and now he was king over both territories. This was the first time that the two territories had been united under one king. Northern Israel was an agriculturally prosperous region of grain in the valleys and both vineyards and olive groves on the hillsides. Judah, however, was a rather desolate region, poor in everything, except goats and a fortress location for Abraham's First National Bank and Pawn Shop. But regardless of what they claim in their fables, modern archaeology proves that the Jews are liars. Small-time bandit chiefs like Saul and David never ruled Israel and Judah simultaneously.

Even according to 2 Samuel 5, Jerusalem had not yet been captured by the Hebrews. The town was so strongly fortified on its rocky spur that the Jebusites who lived safely behind its walls bragged that David "will not get in here. The blind and lame will hold you off." (2 Samuel 5:6.) David captured the city by having his men sneak in through a sewer conduit. At least, this is the explanation that the scribes had for their hero when they wrote the Book of Samuel 200 years later. This is the way they explained how a gang of bandits riding on donkeys and having no siege machines could take a fortified town. But whatever explanation they invented had to conceal the fact that Abraham's First National Bank and Pawn Shop had already been established in that city since the days of Melchizadek.

Abraham's first bribe to Melchizadek – the priest-king of Urusalem (the city of Saleem, the god of the dusk) – was not merely to add to his *asl* the "blessing" of the Most High God of Urusalem. He was there to establish a deposit account in the temple treasury. Abraham did not just leave a tithe and ride off on his donkey. He was in Canaan as the business representative of his father, Terah, and the merchant-moneylender guild of Harran and Ur. By depositing large sums of silver and gold into the treasury of the Most High God of Ususalem, Abraham could operate in Canaan with an assurance that no bandits or sheep rustlers could steal everything he owned; he had "money in the bank," safely on deposit. This put Abraham in a stronger position than the various little towns and wandering shepherds, and it allowed his family of bandits to enter the town at will. The Babylonian moneylenders didn't need a mythical David to sneak into Jerusalem and take it for their own, because they were already there, banking their profits from banditry and loan-sharking behind the secure walls that no other Hebrew tribe could access. That is the only reason the tribe of Judah was supreme, because no matter the fortunes of the other tribes, they alone would always have silver and gold from which to draw upon for investments, loans and the buying of supplies and weapons.

After moving his residence to Jerusalem, David brought his wives and concubines to live there. Eleven more children were born to him in Jerusalem. While there, he was attacked by the Philistines on two further occasions. But after consulting the holy dice, he drove them off to their own territory in Gezer. David was the holy bandit of the Yahweh-god; the great hero of the Jews, who asked his god questions and then threw dice to see if the god answered or not.

2 Samuel 6 brings the Ark of the Covenant into Jerusalem. The entire two-faced fraud of a holy king and a holy priest was now embodied by one Hebrew family in Jerusalem, the City of Holy Lies. The moneylender scribes of Abraham's First National Bank and Pawn Shop tell the story of how King David brought the ark from Kiriath-Jearim, where it had been stored, and installed it in Jerusalem. On the way, according to the scribes, one of the men walking beside the cart touched the ark to steady it. "Then the anger of Yahweh blazed out against Uzzah, and for his crime God struck him down on the spot, and he died there beside the ark of God." (2 Samuel 6:7.) This Yahweh-god really didn't want anybody touching his gold. He was a jealous god, all right – and a greedy and stingy one, too: definitely an appropriate god for a bunch of diabolical bankers and financiers.

Anyway, that was enough to frighten David. Strictly as a scientific experiment to see if it would kill his friend, he stashed this lethal and dangerous ark at a friend's house. After three months, the friend had not been killed by lightning, but had instead found himself "blessed" to still be alive. So, the experiment over, David brought the ark to his citadel in Jerusalem.

Typical of the circumcised goat rustlers, then as they are today, David was very proud of his penis. With his 11 wives he had developed a well-exercised third leg that he was anxious to show off to any other ladies who might be interested. To show the Jews that he had the biggest dong on the mountain, he took the occasion while bringing the ark into the city to show them all how well-hung he was. So, wearing only a loin cloth, David danced and whirled and exposed himself while the ox hide drums, goat horn trumpets and melodious tambourines cranked out the cacophonous noise that passes for music in the Middle East. In this way, David could dance in front of his god and expose his penis at the same time. It was Hebrew prayer in its finest expression. As a big payoff to the gawking bystanders, he splurged in typical Jewish extravagance and gave everybody in the crowd a bread roll, some dates and a raisin cake.

But David's wife, Michal, the daughter of Saul, berated him for exposing himself and flashing his cock at the crowd. So, to punish her for daring to criticize his sexual displays, he refused to ever again have sex with her. This was a good enough excuse to evade the Yahweh-god's command to "Go forth and multiply" and ensure that she didn't have any more children. Hebrew vindictive revenge being what it is, such children of Saul's daughter might be a future threat to his leadership. Besides, he had ten other wives to keep him and his big, nasty, Jewish nubbin busy, while leaving Michal barren.

This story also presents what many would regard as legendary overtones and seems to conflict with information provided elsewhere. If the ark was with the Philistines or at Kiriath-Jearim from the time of Eli's death until David transferred it to Jerusalem, for example, how does it happen to be on the scene at one of Saul's battles and in the hands of one of Eli's descendants (1 Samuel 14:3)? Oh well, what does it matter to the Jews? If two different stories of theirs are both lies, then what does it matter which one you tell? All lies told by the "Holy Chosen Ones of God" are the truth!

2 Samuel 7 once again shows the local nature of the Yahweh-god. Like the other gods of the ancient Near East, Yahweh Sabaoth (God of Armies) "dwelt" in the tent, where the ark was kept. David declared that it was wrong for him to live in a house of cedar, while his god lived in a tent. But the "prophet" Nathan had a dream in which the Yahweh-god said that he liked living in a tent and that it would be one of David's descendants who would build a temple for the god's dwelling place. Furthermore, David was such a loyal gangster that it would be through his descendants that the Yahweh-god would work his magic. Once again, understand that Judaism is a strictly racial program that supports its assertions upon the delusions of a big circumcised *asl*. That is, the Jews claim to be wonderful, because their relatives from 3,000

years ago were supposed to be wonderful and they inherited that wonderfulness. The really wonderful thing about Jewish wonderfulness is that they made it all up.

It should again be noted that the god of the Jewish bandits was "Yahweh Sabaoth," that is, the "God of Armies." Warfare and plunder are traditional sources of Jewish profit, which is why the Jewish bankers today can plunder the world without embarrassment, while pretending to be honest businessmen. As long as other people do the fighting and dying, these devotees of the God of Armies are all in favor of warfare and plunder. As a modern rabbi said, "Wars are the Jews' harvest, for with them we wipe out the Christians and get control of their gold. We have already killed 100 million of them, and the end is not yet." War is the harvest of the Jews.

So, according to the *Hebrew Bible*, the God of Armies chose the Jews to promote warfare, strife and suffering in order to extract profits from the Gentiles. Only the Jews are blessed with such profits, while the Gentiles are cursed forever, to be exterminated by this god of malice and hatred, this "God of Armies," this Yahweh Sabaoth, this god of today's Jews.

2 Samuel 8 tells of the murderous nature of "King" David and his rampages of genocide. He defeated the Moabites, measured out the captured prisoners like cordwood as a form of humiliation, and then executed two-thirds of them, forcing the remainder to pay him tribute. What a mighty Jew! So worthy of the god of genocide!

Big, brave and mighty Jew David attacked Hadadezer from the rear and captured 1,700 charioteers and 20,000 foot soldiers. With malicious cruelty, he cut the leg tendons of all the horses, except 100 teams. Then, in addition to the gold and bronze he captured, he killed 22,000 men of the Aramaeans and forced Aram to pay him tribute. This is what the lying Babylonian scribes claim. But archaeology proves that none of this was possible, since the land of Moab was unoccupied during the time that David allegedly led his gangs of thieves into those territories.

David's bodyguards were Cherethites and Pelethites. These were both foreign mercenaries from Philistia and Greece. So, David's closest personal protection bodyguards were not fellow Jews, but Greek mercenaries. Obviously, he knew that Hebrews could not be trusted. And in this way, he could have foreigners do his killing of political rivals without the worry of having his schemes found out or avenged in the Jewish way of the "avenger of blood."

It should be noted that all of the silver and gold captured by David's army of thieving Jews from Hadadezer, Edom, Moab, the Ammonites, the Philistines, and Amalek was "consecrated to Yahweh," as was the gold, silver and bronze given as a bribe by Hamath (2 Samuel 8:10). This means that the bullion metals were first waved over the fire to be "purified," then they were deposited into the treasury of Abraham's First National Bank and Pawn Shop.

2 Samuel 8 claims that all captured gold and silver should be offered to the God of Armies, who invisibly guards the "Holy of Holies" on the ark before the Holy Treasury. David sets the example. If all future kings want to be

"good kings," they consecrate all gold to the bankers and deposit it safely into the treasury.

2 Samuel 9 claims that David was a kindhearted murderer and pillager who honored the memory of Jonathan by returning all of Saul's land to Meribbaal, one of Jonathan's sons with crippled feet. Thus, he could show what a kindhearted pirate he was by giving some property to one of Saul's descendants – who could never be a threat to him, since he was born a cripple as a result of Jewish incest.

In 2 Samuel 10:17, David "mustered all Israel" to fight the Amorites. "David killed seven hundred of their chariot teams and forty thousand men. When all the vassal kings of Hadadezer saw that they had been defeated by Israel, they made peace with the Israelites and became subject to them. The Aramaeans were afraid to give any more help to the Ammonites." (2 Samuel 10:18-19.)

Some oral sources contain a significant amount of unflattering material about David. "The History of David's Rise" tells of his cooperation with Israel's enemies, the Philistines, his bitter rivalry with Saul, and his conspicuous absence from the fateful battle at Mount Gilboa in which Saul was killed. It concludes with the grisly annihilation of the house of Saul. The "Court" or "Succession History" is a bloody tale of the betrayals and assassinations that eliminated all of Solomon's major competitors for the throne of David.

Such terrible stories are quite unusual among the official chronicles of ancient Near Eastern kings, where the object was generally idealization rather than journalistic accuracy. Many scholars argue that "David's Rise" and the "Court History" were put into writing in the tenth century BC, within or very close to the lifetime of David, when the memories of his alleged crimes and misdemeanors were still vivid. The list of targeted liquidations of northern figures is very long: David is indirectly linked to the death of Abner, the loyal general of Saul (2 Samuel 3:27); to the killing and then beheading of Ishbosheth, the son of Saul (2 Samuel 4:7); to the hanging of seven other members of the house of Saul (2 Samuel 21:7-9); the beheading of the northern rebel Sheba, the son of Bichri (2 Samuel 20:22).

What is not understood by most Bible scholars is that the *Hebrew Bible* is both *a Contract* and *an Operating Manual*. It binds the Jews to the Contract of the Monsters of Babylon. And it shows to them the most criminal and diabolical ways of attaining wealth and property by "walking in the ways" of their wrathful God of Armies against all of Mankind, whom the Jews call the *goyim* (non-Jewish, lowly insects, stupid cattle).

The *Apiru* (bandits) continue to be mentioned as late as 1000 BC. They help explain David's rise to power in a quite down-to-earth way. Put simply, the description of the rise of David in 1 Samuel contains many distinctive parallels to the activity of a typical *Apiru* chieftain and his rebel gang. David and his "mighty men" make their own rules and cynically form shifting political alliances in the interest of survival alone. They live and act in remote villages, on the fringe of the desert, in the rugged Judean wilderness and across the arid steppe land in the south – far from the easy reach of any central authority.

It is clear today that archaeology proves that the conquests of David were fictional stories. Canaanite life in the northern valleys continued uninterrupted well into the tenth century BC. The wave of destruction that had previously been dated to around 1000 BC and attributed to the expansion of the so-called united monarchy in the days of King David actually came later, by almost a century, under kings none of whom were named "David."

Through archaeological dating techniques, we can associate evidence with identifiable biblical characters – primarily the Omride dynasty of the kingdom of Israel, which ruled, according to the biblical and ancient Near Eastern chronology, between 884 and 842 BC. That was several generations *after* the reported time of David and Solomon.

According to 1 Kings 16:15-24, Omri, the dynasty's founder, came to power in a military coup d'état and established his capital on the hill of Samaria, from which he and his son Ahab ruled a vast kingdom. For this, we don't have to entirely trust the *Hebrew Bible*, because we have supporting testimonies from independent, outside sources, confirming the main outlines of the biblical account. This report is substantiated by a number of contemporary inscriptions – the earliest extra-biblical records ever discovered to directly document the existence of biblical characters.

The Assyrians indeed refer to the northern kingdom as "the House of Omri" (never as the kingdom of Israel), confirming the biblical testimony that he, not Saul or David, was the founder of the dynasty and the capital. And the monolith inscription of King Shalmaneser III of Assyria describes a great coalition of kingdoms confronting the Assyrian armies in 853 BC, at the battle of Qarqar, near the Orontes River. One of the most powerful participants in this coalition was a ruler referred to as "Ahab the Israelite," who contributed 2,000 chariots and 10,000 foot soldiers to the anti-Assyrian force. Even if this royal text is typically exaggerated, it still suggests an entirely new scale of military power possessed by the northern kingdom of the House of Omri, the Israelians. At the height of their power, the Omrides apparently extended their rule eastward and northward, into Transjordan and Syria.

Among all the warhorses so highly prized by the Assyrians, none were more sought-after than the famous thoroughbreds from the region of Kush, south of Egypt, along the upper Nile. These Kushite horses were considered the best for chariots and are mentioned in Assyrian texts – as gifts or purchases – from the days of Tiglath-pileser III (745-727 BC) to Ashurbanipal (669-626 BC). Starting in the late eighth century BC, when Assyrian commercial centers had been established in Philistia, along the southern coastal plain, the Assyrians obtained their Kushite horses by direct trade with Egypt.

This is the direct link between the huge Megiddo stables, the Assyrian records, and the lies of the rabbis about the mythical King Solomon. Located in a strategic spot, where the international highway from Egypt to Mesopotamia and to Anatolia descends from the hills into the Jezreel Valley, Megiddo was one of the most important cities of Biblical Israel. Throughout most of the eighth century BC, the northern Israelian kingdom gained great prosperity by being the main importer of the famed Egyptian horses into Assyria. The horses were bred and trained at the stable complex at Megiddo, *the largest known anywhere in the ancient Near East*, and were then sold to Assyria (and possibly other clients) during the reign of Jeroboam II. But by the time of Manasseh there is no evidence of horse-trading in Judah. So, the scribes who wrote the myths about Solomon could get away with their lies by attributing the ruined stables of Meggido to a rich and powerful Solomon who never existed.

Archaeology proves that no one named Solomon ever had anything to do with the great ruined stables that the Jews claimed had been his. The "one thousand four hundred chariots and twelve thousand horses" (1 Kings 10:26) were never owned by a King Solomon, because the stables were the works of Israelian king Omri. The kingdom of Judah had never controlled any part of the Israelian kingdom of Omri, but after Omri was destroyed by Assyria, the priests and the lying rabbis pointed to the 100-year-old ruins of horse stables and claimed that their very own, mythical, glorious, incredibly wealthy and wise-beyond-anybody-else King Solomon had owned it all – and that the Jews were his lucky heirs to it. Once again, modern archaeology proves that the Jews are liars. There was no King Solomon, unless he was the king of a goat farm someplace in Judah, where nobody could read or write – which was actually every place in Judah during the time that he was alleged to have lived. So, if their "glorious history" is a proven lie, what are the Jews other than liars? As for the alleged "Lost Ten Tribes of Israel," we can once again look at the actual evidence, rather than accept the word of the Jews.

The Assyrians appreciated the benefits of deporting defeated populations and replacing them with captives from elsewhere. The resultant social dislocation made it hard for captive peoples to organize resistance. But there was an additional benefit to Assyria. The captured kings and their courts, the wealthy land owners, the generals and upper military echelons, the moneylenders and merchants, as well as the top craftsmen, were all used as administrative arms of the Assyrian government elsewhere in their empire. The captives were not merely carted off as slaves and menial workers, because these captured people had organizational and economic skills useful to Assyria.

The deportees were used as overseers to control the Assyrian people and whatever other conquered people they were tasked to police. In other words, they were given the same occupations that they had had before their exile, as landlords, business administrators, military officers, craftsmen and farm bosses, etc. Because they owed no allegiance to the people they oversaw, they became especially useful to the Assyrian royal moneylenders and merchants in the ruthless exploitation of agriculture, tax farming and commerce. Their only allegiance was to the Assyrian king, who had put them there, and to their own self-interest.

Thus, deportation of captive peoples was not just a method of control, it was a method of commercial exploitation, just as is the immigration of Third World aliens into modern countries. And behind every Assyrian king stood a member of the merchant-moneylenders' guild, acting as "humble advisor." They were also there to remind "the great and mighty king" when the loans he had received from the Guild were due and that he had sworn a mighty oath upon the mighty altar of the mighty gods to repay them in full and on time. If the treasury was empty (and the Sumerian Swindle guaranteed that kings' treasuries were usually empty), then why not go to war against a wealthy country and loot from them what he owed to the moneylenders? Does this sound familiar to modern Readers, whose governments are always at war, whose taxes are always high, and whose economies are always near collapse, while the bankers and financiers are rich?

The Israelian Omride dynasty possessed a strong military force. Shalmaneser III (858-824 BC), one of the greatest Assyrian kings, listed the Battle of Qarqar on one of his victory steles.

Although the Book of Kings depicts Ahab as an idolatrous tyrant, we know from the monolith inscription of Shalmaneser III that he was one of the most energetic opponents of Assyrian domination. While Jehu, the rebel, is pictured in the *Hebrew Bible* as God's instrument to destroy idolatry in Israel, the famous "black obelisk" of Shalmaneser shows him bowing at the feet of the great Assyrian king. Shalmaneser also notes "the tribute of Jehu, son of Omri" and lists a variety of gold and silver objects. So, who is telling the truth? The scribes of Judah or the scribes of Shalmaneser? With such an unbroken record of Jewish lies, why believe the Jews about anything?

The historical Omri Dynasty – and not the mythical Solomon – established the first fully developed monarchy in Israel and in Israel alone, not in the backward state of Judah. What is described in the *Hebrew Bible* as the court of the wise and wealthy King Solomon is actually a description of the royal courts of the Assyrian kings. Solomon was nothing but a fictional character. He was a handy myth for the Jews to brag about; a handy myth whom the rabbis could claim as the founder of the stolen and plagiarized "Jewish Wisdom."

The first obvious challenge in assessing the historical reliability of the David and Solomon stories is to determine the precise date of their reigns. This must be based on evidence within the Bible alone, because nobody in the ancient Near East had ever heard of either one of these characters. At certain points, this list can be checked against contemporary references to the Davidic kings in the chronicles of Assyria and Babylonia. "The Babylonian Chronicle," for example, mentions the siege of Jerusalem during King Jehoiachin's brief reign in the seventh year of Nebuchadnezzar in 597 BC. Manasseh's tribute to Assyria is noted in an inscription of the Assyrian king Esarhaddon in 674 BC. The Assyrian attack on Jerusalem during the reign of Hezekiah is mentioned in the "Annals of Sennacherib" for the equivalent of 701 BC. Ahaz's payment of tribute to Assyria is listed in an inscription of Tiglath-pileser III, dated to 734 BC. Correspondences to the reigns of the northern kingdom – which go back to the Battle of Qarqar in the days of Ahab, in 853 BC – also confirm the reliability of the general framework. Another generally accepted synchronism is the invasion of the country by the Egyptian pharaoh Shishak in the fifth year of Solomon's son Rehoboam – around 926 BC.

When we proceed backward from Rehoboam, the chronology gets considerably fuzzier. Of the 12 kings of Judah from Rehoboam (931-914 BC) to Ahaz (743-727 BC), only three are mentioned in extra-biblical evidence. And, as previously noted, David and Solomon are not mentioned in any contemporary extra-biblical text and hence do not have any reliable, direct anchor to ancient Near Eastern chronology, even though the Jews claim them to be the most powerful, rich, and famous.

Unfortunately, scholars have generally taken these round numbers as precise indications for the dates of the early kings, placing Saul's reign between 1030 BC and 1010 BC, David's between 1010 BC and 970 BC, and Solomon's between 970 BC and 931 BC. To make a long story short, no one knows the exact number of years that David and Solomon each ruled, if they existed at all. The most that can be said is that, if they existed at all, they probably both reigned sometime in the tenth century BC.

Through the proofs of archaeology, we can now say that many of the famous episodes in the biblical story of David and Solomon are fictions, historically questionable, or highly exaggerated. Archaeological evidence shows that there never was a united monarchy of Israel in the way that the Bible describes it. It is highly unlikely that David ever conquered territories of peoples more than one- or two-days' march from the heartland of Judah. Solomon's Jerusalem was neither extensive nor impressive, but rather the rough hilltop stronghold of a local dynasty of rustic tribal chiefs.

As for the "mighty kings" David or Solomon, no one ever heard of them outside of the pages of the lying *Hebrew Bible*, except for one single mention of one single Hebrew phrase, "House of David," on the Tel Dan stela. This is the only "proof" that David ever existed. But Solomon (who was allegedly even greater in wealth and international power) *is not mentioned anywhere, even once, in the archives of the surrounding nations.* We now have the original records of some ancient empires, and a number of important Biblical kings have been identified in Mesopotamian cuneiform archives – the Israelian kings Omri, Ahab, and Jehu and the Judahite kings Hezekiah and Manasseh. But nothing about David or Solomon, who were supposed to be so much greater.

If there were no monuments and no magnificent capitol, then what was the nature of David's realm? The actual dates of such cities as Megiddo, Samaria, Jezreel, Gezer and Hazor are from Omri's Dynasty, not Solomon's era. These dates prove that there was never a united monarchy based in Jerusalem and suggests that David and Solomon were, in political terms, little more than chieftains whose administrative reach remained fairly local, restricted to the hill country. Equally important for understanding the shenanigans of the Jewish scribes, it shows that despite the biblical claims of the uniqueness of Israel, it was only a highland kingdom of a thoroughly conventional Near Eastern type that arose in the north during the early ninth century BC. There was nothing special about those Jews other than their *abracadabra* ability to tell big lies.

David and Solomon, the united monarchy of Israel, and the entire biblical history of Israel is a ruse. For all their reported wealth and power, neither David nor Solomon is mentioned in a single known Egyptian or Mesopotamian text. And the archaeological evidence in Jerusalem for the famous building projects of Solomon is nonexistent. The place where a stupendously wealthy Solomon is supposed to have ruled is only a few goat pens and rude huts.

What do we have so far in the "holy writings and histories" of the Jews? Fraud, deceit, forged documents, counterfeited documents, stolen documents, plagiarized documents, and destroyed evidence. These are the "holy" scriptures of the Jews. And what of the Jewish heroes? The Creation Myth along with Noah and his Ark, the fables of Exodus, the plagues of Egypt, the Passover, the parting of the Sea of Reeds, the murder of Pharaoh and his army, Moses, Joshua, Saul, David and Solomon – all of these are lies and fictional characters. There were no Lost Ten Tribes, no miracles in the desert, no wandering in the desert, no conquest of Canaan, no David killing Goliath, no super-Jew like Samson. There were no "judges," because they were military leaders. There was no United Monarchy under David and Solomon. Jerusalem was not a great city at all, but was the location of a secret temple banking system with Babylon, not Jerusalem, as its hub. So, in short, there is nothing in the *Hebrew Bible* that is true. Everything that the Jews say about Judaism is a lie. There was no Jewish God; the Jews stole a Canaanite God and then claimed that Yahweh was the only god among many. Monotheism was not invented by the Jews, it was an Egyptian belief – a thousand years before there were any Jews to tell lies about God.

And yet, even if the average Christian or other interested researcher believes that the *Hebrew Bible* is true, *then what actual truth does it teach*? Certainly not a knowledge of God, but rather it teaches a celebration of murder, incest, deceit, banditry, and genocide. That is what the *Hebrew Bible* teaches, while making incredible lies that these are what God wants the Jews to practice against all of Mankind.

Of course, you now know that the *Hebrew Bible* is a plagiarized and counterfeited hoax and that it is certainly not "the word of God." But if it is not the word of God, then whose word is it? Whose word is it that demands the dispossession and genocide of Mankind, so that the Jews can steal our property and ensconce themselves in our lands? The *Hebrew Bible* is the word of those who wrote it, of course – the moneylenders, the bankers, the financiers, the Jewish merchants and rabbis who benefit from the betrayal, swindling and extinction of Mankind. If you don't believe this, then look out into the modern world and see who is putting entire nations into poverty and debt, benefiting from warfare, dispossessing people from their homes, enslaving Mankind to loan swindles and credit scams and financial crimes. Look, and you can see them yourself. Behind the corrupt politicians, wars that kill millions, starvation among plenty, diseases that create profits and the destruction of nations, you will always find the banker and financier. Most of them wear beanies and little boxes on their heads during the Jewish holidays where they are safe from serving in the wars that they create. The Monsters of Babylon wrote the *Hebrew Bible*.

CHAPTER 9
THE FRAUDSTERS KNOWN AS THE LATER PROPHETS

WARNING: The interested reader can skip this chapter and go to Chapter 10. But please come back to this chapter later for a more specific insight into the *Hebrew Bible*. This chapter is very boring unless you are a research specialist curious about those hairy-faced, frothing, nasty, goat molesters that the Jews claim were their "inspired prophets." The total message of all of the later Jewish prophets can be summed up in two sentences: "You Israelians are Evil. Come back to the Temple in Jerusalem to feed the priests, pay ten percent of your wealth into the Treasury and then you can be Good, like us Judeans." That is the total message of the Later Prophets. So, go ahead and skip to Chapter 10 and come back later. But for those of you who want every detail of How the Jews Betrayed Mankind, read on.

Next to the Torah and various other Jewish fantasy books, the prophets are the second level of Jewish deceit in regard to the Jews' phony history. A swindler who wants to sell a worthless hole in the ground sprinkles gold nuggets and gold dust among the rocks and debris, so that the fool buys the bulk of rocks based upon the few sparkles that he sees. In the same way, the Jews have increased the apparent value of their scriptures through creative editing and the ravings of their prophetic goat thieves.

This chapter will be a little confusing if you try to link it into a well-ordered history. The various books of the later prophets were always placed in odd chronological order, rewritten from scraps, plagiarized and ghost-written by various rabbinical frauds, then cut-and-pasted together in whatever way best suited the Jewish priests. In correcting this historical literary mistake, I have rearranged the Prophets in their correct chronological order.

There have always been inspired prophets in every religion. The word "prophet" means "to tell forth," in this particular case, a forth-telling of the will of the Jewish priests disguised as the will of God. Every religion, whether mainstream or pagan, has had its prophets. These were men and women who had an immediate experience of God, or at least imagined that they had. These holy ones were supposed to sometimes be able to see the present and the future through the eyes of God; and they would "tell forth" what they saw.

Ahab consulted 400 prophets in 1 Kings 22:5-12. Jezebel, who was a Phoenician native of Tyre, summoned 450 prophets of Baal in 1 Kings 18:19-40. Music was often used to aid in their ecstasy. In the case of the Israelians' neighbors, cuneiform tablets from the 2nd millennium BC tell of prophetic activity at Mari on the Euphrates and at Byblos in Phoenicia.

But the activities of shamans, medicine men, sorcerers, witches, holy men, wise women, religious hermits, monks and prophets are all a part of the religious lore of every peoples, worldwide. All of these spiritual explorers picked methods – meditation, prayer, musical ecstasy, mantras, hallucinatory pharmacopoeia, hypnotism and magic – to attempt to transcend the ordinary earthly experience and to enter into states of super-consciousness. While searching for God with their various spiritual techniques, some succeeded in attaining wisdom and insight, but most became lost in the illusions and delusions of their own minds.

The way to recognize a genuine prophet from all of the fakes, according to the *Hebrew Bible*, is (1) fulfillment of prophesy and (2) agreement with the Laws of Moses. But what can be said about a people whose "Laws of Moses" are counterfeits and forgeries, while their "fulfillment of prophesy" is nothing but delusions and fake "forecasting" based upon those same counterfeits and forgeries? That's Judaism! As you are probably beginning to understand, anybody who believes anything the lying Jews say, is a fool.

That the words of the Jewish prophets have been well-preserved in writing does not mean that there were no other peoples attuned to the ways of God. Indeed, awareness of and prayers toward God, were *the* major features in the lives of *all* peoples in ancient times. The ecstatics and prophets of the ancient Near East were called "nabi," meaning "to be beside oneself."

Another meaning of "nabi" is "to call or proclaim." Thus, the ancient prophets were considered a bit eccentric as they proclaimed their message from God. Usually, those prophets would introduce their message as "Yahweh says this," or "This is the word of Yahweh," or an "Oracle of Yahweh," so that their listeners would pay attention and not think that the words were merely the wild imaginings of a lunatic – even though their words, in most cases, really were the wild imaginings of a lunatic. There were hundreds or thousands of "prophets" among the Jews over the long centuries. Inspired by the *abracadabra* lies of the patriarchs, every goatherd and temple leech who felt the urge to exalt his god and utter a guess about the future was a "prophet." But only those prophecies which closely approximated actual events were ever preserved in writing. Inaccurate prognostications would be discarded, leaving the accurate guesses as "proof."

A man who claims to foresee which horse will win the Kentucky Derby is but one of hundreds of "tipsters" or "prophets" offering their "inside information" about the impending race. All are equally vociferous and adamant. But only the one who actually names the winning horse is considered a prophet. This is how the Jews have picked their so-called "prophets": merely by preserving the writings of the lucky winners, while burning the writings of the lame losers. Under such a system, *one hundred percent of Jewish "prophecies" were true*, simply because the deceiving rabbis burned the writings of the prophets who guessed wrong. And this isn't even counting the fakery practiced by the Hebrew scribes in *backdating* their fake prophecies. A scribe who writes of past events on year ten and backdates the document to year one has a 100 percent chance of correctly "seeing into the future." Such trickery and counterfeiting are found all throughout Jewish literature.

The *Hebrew Bible* really doesn't offer much in the way of valid proofs about anything, since the thousands of prophets who were wrong have not had their writings preserved, while the dozen and a half who prophesied something that turned out to be reasonably accurate have been lauded as the very mouth of God, even though the results could be nothing but statistical chance, no better than a horse race or a toss of the dice. Besides, when all a "prophet" does is vociferate dire warnings and curses, there is no need to be accurate about anything.

These *Hebrew Bible* writings were gathered together by Ezra the Scribe (539 BC) and his accomplices as a means of "proving" the alleged wisdom and foresight of the Jewish prophets, while the thousands of Jewish prophets whose prophecies were wrong and inaccurate were hurriedly consigned to the flames of an all-forgetting fire. Moses, Joshua, Deborah, Gad, Nathan, Ahijah, Jehu ben Hanani, Elijah, Elisha, Jonah, Hulda (the Weasel), Uriah, Shamaiah, Iddo, Azariah, Obed and Samuel are all considered to be prophets.

The prophet of the Babylonian Exile was Ezekiel. With him, the atmosphere changes. Spontaneity and verve decline, visions are grand and very involved, descriptions are meticulous, and interest in the "latter days" increases. In short, the prophesies are frauds perpetrated by the scribes Haggai and Zechariah. The prophets of the Return are entirely concerned with rebuilding the Temple. Then comes Malachi, to point out defects of the Jews. Jonah introduces more lies about getting eaten and regurgitated by a whale.

The actual prophets made up a subculture among the priests of the Temple. They raved while the priests performed empty rituals of slaughter and pantomime. The prophets were like the meditative adepts of any other religion in the ancient Near East in that they immersed themselves in awareness of God's presence. As a continual source of perpetual raving, the prophets served the role of mouthpieces for their god. In this capacity, they were a constant reminder to the Jews that their god was always watching them, ready the convict them of sins that required barbecued goats and gold bars to expiate. All prophets enjoyed the free barbecues, so it paid to rant and rave. Otherwise, they didn't eat. The Temple Scam was set up like this.

Most Bible commentators express the view that the prophets practiced the "three dominant features of Old Testament theology – monotheism, morality, messianism." However, what they do not realize, perhaps because of the blinders of preconceived assumptions, is that the beliefs of the ancient Jews were different than what most Christians assume. And those beliefs were extremely different from those of today's Jews. In *Hebrew Bible* times, the Jews recognized the existence of other gods, but believed that among all the gods, the Yahweh-god reigned supreme. Only at a later date did this idea give way to the notion that Yahweh alone existed while all other gods were but false imaginings. Later still, when the Jewish sect known as "Pharisees" appeared, the Jews recognized He-Who-Must-Not-Be-Named as the top god.

Thus, the so-called monotheism of the Hebrews was actually based on a polytheism which gave one god, named Yahweh, the supreme position. Later, it was declared that Yahweh alone existed. And finally, while they were in Babylon, the Jews discarded Yahweh entirely and began worshiping Satan, He-Who-Must-Not-Be-Named. And even Satan eventually took second place to the self-glorification and self-worship of the diabolical Jews.

As for the alleged "morality" of the Jews, it should be noted that morality was a concept held by all peoples. Every society had its own standards of morality. The Jews had no monopoly on morality, although it was something that they claimed to possess in greater quantity than anyone else. And why not? Claiming to be holy and moral cost them nothing, while they profited much from other peoples actually believing them to be moral. The Jews discovered that taking the moral high road was the best policy as long as other people were convinced that they were actually moral and could not see what frauds they were. More swindling and gathering of gold can be achieved by those who are trusted than by those who are distrusted. So, the Jews have always claimed to possess the highest, greatest moral qualities, both in their religion and in their social habits, since the payoff is so much greater than admitting their crimes. The Jews can swindle much more from those who trust them.

And yet, for all of their grandiose bragging, morality is not something easily ascertained from the *Hebrew Bible*, because so many evil and immoral things are recorded therein as examples of Jewish "virtue." The most basic Jewish teaching is "not to eat of the tree of the knowledge of good and evil." This means that the Jews look at Good and Evil as the same and practice both in whatever manner is most profitable for the Jews. In Judaism, the only "evil" is to not follow the laws of the rabbis as found in the *Hebrew Bible* and, later, in the *Babylonian Talmud*. This actually means that the Jews are lawless, as will be shown below. Thus, for the Jews, the only evil is to be a Gentile, a non-Jew. Being a holy Jew means that all other people are evil and should be treated as such. The Torah is really a demon's book and is, in fact, the Greatest Lie Ever Told. So, it is a fitting scripture for the Jews, the greatest liars and biggest hypocrites who ever walked the earth.

Of course, there are many virtuous sayings and exhortations in the *Hebrew Bible*, but they are always buried and surrounded by murder and an immorality that is claimed to be equally wonderful, since it is so Jewish. And upon further inspection, it is found that the "moral" and "wise" sayings found in the *Hebrew Bible* were stolen from the peoples who inhabited Canaan, Palestine, Egypt and Mesopotamia long before there were any Jews living in those lands. What the Jews claim as their own Scriptures and Wisdom were actually pilfered from earlier peoples, dusted off and written down in Hebrew lettering. The Jews are liars and thieves, and they always have been.

The messianism of the Hebrews had much to do with the belief that no matter how sinful they were, Yahweh would always save a "remnant" of them with which to preserve the swarm. Jewish moneylenders discovered that they could rebuild their fortunes through the magic of the Sumerian Swindle as long as a single moneylender remained who had even a small amount of silver to lend at interest, even after a city was pilfered by war. Isaiah begins this idea of a surviving remnant, then Amos and the subsequent prophets continue it. This eventually contributed to the belief that the "messiah" was the Jewish people themselves, who would gather all the riches of the world into their own possession and kill their enemies with vengeance and thanksgiving; blood and song.

The actual books of the prophets have three attributes. They are (1) "prophetic sayings," which are oracles spoken by the voices in the prophet's head (2) first person narratives where the prophet tells of his experiences, and (3) third person narratives that tell of events in the prophet's life. All three attributes can be mixed, and they were mixed by the scribes of Babylonia under Ezra the Scribe.

There are many alterations to the books of the prophets. Although modern Bible scholars like to think of these alterations as being of "divine guidance and inspiration," this cannot be accepted by anyone interested in truth. A fraud is a fraud, a lie is a lie, and texts written under someone else's authorship are a forgery or a counterfeit. As the *Jerusalem Bible* commentators wrote: "The books of the prophets were kept alive by groups of the devout ... under divine inspiration, either to adapt the books to the spiritual needs of a new generation or to improve them ... these additions could be considerable. By making such alterations, the heirs of the prophets considered that they were at once preserving and maturing the treasure received from their masters." In other words, the Biblical "scholars" of the past 2,500 years accept forgeries as "authentic" as long as they were written under a delusion called "divine inspiration."

What is also not understood by previous Bible scholars, is that changes were made to enhance the power of the rabbis, and not the power of God. The so-called "treasures" which the rabbis didn't actually forge, counterfeit, steal, or plagiarize, were entirely fictitious. The Jews base every, single one of their claims of "holiness" or "chosenness" or "godliness" upon nothing but lies! Internal inspection of their "scriptures" and modern archaeology prove this.

What these Bible scholars do not perceive is that the creative editing for the "spiritual needs of a new generation" or to "improve the prophecies," are not the reasons that the so-called prophecies (or the "forth-telling") were edited. Without understanding the political and economic goals of the priests and rabbis, it is impossible to understand the Bible. After all, if the prophets were really speaking as the mouthpiece of a perfect and all-knowing god, then how is it that the rabbis claim to have the authority to "improve" on such a "divine prophecy"?

All of the prophets were attached to the Temple. Amos is dated from the mid-8th century, about fifty years after the death of Elisha. The age of prophesy lasted about 200 years. But were these actual years or years that the rabbis and the scribes of Ezra in Babylon invented?

Amos 783-743 BC
(Forty Years of Ranting)

It was during the prosperous days under Jeroboam II that the first scathing denunciations of the corrupt and impious aristocracy of the Israelians were expressed by Amos. This shepherd wandered north into Israelian territory and castigated the wealthy for forgetting the Yahweh-god.

His contemporaneous prophet, Hosea, also condemned the Israelians for doing business with Assyria (Hosea 12:1) and not giving a ten percent cut of their profits to the priests in Jerusalem (Amos 8:4-6) who were ready, willing and able to accept all donations and free barbecues in exchange for their holiest grins and blessings. So, Amos and Hosea were agents of the priests in Jerusalem.

Amos was a shepherd of Tekoa on the edge of the desert of Judah. Though he didn't belong to any official priestly cliques, Amos prophesied against the sins of the Israelians from the conviction of his calling, and especially from his direct observation of the swindling, usury, idolatry, prostitution, corruption of judges, use of false weights, money manipulations, produce speculations, oppression of the poor, abandoning of the Laws of Moses, lying, cheating, and extortion: all in all, most of the traditional business practices of the Jews.

He preached around 783-743 BC, during the reign of Jeroboam II of the Northern Kingdom of Israel. He preached against the rich oppressing the poor and against phony liturgical pomp and ceremony. But after so many years of his pointing to the corrupt and rich Hebrews, the Israelians finally kicked him out and sent him back to Judah (Amos 7:12-14). So, he was forced to return to his flocks, where he was probably murdered by the priests of Judah for daring to accuse them in their villainy. He disappeared from history.

His doom-mongering was a threat to the Northern Kingdom. But like all of the books of the Old Testament, the rabbis have forged portions that help them maintain their power. In the case of Amos, where he was mostly an "end-is-near" type of prophet, there is not a lot of tampering with what few pages have survived. There is no way of knowing how much the rabbis burned. As it stands, Amos 9:11-15 seems to have rabbinical fingerprints on it, since it clearly was an editorial addition.

All in all, Amos preached against the shoddy business practices and dishonest avarice of the leading Hebrews of both Israel and Judah. It is clear that the natural disasters such as earthquakes, locusts, warfare and plagues were all attributed to Yahweh's vengeance, and the thunder was thought to be the voice of God. So, Amos was really not so different from the prophets of any other people at the time, except – being a Jew – he considered himself and other Jews to be Chosen Ones of God. That's what Abraham's First National Bank and Pawn Shop claimed they were. And if a Jewish priest says so, it must be true.

Isaiah ~ 765-700 BC
(Forty Years of Malice)

Isaiah was born about 765 BC and he began to prophesy in 740 BC. His preaching spanned forty years. The Book of Isaiah is made up of sixty-six chapters, but only twenty-eight of them were actually his, while thirty-eight were written by the scribes of Babylon. In his prophesies, he foretold the fall of Israel and Judah. At this time, Assyria was expanding its power. Against the armed might of Assyria's king, Tiglath-pileser III, the countries of the Middle East had no equal. But while the Israelians formed defensive alliances with surrounding kingdoms, Ahaz, the King of Judah, sought protection under the Assyrians. Why not? That's where the money was.

So, while Tiglath-pileser III attacked and destroyed the Israelians in 734 BC, the Hebrews of Judah were spared. By 721 BC, Samaria was captured by Shalmanesser, then by Sargon II in 711 BC. The prophet Isaiah pleaded for trust in God, rather than trust in military strength. But the Assyrians had their own mighty gods who were greater than Yahweh, and Sennacherib of Assyria plundered Palestine in 701 BC. Only Jerusalem held out behind its heavy walls and steep ravines, *the only city in the history of Assyria to do so*. Isaiah attributed the capital being saved to the Yahweh-god. But the next king of Judah, Manasseh, murdered Isaiah.

There have been various editorial changes to the Book of Isaiah. The prose in Isaiah 36-39 is allegedly the work of Isaiah's disciples. The oracles against Babylon (Isaiah 13-14), the apocalypse of Isaiah (24-27), and the poems of Isaiah 33-35 are all editorial additions. The second part of the book, Isaiah 40-55, is also a later addition. Those chapters have a historical setting about two centuries after Isaiah. Jerusalem has fallen, the nation is in exile in Babylon, and Cyrus (hailed by the Judeans as the liberator) is almost on the scene. Here's what the *Jerusalem Bible* says about this book:

> "Subsequent investigations have now added weight to the earlier arguments, and a growing number of Catholic interpreters now hold that these chapters are a later addition; not merely because the name of Isaiah is never mentioned but because the historical setting itself is about two centuries after his time. Jerusalem has fallen, the nation is in exile in Babylonia, Cyrus the liberator is already on the horizon. The oracles in the first part of the book were for the most part threatening, and alluded constantly to events under Ahaz and Hezekiah; the oracles of the second part are consoling and remote from this historical context. The style is still very fine, but is different, more rhetorical, diffuse, repetitive. The thought has also developed, and is more theologically expressed. Monotheism is not merely affirmed, but expounded; the impotence of the false gods is used as an argument for their insignificance. Emphasis is laid on the fathom-

less wisdom and providence of God. For the first time religious universalism receives clear expression."

Thus, the historians conclude that these chapters, Isaiah 40-55, were written at the end of the exilic period by someone they think was a disciple of Isaiah. Like every book in the *Hebrew Bible*, the books of Isaiah are full of forgeries. The Biblical commentators know this but accept the fraud as true, because it is "inspired."

Ezra the Scribe wrote the introduction to Isaiah. In the section of the Book of Isaiah which can actually be attributed to him, he is directing his vitriol against the evil Jews, who perform meaningless rituals, make bloody sacrifices, and kill innocent men. But while all of these sins are "like scarlet, they shall be as white as snow" (Isaiah 1:18). Thus, at the earliest times, the Hebrews believed that they could be evil and magically change their evil into good through scapegoating, as well as killing sacrificial animals and pouring their blood onto the putrid altar of Yahweh.

Isaiah tells of a Jerusalem that is filled with assassins and thieves; greed and bribery. He claims that Yahweh will "wield authority over the *goyim* [lowly insects and stupid cattle]" (Isaiah 2:4). He says that among the Hebrews (especially at Samaria) there were many sorcerers, diviners, and soothsayers, and that the people actually shook hands with foreigners and bowed down before idols. The Hebrews are commanded not to forgive those among them who do such things, because touching a non-Jew makes the Jew "unclean." Furthermore, Yahweh will be a terrifying sight and a destructive force against the idolaters. Isaiah decries the arrogant people, the loutish youths and the homosexual acts, but he also attacks the ruler: youthful King Ahaz. He tells the Hebrews how evil they are to cheat, but not to help the poor. Isaiah was one of the poor.

Isaiah 13 and 14, which purport to be a vision of the destruction of Babylon, were not even written by Isaiah, but by his disciples after he had died. Thus, this section is not only a forgery, but it pretends to foresee an event that had already happened while giving their Yahweh-god the credit and holding up Isaiah as a most excellent "visionary." The Jewish test for the validity of a prophet is whether or not his forecasts come true, and Jewish priests considered forging a prophetic document morally acceptable for two reasons. First, they were forging a prophecy for the "greater good" of the Jews. Helping the "holy" Jews was always a noble cause. Second, lying was acceptable, since it furthered the dominance of the Jews over their host peoples. So, lying, deceiving and faking documents is holy and Jewish for these thoroughly immoral people.

In Isaiah 13:1-2, the writer tells how the Jews opened the gates of Babylon to the Persians and led them to the city with hilltop signals. Betrayal is a standard tactic in Jewish warfare. By the devilish teachings of the *Hebrew Bible*, the Jews are instructed to "...gain possession of the gates of their enemies" (Genesis 22:17-18). The Jews position themselves to destroy the people among whom they are allowed to live by opening the gates at critical times.

During both peace and war, the Jewish Fifth Column lets enemies in and lets Jewish criminals escape through the gates that they control. So, even small numbers of Jews can destroy huge cities and populous countries through the Sumerian Swindle's Secret Fraud #21 "Control the choke points and master the body; strangle the choke points and kill the body." Using this ancient technique, the treasonous Jews facilitate the destruction of modern-day Europe and the USA with Third World immigration.

Even in the 700s BC, the Hebrews recognized their Yahweh-god as one god among many, "for Yahweh is a just god." Isaiah 30:18 implies that Yahweh is not like the other gods. Silver and gold idols were common among the Hebrews of Isaiah's day (Isaiah 30:22).

The priests of Yahweh had plenty to say in an attempt to keep their followers giving gifts to the Temple. Yahweh was a terrible demon.

> "See, the name of Yahweh comes from afar, blazing in his anger, heavy his exaction. His lips brim with fury, his tongue is like a devouring fire. His breath is like a river in spate coming up to the neck. He comes to sift the *goyim* with the sieve of destruction, To put the bit of his bridle between the jaws of the *goyim*. Yahweh will make his majestic voice be heard and display his arm falling to strike, in the ferocity of his anger, in the glare of a devouring fire, in cloudburst, downpour, hailstones." (Isaiah 30:27-30.)

If Isaiah was considered to be such a wonderful and accurate prophet, why did he have so many critics (Isaiah 28:7-15)? The answer to this is that Isaiah was wrong more often than he was right. His preaching and prophesying reached the point where plenty of Jews scoffed at him. Great wisdom and foresight could be attributed to the prophet Isaiah merely by telling past histories of the Jews and claiming that he actually foresaw things. Since these scrolls were hand-lettered texts, written with reed pen upon animal skins, they were never very numerous and were easy to destroy. Thus, the original copies were burned, leaving only Ezra's prevarications as examples of historical truth.

The verses in Isaiah 40-55 were not written by anyone even related to Isaiah. They describe events taking place in Babylon and are another attempt by the rabbis to coerce the Jews into obedience to priestly orders. All of the Jews' misfortunes are considered punishments by Yahweh, because the Jews had sinned. "...we had refused to follow his ways and obey his Law" (Isaiah 42:24).

The Promise of the moneylenders is repeated in that Yahweh loves his holy Jews. As supernatural protection, the priests promise the Jews in Isaiah 43:1-13 that they are all Super Jews! And super liars! The scam here is for the Jews to tell all of the lies found in the *Hebrew Bible* to the people of the world as "proof" that it is all true; that – *Abracadabra!* – if the Jews say it's true, then it's true. So, bow down to the mighty god of the Jews and honor His flea-bitten scoundrels.

The chapters of Isaiah 40-55 were written in Babylon, and not by Isaiah, but by what had by this time become that evil sect known as Pharisees. In these chapters, which they claim were written by Isaiah almost 200 years previously, the Jews not only extol the might and power of their god, but actually name Cyrus as their liberator. This is a neat trick. By fooling that Persian king into believing that he was a specially chosen instrument of the Jewish god, they were able to amaze the Jewish crowds with the power and omniscience of Yahweh. Such lies about God even had an impact upon the Christians and Muslims of later centuries, creating some real fools among both.

Dear Reader: suppose someone dug up a time capsule that had been buried for 200 years, and then opened it up to find a book in which your name was mentioned and which described the major actions of your life for the past year. Now, ask yourself, if that happened, how would you feel and what would you think? Certainly, you would be awestruck and amazed. Of course, you would be astounded. Your mind would be in shock as you tried to fathom such an occurrence. "How is this possible?" you would wonder. Here was a book that was 200 years old, and yet it named your name and accurately described the events of the past year of your life. Would you not be shocked? And while in shock, suppose the people who dug up this book told you that they were the very priests and descendants of the prophet who had "foretold these events and named you by name." There is the book and there is your name in the book. Here are the priests claiming that this was proof that they had a special power. And now, they asked you to follow their advice.

Well, this is exactly what the moneylender scribes did to the king of Persia. They took one of the books of one of their prophets, then added things to the chapters designed to amaze and frighten the Persian king. Yes, Cyrus conquered many kingdoms and peoples, but the Jews claimed that he was able to do this only because *their* god, Yahweh, was there to help him do it. The lying Jews flattered Cyrus by telling him how lucky and blessed he was. "See," the scheming Jewish priests told him, "it says right here in our ancient text of prophesy":

> "Thus says Yahweh to his anointed, to Cyrus, whom he has taken by his right hand to subdue the *goyim* before him and strip the loins of kings [murder their children] to force gateways before him that their gates be closed no more [through Jewish Fifth Columns].
>
> "I will go before you leveling the heights. I will shatter the bronze gateways, smash the iron bars. I will give you the hidden treasures [swindled from others], the secret hoards, that you may know that I am Yahweh, the God of Israel, who calls you by your name.
>
> "It is for the sake of my servant Jacob, of Israel my chosen one, that I have called you by your name, conferring a title

though you do not know me. I am Yahweh unrivaled; there is
no other God besides me. Though you do not know me, I arm
you [with loans of silver] that men may know from the rising to
the setting of the sun that, apart from me, all is nothing. I am
Yahweh, unrivaled, I form the light and create the dark. I make
good fortune and create calamity, it is I, Yahweh, who do all
this." (Isaiah 45:1-7.)

And so, the Jews were able to deceive Cyrus and help him conquer Babylon
through the forgery of these chapters in Isaiah. Once Cyrus had captured Babylonia, the Jews offered him their "Jewish Loyalty."

One of the false premises that is relied upon by anyone who searches
scriptures for the secrets of God, is that these scriptures are based upon and
written by other seekers of Truth, Wisdom and Godliness. But such a assumption is false. To draw this false conclusion in regard to the *Hebrew Bible* of the
Jews is a very serious mistake. Part of the problem is that most people think
the *Hebrew Bible* was written in a linear timeline and was a record of ancient
adventures by very ancient Hebrews. But as modern archaeology and historical
analysis quite plainly show, the *Hebrew Bible* is really a montage of records
pieced together by the ancient Hebrews in a way that shows themselves in the
best possible light. The Jews lie about history and they lie about God and they
lie about themselves.

The practice of psychological warfare can be seen taking place in the
pages of the Book of Isaiah. As another example that is repeated throughout
history, the Jews betrayed the Babylonians to their enemies from Persia. "Your
descendants shall gain possession of the gates of their enemies. All the nations
of the earth shall bless themselves by your descendants, as a reward for your
obedience" (Genesis 22:17-18). The Jews opened the gates of Babylon to Cyrus. Following their rabbis in welcoming Cyrus to Babylon, the treasonous
Jews sang and danced and celebrated its capture. Before the ink was dry, the
Jewish priests rolled out more "ancient prophecies of Isaiah," who conveniently "foretold" not only that Cyrus would capture Babylon, but that he did so
only because he had the Jewish god giving him that conquering power. Thus,
they claimed that *their god* captured Babylon, using Cyrus as His servant and
with the help of the Jewish priests. Thus, the Bankers of Babylon made themselves into the priests of Judaism.

Since these "ancient prophecies" were so "accurate," how could Cyrus
not be amazed? And while he was amazed at these "ancient predictions" that
were alleged to be 200 years old – even naming him by name – the rabbis set the
hook hidden in their phony prophecies and caught this deceived king like a fish.

"My name is Yahweh," thundered the god, not from the skies but from
the pages of the Jewish manuscripts. "I will not yield my glory to another, nor
my honor to idols. See how my former predictions have come true. Fresh
things, I now foretell; before they appear I tell you of them" (Isaiah 42:8-9).

Oh? What are these "fresh things" that this mighty god of the Jews "pre-dicted" 200 years earlier? Why, nothing less than another Jewish swindle! Cy-rus had been able to enter Babylon with the help of the Jews opening the gates of that mighty city. He was grateful for this. Cyrus was met by dancing and singing Jews who celebrated his victory with elaborate feasting and merrymak-ing while offering the conquering king their "Jewish Loyalty." The Jewish priests solemnly read to Cyrus the so-called "ancient" prophecies of Isaiah, who "foretold" Cyrus' victory over Babylon. They bragged that Cyrus was the beloved "anointed one" of the Jewish god, convincing him that he had fulfilled his destiny and walked in the immortal paths of the god. But there was more!

The Hebrew rabbis continued to read to Cyrus from their "ancient" prophesies that still had fresh ink on them, where Yahweh says:

> "Thus says Yahweh, the Holy one, he who fashions Israel: Is it for you to question me about my children and to dictate to me what my hands should do? I it was who made the earth, and created man who is on it. I it was who spread out the heavens with my hands and now give orders to their whole array. I it was who roused Cyrus to victory, I leveled the way for him. He will rebuild my city, and will bring my exiles back without ransom or indemnity, so says Yahweh Sabaoth." (Isaiah 45:11-13.)

And so, Cyrus, the mighty king, the great conqueror, had now been out-maneuvered in the realm of psychological warfare. Instead of Cyrus giving the orders, it is the "god of the Jews" who was giving them.

According to the Jews, the Yahweh-god had thundered this ancient "manuscript" into the ear of Isaiah (Isaiah 45:7-8). So, Cyrus had better be careful to do everything that the Jews demand. Cyrus was commanded by this mighty Canaanite god, who had adopted the merchant-moneylenders as his own special people, to rebuild Jerusalem and send the Jews back for free.

What's even more, the rabbis made their "ancient prophet" Isaiah claim that Cyrus was also the beloved of Yahweh, *predestined* to do the bidding of this god and his whining Jews. Not only was Cyrus commanded to destroy the Babylonians, but also to wreak vengeance upon the enemies of the Jews. "My beloved will perform my pleasure with Babylon and the offspring of the Chal-deans" (Isaiah 48:14).

Thus, not only did the Bankers of Babylon cynically and hypocritically raise Cyrus up on a pedestal so that they could honor him and praise him as the very highest of mighty men, but they simultaneously put him under the power of their Jewish god. While the hypocritical and subversive Jews were bowing at the feet of Cyrus and singing and dancing and serving him with all of the submissiveness of worshipful and "loyal" subjects, the rabbis were whispering into his ear the latest "prophecies" and commands of the Yahweh-god. Thus, the Jewish Double-Whammy was invented. That is, the vast hordes of little Jews would scrape and bow to the erstwhile "leader," setting the example for the non-Jew populace, while the big Jews and rabbis and bankers in the background gave the orders, which the non-Jewish populace had to obey, since these orders seemed to come from the mouth of the king himself. These Monsters of Babylon had their every wish come true – the lying priests commanded whatever the scribes wrote in their goatskin fables and the king commanded whatever the merchant-moneylender-priests whispered into his ear. And all of the Jews, both big and little, offered the king their undying "Jewish Loyalty." This is the Tick-Behind-the-Ear technique that the Jews have used for 2,500 years to their great, demonic advantage, and to the great disadvantage of the Gentiles everywhere, as you shall see in the following chapters.

Anyway, the Jewish god foretold that Cyrus would "perform my pleasure" with the Babylonians. So, how could Cyrus refuse to go along with the fraud? Here he had the entire Babylonian Empire handed to him without a fight, through the treachery and hypocrisy of the Jews. Here he had the apparently "ancient" prophesy of Isaiah "foretelling" from some 200 years earlier that he, Cyrus himself, would be the "beloved" of this god of the Jews. Here he had thousands of little prancing and fawning Jews begging to touch his footprints, kneeling at his feet with sham looks of awestruck adoration, and fighting among themselves for the honor of serving him a bowl of fruit or holding up a palm leaf to give him shade. Here he had thousands of little Jews cheering and dancing and singing in unison as his chariot drove through the streets and villages. And here he had the Jewish priests loudly making a show of saying prayers to their god in thanksgiving and "blessing" him with the rabbis' splayed-devil-claw hand salute.

So, what could the very flattered and pleased King Cyrus do, but ask the obvious question, which was: "If the god of the Jews foretold that I would be the beloved one to perform my pleasure with the Babylonians and their offspring, what, pray tell, is that pleasure to be?"

Well now! Glad that he asked, the rabbis just happened to have a long list of what Cyrus could do to make himself pleasing to the Jewish god. And who else would know what would make a Jewish god happy, except a Jewish rabbi? So, first they presented the rabbinical idea that the Holy Children of God – namely, themselves – were very much like their god. In fact, they were made in His image! It says so in these holy hoaxes known as the Torah, so it must be true! And since the god of the Jews was a god of Vengeance – well, now! – the first order of business was to take vengeance upon the enemies of the Jews among the Babylonians, who had destroyed Abraham's First National Bank and Pawn Shop in Jerusalem and carted them all off to Babylon to get honest jobs.

When Nebuchadnezzar deported the Jews from Jerusalem and Judah in 586 BC, he did not enslave them. They were the chief administrators, priests, artisans and farm foremen, chief merchants and military officers whom he wanted to employ in the Babylonian Empire. He could not give them the positions of his nobles and high Babylonian officials, but he did give them profitable employment in the lower echelons of Babylonian society, overseeing the Babylonian people who were the Have-Nots. But this was an insult to the

Jews, who always expected to be treated with the greatest honor and have the best places at the dinner tables and the highest positions of authority – a great insult to God's Chosen People! For this, and for the Babylonian destruction of Jerusalem, they wanted their never-ending, eternally burning revenge! Thinking that the Jews were just like all of the other captives who were willing to work for the greater good of Babylonia, the Babylonians made a place for the newly arrived Jews and welcomed them as new additions to the great Chaldean Empire. For their part, the Jews kept their hatred for the *goyim* (non-Jewish, lowly insects, stupid cattle) to whom they now owed their livelihood carefully concealed, while they accepted every good thing offered to them.

But at the first opportunity, the big Jews and the little Jews came to Cyrus on bended knees, lamenting, moaning, wailing, and whimpering about the "persecutions" and "indignities" that they had suffered at the hands of the various Babylonians – at whom they were not at all shy about pointing their fingers and naming by name. The Jews pointed their accusing fingers at any and all of the Babylonians who had given them trouble, as well as at those whose only "sin" was not being Jewish. *Lex talionis*: the Semitic eye-for-an-eye revenge for whatever "slight" or insult the "Holy Ones of God" had allegedly suffered. The Jews had had sixty years to learn who owned what and who had the most power in Babylonia, and they were now repaid with Jewish vengeance. Following the teachings of their evil priests ("Even the best of *goyim* should be killed"), the Jews pointed out to Cyrus the best and the wealthiest and the most intelligent Babylonians for slaughter.

The Babylonian leaders were the first to be executed. The mayors of the towns, the cuneiform teachers, the captains of the guard, the princes, the tax collectors, the richest merchants, the keepers of the inns, the cattle dealers, the millers and wine makers, the boat captains and ferrymen, the gold and silver smiths, the money changers and the biggest farmers with the richest farms: they and their entire families were executed or sold into slavery because, as the rabbis decreed, this would be pleasing to the Jewish god. All of these wealthy and well-educated people had "insulted" the "Holy Chosen Ones of God," the mighty god who had named Cyrus by name in the forged Jewish scriptures.

After Cyrus had had all of these Babylonians removed from the land – well, now! – who was better qualified to take their places than the loyal Jews who had lived in Babylon for fifty or sixty years? Who could Cyrus find better qualified to collect taxes from the now-terrified Babylonians than the Jews who knew the Babylonian people so well? Who could Cyrus find who were better qualified to be the mayors of the towns, the teachers of the children, the captains of the guard, the tax collectors, the merchants, the innkeepers, cattle dealers, millers and wine makers, the boat captains and ferrymen, the gold and silver smiths, the money changers and the bailiffs of the large farms? And with music and songs of praise to their god and blessings to Cyrus, the Jews were quick to move into these now-vacant positions, following in the "ways" of their thieving goat-rustler god, taking what they did not work for and feeding off of the labor of others in "a land with large, flourishing cities you did not build, houses filled with all kinds of good things you did not provide, wells you did not dig, and vineyards and olive groves you did not plant" (Deuteronomy 6:10-11).

But the Bankers of Babylon and their scheming priests of the Yahweh-god could not merely flatter and deceive Cyrus into doing their bidding and leave it at that. They also had to build up the morale of the evil Jews whom they wanted to turn into the demons that we know so well today. Those Jews, whom the rabbis needed as their loyal disciples and faithful followers, had to be given a spirit of subversive conquest and indignant rebellion. The moneylenders of Babylon did not want them to merely trudge back to Jerusalem as weary captives returning home. No, they wanted to rebuild their treasure temple and its bullion vaults. For this, they needed willing and animated labor.

So, Ezra the scribe and his office of priests wrote up some more "ancient" prophesies and put Isaiah's name on them. Thus, out of the masses of deceived Hebrews, the rabbis created a type of people who were not only deluded by their lies, but also malevolent; a people who, through the example of the rabbis, understood that deceit and trickery gained them wealth and power. Through the lies of the rabbis, the Jews learned that if they could hold together and play the charade as an organized, conspiring gang, they could undermine, subvert, destroy and plunder peoples greater than themselves. But they had to conspire together to do it.

With their betrayal of the Babylonians and deceiving of Cyrus, the Jews realized that even mighty kings could fall victim to Jewish intrigues, just so long as the Jews could maintain the Jewish illusion as an organized and coordinated conspiring gang of liars and swindlers. The Jews learned in Babylon that, without armies or force of arms, they could conquer great nations using only the lies on their lips and the unending malice in their hearts, financed by the river of gold and silver supplied by their Sumerian Swindle.

The Jews learned in Babylon how to manipulate large masses of non-Jewish peoples simply through coordinated fraud, conspiring malice, hatred and perfidious subterfuge – by dancing in unison, by moaning and whining in chorus, by destroying their enemies with whispered slanders, by flattering kings and politicians with extravagant praises, and by exterminating four generations of their opponents. By rotting societies from within, the Jewish culture could thrive like mold on an apple. But the Jews were not parasites like most parasites found in Nature. No, there was nothing natural about the Jews. They were not passive parasites. They were (and are) predatory parasites. They actively sought out and attacked their hosts.

With this knowledge and by using these techniques, the moneylenders of Babylon promised their Jews, through the still wet ink of Isaiah's phony "prophecies" that:

> "Kings will be your foster fathers, their queens your nursing
> mothers. They will fall prostrate before you, faces to the ground,
> and lick the dust at your feet. And then you shall know that I am

Yahweh; And that those who hope in me will not be put to shame. ... I myself will fight with those who fight you, And I myself will save your children. I will make your oppressors eat their own flesh, they shall get as drunk on their own blood as on new wine. Then all mankind shall know that I, Yahweh, am your savior. And that your redeemer is the Mighty One of Jacob." (Isaiah 50:23-26.)

And who was Jacob other than a thieving, Hebrew-Hyksos goat rustler, roaming a dusty desert while robbing and murdering his neighbors? Thus, the scheming rabbis, scribes and priests of Abraham's First National Bank and Pawn Shop wanted their Jews to return to Jerusalem in proud triumph, not in drooping exhaustion (Isaiah 52:11-12), and to return with their wealth intact, like conquering bankers fat with the swindled wealth of their betters.

But some of the older and smarter Hebrews who remembered their earlier days in Babylon undoubtedly asked, "How is it that these prophesies were not read to them *before* their captivity in Babylon?" The ready lie of the rabbis was that these prophesies had been kept secret for two centuries because they could only be revealed at the right time, *after the captivity had occurred* and (here is the kicker) because of the "unbelief and sins of your fathers and of yourselves." It was a continuing rabbinical deceit to spur the Jews to greater exertions by claiming that their many sins needed purging. And who could have more sins than the thieving, murdering, betraying, lying Jews of Abraham's First National Bank and Pawn Shop of Jerusalem?

After having seduced and deceived King Cyrus, the rabbis realized that they had discovered a method of conquest that was subtle in the extreme. It was a subtle application of Secret Problem #10 of the Babylonian Moneylenders: "Kings are targets, so it is better to hold the target in your hands than to be a king." Their method was not based upon military power, although military power was one of their options as long as *someone else* was paying for the military and risking their lives in battle. The Jewish method was based upon financial bribery, purchasing power, and the false claims of a religious hoax, not upon goodness or superior virtue, although goodness and superior virtue was what they at all times cloaked themselves with, like the gossamer tube that cloaks the gnarly spider. The method of the rabbis was based upon cloaking themselves in the highest and most virtuous moral precepts as an outer covering and deceitful facade, while employing the most evil and treacherous techniques that could be devised by either man or demon. Thus, it was in Babylon that the rabbis developed a system of political and monetary warfare that became known as Judaism. To strengthen and motivate their Jews, they added to the Book of Isaiah the "prophesy" that "Your race will take possession of the *goyim* and people the abandoned cities" (Isaiah 54:3). It was a race-based system of dispossession, treason, pillage and genocide, financed by the Sumerian Swindle and directed by the evil rabbis of Judah.

And so, with gladness and singing, some (but not all) of the Jews prepared to leave Babylon and move back to Jerusalem. The lying rabbis read them words from the still-wet ink of the so-called "ancient prophesies of Isaiah," where the chief banker of the moneylenders calls himself "the god of the whole earth" (Isaiah 54:4-5).

To further consolidate their swindle, the rabbis made sure that they could use the ancient "promises" of the lying Yahweh-god by having their newly inked "prophesies of Isaiah" state that, yes, the Yahweh-god broke his promises once again and destroyed the Jews out of anger, but now he is once again promising to be a good god and love them forever. So, now they can trust him again (Isaiah 54:7-10).

Through the wet ink of Isaiah, the rabbi-priest-moneylenders told their Jews that they could go home to Judah while all of creation celebrates the Jews, who are so holy that the "mountains and hills will break into joyful cries before you and all the trees of the countryside clap their hands" (Isaiah 55:12-13). Yes, all of the world is so lucky to be lied to, deceived, betrayed, swindled, destroyed and dispossessed by the holy Jews! And so, out of Babylon came a people who were led by devils dressed as rabbis and who, with gladness and singing, offered themselves as willing servants to whatever lies and frauds destroyed the largest number of hated *goyim* or gave them the highest profits. The pages of Isaiah from chapter 40 through 55 were counterfeited and added to the books many hundreds of years after that old Hebrew goat molester had died.

Isaiah chapters 56-66 were written in Babylon and edited after the return to Jerusalem. Thanks to their successes in fraud and forgery, the Jews now had many non-Jews who had heard how the so-called "ancient prophesies of Isaiah" had predicted that Cyrus would release the Jews from Babylon. The non-Jews had heard the amazing lies about Moses, so they were very anxious to know more about this powerful god of the Jews. The Jews thus had an abundance of non-Jewish fools who had fallen into the swindle and wanted to be included among the self-proclaimed "Chosen Ones of God." They also wanted to share in "the Promise."

So, quite conveniently, the wicked rabbis trotted out another "ancient prophecy of Isaiah" dripping with wet ink. In Isaiah 56, Yahweh tells how to accept more converts to his worship and to the Jewish religion. Thus, the rabbis were able to not only increase the numbers of their Jews, but also to increase the numbers of roasted fowls, sheep, goats and cattle that were sacrificed upon the fly-swarming altar of Yahweh (Isaiah 56:6-8), along with the cash donations, of course.

Who was it among the Jews who offered child sacrifices and performed sexual acts under the sacred trees? The leaders of Judah, the kings, princes and administrators, of course! Isaiah said, "Our watchmen are all blind, they notice nothing ... Devout men are taken off [and killed] and no one gives it a thought .... But you, you sons of a witch ... sacrifice children in the wadis and in rocky clefts .. etc." (Isaiah 56-57.) Who did Isaiah preach against? The Jewish leaders! (Isaiah 59:5-8.) Once Cyrus had been flattered and deceived to the point of complete subjugation to the wishes of the wicked priests of Yahweh, he could not say "no" to whatever they claimed that their powerful god wanted. And Yahweh wanted quite a lot!

For their services to Cyrus of betraying the Babylonian Empire and opening the city to him, the treasonous Jews were able to insinuate themselves into Cyrus' court as advisors, merchants and moneylenders, dream analyzers, physicians, demon exorcists, and "holy prophets." As a reward for their treason and treachery against Babylonia, the Jews were able to acquire complete economic and administrative control of the former Babylonian empire, choosing the richest lands and the most profitable positions after having had the former Babylonian owners executed. In addition, the mighty god of the Jews, speaking through the wet ink of Isaiah, proclaimed that Cyrus would also give back to the Jews all of their former lands in Judea.

It was after these acts were decreed and finalized that, in triumph, the rabbis realized that they had perfected the perfect swindle. It was here that the wet-ink prophesies of Isaiah were read to the Jews. And it was at that point that the Jews became a Holy Vampire Nation, while the rabbis chanted the Books of Isaiah, chapters 60-62. The Jews believed that they were God's Chosen and beloved people who deserved the worship by all of Mankind while they swindled, dispossessed, murdered and enslaved all of Mankind. And they assumed the posture and attitude of expecting all non-Jews to treat them this way. The arrogant, bloodsucking, obnoxious, greedy Jew was sired in Babylon and created in Babylonia.

> "And your gates will lie open continually, shut neither by day nor by night, for men to bring you the wealth of the *goyim* with their kings leading them; for the *goyim* and kingdom that refuses to serve you shall perish, such *goyim* shall be utterly ruined." (Isaiah 60:11-12.)

> "You will feed on the wealth of *goyim* and array yourselves in their magnificence." (Isaiah 61:6.)

Does Judaism teach the Jews to become a better people? Not at all. "Walking in the ways" of their demon god, the Jews are urged to *array themselves in the magnificence of other people*. The Jews themselves have never, ever added to the Civilization of Mankind, because they are robbers and parasites. Like their "holy" scriptures which they counterfeited, whatever "magnificence" the Jews exhibit is nothing but exhibiting what they have robbed from other people. No Jew has ever owned anything that was not swindled or burglarized from others. Look at the swindling, super-wealthy, Jewish financiers and bankers and tycoons in modern times, and you will see that their wealth is really the magnificence of others – just as it has always been. But "just as it has always been," *does not mean that that is how it should continue.*

The proof that these wet-ink "prophesies" were neither from God nor from Isaiah is found within them. Isaiah 62:8 shows their flawed and human origin, since history proves that these were just more lies from a Yahweh-god who was nothing more than a figment of rabbinical imagination. God never did any of the things that the Jews claim he did. And the actual Yahweh-god of the Jews, lying through the mouths of the Jewish priests, broke every promise that he ever made. But the Jews believed it. Indeed, they didn't have much choice, since the rabbis killed any Jew who questioned the truth of their "holy" lies. In the realm of rabbinic sorcery – Abracadabra! – as long as you believe what the rabbi says, you will be his devoted servant.

For the Jews, Yahweh was a terrible monster of a god. For extra terror, while in Babylon, the rabbis wrote Isaiah 63, describing Yahweh as a monster who crushes Jews who are not obedient to Him, like a man stomps on grapes to make red wine (Isaiah 63:3-6). Immediately after this literary terrorism, the rabbis wanted the Jews to praise Yahweh and bring his rabbis and priests gifts. So, they had Isaiah say:

> "Let me sing the praises of Yahweh's goodness, and of his mar-
> velous deeds, in return for all that he has done for us and for the
> great kindness he has shown us in his mercy and in his bound-
> less goodness." (Isaiah 63-7.)

Excuse me? Even while singing this psalm the Jews are lying, because their Yahweh-god has none of these attributes, and is rather quite the reverse of good and kind. As their own writings prove, the Yahweh-god of the Jews is a monster – a terrible monster of a god. No lies of the rabbis can erase that fact. The Jews sing their praises for a demon who destroys the world and all of its people, using the Jews as his servants and rewarding them with booty, as Isaiah 65 claims. Further threats from the priests make sure the Jews are good "servants" and provide the rabbis with plenty to eat and plenty of gold to invest and spend.

The total number of chapters in Isaiah is sixty-six. Of these, thirty-eight were written by the rabbis as part of the scheme to get out of forced residence in Babylon. Thus, fully fifty-eight percent of the chapters in Isaiah were not even written by Isaiah, but were composed by the rabbis in Babylon who claim that it was all Isaiah's work. Once again, their own writings prove that the Jews are liars and deceivers, just like Jesus said that they are.

Hosea 743-724 BC
(Twenty Years of Threats)

Hosea begins with a false date. This shouldn't be so surprising, since just about everything in the *Hebrew Bible* and in Judaism is false. It is claimed to have been written when Jeroboam was king of the Israelians. But it is clear that Hosea did most of his preaching during the reign of the last kings of the Israelians: Menahem (743-738 BC), Pekahiah (738-737 BC), Pekah (737-732 BC) and Hoshea (732-724 BC).

Hosea was a contemporary of Amos and he was from the Northern Kingdom of the Israelians. During those times under king Jeroboam II in 783-721 BC, Assyria was the greatest power of the region. He may have lived through Assyria's defeat of Samaria in 721 BC.

True to the Circumcised Penis Cult of Judaism, Hosea uses sexual imagery in his descriptions of the relationship between their god and the Hebrews. The Jewish god's relationship with Israel is that of a husband and wife. In this case, the Yahweh-god is the screwer and the Hebrews are the screwees. But he also attacks the worship of Yahweh at Bethal, where Baal and Astarte are also worshiped. It should be noted that the Yahweh-god had a wife. And this wife was none other than the Babylonian goddess Astarte (Ishtar). In the Canaanite religion, the son of Yahweh was the god Baal.

The priests of Jerusalem added their self-promotional blurbs. When Hosea said of the House of Israel (the Israelians in the north): "No more love shall the House of Israel have from [God] in future, no further forgiveness" (Hosea 1:6), the rabbis added "But my love shall go to the House of Judah and through Yahweh their God I mean to save them – but not by bow or sword or battle, horse or horseman" (Hosea 1:7).

The Israelians also worshiped the Canaanite Baals, the fertility gods whom they believed gave them as much produce and livestock as did Yahweh. As there were thousands of prophets, all shouting, "It is God who is speaking through my mouth!" only those prophets who benefited the priests of the Abraham Temple Cult have been preserved in writing.

It is the brainwashing refrain from their hairy-faced prophets that really got the Hebrews all worked into an ecstasy. Speaking through the garlic and fishy breaths of Hosea, Yahweh says, "You are my people." And the Hebrews reply, "You are my god" (Hosea 2:23). This leads to enthusiastic fornication among the circumcised Jews who have Hosea's sexual promises ringing in their ears: "the number of the sons of Israel will be like the sand on the sea-shore, which cannot be measured or counted" (Hosea 1:10).

Because he is preaching to the Israelians, the Northern Kingdom, Hosea enumerates the ways of these Hebrews. He states that among them, "there is no fidelity, no tenderness, no knowledge of God in the country, only perjury and lies, slaughter, theft, adultery and violence, murder after murder" (Hosea 4:1-2). In short, Hosea is showing what the Jews were like in those days. Descended from the thieves and cutthroats of an earlier era, they had not changed their evil ways much at all, except now they were becoming wealthy from various business enterprises with the merchant-moneylenders of Assyria.

The Hebrew priests themselves were even worse than the ordinary Hebrews. After all, when a Hebrew did an evil act and felt bad about it, he would go to the temple with a goat or lamb to sacrifice in atonement. The demonic priests poured out the blood of the victim on the fly-encrusted altar, and after burning some of the animal in the fire, would roast and eat the rest of it. So, the more sinful the wicked Hebrews were, the fatter the priests became.

From the inception of the Northern Kingdom to the year 737 BC, seven of its kings were murdered. The Hebrew bandits were cunning and treacherous, according to Hosea. "Deceit is their principal behavior" (Hosea 7:1) and they "consume the men who rule them" (Hosea 7:7). One Hebrew made these observations of his fellow Hebrews during the 700s BC. At that time, the Hebrews were still the active thieves and murderers that they had been from the very earliest times. They had not yet learned to be scheming Jews and murder people with stealth and cunning.

Micah 740-687 BC
(Fifty-Three Years of Violent Shouting)

Micah was a Judean who preached during the reign of kings Jotham, Ahaz and Hezekiah from between 740-687 BC. This was before and after the fall of Samaria in 721 BC. He was a contemporary with both Hosea and Isaiah. He was a country man, not a city dweller. So, his words were sometimes coarse.

Like most of the biblical books, Micah has been methodically edited by the rabbis. That there are only seven chapters to the book of a prophet who preached for forty or fifty years shows how the rabbis kept only what benefited their power.

Micah was most vehement in his condemnation of rich capitalists, avaricious priests and prophets, tyrants and venal judges, violent and rich men, social injustice, relentless usurers, swindling tradesmen, liars, fighting and inharmonious families, and those who used fraudulent measures or confiscated property for debt payment – in other words, the typical Chosen Ones of Abraham's First National Bank and Pawn Shop. He knew quite well the ways of the Jews, as he wrote:

> "Now, listen to this, you princes of the House of Jacob, rulers of the House of Israel, you who loathe justice and pervert all that is right, you who build Zion with blood, Jerusalem with crime. Her princes pronounce their verdict for bribes, her priests take a fee for their rulings, her prophets make divinations for money." (Micah 3:9-11.)

In these pronouncements, it is easy to see that in this modern-day world, the Jews have not changed at all. It is "business as usual" for the Jewish hypocrites who commit crimes while using religion as a mask for their evil.

The rabbis inserted some of their propaganda into Micah, which is identical to Isaiah 2:2-5. In this, the rabbis promote the idea of the "greatness" of their laws and oracles so that all the people of the earth will want the rabbis to teach them and guide them in the demonic ways of the Jews.

Much of Micah was written by the Jews after he had died. These prophesies of disaster are all designed to show the "god-given foresight" of the prophets. But the really tricky part is the "prophesy" that Jerusalem will once again rule over Israel (Micah 4:8). Thus, from their captivity in Babylon after 587 BC, the rabbis edited in their own favor the prophesies of Micah from 150 years earlier. They had plenty of old scrolls from which to "cut and paste." And to ensure the primacy of their tribal totem, the lion, the rabbis had Micah say:

> "Among the many peoples, the remnant of Jacob will be among
> the *goyim*, like a lion among beasts of the forest, like a young
> lion among flocks of sheep trampling as he goes, mangling his
> prey which no one takes from him." (Micah 5:7-8.)

The rabbis wanted their tribes of thieves and murderers to continue with their depredations among the people of the world. The Jews were to be as wild lions among the people of the earth, and destroy all nations. This is the rabbis' interpretation of these lines and it is why every country in which the Jews have been allowed to settle, soon become diseased, betrayed and broken societies, eaten from within by these betrayers of Mankind. Further, the god of the Jews through Micah says:

> "I will take revenge in anger and fury on the *goyim*
> that would not obey" (Micah 5:14).

And what are the various peoples of the world to obey? Why, the dictates of the Jewish merchant-moneylenders and rabbis, of course! These vicious, cunning rabbis and their perfidious people have decided that they will tear up like lions all the people in the world who do not bow down to them and their Jewish God of Lies, seated in the treasury of Abraham's First National Bank and Pawn Shop. The Jews have no power to do this, other than with the malice in their hearts driving the wealth of their swindles. They are demons.

At the end of the Book of Micah, the rabbis counterfeit a few extra verses to give Micah even more "prophetic foresight." To show the Jews how to treat their enemies, the wet ink of the rabbis in Babylon added, "My eyes will gloat" over my enemies who "will be trampled underfoot like mud in the streets" (Micah 7:10). Remember, the Yahweh-god of the Jews demands that they "walk in his ways." Thus, the Jews desire to trample underfoot the people of the world so that they feel "holy" and "chosen". This Jewish teaching was reflected in more modern times in the 19th century AD, when the Jewish banker Alphonse Rothschild in 1866 was asked by a friend after dinner, "Why, when he was so rich, he worked like a negro to become more so. 'Ah!' Alphonse replied, 'You don't know the pleasure of feeling heaps of Christians under one's boots.'" Alphonse Rothschild was one of the Monsters of Babylon. You will meet more of them in Volume III: *The Bloodsuckers of Judah*.

After their return from Babylon to Jerusalem in 538 BC, the rabbis added verses 7:11-20 to Micah, just to make sure that their brand of Jewish beliefs were based on "ancient and accurate prophesies" counterfeited from 150-200 years earlier. Yes, the Jews had some "mighty" prophets who looked into the distant future and regardless of what they claimed that they saw, the rabbis wrote down an improved, kosher version of it later, complete with antedated time frames and post-dated prophesies. With lies such as these, told in those far away times and honed to perfection by the Jewish rabbis and "scholars," they built a foundation for the deception of the entire world, a deception that is still being promoted today by the world's most horrible people, the Jews.

Zephaniah 640-630 BC
(Ten Years of Violent Protests)

Zephaniah did his preaching in Judah between 640 and 630 BC, while Josiah was still a child and before the reforms inaugurated upon the "discovery" of the counterfeited Book of Deuteronomy.

Zephaniah threatened almost everybody. Those who prayed to any god except Yahweh were, of course, first on his list of those that Yahweh intended to slaughter. That it took thirty to forty years for his prophesies to come about doesn't seem to matter much to those who believe the lying, old Jewish vermin. With the continual rise and fall of nations, a prophesy of doom can be given to any of them and if you wait long enough, the prophesy will be fulfilled.

But Zephaniah was after more than just those who prayed to foreign gods, he also threatened anyone who dressed in foreign fashions. You see, even in those days, the Jews controlled the garment industry in Judah and Israel. And they didn't appreciate anyone not buying clothes from them. But instead of merely putting foreign competitors out of business with boycotts, arson, lawsuits and refusal of advertising, like the Jews of today due to their competitors, those old Judeans had their prophets call down the thunderbolts of Yahweh on them (or threaten to do so) for not dressing like a Judean complete with untrimmed beard, sidelocks, fringed shawl, and circumcised penis.

As Zephaniah rants: "I will punish the ministers, the royal princes, and all those who dress themselves in foreign style" (Zephaniah 1:8). But of course, the clothes of the Jews were also gang colors. By their hair style and clothes, the Jews could spot each other instantly. In this way, Jewish merchants could travel without being attacked and killed by Jewish thieves. Jewish swindlers could be sure to pick a non-Jewish mark for their con jobs. Jewish merchants could use false weights on the non-Jews without censure. And non-Jewish women could be raped and sold into slavery without the rabbis interfering with the Jewish slave masters. For these and a thousand other reasons related to their criminal gang mentality, the rabbis insisted on a Jewish dress code. It saved time, since Jewish merchants wouldn't try to swindle those whom they didn't know were Jews. They could just swindle those who didn't dress like Jews.

All in all, the few pages that compose the Book of Zephaniah were probably written by the rabbis in Babylon, with the last two paragraphs having been added after their return to Jerusalem. So, once again, the wet ink histories written in future tense gave the lying rabbis another slimy hold upon the credulity of the Jews, as well as upon the gullible people of the world. All in all, Zephaniah is another Jewish fraud.

Jeremiah 626-598 BC
(Twenty-Eight Years of Whining)

Jeremiah was born into a priestly family in about 646 BC. Naturally, his only education came from the Operating Manual of Abraham's First National Bank and Pawn Shop in Jerusalem. His father was one of the Temple loafers whose only occupation was to get free barbecued goats, bread and wine, and shekels of silver from the Hebrews whom the Levite Police had caught in the act of "sinning."

Who was Jeremiah prophesying against? Why, the wicked Jews of Jerusalem and all of Judah, because they worshiped idols (Jeremiah 1:16). Also, against the king of Judah, its princes, its priests and prophets and the Hebrews in the countryside (Jeremiah 1:18); against the Hebrew kings and prophets who had followed the god, Baal (Jeremiah 2:8 and Jeremiah 2:25); against those who committed murder while pretending to have caught the victims attempting a burglary (Jeremiah 2:34). In fact, against everybody. The inbred Jews were obviously genetically predisposed toward crimes of every sort, even in the old days when the Levites kept careful watch over them.

The prophets always had a ready supply of invaders for threatening the Hebrews. When Jeremiah began his threatening prophecies in 626 BC, he had the Scythians who had invaded the Syrian-Palestine frontier between 630-625 BC. And the Chaldeans kings were very powerful in Babylonia, capturing Nineveh in 612 BC.

Jeremiah condemns the people of Judah, all of them, with idolatry, atheism, sensuality, exploitation of the poor, and adultery, all of which he blames on the ruling classes, the kings, princes, priests and prophets. Not even one man in all of Jerusalem was righteous (Jeremiah 5:1), except Jeremiah, of course. They were the wild and woolly Hyksos-Hebrews.

Jeremiah mentions the Jews in his "prophecy" in this manner: "Monstrous, horrible things are happening in the land: the prophets prophesy falsely, the priests teach whatever they please" (Jeremiah 5:30-31). These priests were the evil priests of the Yahweh-god. They and the kings, princes, and priests worshiped the sun, moon and stars and practiced divination (Jeremiah 8:2) So, you see, these Jews were some extremely nasty critters. They could claim a degree of "holiness" only by lying about it.

Jeremiah condemns the Judeans of Jerusalem for exploiting non-Jews, orphans and widows, for stealing, for being wicked slanderers, deceivers, liars, and corrupt frauds (Jeremiah 9:4-8) as well as for murder, adultery, perjury and idolatry with Baal (Jeremiah 7:6). He also preaches against the Jewish tradition of the priests that allowed the worship of idols, as long as only a part of the worship was performed. So, even at this early time, the wicked priests of Judah were scheming about ways of evading the Mosaic Laws of their own religion, just like the modern-day rabbis do!

> "Cannot you see what they are doing in the towns of Judah and in the streets of Jerusalem? The children collect the wood, the fathers light the fire, the women knead the dough, to make cakes for the Queen of Heaven." (Jeremiah 7:17-18.)

This shows that even at that early time, the Pharisee sect of Judaism was already rearing its monstrous head. Such teaching of the Pharisee rabbis is that only a complete action is a sin. But if each Jew only does a small part, none of them are guilty. The Queen of Heaven was *Ishtar*, the Assyrian goddess of fertility, known in Canaan as *Asherah*, the wife of *Yahweh*. The Hebrews were sacrificing their sons and daughters to a Canaanite god (Jeremiah 7:31).

This was the wild and lawless city of Jerusalem after the Hebrews had taken it. So, one must wonder why all of these stories written by the rabbis about Moses, Joshua, David and Solomon had such little effect on these idiot Hebrews? Could it be that the rabbis hadn't written the Torah, yet, since they hadn't yet been carted off to Babylon, where they had more leisure time to imagine things and write them down?

During their stay in Babylon, the evil rabbis had gathered up the scrolls of the prophesies of Jeremiah and added some of their own writings. Jeremiah 10:1-16 was added to keep the Judean Hebrews aware of Yahweh, so that they would not go running after the idols of Babylon. During Jeremiah's time, King Josiah began some religious reforms, because during renovations of the Temple, the Book of Deuteronomy was – *Abracadabra*! – "found." Either it had been hidden and forgotten during the previous reign of the evil King Manesseh (687-642) or it hadn't been written yet. But since only forty-seven years had passed since Manesseh began his rule and the pious King Josiah (640-609 BC) began his own rule, it seems rather impossible that the laws and rules of Deuteronomy could have been overlooked or forgotten in so short a time, what with the priests insisting on always following tradition.

What is more likely is that these rules were written, not in the ancient times and forgotten, but rather with the wet ink forgeries and counterfeits of the priests under Josiah's reign. Furthermore, there are astonishing similarities between some of the clauses in the Code of the Covenant or in Deuteronomy and those in the Mesopotamian codes, in the Collection of Assyrian Laws, and in the Hittite Code. Although Biblical commentators all try to uphold their belief in the God-ordained source of the Jewish Laws, in fact, the thieving rabbis of Jerusalem and swindling bankers of Babylon, directly purloined whatever laws they could from whatever sources suited their purposes.

Thus, the Laws of Deuteronomy can best be understood as the works of the temple priests, such as Jeremiah and his father, trying to solidify their control and monopoly of Temple worship. This was not only a religious practice for them, but a lucrative profession that brought in silver and gold. Silver was brought to the Temple as an offering and it was also collected from the people by the keepers of the threshold as an entry fee. This same practice is seen in modern synagogues where, especially during holidays, tickets are sold to get in! The keepers of the threshold were themselves priests, but not your ordinary fat Pharisees. They were chosen for this particular guard duty because they were big and strong, and could beat up or kill anyone who broke the rules or tried to enter for free. In addition, fat goats and calves were sacrificed on the fly-swarming altar of Yahweh and later eaten by the sacrificer, the priests and the large families of the priests. The entire Temple Scam was carefully orchestrated. So, it isn't likely that a book like Deuteronomy would have been forgotten. It is more likely that it was forged in secret in order to gain full control over the boy-king Josiah and greater power over the people of Canaan for the priests of Yahweh.

In 640 BC, Josiah became king of Judah. He was only eight years old at the time (2 Kings 22:1), so he came immediately under the influence of the priests, prophets and scribes. Of course, they were able to teach him their ways and he became a devout follower of the priests of Abraham's First National Bank and Pawn Shop. As a young boy, he was easily deceived by all of the rabbinical and priestly lies about Moses, Joshua, David and Solomon.

Jeremiah came from a priestly family and Josiah was tutored and advised by the priests. Jeremiah was about twenty years old in 626 BC, when he began prophesying. At that time, King Josiah was only about twenty-one years old. So, the two of them would naturally have a certain rapport that equally-aged youths have together among their older advisors and administrators. The two of them had been acquaintances for at least four years before the fraud of Deuteronomy was perpetrated by the High Priest. Jeremiah had been ranting at the Judeans between his first prophesy in 626 BC and the so-called "discovery" of the Book of Deuteronomy in 622 BC, making him about twenty-four years old and King Josiah about twenty-six years old.

This so-called "discovery" of Deuteronomy allowed the Yahweh Cult to triumph over the other religions in the region by killing and burning down everything that wasn't Jewish. It was eighteen years of genocide before the priests of the Temple of Yahweh were able to regain dictatorship over the religious practices in Jerusalem and finally in all of Judah and Samaria. It is a rather lengthy list of temples, high places, sacred groves and altars destroyed and priests murdered by Josiah throughout his realm. The entire chapter of 2 Kings 23 reads like a Who's Who in ancient religions of the Middle East. The Hebrews obviously prayed and sacrificed to every devil and god in the lands, and ended up being forced to pray to the biggest devil of them all, the Yahweh-god of the Jews.

If you will take a time out here from this book and read 2 Kings 23:1-30, you can see that the priests of the Yahweh Cult had lots and lots of competition in getting what they considered their fair share of the money and the sacrificial meat. In this long list of various Canaanite cults and religious practices, the rabbis try to give the impression that this was all a result of "backsliding" away from the allegedly "ancient and traditional religion of Yahweh." But Judaism is a huge fraud. It was not a religion that was given to "the descendants of Abraham who escaped from Egypt and who followed the Laws of Moses." Not at all! The alleged "backsliding" of the Israelites into idolatry *was actually normal for them*.

Archaeology shows that the age of tribal and Davidic fidelity to the Yahweh-god was a late religious ideal, not a historical reality. The idolatry of the people of Judah was not a departure from their earlier alleged monotheism. Idolatry was actually the way the people of Judah had worshiped from their earliest times. The Contract that the Banker's Guild of Babylon was trying to inveigle the Hebrews to accept is not what the early Hebrews actually believed in. It was what the Babylonian moneylenders of Abraham's First National Bank and Pawn Shop *wanted* the Hebrews to believe.

It is well-known today of the strong disagreements between religious groups. The history of all of Mankind is replete with murders, wars, betrayals, and various lies and swindles, all in the name of one religious group trying to serve the god of their choice and defeat the peoples who pray to different gods. The scribes and priests of Yahweh were certainly no different in this respect. What has differentiated these Jews from the followers of other gods is the subtlety and deviousness of their attack strategy. In addition, the Jews had a tactical advantage over their idol-worshiping adversaries. It is appropriate here to consider this thing called idolatry or the worship of idols. We have some excellent examples of this practice even in modern times, among the Hindus of India.

The Hindu people have statues of all sizes of their various gods and goddesses: the blue-complected Krishna and his consort, multi-armed Siva and Vishnu, demon statues of fang-toothed Kali with garlands of human heads, the Siva lingam, elephant-headed Ganesh, monkey gods, and the list goes on. Today's ignorant Hindus pay the highest respects to these statues while bathing them in milk or warm, scented water, fanning them on hot days, dressing them in fine clothes and garlands of flowers, offering them food and drink, and bowing down to them in complete and utter obeisance and worship. The sacrifice of animals to these statues is still a big part of many Hindu sects to this very day.

So, we can see for ourselves what idol worship is all about today, just as in ancient times. However, what is not generally understood by Western Man is that modern-day Hindus are not usually praying to the statues themselves. What the Hindus believe is that the idol *represents* the actual god that they pray to and that this god actually and invisibly descends and enters into the statue and looks out of the eyes of the statue to see and enjoy the obeisance and gifts that are offered. And these gods from inside the statues listen to and perhaps grant the prayers and requests that are made by the believing worshipers.

Yes, the Hindus know that the idol is made of wood or stone. But it is the god that the idol *represents* to whom he offers his prayers. It is the god within the idol whom they worship.

In any case, the priests of the cult of Yahweh had a handy attack and a ready defense in their assault on idolatry. Their god was both invisible and all-knowing, so they could pray to him without idols. Plus, they could ridicule idol worship as the primitive and ignorant thing that it is. Their argumentative trick was that since the idols were obviously man-made of wood or stone, they were really quite false as gods. Therefore, they reasoned, since these were false gods, the Cult of Yahweh must be true. The idolaters could not prove the invisible Yahweh false, and there was nothing substantial to cling to. Yahweh wasn't inside an idol. He was sitting invisibly on his "thrown of mercy" or living invisibly behind the Temple Veil or sending his giant nostril down to smell the "sweet savor" of burning dead animals.

All of the sects and religions that were practiced in Canaan and Judah during the time of Jeremiah were idolatrous religions. As can be seen in 2 Kings 23:1-30, some of these were even practiced within the Temple itself. So, there is little wonder that the priests of Yahweh were rather pressed for space and jealous of their reduced privileges. Indeed, their god was a jealous god and so were his wicked priests. The kings of Israel were not helpful, since they had set up the idols themselves. After all, it was part of the politics of those days for kings to show respect to the gods of visiting kings and dignitaries.

And so, once they had a king such as Josiah in power whom they could control totally deceive, the rabbis pretended to find the book that they had written and hidden in the Temple wall. This was the Book of Deuteronomy. And while writing their ancient manuscript called Deuteronomy, the scribes were careful to make sure that only the Jewish priests would have the monopoly on the worship of Yahweh. They wrote into Deuteronomy a law making Jerusalem alone a unique sanctuary.

As a king who had been raised by the priests since boyhood, Josiah was a malleable tool in the hands of the rabbis. Brainwashed since childhood with the lies of the priests of Abraham's First National Bank and Pawn Shop, Josiah obediently destroyed all other centers of worship, not merely the foreign gods' altars but even the altars devoted to Yahweh himself, which were tended by the country priests. The country priests were required to live in Jerusalem and attend the one Temple, there eating their "temurah," the food left on the altar. Or else they were killed. And what better way could a good Jewish priest eliminate competition than by having the king kill them all?

When he had finished this work of "cleansing" the land of idolatry, King Josiah ordered a celebration of Passover "as prescribed in the book of the covenant." No Passover like this one had been celebrated since the days when the judges ruled Israel. The eighteenth year of King Josiah was the only time when such a Passover was celebrated in honor of Yahweh at Jerusalem.

Josiah was named by all the rabbis as the most religious of all kings. But for all of Josiah's Jewish zeal, the lying god of the Jews didn't protect him from being killed in battle with the Egyptians on their way to offer their assistance to Assyria against Babylonia. That the wicked Jewish priests could fool their own people is wonder enough. That they could fool all of the people of the Western world for 2,500 years is beyond wonder!

According to Jeremiah, all the *goyim* (non-Jewish, lowly insects, stupid cattle) must learn the ways of the Jews (Jeremiah 12:16-17). Jeremiah was just as evil a Jew as our modern variety. If the People actually knew how evil the Jews are, they would rise up and kill them all. Knowing this, the Jews lie to us about what their religion actually teaches and what their actual methods and goals are. While lying and claiming a "higher morality," the Jews practice the most diabolical treason upon all of Mankind.

When Nebuchadnezzar led away the captives of Jerusalem, he took with him all the ruling elite, the king's court, the high priests, the wealthy merchants, and the property owners of Judah, along with the blacksmiths and metalworkers (Jeremiah 24:1). Remember, the Laws of Moses only allowed the wealthy to own property inside the city walls. Thus, the ones who were carted off to Babylonia were the rich moneylenders, high priests and members of the king's court as well as artisans and metal workers, that is, most of the city dwellers of Jerusalem, leaving the city open to whomever wanted to take up residence in the homes of the rich. *Three-quarters of the population of Judah remained on the land.* Nebuchadnezzar needed them to pay taxes in grain, olive oil and silver. Nothing would be gained by deporting them all to Babylonia where he already had plenty of farmers and debt slaves.

It was these classes of wealthy elite and priests of Jerusalem who schemed to get their property back by figuring out a way to be released from captivity. The Babylonian merchant-moneylenders and evil priests of Abraham's First National Bank and Pawn Shop had a successful scam going with Judaism. For nearly a thousand years, this sect of international merchants and moneylenders had profited from their monopoly over the secure treasury temple in Jerusalem. Wherever those swindlers traveled, they were immune from taxes and military duty. And they were free to do business and voraciously collect interest without the interference from the human sentiments of the foreign priests. With their own moneylender religion, they were outside the moral bounds of all other peoples and were free to do as they wished, regardless of any consideration other than profits and their own self- interest. In fact, their "holiness scam" was so successful in both profits and prestige that the "Holy Ones of God" could look down upon all other people as *goyim* (non-Jewish, lowly insects, stupid cattle).

The Jewish moneylenders of Jerusalem had plenty of help from their fellow guild members, internationally as well as from within Babylonia itself. Theirs was a system of commerce and loan-sharking concealed within a religious fraud that kept their profits well-protected. To lose their main Jerusalem treasury would be a disaster. But to lose the protecting religious fraud that surrounded the treasury would be worse. How could they maintain the illusion of being worshipers of a "mighty god," if that god's temple was abandoned and under non-Jewish rule? How could they guarantee safe deposits to their membership without a secure treasury? How could they run their bill discounting scam without a bank? Wealth requires a place to store that wealth and a place to store the records of that wealth, such as loan contracts, mortgages, letters of credit, and ownership documents of all sorts. How could they maintain their domestic and international properties without secure city walls and a temple treasury strong room?

In 589 BC, records were still being kept on clay tablets as well as parchment scrolls and papyrus. A secure place was necessary to store these heavy and valuable documents, not to mention the tons of gold and silver that their businesses generated. A temple and a walled city were the necessary basic technology for successful international commerce and trade in the ancient world. And now Nebuchadnezzar had ruined their plans, confiscated their wealth, kidnapped them and their families and located them all in Babylonia where – as educated merchants and administrators – they were required to work as land overseers, accountants, tax farmers, slave masters, clerks and assistants for the Babylonian aristocracy.

They could still keep their military deferment from Nebuchadnezzar's army as long as they clung to their weekly Sabbath rituals and refused to work, wailing and cringing beneath the lashes and kicks of the soldiers with the excuses that: "It isn't our fault. We would be glad to serve in the army, but our god would be angry and give us leprosy if we did so. And then all of your army would also catch leprosy. Or the earth would open up and swallow us along with your armies. Here take a bribe to let us keep our deferment." And by keeping their Sabbath, they had every excuse for gathering all of these scheming moneylenders, slave drivers, pimps, property owners and royal administrators together into one gang, once a week for fifty years, and plenty of time to come up with a solution to their predicament and transmit that solution through their Kehillah spy system into Persia.

First on their agenda, the wealthy merchant-moneylenders and priests of Jerusalem who were carted off to Babylon were not going to allow their countrymen to fill their vacant positions and occupy their houses and properties. If the Jerusalem moneylenders were going to get out of Babylonia and return to Jerusalem, they had to have a place to go back to. So, they had Gedaliah, the Hebrew who had been appointed governor by Nebuchadnezzar, as well as his close advisors, murdered. To assure their return to power, the evil priests of the Temple had their mouthpieces, the prophets, tell more lies to both the Babylonian captives and to those still in Jerusalem and say that God loved them best. For example, Jeremiah 24 claims the deportees to be the "good figs." And that the glory of Yahweh flew off with Ezekiel to Babylon (Ezekiel 11). Jeremiah 31:3 claims that Yahweh tells him, "I have loved you with an everlasting love, so I am constant in my affection for you." Yeah! Right! The lying god of the Jews, still telling the same lies.

Based upon the *asl* of Abraham, one of the many insane beliefs of the Jews is that their god eternally loves them no matter what evils they do. Even when they do all sorts of evil, their god will still love them, no matter what. Even if they do evil and murder millions of people (as they have done) and steal all the wealth on Earth (as they are presently doing), the Jews believe that even if their god does not approve of their actions, he will still love them if, for no other reason, then the "virtue" inherited from Abraham's big *asl*. The Jews set themselves up as eternally blessed and impervious to hellfire. Even if they give the people of the entire world a life of hell, they consider themselves blessed angels and specially chosen by their god for wealth and plenty to eat. Many must suffer and die so that a few Jews may live in luxury.

The Jews were still sacrificing their children to Molech as late as 587 BC. Jerimiah 32:35 plainly shows this. Later, under Ezra the scribe, the wicked priests of Judah added to the Book of Jeremiah. They wanted to make sure that their position was assured as priests of Yahweh. If the disasters that Jeremiah foretold had truly been a result of the wickedness of themselves, then they didn't want the Jews to question whether or not they and their sons were qualified as leaders. So, they added their wet ink to Jeremiah's prophesies and thus had God Himself proclaim that the priests, the Levites, and their wicked sons were guaranteed to be restored to their former positions.

Whole sections of the Book of Jeremiah were written by the rabbis while they were in Babylon. One section of note is the story of one Ebed-Melech, who was a eunuch and a Cushite attached to the royal palace. This Black eunuch is given the credit of saving Jeremiah from imprisonment and death in a well. Later, as the story goes, Yahweh prophesies through Jeremiah to Ebed-Melech that because he put his trust in Yahweh, he would escape with his life. But whether he actually escaped or not isn't told. Only the wet-ink promise of the rabbis is recorded. But it was a good lie to tell the various slaves and servants in the palace of Nebuchadnezzar, how they could also obtain the blessing of the Yahweh-god, if only they would help the Jews get back to Jerusalem.

Working with their busy writing tools in Babylon, the rabbis added more to the Book of Jeremiah that would further their goals of total fear and dictatorial power. They put the story of Gedaliah's assassination (Jeremiah 39-43) into the context of another threat of what happens when the Jews do not obey the orders of their rabbis.

Writing from the comfortable position of forecasting-after-the-fact, these Jewish sorcerers were able to squeeze another lesson for their followers out of the Book of Jeremiah. In this, Nebuchadnezzar's successful expedition against Egypt in 568-567 BC allowed the rabbis to conveniently kill off the Hebrews who sought the protection of Pharaoh, rather than the protection of Yahweh. Working the trade route along the Nile, there was already a large Jewish colony in Memphis of Lower Egypt, Pathos of Upper Egypt and Elephantine by 569 BC when Nebuchadnezzar invaded. It didn't matter whether or not those Jews actually perished; all that mattered was that the scribes erased them from history with their pens. *Abracadabra!*

Nebuchadnezzar had had to war against the Jews twice. And after king Zedekiah had sworn fealty to Nebuchadnezzar the first time and then betrayed him by allying with Egypt, Nebuchadnezzar had had enough of the perfidious Jews. So, he had king Zedekiah's family and all of his sons killed before his very eyes. Then, so that his murdered family was the last thing he ever saw, Nebuchadnezzar had Zedekiah's eyes forever blinded with red, hot spikes. Then, he was led away in chains to Babylon. Thus ended the line of the kings of Judah of the House of David, and Yahweh is caught in another lie.

Who, then, remained as leaders of the Jews? Only the priests and the scribes were left with any authority. But these, too, were deported to Babylon with all of the upper-class Jews, merchants, metal smiths and craftsmen, where they were to work for the greater glory of Nebuchadnezzar and the Babylonian Empire.

Both text and archaeology contradict the idea that between the destruction of Jerusalem in 586 BC and the return of the exiles after the proclamation of Cyrus in 538 BC, Judah was in total ruin and uninhabited. When we total the population of Judah in the late 7th century, *before* the destruction of Jerusalem, we can gain an idea of the scale of the deportations. From data collected during intensive surveys and excavations, Judah's population can be quite accurately estimated at about 75,000, with Jerusalem comprising at least twenty percent of this number – 15,000 – and another 15,000 probably inhabiting its nearby agricultural hinterland. Thus, even if we accept the highest possible figures for exiles (20,000), it would seem that they comprised *at most* a quarter of the population of the Judahite state. That would mean that at least seventy-five percent of the population remained on the land. This community included not only poor villagers, but also artisans, scribes, priests, and prophets.

When the Chaldeans had deported the metal smiths, merchants, craftsmen, nobles and priests to Babylon, they left behind most of the farmers and the humbler people. These were allowed to occupy the farms, businesses and properties of the upper-class Hebrews who had been deported. Thus, the remaining poor Hebrews suddenly became immensely rich in land, grain, wine grapes and summer fruits. For the poor farmers, suddenly getting rid of the extortion of the Temple priests and the taxes of the king, and being relieved of the anxiety caused by following the ridiculous Laws of Moses under penalty of death, must have been an occasion of great rejoicing. No more Jews! Hooray!

Gedaliah was appointed governor of Judea by Nebuchadnezzar. There were Hebrews living among the Ammonites and at Moab (Jeremiah 40:11). These now returned for a share of the abandoned property. With the rich Jews and the rabbis all carried off to Babylon, there were plenty of goods and the best land available to whatever Hebrew wanted to take it for his own.

Although Jeremiah was left behind in Jerusalem, he knew that if the remainder of Hebrews were to look for leadership, it would have to be toward the captives in Babylon. But Nebuchadnezzar and his Chaldeans had appointed Jeremiah's friend, Gedaliah, to be governor of Judea. From being a low-level official, Gedaliah became the top official in Judea and at Jerusalem. He alone was only responsible to Nebuchadnezzar for the lands of Judea now under Babylonian conquest. With the murdered family and blinded eyes of Zedekiah, the previous king, forever fresh in his mind, he certainly had no intention of doing anything but his very best as the servant of Nebuchadnezzar, the King of Babylonia.

At Jerusalem, the Temple was burnt, but still stood as a focal-point of Hebrew worship. Thus, there was the danger to the rabbis in Babylonia that given enough time, Gedaliah would be accepted as a king of Judea and the worship at the Temple would be resumed by the small-town priests and itinerant scribes. This would mean that those rabbis in Babylon would never be able to regain their power, since their places at the Temple would be taken and their monopoly powers over the Temple treasury and the ceremonies likewise would be replaced by the lower-echelon priests. So, the rabbis hired some mercenaries to assassinate Gedaliah.

In the Book of Jeremiah, it says that "Baalis, king of the Ammonites, has sent Ishmael, son of Nethaniah to murder" Gedaliah (Jeremiah 40:14). But literary analysis proves that this section of Jeremiah was written by the rabbis at Babylon and not by Jeremiah. The lies of those wicked rabbis are not, in this case, very well hidden. The Jews always try to establish a patsy or a scapegoat to take the blame for their own crimes.

There were quite a lot of Jews "living in Moab and among the Ammonites" (Jeremiah 40:11). So, it wasn't likely for the Ammonites to be antagonistic to the Judeans at this time, since they had been living together peacefully. What's more, the Ammonites and Judeans had been allies against Babylon, so why would the Ammonite king want to assassinate Gedaliah? The Ammonites were still holding out against the armies of Babylon and though Jerusalem had fallen, it would weaken the Ammonites even more to kill Gedaliah. As the rabbis wrote, if Gedaliah was killed, "It would mean that all the Judeans who have rallied around you [Gedaliah] would be scattered again. Why should the remnant of Judah perish?" (Jeremiah 40:15.) To kill the representative of Nebuchadnezzar would be an attack on the sovereignty of this great king and would bring down his wrath upon both the guilty and the innocent. So, for the Ammonites or the Judeans themselves to kill Gedaliah would be a stupid and ridiculous act. Thus, it was obviously the work of mercenaries. And who, other than the power-hungry priests held captive in Babylon, would have the motive to hire mercenaries to kill Gedaliah?

This is a theme that you will see repeated countless times throughout history. Great men and great leaders are killed or die mysteriously, and around them are countless Jews pointing their fingers at some scapegoat or patsy. But regardless of *who the scapegoat is*, and regardless of what the alleged "proofs" are, it remains true that when those people were murdered or died on the operating table, or when those people had fatal "accidents," that the only ones benefiting from those tragedies were the Jews, the very same "innocent Jews" who stood around pointing their accusing fingers at someone else. So, it can also be seen in this ancient murder mystery, written into the Book of Jeremiah, the accusing finger of the rabbis pointing at Baalis and the Ammonites, a group that could only lose with Gedaliah's assassination.

But who could possibly have benefited from the murder of Gedaliah? The rabbis and moneylenders held captive in Babylonia! They alone! They paid Ishmael to kill Gedaliah along with any witnesses to the murder. Of course, the murderers stole whatever valuables that they could find. But "Ishmael son of Nethaniah, son of Elishama, who was of royal descent" (Jeremiah 41:1) and one of King Zedekiah's chief officers was not merely interested in killing the man who had been made governor and put in the king's place by Nebuchadnezzar, he was *also interested in destroying anyone who recognized the authority of Temple worship without the high priests.* The murderers were not sent just against the governor, but also against the lower-level priesthood. In his actions after the murder of Gedaliah, Ishmael shows the conspiracy behind his crimes. He was hired not merely to assassinate the governor, but to strike a blow against anyone who dared to infringe upon the power of the rabbis and High Priest, who were then held captive in Babylon.

The day after the murder of Gedaliah, Ishmael went out to a group of eighty worshipers who were traveling to the Jerusalem Temple to pray. They were unarmed, they had gashed their bodies in the pagan fashion, shaved off their beards and tore their garments in mourning for the defeat of Jerusalem. They were going to offer incense and pray at the Temple in Jerusalem. As you know from other accounts in the *Hebrew Bible*, only the High Priest may offer incense to the Yahweh-god under pain of instant blasting with fire and the earth swallowing up such transgressors.

Ishmael met them on the road and invited them to visit Gedaliah, whom he had already murdered. But once they were within the town gates, he and his men killed all of them, except for ten. It is interesting to see how the lying rabbis have worked into their story this power of ten Hebrews. This is a lesson for the Jews. The tale is told in this manner:

> "But once they [the eighty mourners] were well inside the town, Ishmael son of Nethaniah slaughtered them, with the help of his men, and threw them into a cistern. There were ten of them, however, who said to Ishmael, 'Do not kill us: we have stocks of wheat and barley, oil and honey, hidden away in the fields.' So he spared them and did not kill them with their brothers." (Jeremiah 41:7-8.)

The power of the bribe is thus taught in the Operating Manual of the Jews. But another lesson is also taught as well. It is important here to note that these ten were of the same *minyan*. A *minyan* is the minimum number of Jews that the rabbis have decreed to be necessary before they are allowed to pray. This group of ten can often be seen in old photographs or drawings of groups of Jews. Standing in a circle, facing inward, they are alleged to be praying or chanting from whatever books they hold in their hands. Whether they are praying to a God or to a Devil, depends upon the individual group of Jews and who they hold to be the most powerful. But this circle of Jews with their backs turned to outside observation and their circle closed with shoulder-to-shoulder solidarity has been used since ancient times as a means of generally gossiping, trading information about business and the local *goyim* (non-Jewish, lowly insects, stupid cattle), passing along packages of money or smuggled contraband and, in general, taking the opportunity to secretly undertake affairs that are secret to even the Jews outside of the *minyan,* but *especially* secret from all non-Jews. Much smuggling of valuables, exchanging of monies and sharing of business information can be hidden from non-Jews whenever the Jews pretend to be praying in their group of ten.

So, out of those eighty Judeans being attacked by Ishmael, during the screams and curses, the shouting and the slaughter, a single group of ten was spared. Those ten, obviously being of the same *minion*, quickly formed a circle and asked, "What can we do?" and in unison replied, "We have wealth! Let us offer a bribe to be spared from death." And that is what they did.

But the main lessons that the rabbis wanted the Hebrews to learn from the Book of Jeremiah were again repeated when the Jews who remained after Gedaliah's murder fled to Egypt. Jeremiah is alleged to have warned them to stay and not flee. But they disobeyed and ran off to Egypt. This is a rabbinical addition, but the lesson that was written for the training of future Jews was: Do what your rabbi, scribe or prophet tells you to do and don't ask questions.

To completely hide their own complicity in Gedaliah's murder, the hypocritical Jewish priests of Babylonia declared a special day every year to mourn Gedaliah, a day of mourning that the Jews still celebrate to this day, a special Jewish holiday to celebrate how clever they are at killing their opponents. Dancing on their enemies' graves, singing songs celebrating the slaughter of the Egyptians' first born, and hypocritically mourning for someone they have just murdered are all attributes of the Jews: those evil, perfidious and most horrible people.

One of the methods used by the rabbis to hide their forgeries was to put various chapters of the biblical books out of chronological order. This confuses the reader. The Book of Jeremiah is an example of this technique. But as for chasing down and classifying this chronological shuffling, I will leave it to other researchers who have an interest for such a project. Such details are not relevant to the present history.

"Every man after his own heart," was a phrase used constantly throughout the *Hebrew Bible*. This rabbinical complaint was meant to give the illusion that the Jews should be ashamed of following their own will and logic and should, instead, follow the dictates of the rabbis, priests and scribes. In 569 BC, the rabbis and scribes had been living in Babylon for about eighteen years. Keeping the Hebrews loyal to themselves and to their Yahweh-god took up a lot of their energy, because in strange lands, one god looked as good as another. Those evil priests knew that if they were ever again to have any real power, it had to be in the land of their myths about Moses in Palestine. So, their main goal was to use whatever cunning tricks they could, to keep the Hebrews concentrating on what they called "the Holy Land."

Jeremiah 44 is a good example of the fear, threats and promises that the rabbis were capable of using. They put Jeremiah's name on a document addressed to the Hebrews living in Migdol, Tahpanes, Noph, Memphis in Lower Egypt, and Pathos (Upper Egypt and Elephantine). This booklet is nothing but another warning to only pray to Yahweh and to return to Judah, for the rabbis were already hatching a plan for escaping the captivity and they wanted to make sure that as many Hebrews as possible would move back to Judah, so as to be able to rule over them, gather in their tithes and get their international banking business reestablished.

In their lust for power, the rabbis used the deceitful method of *writing in the present about the past to pretend to foretell the future*. For example, Jeremiah 44 was written by the rabbis in Babylon soon after 569 BC. In that year, the Pharaoh Hophra (who succeeded Neco in 588 BC) was dethroned and executed by Amasis. As so-called "proof" that this falsified Jeremiah 44 was actually genuine, soon after Hophra was executed, the rabbis put an earlier date on the manuscript and sent it off as a "prophecy" of what would happen to Hophra in the "future." The rabbis are experts at lies and deceits of this nature, even to this very day. Even a casual perusal of their ridiculous *Babylonian Talmud* proves this statement without doubt.

At the time of the writing, the prophet Jeremiah had died in Egypt and since the writer, Baruch, was alive in Babylon, it isn't difficult to figure out who wrote the so-called "prophesies" of Jeremiah 44 – the evil and lying Judean scribes and rabbis! They claimed that it was a "prophecy" delivered in 605 BC but, strange to say, when they delivered it to the Jews in Egypt twenty-five years later, the ink was still fresh. In the West, we call that a counterfeit, a swindle and a forgery. But the rabbis don't call it that. They raise their eyes over the wet ink and gaze off into heaven with a look of wonder on their hypocritical faces and say, "Wet ink on such an old document! It's a miracle!"

While they were in Babylon, the rabbis forged several of Jeremiah's "prophecies" as a means of preparing the Hebrews for their return to Jerusalem and rabbinical dictatorship. By using the long-dead Jeremiah as their mouthpiece, they could avoid the punishment that the Babylonians would certainly mete out, if it were known that those curses, such as one found in Jeremiah 50 and 51, actually came from living rabbis instead of a dead prophet. One of the proofs for the false Babylonian authorship of these so-called "prophesies" is the use of the cryptogram "Leb-kamai" (Jeremiah 51:1) as a code word for Chaldeans. Thus, the rabbis could read these allegedly ancient "prophesies" aloud in the synagogues of Babylon without fear that any Chaldeans would overhear and know that they were being purposely subverted and cursed. In the ancient times, a curse was taken as a very serious thing indeed, and not to be lightly accepted. Such cutting and pasting of Jeremiah 6:22-24 into Jeremiah 50:42 are other proofs of rabbinical forgery.

So, what we have in Jeremiah 50 and 51, are not examples of prophetic "vision" or "foreknowledge." What we have are examples of the rallying propaganda used by the rabbis to prepare the Jews for the undermining and betrayal of Babylon to her enemies. Also, this is part of the deceiving of Cyrus and the Persians. By presenting books such as Isaiah and Jeremiah as old manuscripts that foretell the future, the rabbis could convince the Persians that their victory was certain. Against a powerful and ambitious king, such a "prophecy of ancient lineage" would not be an easy inducement to resist. Additionally, with the backing of the international moneylenders' monopoly in silver bullion, Cyrus would be well-provisioned in arms and men for his assault upon Babylon.

Jumping from one lie to another, the rabbis quickly muffled the reasons that they gave for Babylon defeating Judah. The sins of the Jews were now forgiven. Now, their conveniently adroit Yahweh-god wanted to destroy Babylon because of "the vengeance of Yahweh, the revenge for his Temple" (Jeremiah 51:1). That capricious Jewish god has now forgotten that he had the Babylonians destroy his own Jerusalem Temple as punishment for the sins of the Jews in the first place! Now, he wants to destroy Babylon because they destroyed his temple. Perfect Semitic logic! Perfect logic for targeting the hatred and malice of the Jews against the Babylonians.

However, the rabbis could not know that there would be people 2,500 years later who would be experiencing their depredations and reading about their lies, and who would deal with the Jews regardless of their lying boogeyman of a god, who they attempted to call up. Though they make claims (Jeremiah 51:5-19) that their god made everything and can do anything, these dark little beetle-eyed rabbis are themselves nothing more than little wizards pulling the hidden wires in the Land of Oz. In this case, they wrote curses against Babylon *after* they had safely returned to Jerusalem and put the name of a 100-years-dead prophet on those curses, so as to bolster their own fake occult power and prestige among the returnees from Exile.

The rabbis who wrote Jeremiah 52 divulged what the Jews have practiced from the earliest days. The Jews love to be exalted and honored as if they are actually worthy of honor. So, in Jeremiah 52, the rabbis wrote that after Nebuchadnezzar died, Evil-Merodach came to the throne of Babylon. He pardoned King Jehoiachin, treated him well and gave him an exalted position above all of the other captive kings kept at Babylon. They like to give the impression that treating Jews well is the normal thing to do. They leave this honoring of Jehoiachin as a fact of history that other kings should repeat with other captured Jews.

However, these wicked rabbis don't mention that while Nebuchadnezzar was on the throne, the Jews were busy giving gifts and gold to those Babylonian princes who were in the line of succession. Certainly, the rabbis had plenty of gold stashed away among their international fraternity of moneylenders and merchants. And they had lusty, nasty Jewish daughters imagining themselves to be another Sarah, willing to serve the Yahweh-god by seducing the leaders of Babylon.

Evil-Merodach, who had been treated with special attention and financial gifts by the Jews, and who had been treated to special sexual tricks by all of the Monica Lewinskys among the Jewesses, was well-inclined to give Jehoiachin an honored place at his table. From this honored place, Jehoiachin was able to more than repay the rabbis by providing intimate details and advanced knowledge of Babylonian political and military intelligence. Thus, *by bribing and flattering a key political figure of Babylon*, the Judeans were able to destroy the entire society. They bribed a king and then claimed that he loved the Jews because of their great "virtue."

To cover their fraud, the rabbis attached to their literary counterfeit, Jeremiah 50 and 51, an example of rabbinical sorcery. Here, they relate how their mighty wet-ink prophet Jeremiah cursed Babylon and then had the curses read aloud to the town before the parchment was tied to a stone and thrown into the Euphrates River with the words, "So shall Babylon sink, never to rise again from the disaster with which I am going to overwhelm her" (Jeremiah 51:64). But all in tune with the lies that the prophets of the lying god of Judah told, Babylon lasted more than another 250 years, before Alexander the Great brought Hellenism to the ancient Near East and Babylon gave up its ancient reign. Two-hundred fifty years later makes not much a prophesy out of that one. But that's Judaism, always ready with a curse based on lies.

Nahum 612 BC
(One Year of Hatred)

The three pages of hatred written by Nahum in 612 BC were not much of a prophecy against Nineveh. Again, the tenses were changed by the rabbis to give the impression that this vengeful poem was a prophecy for the future. Even if it was written before the fall of Nineveh, the poem is merely an outpouring of Jewish curses and hatred toward Assyria.

However, it is interesting to note not only the attributes that the Jews recognize in their god, but also the attributes that the Jews personally express in their own characters and actions. After all, the Jews believe that they were created "in the image of God." So, they reason that they must be the same as they imagine their god to be.

Nahum writes: "Yahweh is a jealous and vengeful God, Yahweh avenges, he is full of wrath; Yahweh takes vengeance on his foes, he stores up his fury for his enemies" (Nahum 1:2), "*Those who defy him he will destroy utterly*, he will pursue his foes into the darkness" (Nahum 1:8), and "He it is who utterly destroys: oppression will not lift its head a second time. They will be consumed like a thicket of thorns, like dry straw, utterly" (Nahum 1:9-10). And so, in these lines, we can see not only the type of devil-god that the Jews worship even today, but also the characteristics that the Jews make part of their personal characters as they "walk in the ways of their god."

So that you realize these old stories are relevant to modern times, this sort of vengeful, evil and ruthless behavior can be seen in the ways that the modern Jews persecute their enemies in order to destroy them completely and forever, even unto four generations! Old ex-Nazis sixty years after the end of World War II, elderly and bent with age, are at the time of this writing in 2014 AD, a target of the various Jewish hate groups such as the Anti-Defamation League of B'nai B'rith. The actual translation of the name of this Jewish hate group means "The Anti-Defamation League of the Circumcised Penis" – that's just how the Jews brag to let everybody know that they all have Jewish members and you'd better not turn your back on them, because they are there to screw you one way or another. It doesn't matter to the Jews that the Nazis lost the war after a fair fight and that everyone on earth follows the dictum to "let bygones be bygones" or to "forgive and forget." These modern Jews with their ancient circumcised penises "walk in the vindictive ways of their demon-god" to this very day, eternally wrathful and vengeful and full of hatred to the people of the world. For the Jews to terrorize all of Humanity so that all Peoples have a "fear of the Jews," it is necessary for the Jews to maintain a never-ending, relentless oppression and persecution of their enemies both real and imagined. It is a demonic hatred by a demonic people.

John Demjanjuk is a good example of an imagined enemy. The Jews falsely accused him of being a notorious Nazi prison guard who was nicknamed "Ivan the Terrible." Not only did the Jews falsely accuse this American citizen, but *they falsified evidence to convict him and withheld evidence that would prove him innocent*. They ruined his life and had him deported from America to Israel to stand trial. And even after he was proven innocent, the bloodlust and hatred of the Jews was not quenched. They are the very voice of God, to hear them tell it.

The Jews continued their persecution in order to cover up the fact that they were wrong. Since the Jews maintain the lie that they are perfect "Chosen Ones of God," they could not be wrong. Otherwise, if Demjanjuk had escaped, *people might begin to question whether there are other issues in which the Jews are wrong*. So, they continued to destroy him by picketing his house, threatening his physical safety, filling their monopoly news media with slanders and smears against him, and in general making his life miserable.

John Demjanjuk was not important to them. What was important for the Jews was to terrorize the minds of the People of the world with the idea that it is not God, but the Jews who are to be feared in their wrath. They claim to be made in the so-called "image of God" and therefore they are a "jealous and vengeful" people. They "avenge" and are "full of wrath." The Jews take "vengeance upon their foes" and "store up fury" for their enemies. Those who defy the Jews, they try to destroy utterly. They will pursue their foes into the darkness. Their enemies will be consumed like a thicket of thorns, like dry straw, utterly. All of this, they assume to be their own attributes, because these are the same attributes that their furry-faced old gibbering prophets gave to the god whom they try to emulate. But Jesus proved that the Jews are devils, and the actions of the Jews themselves prove that they are devils.

John Demjanjuk defied the false accusations of the Jews and won. If he had been convicted by the Jewish lies, they would have executed him by hanging, which they almost accomplished in his first trial and conviction. But since he was innocent and escaped execution, the "pious and holy" Jews wanted to kill him anyway. And why? *Because he dared to defy the Jews! And to defy the Jews is the same as defying the Jewish God*. And those who defy the Jewish God, "he will destroy utterly." Therefore, according to the rabbis, it is "within their rights" to kill any and all non-Jews who defy them. With this kind of belief and actions based on it, is it any wonder that Jesus said the Jews are children of the devil? Why have the Jews been hated wherever they go? Because they deserve it. That's why.

And who are the Jews? According to them, they are God's Chosen People, made in His likeness, in the very image of God, walking in His ways. As the rabbis teach:

> "If a non-Jew smites a Jew, he is worthy of death for it is written, And he looked this way and that way, and when he saw that there was no man, he slew the Egyptian. Rabbi Hanina also said: He who smites an Israelite on the jaw, is as though he had thus assaulted the Divine Presence; for it is written, one who smiteth an Israelite attacketh the Holy One" (*Babylonian Talmud*, Sanhedrin 58b).

Thus, the rabbis teach the Jews to kill anyone who dares to strike them, even if they deserve it! But they avoid any witnesses for their crimes, like Moses who killed the Egyptian after first looking around to check for witnesses (Exodus 2:12). The Jews are gangsters. They are trained to be criminals by their Training Manual of Criminality and Sociopathy, the *Hebrew Bible*, and by their demon rabbis.

With all of the curses and hatred that Nahum expends on Assyria, the joke was on him as well as on anyone who believes that the lies of the Jews are true. He was a lousy prophet, since he "prophesied" the fall of Assyria but failed utterly to "foresee" the fall of Jerusalem only fourteen years later. Thus, Nahum was only a chronicler of the fall of Nineveh. He was not a prophet. But his words were edited by the rabbis to give the impression that the Jewish prophets were genuine seers of the future, instead of the mere trumpets for the rabbis' deceit that they actually were. The Jews are many and all bad things, but at forgery, deceit, counterfeiting and lies, they are master criminals. The *Hebrew Bible* is a prime example of their work.

Habakkuk 605-597 BC
(Eight Years of Fakery)

Habakkuk did his preaching between 605 BC and 597 BC. It was in 605 BC that Nebuchadnezzar won the battle of Carchemish to become the greatest power in the Middle East. And in 597 BC, he besieged Jerusalem. With these threats in mind, Habakkuk does the usual ranting and raving of the old prophets, pointing his finger at his own people and accusing them of not following the rabbis' advice. So, in this case, Habakkuk is nothing special.

However, one interesting thing is that the very words of his five imprecations (Habakkuk 2:5-17) precisely fit the fate of today's Jews. It fits what will happen to today's Jews as the people of the world discover their evil treachery. The Final Solution has arrived for the Jews.

Ezekiel 593-571 BC
(Twenty-Two Years of Malice)

According to the internal chronology of Ezekiel, his entire ministry was "among the exiles in Babylon between 593 BC and 571 BC." But all of his so-called "prophecies" occur in Jerusalem before and after the fall of that city in 587 BC. How is this explained?

The entire Book of Ezekiel "appears to be a well-constructed whole." However, there are enough irregularities of time, place and duplicate passages to show that the book was another Jewish custom-made forgery by the rabbis.

Ezekiel was, no doubt, one of the many "prophets" who were attached to the Temple. Their official duty, for which they were paid in barbecued goat meat and silver, was to go into a catatonic fit, roll their eyes and talk gibberish, preach death and destruction, froth at the mouth, tear their clothes like maniacs, and urge the Jews to obey the priests or suffer the fate of Sodom and Gomorrah.

In India today, there is no end to the number of religious fanatics who feel the urge to do weird things for the sake of penance for their sins or for some sort of religious merit or countless other reasons not even known to them. Holding a single arm straight up in the air for fifty years until the muscles atrophy, sitting on a bed of nails, walking only on their hands, crawling instead of walking, eating only filthy food, going about totally naked, etc., are practices that can today be seen carried out by people in India who have these urges toward religious expression – that is, for idiot Indians, it is religious expression. To other people, it appears to be lunacy in the extreme. So, some of Ezekiel's statements and actions were written down in Jerusalem and later combined during the Babylonian Exile in whatever way the scribes deemed appropriate for realizing their dark goal of returning to Jerusalem.

Such strange actions by religious fanatics were no different in the ancient times anywhere in the world – including Jerusalem, with its scores of gibbering lunatics with boxes tied to their furry heads and their foreskins cut. Those "prophets" were attached to and dependent upon the Temple and its delicious roasted holocausts. Ezekiel was one of those fanatics whose job it was to threaten the Jews with God's vengeance *if they didn't obey the rabbis.* Some prophets preached peace, some preached hellfire.

The Book of Ezekiel was written by the rabbis in Babylon. Once again, the rabbis stitched together various writings by Ezekiel, as well as some anecdotes about him, to counterfeit the book and "prove" the fake holiness and power of the Jewish prophets, priests and rabbis. They did this to terrorize and subjugate their Jewish gangs, so that they could maintain their power over them during the Babylonian Captivity. By repeating over and over again the same refrain that the Hebrews were "stiff-necked and rebellious" against the Laws of Yahweh, these evil rabbis could reemphasize the lesson that only by following the priests could the Jews even draw breath and not die.

Even though both "prophets" allegedly knew each other, it was not necessary for Ezekiel and Jeremiah to mention each other in "their" books, as some commentators question, because neither of them wrote the books that carry their names. These were written by the priests and scribes of Babylon. The chief goal of these rabbis was not historical accuracy, but religious and political power. Ezekiel's style is monotonous, because it is a result of the workings of a scribal committee and not of a single man's experience.

The rabbis were attempting to transfer the power of the Yahweh-god from the Temple to themselves. They continued the same process with Ezekiel as they had begun with Jeremiah. They concentrated power into their own hands by claiming that all of their troubles came from the Jews "following their own hearts," instead of following the rabbis.

By emphasizing such things as "legal purity" rather than *actual* purity, and detailed rituals rather than any sort of *actual* spiritual attainment, the rabbis built the hypocritical hoax of Judaism. They used such forgeries as the Book of Ezekiel as a foundation for their Jewish Cult. Weird imaginings, fraudulent writings, forged documents and rabbinical evil schemes, all make up the Book of Ezekiel and give him the title as "the father of Judaism."

Why should Ezekiel be called the "father of Judaism"? What happened to Moses? Certainly, every religion on earth, as well as the countless sub-sects and the individual shamans, sorcerers, witch-doctors, hermits, monks, nuns, yogis, and sadhus have had visions. Among all of the religions on earth, amazing stories are told of people flying through the air, walking on water, foreseeing future events, seeing fantastic sights of gods and goddesses and wondrous places replete with fantastic and colorful animals and scenery. So, why should more weight be given to the likes of Ezekiel and his criminal gang of rabbis than to the visions of other saints from other religions?

Before you think that I am mocking and disbelieving the tales of these religious visionaries, I want to pause here and explain something. I know that the more sensitive and religious members of Mankind are capable of wondrous feats and incredible insight. What the ordinary person can only explain as a "miracle," is often just a simple and ordinary day in paradise to some of these religious adepts. I do not dispute that the Universe is full of wonders. And I do not dispute that the human Mind and Spirit are capable of fantastic feats of Power. To me, these are simply gifts of Knowledge of God that are discovered by any sincere Seeker of Truth or Seeker of God. Many of the saints and sages from the various cultures of Mankind have exhibited gifts of Power and Knowledge that they have unlocked from within themselves. As Jesus taught, anyone who tries can attain those powers.

But the question which more people need to ask is this: why, among all the peoples of the Earth, do the Jews believe that only *their* prophets and rabbis have had True Vision, while the spiritual teachers of other peoples have all been false? The answer to this is very simple and it will unfold during the course of this book. However, it is not simply that the rabbis and Jews are liars, deceives, forgers, frauds, destroyers of documents, counterfeiters, murderers and thieves. The fact is that the Babylonian priests of Abraham's First National Bank and Pawn Shop are actually con artists posing as holy men who have hijacked a spiritual path and made it into a spiritual perversion known as Judaism. Does this sound too astonishing or too blunt? As you will see by what follows, this is the correct assessment of the Jewish demons. Later, the same phony Semitic con was used by Mohammad, the false prophet of Arabia.

One way that the rabbis constructed their pseudo-religion was with the literary method of *biased choices*. Those of their prophets who could be used for promoting the Pharisaic deceits have been retained. Those whose works did not promote the rabbinical hoax were destroyed.

One of the rabbis' editorial additions in Ezekiel contains some serious backpedaling. After all of the cursing of their neighbors for sacrificing their firstborn sons to the various gods, Ezekiel lamely claims that Yahweh also had decreed that they must offer their firstborn sons as human sacrifices. Here is that law in Exodus:

> "You must give me the first-born of your sons; you must do the same with your flocks and herds. The first-born must remain with its mother for seven days; on the eighth day you must give it to me." (Exodus 22:29-30.)

Yahweh demands the human sacrifice of the first born or else the parents may "redeem" the child by paying the priest, a sort of Semitic protection racket. But these "eternal laws of Yahweh," according to the lies of Ezekiel, were laid down because Yahweh wanted to punish the Jews by giving them some "laws that were not good." So, this lying rabbi of the Abraham's First National Bank and Pawn Shop claimed that Yahweh was talking through Ezekiel's mouth and said:

> "I even gave them laws that were not good and observances by which they could never live, and I polluted them with their own offerings, making them sacrifice all their first-born, which was to punish them, so that they would learn that I am Yahweh." (Ezekiel 20:25.)

The falsity of the Jewish rabbis' political theology becomes increasingly clear with Ezekiel. Here we do not have the omniscient and omnipotent Yahweh-god decreeing his eternal and pristine Laws for the benefit of the Jews. But instead, we have Yahweh speaking through his medium, Ezekiel, and claiming that "Whoops! I gave you some Laws that were not so good because I wanted to punish you." The lying god of the Jews is a mighty fraud.

Throughout the *Hebrew Bible*, the rabbis, prophets and priests condemn the Hebrews for sacrificing their children to Baal and Molech, while the priests themselves were sacrificing the firstborn sons of the Hebrews to Yahweh. Throughout the *Hebrew Bible*, we read the refrain that Yahweh is a "jealous god." Now we can understand that his alleged "jealousy" included the coveting of those human sacrifices for Yahweh alone.

This is just one more of countless reasons why it is false to assume that Judaism was or is a monotheistic religion with a "higher morality." From the earliest times, other gods were recognized as existing. Only at a later date did the rabbis insist that only Yahweh was real and all of the other gods were unreal.

This Yahweh-god of Moses commanded human sacrifice in Exodus, but now Ezekiel is saying, "It was all a joke, because Yahweh is so wonderful that all he wanted to do was have you kill your children as punishment for not following the Laws of Moses and to prove that he is a great god." The phony Jews have been following this kind of murderous, fraudulent deceit and phoniness for 2,500 years!

The priest Ezekiel was careful to protect the priests' monopoly on free gifts. So, he has Yahweh speak through his mouth and say

> "For on my holy mountain, on the high mountain of Israel – it is the Lord Yahweh who speaks – is where the whole House of Israel, resettled in the country, will worship me. There I will welcome you, and there expect your presents, your choicest gifts and all your holy offerings." (Ezekiel 20:40-41.)

Yes, that invisible god who created the entire universe and then fasted for ten billion years before any Jews decided to feed him, really needs that gold and silver and those barbecued goats. So, don't be late, because the priests and rabbis expect a timely supper. Judaism is a complete fraud.

The priests and rabbis of Israel were so double-crossing to their own people that they acted as spies and betrayers to the very enemies who would destroy their own people. For example, while Nebuchadnezzar was besieging Jerusalem, the prophet Jeremiah (Jeremiah 39:11 and Jeremiah 38:24) was undermining the morale of the citizens with his doom-mongering. So much so, that Zedekiah had him arrested. In like manner, Ezekiel went out to the crossroads to put up road signs pointing to Jerusalem, so that Nebuchadnezzar would be able to easily find his way to the attack (Ezekiel 21:18-28). And after being defeated by the Babylonians, it was these same priests who offered their "Jewish Loyalty" to the Babylonians and who received welcome in the temples of Babylon. Treason is a Jewish trait, built right into Judaism. The Jews betray all other people. And it is why the treasonous Jews themselves consider "informers" and "traitors" within the Jewish community as their most dangerous enemy. The Jews know only too well the practice of treason and its power for destruction, because all Jews are traitors, so they are especially vigilant of other Jews.

The Old Testament really has some rather nasty and crude pornography in it, which is reflected in the filthy mind of today's Jews (Ezekiel 23:19-22).

How could it be otherwise among a people who are obsessed with their circumcised penises, their menstruating women, their sodomizing of little children, their scriptures that order them to "go forth and multiply," and where nearly every Jewish book declares the holiness of what "comes forth from their loins" (their sexual organs)? This is what they are constantly reminded of as they study their demon books of murder, rape and pillage, which they claim as the "holy" *Hebrew Bible*. Such Jewish filth is carried over and amplified in the *Babylonian Talmud*, as you shall see in the following chapters.

Free choice was something that the rabbis claimed did not exist for the Jews. The Jews were forbidden to study other religious views and choose to follow one over another, because the swindlers of Babylon stated that "the Hebrews did not choose Yahweh, Yahweh chose the Hebrews."

"No," the rabbis insisted, as they counted the dwindling numbers of silver coins that were contributed by pious Hebrews. "No!" the rabbis screamed as they received fewer cows, goats, sheep, incense, oil, grain, vegetables, fine linen and woolen gods with which to support themselves and their huge, ravenous families. "No!" these sly priests dictated to the Hebrews through their prophets such vociferating as "Yahweh is a jealous god. And if you don't follow the ways and the laws that we priests claim that Yahweh desires, then Yahweh will curse you with plague, drought, warfare, thunder and lightning, invasion of murderous pagans, locusts and earthquake. No!" The study of other religions was prohibited. And why? Because the Hebrews might find something better? No, because as a religion, Judaism is a lie. *All other religions – including idol worship – are better and more truthful than Judaism.* Judaism and its demented, Semitic son, Islam, are both false religions and lies. To allow their adherents to even look into other religions, is to expose the lies of the Semites to the truths of real religion.

Certainly, there are powerful and terrible calamities even in modern times. But it was the malevolent cleverness of the rabbis to blame all of these disasters, not upon their Yahweh-god, but upon the many sins of the Hebrew people. Since all of these natural and simple-to-understand calamities were misunderstood, the ruse worked perfectly. The rabbis had at their command entire tribes of people who cowered in fear not only of the thunder clap, but also at the roar of a rabbi whose voice was believed to reach the very high heavens of the Yahweh-god Himself. The rabbis were quick to threaten godly retribution for Hebrews who strayed from the precise letter of the Laws which the lying priests had written themselves, but which they had attributed to God. God is great. And God is true. But what the Semites (both Jews and Muslims) have written and taught about God are lies. God never did any of the things that the Semites claim that He did. The Jews (and Muslims, as you will see in later chapters) are proven to be liars – all of them. And who tells lies about God other than demons?

And so, when the thunder roared over Jerusalem or the rains failed, the rabbis would stride through the crowds calling out, "Sin! There is sin in Israel! Who is it? Who is breaking the Laws of Yahweh Sabaoth!?" And since the rabbis had legislated to themselves the power to whip, stone, burn and hang anybody whom they could prove had broken one of the Laws of Moses or one of the unwritten, oral laws known as the "Tradition of the Elders," those thickly bearded, lust-filled, stinking old frauds were an unending cause of terror among the Hebrews. Even a glance from the Evil Eye of a Jewish priest or rabbi, turned strong Hebrew men into cowering slaves. The *feeling of power that this terror gave them*, was something that became the focal point of their lives. Power! Power to have the Hebrews shiver and bow at their mere glance! The Power that caused the Hebrews to always greet them with smiles and gifts and the best places at the supper tables. The rabbis learned to wield this power with ruthlessly selfish determination, even to the point of having men, women and even children seized and put to death in various horrible ways, because they had not followed the multitudinous Mosaic laws to the letter or had said something disrespectful to a rabbi.

Against the claim that the Jews were a great and prosperous nation, what proof is there except the word of the rabbis? Greatness is relative. An ant is great compared to a microbe. A mountain is great compared to a speck of dust. That the rabbis claimed that the insignificant group of tribes inhabiting the highlands of Palestine were "a great nation" is simply ludicrous. Archaeology proves their deceits. But it played well both among the Hebrew goatherds and farmers, as well as for the credulous ears of the Babylonian kings and princes.

In Ezekiel's listing of the kinds of wealth that were traded among all of the nations with the Phoenicians at Tyre, Judah was listed as having to trade only such things as "grain, wax, honey, tallow and balm" (Ezekiel 27:17). These were not the products of a great nation. These were the products of a bunch of ignorant, but crafty, thieves who had exchanged a life of wandering gangs for the life of settled farmers and herdsmen. As you will see, holding themselves up as great people while hiding their infamy and crimes is one of the secrets to the success of the Jews to this very day. Wall Street and the City of London are full of them.

One great talent of the rabbis has always been to make every claim of the great power for their god. Wherever Jews were allowed to live, no other people were allowed to have any religions or any gods by the Semitic laws of the Jews. Only the god of the Jews existed. And not only did He exist, but He loved only the Jews and no one else, just as the Semitic god, Allah, loves only the Muslims and no one else. This is certainly an appropriate god for a people raised on banditry, for a people devoted to acquiring the material possessions of others through theft and murder or the larceny of moneylending, because such a god reflects the basic interests of the Semites themselves – complete ownership and unyielding, greedy ruthlessness. So, for Yahweh to demand complete ownership and obeisance of the Jews to Himself was only a reflection of the demands of the Jews for complete ownership and obeisance of other peoples towards themselves, the holy chosen ones of Abraham's First National Bank and Pawn Shop with main offices in Jerusalem.

If other people say, "Ah! the sun is so warm and nice. It is Zeus (or Thor or Ammun or Chemosh or any other named god) whom we must thank for it," then the rabbis would scoff (since they are such experts at scoffing), "No! The sun was made by *our* god, not yours! If you pray, it must be to Yahweh alone! And if you do not pray to Yahweh, then we will kill you and take your possessions." Mohammad would later use the same lies about God to lead the Muslims into hell.

A main trick in this Jewish swindle has always been to conceal their banditry by pleading – with all of the appropriate whining and moaning – that they, the innocent Jews, are forced to be the way they are, not out of their own greed and malice, but because it is the will of their Yahweh-god who demands it of them. Thus, the pointing finger of the Jews draws the ire of their victims away from their own infernal bosoms and directs it toward the empty skies wherein dwells their mighty god, Yahweh. The amazing thing about this swindle which has persisted for so many centuries, is that the naive victims of the Jews actually *want* to believe the incredible stories about God that the lying Jews tell. The people *want to believe* that such fables about God as told in the *Hebrew Bible* are true. Thus, they are deceived. God never did any of the things that the Jews claim that He did. And who else lies about God other than devils? The Jews are lying devils, as are those other Semitic frauds, the Muslims.

In Ezekiel 24:1, the rabbis of Babylon were careful to write down the date of the beginning of the siege of Jerusalem, so as to swindle the readers into believing that these were "prophecies" of *future events* rather than the *histories* of past events that they actually were. In the same manner, the rabbis lamely gave excuses when their god failed to hold up his end of the "prophesy." In Ezekiel 26:1, the rabbis wrote that because Tyre "jeered at Jerusalem," their Yahweh-god was going to demolish it. But that was in 587-586 BC, when these Jewish curses were cast. Ten years later, Nebuchadnezzar was having trouble. He still hadn't taken Tyre and he had to pay his army with silver that he didn't have. So, the god of the Jews said through Ezekiel, "since he has been working for me," his efforts against Tyre will be rewarded by handing the wealth of Egypt over to him (Ezekiel 29:20). The dreadful rabbis never even blink when telling a lie. If one lie doesn't work, they quickly tell another.

It was during the Babylonian Captivity that the priests were finally able to get total control of the Hebrew people and create Judaism. Before this time, there were only Hebrews and wicked priests. After this time, there were only evil Jews and wicked priests. The priests created an all-powerful theocracy which did not allow for the return of a monarchy after the Jews had been released back into Jerusalem.

Ezekiel 38-39 is the earliest example of apocalyptic writing. It was a form of terrorism developed to whip the Jews into submission to the priests. Other examples are Isaiah 24-27, Deuteronomy 7-12 and Zechariah 9-14. The 2nd century BC had the most vigorous production of these bad dreams and nightmares written onto parchment and papyrus. But in the dream of this old, hairy prophet Ezekiel, the Jews excel in their methods of slaughtering other people while praying to their god of genocide, Yahweh.

This Yahweh-god of the Jews delights in barbaric acts of bloodshed and destruction so that He can make his name famous. After He causes Israel to slaughter the army of Gog from the north, so that the animals of the fields "eat flesh and drink blood," "eat the flesh of heroes," and "drink the blood of princes of the world" (Ezekiel 39:17-20), Yahweh says through his mouthpiece, Ezekiel,

> "That is how I shall display my glory to the nations, and all nations will feel my sentence when I judge, and feel my hand when I strike them." (Ezekiel 39:21.)

And so, in butchery and warfare, the god of Israel rejoices. The Yahweh-god of the Jewish bankers was made in their own image, because nothing is so profitable or so rejoicing to a banker than warfare. And His Jews were made in this same image, *according to their own declarations*, to "walk in his ways." In His image and with His ferocity, the Jews believe that they have been commissioned to enslave, steal from, dispossess and kill off the people of the entire world. O such a happy god, and such nice and benevolent Jews! Not much different, this Jewish Cult, from that Old India Cult of the Thugees (see Volume 1, Appendix A).

While in the Babylonian Captivity, the rabbis had plenty of time to plot their return to power. They no longer had to contend with the kings of Judah, since both king and people were captives in Babylon, where the last king of the line of David died. This proved once again that Yahweh was a god of lies and broken promises. The rabbis had been able to murder Gedaliah while putting the blame on the Ammonites and eliminating any leadership in Jerusalem that they themselves could not control. Thus, the only possible leaders left to the Jews were the priests of Yahweh, the bloody god of Israel, then residing in Babylon with his "holy" moneylenders and scheming priests.

The rabbis and scribes had been granted the same privileges as all of the other captive peoples in Babylon to worship their own gods. But what Nebuchadnezzar and his son, Belshazzar, didn't know, was that the god of the Jews was a god of vengeance, and the Jews, who believed that they had been made in His own image, followed this vengeful god's terrible methods. So, while all of the other peoples who had been gathered to Babylonia were working toward a prosperous Babylonian Empire, the Hebrew priests were vengefully working toward the destruction of their hosts. While Jewish kings and councilors were bowing at the feet of their Babylonian overlords, they were secretly investigating and spying upon the power and wealth of both Babylon and the countries around Babylon. While the rabbis were discussing and studying religion with the priests from other countries and stealing their ideas for later use, they were also rewriting the Torah and prophetic books to better empower themselves and to perfect their system of lies, all while claiming a moral high ground from the religions around them. It was in Babylon that they learned about the Aryan religions of India and its gods of Universal power. Here, they recreated their Cult of Yahweh from an international moneylenders' deity to God of the Universe.

One such effort is Ezekiel 40-48. This was written by rabbinical committee upon which they placed Ezekiel's name and wrote that God Himself showed them the measurements for the new Temple that they were planning to build. How could these priests living in Babylonia plan to build the Second Temple unless they had the financial backing to do so? As previously stated, the center of Judaism has never been the Temple or Jerusalem, it has always been where the center of finance was. And in the 6th century BC, the financial center of civilization was Babylonia (Iraq), soon to be shifted to Persia (Iran) where the big bankers and financiers lived in luxury.

The new Temple design had ample space for making bloody sacrifices among the swarms of flies and the stench of animal dung and rotted meat – roast beef for the priests, lamb stew for the priests, doves, pigeons, goats and lambs, all to sacrifice for sin offerings and reparation offerings to be eaten by the priests and their hungry families numbering as many as forty wives and their scores of children. The priests could afford to follow their dictum to "Go forth and multiply." Sex was a means of feeling that they were especially holy. This vile religion of demons was well-suited to setting up all of the laws necessary to provide themselves with the very best of everything. And all for free!

Besides the measurements of this temple, an interesting feature on the walls "were carved cherubs and palm trees … each cherub had two faces – the face of a man turned toward the palm tree one side and the face of a lion towards the palm tree the other side, all round the Temple" (Ezekiel 41:18-19). This lion face was to represent the animal totem of the tribe of Judah, the lion. So, the first Jews pictured themselves with two faces, one human and one a fierce animal. Two-faced Jews! Grinning human and devouring beast, all in one! How appropriate!

Provision was made for plenty of guardrooms to protect the Temple and its treasury from non-Jews and other undesirables. The guards acted as the personal goons of the priests to arrest any Jews who broke the ever-increasing number of Oral Laws. Even into Roman times, several hundred years later, any non-Jew who entered the inner parts of the Temple would be murdered. There was even a sign posted with such a warning.

In Ezekiel 43, the rabbis announced through the mouth of Yahweh that they no longer wanted any kings ruling them. They themselves would rule. As Yahweh is claimed to say through the rabbinical writings under the name of Ezekiel, "From now on they [the Jews] will banish their whorings and the corpses of their kings from my presence and I shall live among them forever" (Ezekiel 43:9). How many times has this lying god made these same claims over the centuries? But the promise only lasted as long as there was plenty of animal blood sprinkled and poured on the fly-encrusted altar and lots of meat for the priests and their huge families to engorge themselves. Then, this god of the universe would feel comfy.

However, in their subtle, Jewish, legal manner, they mention that no one may eat at the outer, east gate of the Temple sanctuary except the prince. But what do the rabbis mean by this, since they have already had their God announce the end of all further kings? The prince is the head banker of Abraham's First National Bank and Pawn Shop. We will see this term used often throughout history. A "prince of Judah" is always a banker or a super-wealthy merchant. God is the king of Israel and the prince of Israel is a banker. Thus, Judaism began in Babylon as a scheme by Terah, the patriarch of the money-lender guild of Ur, and it reached its demonic perfection in Babylon as a power grab by the rabbis who rewrote all scriptures to empower themselves and to benefit their prime contributors, the Jewish moneylenders and merchants. From Babylon, the Monsters were born, showing themselves as honest bankers, simple merchants and holy priests; and all of them were Jews.

Even the Levites who used to hold high office under the first Temple, the so-called Temple of Solomon, were reduced in status to guard duty and the killing of the sacrificial animals. So, it was in Babylon that the Levitical priests of Zadok made themselves masters of the Temple (Ezekiel 44:22-23 & 44:28-31). These priests made themselves quite comfortable. They had a superstitious people bowing at their feet, bringing them the choicest foods and wines, the finest linen and wool, the freshest garden produce, expensive incense and, of course, gold and silver offerings. They had virgins to marry, sometimes as many as twenty or forty, depending upon how high in the priesthood they could climb. And they had a nice, new Temple to live in as well as a piece of land totaling 25,000 cubits by 20,000 cubits for priestly houses and living space. Plus, they were able to forge even more decrees from Yahweh so they could tax the people in even more oil, produce, livestock and wine.

While they were in Babylon, the rabbis studied Babylonian law, religion, magic, demonology and sorcery. The rabbis accepted the Babylonian calendar along with its astrology based on celestial constellations. The Babylonian Calendar is still the standard Jewish calendar today. They studied Babylonian astrology and made it into the devil-worship and sorcery that the Jewish Kabbalists, rabbis and Hassids practice today. Offering their "Jewish Loyalty" as advisors to Nebuchadnezzar, they were sent on political missions to other countries where they contacted other members of the International Cult.

Especially in Persia, did they find fertile possibilities for fomenting revolution and warfare against Babylon. While acting as emissaries of Babylon, the Jews practiced their arts of the spy and double-agent for Persia. So, while bowing at the feet of Nebuchadnezzar, and while proclaiming their undying "Jewish Loyalty" and devotion, they were arranging for his destruction behind his back. It was in Babylon that they perfected their treachery on an International level for deceiving the wise and enslaving the foolish. As arch deceivers of Mankind, the Jews have deceived and betrayed *both* the wise and the foolish. And they are doing so today.

Lamentations
(Fall of Jerusalem After 587 BC)

Lamentations is traditionally ascribed to the prophet Jeremiah, but it was actually written *after* the fall of Jerusalem in 587 BC. With a lot of whining and crying, Lamentations is read during the Jewish fast that commemorates the conquest of Jerusalem in 587 BC. The Jews whine and cry a lot in the belief that they can fool Yahweh with their lamenting so that he will give them more blessings. So much of Judaism is a carnival sideshow that to hear the rabbis and cantors moaning their way through the reading of Lamentations, is just like listening to Grade-B actors swooning. It is all acting.

When the Jews were defeated by Nebuchadnezzar, "the neighboring peoples of Edom, Moab and Ammon not only refused help but were actively hostile." So, it is easy to see that the Jews were not very popular with their next-door neighbors. Hatred of the Jews is found wherever people have had a long enough time to know and to experience Jews. Where there are no Jews, there is no hatred for them. The Jewish-named phenomenon which they call "anti-Semitism" does not exist anywhere in the world until the Jews arrive on the scene. Once people come into contact with Jews, they become anti-Semitic.

Modern day Jews insist that the people who hate Jews are mentally ill. But the question never seems to center on the fact that the people were perfectly normal until the Jews moved in, and then they became rabidly anti-Jewish. Doesn't this mean that if anti-Semitism is a sort of disease as the Jews claim, then the Jews themselves are the carriers of the disease? You only catch anti-Semitism because it is a disease carried and spread by the Jews themselves. So, like any disease vector, the disease is eliminated when the vector is removed.

Haggai 520 BC
(1 Year of Sniveling)

The last, the post-exilic, period of prophecy opens with Haggai. The change is striking. Before the Exile, the watchword of the prophets was Punishment. During the Exile, it became Consolation. Now it is Restoration. Haggai was one of the priests who returned with the exiles from Babylon to Jerusalem. By this time, they were all dyed-in-the-wool Jews. They had been brainwashed by the wicked rabbis to the point where all a rabbi had to do was roll his eyes back in his head, foam at the mouth and say, "Thus, says Yahweh!" and the Jews would tremble and urinate in their robes.

The Jews who came out of Babylon were an evil and greedy lot. Through their treachery, bribes and treason, they had managed to subvert administrative control of Babylon under Cyrus. Those who stayed behind in Babylon were well satisfied with their wealth and privileges. Those who returned with Ezra the Scribe and the various priests, did not return out of religious conviction. As Habakkuk writes, the Jews returned in order to get back the lands and properties, the farms and town houses, that their fathers had been forced to abandon under Nebuchadnezzar. Thus, Habakkuk the priest rebukes the returning Jews.

Since there was a drought followed by mildew of the stored crops, Habakkuk claims that Yahweh did this because the greedy Jews built their own houses, but did not rebuild the Temple for Yahweh's delight and for the priests' comfort. So, his prophecies are really a lot of cheerleading for priestly interests. His one-page "prophecy" is dated August, 520 BC. The Jews had returned from Babylon and had been living in Jerusalem for eighteen years. But they had not rebuilt the Temple. This speaks eloquently about their priorities and their so-called "piety." And what a coincidence! In this "prophecy," he blames the drought and the small harvests on Yahweh being unhappy that the Jews had not rebuilt the Temple for Yahweh and his hungry priests.

In October, 520 BC, Haggai coughs up another prophecy using the voice of Yahweh. This time promising to make the Temple, which Yahweh wants the Jews to rebuild, a place where all the silver and gold of the world will flow in, Haggai says:

> "For Yahweh Sabaoth says this: A little while now, and I am going to shake the heavens and the earth, the sea and the dry land. I will shake all the nations and the treasures of all the nations shall flow in, and I shall fill this Temple with glory, says, Yahweh Sabaoth. Mine is the silver, mine the gold!"
> (Haggai 2:6-8.)

Such were the priorities of the god of the merchant-moneylenders, the scheming bankers, and the priests in Babylon and their God of Lies, all greedy for gold. So, who do you suppose wrote the "scriptures" of Judaism, holy bandits or holy bankers? Oy! Such a choice! Judaism is truly a religion of the merchants and moneylenders! Fresh from their victory in deceiving Cyrus, the moneylenders now needed a secure temple in which to stash their loot and to serve as the focal point for the world's biggest banking and religious fraud.

Haggai certainly knew how to get the attention of the Jews. By promising to shake all the gold and silver in the world out of the non-Jews and into the hands of the Jews, Haggai rallied his Jews into the religious zeal that the Jews are so famous for, the religion of getting free stuff and hoarding gold. Even after eighteen years, building a temple for their god they didn't care about. But building a temple to store all the gold and silver in the world! Now, that's the kind of promise to stir the religious zeal in the heart of every kike. The Jews rallied around this call to the faithful and rebuilt the Temple in praise of a god that would promise them not eternal life, not spiritual comfort, not holy bliss, but all of the gold and silver in the world! Now that's the kind of god that the Jews would die for, a rich and generous god who would steal from the non-Jews and give to the Jews. That was the god of Israel! Hallalu-Yah!

Because the priests wanted the Temple built as soon as possible, their god gave a special message to Zerubbabel, the Babylonian governor, promising him that Yahweh would shake up the heavens and the earth, destroy the nations, and in general smash up everything. Then to make sure that Zerubabbel was terrified, as well as honored and flattered, to the maximum, Haggai adds, using the voice of god,

> "When that day comes – it is Yahweh Sabaoth who speaks – I will take you, Zerubabbel son of Shealtiel, my servant – it is Yaweh Sabaoth who speaks – and make you like a signet ring. For I have chosen you – it is Yahweh Sabaoth who speaks." (Haggai 2:23.)

By this time, the rabbis and prophets had learned that they could tell any lie, claim that it came from Yahweh, and the people would believe them! After all, everybody believed the stories that they told in the Torah and all the counterfeited messages in their books of prophets. So, why not tell some lies vocally instead of just writing them all down and claiming that they were ancient prophesies? You can be sure that Zerubabbel was properly impressed, or rather, terrified to have a message like that delivered by the "holy messengers" of god. Zerubabbel began work on the Temple without delay and with fear and trembling, which is exactly how the rabbis like people to act toward their fraudulent selves.

But there is another aspect of Yahweh that the priests learned from Babylon and India and which Habakkuk introduced to the Jews. That is the idea that *their* god is the supreme one.

> "His majesty veils the heavens, the earth is filled with his glory ... Plague goes in front of him, fever follows on his heels. When he stands up he makes the earth tremble, with his glance he makes the *goyim* quake." (Habakkuk 3:3-6.)

Thus, the Jews stole the might of the gods from other countries and conferred it upon their own Canaanite god and, of course, upon themselves. And what a great god of the Jews! A god of plague and fevers! A god who destroys nations! A god to be emulated by the Jews who "walk in his ways" in bringing about these disasters upon Mankind! And, in modern times, when those whose job it is to prevent, stop and cure plagues and fevers, are doctors; and those doctors are Jews who love gold and silver more than they love God, then you can be sure that the cost of medicine will always be high and no plagues or fevers will ever be cured by those who "walk in the ways" of the demon-god of the Jews.

Zechariah 520-518 BC
(Two Years of Excuses)

In October of 520 BC, two months after Haggai started messing with their minds, Zechariah butted in with his own "prophesies." The priests were tired of the burned-out and broken-down ruins in which they had been living and they wanted the Jews to start rebuilding the Temple. By this time, the rabbis had completed all rewriting and counterfeit work on the Torah and there was a good supply of prophets with whom to browbeat the Jews into obedience. Zechariah draws upon these myths and stories with an "I told you so" sort of glee. He reminds the Jews that their ancestors were all punished by Yahweh, so they had better get to work on the Temple real fast if they know what's good for them!

Zechariah is also an apologist for Yahweh, because the rabbis wanted the Jews to love Yahweh and not think that their god was such a bad fellow. After all, Judah had been plundered and carried off into exile by the Babylonians for sixty years. All of the harm that the Jews had suffered, the priests had at first blamed on the Jews, because they weren't following rabbinical rules. Therefore, the accusing fingers of the rabbis pointed at the Jews as being the cause of their own bad luck. Then, after they had returned to Jerusalem, the rabbis pointed their lying fingers, not at the Jews who were at the moment supposedly totally forgiven by Yahweh, but they pointed at all of the people of the world! The scapegoat for Jewish suffering was now everybody on earth! The scribes had their prophet Zechariah write:

> "Yahweh Sabaoth [God of Armies] says this: I feel most jealous love for Jerusalem and Zion, but very bitter anger against the proud *goyim*; for my part I was only a little angry, but they have overstepped all limits." (Zechariah 1:14-15.)

Ooh, scary stuff, indeed! To keep the hatred of the Jews concentrated and directed toward all non-Jews, the rabbis showed them that their god was not such a destructive and malevolent god after all.

Now it was not the "sins" of the Jews that was at fault. Now *it was the malicious neighbors of the Jews* who were at fault. Thus, in dealing with their neighbors, the Jews were directed to once again use self-righteous indignation, malice, hatred, anger, greed, slanders and their whole evil arsenal of Semitic weapons for again seizing property and valuables from the surrounding peoples, as if everybody in the world owed all of their goods, proffered with humility on bended knee, as gifts for the "Holy Chosen Ones of God." Truly, the Jews would make the world biggest clowns except for the fact that they take their incredible vindictive greed so seriously – clowns, with the hearts of swine, posing as saints! The Jews are a type of creature, not quite a human being, but a type of bizarre clown imagining themselves as angelic beings.

In addition, the rabbis promised the Jews that not only would they be able to shake all the gold and silver out of the *goyim* (non-Jewish, lowly insects, stupid cattle), but the *goyim* of the world would also worship Yahweh, the god of the moneylenders. To make sure that the Jews were properly impressed with the "holiness" of the High Priest, Joshua, Yahweh puts in a good word for Joshua in Zechariah's fourth "vision" where he allegedly says of

Joshua, "If you walk in my ways and keep my ordinances, you shall govern my house." That is, the Jews were reminded that the Law was God's law, and not something invented by lying rabbis. But the lying rabbis were clever enough to authorize themselves total power by having one of their own "prophets" speak with the voice of Yahweh and claim that performing the empty rituals in the Laws of Moses automatically legitimatized the High Priest as ruler over the Jews. This not only kept them entrapped by the rabbis, but it gave Joshua the edge that he needed to scream and throw fits whenever work on the Temple lagged.

But to really solidify their theocratic schemes, the Jewish priests had Zechariah dream up a fifth "vision" whereby Yahweh has seven eyes that see the whole world. He is called the god of the whole world. And he is served by two equal leaders, a priest and a civil servant. Joshua was the priest and Zerubabbel was the governor of Judea.

To give a good scare to the populace, the rabbis used a bit of sorcery in Zechariah's sixth "vision" of a flying scroll, which was a curse that would magically settle over all of Palestine and enter the houses of thieves and anyone who swears falsely by Yahweh's name. This curse would consume the whole house, timber, stone and all. And Yahweh was going to let it loose! Run for your lives! Or to prevent that curse, bring a goat to the Temple, cut its throat, pour out its blood, burn the fat so that the giant invisible nostril of Yahweh can smell a sweet savor of burning goat fat. Then and only then, will all be well, as the priests and rabbis lick the grease from their beards with darting tongues.

Certainly, the rabbis were pulling out all stops on this particular "prophecy." Since they couldn't physically force the Hebrews to rebuild the Temple, they could scare them into doing it. The flying scroll was to curse anyone who had sworn to rebuild the Temple while they were in Babylon, but who continually put off doing any work for these eighteen years.

To purify the land of the Jews and to curse the land of Babylon, Zechariah had another "vision." The seventh vision was of wickedness, which was carried off to Babylon.

Finally, the rabbis do some of their wet ink transcriptions in Zechariah's eighth "vision." In this one, the gold that is given to the Temple is to be made into a crown for Zerubbabel. A gold crown might seem like a big gift, but compared to the huge hoard of gold within the Temple it was nothing to the priests and money changers who owned the Temple. Later, after the greedy priests had become the religio-political leaders, the wet ink was applied so the gold crown was ordained for the priest Joshua. Thus, the rabbis give and the rabbis taketh away. Bow down and kiss the hellish cloven hooves of the scheming rabbis.

By 518 BC, the Temple was finally being rebuilt. It took twenty years for the ever-so-pious Jews to take a pause from making money and to start building a treasure house for their god. The rabbis had succeeded in arranging and editing their Torah and "prophets" in such a way that all events in the history of the world were credited to the god of the Jews. The myths, lies, plagiarisms, frauds and forgeries of the Jews were by this date being promoted as the "holy truth" and the "sacred" texts. But having only Truth alone serve them was never a technique of the lying rabbis who additionally wanted deceit and forgery to serve them as well. After all, those evil priests believed that since God had given Abraham's First National Bank and Pawn Shop the entire world including all of the seas, mountains and people thereon, then it only made sense for the rabbis to also own all of the devils and demons as well.

Their Big Book of Lies (the *Torah*) claimed that the Yahweh-god prohibited them to "eat of the fruit of the tree of the knowledge of good and evil." To the rabbis, this meant that no deed was too good or too evil. They could do either as it profited them, just as long as they practiced the empty and ridiculous Laws of Moses, so as to "purify" and "make clean" themselves through ritualistic magic. The Mosaic Law did not discuss morality, truth or goodness; it was merely a one-way Contract of obligations to the priests who served the invisible Yahweh-god his supper. Whether the Jews used Truth or Lies didn't matter, since they considered themselves above the angels in holiness and above both Good and Evil in all of their actions. All that mattered to the Jews was obtaining total power and wealth for its own sake. The getting and hoarding of treasure was a sign from God that they were being blessed by the god who loves gold.

So, writing more of their wet ink "prophecies," the rabbis in about 333 BC added six more chapters to Zechariah, claiming that these had been written by him 185 years previously. This was a standard procedure of the rabbis, who had had plenty of practice over the centuries in this line of forgery. If anyone questioned the veracity of these various documents, the lying rabbis would tear their own clothes, howl to the skies and have the questioner stoned to death or strangled. So, there was little dissent among the Jews.

Zechariah 9 through 14 are an odd collection of various writings with no names or dates. But since they contained the name of Yahweh written on them, the stupid rabbis could not just throw them away. So, they pasted them onto the end of the Book of Zechariah, from where they have caused confusion for over 2,300 years.

The Jews believed every word that their rabbis and prophets wrote. So, the Jews from the earliest times found that believing the lies of the rabbis was better than not believing them and then having molten lead poured down their throats by these same old devils. Believing what the rabbis wrote long ago has caused the modern Jews to find a sort of twisted solace and perverted safety in such horrors as biological warfare.

> "And this is the plague with which Yahweh will strike all the *goyim* who have fought against Jerusalem; their flesh will moulder while they are still standing on their feet; their eyes will rot in their sockets; their tongues will rot in their mouths." (Zechariah 14:12.)

It is for such reasons, that the Jews of modern day Israel have the world's largest supplies of biological weapons ready for use upon Mankind. But you *goyim* should not fear, because all who survive having your flesh rot will be among the non-Jews who will go to Jerusalem and celebrate the Feast of Tabernacles. Oh joy!

Henry Kissinger no doubt had such teachings in mind when he, while in the Nixon White House, ordered the production of the AIDS virus. (See Volume III, *The Bloodsuckers of Judah*) Spreading plagues among Mankind is what pious Jews do. Do you like sugar? Or how about Ebola?

Chronicles, Ezra, and Nehemiah
(All Written by One Author, 538-515 BC)

Ezra wrote the books entitled, Chronicles, Ezra, and Nehemiah. I will only comment on Ezra, since it contains some special information useful to this study, although more proofs that Judaism is designed as a military organization serving its "god of hosts" is found in Chronicles. Judaism is not a religion; it is a system of organized crime where every Jew is a foot soldier in an army of inbred, genealogically connected criminals. It's a gigantic crime family. Chronicles, written in the mid-to-late 4th century BC, shows its racial and military basis.

Ezra begins with the thoroughly deceived Persian King Cyrus decreeing that the Jews could go back to Jerusalem. As you saw in such counterfeits as Jeremiah and Ezekiel, Cyrus had been deceived into thinking that the wet-ink "prophesies" that the Jews had presented to him were genuine fortune-telling documents. He admits in his proclamation that the Yahweh-god had ordered him to rebuild the Temple in Jerusalem just as the fake prophesies demanded. Cyrus expresses the usual Near Eastern belief that the Yahweh-god had his residence in Jerusalem. Cyrus wanted that god to stay there and not wander around causing him trouble.

The two ancient conspiring gangs of Judah and Benjamin are cited in Ezra. "Then the heads of families of Judah and Benjamin, the priests and the Levites" (Ezra 1:5) went off to Jerusalem to rebuild. The administrative structure had not changed. The priests of Abraham's First National Bank and Pawn Shop were still in control. The so-called "promises" to David had evaporated with the last of the Davidic kings dying in Babylon. And the tribe of Benjamin was still obediently serving the priests of Judah who gave them their orders.

The only difference with Benjamin now, was that its members were totally submissive and obedient. As you will remember, besides the tribe of Judah, only the Benjamites knew how Abraham's family had defrauded the Canaanites of their land, hijacked their god and stolen their property in order to establish a fake religious facade for a treasury. To wipe out these eyewitnesses, all of the women and children and almost all of the men of the entire tribe of Benjamin had been massacred at the instigation of the Levitical priests. Those leaders who knew their actual history as mercenaries for Abraham's father had been killed. The few lower-level soldiers who remained were married off to new Jewish wives who replaced their slaughtered families. These survivors had been cowed into silent obedience to the rabbinical line of myth. Instead of a tribe of uncontrolled Babylonian perverts and wild cutthroats, the Benjamites were now under priestly control. With the elders and leaders of their tribe exterminated along with their history, the Benjamite survivors now actually believed the lies of the Torah!

To see off these returnees to Jerusalem, the rich Jews living in Babylonia gave them plenty of gold and silver for the rebuilding job. There were a lot of rich Jews living in Babylonia, which might seem a bit strange for a people who whine and cry so much about how poor and oppressed they were. Under Nebuchadnezzar, the Jews had been given jobs as befitted their occupational skills – as administrators, merchants, tax-farmers, artisans, etc. Under Cyrus, the Jews had inherited the properties of the Babylonians whom they had had Cyrus execute. Cyrus even gave them back the golden vessels of the Temple which Nebuchadnezzar had confiscated.

> "...to Sheshbazzar, the prince of Judah. The inventory was as follows: thirty golden bowls for offerings, one thousand and twenty-nine silver bowls for offerings, thirty golden bowls, four hundred and ten silver bowls, one thousand other vessels. In all, five thousand four hundred vessels of gold and silver." (Ezra 1:7-11.)

This is a very telling sentence on two levels. First, the title "prince of Judah" has a lot more depth to it than merely being a son of some dethroned king. A "prince of Judah" is an honorific that we will find often in later centuries, as you will see. To the Jews, a "prince of Judah" is usually a banker, a rich moneylender or a fabulously wealthy businessman and is the head of the Kehillah, that secretive system of Jewish spying and subversion. So, Sheshbazzar represented not a king, but a chairman of the board of a commercial combine. He was the "prince" of the international criminal conspiracy of Jewish merchants and moneylenders posing as saints. That is what the "Prince of Judah" or Director of the Kehillah is. He was the leader of *international* Jewry.

Second, what other religion has such an interest in the silver and gold ornaments on its temple altar as does the money-grubbing religion of the Jews? They did not worship actual bricks of bullion because that would be too obviously idolatry and it would not sufficiently conceal the precious metals, themselves. Instead, using hocus-pocus misdirection, these clever bankers melted the bullion and cast it into the shapes of bowls and candle sticks (menorah) and decorated Abraham's First National Bank and Pawn Shop with these. The shape-shifting gold and silver bullion was still there on deposit but it was hidden in plain sight in the shape of "holy" offering bowls which were "sacred"

(Ezra 8:28) and therefore, not to be touched or stolen unless you wanted to catch leprosy.

It is not the shape of the metal that makes it valuable, but its purity and weight. Ezra, being a typical Jewish scribe and accountant, delighted in listing the totals that he sent to Jerusalem.

> "So I weighed out and handed over to them six hundred and fif-
> ty talents of silver, one hundred silver vessels worth two talents,
> one hundred talents of gold, twenty golden bowls worth a thou-
> sand darics, and two vessels of fine gilded bronze which were as
> valuable as gold." (Ezra 8:26-27.)

A *talent* weighed 30 kilograms. A *daric*, which was a Persian coin, weighed 130 grains. So, the total that Ezra transferred to Jerusalem was 652 talents of silver (19,560 Kilograms or 43,122 pounds), 100 talents of gold (3000 kilos or 6614 pounds) plus 271 Troy ounces in coined darics (8.4 kilos or 18.6 pounds).

All of this totals 43,122 pounds of silver and 6,633 pounds of gold that Ezra sent to the temple in Jerusalem. You can figure out how much this is in modern money based on present gold and silver valuations. But whatever the dollar amount is, 21.6 tons of silver and 3.3 tons of gold is quite a lot in any-body's estimation. Enough to establish a well-funded bank inside of the temple treasury!

In all, Ezra claims that 42,360 Jews returned to Jerusalem in the first batch, not counting slaves and servants nor their thousands of donkeys and camels to haul their loot, which Ezra is only too happy to brag about and list. These were some very rich Jews who had certainly not been slaves in Babylon for the past sixty years but had made a lot of money while there.

To show this, Ezra claims that *out of just a few of the families,*

> "... a certain number of heads of families made voluntary offer-
> ings for the Temple of God, for its rebuilding on its site. In ac-
> cordance with their means, they gave 61,000 gold drachmas,
> five thousand silver minas and 100 priestly robes to the sacred
> funds." (Ezra 2:68-69.)

Yes, these "poor, innocent, oppressed captives" of Nebuchadnezzar in their horrible Exile from their beloved holy treasury in Jerusalem, had eked out a miserable slave's existence in Babylonia. In their "extreme poverty" under the "oppressive dictatorship" of the Babylonians, they had only been able to scrap together a measly 806 pounds or so of gold, a paltry 2.8 tons of silver and 100 priestly robes made of expensive purple and red dye, with gold bells sewn to the hems. This blessed gold and divine silver *was added* to the "sacred funds."

Also, it can be noted that the assassination of Gedaliah had paid off. The small-time Jews who had remained in Judah made no objection at all when this gang of rich, murdering kikes moved back into the neighborhood after a sixty-year absence. They simply made way for them without complaint and gave up their homes and buildings. "The priests, Levites and part of the people settled in Jerusalem; the gatekeepers, cantors, oblates and all the other Israelites, in their own towns" (Ezra 2:70). The big Jews were back in business and the little Jews stepped out of their way to avoid being murdered.

However, the people of Samaria, the Israelians, knew the Jews only too well and tried to warn the Persian king Artaxerxes about the Jews rebuilding "that rebellious and wicked city" (Ezra 4:11-16). Finding the accusations true (that the Jews were seditious and rebellious), the king ordered all work to stop. But the frantic prophets Haggai and Zechariah began to rant and rave about Yahweh, frightening the Jews enough that the work began once again after it was determined that they had had the authorization of King Darius to do the work.

When the Temple was finally rebuilt, Ezra the Scribe came up from Babylon with the freshly written "ancient scriptures" that he and his scribal forgers had completed. "For Ezra had devoted himself to the study of the Law of Yahweh, to practicing it and to teaching Israel its laws and customs" (Ezra 7:10). He also carried with him and his entourage of priests and Levites,

> "...the silver and gold which the king and his councilors have
> voluntarily offered to the God of Israel who dwells in Jerusalem
> as well as all the silver and gold you find in the whole province
> of Babylonia, together with those voluntary offerings given by
> the people and the priests for the Temple of their God in Jerusa-
> lem." (Ezra 7:15-17.)

Criminals always find ways of evading the law. The Jewish priests, rabbis and moneylenders are no different. They had written the laws of the *Hebrew Bible* that guaranteed a self-financed Temple organization complete with military deferment for all members and a built-in banking system. But even these laws – that they had written themselves and signed God's name to – were still too restrictive for their criminal intention to defraud the world. So, among the returning priests and Levites was a new breed of Jewish lawyer who specialized in double-talk, deceit, and rambling discombobulation. These rabbis were experts at evading even their own laws, and through blatant lies could turn the Mosaic Laws upside down, inside out and backward, using nothing more than their rubbery lips and evil minds. In later days, they became known as Pharisees.

You already know that the entire *Hebrew Bible* is a fraud because modern archaeology and literary analysis prove it. But ancient people did not know this. In a world with so many belief systems and gods and goddesses, one more religion claiming to speak for a mighty god sitting in a temple was not unique. So, the lies of Judaism went unnoticed among the other peoples of the ancient Near East, who were just as mystified about how their wealth disappeared and why their children went off to war as modern people are. That the Temple scam of Judaism was designed as a banking system, was not at all obvious – and purposely so. If the ancient people inquired of the Jewish priests about the beliefs of the Jews, they were told all the usual fairy stories written down in the Biggest Lie Ever Told, all embellished with bragging about how "moral" and "upright" Judaism was supposed to be. The actual mechanisms of Judaism remained hidden from non-Jews for the very reason given by a more modern rabbi: "To communicate anything to a goy about our religious relations would be equal to the killing of all Jews, for if the goyim knew what we teach about them, they would kill us openly." The Gentiles paid their interest payments to the Jewish moneylenders, lost their farms through foreclosure, had their wives and children carted off into slavery and joined the army for three meals a day and a pittance – just as it had always been – while the Jews stayed safely behind the lines, counted the profits and sneered at them as being "non-Jewish, lowly insects and stupid cattle."

It was only after Ezra the Scribe and his gang of specialized Pharisee lawyers returned from Babylon, that the ordinary people such as the Canaanites and Samaritans began smelling a Jewish rat. Not only were the Jews just as ruthless as they had always been, but after 539 BC, they were even worse. The reason for this is found in this new breed of Pharisee lawyers.

In Babylon, the greedy Jewish bankers and evil Jewish priests had realized that as great a system as Judaism was for making money and keeping it, they were restricted in their acquisitive covetousness by the very laws that they had written, laws that they claimed had been dictated by God, Himself. As master criminals, the bankers and priests wondered how they could evade such laws for their own benefit and still enjoy the perquisites that the Temple Scam offered its adherents. For example, how could they steal a non-Jews property or murder his entire family, if their own laws commanded "Thou shalt not steal" and "Thou shalt not kill"? Wouldn't the *goyim* start wondering about the great difference between what the Jews preached and what they practiced, and begin to look more carefully at their hoax?

The solution to this "holy" banking problem is the same solution that the Jews use to this very day. It was simple. The Pharisees claimed that the *Hebrew Bible* was the "word of God" and *was given only to the Jews and not to anybody else*. Therefore, "Thou shalt not steal" meant "Do not steal from a Jew" but God's holy law said nothing about "Do not steal from a Gentile." "Thou shalt not kill" meant that the God of the Jews (who hated all of Mankind but loved the Jews) wanted them not to kill each other, but it was perfectly okay to kill non-Jews. Otherwise, why did God not actually command, "Thou shalt not kill non-Jews"?

This same twisting of the Mosaic Laws was used in every single line of the *Hebrew Bible* – plus tens of thousands of other rules, laws, methods and demonic advice, which the Pharisees brought with them from Babylon and continuously developed for the next thousand years. They called their *abracadabra* system "The Tradition of the Elders" and claimed that God had whispered these secret "laws" into Moses' ear and they were passed down orally from Moses and Aaron to themselves. How could anyone argue with perfect lies like this? The Jews could still promote the laws of Moses as the "word of God," but could refute, reverse and change them in any way that suited them. They could negate every single one of those laws by claiming the "authority" of the secret "Oral Law," which only they knew. So, pay a little extra to the Pharisee lawyer and have your sins expunged. In this way, the Pharisee rabbis became popular with the ordinary Jews since they could always evade the Mosaic Law and its penalties of "sin" offerings. Through the Pharisees, the Jews were always declared to be "sinless" by finding a loophole for their Crimes against Mankind as well as against each other.

The lies of the Jews had gained them their release from "captivity." And now the terrifying tales that the Jews told in their Torah and prophets, had the Persians quaking in their sandals and offering to the Jews their first love in abundance – gold and silver. In addition, the ultimate wish of the Jewish priests was also granted to them by Artaxerxes, namely, that the Jewish priests could kill anybody who didn't believe them.

> "And you, Ezra, by virtue of the wisdom of your God, which is in your possession, you are to appoint scribes and judges to administer justice for the whole people of Trans-Euphrates, that is, for all who know the Law of your God. You must teach those who do not know it. If anyone does not obey the Law of your God – which is the law of the king – let judgment be strictly executed on him: death, banishment, confiscation or imprisonment." (Ezra 7:25-26.)

In other words, the priests were given back all of their old dictatorial powers *plus* all of the gold in Babylonia, *plus* the "right" to murder any non-Jew who didn't believe their lies. It was the Devil's Truth! Not a bad profit for such "oppressed" moneylenders and merchants!

One of the first "problems" confronting Ezra when he reached Jerusalem was that the Hebrews had married into families of Canaanites so that "the holy race has been mingling with the *goyim*" (Ezra 9:2). At this news, what did the famous Jew do?

> "At this news, I tore my garment and my cloak; I tore hair from my head and beard and sat down, quite overcome. All who trembled at the words of the God of Israel gathered around me, when faced by this treachery of the exiles." (Ezra 9:3-4.)

The street theater of the rabbis once again! By making a show of insanity, he had all the Jews around him trembling in fear. Marrying other people who were not also members of the Jewish "holy race" was considered to be treason. He didn't stick a spear in the crotch of every Hebrew and his *goyim* wife like Phineas the priest ... but almost. After much weeping at prayers, the other

Jews agreed to divorce their non-Jewish wives. They didn't want to heap such a terrible sin of marrying a non-Jew on top of all of their other sins. The Jews are always moaning about their sins, because they always have so many of them! But they have a god who forgives even their most gruesome crimes for nothing more than a barbecued goat. What a miracle!

In summation: the *Hebrew Bible* came out of Babylon, carried by Ezra and his entourage. These scriptures claimed that Terah, Abraham, Isaac and Jacob were all Babylonians who had incestuously married Babylonians from which all of the Hebrew tribes were descended. The *Torah* was composed by the descendants of Babylonian moneylenders who had established Abraham's First National Bank and Pawn Shop in Jerusalem. It was back into Babylonia during the Exile that Nebuchadnezzar brought the Hebrews along with their various tribal histories and religious texts. Hebrews and Judeans went into Babylon and after sixty years, Jews came out again, more wicked than before. It was during this long time that the scribes rewrote the various books and added to them whatever they found of use from the cuneiform libraries of Babylon. Astrology, the Babylonian calendar, the wisdom literature of the Babylonians, Assyrians, Sumerians and the Egyptians were sources of their literary plagiarism. And it was with Ezra the Scribe that Judaism was firmly and irrevocably declared to be a racist religion at odds with all other races whom the Jews referred to as "lowly insects and stupid cattle," the *goyim*.

By 539 BC, the Jews had declared a racial war against all of Mankind based upon the fake scriptures that they, themselves, had forged. In their racist demonic religion, they claimed themselves to be "the Chosen Ones" of a demonic god who hated all of Mankind and who therefore commanded the Jews to "walk in his ways" by impoverishing and committing genocide against the people of the world. And the greedy and malicious Jews were very happy to obey, because that meant more wealth for them. Many must suffer and die so that a few Jews may live in luxury.

Jonah ~ 400-500 BC
(After the Exile)

By the time the Book of Jonah was written, the rabbis were confident enough in their *abracadabra* that *any* lie that they told would be believed. As an example of how literary and biblical analysis works, it does not take an expert in English literature to be able to distinguish when a piece of literature was written. Even a person with an ordinary education can tell the difference between and give the approximate date of something written in Shakespeare's time (the 1600s AD), and something written in the 1900s AD in the United States. The language used, the words selected, the events alluded to, and the types of thoughts expressed, all date a work of literature for even an average reader, even if no author or publishing date is given. So, how much more accurately can a piece of literature be dated when it is read not by an average reader but by a real expert of the language? This is true of all languages. Experts in each language can tell the approximate date of any piece of work that they read.

In the same way, experts of ancient languages can learn when something was written, even if a false date is affixed to it. Now, the old devils who invented Judaism were not aware of this literary science nor did they care about it. When the rabbis wrote the Book of Jonah, they were interested in immediate problems and immediate results. The rabbis thought that their lies could never be discovered. After all, it was a matter of belief or non-belief. Either you believed their lies or you didn't. If you were a Jew who didn't believe the rabbis, they would kill you because Jewish lies are the Devil's Truth. If you were a Gentile who didn't believe the lies of the rabbis, they would call you dirty names, besmirch your character, try to get you fired from your job, and declare you to be a sinner who was going to hellfire and then kill you. They never imagined that millennia later, there would be sciences that – believe it or not – could prove them all liars.

Although the Book of Jonah is supposed to have been written sometime between 783 and 743 BC during the reign of Jeroboam II, the language experts know that it was written after the Exile, and probably during the 5th century BC. So, once again we have a situation where the rabbis have presented their lies with great fanfare and bluster, claiming them to be true. But why did they do this? With Christian charity and innocence, the editors of the *Jerusalem Bible* claim that Jonah was written "to amuse and instruct." One must consider the social situation in Jerusalem during the time between 500 and 400 BC.

It was during this time that the rabbis were very busy wielding their power over the Jews. The Second Temple had been rebuilt by 515 BC. And there was a growing population of Jews and especially non-Jews who were living in Palestine. As these non-Jews were told the ancient myths and lies about Moses, Abraham and Yahweh, these non-Jews became interested in converting to Judaism. After all, in feats of power, what other god could compare with the lies that the rabbis told about Yahweh? And since the rabbis had already written and edited "The Greatest Lie Ever Told" when they had assembled their *Hebrew Bible*, they felt confident that they could tell more lies and not be found out. After all, if people would believe that Yahweh and Moses could part the seas and kill all the firstborn sons of Egypt, or if Joshua could have God stop the sun in the sky for a whole extra day, then why not believe the story of Jonah in the belly of a fish?

So, the Book of Jonah was written. It was sufficient for the rabbis' goals at the time, but the language experts of modern times know that it is falsely dated, while the archaeologists know that the history told is false history; and yet, this Jewish fairy tale is accepted by Jews and Christians alike as "inspired truth." Such is the blindness of men who do not look carefully at the Jews and their lies.

Anyway, the editors of the *Jerusalem Bible*, language experts that they are, have stated: "The hero of this droll adventure is a prophet mentioned in 2K14:25, who lived in the reign of Jeroboam II. The book, however, does not claim to be his work and certainly cannot be by him.... thought and phrases are borrowed from Jeremiah and Ezekiel; the language of the book is late. All point to a date after the Exile, somewhere in the 5th century.... This late date is warning enough against any interpretation of the book as history. This is excluded by other arguments as well. There is no trace in Assyrian or biblical documents of a conversion of the king of Nineveh with all his people to the God of Israel." But even while writing this, the editors don't see anything wrong with believing in a book that on all points is false.

But what is it that the rabbis wanted to accomplish by writing yet another hoax? Didn't Judaism have hoaxes in plenty already? First, you must understand the mindset of the rabbis and the Jews. In their secret Talmudic Law, the rabbis teach that if a fraud can be achieved without anyone discovering it, then it is perfectly legitimate and – *Abracadabra*! – it becomes true. In the 400s BC, Nineveh had already been rubble and ruin for over 200 years.

No rabbis could foresee that the archaeologists of the 19th and 20th centuries AD would know more about Nineveh than they did. No ancient rabbi could imagine anyone actually digging up and sifting for buried clues through the wreckage and the thousands of tons of dirt and broken pottery for the buried cuneiform libraries. And so, just like their Egyptian historical swindles concerning Moses, the rabbis believed that no one would be able to discover their literary and religious crimes. The Jews were master criminals by this time, but they could not foresee modern archaeology and forensic analysis proving their guilt. The lying rabbis once again told tales about their wonderful god which all other peoples of the world should believe in and worship and make donations. With such a great god, all the people of the world would want to worship at the Temple in Jerusalem and make sacrifices and offer gifts to the holy priests of Yahweh. It was even better than Disneyland, because what the Temple of Yahweh offered was totally imaginary.

The Book of Jonah was written not so much for the Jews, but for the pagans who were just as happy worshiping one idol as another. Only now, the rabbis wanted the pagans to worship and sacrifice to Yahweh. So, they wrote how the pagan "sailors were seized with terror" (Jonah 1:10) that Jonah had disobeyed Yahweh. The sailors were "seized with dread of Yahweh; they offered sacrifice to Yahweh and made vows" (Jonah 1:16). And when Jonah preached in Nineveh, all of the pagan people "believed in God" and repented (Jonah 3:5). And to let both Jews and pagans know that the conveniently useful god of the rabbis could make or break promises at a whim, the rabbis wrote: "Who knows if God will not change his mind and relent, if he will not renounce his burning wrath, so that we do not perish?" (Jonah 3:9.) Thus, the Book of Jonah was written to lure more pagans into enriching the Jews with their contributions to the Temple, while apologizing for the unreliable and capricious nature of their lying god.

With the Book of Jonah, the rabbis closed off the objections by some Jews that Yahweh very often broke his promises by saying that Yahweh could change His mind if He wanted to. And by opening the doors of the Temple treasury so that even non-Jews could throw their wealth inside, the clever rabbis assured everyone worldwide whether Jewish or non-Jewish that in return for their gold and silver, their livestock and corn, in return for their oil and wine, their woven cloth and embroidered linens, in return to their precious stones and sweet incense, their baked bread and sweet honey, in return for their best and finest wealth given into the Jewish Temple with feelings of religious piety, that, for all of this, the rabbis would give their splayed-lizard-claw salute and say, "May the god of Israel bless You," while flicking their tongues across their sucking lips. Judaism was a very profitable swindle.

In their diabolic evil, the rabbis from the time of Ezra forward, never again said the name of their God. To repeat the name of God aloud is decreed by the evil rabbis to be a death sentence to anyone who uses that name. It is from this time onward that the Devil finally gained complete control over the Jews so that they could now repeat the name of Lucifer, but they were forbidden to say the name of God. And so, the fictitious Book of Jonah completes the swindle. It was the last book added to the *Hebrew Bible*, because it completes and perfects the Greatest Lie Ever Told and puts the kosher seal of approval upon the world's most perfect organized crime unit. And that organized criminal conspiracy is known as Judaism, a Cult based entirely upon lies.

Obadiah ~ 400-500 BC

This book was probably written long after 587 BC, when Jerusalem had been destroyed, and even after 312 BC when Edom was conquered by the Nabataeans. This 275-year span leaves a lot of time for Yahweh to work his evil.

> "The book has affinities with the maledictions against Edom, current after 587 BC, in Psalms 137:7, Lamentations 4:21-22, Ezekiel 25:12; Malachi 1:2 and Jeremiah 49:7: the Edomites had taken advantage of the destruction of Jerusalem to invade southern Judah."

But there are two things about Jewish "prophesies" that are not generally understood. First, most of them were written after the fact. So, they were actually fraudulent. However, many of them were not actually prophesies of the future, but were actually curses. The old rabbis would curse their enemies with all of the things that they wanted to happen. Obadiah is such a curse. That only a few of these "prophetic" events actually occurred, did not prevent the later rabbis from holding up such books as Obadiah as "proof" of how wise and far-seeing their fellow priests were. It was the custom of the rabbis to never throw away or burn any writings that had the tetragrammaton written on it. So, a book of curses like Obadiah would sit in the Temple archives for 275 years. And when finally the Edomites were conquered, these curses would be pulled out, dusted off and proclaimed to be prophesies! This is merely one example of Jewish sorcery and deceit.

Malachi ~ 445 BC

The rabbis didn't have any prophets handy around 445 BC, so they had to invent one to give legitimacy to their further demands upon the Jews. "Malachi" means "my messenger." The book is named from the word "Malachi" that is used in the first sentence.

The Book of Malachi is nothing but shameless extortion. The evil priests of Judah had set up for themselves an efficient and profitable religious scam which they had put into action once they had returned to Jerusalem. But the Jews could see that their tithes and animal sacrifices went to making the greedy rabbis fat and wealthy. So, being cheap Jews, they tried to reduce their losses to the priests, rabbis, prophets and the numerous children of these professional leeches. Some of the Hebrews tried to save their best livestock for their herds. So, rather than taking the best of their animals to be slaughtered and eaten by the priests, they took lame, diseased or stolen animals to the Temple. In response, the rabbis wrote up a prophet that they named Malachi to tell the Jews to give them better service.

Keeping their deception well-concealed as always, the rabbis made sure that the warnings from "God" were directed toward themselves. Their charade would be too transparent to the wily Jews if they didn't include themselves in the warning from "God" since the Jews knew what a crafty bunch of loafers the priests really were. So, they added a warning from God to themselves to be sure to stand in fear and trembling before the fly-encrusted altar of Yahweh and to stand in awe of his name. This was not difficult for them to do and it added to their act by approaching the altar while trembling and cowering, wide-eyed and terrified. Of course, ordinary Jews would be duly impressed with such quality acting.

The rabbis wrote for the Jews to hear and for themselves to profit from, these words: "The lips of the priest ought to safeguard knowledge; his mouth is where instruction should be sought, since he is the messenger of Yahweh Sabaoth" (Malachi 2:7). Thus, they reemphasize to the Jews that the priests are the supreme authority between the Jews and God, and that whatever lies spew out of their ravenous mouths should be considered "knowledge." And now to add spice to their acting ability, they quivered and quaked in pretended fear and awe, so that the Jews would stand in fear and awe without pretending.

At this time, after so many centuries of priestly greed, the Jews had gotten a pretty good idea of the fraudulent aspect of their Temple priests. So, the rabbis added to this "prophecy" of Malachi these words to the priests: "You have strayed from the way" (Malachi 2:9). And what was this "way"? Why, it was all of the Laws that the priests had invented to ensnare their subjects. Thus, the Book of Malachi further emphasized that the priests must enforce the laws that they had made in order to keep the power that they had swindled.

To rope the Jews further into their conspiracy, the rabbis wrote in Malachi to not divorce their wives and not to "break faith with the wife of your youth" (Malachi 1:15). Certainly, the women would back up and believe the

Book of Malachi with a "prophesy" such as this, since divorce was very harsh on Jewish women. But the reasoning of the perfidious rabbis was even more demonic than merely to have the women take their prophesy at face value.

The reason that the rabbis wanted the Jews to keep the "wife of their youth" was because Jewish marriages were then and still are today (though less so than in ancient times) arranged marriages. A Jewish man whose family had arranged a marriage that enriched or promoted their social status might find that the Jewish princess he had married was a terrible shrew and want a divorce. Since these arranged marriages for wealth and political power made a more corporately strong Judaism, the rabbis wanted to snuff out any individual choice in marriage.

In addition, the rabbis had finally developed in full their method of subverting the men by controlling the women. The women would naturally rally to the message that divorces were forbidden by God and insist that their husbands also accept it, and by accepting this part of the "prophecy," they would also have to accept the part about giving the priests better food and wine. It was a clever trick by those cunning loafers, the priesthood of rabbis. It would be a trick often repeated in modern times. Many of the laws and regulations that are written into U.S. and European law use this method of wrapping a bitter law inside of a sweet one, all on the same piece of paper. Modern laws are based on fraud and deception, because they are written by Jewish lawyers. Modern laws can only be corrupt, because they are written by the most evil people who ever lived. Any law either written or promoted by Jews is automatically null and void.

Joel ~ 400 BC

The Book of Joel was written about 400 BC. Joel had a problem. The rabbis at this time had gained full power over the Jews by claiming that if they followed the Laws of Moses, then all would be well for Israel. However, a plague of locusts ate every green leaf in all of the country. This is very embarrassing for the priests. They had already had all of their so-called "prophets" put the blame for every disaster upon the shoulders of the Jews, upon themselves or upon the shoulders of the surrounding non-Jewish neighbors of Judah and Israel. According to the rabbis, every disaster was the result of Jewish sins against the Laws of God resulting in divine punishment.

So, now at 400 BC, after the Jews had been totally frightened into unquestioning submission to rabbinic laws, what could the rabbis tell their followers? That the locusts were sent because they had sinned? No, that song had been played so many times that the Jews were weary of it, especially since it was no longer true for their obedient and unquestioning service to the rabbis and their Temple regulations and taxes.

Certainly, when the sky was darkened with locusts and all of the food was devoured by those ravenous insects, the rabbis could order a fast (Joel 1:14) and assemble everyone in the country for prayers and weeping before the putrid, odoriferous altar of Yahweh, but how could they explain the plagues of locusts since the Jews all followed the priestly laws? Ever ready with a scheme, the rabbis first gave their usual response to the Jews through Joel:

> "But now, now – it is Yahweh who speaks – come back to me with all your heart, fasting, weeping, mourning. Let your hearts be broken, not your garments torn, turn to Yahweh your God again, for he is all tenderness and compassion, slow to anger, rich in graciousness, and ready to relent. Who knows if he will not turn again, will not relent, will not leave a blessing as he passes, oblation and libation, for Yahweh your God?" (Joel 2:12-14.)

So what are the rabbis saying here? They are saying that this vengeful, wrathful, terrible god who has sent the plague of locusts (even though the Jews have followed the laws of the rabbis) is tender and compassionate as long as the Jews go into their act of "weeping and mourning," and (oh yes, by the way) as long as they leave a libation of wine and oil and an oblation of grain and meat for both god and priest to eat – then all will be well for the Jews, according to the rabbis who wrote those prophesies. That is, even though the locusts have eaten everything, be sure that the priests are well-fed.

But the alleged "prophecy" of Joel states that after the locusts leave, Yahweh says, "Never again shall I make you a thing of shame for the nations" (Joel 2:19). So, either the rabbi-prophet Joel is lying or the god of the Jews is lying, since his "promise" had already been broken countless times in the past and would be broken countless times in the future. The Jews have always been a thing of shame for all people, for it is a shame that the Jews are as evil and perfidious as they are to all other people worldwide. It is especially shameful that they are allowed to escape their just rewards.

Since the rabbis couldn't explain the locusts as just an ordinary phenomenon since they claimed that their almighty god was the cause of all events, and since they couldn't blame the locusts on the Jews as a punishment for sin, Yahweh apologized and said:

> "I will make up to you for the years devoured by grown locust and hopper, by shearer and young locust, my great army which I sent to invade you. You will eat to your heart's content, will eat your fill, and praise the name of Yahweh your God who has treated you so wonderfully." (Joel 2: 25-26.)

In modern terms, these sly rabbis would be called "spin doctors," or if you wish to use an older term, you can call these rabbis blatant liars and frauds.

So, in the first two chapters of Joel, we can see how the rabbis maintained their power over the superstitious Jews even in the face of an inexplicable plague of locusts. This improvisational aspect of Judaism whereby any deceit or trick is allowable as long as Judaism gains the upper hand, is a trade-mark of the rabbis.

The commentary in *The Jerusalem Bible* says, "… it is also possible that chapters 3-4 were added by another inspired author." This is rather amazing to me that the Christians so easily overlook the errors, inconsistencies and forger-ies of the Old Testament for the sake of blind belief by calling sly subterfuges and blatant Jewish lies by the name, "inspired."

The obvious difference between Joel 1-2 with Joel 3-4, is quite striking. It was probably written by a later author and added to Joel to make Joel a more powerful part of Jewish racist imperialism. Found in chapters 3 and 4, are the fire and thunder and dark days of apocalyptic destruction. All of this fire and brimstone of chapter 3 is written to get the mind of the Jews off of mere disas-ter by locust and back onto disaster by Yahweh. But this is just the warm-up.

Joel 4 is where the rabbinical finger points, not at the Jews, and not at Yahweh, but *at the non-Jewish people of the world*! The hatred of the Jews for all the nations on earth is once again revealed in chapter 4. Again, this was an embarrassing time for the rabbis. They had a plague of locusts to explain be-fore crowds of Jews who had followed all of the rabbinical laws and yet were still left without either their crops or an explanation. So, what can a pious and holy rabbi do in a situation like this? Lie? They already did that in the first two chapters. Blame the sins of the Jews? No, this was and would forever be a convenient ploy but it wouldn't work this time around. Blame somebody else? Of course! This would solve the rabbis' dilemma. By using all of the non-Jews of the world as their scapegoat, the rabbis could take away the puzzlement of the Jews and turn it into a self-righteous indignation, malice and hatred.

So, the rabbis wrote chapters 3 and 4 and added them to Joel. It is now explained that these locusts were no longer locusts but were really just a lesson from the Yahweh-god as to how the Jews should treat all of Mankind. And why should the Jews be like locusts, eating up the wealth and consuming the property of all of Mankind, you may ask? And the answer is, as revenge for the punishment that the Jews had received for their own sins! Now, I ask you, Dear Reader, is this logical? No. Is this fair to Mankind? No. But this is an example of demonic rabbinical thinking. Forgive the evils of the Jews and blame the rest of Mankind for the crimes of the Jews, so that the Jews can count themselves free of sin and holy and all other people wicked and damned. You've got to admit that these Semitic rabbis are clever devils to have devised such a lie. And the stupid Jews must believe the rabbis, or else the rabbis will kill them!

In these chapters, the rabbis claim that the Yahweh-god promises to pun-ish all the *goyim* on earth as revenge for what they did to the poor, innocent, Chosen Ones. In other words, even when the Jews are guilty of their crimes, they are really innocent, because their crimes are the fault of the Gentiles! All of their evil is forgotten, just as the Jews of today are always happy to forget their own sins and to blame their bad treatment on other people. So, here is a part of Jewish criminal pathology as found in the Book of Joel. The Jews have always treated other people with malicious hatred, because of such teachings that blame the Gentiles for all Jewish losses. Such teachings have created an entire Jewish culture of sociopaths and psychopaths, and some very dirty rats; a culture of Jews maliciously enthusiastic about betraying all of Mankind.

To take their minds off of the fact that the rabbis are powerless before a capricious and untrustworthy god who destroys the Jews on a whim, the rabbis point their accusing fingers at all other people and all nations on earth as being full of wickedness. Now, it is the people and the nations of the world that the god of the Jews wants to punish. And what is the crime of the non-Jewish Gentiles? Why, it's obvious what their crimes are! They aren't Jews, of course! What greater crime could there be? So, this demon god of Abraham's First National Bank and Pawn Shop will use his willing and malicious Jews to punish Mankind for the sin of not being Jewish.

Thus, a war cry is issued. In this case in Joel 4, the rabbis unify the Jews once again in their demonic goal of making war on the people of the entire earth. But it is not a blatant war of force, because the Jews are too few in number to go to war with the whole world. So, it is a sinister and secret war of treachery, treason, lies, fraud, subversion, secret murder, impoverishment, poisoning and starvation, all waged from a safe distance and from behind the scenes, hidden from within the safety of an illusion of religion of the mighty god of bankers and armies – and financed with the money that the Jews swindled from their victims!

Furthermore, this warfare on all the people on earth is described as a "holy" undertaking: "Sanctify the war!" (Joel 4:9.) In Joel, the monopoly on slavery by the Jews was sanctified before the fly- and maggot-infested altar of Yahweh. After all, the sins of the Jews, their Crimes Against Humanity, are totally forgotten (as usual) and only Yahweh's hatred for non-Jews is expressed. Yahweh and the Jews want vengeance for all of the woes that the Jews have suffered; for all of the thefts for which they have been caught and punished; for all of the murders for which the Jews have been caught and punished; for all of the insults and slanders that the Jews have meted out and received punishment in return. The god of the Jews wants revenge, never-ending revenge, because his holy criminals have been caught in their crimes! The Pharisee rabbis who wrote Joel wanted to exonerate the Jews from their crimes while convicting all of Mankind for not being born as innocent Jews!

These are the holy, chosen ones of God Almighty, Himself! They and their Sumerian Swindle of usury and banking are given to the whole world by the Yahweh-god of the moneylenders. Why should the Gentiles object to being swindled and robbed by such holy Jews? It is a gift of the very God of the Whole Universe for the Jews to steal from, defraud, betray and murder the non-Jews. They are this Demon's holiest servants, so they deserve it! Therefore, in the twisted Semitic logic of this religion of bankers and bandits, if they are caught in their crimes and punished by the Gentiles, then that is an insult to God. Therefore, the Jews must take revenge for being punished for their crimes – typical gangster mentality of hating the cops for stopping their crimes!

This was all music to the ears of those descendants of the *Apiru*, those old Hyksos cut-throats and bandits of the deserts. So, here by 400 BC, we see the Jews, believing in the prophetic power of the wet-ink prophets created by a lying, crafty and demonic priesthood of scribes and rabbis. The Jews were here beginning their long march of destruction and desolation among the peoples of the world, not by using the power of a god, but by using the power of the merchants and moneylenders – many little fleas sucking the blood of people greater than themselves.

In Joel 4:8, the god of the Jews allegedly says to the Gentiles:

"I am going to sell your sons and daughters into the hands of the sons of Judah, and they will sell them to the Sabaeans [the Arabs], to a distant nation: Yahweh has spoken." (Joel 4:8.)

And so, the religious sanction for the international slave trade that was a monopoly of the Sumerian Swindle throughout the ancient Near East is here revealed. This was not a slave trade that was only developed in ancient times, but has been a standard part of Judaism into modern times: both actual slavery and wage slavery, as well as the Jewish prostitution business.

In modern times, with the Jews controlling the gates of immigration, with the wholesale immigration of Muslim demons into the White nations of the globe, the nasty kikes of Yahweh use immigration to wage war. Among easily frightened and completely superstitious people that the Jews had become by this time, these words in the Book of Joel were the god-sanctioned permission to wage war on all people in the world and enslave them. From little lies great harm can come. But from giant lies of the rabbis, destruction and the Demon are visited upon all of Mankind. We can properly thank the Jews for all of this, along with the ones who provide the Jews with our money – the International Bankers and Financiers, every one a criminal and most every one a Jew.

Baruch ~ 200-100 BC

The Book of Baruch is not a part of the *Hebrew Bible*, but it is included in the Christian Bible. Why did the Jews not want to include this among their so-called "sacred" writings? And why would the Christians decide to include it in their own Old Testament? In the first place, Baruch may have been written as late as the 2nd or 1st century BC. So, Baruch would not be what it claims to be, which is a book written in Babylon during the Exile. It thus joins every book of the *Hebrew Bible* in not being what they claim it to be. But whatever its actual time of composition, its contents are what matter in this case.

The main reason why the Jews deleted Baruch from the *Hebrew Bible* is that it shows that the Jews in Babylon were really not the poor, pitiful slaves that the Jews have consistently claimed that they were. In fact, Baruch shows that they were really quite wealthy.

Claimed to have been written in 582 BC, *after only five years in Babylon*, Baruch shows that the Jews had ample amounts of gold and silver. They contributed enough money to send to Jerusalem to support "the priest Jehoiakim son of Hilkiah, son of Shallum, and the other priests, and for as many people as were with him in Jerusalem" (Baruch 1:7) as well as money "with which to pay for holocausts, offerings for sin, and incense" (Baruch 1:10). So, they were doing quite well in Babylon and elsewhere in the Middle East, since they could afford to do all of these things. After all, Judaism was then, as it is today, an international criminal conspiracy. The members of Abraham's First National Bank and Pawn Shop were well-entrenched wherever silver and gold changed hands for commerce. So, when the Exiles reached Babylon, they were greeted by their fellow Jews, who were already in control of the commerce of the entire ancient Near East.

But mainly, the Jews did not include Baruch in their Old Testament for four reasons. Firstly, Baruch shows one of the secret methods that the Jews use in destroying nations. I call it the "tick behind the ear technique" and it is still in use to this very day. Just as a tick cannot live on a cat or dog unless it lodges itself behind the ear or on the neck where the teeth and claws of the unfortunate critter cannot dislodge it, so too are the Jews adept at lodging themselves behind the leader of a targeted group. By first befriending and then attaching themselves to kings, presidents, chairmen of the board, mayors, and leaders in every segment of society, the Jews have learned how to manipulate entire organizations and entire countries merely by manipulating the leaders of those organizations and countries. By standing behind men of influence and power, the Jews cannot be easily dislodged by those whom they swindle and betray because they have the protection of the man in power. By being able to manipulate these powerful men, the Jews are able to manipulate entire societies. Thus, do I call this Jewish method, the "tick behind the ear technique."

The Book of Baruch shows this technique which begins with flattery and praise for their victim. Although they were kept in Babylon, Baruch says,

> "Pray for the long life of Nebuchadnezzar king of Babylon, and
> of his son Belshazzar, and that their days on earth may endure as
> the heavens; pray that the Lord may give us strength and clear
> understanding so that we may lead our lives under the protection
> of Nebuchadnezzar king of Babylon and of his son Belshazzar,
> and by our long service win their favor." (Baruch 1:11-12.)

What is revealed here is an example of "sucking blood from the neck." The Jews try at every opportunity to seduce the leaders of nations. By controlling the leader, the Jews can rule entire nations. Not only is this method revealed in Baruch, but the fact is that after only five years in Babylon, the Jews were prosperous and protected by Nebuchadnezzar. In this, their international monopoly of silver bullion played a major part in Nebuchadnezzar's kindness toward these scheming Jewish moneylenders.

The second reason the Jews didn't include Baruch in the *Hebrew Bible* is because it demonstrates that, even though they were separated from Jerusalem and the Temple, it was the exiled priests in Babylon who still maintained control of the priests in Jerusalem and supported them financially. It was important to suppress the Book of Baruch, because it reveals the power structure and the cooperation among the rabbis over long distances and across countries.

Third, Baruch reveals the revenge-motive of the Jews. While hypocritically praying for Nebuchadnezzar's well-being, they were plotting his demise.

> "Your enemy has persecuted you, but soon you will witness his destruction and set your foot on his neck." (Baruch 4:25.)

Fourth, the method that the rabbis used for legitimizing their swindles is revealed. Speaking about the Babylonian priests, Baruch states:

> "Whatever is sacrificed to them, the priests resell and pocket the profit; while their wives salt down part of it, but give nothing to the poor or to the helpless." (Baruch 6:27.)

Giving a small percentage of Temple profits to the poor is an ancient scam that has allowed the rabbis to pocket the greater share for themselves while appearing to be kindly and generous. That Baruch accused the Babylonian priests of exactly what the rabbis and their wives were also guilty of, was not something that the rabbis, priests and scribes wanted to advertise. Baruch was left out of the *Hebrew Bible* so that they would appear to be what they were not – generous and virtuous. Besides all of the above, the Book of Baruch is a lot of Jewish whining and crying, with little else to commend it.

So, why would the Christians want Baruch included in the Old Testament? For two reasons: One, it shows the sinful ignorance of the Jews in their refusal to do good and, two, it demonstrates (although it does so fraudulently) of how God promised to return the Jews to Jerusalem. Even though the verses in Baruch 3:9-5:9 were written long after the Jews returned, the fact that it was written by a lying Jew and proclaimed to be a "wondrous prophesy fulfilled" seemed good enough for the gullible Christians. So, the Christians put Baruch in their Bible as "the gospel truth," once again proving that the Christians do not believe Jesus, they believe the lying Jews instead.

Daniel 167-164 BC

It is difficult to determine which books in the *Hebrew Bible* are the most fraudulent, since they all clamor for that distinction in various ways. Certainly, the Book of Daniel can be rated among the top contenders.

In Ugarit, the clay tablets containing the "Tale of Aqhat" were unearthed in 1930-31 by French archaeologists. These tablets tell of an Ugaritic man named Daniel and a youth named Aqhat, and can be accurately dated to the second quarter of the 14th century BC. "Daniel" means "El judges" or "God judges." One of the great fraudulent heroes of the Jews is a fictional character named after a Canaanite god, *El*.

The verses in the Book of Daniel (4:28-33) that attribute to Nebuchadnezzar a period of madness are clearly a corruption of the stories about Nabonidus. Indeed, a fragment from the recently discovered Qumran scrolls shows that other Jewish traditions assigned Nabonidus' long sojourn in the desert to the correct Babylonian king, ascribing to him a seven-year illness brought on by divine wrath. But as I demonstrated in Volume One, Nabu-Na'id (Nabonidus) stayed in the desert of Northern Arabia mainly out of religious conviction and as a way to avoid the power of the Babylonian priests.

The Book of Daniel is written in two languages, Hebrew and Aramaic. The reason for this is twofold. First, by writing the introduction to the book in Hebrew, the root language of the story is established as a Hebrew story about Hebrews. But most of the story is written in Aramaic, which was the international language of business from Egypt to Persia and throughout the entire ancient Near East. Anywhere there were silver shekels to be made, were found the Aramaic-speaking Jewish merchants and moneylenders.

At that time, the common Jews did not speak or understand Hebrew. They only spoke Aramaic. So, the priests showed off their learning by beginning the story in a language that the common people would have to ask them to translate, and then continuing the bulk of the story in a language that they all understood. By having the Jews come to the rabbis to ask what the beginning portion in Hebrew meant, the rabbis had an opportunity to verbally and secretly impress upon the Judeans the importance of repeating these fabrications in the Book of Daniel to the Greeks, the Babylonians, and any other non-Jews that they could. In this way, the gullible non-Jews would stand in awe of the Jews and give them political and business positions and other advantages. "Prestige" was a valuable robe that every Jew could wear simply by telling the lies found in the *Hebrew Bible* and claiming to be a "Chosen One of God."

The Book of Daniel was directed to all of the Jewish communities in the Middle East, all of whom spoke Aramaic. When such a story of a super-Jew like Daniel is repeated by thousands of Jews to the trusting and gullible peoples of the Middle East, there is certainly wealth and social advantage to be gained. When it was repeated to the Greeks, who were the ruling power at that time, there could be no doubt that many Greeks of high social and political standing would want Jews to delve into their dreams and advise them about the future. While delving, the Jew could learn about business dealings, political connections and blackmail possibilities admitted to every dream wizard.

One of the most interesting things about the Book of Daniel is that the Christians *know for a certainty* that it's a work of fiction and yet they accept it as "inspired," "Biblical" and "godly." The Jewish rabbis know that it comes from their many lies and fairy tales about Yahweh, but they include it in their "holy book" because the Book of Daniel furthers the aim of the rabbis. Those aims are total power and complete domination of the world, with themselves as the ultimate beneficiaries. And of course, the Muslims believe the Book of Daniel is genuine, but they don't read it, so they don't know what it says, which leaves them free to make up their own stories about it. These are the three major Semite-based religions of the world, all telling you "the Truth" based on their own lies and ignorance!

The Book of Daniel was written between 167 and 164 BC, when Alexander's Greeks had full military and political control of the entire Middle East. Also by this date, Judaism was a fully developed subversive, criminal hoax, with agents operating out of every synagogue in nearly every country. Daniel pretends to have been written during the Babylonian Captivity 200 years previously, but for it to have been written then is an impossibility. But when confronted with the proofs of their lies, the Jewish rabbis can always say that even though it looks like it never happened according to history and according to all evidence, it *did* in fact happen because, first, the rabbis *said* that it happened and, second, it was *a miracle* – and who can explain a miracle? No matter what kind of proof stands against them for being actual lies, the rabbis argue that the stories found in the Book of Daniel are true accounts of miracles, which happen against all human understanding. These are the "wise" rabbis. Such liars!

That many of the statements in Daniel did not correspond with known and provable historical events didn't matter to the rabbis who wrote those fables, because they believed that no one would be able to catch them in their lies. Belshazzar was the son of Nabonidus and not as the book says, of Nebuchadnezzar, nor was he ever king. Darius the Mede is unknown to historians, nor is there room for him between the last Chaldean king and Cyrus the Persian, who had already conquered the Medes. The Neo-Babylonian background is described in words of Persian origin; the instruments in Nebuchadnezzar's orchestra are given names translated from the Greek. The dates given in the book agree neither among themselves nor with history, and they seem to have been placed at the chapter heads without much care for chronology. All in all, Daniel is another Jewish hoax.

Knowing this, the commentators on the "history" of Daniel jump to the very same false conclusion that most other Christian believers have jumped to over the past 2,000 years. By not understanding that all Jews are liars, the Christians have been fooled into believing that the Old Testament is the "word of God." So, the Christians end up believing the most incredible Jewish cons. But if we look at what was happening in Palestine during the years when Daniel was written, then it is very easy to see why the Book of Daniel was written in the first place.

At that time, the Greek Ptolemies and Seleucids held sway over the Middle East. These generals from the armies of Alexander the Great were spreading Greek arts, sciences, philosophies, religion and Greek Culture wherever they ruled. All of this was a very powerful challenge to the rabbis. After all, the Greeks asked for human logic, reason and truth in their dealings with men and with gods. But the rabbis demanded blind obedience and fanatical belief in the stories, fables, myths and lies that they taught. By Jewish law, any Jew who questioned the word of a rabbi could be stoned to death. The sheer terror that the rabbis, scribes and priests inflicted over their ignorant and superstitious Jews was directly challenged by this new learning of Greek logic and philosophical inquiry. Truth and logic were concepts alien to the lying *abracadabra* of the Semites. The rabbis did not dare to tell the truth, otherwise the entire structure of Judaism would collapse.

What could the rabbis offer the Jews in the face of Greek superiority? The Greek armies had wiped out the Jewish opposition quite easily. The Greek athletes walked about in well-muscled beauty that was derived from their gymnasium and sports field workouts, wrestling, foot races, boxing, etc. The Greek philosophers could defeat every rabbi in logic, philosophy and wisdom to an embarrassing degree. Aristotelian thought enabled the Greeks to invent great machines, ships, buildings and explanations of physical and metaphysical phenomena.

What did the flabby, fat, bearded, stinking, lice-infested and superstitious Jewish priests and rabbis, surrounded by clouds of flies, have that could compare with or excel the gifts of Greek civilization? Actually, they had nothing at all that was superior, except for one thing: their Semitic ability to lie and deceive on a grand scale. And so, the evil genius of the Jewish rabbis was pooled to produce the fake and fraudulent Book of Daniel.

In this book, they present Daniel as a perfect Jew, without blemish, of good appearance, true to Jewish kosher food laws and Jewish traditions, trained in all wisdom and quick to learn. In other words, Daniel and his buddies (Shadrach, Meshak and Abednego) were Super Jews. According to the story, they were trained by the Babylonians as scribes, translators, archivists, scholars, astrologers and for other important duties in the Babylonian civil services. These were the usual easy and high-paid jobs that Jews relish in positions where they can gather information on lucrative business opportunities and spy upon their employers.

Not only were Daniel and the other Super Jews allegedly in better health than the boys who ate pagan food, but as a reward for staying kosher (eating food that the rabbis had "blessed" by charging everybody a special stamp tax),

> "God favored these four boys with knowledge and an intelligence in everything connected with literature, and in wisdom; while Daniel had the gift of interpreting every kind of vision and dream." (Daniel 1:17.)

So, the lying rabbis taught that these Jews could surpass the Greeks in "knowledge." And of course, "knowledge" is defined by the stinking rabbis as the "Torah." The Super Jews were intelligent in "everything connected with literature." Of course, the fly-speckled rabbis defined "literature" as "Torah." And when the Jews study the lies of the Torah, they get "wisdom." Calling

themselves "scholars," the deceiving rabbis can certainly make up any definition that suits their purposes. Right?

We should also look carefully at this Jewish fondness for using their
"special, holy, Jewish gift" in wanting to interpret other peoples' dreams, because it is an ancient swindle that the Jews still practice in modern times under
the auspices of psychology.

The rabbis took their clue from the earlier Jewish lies of Joseph interpreting Pharaoh's dream. They knew that dreams sometimes have meanings and
that whoever could put himself into the position of interpreting the dreams of
kings or important officials, could influence the destinies of entire nations
merely by "capturing the gates" to the king's mind. In addition, anyone who
could interpret dreams was considered to have the spirit of God inside of him.
Thus, the powers that he was *believed* to have, could open doors of wealth and
influence. Oy! Wealth and influence! The dreams of every Jew! Thus, it has
always been the goal of the Jews to put themselves into such a position as
dream interpreters or seers. Pompously advertising themselves as "very wise,"
the rabbis themselves did not have any political power, but the kings whose
dreams they could interpret *with Jewish interpretations* had power. So, the
rabbis endeavored to place themselves at the forefront, as physicians, sorcerers, wizards, seers and witches: as unrivaled dream interpreters. If there happened to be any sorcerers, wizards, seers or witches who actually did have a
skill in dream interpretation, the rabbis merely had them stoned, burned or
murdered on the highways so as to keep the field as their own monopoly. They
were commanded to do so by their Yahweh-god. The murder of a non-Jew by
a Jew was counted as a "pious" deed.

As an antidote to the superior knowledge, martial and athletic skills of
the Greeks, and as a way of getting themselves hired as "dream interpreters,"
the rabbis invented this Super Jew, Daniel, whom Nebuchadnezzar found to be
"ten times better than all the magicians and enchanters of his entire kingdom"
(Daniel 1:20). The rabbis state that Daniel stayed with Nebuchadnezzar until
the first years of King Cyrus, which was impossible since Nebuchadnezzar
(605-562 BC) was long dead by the time Cyrus (538-530 BC) entered Babylon
with Jews opening the gates for him.

Although the Book of Daniel was directed toward the Jews in general, it
was written for the young Jewish boys in particular. For their part, the Jewish
children could see how beautiful the Greek youths were; how healthy and
strong; how logical and clear they were in their reasoning and how elegant
they were in their speech. All of the beautiful sculptures, buildings and science
of the Greeks were attractive to these Jewish boys, as well as to the more intelligent of the Jewish administrators and scholars. All of this was a direct threat
to the power of the lying, demon rabbis. Whatever was a threat to their power
and wealth, was deemed by them to be "evil" and an "anathema," as opposed
to what they considered to be the only real and genuine good – namely, themselves, preaching the Lies of Moses.

So, the rabbis resorted to their oldest and most successful ploy and the greatest power of the Jews – they lied. The rabbis had attained total power over the Jews. They considered themselves to be not only holier and higher than the angels, they believed that as the image of God, they could create events merely by opening their mouths and saying whatever they pleased. They could curse enemies, bring forth demons, give blessings and interpret the laws of their mythical Moses in any way that they wanted. So, for the rabbis and priests to fabricate another "holy" text was no great feat, especially since so many of the books in their *Hebrew Bible* were cobbled together by them according to their political, religious and monetary needs. For these rabbis, if God could create reality merely by speaking it into creation, then they could do the same as God did. As long as no one knew that they were inventing their lies from empty air, then there could be no proof that they were telling lies. Without proof that they were liars, then the people would have to believe them.

In Semitic culture and reasoning, "intelligence" is less important than "craftiness." Fooling someone with clever lies is considered by the Semites (both Hebrews and Arabs) to be a wondrous power. If those lies are used to further one's own ends, and those ends are claimed to be in the service of God, then the wicked rabbis believed that their lying deceitfulness and treasonous betrayals of truth was a holy power. Don't you know? Jewish lies are *almost* the power of God, they are so clever! Telling wondrous tales of past events, even if the tales are lies, makes them true, because no one can prove that they are false! Telling lies while destroying all opposing proof makes the lies true. If no one can prove that they are false, then of course they have to be true. Right? And since the fables happened in the past, and the past is over with forever, then the fables are true and that's that and that's the end of the story. How can you be so stupid not to trust and believe a Holy Chosen One of God?

The rabbis around 167 BC desperately needed to deny and denigrate the teachings of the Greek philosophers and reemphasize their own traditions. The same methods that they had used to undermine Nebuchadnezzar and the Babylonians were subtly taught to the Jewish youths through the Book of Daniel. This teaching was basically that if youths adhered to the lies of the rabbis, they would become Super Jews who could foretell the future, interpret dreams, become immune to fire and wild animals, and attain vast wealth and power over the world and its occupants. Who needed truth, logic, philosophy, medicine and science from the Greeks when, by being a follower of the Traditions of the Elders and a student of the rabbis, the youths of Judah could become Super Jews like Daniel, Shadrach, Meshach and Abednigoh? They could have the whole world simply by lying and deceiving.

Thus, the rabbis taught that the four, Super Jew boys – Daniel, Hananiah, Mishael, and Azariah – were so kosher, so smart, so wise and "ten times better than all the magicians and enchanters" (Daniel 1:20), that Nebuchadnezzar made them members of his royal court.

This is the first principle of Jewish Power that the rabbis revealed in the Book of Daniel to their little *kikenvermin*; a lesson learned through long centuries of selling spices, pearls and little knickknacks. *The first step in attaining power over other people is to gain access to the rulers and the administrators of that people.* If the rulers can be controlled by the Jews, then the entire people can be controlled through those Jewish-corrupted leaders. It is similar to controlling a horse. A horse is very much stronger than a man. But if you can get control of its head, the strong body will go wherever the weak head looks. A horseman controls the head of a horse through the bit and bridle. A Jew controls the head of a people through bribes, blackmail, and sexual entrapment of the leaders. As the nations of the West have learned to our woe, when Jews are in government, it matters not who the elected official is or who the dictator is because behind the scenes, it is the Jew who pulls the strings and controls the head of, and the leader of, the betrayed people.

Now, one of the methods for controlling the leader of a country, obviously, is to control his very mind. The unique sorcery of the Jewish rabbis, in this area, has been to boast and brag about their powers of interpreting dreams. To do this, it is not necessary to accurately be able to interpret. All that is necessary is to *claim* that you are the greatest expert in dream interpretation and to be able to convince the victim that your interpretation is the correct one. This is where spies and gossip-mongers have served the Jews so well over the centuries in gathering advanced intelligence and tidbits of personal knowledge. To know the intimate details of the victim's life, which he doesn't know that you know, and to be able to weave these into the fabric of the alleged "interpretation" of his dream, has led many seekers of knowledge to their doom and sorrow at the hands of Jewish interpreters of dreams. This Jewish swindle was used many times in Biblical literature such as between Joseph and Pharaoh or between Daniel and Nebuchadnezzar or 2,000 years later between the Jew, Sigmund Freud, and the non-Jewish fools of Europe and America.

The Book of Daniel isn't a book of history, it is a book of Jewish propaganda teaching the lessons of subversion to the Jewish youths. Not only is the super-Jew, Daniel, able to interpret dreams because he is so smart, but he is even able to interpret dreams *before* the dream is even told to him! Rather than understanding that this is a work of fictional fantasy, the Book of Daniel has been passed down as "inspired scripture" to 2,200 years of gullible readers. That is, the Book was accepted by the gullible readers or else those who did not believe these fables were hauled before the Jewish priests and either stoned to death, strangled, decapitated or had molten lead poured down their throats. These were the "permitted" methods of execution for anyone who did not believe the rabbis or the lies that they published. Thus, over the centuries the rabbis weeded out the intelligent Hebrews by killing them and allowed to live the most devoutly gullible and fanatical of the Jews under their control.

When the Book of Daniel was first read to the Jews in Jerusalem, you can rest assured that the priests, scribes and Pharisee rabbis made a big show of it. After all, it was the operational instructions for all Jews in their assault upon Greek Culture. The usual sacrifices were made; innocent animal blood was poured out and sprinkled on the reeking altar of Yahweh among the swarms of buzzing flies and the incantations of the priests.

However, by this time there were two classes of Jews in Jerusalem. These two classes of Jews have been a secret part of Judaism since their return from Babylon. These I call the inner-door Jews (the Big Jews) and the outer-door Jews (the Little Jews).

The Big Jews were directly descended from the original Jews who returned to Jerusalem with Ezra and his wizards. They were a closed clique who had their family-related stories about their years in Babylon. They were all members of a socially elite group of priests and their lackeys, who controlled most of the religious, political and mercantile enterprises in and around Judah. They all spoke Aramaic as well as Hebrew. But the Jews who still lived in Mesopotamia spoke Aramaic.

The Little Jews were composed of the ones who had remained in Judah, the poor and uneducated as well as the petty officials and farmers. These were the outer-door Jews who could only hope to enter the ranks of the exclusive ruling inner-door Jews through marriage. These spoke only Aramaic and actually worked for a living.

Thus, the Book of Daniel was read to all of the Jews throughout the Middle East, all of whom spoke Aramaic. Daniel was their refresher course in international intrigue. It should be noted how the instructions in Daniel are for the Jews to use "shrewd and cautious words" (Daniel 2:14) when they speak to foreign superior officials. And when selling their line of deceit to kings such as Nebuchadnezzar, they are to emphasize their own sham humility before the magnificent, egotistical self-interest of the kings and officials that they are attempting to deceive.

Daniel pretends to be the perfect servant as he says to Nebuchadnezzar,

> "This mystery was revealed to me, not that I am wiser than any other man, but for this sole purpose: that the king should learn what it means, and that you should understand your inmost thoughts" (Daniel 2:30).

Of course, there is no mention that the dream interpreter would *also* know the king's innermost thoughts. And how great an advantage it is for anyone, especially if they have the ability to act on this knowledge, to understand the innermost thoughts of a king, a president or a dictator! Learning the innermost thoughts of the leaders of the country has been a prime goal of Jews and Judaism to this very day. How else can this organized criminal conspiracy commit perfect treason and lead nations to ruin?

Even in modern times, the Jews always claim to be totally self-effacing and to be interested only in the welfare of the non-Jews. But this Jewish "kindness" is like the farmer who is kind to his cows and sheep for many years with the sole aim to kill them and eat them or sell them for money. The Jews consider non-Jews to be no better than cattle. This is what "goyim" means, "non-

Jews, lowly insects, stupid cattle." They brag about it in their own writings, but they lie about it when confronted with these same writings.

The interpretation that is given in Daniel 2 of the king's dream was the outer-door teaching. The idea was to further convince the ordinary Jews and converts of the foresight and power of the Jewish prophets. That Daniel was written 400 years after the fake prophecy was not something that the perfidious rabbis desired to publish. Their goal, as always, was obedience and worship from their Jews. For the ordinary Jews, the Book of Daniel showed that Daniel's prophetic power was given to him by the mighty Yahweh-god. So, for these stupid Jews, the interpretation of Nebuchadnezzar's dream seemed both accurate and inspiring. It gave the illusion of accuracy because it spoke of the four kingdoms since the time of Nebuchadnezzar as if these had been predicted in advance. Babylon was the head of gold, Medes was the chest and arms of silver, Persia was the belly and thighs of bronze and Greece was the legs of iron with feet part iron and part earthenware.

Thus, the Little Jews (proselytes and mamzers) were taught that these allegories were meant to represent the kingdoms that had controlled the Middle East up until the time of 167 BC. For the outer-door Jews, it was enough to be told that these kingdoms were all doomed before the rock of Judaism, which would shatter them and become a kingdom that would last forever. Thus, by naming real kingdoms that had appeared and disappeared in history, followed by the appearance of Greece in their own time and then by the promise of an eternal Israel, the common Jews were once again deceived by the rabbis into becoming martyrs and soldiers of the Big Jews, a wicked and demented class of Jewish merchants, bankers, rabbis and priests. The Little Jews were filled with renewed belief in the power of their god and in the foresight and wisdom of his prophets who could "see into the future" by simply backdating all of their stories. With this kind of belief, the threat to the rabbis offered by Greek philosophy and logic was thwarted while their own power was increased. And it was all done with the Big Lie Technique that they had been honing for over a thousand years. But this was only one level of rabbinical strategy and devil-craft in the Book of Daniel.

The rabbis had cultivated the idea that they were powerful, wise, knowledgeable and privy to the secrets of God. This reputation kept the superstitious Jews fearful, obedient and prompt with the daily offerings of meat, vegetables and wine and the choicest gifts for the Temple and its ravenous rabbis. The Book of Daniel was written by the rabbis to promote this perpetually unmerited, but profitable, worship.

The inner-door secret to this tale in Daniel was simply that the four metals represented a single kingdom composed of four castes. At the top, made of gold, was the king (with a priest whispering in his ear). The arms and chest of silver represented the administrators, soldiers, guards and police, who were the arms of the priests. The belly and thighs of bronze represented the merchants. And the legs of iron represented the laborers and farmers. It is these laborers and farmers upon whom the entire society depends, just as the legs of a man carry his whole body. But the legs have feet partly of iron and partly of earthenware and they represent the basic laborer and the family unit, the father and the mother. These feet are the foundations of every nation and every people. The family unit and the masses of workers are what support the entire society. If the laborers of a nation are shattered and destroyed or if the families of a nation are shattered and destroyed, then that nation will fall into the dust. And even a small stone – just a few Jews (controlling the gates) – could destroy a *goyim* family (lowly insects, stupid cattle). And *just a few Jews* could destroy the labor power of a nation and the entire nation would come crashing down – workers, farmers, merchants, police, guards, soldiers, administrators, king, everybody except the Jews. As the families of the non-Jews were smashed, as the laboring masses of a nation were smashed, more Jews could move in and soon, out of the rubble of destroyed families and workers, the Jews could grow into a mighty mountain. The Jews are commanded by their demon-god to be destroyers; many must suffer and die so that the Jews may live in luxury, eating food they did not grow, living in houses they did not build – predatory, bloodthirsty, parasites, killing the host and feeding off of its remains while avoiding detection through the mimicry of religious poses and pious posturing.

The feet, the foundation, the workers, the family unit – these were the weakest part of the mighty statue of Nebuchadnezzar's dream. The rock that shattered these brittle feet and caused the entire statue to fall into dust was the rock of the Jews and their demon religion of merchants and moneylenders. Furthermore, it was only a small stone when it shattered the statue's feet. After the statue crumbled into dust, the stone grew into the mighty mountain of demonic Judaism, sucking up the wealth and life force of a destroyed society, like a poison mushroom grows from the debris of fallen trees in a forest.

And so, the secret teaching that was passed along to the administrators of Judah was that in order to destroy their enemies, they would have to attack the feet with all of their puny power. Certainly, going after the gold and silver and bronze was to be striven after, since all levels of society were to be the target of the Jews in their future assaults upon Mankind. But the feet, the underpinnings of any nation, could be attacked and shattered and not by any great force but merely by a small stone, a small number of Jews grouped together in collusion. Once the non-Jewish people (the lowly insects, stupid cattle) were reduced to chaos and rubble, then a small number of Jews could grow through high birth rates and the immigration of foreign Jews. And together, they could suck up the fallen wealth and grow into a mighty mountain to last forever! This is what the rabbis taught to the Jews in secret as the meaning in the Book of Daniel

Any nation that loses the loyalty and efforts of its laboring class, will soon crumble into ruin. Any nation whose farmers become disenfranchised from the land, who become overburdened with taxes and confiscations, whose labors become excessive, those nations will die. And so, it has been the primary objective of the Jews to gain control of the leadership so as to be able to destroy the little people of a non-Jewish nation first, to create hardship, pov-

erty, disease, taxation, broken families, alcoholism, debauchery and hopeless-
ness among the lower classes. Then, the Jews can pick up the pieces and grow
wealthy and strong from the chaos that they create. First, through dispossession of the people and, once the people are too hungry and poor to resist, then
through extinction, can the evil worshipers of the God of Genocide grow into a
"mighty mountain."

2,300 years later, these same secret teachings from the rabbis' demonic
soul reached their final fulfillment when the Jews invented Communism and
murdered 100 million non-Jews worldwide. And you can see these same
teachings being applied in modern Europe, the USA and Australia by these
same Jews – the People dying, impoverished, dispossessed and tilting towards
extinction while the Jewish bankers and financiers grow ever fatter (See Volume III: *The Bloodsuckers of Judah*).

For the ordinary Jew, it was enough for him to read in Daniel 2 that Nebuchadnezzar, the king of kings, was so amazed with the Super Jew Daniel that
he "fell prostrate before Daniel" and gave him riches of the whole province of
Babylon and made him head of all the sages of Babylon. (Daniel 2:46-49).
This was certainly enough to make any Jew's heart glad; to have kings bow at
his feet and give him wealth and power. And what did the Jews have to do to
gain all of this? Why, simply to follow the teachings and orders of the "holy
and wise" rabbis! These same lying rabbis, however, "forgot" to mention that
the Jews of Babylonia had "riches and governorships" in Babylonia, not because of their "wisdom," but because of their betrayal of the Babylonians to
the Persians. It was not Nebuchadnezzar, the same Babylonian king who had
destroyed Jerusalem and shipped them off to Babylon, who gave them riches. It
was Cyrus the Persian who rewarded them for their treason against Babylonia.

It is here in the Book of Daniel that the rabbis covered their tracks, wiped
off their fingerprints, and with their lying *abracadabra* protected their treasonous fellow Jews in Babylon. The Jews of Babylon had gained their various
official positions as a result of their betrayal of Babylonia to Persian king Cyrus. Any Babylonian who objected to their rule was either executed or murdered or his children were kidnapped and sold into slavery. So, the rabbis hid
all of these crimes by having the fictional hero, Daniel, for his "great wisdom
and service" to the Babylonian king, gain the administration of Babylon's
provinces. In league with the three Jew-boys who did a Jewish name-change
from Jewish-names to the Babylonian names of Shadrach, Meshach and
Abednego.

Thus, if the peoples of the ancient world in 167 BC, whether Greeks or
Babylonians, were to ask, "Why is it that there are so many Jews controlling
the affairs of Babylonia?" then the Jews could point to the "great prophet"
Daniel and say, "It is our reward for being so wise and holy." And why not?
The cuneiform tablets were purposely destroyed or buried under rubble. After
four hundred years, if the rabbis claimed that the Jews controlled Babylonia
through "wisdom" rather than through treachery, then who would know that
they were lying? No one could possibly know Archaeology was another two

millennia away. And the "word of the Jews" was the only "history" that any-one could depend upon.

Once you understand the historical background to the Book of Daniel, the reason that the rabbis wrote it and the lessons that they were teachings their Jews, then the Book of Daniel takes on a rather shoddy appearance. In Daniel 3, the rabbis show Shadrach, Meshach and Abednego, trusting in their Jewish god and being thrown into the fiery furnace. But being protected by an angel, they walk out unharmed. Then, the rabbis convert Nebuchadnezzar to Judaism, and have him say, so that the Greeks would know who they were dealing with,

> "Blessed be the god [of the Jews] …he has sent his angel to res-cue his servants who, putting their trust in him, defied the order of the king, and preferred to forfeit their bodies rather than serve or worship any god but their own. I therefore decree as follows: Men of all peoples, nations and languages! Let anyone speak disrespectfully of the God [of the Jews] and I will have him torn limb from limb and his house razed to the ground, for there is no other god who can save like this! Then the king showered favors on Shadrach, Meshach and Abednego in the province of Babylon." (Daniel 3:28-30.)

It has been a never-ending desire of the Jews in all ages to have the gov-ernment pass laws giving them the right to lie and deceive the people. From the most ancient times, this was Secret Fraud #17 of the Sumerian Swindle: "Kings are required to legitimatize a swindle, but once the fraud is legalized, those very kings must be sacrificed." The Laws of Hammurabi did this with the *tamkarum* (merchant-moneylenders). The Laws of Moses did this for the rabbis. And here, the lying rabbis claimed that Nebuchadnezzar passed such laws to protect the Jews from any Greeks who laughed at their fables. And in 167 BC, there were plenty of Greeks laughing at the ridiculous Jews and their fables.

With such insane desires to "legalize" their perfidious crimes, who knows whether maybe someday in the future, the governments of the world will be bribed by the Jews into making it a crime to question the lies of the Holocaust or a crime to question why the 9/11 attacks on America, an event where only non-Jews died and where only Jews controlled all the gates of ac-cess and information? Or under such rabbinical deceit, ludicrous laws might be passed making it a hate crime to "speak disrespectfully of the Jews." But no, I must be too engrossed with these ancient swindles. None of this ancient history could possibly ever be repeated today in modern times. Modern people are too intelligent to be deceived by such blatant lies of the Jews, where only Jews are doing the talking. Right? Surely, the Jews have improved on the ways that they practice their ancient religion. Now, in modern times, surely the Jews have turned into good people at long last. One can only hope. But such hopes are in vain for the World's Oldest Organized Criminal Conspiracy of Jewish demons.

Anyway, Daniel was potent propaganda among a people who had no way of verifying the lies that the rabbis wrote. When Daniel was written, Nebuchadnezzar had already been dead for over 400 years and the Babylonian Empire had been buried in the dust of Iraq, leaving Jews to give their "Jewish Loyalty" first to the Persians and then to the Greeks, while betraying both.

Further in Daniel 4, the god of the Jews makes Nebuchadnezzar go mad for seven years until he admits that the god of the Jews is the Most High God and the King of Heaven. Modern archaeology shows that there is no record of this happening in the archives of the Babylonians. The people of those days could only trust the lying words of the Jews since the Babylonian archives were buried under tons of rubble. That the rabbis could tell lies that could not be disproved gave them an evil power that is still among us to this day wherever Jews and rabbis are found. So, who was alive in 167 BC Jerusalem, who could claim that the rabbis' stories were false? The archives of Babylon and Assyria were waiting silently for the spades and whisk brooms of modern archaeologists. *Lies that are not opposed and disproved, remain standing and masquerading as "truth."* Thus, for over 2,000 years have the people of the world been deceived by the Jews.

The Book of Daniel is also incorrect in its enumeration of the Babylonian kings. That the rabbis would make such a mistake reflects their supreme confidence that the cities and archives of Babylon were forever destroyed, so they were free to tell whatever lies would benefit themselves and their religious swindle. The Book of Daniel says that Belshazzar was the son of Nebuchadnezzar, but he was actually the son of Nabonidus; and he was never a king of Babylon. Daniel claims that someone named Darius the Mede became king of Babylon, but this was not true, since such a king never existed. These were details unknown to the Jews, but it didn't matter for the purposes of their fabulous fairy tales in the Book of Daniel. Who could naysay the lying rabbis?

After the conquests of Alexander, the Greeks had full control of the entire Middle East and Egypt. Greek writing, philosophy and culture were dominant everywhere. The reason for writing Daniel was to encourage the Jews to resist Hellenization even unto death and torture. So, they used the long-dead and unverifiable kings of Babylon as their foils in order to "prove" the superiority of Yahweh to all other gods. They wanted to teach the Jews that as a reward for their diligence, they could receive high position, wealth and power in the royal courts of their enemies. Daniel is a book not only of subterfuge, but also of subversion.

According to the rabbis, super-Jews like Daniel and his three buddies are protected from fiery furnaces and a den of lions, because they are virtuous and clever. So, they always get rich rewards and have kings bowing at their feet. Of course, as befits the followers of the God of Vengeance, all of Daniel's accusers always meet a gruesome and vengeful end. Thus, the dreams of every Jew are realized in Daniel – wealth, prestige, power and vengeance. All they have to do to get all of this is follow the teachings of the rabbis. How convenient for the rabbis!

After the kings such as Nebuchadnezzar, Belshazzar and Darius realize that the god of the Jews is the top god, the rabbis have them decree to all the peoples of the world that "in every kingdom of my empire let all tremble with fear before the god [of the Jews]" (Daniel 6:26). Thus, the Book of Daniel became an excellent propaganda piece and psychological warfare tool for the rabbis to shove under the noses of the Greeks, puff themselves up with theatrical pride and fake "prestige," and get what they wanted.

Remember, the ancient peoples very much believed in the gods. Religion was a very large part of their social investment of time and property. So, for the Greeks to be faced with what appeared to be an ancient document telling wondrous tales of the Jewish god making toys out of the great empires and kings of antiquity, was serious. Could they really afford to push around the Jews and then be visited with hailstorms, earthquakes, famine, plague, blindness, locusts and myriad other disasters? Should the Greeks take the cautious approach and do what the Jews wanted; make the Jewish rabbis happy with gifts and special privileges? These were questions of great state importance and national security. Although laughable to us in modern times, these were extremely serious questions to the ancient peoples. And these were questions that the rabbis were only too willing to help the Greek kings decide with their self-proclaimed skills at dream evaluation, sorcery and medical quackery.

Daniel 8-12 revert to the Hebrew language and use the recent history of Judah, written in the prophetic future tense, so as to deceive the Jews and make them believe in the power and wisdom of their god, their prophets and, most importantly, their rabbis. Writing in Daniel 9, they were able to "substantiate" that the rabbi-written prophesy of Jeremiah was not a fake, but was really true and actually written by Jeremiah. So, the rabbinical method of using two lies to create a Jewish truth is brought into play here.

Among the wet ink of their "prophesy of Daniel," the rabbis placed a cookie for their Jews to bite on. This was the promise of bodily resurrection after death. Daniel 12:2-3 states:

"Of those who lie sleeping in the dust of the earth many will awake, some to everlasting life, some to shame and everlasting disgrace. The learned will shine as brightly as the vault of heaven, and those who have instructed many in virtue, as bright as stars for all eternity."

Thus, the lying rabbis promise the Jews eternal life while, of course, putting themselves first as the "learned" and as instructors of "virtue," even though the "knowledge" of the rabbis is falsehood and their "virtue" is the most knavish wickedness.

To be sure that all of their phony predictions would be believed, at the end of the Book of Daniel, they have an angel say: "these words are to remain secret and sealed until the time of the End" (Daniel 12:9). Daniel 12 ends the Hebrew version of the Book of Daniel and conveniently covers the fact that none of the Jews had ever heard of the "ancient" Book of Daniel until after the death of the Greek general and king, Antiochus Epiphanes in 164 BC.

Daniel 13 and 14 are later additions which are not included in the *Hebrew Bible*, but were added in Greek – a couple of weak stories glorifying Daniel and the god of the Jews. Regardless of the alleged "virtues" of Daniel and his co-conspirators, the rabbis made sure that everyone knew that only Jews have supernatural powers and all other people are to be vilified and slandered. So, the various names used for Daniel's competition are "sorcerers, magicians, enchanters, Chaldeans (that is, divination originating in Babylonia), sages and wizards." This talent that the Jews have for vilifying anyone who is not of their own holy and angelic breed, was developed at a very early age, but it has not diminished at all into modern times, as can be seen in any publication or other media where only the Jews are doing the talking.

Because the Book of Daniel is a piece of propaganda written in about 167 BC, it really has a lot to teach about the Jewish goals at that time. It is presented like so many other Jewish frauds throughout the centuries, as an ancient prophecy come true. So, it was easy for the symbolism of Nebuchadnezzar's dream to come true, since all of the events had already occurred before the "prophecy" was made. However, it is interesting to read exactly what it was that the rabbis wanted all of the Jews to believe at that time, because this shows how truly insane those old, bearded, rabbinical perverts really were – and still are today.

The Book of Daniel describes the belief system that the rabbis were using. In both Hebrew and Aramaic, the rabbis of Jerusalem let their strategy and tactics be known to the other rabbis throughout all of the Jew-infested countries. By 167 BC, Judaism had finally become the perfect crime. The Jews had betrayed the Babylonians, deceived the Persians, and swindled the Greeks. And now, with this Book of Daniel the rabbis were tightening their hold on their Jews with this psycho-political assault on Greek Culture. With Greek Culture came an understanding of True Money. With such knowledge spreading, the people of the world could not be swindled with Jewish gold and Jewish silver.

By Daniel, Chapter 2, the rabbis, writing in Aramaic, described under the guise of an "ancient prophecy" what they wanted their Jews to do. One thing that they wanted of utmost importance to them, was for the Jews to follow the rabbinical teachings and avoid Greek knowledge or Greek thought. To the rabbis, reason and logic were poison. What they wanted was blind obedience and fanatical belief. And to get these, they required, not the heroes of the living Greek philosophy, but the heroes composed of Super Jews protected by a mighty god living in a mythical, ancient Babylonia that no one had ever heard of. *Abracadabra*! It was true, because a holy rabbi said so. And any Jews who didn't believe them, would be killed, leaving us with what we have today – the Devil's Truth, promoted by grinning liars wearing beanies and holding their holy penises with a cloth, so that they aren't tempted to abuse themselves. Yes, they are God's Chosen People, to hear them tell it.

www.ingramcontent.com/pod-product-compliance
Lightning Source LLC
Chambersburg PA
CBHW021601120626
46545CB00001B/21